THE
BARBOUR
BIBLE
REFERENCE
COMPANION

THE
BARBOUR
BIBLE
REFERENCE
COMPANION

GEORGE W. KNIGHT
RAYBURN W. RAY

BARBOUR BOOKS

An Imprint of Barbour Publishing, Inc.

Published by Barbour Books, an imprint of Barbour Publishing, Inc., P.O. Box 719, Uhrichsville, Ohio 44683, www.barbourbooks.com

Our mission is to publish and distribute inspirational products offering exceptional value and biblical encouragement to the masses.

 Member of the
Evangelical Christian
Publishers Association

Printed in the United States of America.

To all my Bible teachers and students,

past and present,

who have sparked my commitment

to a lifetime of study

of God's Word

Table of Contents

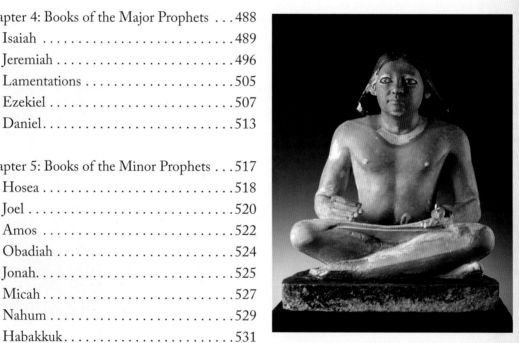

Acknowledgments

A book this comprehensive in scope doesn't happen without the encouragement and support of many people. My special thanks to those who have played a major role in its creation.

Paul K. Muckley, senior editor for non-fiction at Barbour Publishing, served as cheerleader and problem solver for the entire project. He worked under an impossible schedule to make sure all the pieces came together in the right order. My thanks to him for a job well done.

As an editor myself, I realize that behind-the-scenes book-publishing professionals seldom get the recognition they deserve. So let me say a special "thank you" to those creative professionals on the production team who assisted Paul so capably: Steve Miller, photo researcher; Jason Rovenstine, design director; Robyn Martins, page designer; Lauren Schneider, proofreader; Connie Troyer, indexer; and others who played smaller but very important roles in the process.

I am also grateful to my friend and colleague, Rayburn Ray, who worked with me several years ago to cowrite the Bible dictionary part of *The Barbour Bible Reference Companion*. This was the flagship book that led to several other books in the "Layman's" series of Bible reference titles, published by Barbour since 1998. My thanks for Rayburn's contribution to this project and his continuing friendship.

Finally, I express the warmest "thank you" of all to my wife, Dorothy. For more than forty years she has encouraged me in my writing efforts. She has tolerated my "creative moodiness," never complaining about the hours I spend at the typewriter or word processor. In recent years, she has even gone the second mile by helping me with some of the "grunt work" required for the creation of a reference book such as this—checking Scripture references, doing proofreading, and compiling indexes. King Solomon, author of the book of Proverbs, described her well: "She openeth her mouth with wisdom; and in her tongue is the law of kindness…let her own works praise her in the gates" (Prov. 31:26, 31).

Introduction

As an average, everyday student of the Bible, you deserve biblical study tools that are handy, affordable, and easy to understand. And that's exactly what you get in *The Barbour Bible Reference Companion*.

In this single volume, you have access to four separate Bible study aids—a virtual Bible study library—in one easy-to-use package. For your convenience, these four study tools are grouped into two major sections: (1) Bible Dictionary with Concordance, and (2) Bible Handbook with Notes on Customs and Curiosities (see contents page).

The Bible Dictionary section of the book contains articles on the most important persons, places, objects, and doctrines mentioned in the Bible. Concordance entries of key Bible words and phrases are placed alphabetically among the dictionary articles. The book's Bible Handbook section gives an overview and a summary of all sixty-six books of the Bible. Notes on customs of Bible times that help you understand God's Word better are placed in the handbook at the appropriate biblical passages where these customs are described.

This four-books-in-one approach should make your Bible study time more productive. No longer will you have to turn to a dictionary, a concordance, a handbook, and a book on Bible customs to find answers to your questions about God's Word. They are right here between the covers of this one book. The thorough index at the back of *The Barbour Bible Reference Companion* is designed to help you narrow your search if you are looking for a specific topic or subject.

Another handy feature is the maps section at the back of the book. Whenever a city, a nation, or other biblical place name is mentioned, these places are cross-referenced in the text to the appropriate maps. This valuable visual aid should give you a better understanding of biblical geography.

Speaking of visual aids, your study and research will also be enhanced by the drawings and photographs—most of them in full color—of Bible places and personalities throughout the book. These art pieces were specifically selected to make the Scriptures come alive for students of God's Word.

You will also enjoy the abundance of Scripture references included in the dictionary articles and summaries of Bible books. These are included to encourage you to dig deeper in your study of the Bible. The copious cross-references to related subjects in the dictionary articles also serve this same practical purpose.

How is it possible to put all this valuable information into one affordable book of about 700 pages? It's possible because the authors carefully selected the content according to biblical significance. *TThe Barbour Bible Reference Companion* includes only the most vital and essential information, written in a terse, no-nonsense style. The Concordance section, for example, majors on biblical words with theological significance, including "Adoption," "Confess," "Love," "Mercy," "Peace," and "Redemption," and key phrases such as "Eternal Life," "Gift of God," and "Signs and Wonders." The book is not intended for scholars but for lay students and casual readers who want to get to the heart of the Bible quickly and easily—without wading through a lot of verbiage.

The translation on which this book is based is the familiar Authorized, or King James Version. But variant readings are cited from the New International Version and the New Revised Standard Version to clarify obscure words and phrases.

In the Bible Dictionary section, variant readings for a key word from the NIV and NRSV are included in parentheses immediately following that word. For example: **FIRMAMENT (EXPANSE, DOME).** The word *firmament,* the key word for this article, is from the KJV. *Expanse* and *Dome* are how the word *firmament* is rendered by the NIV and the NRSV in the account of creation in Genesis 1:6. This helpful format makes the book usable with these two modern translations, in addition to the King James Version.

Another helpful feature of the Bible Dictionary section is the inclusion of all variant names for a person or place recorded in the King James Version itself. For example, the ancient kingdom of Babylonia is also referred to in the KJV as Sheshach, Shinar, and Chaldea. This is how the key word is listed in the entry on Babylonia: **BABYLONIA/SHESHACH/SHINAR/CHALDEA.** The slash marks between these words indicate these are variant names for Babylonia that occur at different places in the KJV. These variant names are also cross-referenced to Babylonia at the appropriate places in the dictionary text. Example: **SHESHACH.** See *Babylonia.* This helpful feature should clear up some of the confusion about variant biblical names in the King James Version for serious students of the Scriptures.

My prayer is that *The Barbour Bible Reference Companion* will serve as a valuable source of information for all students who, like the citizens of Berea in the New Testament, are eager to learn more about the Bible, studying expectantly and "with all readiness of mind" (Acts 17:11).

George W. Knight
Nashville, Tennessee

Bible Dictionary

with

Concordance of Key Bible References

List of Abbreviations (for Bible references)

Biblical books noted in *The Barbour Bible Reference Companion* will be abbreviated as follows:

Old Testament

Gen. . . . . Genesis
Exod. . . . . .Exodus
Lev. . . . . Leviticus
Num. . . . . Numbers
Deut. . . . . Deuteronomy
Josh.. . . . . Joshua
Judg. . . . . Judges
Ruth . . . . Ruth
1 Sam. . . . . 1 Samuel
2 Sam. . . . . 2 Samuel
1 Kings . . . . 1 Kings
2 Kings . . . . 2 Kings
1 Chron. . . . . 1 Chronicles
2 Chron. . . . . 2 Chronicles
Ezra. . . . . .Ezra
Neh. . . . . Nehemiah
Esther . . . . Esther
Job. . . . . .Job
Ps./Pss. . . . . .Psalm/Psalms
Prov. . . . . .Proverbs
Eccles. . . . . Ecclesiastes
Song of Sol.. . . . Song of Solomon
Isa.. . . . . .Isaiah
Jer.. . . . . Jeremiah
Lam. . . . . Lamentations
Ezek.. . . . . .Ezekiel
Dan. . . . . Daniel
Hosea . . . . Hosea
Joel . . . . Joel
Amos. . . . . .Amos
Obad. . . . . Obadiah
Jon. . . . . .Jonah
Mic.. . . . . Micah
Nah. . . . . Nahum

Hab. . . . . Habakkuk
Zeph.. . . . . .Zephaniah
Hag. . . . . .Haggai
Zech.. . . . . Zechariah
Mal.. . . . . Malachi

New Testament

Matt. . . . . Matthew
Mark . . . . Mark
Luke . . . . Luke
John. . . . . .John
Acts. . . . . Acts
Rom. . . . . Romans
1 Cor. . . . . 1 Corinthians
2 Cor. . . . . 2 Corinthians
Gal. . . . . Galatians
Eph. . . . . Ephesians
Phil.. . . . . Philippians
Col. . . . . Colossians
1 Thess. . . . . 1 Thessalonians
2 Thess. . . . . 2 Thessalonians
1 Tim. . . . . 1 Timothy
2 Tim. . . . . 2 Timothy
Titus . . . . Titus
Philem. . . . . .Philemon
Heb. . . . . Hebrews
James. . . . . .James
1 Pet. . . . . .1 Peter
2 Pet. . . . . .2 Peter
1 John . . . . 1 John
2 John . . . . 2 John
3 John . . . . 3 John
Jude. . . . . .Jude
Rev.. . . . . Revelation

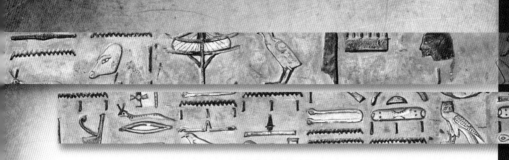

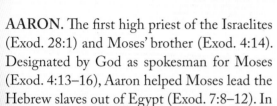

AARON. The first high priest of the Israelites (Exod. 28:1) and Moses' brother (Exod. 4:14). Designated by God as spokesman for Moses (Exod. 4:13–16), Aaron helped Moses lead the Hebrew slaves out of Egypt (Exod. 7:8–12). In the wilderness, he was consecrated by God as Israel's first high priest, and his sons inherited this position from their father (Num. 3:38). Like Moses, Aaron was not allowed to enter the Promised Land because of his act of unfaithfulness in the wilderness (Num. 20:6–12). His earthly priesthood is compared unfavorably to the eternal priesthood of Christ (Heb. 5:4; 7:11). See also *High Priest; Priest.*

AARON. Aaron, older brother of Moses, became Israel's first high priest— starting a family dynasty of priests that lasted more than a millennium.

AARONITES. Descendants of Aaron who were a part of the priestly tribe of Levi. A large force of Aaronites fought with David against King Saul (1 Chron. 12:23–27).

AB. The fifth month of the Jewish year, roughly equivalent to our modern August. This month is referred to, though not specifically by name, in Num. 33:38.

ABADDON/APOLLYON. A Hebrew word meaning "destruction," used to characterize the angel of the bottomless pit (Rev. 9:11). *Apollyon:* Greek form.

ABANA RIVER. A river of Syria that flowed through the

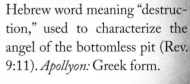

city of Damascus. It was mentioned by Naaman the leper as more favorable for bathing than the Jordan River (2 Kings 5:12). See also *Pharpar.*

ABARIM. A rugged mountain range east of the Jordan River in Moab from which Moses viewed the Promised Land before his death (Deut. 32:48–50).

ABASE [D]
Ezek. 21:26 exalt him that is low, and *a* him that is high
Luke 18:14 every one that exalteth himself shall be *a'd*
Phil. 4:12 I [Paul] know...how to be *a'd*...how to abound

ABBA. An Aramaic word meaning "father," used by Jesus while praying in Gethsemane (Mark 14:32, 36). It was also used by Paul to express the Christian's sonship with God the Father (Rom. 8:15).

ABDON. A minor judge of Israel who ruled for eight years (Judg. 12:13–15). See also *Judges of Israel.*

ABED-NEGO/AZARIAH. One of Daniel's three friends. Thrown into the fiery furnace by King Nebuchadnezzar of Babylonia (Dan. 3:13–27), he was later promoted by the king after his miraculous deliverance at the hand of God (Dan. 3:28–30). *Azariah:* Hebrew form (Dan. 1:7).

ABEL
1. Second son of Adam and Eve (Gen. 4:2). Abel's animal sacrifice was pleasing to God (Gen. 4:4). Abel was then killed by his brother Cain in a jealous rage (Gen. 4:5, 8). Jesus regarded "righteous Abel" as the first martyr (Matt. 23:35). Abel's works were called "righteous" (1 John 3:12), and his sacrifices were commended as a testimony of faith (Heb. 11:4).

2. A fortified city in northern Israel where Sheba sought refuge during his rebellion against David. The citizens of Abel killed Sheba to end the siege by the king's army (2 Sam. 20:14–22).

ABIA. See *Abijah.*

ABIAH. A son of Samuel and corrupt judge of Israel. Abiah's dishonesty, along with that of his brother Joel, led the people to ask Samuel to appoint a king to rule the nation (1 Sam. 8:2–5). See also *Joel,* No. 2.

ABIATHAR. A high priest under David who remained faithful to the king during Absalom's rebellion (2 Sam. 15:24–35). He was later banished from the royal court by Solomon for supporting Adonijah as king (1 Kings 1:7–25; 2:22–35).

ABIB/NISAN. The first month of the Hebrew year, the time when barley opened (Exod. 13:4). Roughly equivalent to our modern April, this month was known as *Nisan* after the Babylonian Exile (Esther 3:7).

ABIDE [ING, TH]
Ps. 91:1 *a* under the shadow of the Almighty
Luke 2:8 shepherds *a'ing* in the field
John 3:36 believeth not the Son...wrath...*a'th* on him
John 14:16 another Comforter...may *a* with you for ever
John 15:5 He that *a'th* in me [Jesus]...bringeth...fruit
1 Cor. 13:13 *a'th* faith, hope, charity
1 John 2:10 He that loveth his brother *a'th* in the light
1 John 2:17 he that doeth the will of God *a'th* for ever

ABIGAIL. A wife of David and the mother of Chileab (2 Sam. 3:3). While married to Nabal, Abigail appeased David's anger after Nabal rejected David's servants (1 Sam. 25:14–35). See also *Nabal.*

ABIHU. One of Aaron's four sons. Abihu and his brother Nadab offered "strange fire," or a forbidden sacrifice, to God—an act for which they were destroyed by fire from God (Lev. 10:1–7). See also *Nadab*, No. 1.

ABIJAH/ABIJAM/ABIA. The son and successor of Rehoboam as king of Judah (reigned about 913–911 B.C.; 2 Chron. 11:20–22). *Abijam:* 1 Kings 14:31; *Abia:* Jesus' ancestry (Matt. 1:7).

ABILENE. A province of Syria governed by the tetrarch Lysanias during the ministry of John the Baptist (Luke 3:1–2). See also *Lysanias*.

ABIMELECH

1. A Philistine king of Gerar in Abraham's time. He took Sarah, Abraham's wife, into his harem, then returned her to Abraham when he was informed in a dream that she was married (Gen. 20:1–18).

2. A rebellious son of Gideon who killed all his brothers after his father's death in an attempt to become king over all Israel (Judg. 9:5–22). He was killed by his armorbearer after a woman dropped a stone on his head from a city wall (Judg. 9:50–54).

ABINADAB

1. A man of Kirjath-jearim whose household kept the ark of the covenant for twenty years after it was returned by the Philistines (1 Sam. 7:1–2).

2. A son of King Saul killed at Gilboa, along with Jonathan (1 Chron. 10:1–6).

ABIRAM. A rebel against Moses in the wilderness who died in an earthquake because of his disobedience (Num. 16:1–33).

ABISHAG. A young woman who served as David's nurse in his old age (1 Kings 1:1–15).

David's son Adonijah was killed by Solomon for desiring to marry her after David's death (1 Kings 2:13–25).

ABISHAI. The deputy commander of David's army (2 Sam. 10:9–10). Loyal to David in Absalom's rebellion (2 Sam. 16:9–12), he also saved David's life by killing a giant (2 Sam. 21:16–17).

ABISHALOM. See *Absalom*.

ABLUTION. The ceremonial washing of a person's body or clothing to make him pure. Such washing was commanded in the O.T. Law (Exod. 40:12–13). True cleansing is found only in the blood of Christ (Rev. 1:5). See also *Clean*.

ABNER. The commander-in-chief of Saul's army. He introduced David to King Saul (1 Sam. 17:55–58) and established Saul's son Ish-bosheth as king after Saul's death (2 Sam. 2:8–10). Later he shifted his loyalty to David and persuaded all the tribes of Israel to follow David's leadership (2 Sam. 3:17–21).

ABOLISH [ED]
Isa. 2:18 the idols he [God] shall utterly *a*
Isa. 51:6 my [God's] righteousness shall not be *a'ed*
2 Tim. 1:10 Jesus Christ, who hath *a'ed* death

ABOMINATION. Something considered repulsive by the Hebrews. Examples of these despised practices are heathen idolatry (Deut. 7:25–26), blemished animal sacrifices (Deut. 17:1), sexual transgressions (Lev. 18), child sacrifice (Deut. 12:31), and the practice of witchcraft, magic, and spiritism (Deut. 18:9–12).

ABOMINATION OF DESOLATION. The action of Antiochus Epiphanes in sacrificing a pig in the Jewish temple about 165 B.C. This despised act of the Syrian ruler is considered fulfillment of Daniel's prophecy (Dan. 9:24–27; Matt. 24:15). See also *Antiochus IV Epiphanes; Maccabees.*

THINGS CONSIDERED ABOMINABLE BY THE LORD

1. Graven images, or idols (Deut. 7:26)
2. The froward, or wicked (Prov. 3:32)
3. Cheating with a false balance (Prov. 11:1)
4. Lying lips (Prov. 12:22)
5. Sacrifice of the wicked (Prov. 15:8)
6. Thoughts of the wicked (Prov. 15:26)
7. Vanity and pride (Prov. 16:5)

ABOUND [ED]

Rom. 5:15 grace of God...*a'ed* unto many
Rom. 5:20 grace did much more *a*
Rom. 6:1 continue in sin, that grace may *a*?
Rom. 15:13 *a* in hope, through the...Holy Ghost
Eph. 1:8 he [God] hath *a'ed* toward us in all wisdom
Phil. 4:12 I [Paul] know...how to be abased...how to *a*

ABOVE

Gen. 1:7 God...divided the waters...*a* the firmament
Deut. 7:6 chosen thee to be a special people...*a* all people
1 Chron. 16:25 great is the LORD...to be feared *a* all gods
Ps. 95:3 the LORD is...a great King *a* all gods
Prov. 31:10 a virtuous woman? For her price is far *a* rubies
Jer. 17:9 heart is deceitful *a* all things
Matt. 10:24 The disciple is not *a* his master
1 Cor. 10:13 God...not suffer you...tempted *a*...ye are able
Eph. 4:6 One God...who is *a* all, and through all
Phil. 2:9 given him [Jesus] a name...*a* every name
Col. 3:1 seek those things which are *a*
James 1:17 Every good...and...perfect gift is from *a*

ABRAHAM/ABRAM. The father of the nation of Israel (Ps. 105:6, 9). A native of Ur in southern Babylonia, he married Sarah and went to Haran (Gen. 11:26–31). Later he obeyed God's call to leave Haran for a "land

that I will shew thee" (Gen. 12:1–5). God made a covenant with Abraham to bless all nations of the world through him (Gen. 12:2–3). The land of Canaan was also promised to Abraham's descendants (Gen. 12:7; 13:14–18).

Although Abraham and Sarah were childless at an advanced age, God promised Abraham a son (Gen. 15:1–4; 17:19). At Sarah's urging, Abraham fathered Ishmael by Sarah's servant Hagar (Gen. 16:1–4, 15). God changed the names of Abraham and Sarah from *Abram* and *Sarai* (Gen. 17:5, 15) and established circumcision as a covenant sign (Gen. 17:10–14). The covenant was to be fulfilled through Isaac rather than Ishmael (Gen. 17:20–21; Gal. 4:22–31). Isaac was born in the couple's old age (Gen. 21:1–7).

As a test of faith, God asked Abraham to sacrifice Isaac (Gen. 22:1–13). Then God Himself intervened to save Isaac and again promised to bless Abraham for his unwavering faith (Gen. 22:16–18). Abraham died at 175 years of age and was buried beside Sarah near Hebron (Gen. 25:7–10).

Abraham remains a model of righteousness and faith for all believers (Gen. 26:24; Ps. 47:9; Isa. 41:8). An ancestor of Christ, he is viewed as a spiritual father of all who share a like faith in Christ (Matt. 1:1; 3:9; Gal. 3:6–9). See also *Sarah.*

ABRAHAM'S BOSOM. A symbolic expression for the blissful state after death (Luke 16:22). The Jews believed they joined their forefathers, particularly "father Abraham," upon their death (Gen. 15:15).

ABSALOM/ABISHALOM. The vain, rebellious son of David (2 Sam. 3:3). He killed his brother Amnon for molesting their sister Tamar (2 Sam. 13:22–33). Absalom conspired against David and seized Jerusalem

(2 Sam. 15:1–29). Massing an army against David (2 Sam. 17:24–26), he was killed by David's commander Joab after his hair was tangled in a tree (2 Sam. 18:9–18). David mourned grievously at Absalom's death (2 Sam. 18:19–33). *Abishalom:* 1 Kings 15:2, 10. See also *David.*

ABSTINENCE. To refrain from eating or drinking harmful substances or participating in sinful acts. Priests and Nazirites abstained from strong drink (Num. 6:1–4). Gentile Christians were advised to abstain from fornication and idolatry (Acts 15:20). All believers are counseled by Paul to refrain from any practices that might offend a weak brother (Rom. 14:21). See also *Moderation; Temperance.*

ABUNDANCE

Ps. 37:11 meek shall...delight...in the *a* of peace
Eccles. 5:12 *a* of the rich will not suffer him to sleep
Matt. 12:34 out of the *a* of the heart the mouth speaketh
Luke 12:15 life consisteth not in the *a*...he possesseth

ABUNDANT

2 Cor. 4:15 *a* grace might...redound to the glory of God
2 Cor. 11:23 in labours more *a*, in stripes above measure
1 Tim. 1:14 grace of our Lord was exceeding *a* with faith

ABYSS/BOTTOMLESS PIT. A word translated literally as "bottomless pit" in the book of Revelation, indicating the place where Satan dwells (Rev. 9:1–2, 11).

ABRAHAM. In a test of faith, God asked Abraham to sacrifice his son Isaac. An angel stops Abraham at the last moment, and Isaac grows up to become one of the fathers of the Jewish nation.

ACACIA. See *Shittah.*

ACCAD (AKKAD). A fortified city built by Nimrod, a descendant of Noah (Gen. 10:8–10), in the land of Shinar—an ancient kingdom between the Tigris and Euphrates rivers. *Akkad:* NIV.

ACCEPT [ED]
Job 42:9 the Lord also *a'ed* Job
Jer. 37:20 my supplication...be *a'ed* before thee [God]
Amos 5:22 burnt offerings...I [God] will not *a* them
Luke 4:24 No prophet is *a'ed* in his own country
Acts 10:35 feareth him [God]...is *a'ed* with him

ACCEPTABLE
Ps. 19:14 meditation of my heart...*a* in thy [God's] sight
Prov. 21:3 To do justice...is more *a*...than sacrifice
Isa. 61:2 To proclaim the *a* year of the Lord
Rom. 12:1 bodies a living sacrifice...*a* unto God
Eph. 5:10 Proving what is *a* unto the Lord
1 Tim. 2:3 good and *a* in the sight of God
1 Pet. 2:5 spiritual sacrifices, *a* to God by Jesus Christ

ACCESS
Rom. 5:2 By whom [Jesus]...*a*...into this grace
Eph. 2:18 through him [Jesus]...*a*...unto the Father
Eph. 3:12 In whom [Jesus]...*a* with confidence

ACCHO/ACRE (ACCO). A coastal city near Mount Carmel in the territory of Asher (Judg. 1:31). This is the same city as N.T. *Ptolemais* (Acts 21:7). It is known today as *Acre. Acco:* NIV, NRSV.

ACCOMPLISHED
Isa. 40:2 Jerusalem...her warfare is *a*
Luke 2:6 days were *a* that she [Mary] should be delivered
John 19:28 Jesus knowing that all things were now *a*

ACCORD
Acts 1:14 These all continued with one *a* in prayer
Acts 2:1 Pentecost was...come, they were all with one *a*
Acts 2:46 one *a*...and breaking bread from house to house
Phil. 2:2 having the same love, being of one *a*

ACCOUNT [ED]
Ps. 144:3 son of man, that thou makest *a* of him!
Matt. 12:36 idle word that men...speak, they shall give *a*
Luke 21:36 *a'ed* worthy to...stand before the Son of man
Rom. 14:12 every one...shall give *a* of himself to God
Gal. 3:6 Abraham believed God...*a'ed*...for righteousness
1 Pet. 4:5 give *a* to him...ready to judge...the dead

ACCOUNTABILITY. The biblical principle that each person is answerable to God and responsible for his or her actions (Rom. 14:12). Accountability also involves the obligation to act with love toward fellow believers (Rom. 14:15–19).

ACCURSED
Josh. 7:1 For Achan...took of the *a* thing
Rom. 9:3 myself [Paul] were *a* from Christ for...kinsmen
1 Cor. 12:3 no man speaking by the Spirit...calleth Jesus *a*

ACCUSATION
Matt. 27:37 his *a*...Jesus the King of the Jews
Luke 6:7 watched him [Jesus]...find an *a* against him
John 18:29 Pilate...said, What *a*...against this man [Jesus]

ACCUSE [D]
Matt. 12:10 heal...sabbath day...might *a* him [Jesus]
Matt. 27:12 *a'd* of the chief priests...he [Jesus] answered nothing
Luke 23:2 *a* him [Jesus]...perverting the nation

ACELDAMA (AKELDAMA, HAKEL-DAMA). A field near Jerusalem purchased with the money that Judas was paid to betray Jesus. The name means "field of blood" (Acts 1:15–19). *Akeldama:* NIV; *Hakeldama:* NRSV.

ACHAIA. A province of Greece visited by the apostle Paul (Acts 18:12). Christians at Achaia contributed to their impoverished brethren at Jerusalem (Rom. 15:26).

ACHAN/ACHAR. A warrior under Joshua who was stoned to death for withholding the spoils of war (Josh. 7:16–25). *Achar:* 1 Chron. 2:7.

ACHAZ. See *Ahaz.*

ACHISH. A Philistine king of the city of Gath who provided refuge to David when he fled from King Saul (1 Sam. 21:10–15; 27:5–7).

ACHMETHA (ECBATANA). The capital city of the empire of the Medes and later one of the capitals of the Persian Empire (Ezra 6:2). *Ecbatana:* NIV, NRSV.

ACKNOWLEDGE
Ps. 51:3 I *a* my transgressions...my sin is ever before me
Prov. 3:6 ways *a* him [God], and he shall direct thy paths
Jer. 14:20 *a*, O LORD, our wickedness...sinned against thee

ACRE. See *Accho.*

ACTS
Deut. 11:7 eyes have seen all the great *a* of the LORD
Ps. 103:7 his [God's] *a* unto the children of Israel
Ps. 150:2 Praise him [God] for his mighty *a*

ACTS OF THE APOSTLES. The one book of history in the N.T. that traces the expansion and development of the early church from the ascension of Jesus to Paul's imprisonment in Rome—a period of about thirty-five years. Written by Luke as a companion or sequel to his Gospel and addressed to Theophilus (see Luke 1:3–4; Acts 1:1–2), Acts shows clearly how the Christian witness spread in accordance with the Great Commission of Jesus (see Acts 1:8): (1) in Jerusalem (1:1–8:3), (2) throughout Judea and Samaria (8:4–12:25), and (3) to the entire world (12:26–28:31). See also *Luke.*

ADAM. The first man. Created in God's image (Gen. 1:26–27), Adam was an upright and intelligent being (Gen. 2:19–20)—the first worker (Gen. 2:8, 15) and the first husband (Gen. 2:18–25). He received God's law (Gen. 2:16–17) and knowingly sinned, along with Eve (Gen. 3:6). Their sin resulted in broken fellowship with the Creator (Gen. 3:8) and brought God's curse (Gen. 3:14–19) and eviction from Eden (Gen. 3:22–24). Adam fathered Cain and Abel (Gen. 4:1–2), Seth (Gen. 4:25), and other children (Gen. 5:3–4). He died at age 930 (Gen. 5:5).

As head of the human race, Adam introduced sin into the world. He represents the lost and dying condition of all unrepentant sinners (Rom. 5:12–19; 1 Cor. 15:22). But Christ, referred to in the N.T. as the "second Adam," offers deliverance from the curse of sin and death (Rom. 5:14–19; 1 Cor. 15:22). See also *Eden, Garden of; Eve; Fall of Man.*

ADAR. The twelfth month of the Jewish year, roughly equivalent to parts of our modern February and March. Haman ordered the massacre of the Jews on the thirteenth day of this month (Esther 3:13).

ADAMANT. A precious stone, possibly corundum (Ezek. 3:9; Zech. 7:12).

ADDER. See *Asp.*

ADMAH. One of the five cities near the Dead Sea destroyed with Sodom and Gomorrah (Gen. 10:19; Deut. 29:23). See also *Cities of the Plain.*

ADMONISH [ING]
Rom. 15:14 ye also are...to *a* one another
Col. 3:16 *a'ing* one another in psalms and hymns
2 Thess. 3:15 not as an enemy, but *a* him as a brother

ADONAI. The Hebrew name for God, translated "Lord" (Ezek. 11:8). See also *God; Lord.*

ADONIJAH. David's fourth son and rival of Solomon for the throne (2 Sam. 3:4; 1 Kings

1:5, 30). Adonijah was executed by Solomon (1 Kings 2:19–25).

ADONI-ZEDEC. One of five Amorite kings who joined forces to oppose Joshua's army at Gibeon. He was defeated and killed by Joshua (Josh. 10:1–26).

ADOPTION. The legal act of giving status as a family member (Exod. 2:9–10; Esther 2:7). Paul spoke of adoption in symbolic, spiritual terms (Rom. 11:1–32; Gal. 4:4–7). Adoption as God's children is made possible by faith in Christ (Gal. 3:24–26). See also *Inheritance.*

Rom. 8:15 Spirit of *a*, whereby we cry, Abba
Rom. 8:23 waiting for the *a*...redemption of our body
Eph. 1:5 predestinated us unto the *a* of children by Jesus

3
C
6

ADORAM. A city in southwest Judah rebuilt and fortified by King Rehoboam, son of Solomon (2 Chron. 11:5, 9). Now known as *Dura,* it is located five miles southwest of Hebron.

ADRAMMELECH. A pagan god worshiped by Assyrian colonists who settled in Samaria after the fall of the Northern Kingdom. Children were offered as sacrifices to this god (2 Kings 17:31).

ADRAMYTTIUM. An important seaport in the Roman province of Asia. Paul boarded a "ship of Adramyttium" to begin his voyage to Rome (Acts 27:2).

4
D
3

ADRIA/ADRIATIC SEA. A name for the central part of the Mediterranean Sea, south of modern Italy. Paul was shipwrecked here during his voyage to Rome (Acts 27:27). *Adriatic Sea:* NIV.

3
C
6

ADULLAM. A royal Canaanite city conquered by Joshua (Josh. 12:7, 15). In later

years David sought refuge in a cave near here (1 Sam. 22:1–2).

ADULTERY. Sexual intercourse with a person other than one's husband or wife. Adultery is specifically prohibited by the seventh of the Ten Commandments (Exod. 20:14). Jesus expanded the concept to prohibit the cultivation of lust and desire that leads to adultery (Matt. 5:28). See also *Fornication.*

Deut. 5:18 Neither shalt thou commit *a*
Prov. 6:32 committeth *a*...destroyeth his own soul
Mark 10:11 put away his wife, and marry another, committeth *a*
John 8:3 brought unto him [Jesus] a woman taken in *a*
Gal. 5:19 works of the flesh are...*A*, fornication

ADVENT OF CHRIST, THE FIRST. The birth of Jesus Christ in human form to the virgin Mary. His coming was foretold in the O.T. (Isa. 7:14; 9:6). Joseph was reassured by an angel that Mary's pregnancy was supernatural (Matt. 1:20–21). The angel Gabriel announced His coming birth to Mary (Luke 1:26–35).

Jesus was born to Mary in Bethlehem (Matt. 1:25; 2:1). His birth was revealed to shepherds (Luke 2:8–16). Wise men from the East brought gifts to the Christ child (Matt. 2:1–11). His birth was defined as a redemptive mission (Matt. 1:21–23; Luke 2:10–11). It nullified the O.T. ceremonial system (Heb. 9) and introduced the gospel age (Acts 3:20–26). See also *Incarnation of Christ; Virgin Birth.*

ADVERSARY. An active opponent; a term descriptive of Satan (1 Pet. 5:8). God's wisdom is promised to believers when they face the adversary (Luke 21:15). God's judgment will ultimately fall on His enemies (Heb. 10:27).

ADVERSARY [IES]
Deut. 32:43 he [God] will...render vengeance to his *a'ies*
Ps. 69:19 mine *a'ies* are all before thee [God]
Ps. 109:29 Let mine *a'ies* be clothed with shame

ADVENT OF CHRIST, THE FIRST. Displayed on a wall in Bethlehem's Church of the Nativity is this reminder of why the world's oldest church exists. An angel tells shepherds to go into the village to see the newborn Christ. An ancient tradition says Jesus was born in a cave beneath this very church.

Nah. 1:2 Lord will take vengeance on his *a'ies*
Matt. 5:25 Agree with thine *a*...in the way with him
1 Cor. 16:9 great door...is opened...many *a'ies*

ADVERSITY. Difficult or unfavorable circumstances, perhaps caused by sin (Gen. 3:16–17) or disobedience toward God (Lev. 26:14–20). Adversity may also be used by God to test our faith (1 Pet. 1:6–7) or to chasten and correct (Heb. 12:5–11). See also *Suffering; Tribulation.*

Prov. 17:17 a brother is born for *a*
Prov. 24:10 faint in the day of *a*, thy strength is small
Isa. 30:20 bread of *a*, and the water of affliction

ADVOCATE. One who pleads the cause of another (1 John 2:1). As the advocate, the Holy Spirit provides power for worldwide evangelism (Acts 1:8) and will abide with believers forever (John 14:16). See also *Comforter; Counsellor; Holy Spirit; Paraclete.*

AENON. A place near Salim, exact location unknown, where John the Baptist baptized. It was probably near the Jordan River, "because there was much water there" (John 3:23).

AFFECTION
Rom. 1:31 Without understanding...without natural *a*
Col. 3:2 Set your *a* on things above
Col. 3:5 uncleanness, inordinate *a*
2 Tim. 3:3 Without natural *a*, trucebreakers

AFFLICT [ED]
Exod. 1:12 more they *a'ed* them [Israelites]...more they...grew
Job 34:28 he [God] heareth the cry of the *a'ed*
Ps. 88:15 I am *a'ed* and ready to die
Isa. 49:13 Lord...will have mercy upon his *a'ed*

Isa. 53:4 him [God's servant] stricken...smitten...*a'ed*
Lam. 3:33 he [God] doth not *a* willingly nor grieve
Matt. 24:9 *a'ed*, and shall kill you...for my [Jesus']...sake
James 4:9 Be *a'ed*...your laughter be turned to mourning
James 5:13 any *a'ed*? let him pray

AFFLICTION. Any condition that causes suffering or pain. Affliction may come as a result of God's judgment on sin (Rom. 2:9), or it may be an instrument of purification and perfection for believers (Rom. 5:3–5; 2 Thess. 1:4–7). See also *Anguish; Persecution; Suffering.*

AFFLICTION [S]
Exod. 3:7 I [God] have...seen the *a* of my people
Deut. 16:3 unleavened bread...the bread of *a*
Ps. 34:19 Many are the *a's* of the righteous
Isa. 30:20 bread of adversity, and the water of *a*
2 Cor. 4:17 light *a*...worketh for us...exceeding...glory

2 Tim. 4:5 endure *a's*...make full proof of thy ministry
Jas. 1:27 visit the fatherless and widows in their *a*

AFRAID
Gen. 3:10 I [Adam] was *a*...and I hid myself
Exod. 3:6 Moses...was *a* to look upon God
Josh. 1:9 be not *a*...for the Lord...is with thee
Job 5:21 neither shalt thou be *a* of destruction
Ps. 56:3 What time I am *a*, I will trust in thee [God]
Isa. 12:2 not be *a*...Jehovah is my strength
Jer. 2:12 Be astonished...be horribly *a*...saith the Lord
Matt. 14:27 Jesus spake...it is I; be not *a*
Luke 2:9 and they [shepherds] were sore *a*
John 14:27 Let not your heart be troubled, neither let it be *a*

AFRICA. See *Libya.*

AGABUS. A Christian prophet who warned Paul in Antioch of Syria of a worldwide famine

AFFLICTION. Jesus heals a man born blind. Famed for His healing miracles and His message of hope, Jesus seemed constantly surrounded by crowds of sick and disheartened people.

(Acts 11:28). At Caesarea, Agabus used a symbolic demonstration to predict Paul's impending arrest (Acts 21:10–11).

AGAG

1. A king of Amalek in Balaam's prophecy. Balaam predicted that Israel's king would be more powerful than Agag (Num. 24:7)

2. An Amalekite king spared by King Saul in disobedience of God's command. Saul's disobedience led to his rejection as king of Israel by the Lord (1 Sam. 15:8–23). This may be the same king as *Agag,* No. 1.

AGAPE. A Greek word for selfless love, the type of love that characterizes God (John 15:13; 1 John 3:16). Agape is primarily an act of the will rather than the emotions (John 3:16; Rom. 5:8). Agape love for others is a badge of discipleship (John 13:34–35). This love is the greatest and most enduring of all Christian virtues (1 Cor. 13). See also *Love.*

AGAR. See *Hagar.*

AGATE. A precious stone in the breastplate of the high priest (Exod. 28:19), probably a distinct variety of quartz. See also *Chalcedony.*

AGORA. See *Marketplace.*

AGREE [D]
Amos 3:3 two walk together, except they be *a'd*
Matt. 5:25 *A* with...adversary quickly
Matt. 20:13 not thou *a* with me for a penny?

AGRIPPA. See *Herod,* No. 5 and No. 6.

AGUE. See *Burning Ague.*

AGUR. The author of Proverbs 30. Nothing else is known about Agur.

AHAB. The wicked king of Israel (reigned about 874–853 B.C.) and husband of Jezebel. Ahab was known as an aggressive builder (1 Kings 22:39). Influenced by Jezebel, he introduced Baal worship into Israel (1 Kings 16:31–33). His pagan practices were denounced by the prophet Elijah (1 Kings 17:1). Ahab waged war against King Ben-hadad of Syria (1 Kings 20) and was killed in a battle at Ramoth-gilead (1 Kings 22:34–38). See also *Jezebel.*

AHASUERUS. A king of Persia who married Esther and listened to her counsel regarding the Jewish people. He ordered his aide Haman executed—an act that saved the Jewish people from destruction (Esther 7). Most scholars agree that this Ahasuerus is the same person as King Xerxes I of Persian history (reigned 485–464 B.C.). See also *Esther; Haman.*

AHAVA/IVAH (IVVAH). A town in Babylonia where the Jewish exiles gathered after their deportation to this pagan nation. Ezra camped near a stream with this name before leading a group of exiles back to Jerusalem (Ezra 8:15–31). *Ivah:* 2 Kings 18:34; *Ivvah:* NIV, NRSV.

AHAZ/ACHAZ. A king of Judah (reigned about 742–727 B.C.) who practiced idolatry. Ahaz defended Jerusalem against Rezin of Syria and Pekah of Israel (2 Kings 16:5–6), but he was eventually defeated and many citizens of Judah were taken captive (2 Chron. 28:5–8). He foolishly paid tribute to the king of Assyria (2 Kings 16:7–9). *Achaz:* Jesus' ancestry (Matt. 1:9).

AHAZIAH

1. A king of Israel (reigned about 853–852 B.C.) and son of Ahab. A Baal worshiper

(1 Kings 22:52–53), he was injured in a fall from the balcony of his palace. After consulting a pagan god for help, he died, in fulfillment of Elijah's prophecy (2 Kings 1:2–17).

2. A king of Judah (reigned about 850 B.C.). The son of Jehoram and Athaliah, he followed in their evil ways by practicing idol worship. He was eventually assassinated by Jehu (2 Kings 9:27–28). *Jehoahaz:* 2 Chron. 21:17; *Azariah:* 2 Chron. 22:6.

AHIJAH. A prophet who revealed to Jeroboam the forthcoming split of Solomon's united kingdom (1 Kings 11:29–31). Later, Ahijah foretold the death of Jeroboam's son and the elimination of his line from the kingship (1 Kings 14:1–11). See also *Jeroboam,* No. 1.

AHIKAM. A royal official who protected the prophet Jeremiah from the persecution of King Jehoiakim (Jer. 26:24).

AHIMAAZ. A son of Zadok the high priest (1 Chron. 6:8–9) who warned David of Absalom's plans for rebellion. Ahimaaz also reported Absalom's defeat and death to David (2 Sam. 18:19–30).

AHIMELECH. The high priest at Nob during the reign of Saul (1 Sam. 21:1). He befriended David during his flight from Saul (1 Sam. 21:2–9). Ahimelech was killed at Saul's command (1 Sam. 22:16–19).

AHITHOPHEL. One of David's aides who joined Absalom's rebellion (2 Sam. 15:12, 31). He committed suicide when he realized Absalom's plot was doomed (2 Sam. 17:23).

AI/AIATH/AIJA/HAI. A royal Canaanite city that first defied Joshua and then later was defeated and destroyed by the invading Israelites (Josh. 7:2–5; 8:18–21). *Aiath:* Isa. 10:28; *Aija:* Neh. 11:31; *Hai:* Gen. 12:8.

AIJALON/AJALON. A city in the territory of Dan (1 Sam. 14:31) where Joshua battled the five Amorite kings. During this battle the sun stood still (Josh. 10:12–13). *Ajalon:* Josh. 19:42.

AIJELETH SHAHAR. A musical term in the title of Ps. 22, probably indicating the melody to be sung.

AJALON. See *Aijalon.*

AKELDAMA. See *Aceldama.*

AKKAD. See *Accad.*

ALAMOTH. A musical term in the title of Ps. 46, perhaps referring to a choir of women's voices (1 Chron. 15:20).

ALEXANDER THE GREAT. Greek ruler and world conqueror. He took the throne in 336 B.C. and extended his empire from Greece around the Mediterranean Sea to Egypt and then to India. Although he is not mentioned by name in the Bible, Alexander is perhaps the "mighty king" of Dan. 11:3–4. (See also Dan. 7:6; 8:21.)

ALEXANDRIA. A city of Egypt founded by Alexander the Great that was a cultural center and capital city of Egypt in N.T. times. Citizens of Alexandria opposed Stephen (Acts 6:9). Apollos was a native of this city (Acts 18:24). Paul left Malta for Rome on a ship from Alexandria (Acts 28:11). Seventy Jewish scholars were commissioned in this city to translate the O.T. from Hebrew to Greek—the famed version of the Bible known as the Septuagint.

Alexandria was well known for its extensive library, which drew scholars from throughout the ancient world. See also *Septuagint*.

ALGUM/ALMUG. A tree imported from Lebanon (2 Chron. 2:8). Its wood was used in Solomon's temple in Jerusalem. *Almug:* 1 Kings 10:11–12.

ALIEN. A foreigner or stranger from a country other than Israel (Exod. 18:3). Regarded as Gentiles, aliens did not enjoy the rights of the citizens of Israel (Deut. 14:21; Job 19:15). See also *Foreigner*.

ALIVE
Gen. 7:23 Noah only remained *a*
Luke 15:24 my son was dead, and is *a* again
Acts 1:3 he [Jesus] showed himself *a*
1 Cor. 15:22 in Christ shall all be made *a*
Rev. 2:8 first and the last, which was dead, and is *a*

ALLEGORY. A story that communicates an important truth in symbolic fashion. Paul spoke of the births of Ishmael and Isaac in allegorical terms (Gal. 4:22–26).

ALLELUIA. The Greek form of the Hebrew word *Hallelujah*, meaning "praise ye the Lord" (Rev. 19:1–6).

ALLIANCE. A treaty between nations or individuals. Alliances with conquered Canaanite nations were forbidden (Exod. 23:32; Deut. 7:2–5). The prophets warned Israel against forming alliances that might replace their dependence on God (Jer. 2:18).

Nevertheless, alliances between O.T. personalities and foreigners were common. Examples are (1) Abraham with Abimelech of Gerar (Gen. 21:22–34); (2) King Solomon with Hiram of Tyre (1 Kings 5:1–12); and

ALMOND. Bursting into springtime bloom, an orchard of almond trees awakens the colors of a small field in Israel.

(3) Solomon's many marriage alliances (1 Kings 3:1; 11:1–3). See also *League*.

ALMIGHTY. A title of God that indicates His absolute power and majesty. God used this term to identify Himself as He talked to Abraham (Gen. 17:1). Ezekiel portrayed God in this light in his vision of God's glory (Ezek. 1:24; 10:5). "Almighty" is also used of Christ (Rev. 1:8; 19:15). See also *Sovereignty of God*.

ALMOND. A small tree known for its early spring blossoms. Jeremiah visualized an almond branch as a sign of God's rapidly approaching judgment against the nation of Judah (Jer. 1:11–12). See also *Hazel*.

ALMS. Voluntary gifts to the needy. The Israelites were commanded to be generous to the poor (Deut. 15:11; Luke 12:33). Jesus cautioned His disciples not to give alms for show or the praise of others (Matt. 6:2–4). See also *Beggar; Poor*.

ALMUG. See *Algum*.

ALOES. A spice for embalming the dead, used by Joseph of Arimathea and Nicodemus on the body of Jesus (John 19:38–39).

ALONE
Gen. 2:18 not good that the man should be *a*
Isa. 2:11 the Lord *a* shall be exalted
Luke 5:21 Who can forgive sins, but God *a*?
James 2:17 faith, if it hath not works, is dead, being *a*

ALPHA AND OMEGA. The first and last letters of the Greek alphabet. Symbolic of the eternity of Christ, this title is applied to God the Father and God the Son (Rev. 1:8; 21:6). The risen Christ described Himself in this fashion, indicating He is the Creator, Redeemer, and Final Judge of all humankind (Rev. 22:13).

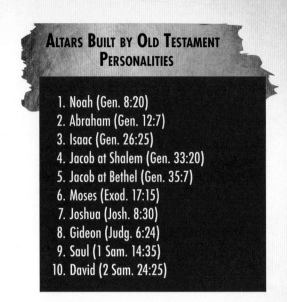

ALTARS BUILT BY OLD TESTAMENT PERSONALITIES

1. Noah (Gen. 8:20)
2. Abraham (Gen. 12:7)
3. Isaac (Gen. 26:25)
4. Jacob at Shalem (Gen. 33:20)
5. Jacob at Bethel (Gen. 35:7)
6. Moses (Exod. 17:15)
7. Joshua (Josh. 8:30)
8. Gideon (Judg. 6:24)
9. Saul (1 Sam. 14:35)
10. David (2 Sam. 24:25)

ALTAR. A platform, table, or elevated structure on which sacrifices were placed as offerings. Altars were originally made of earth or rocks (Exod. 20:24–25), but they evolved into more sophisticated structures after the construction of the tabernacle (Lev. 9:24). Pagan Canaanite altars were often called "high places" because they were built on hills or high platforms (Num. 33:52). See also *High Place*.

ALTASCHITH. A word of uncertain meaning in the titles of Pss. 57, 58, 59, and 75.

ALWAYS
Gen. 6:3 My [God's] spirit shall not *a* strive with man
Prov. 5:19 be thou ravished *a* with her love
Mark 14:7 me [Jesus] ye have not *a*
Luke 18:1 men ought *a* to pray
Acts 7:51 ye do *a* resist the Holy Ghost
2 Cor. 4:10 *A* bearing about...the dying of the Lord

AMALEK. The son of Eliphaz, grandson of Esau, and ancestor of the Edomites (Gen. 36:9–12).

ALTAR. A restored sacrificial altar in Beersheba where Abraham once lived. The altar's four corners, called horns, may have helped keep the burning wood and animal sacrifice from falling off.

his army, Amasa was killed by Joab (2 Sam. 20:9–12).

AMAZED

Matt. 12:23 people were *a*...Is not this the son of David?

Matt. 19:25 disciples heard it, they were exceedingly *a*

Mark 9:15 people...were...*a,* and...saluted him [Jesus]

Luke 9:43 they were all *a* at the...power of God

Acts 2:7 they were all *a*...are not all these...Galilaeans?

AMAZIAH. A king of Judah (reigned about 796–767 B.C.; 2 Kings 14:1–20). He assembled an army to attack Edom and embraced the false gods of Edom (2 Chron. 25:5–15). Amaziah was assassinated by his political enemies (2 Chron. 25:25–28).

AMBASSADOR. A messenger, spokesman, or representative of a ruler or king. Paul considered himself an ambassador for Christ (Eph. 6:20) and applied this term figuratively to all believers (2 Cor. 5:20).

AMALEKITES. A tribal enemy of the Israelites. Their animosity against the Hebrews apparently began during the years of wilderness wandering with an unprovoked attack (Exod. 17:8–16). Saul battled this tribe as well (1 Sam. 14:48), and they suffered a major defeat at the hands of David (1 Sam. 30).

AMASA. David's nephew and commander of Absalom's rebel army (2 Sam. 19:13). Later forgiven by David and appointed to command

AMBER. A gem or precious stone known for its yellowish-orange brilliance. The prophet Ezekiel compared God's glory to amber (Ezek. 1:4, 27; 8:2).

AMEN. A solemn word used to express approval (Neh. 8:6), confirm an oath (Neh. 5:13), or close a prayer (1 Cor. 14:16). Jesus is called "the Amen," meaning He is true and reliable (Rev. 3:14).

AMETHYST. Violet-colored amethyst was one of twelve precious stones worn on the breastplate of Israel's high priest. Each stone represented a tribe of Israel.

AMETHYST. A violet-colored precious stone in the breastplate of the high priest (Exod. 28:19), also used in the foundation of New Jerusalem (Rev. 21:20).

AMMONITES. A race or tribe descended from Ammon who became enemies of the Israelites during the Exodus (Deut. 23:3). Their chief pagan god was Chemosh (Judg. 11:24), and the Israelites often indulged in their idolatrous practices (Ezra 9:1). Tobiah, an Ammonite, tried to prevent Nehemiah from rebuilding the walls of Jerusalem (Neh. 2:10, 19).

AMNON. A son of David. Amnon assaulted his half sister Tamar—an act avenged with his death at the hand of her brother Absalom (2 Sam. 3:2; 13:1–29). See also *Tamar*, No. 2.

AMON. An evil and idolatrous king of Judah who reigned for only two years, about 643–641 B.C. Assassinated by his own servants, he was succeeded by his son Josiah after his assassins were killed by the people of Judah (2 Kings 21:18–26).

AMORITES. One of the tribal groups of Canaan defeated by the Israelites. Descendants of Ham through his son Canaan (Gen. 10:6), the Amorites were a formidable enemy, but Joshua broke their strength with victories over the armies of Sihon and Og (Josh. 12:1–6). Remnants of the Amorites were reduced to servitude under King Solomon (1 Kings 9:19–21). See also *Canaan*, No. 1.

AMOS. A herdsman from Tekoa in the Southern Kingdom (Judah) who prophesied against the Northern Kingdom (Israel) during the tenure of King Jeroboam II (Amos 1:1; 7:14–15). Known as the great "prophet of righteousness" of the O.T., he condemned the rich and indulgent for oppressing the poor (Amos 8:4–6) and foretold Israel's collapse and captivity by Assyria (Amos 7:17). Amos was a contemporary of the prophets Isaiah and Hosea.

AMOS, BOOK OF. A prophetic book of the Old Testament written by the prophet Amos about 760 B.C. to call the wayward people of the Northern Kingdom back to worship of the one true God.

A short book of only nine chapters, Amos falls naturally into three major divisions: (1) pronouncement of judgment on surrounding nations and Israel (1:3–2:16); (2) three sermons of judgment against the idolatry, corruption, and oppression of Israel (3:1–6:14); and (3) five visions of God's approaching judgment against the nation (7:1–9:10).

Perhaps the greatest contribution of the book is the concept that religion demands righteous behavior. True religion is not a matter of observing rituals and feast days, Amos declared. It consists of following God's commands and treating others with justice: "Let judgment run down as waters, and righteousness as a mighty stream" (Amos 5:24).

AMOS THE HERSDMAN AND FARMER

Amos insisted that he was not a prophet by profession but only "an herdman, and a gatherer of sycomore fruit" (Amos 7:14). The sycamore was a type of fig that grew in his native Judah. The "summer fruit" in Amos's vision (8:1-2) probably included figs.

ANAK. The son of Arba and ancestor of a tribe of giants (Deut. 9:2), or men of renown.

ANAKIMS (ANAKIM, ANAKITES). A tribe of giants, descended from Anak, who inhabited Canaan and were greatly feared in Joshua's time (Num. 13:28, 33; Deut. 9:2). The term may also refer to prominent people, or men of renown. Joshua divided their forces and captured their major walled city, Hebron, or Kirjath-arba (Josh. 14:12–15). The remnants of the Anakim may have been absorbed into the Philistine people. *Anakim:* NRSV; *Anakites:* NIV. See also *Emims.*

ANAMMELECH. A false god worshiped at Samaria by foreigners who settled the land after the defeat of the Northern Kingdom by Assyria (2 Kings 17:24, 31).

ANANIAS

1. An early believer at Jerusalem struck dead for lying and withholding money he had pledged to the church's common treasury (Acts 5:1–11). See also *Sapphira.*

2. A believer at Damascus who ministered to Paul after the apostle's dramatic conversion (Acts 9:10–18).

ANATHEMA. The transliteration of a Greek word that means "accursed" or "separated." In 1 Cor. 16:22, anathema expresses the concept of excommunication, or a cutting off of the offending party from the church.

ANATHOTH. A village about three miles north of Jerusalem and the birthplace of the prophet Jeremiah (Jer. 1:1).

ANCIENT OF DAYS (ANCIENT ONE). A title for God used by the prophet Daniel to show His ruling authority over the world empires of his day (Dan. 7:9–22). *Ancient One:* NRSV.

ANDREW. One of the twelve disciples of Jesus and brother of Simon Peter. A fisherman from Bethsaida (John 1:44) on the shore of the Sea of Galilee, Andrew was a follower of John the Baptist before he became a disciple of Jesus (John 1:35–40). He was known as one who introduced others to Jesus, including his brother Simon (John 1:41–42), the boy with the loaves and fish (John 6:5–9), and certain Greek

ANGEL APPEARANCES

1. To Hagar during her pregnancy with Ishmael (Gen. 16:7–11)
2. To Lot (Gen. 19:1)
3. To Hagar and Ishmael in the wilderness (Gen. 21:17)
4. To Abraham (Gen. 22:11, 15)
5. To Jacob at Haran (Gen. 28:12; 31:11)
6. To Jacob at Mahanaim (Gen. 32:1)
7. To Moses (Exod. 3:2)
8. To Balaam (Num. 22:22–35)
9. To Gideon (Judg. 6:11–22)
10. To Samson's mother and father (Judg. 13:3–21)
11. To Elijah (1 Kings 19:5, 7; 2 Kings 1:3, 15)
12. To David (1 Chron. 21:16)
13. To Gad (1 Chron. 21:18)
14. To Ornan (1 Chron. 21:20, 27)
15. To Shadrach, Meshach, and Abed-nego (Dan. 3:24–28)
16. To Zechariah (Zech. 1:9)
17. To Joseph in Nazareth (Matt. 1:20)
18. To Joseph in Bethlehem (Matt. 2:13)
19. To Joseph in Egypt (Matt. 2:19)
20. To Zacharias (Luke 1:11–29)
21. To Mary (Luke 1:26–38)
22. To shepherds at Jesus' birth (Luke 2:9–13)
23. To Jesus in the Garden of Gethsemane (Luke 22:43)
24. To Jesus at the resurrection (Matt. 28:2)
25. To women at the tomb (Matt. 28:5)
26. To Mary Magdalene at the empty tomb (John 20:11–12)
27. To the apostles (Acts 5:19)
28. To Philip (Acts 8:26)
29. To Cornelius (Acts 10:3)
30. To Peter in prison (Acts 12:7–11)
31. To Paul (Acts 27:23–24)
32. To John on the isle of Patmos (Rev. 1:1)

citizens who came to talk with Jesus (John 12:20–22). See also *Twelve, The.*

ANGEL. A spiritual or heavenly being whom God sends as His special messenger or helper to human beings. Angels are not the same as God, since He created them (Ps. 148:2, 5). They serve under His direction and obey His commands (Ps. 103:20). Special functions of angels are delivering God's message to human beings (Luke 1:13), protecting God's people (Dan. 3:28), relieving human hunger and thirst (Gen. 21:17–19), and praising the name of the Lord (Ps. 103:20–21).

Before the creation of the world, certain angels revolted against God and were cast out of heaven. The ringleader of this revolt was Satan (Rev. 12:7–9). Another of these fallen angels is Abaddon or Apollyon, "the angel of the bottomless pit" (Rev. 9:11). See also *Angel of the Lord; Gabriel; Michael,* No. 2.

ANGEL OF THE LORD. A heavenly being sent by God to human beings as His personal agent or spokesman. This messenger appeared to Hagar in the wilderness (Gen. 16:7–12), to Moses (Exod. 3:2–3), and to Gideon (Judg. 6:11–12).

ANGELS

Ps. 8:5 thou [God] hast made him [man] a little lower than the *a*
Luke 15:10 joy in the presence of the *a*...over one sinner
1 Cor. 13:1 tongues of men and of *a*, and have not charity
Heb. 13:2 some have entertained *a* unawares

ANGER. A strong feeling of displeasure. God is sometimes pictured as slow to anger (Nah. 1:3). Jesus condemned anger without cause (Matt. 5:22). See also *Wrath.*

Ps. 6:1 Lord, rebuke me not in thine *a*
Ps. 30:5 his [God's] *a* endureth but a moment
Ps. 103:8 Lord is merciful...slow to *a*
Prov. 16:32 He that is slow to *a* is better than the mighty

ANOINT. As his older brothers watch, young David is anointed with oil by the prophet Samuel, marking David as Israel's future king—also known as the "anointed one."

Jer. 4:8 fierce **a** of the Lᴏʀᴅ is not turned back
Mark 3:5 he [Jesus] looked...with **a**...for the hardness of their hearts
Col. 3:8 put off all these; **a**, wrath, malice
Col. 3:21 Fathers, provoke not your children to **a**

ANGUISH. Mental or emotional stress caused by physical pain (2 Sam. 1:9), conflict of soul (Job 7:11), or physical hardships (Exod. 6:9). See also *Affliction; Suffering.*

ANISE (DILL). A common plant of little value used for seasoning food and for medicinal purposes. Jesus condemned those who tithed this insignificant plant but overlooked more important matters, such as judgment, mercy, and faith (Matt. 23:23). *Dill:* ɴɪᴠ, ɴʀsᴠ.

ANNA. An aged prophetess who praised God at Jesus' presentation as an infant in the temple at Jerusalem (Luke 2:36–38).

ANNAS. A Jewish high priest who presided at the trial of Jesus. He questioned Jesus about His disciples and His doctrine. After interrogation, Annas sent Jesus bound to Caiaphas (John 18:12–24). The apostles Peter and John also appeared before Annas (Acts 4:6–7).

ANOINT. To set a person apart for a specific work or task. In O.T. times kings, priests, and prophets were anointed by having oil poured on their heads (Exod. 29:7). Anointing for healing was practiced in N.T. times with the application of oil (Mark 6:13). See also *Oil*.

ANOINT [ED, EST, ING]

Exod. 30:30 *a* Aaron and his sons
Judg. 9:8 trees went forth...to *a* a king
2 Sam. 2:4 they *a'ed* David king over...Judah
Ps. 23:5 thou [God] *a'est* my head with oil
Isa. 61:1 Lord hath *a'ed* me [God's servant]...to proclaim liberty
Mark 14:8 come...to *a* my [Jesus'] body to...burying
John 12:3 Mary...*a'ed* the feet of Jesus
James 5:14 *a'ing* him with oil in the name of the Lord

ANOINTED ONE. See *Jesus Christ; Messiah*.

ANSWER

Ps. 27:7 have mercy...and *a* me
Prov. 15:1 A soft *a* turneth away wrath
Prov. 26:4 *A* not a fool according to his folly
Luke 21:14 not to meditate before what ye shall *a*
1 Pet. 3:15 give an *a* to every man that asketh you a reason

ANT. A small insect cited as an example of hard work (Prov. 6:6–8).

ANTEDILUVIANS. Persons who lived before the great flood. All except Noah were condemned for their wickedness (Gen. 6:5–8). See also *Flood, The*.

ANTHROPOMORPHISMS. Human attributes ascribed to God. For example, God is described as having an arm of deliverance (Exod. 6:6), eyes too pure to look upon evil (Hab. 1:13), and a nature that is provoked to anger and jealousy by idolatry (Ps. 78:58).

ANTICHRIST. The archenemy of Christ and all Christians who will be defeated in the endtime. Rooted in the prophecies of Daniel (Dan. 7:7–8), the Antichrist receives his authority and power from Satan (Rev. 13:4). He is lawless and deceitful (2 Thess. 2:3–12; 2 John 7).

APOCALYPSE. Four horsemen of the apocalypse stampede the earth with death and destruction, as envisioned by John in the book of Revelation.

Characterized as a "beast," the Antichrist will appear before the return of Christ to wage war against Christ and His people (Rev. 13:6–8). However, he will be defeated by Christ and cast into a lake of fire (Rev. 19:20; 20:10). See also *Dragon*.

ANTINOMIANISM. The concept that grace exempts a person from the moral law. According to Paul, this idea is based on an erroneous view of grace (Rom. 6:1–2). Inconsistent with life in the spirit, antinomianism may cause a weak brother to stumble (1 Cor. 8:9). Abuse of Christian liberty violates the spirit of brotherly love (Gal. 5:13–16).

ANTIOCH OF PISIDIA. A city of Pisidia, a district in Asia Minor. Paul preached in the synagogue in this city, where resistance to the gospel caused him to redirect his ministry to the Gentiles (Acts 13:14–51). See also *Pisidia*.

ANTIOCH OF SYRIA. A city in Syria and site of the first Gentile Christian church that sent Paul on his missionary journeys (Acts 13:1–4; 15:35–41). Believers were first called Christians in this city (Acts 11:26). The church at Antioch was troubled by Judaizers who insisted that Gentile believers be circumcised (Acts 15:1–4).

ANTIOCHUS IV EPIPHANES. The cruel ruler of the Seleucid dynasty in Syria (ruled about 175–164 B.C.) whose atrocities led the Jewish people to revolt. He is not mentioned by name in the Bible, but see *Abomination of Desolation; Maccabees*.

ANTIPATRIS. A city between Jerusalem and Caesarea where Paul was lodged as a prisoner while being transported to Caesarea (Acts 23:31).

ANVIL. A block of iron on which metal was shaped by a blacksmith (Isa. 41:7).

APE. A type of monkey, perhaps a baboon or chimpanzee, imported into Judah by King Solomon (1 Kings 10:22).

APOCALYPSE. A Greek word translated "revelation" that refers to an unveiling of the hidden things known only to God (Gal. 1:12). The book of Revelation depicts the end of the present age and the coming of God's future kingdom through symbols, visions, and numbers. This imagery was probably used to hide the message in a time of persecution.

Other examples of apocalyptic writing in the Bible are Dan. 7–12, Isa. 24–27, Ezek. 37–41, Zech. 9–12, Matt. 24, and Mark 13. See also *Revelation of John*.

APOCRYPHA. A group of sacred books written about 150 B.C. to A.D. 70 and included in the Bibles of some religious groups. These books are generally not considered authoritative in the same sense as the universally recognized books of the Bible.

The books of the Apocrypha are Baruch; Bel and the Dragon; the Wisdom of Jesus, the Son of Sirach; the First and Second Books of Esdras; Additions to the Book of Esther; Epistle of Jeremiah; Judith; First and Second Maccabees; Prayer of Azariah and the Song of the Three Young Men; Prayer of Manasseh; Susanna; Tobit; and Wisdom of Solomon.

APOLLOS. A Jewish believer from Alexandria in Egypt who worked with the church at Ephesus after it was founded by Paul. Eloquent and learned, Apollos was a disciple of John the Baptist (Acts 18:24–25). Aquila and Priscilla instructed him in the true doctrines of the faith, and he became an effective church leader, preaching also in Achaia and Corinth with great success (1 Cor. 3:4–6, 22). Paul mentioned Apollos as one whom a faction of the Corinthian church favored (1 Cor. 1:12). See also *Aquila*.

APOLLYON. See *Abaddon*.

APOSTASY. A falling away from the truth or renunciation of one's faith in Christ (Heb. 3:12). Apostasy is caused by Satan (Luke 22:31–32) and influenced by false teachers (2 Tim. 4:3–4). Professed believers may fall away because of persecution (Matt. 13:21) or love of worldly things (2 Tim. 4:10). Apostasy will not occur if believers are grounded in the truth (Eph. 4:13–16) and depend on God's protective armor (Eph. 6:10–18).

APOSTLE. A person personally commissioned by Christ to represent Him (Matt. 10:1–4). The original twelve apostles or disciples were chosen by Jesus after He had prayed all night (Luke 6:12–16). Apostles are persons sent with a special message or commission (John 15:16). Jesus empowered His apostles to cast out evil spirits and to heal (Matt. 10:1).

Paul regarded himself as an apostle because of his encounter with Christ on the Damascus Road and his personal call by Jesus to missionary work (1 Cor. 15:8–10). In Paul's letters, persons who saw the risen Christ and who were specially called by Him are regarded as apostles (1 Cor. 15:5–8). See also *Disciple; Twelve, The*.

APOSTLE [S]
Acts 2:43 wonders and signs were done by the *a's*
Acts 8:1 they [believers] were...scattered...except the *a's*
Rom. 11:13 I [Paul] am the *a* of the Gentiles
1 Cor. 12:29 Are all *a's*? are all prophets?
Eph. 2:20 built upon the foundation of the *a's*
Eph. 4:11 gave some, *a's*; and some, prophets
Heb. 3:1 *A* and High Priest of our profession, Christ Jesus

APOTHECARY (PERFUMER). A person who made perfumes, which were used in worship ceremonies or to anoint the bodies of the dead (Exod. 30:25–35). *Perfumer:* NIV, NRSV.

APPEAR [ED, ETH, ING]
Gen. 1:9 let the dry land *a*: and it was so
Ps. 42:2 when shall I come and *a* before God?
Ps. 102:16 the LORD...shall *a* in his glory
Matt. 17:3 *a'ed*...Moses and Elias talking with him [Jesus]
Mark 16:9 Jesus...*a'ed* first to Mary Magdalene
Mark 16:14 he [Jesus] *a'ed* unto...eleven
Luke 1:11 there *a'ed* unto him [Zacharias] an angel
2 Cor. 5:10 all *a* before the judgment seat of Christ
1 Tim. 6:14 keep this commandment...until the *a'ing* of our Lord
2 Tim. 4:1 judge the quick and the dead at his *a'ing*
James 4:14 It [life] is...a vapour, that *a'eth* for a little time

APPII FORUM (FORUM OF APPIUS). A station on the Roman road known as the Appian Way about forty miles south of Rome. Paul's friends traveled here to meet him as he approached the Roman Empire's capital city (Acts 28:15). *Forum of Appius:* NIV, NRSV.

APPOINT [ED]
Num. 1:50 *a* the Levites over the tabernacle
Ps. 104:19 He [God] *a'ed* the moon for seasons
Luke 10:1 Lord *a'ed* other...and sent them two and two
Acts 6:3 seven men...may *a* over this business
2 Tim. 1:11 I [Paul] am *a'ed* a preacher
Heb. 9:27 *a'ed*...once to die, but after this the judgment

AQUILA. A Christian believer who, with his wife, Priscilla, worked with Paul at Corinth (Acts 18:2) and continued Paul's work at Ephesus (Acts 18:24–26). They were also associated with the church at Rome (Rom. 16:3).

ARABAH. The valley on both sides of the Jordan River that stretches for about 240 miles from Mount Hermon in the north to the Red Sea in the south (Josh. 18:18).

ARABIA. A hot, dry, and sparsely inhabited desert area southeast of Palestine about 1,400 miles long by 800 miles wide. The queen of Sheba came from Arabia, bringing gold and precious jewels to King Solomon (1 Kings 10:2–15).

ARAM. See *Syria*.

ARARAT, MOUNT. A mountainous region where Noah's ark landed (Gen. 8:4). The location of this mountain is uncertain. Several unsuccessful expeditions to find the ark on Mount Urartu in eastern Armenia (modern Turkey) have been undertaken. See also *Ark, Noah's*.

ARAUNAH/ORNAN. A Jebusite from whom David bought a threshing floor as a place to build an altar (2 Sam. 24:16–24). This plot of ground was the site on which Solomon's temple was built in Jerusalem in later years (2 Chron. 3:1). *Ornan:* 1 Chron. 21:15; 2 Chron. 3:1.

ARBA. The father of Anak and ancestor of a tribe of giants known as the Anakims or Anakim (Josh. 14:15). See also *Anakims*.

ARCHAEOLOGY OF THE BIBLE. The study of remains of past civilizations in an attempt to understand the life and times of biblical peoples. Archaeology involves scientific excavations, examination, and publication by museums and laboratories. Fragments of ancient writings as well as bones, metal, stone, and wood are studied. The focus area for N.T. archaeology largely coincides with the ancient Roman Empire. For the O.T. period, the focus of archaeology includes Palestine (Canaan), Syria, Egypt, the Mesopotamian Valley, and Persia (modern Iran).

Major methods of establishing dates for archaeological finds are (1) examination of the layers of soil in mounds or "tells" (stratigraphy), (2) the study of pottery materials and designs (typology), and (3) measurement of the

ARARAT, MOUNT. Snow-topped Mount Ararat rises nearly seventeen thousand feet, higher than any other mountain in the Ararat range. Neighboring Little Ararat rises about thirteen thousand feet.

radioactivity of an object's carbon content (radiocarbon dating).

Archaeology helps us understand the Bible better by revealing what life in biblical times was like, throwing light on obscure passages of Scripture, and helping us appreciate the historical setting of the Bible. For example, exploration of the city of Ur revealed that the home of Abraham was a thriving city of industry and idolatry in O.T. times. The Dead Sea Scrolls, the greatest manuscript discovery of modern times, includes a complete scroll of the book of Isaiah and fragments of most of the other O.T. books. See also *Dead Sea Scrolls*.

ARCHANGEL. A chief angel or perhaps a spiritual being next in rank above an angel. In the end times Michael the archangel will contend with Satan (Jude 9) and proclaim the Lord's return (1 Thess. 4:16). See also *Angel; Michael*, No. 2.

ARCHELAUS. See *Herod*, No. 2.

ARCHEVITES. Foreign colonists who settled in Samaria after the Northern Kingdom fell to Assyria (Ezra 4:9–16). See also *Samaritan*.

ARCTURUS. A constellation of stars cited as evidence of God's sovereignty (Job 9:9).

AREOPAGUS. A council of Greek philosophers in Athens before whom Paul appeared to defend his claims about Jesus and His resurrection (Acts 17:19). The hill on which these philosophers met was apparently called *Mars' hill* (Acts 17:22). See also *Athens*.

ARGOB. A district of Bashan included in Solomon's kingdom. Argob contained sixty fortified cities (1 Kings 4:13).

ARIEL. A symbolic name for the city of Jerusalem, meaning "lion of God" (Isa. 29:1–2, 7). See also *Jerusalem*.

ARIMATHAEA (ARIMATHEA). A city in the Judean hills about five miles northwest of Jerusalem and home of the Joseph who buried the body of Jesus in his own tomb (John 19:38). *Arimathea:* NIV, NRSV. See also *Joseph*, No. 3.

ARISE
Josh. 1:2 now...*a*, go over this Jordan
Prov. 31:28 children *a* up, and call her blessed
Isa. 60:1 *A*, shine; for thy light is come
Mal. 4:2 Sun of righteousness *a* with healing in his wings
Matt. 24:24 shall *a* false Christs
Acts 11:7 *A*, Peter; slay and eat
Acts 20:30 men *a*, speaking perverse things

ARISTARCHUS. A Christian who accompanied Paul on the third missionary journey (Acts 20:4). Later he traveled with Paul to Rome (Acts 27:2).

ARK, NOAH'S. A large wooden ship in which Noah and his family and selected animals were delivered by the Lord. The ark was necessary because God wished to preserve righteous Noah and his family while destroying the rest of humankind because of their wickedness.

Noah built the ark according to God's directions (Gen. 6:14–16). Then he and his family entered the ark, along with a pair of all living creatures (Gen. 6:19–20). Rain fell for forty days (Gen. 7:17), and water covered the earth for 150 days (Gen. 7:24).

Finally, God sent a wind to restrain the water (Gen. 8:1–3) and the ark rested on a mountain in Ararat (Gen. 8:4). Noah and his passengers were delivered safely to dry land (Gen. 8:18–19). Upon leaving the ark, Noah built an altar and offered sacrifices to God for their deliverance. God promised Noah that the

ARK, NOAH'S. Noah's ark stretched longer than a football field, end zones included. Looking a bit like a floating warehouse, this covered barge—for about one wet year—became home to Noah's family and pairs of land animals.

earth would not be destroyed by water again (Gen. 8:20–22).

The ark is symbolic of baptism (1 Pet. 3:20–21) and God's preserving grace (Luke 17:26–27; Heb. 11:7). See also *Ararat, Mount; Noah.*

ARK OF THE COVENANT/ARK OF THE TESTIMONY. A wooden chest containing two stone tablets on which the Ten Commandments were inscribed. The ark symbolized God's presence to the nation of Israel (Deut. 10:3–4). It was taken into battle by the Israelites (1 Sam. 4:4–5) and captured by the Philistines (1 Sam. 4:10–11).

After its return to Israel (1 Sam. 6:1–15), the ark was later placed in the temple in Jerusalem (1 Kings 8:1–9). It was probably carried away by King Nebuchadnezzar of Babylonia along with other treasures after the fall of Jerusalem in 587 B.C. (2 Chron. 36:7, 18). *Ark of the Testimony:* Exod. 25:22.

ARMAGEDDON. A Greek word for the valley between Mount Carmel and the city of Jezreel. This valley was the site of many battles in Bible times due to its strategic location on two major trade routes. Because of its bloody history, this region became a symbol of the final conflict between God and the forces of evil, and of God's ultimate victory (Rev. 16:16). See also *Megiddo.*

ARMENIA. A mountainous land north of Syria formerly known as Ararat (Isa. 37:38). See also *Ararat, Mount.*

ARMOUR. Defensive covering used as protection during battle. The word is also symbolic of God's spiritual protection (Eph. 6:11).

ARMOURBEARER. An aide or attendant who carried the armor and weapons of a military officer or warrior of high rank (Judg. 9:54).

ARNON. A swift river that runs through the mountains east of the Jordan River and into the Dead Sea (Josh. 12:1).

AROMATIC CANE. See *Calamus.*

ARPHAXAD. A son of Shem born after the great flood (Gen. 11:10–13).

ARROW. A projectile shot from a bow. This word is also used symbolically to denote a calamity inflicted by God (Job 6:4) or to signify something injurious, such as false testimony (Prov. 25:18).

ARTAXERXES I. The successor of Cyrus as king of Persia and the king in whose court Ezra and Nehemiah served (Ezra 7:1, 7). About 458 B.C. Artaxerxes authorized Ezra to lead a large

A

group of Jews back to Jerusalem for resettlement (Ezra 7). About thirteen years later he allowed Nehemiah to return to rebuild the walls of Jerusalem (Neh. 2:1–10; 13:6). See also *Ezra; Nehemiah.*

ARTEMIS. See *Diana.*

ARTIFICER. A workman especially skilled in metalworking. Solomon hired craftsmen from Tyre with these skills to help build the temple in Jerusalem (2 Chron. 2:3, 7). See also *Smith.*

ASA. Third king of Judah (reigned about 911–869 B.C.) who led in a national religious revival. He destroyed the places of idol worship (2 Chron. 14:2–5) and fortified Judah to usher in a period of peace (2 Chron. 14:6–8). Reproved by Hanani the prophet for not relying on the Lord, he died from a foot disease (2 Chron. 16:7–14).

ASAHEL. David's nephew and a captain in his army (1 Chron. 27:7). Asahel was killed by Abner, commander in Saul's army (2 Sam. 2:17–23).

ASAPH. A Levite choir leader and writer of psalms mentioned in the titles of Pss. 50 and 73–83.

ASCEND [ED, ING]
Ps. 24:3 who shall *a* into the hill of the LORD
Ps. 68:18 hast *a'ed* on high...led captivity captive
John 1:51 angels of God *a'ing*...upon the Son of man
John 20:17 I [Jesus] am not yet *a'ed* to my Father

ASCENSION OF CHRIST. Jesus' return to His Father after His crucifixion and resurrection (Luke 24:50–51). Foretold in the O.T. (Ps. 68:18), the ascension occurred forty days after the Resurrection (Acts 1:2–11). Christ

will return to earth as surely as He ascended to heaven (Acts 1:11).

ASENATH. The Egyptian wife of Joseph and mother of Manasseh and Ephraim (Gen. 46:20). The pharaoh of Egypt approved this union and probably arranged the marriage (Gen. 41:45). See also *Joseph,* No. 1.

ASHAMED
Gen. 2:25 both [Adam and Eve] naked...and were not *a*
Mark 8:38 of him also shall the Son of man be *a*
Rom. 1:16 I [Paul] am not *a* of the gospel
2 Tim. 2:15 workman that needeth not to be *a*
1 John 2:28 not be *a* before him [Jesus] at his coming

ASHDOD. A major Philistine city (Josh. 13:3) and center of Dagon worship (1 Sam. 5:1–7). It was called Azotus in N.T. times (Acts 8:40). See also *Dagon; Philistines.*

ASHER/ASER. A son of Jacob by Zilpah (Gen. 30:12–13) and ancestor of one of the twelve tribes of Israel (Deut. 33:24). Asher's tribe settled in northern Canaan. *Aser:* Greek form (Luke 2:36). See also *Tribes of Israel.*

ASHES. Residue from burning. A symbol of mourning and repentance, ashes were also used for purification (Heb. 9:13).

ASHIMA. A false god worshiped by foreign colonists who settled in Samaria after the fall of the Northern Kingdom to Assyria (2 Kings 17:30).

ASHKELON/ASKELON. One of five major cities of the Philistines (Josh. 13:3) and a pagan center denounced by the prophet Amos (Amos 1:8). *Askelon:* Judg. 1:18. See also *Philistines.*

ASHTAROTH/ASHTORETH. A pagan fertility goddess worshiped by the Philistines and also by the Israelites soon after the death of

ASCENSION OF CHRIST. Jesus ascended to heaven from this very spot on top of the Mount of Olives, according to an ancient tradition. In this tiny chapel—the Dome of the Ascension—rests a small rock with an indentation said to have been made by Christ's departure. Once a church, this memorial was captured by Muslims in the 1100s and remains in their control.

Joshua (Judg. 2:13). Her symbol was an ever-green tree, a pole, or a pillar near a pagan altar. *Ashtaroth* and *Ashtoreth* are plural forms of her name (1 Sam. 7:4; 1 Kings 11:33). Her name in the singular form was *Asherah*.

ASIA. A Roman province in western Asia Minor that included the cities of Ephesus, Smyrna, and Pergamos—the first three cities mentioned in the book of Revelation (Rev. 1:11; 2:1–17). At first forbidden by a vision to enter Asia (Acts 16:6), Paul later did extensive evangelistic work in this province, and his message was well received (Acts 19:10).

ASK
Matt. 6:8 Father knoweth what...ye...need...before ye *a*
Matt. 21:22 shall *a*...believing, ye shall receive
Luke 11:13 Your...Father give the Holy Spirit to them that *a* him
John 16:24 *a*, and ye shall receive
Eph. 3:20 abundantly above all that we *a*
James 1:5 lack wisdom, let him *a* of God
James 4:2 ye have not, because ye *a* not

ASKELON. See *Ashkelon*.

ASNAPPER (ASHURBANIPAL, OSNAP-PAR). The last of the great kings of Assyria (reigned about 668–626 B.C.), called the "great and noble" (Ezra 4:10). Asnapper required King Manasseh of Judah to kiss his feet and pay tribute to him. This is probably the same king as the Ashurbanipal of Assyrian history. *Ashurbanipal:* NIV; *Osnappar:* NRSV. See also *Assyria*.

ASP. A deadly snake of the cobra variety that is symbolic of man's evil nature (Isa. 11:8). This is probably the same snake as the *adder* and *viper*.

ASS. A donkey; a common beast of burden in Bible times (Gen. 22:3). Jesus rode a young donkey rather than a prancing warhorse into Jerusalem to symbolize His humble servanthood

and the spiritual nature of His kingdom (Luke 19:30–35). See also *Foal*.

ASSEMBLY. A gathering or congregation of people for worship. God directed Moses to assemble the Israelites at the door of the tabernacle (Num. 10:2–3). The psalmist gathered with God's people for worship and praise (Ps. 111:1). Assembling for worship is enjoined for all Christians (Heb. 10:25). See also *Congregation; Church*.

ASSHUR. A son of Shem and ancestor of the Assyrians (Gen. 10:22). See also *Assyria*.

ASSUR. See *Assyria*.

ASSURANCE. Complete confidence in God's promises. Our spiritual security is based on our adoption as God's children (Eph. 1:4–5). Believers are secure in the grip of the Father and Son (John 10:28–30).

ASSYRIA/ASSHUR/ASSUR. An ancient kingdom between the Tigris and Euphrates rivers that became the dominant power in the ancient world from about 900 to 700 B.C. The aggressive and warlike Assyrians were known for their cruelty in warfare, often cutting off their victims' hands or heads and impaling them on stakes. For this cruelty and their pagan worship, they were soundly condemned by the O.T. prophets (Isa. 10:5; Ezek. 16:28; Hosea 8:9).

The region that developed into Assyria was originally settled by the hunter Nimrod, a descendant of Noah (Gen. 10:8–12). An early name for Assyria was *Asshur*, after a son of Shem who was connected with their early history (Gen. 10:11).

About 722 B.C. King Shalmaneser of Assyria overthrew the Northern Kingdom of Israel, enslaved many of its inhabitants, and resettled the region with foreigners (2 Kings 18:10–11). Several years later Sennacherib invaded Judah (2 Kings 18:13) and exacted tribute from King Hezekiah (2 Kings 18:14–16). *Assur:* Ezra 4:2. See also *Asshur; Nineveh.*

ASTROLOGER. A person who studied the stars in an attempt to foretell the future—a practice especially popular among the pagan Babylonians (Isa. 47:13). See also *Wise Men.*

ASWAN. See *Sinim.*

ATHALIAH. The daughter of Ahab and Jezebel who murdered the royal heirs of Judah and claimed the throne (reigned as queen of Judah about 841–835 B.C.; 2 Kings 11).

ATHEISM. The denial of God's existence. This defiant attitude is illustrated by the Egyptian pharaoh's refusal to release the Hebrew slaves (Exod. 5:2). The psalmist declared that disbelief in God is a characteristic of the foolish (Ps. 14:1). God's clear revelation of His nature and His intent for humankind leaves unbelievers without excuse (Rom. 1:18–25). See also *Infidel; Unbelief.*

ATHENS. The capital city of ancient Greece where Paul debated with the philosophers about Christ and Christianity during the second missionary journey. Known as the center of Greek art, literature, and politics, Athens also struck Paul because of its idolatry, with shrines erected to numerous deities, including the "unknown god" (Acts 17:23). See also *Areopagus.*

8
B
3

ATONEMENT. Reconciliation of God and man through sacrifice (Rom. 5:11). In O.T.

ATHENS. A temple to the Greek goddess Athena towers above the Acropolis hilltop in Athens. This temple was more than four hundred years old by the time Paul arrived with his message about the "Unknown God."

times such reconciliation was accomplished through animal sacrifices symbolic of the people's repentance. But true reconciliation is made possible by Christ's atoning death and resurrection (Rom. 5:1; Eph. 1:7). Man's justification in God's sight is made possible by repentance and faith (Eph. 2:8).

God's righteousness is imparted through Christ's sacrifice (2 Cor. 5:21). His atonement is the foundation for genuine peace (Eph. 2:13–16). All who are redeemed through their acceptance by faith of the sacrifice of Christ are called as ministers of reconciliation (2 Cor. 5:18–21). See also *Atonement, Day of; Justification; Reconciliation.*

ATONEMENT, DAY OF. A Jewish holy day (Yom Kippur) on which atonement was made for all Israel (Lev. 16:29–30; 23:27–28). Preceded by special sabbaths (Lev. 23:24) and fasting, this event recognized man's inability to make atonement for himself. On this day the Jewish high priest made atonement first for himself and then for the sins of the people by sprinkling the blood of a sacrificial animal on the altar (Lev. 16:12–15). The scapegoat, representing the sins of the people, was released into the wilderness to symbolize pardon (Lev. 16:21–23). See also *Atonement; Scapegoat.*

A SUPERIOR ATONEMENT

The Day of Atonement was a time when all the people of Israel sought atonement for their sins (Lev. 16). The writer of Hebrews in the New Testament declared that this ritual is no longer necessary because Christ laid down His life as a permanent, once-for-all sacrifice to make atonement for our sins (Heb. 10:1–10).

ATTAIN [ED]
Ps. 139:6 knowledge is too wonderful...I cannot *a*...it
Phil. 3:12 as though I [Paul] had already *a'ed*
Phil. 3:16 already *a'ed*, let us walk by the same rule

AUGUSTUS. A title of honor, meaning "his reverence," bestowed upon the emperors of the Roman Empire (Luke 2:1). See also *Caesar; Roman Empire.*

AUL. See *Awl.*

AUTHORITY
Prov. 29:2 righteous are in *a*, the people rejoice
Matt. 8:9 a man under *a*, having soldiers under me
Mark 1:22 he [Jesus] taught them as one that had *a*
Luke 9:1 he [Jesus]...gave them...*a* over all devils

AUTUMN RAIN. See *Former Rain.*

AVA. An Assyrian city whose citizens settled in Samaria after the Northern Kingdom fell to Assyria (2 Kings 17:24–31). This is perhaps the same place as Ahava. See also *Ahava; Samaritan.*

AVEN. See *On, No. 2.*

AVENGER OF BLOOD. The closest of kin to a slain person who was expected to kill the slayer. Cain feared the avenging relatives of his brother after he murdered Abel (Gen. 4:14). Six cities of refuge were established throughout Israel to provide a haven for those who had accidentally taken a human life (Num. 35:12). Jesus counseled against such vengeance, calling for love of one's enemies and unlimited forgiveness instead (Matt. 5:43–44). See also *Cities of Refuge; Manslayer.*

AWL/AUL. A tool used by carpenters and leather workers to punch holes. *Aul:* Exod. 21:6; Deut. 15:17.

AXE. A tool for cutting wood (Deut. 19:5).

AZARIAH

1. Another name for Ahaziah, king of Judah. See *Ahaziah*, No. 2.

2. A prophet who encouraged King Asa of Judah to destroy all idols in the land (2 Chron. 15:1–8).

3. The Hebrew name of Abed-nego. See *Abed-nego.*

4. Another name for Uzziah, king of Judah. See *Uzziah.*

AZAZEL. See *Scapegoat.*

AZOTUS. See *Ashdod.*

AZZAH. See *Gaza.*

B

BAAL. *Baal, the Canaanite god of rain and fertile land, holds a spear that resembles lightning or a blossoming branch.*

BAAL/BAALIM. The chief Canaanite god (Judg. 2:13) who, as the god of rain, was thought to provide fertility for crops and livestock. Baal worship was associated with immorality (Hosea 9:10) and child sacrifice (Jer. 19:5)—pagan rituals considered especially offensive to the one true God of the Israelites.

During their history, the Hebrew people often committed idolatry by worshiping this god of their Canaanite neighbors. The prophet Elijah denounced the prophets of Baal, and the God of Israel won a decisive victory over this pagan god on Mount Carmel (1 Kings 18:17–40). *Baalim:* plural form (1 Sam. 12:10).

BAALAH. See *Kirjath-jearim.*

BAAL-BERITH. A name under which the pagan Canaanite god Baal was worshiped at Shechem in the time of the judges (Judg. 9:4). See also *Baal.*

BAALIM. See *Baal.*

BAAL-PEOR. A local manifestation of the pagan Canaanite god Baal. Baal-peor was worshiped by the Moabites (Deut. 4:3). See also *Baal.*

BAAL-PERAZIM/PERAZIM. A place in central Palestine where David defeated the Philistines (2 Sam. 5:18–20). *Perazim:* Isa. 28:21.

BAAL-ZEBUB/BEELZEBUB. A name under which the pagan Canaanite god Baal was worshiped by the Philistines at Ekron (2 Kings 1:2). The N.T. form of this name was *Beelzebub*, used as a title for Satan, meaning "prince of devils" (Matt. 12:26–27).

BAASHA. A king of the Northern Kingdom (reigned about 909–886 B.C.) who gained the throne by killing King Jeroboam's heirs (1 Kings 15:16–30).

BABEL, TOWER OF. A tall structure known as a ziggurat built on the plain of Shinar in ancient Babylonia as a show of human pride and vanity. God confused the language of the builders so they could not communicate. After they abandoned the project, they were scattered abroad (Gen. 11:1–9). See also *Ziggurat*.

BABOON. See *Peacock*.

BABYLON. The capital city of the Babylonian Empire, built by Nimrod the hunter (Gen. 10:9–10). Site of the tower of Babel, Babylon was a magnificent city-state that attained its greatest power under Nebuchadnezzar (Dan. 4:1–3, 30). The Jewish people were taken to Babylon as captives after the fall of Jerusalem in 587 B.C. (2 Chron. 36:5–21).

BABYLONIA/SHESHACH/SHINAR/CHALDEA. A powerful nation in Mesopotamia that carried the Jewish people into exile about 587 B.C. Also called *Sheshach* (Jer. 25:26), *Shinar* (Isa. 11:11), and the land of the *Chaldeans* (Ezek. 12:13), Babylonia reached the zenith of its power under Nebuchadnezzar (reigned about 605–560 B.C.). The nation was a center of idolatry dominated by worship of Merodach, the Babylonian god of war (Jer. 50:2).

After holding the Jewish people captive for many years, the Babylonians were defeated by the Persians about 539 B.C., fulfilling the prophecies of Isaiah and Jeremiah (Isa. 14:22; Jer. 50:9). See also *Mesopotamia; Sumer.*

BABYLONISH GARMENT. An expensive embroidered robe kept by Achan as part of the spoils of war after the battle of Jericho (Josh. 7:21).

BACKBITING. The act of reviling, slandering, or speaking spitefully of others—behavior considered unworthy of a Christian (2 Cor. 12:20).

BACKSLIDING. The act of turning from God after conversion. The causes of backsliding are spiritual blindness (2 Pet. 1:9), persecution (Matt. 13:20–21), or love of material things (1 Tim. 6:10). This sin separates the backslider from God's blessings (Isa. 59:2). But confession and repentance will bring God's forgiveness (1 John 1:9) and restoration (Ps. 51).

BACKSLIDING [S]
Jer. 3:14 Turn, O *b* children, saith the LORD
Jer. 14:7 our *b's* are many; we have sinned
Hosea 4:16 Israel slideth back as a *b* heifer
Hosea 14:4 I [God] will heal their *b*

BADGER (HIDES OF SEA COWS). An animal whose skins were used as the covering for the tabernacle (Exod. 25:5). *Hides of sea cows:* NIV. See also *Coney.*

BAG. See *Scrip.*

BALAAM. A soothsayer or magician hired by the king of Moab to curse the Israelites to drive them out of his territory. Prevented from doing so by an angel, Balaam blessed the Israelites instead (Num. 22–24). See also *Balak.*

B

BALAK/BALAC. The king of Moab who hired Balaam the soothsayer to curse the Hebrews as they crossed his territory. His scheme failed when God forced Balaam to bless them instead (Num. 22–24). *Balac:* Greek form (Rev. 2:14). See also *Balaam.*

BALANCE (SCALES). An instrument with matched weights, used by merchants to weigh money or food in business transactions (Prov. 11:1). *Scales:* NIV.

BALANCE [S]
Lev. 19:36 Just **b's,** just weights, a just ephah
Job 31:6 Let me be weighed in an even **b**
Dan. 5:27 Thou [Belshazzar] art weighed in the **b's**

BALM OF GILEAD. An aromatic gum or resin exported from Gilead in Arabia. It apparently was used as an incense and for medicinal purposes (Jer. 8:22).

BALSAM. See *Mulberry.*

BAND [S]
Jer. 2:20 I [God] have...burst thy **b's**
Hos. 11:4 I [God] drew them...with **b's** of love
John 18:12 the **b**...took Jesus, and bound him
Acts 10:1 Cornelius...of the **b** called...Italian **b**

BANNER. See *Standard.*

BANQUET. An elaborate and sumptuous meal, usually served on a special occasion. Esther exposed the plot of Haman to destroy the Jews during a banquet (Esther 7:1).

BAPTISM. A rite signifying a believer's cleansing from sin through Christ's atoning death. John the Baptist baptized converts to signify their repentance (Matt. 3:6–8). Jesus was baptized by John in the Jordan River to fulfill all righteousness and to set an example for us (Matt. 3:15).

In the N.T. church, Gentiles who received the Holy Spirit were promptly baptized (Acts 10:44–48). Christian baptism memorializes the death, burial, and resurrection of

BAPTISM. A minister visiting the Holy Land baptizes a fellow visitor in the Jordan River. Many Christian pilgrims follow the footsteps of Jesus by being baptized in the same river where he was baptized by John the Baptist.

Christ (Rom. 6:3–5). For the believer, baptism is a testimony of faith and a pledge to "walk in newness of life" with Jesus Christ (Rom. 6:4).

Matt. 20:22 the *b* that I [Jesus] am baptized with
Matt. 21:25 The *b* of John, whence was it
Mark 1:4 John did...preach the *b* of repentance
Eph. 4:5 One Lord, one faith, one *b*
Col. 2:12 Buried with him [Jesus] in *b*
1 Pet. 3:21 The like figure...*b* doth...save us

BAPTIZE [D, ING]

Matt. 3:11 he [Jesus] shall *b* you with the Holy Ghost
Matt. 3:13 Jesus... to be *b'd* of him [John]
Matt. 28:19 teach all nations, *b'ing* them
John 4:1 Jesus made and *b'ed* more disciples than John
Acts 2:38 Repent, and be *b'd*...in the name of Jesus
Acts 8:12 they [the Samaritans] were *b'd*
Acts 8:36 what doth hinder me [the eunuch] to be *b'd*
Acts 9:18 he [Paul] received sight...arose, and was *b'd*
Acts 16:15 she [Lydia] was *b'd*, and her household
Acts 16:33 he [Philippian jailer]...was *b'd*
Acts 22:16 arise, and be *b'd*, and wash away thy sins
Rom. 6:3 into Jesus Christ were *b'd* into his death
1 Cor. 12:13 by one Spirit are we all *b'd* into one body
Gal. 3:27 many of you as have been *b'd* into Christ

BARABBAS. A notorious prisoner, guilty of murder and insurrection, at the time when Jesus appeared before Pilate (John 18:40). Incited by Jewish leaders, the mob demanded that Barabbas be released instead of Jesus (Mark 15:9–11).

BARAK. A general under Deborah and judge of Israel. He and Deborah were victorious against the Canaanites (Judg. 4). See also *Deborah*.

BARBARIAN. A word meaning "uncivilized" and a title used by the Greeks to designate foreigners, or citizens of other nations besides Greece (Rom. 1:14).

BAR-JESUS/ELYMAS. A sorcerer and false prophet who opposed Paul and Silas at Paphos during the first missionary journey (Acts 13:6–12). *Elymas:* Acts 13:8.

BAR-JONA. The surname of the apostle Peter, meaning "son of Jonah" (Matt. 16:17). See *Simon*, No. 1.

BARLEY. A grain similar to oats, used as food for livestock (1 Kings 4:28) and also ground into bread by poor people (John 6:13).

BARNABAS/JOSES. A Jewish Christian who befriended Paul after Paul's conversion, introduced the apostle to the Jerusalem church (Acts 9:27), and traveled with Paul during the first missionary journey (Acts 11:22–26). *Joses:* Acts 4:36.

BARRACKS. See *Castle*.

BARREN. Unable to bear children. In the O.T., barrenness was seen as a sign of God's judgment (1 Sam. 1:5–7). Women in the Bible who had this problem—but who were eventually blessed with children—were Sarah (Gen. 11:30), Rachel (Gen. 29:31), Hannah (1 Sam. 1:5), and Elisabeth (Luke 1:7). See also *Children; Womb*.

BARRIER. See *Middle Wall of Partition*.

BARTHOLOMEW. One of the twelve apostles of Jesus (Mark 3:18). Some scholars believe he is the same person as Nathanael (John 1:45–49). See also *Twelve, The*.

BARTIMAEUS. A blind beggar healed by Jesus on the road to Jericho (Mark 10:46–52).

B

2
E
2

BARUCH. The friend and scribe of the prophet Jeremiah. Baruch recorded Jeremiah's messages warning of the impending defeat of the nation of Judah (Jer. 36:4–32). Like Jeremiah, he fled to Egypt after the fall of Jerusalem (Jer. 43:1–7). See also *Jeremiah.*

BARZILLAI. An aged friend of David who helped the king during his flight from Absalom (2 Sam. 17:27–29).

BASHAN. A fertile plain east of the Jordan River conquered by the Israelites (Num. 21:33) and allotted to the half-tribe of Manasseh (Josh. 13:29–30).

BASKET [S]
Jer. 24:2 One *b* had very good figs
Amos 8:1 behold a *b* of summer fruit
Matt. 14:20 fragments that remained twelve *b's* full
Acts 9:25 disciples...let him [Paul] down...in a *b*

BASON (BASIN, BOWL). A container used in the home (2 Sam. 17:28) and as a ceremonial vessel in the temple or tabernacle (Exod. 24:6). *Basin:* NRSV; *bowl:* NIV. See also *Bowl; Laver.*

BAT. A nocturnal flying mammal, considered unclean by the Hebrews (Lev. 11:19).

BATH. The standard Hebrew measure for liquids, equivalent to about six gallons (1 Kings 7:26).

BATHING. A washing of the body to make it ceremonially clean and pure (Lev. 15:5, 16). See also *Clean; Wash.*

BATH-SHEBA/BATH-SHUA. The wife of Uriah who committed adultery with David and became his wife (2 Sam. 11:2–27). Because of their sin, Bath-sheba's first child died. She later gave birth to four sons, including Solomon,

who succeeded David as king. *Bath-shua:* 1 Chron. 3:5. See also *David; Solomon.*

BATTLEMENT (PARAPET). A railing around the roof of a house, required by law to prevent falls (Deut. 22:8). *Parapet:* NIV, NRSV.

BDELLIUM. A word that probably refers to a fragrant gum resin (Num. 11:7) as well as a precious stone (Gen. 2:12).

BEAR. A large animal similar to our brown bear that was common in Palestine in Bible times. David killed a bear to protect his father's sheep (1 Sam. 17:34–37).

BEAR [ETH, ING]
Gen. 17:19 Sarah thy [Abraham's] wife shall *b*...a son
Exod. 20:16 not *b* false witness against thy neighbour
Deut. 32:11 eagle...*b'eth* them [her young] on her wings
Ps. 91:12 *b* thee up...lest thou dash thy foot against a stone
Isa. 7:14 virgin shall...*b* a son...Immanuel
Ezek. 18:20 father *b*...iniquity of the son
Matt. 3:11 whose [Jesus'] shoes I [John the Baptist] am not worthy to *b*
Mark 15:21 compel one Simon...to *b* his [Jesus'] cross
Luke 4:11 they [angels] shall *b* thee [Jesus] up
Luke 13:9 if it *b* fruit, well: and if not...cut it down
Luke 14:27 doth not *b* his cross...cannot be my disciple
John 1:7 came for a witness, to *b* witness of the Light
John 10:25 works that I [Jesus] do...*b* witness of me
John 16:12 many things to say...but ye cannot *b* them
Rom. 8:16 Spirit itself *b'eth* witness with our spirit
Rom. 15:1 strong...*b* the infirmities of the weak
1 Cor. 13:7 [charity] *b'eth* all things
Gal. 6:2 *B* ye one another's burdens
Gal. 6:17 I [Paul] *b* in my body the marks of the Lord Jesus
Heb. 9:28 Christ was once offered to *b* the sins of many
Heb. 13:13 Let us go forth...*b'ing* his [Jesus'] reproach

BEARD. Trimmed and groomed facial hair— a mark of pride among Jewish men. To shave one's beard or pull out the hair was a gesture of anguish and grief (Jer. 48:37–38).

BEAT [ETH]

Isa. 2:4 shall *b* their swords into plowshares
Isa. 3:15 ye *b* my [God's] people to pieces
Joel 3:10 *B* your plowshares into swords
Matt. 7:25 winds...*b* upon that house
Acts 16:22 commanded to *b* them [Paul and Silas]
1 Cor. 9:26 so fight I [Paul], not as one that *b'eth*
    the air

BEATITUDES. Pronouncements of blessing at the beginning of Jesus' Sermon on the Mount. God's special reward is promised to those who recognize their spiritual need (Matt. 5:3); those who mourn (5:4); those who are humble (5:5), obedient (5:6), merciful (5:7), and pure in heart (5:8); those who practice peacemaking (5:9); and those who are persecuted for Jesus' sake (5:10–11). See also *Sermon on the Mount.*

BEAUTIFUL

1 Sam. 16:12 he [David] was...of a *b* countenance
2 Sam. 11:2 David...saw a woman...very *b*
Eccles. 3:11 He [God] hath made every thing *b*
Matt. 23:27 ye [scribes and Pharisees]...appear *b*
    outward
Rom. 10:15 as it is written, How *b* are the feet of
    them

BEATITUDES. From the Chapel of the Beatitudes near the Sea of Galilee, visitors can look down over a sloping hillside where tradition says Jesus preached his famous Sermon on the Mount.

BEAUTIFUL GATE. A gate that served as one of the main entrances into the temple area in Jerusalem in N.T. times (Acts 3:2).

BEDAN. A minor judge of Israel who served after Gideon and before Jephthah. His name is not recorded in the book of Judges (1 Sam. 12:11). See also *Judges of Israel.*

BEDCHAMBER (BEDROOM). The sleeping room in houses of Bible times (2 Sam. 4:7). *Bedroom:* NIV.

BEELZEBUB (BEELZEBUL). *Beelzebul:* NRSV; see *Baal-zebub.*

BEER-SHEBA. The name of a well in southern Judah that Abraham and Abimelech dug to seal their covenant of friendship (Gen. 21:31). The name was also applied to the surrounding wilderness (Gen. 21:14) and an important city that grew up around the well (Gen. 26:32–33; Judg. 20:1). See also *Well.*

BEGAN

Gen. 6:1 men *b* to multiply on...the earth
Matt. 4:17 Jesus *b* to preach, and to say, Repent
Mark 6:7 he [Jesus] called...the twelve...*b* to send them forth
Mark 8:31 he [Jesus] *b* to teach them...Son of man must suffer
Luke 14:18 they all with one consent *b* to make excuse
Luke 19:45 he [Jesus]...*b* to cast out them that sold
John 13:5 he [Jesus]...*b* to wash the disciples' feet

BEGGAR. One who lives by handouts (Luke 16:3). The Israelites were commanded by God to care for the poor (Deut. 15:7–11). See also *Alms; Poor.*

BEGINNING

Gen. 1:1 the *b* God created the heaven
Job 42:12 Lord blessed the latter end of Job more than his *b*
Ps. 111:10 The fear of the Lord is the *b* of wisdom
Eccles. 7:8 Better...end of a thing than the *b*
Matt. 20:8 give them their hire, *b* from the last
John 1:1 In the *b* was the Word
Col. 1:18 he [Jesus] is the *b*, the firstborn from the dead
2 Thess. 2:13 God hath from the *b* chosen you to salvation
Heb. 7:3 [Melchisedec] having neither *b* of days
2 Pet. 3:4 all things continue as they were from the *b*
1 John 1:1 That which was from the *b*...we have heard
Rev. 22:13 Alpha and Omega, the *b* and the end

BEGOTTEN. A word that describes Christ as the only and unique Son of His heavenly Father (John 3:16–18).

BEHAVE [D]

1 Sam. 18:14 David *b'd* himself wisely
1 Cor. 13:5 [charity] doth not *b* itself unseemly
2 Thess. 3:7 we *b'd* not ourselves disorderly

BEHEADING. To cut off a person's head; a form of execution or capital punishment. John the Baptist was put to death in this manner (Matt. 14:10).

BEHEMOTH. A large beast mentioned by Job (Job 40:15–24), probably referring to the elephant or the hippopotamus.

BEHIND

Matt. 16:23 he [Jesus]...said unto Peter, Get thee *b* me
Phil. 3:13 forgetting those things which are *b*
Col. 1:24 fill up that which is *b* of the afflictions of Christ
Rev. 1:10 I was in the Spirit...and heard *b* me a great voice

BEHOLD [EST, ING]

Ps. 119:18 *b* wondrous things out of thy [God's] law
Prov. 15:3 eyes of the Lord...*b'ing* the evil and the good
Isa. 7:14 *B*, a virgin shall conceive, and bear a son
Luke 1:38 Mary said, *B* the handmaid of the Lord
Luke 6:41 why *b'est* thou the mote...in thy brother's eye
John 1:36 he [John the Baptist] saith, *B* the Lamb of God
2 Cor. 5:17 *b*, all things are become new

BEKAH. A Hebrew weight equal to one-half shekel, or about one-quarter ounce (Exod. 38:26).

BELA. See *Zoar.*

BELIAL. A word for wickedness or wicked people (1 Kings 21:10). The word also means wickedness personified—a reference to Satan (2 Cor. 6:15). See also *Satan.*

BELIEVE. To accept or trust fully. Belief or trust in Christ is necessary for salvation (Acts 16:31) and essential to righteousness (Gal. 3:6). See also *Faith; Trust.*

BELIEVE [D, TH]

Gen. 15:6 he [Abraham] *b'd* in the Lord
Mark 5:36 he [Jesus] saith...Be not afraid, only *b*
Mark 9:24 Lord, I *b*; help thou mine unbelief
John 3:36 He that *b'th* on the Son hath everlasting life
John 4:48 Except ye see signs and wonders, ye will not *b*
John 11:26 whosoever...*b'th* in me [Jesus] shall never die
John 14:1 ye *b* in God, *b* also in me [Jesus]
John 20:29 they that have not seen, and yet have *b'd*
Rom. 1:16 power of God...to every one that *b'th*
Rom. 4:3 Abraham *b'd* God...counted...for righteousness
Rom. 6:8 we *b* that we shall also live with him [Jesus]
Rom. 10:14 call on him in whom they have not *b'd*
Rom. 13:11 salvation nearer than when we *b'd*
1 Cor. 1:21 foolishness of preaching to save them that *b*

1 Cor. 13:7 [charity] beareth all things, **b'th** all things
1 John 3:23 we should **b** on the name of his Son Jesus
1 John 5:1 **b'th** that Jesus is the Christ is born of God

BELIEVERS. A term for Christian converts (Acts 5:14). Paul encouraged Timothy to serve as an example for other believers (1 Tim. 4:12). See also *Brother.*

BELLOWS. A blacksmith's tool, used to force air onto a fire to make it hot enough to work metal (Jer. 6:29). See also *Smith.*

BELONG [ETH]
Ps. 3:8 Salvation **b'eth** unto the LORD
Ps. 94:1 LORD God, to whom vengeance **b'eth**

Dan. 9:9 to the Lord our God **b** mercies
1 Cor. 7:32 unmarried careth for the things that **b** to the Lord

BELSHAZZAR. The son or grandson of Nebuchadnezzar and the last king of the Babylonian Empire (Dan. 5:1–2). Daniel interpreted a mysterious handwriting on the wall for Belshazzar as a prediction of doom for the Babylonians (Dan. 5:17). That night, Belshazzar was killed when the Persians captured Babylonia (Dan. 5:30–31). See also *Babylonia.*

BELT. See *Girdle.*

BELSHAZZAR. Babylonian ruler Belshazzar is terrified as he watches a disembodied hand write on the palace wall. The prophet Daniel interpreted the cryptic message, which revealed Belshazzar had reason to fear. Invaders killed him that same night.

BELTESHAZZAR. See *Daniel*, No. 1.

BENAIAH. A loyal supporter of David and Solomon. A commander of David's bodyguard (2 Sam. 20:23), he later became commander-in-chief of Solomon's army (1 Kings 2:35).

BEN-AMMI. Lot's son by his youngest daughter. Born in a cave near Zoar (Gen. 19:30–38), he was the ancestor of the Ammonites. See also *Ammonites; Lot.*

BENEDICTION. A prayer for God's blessings upon His people. The benediction that priests were to use was spoken by God to Aaron through Moses (Num. 6:22–26). See also *Bless.*

BENEVOLENCE. Generosity toward others. Paul commended generosity toward the needy (Gal. 2:10). Christian benevolence should be shown toward God's servants (Phil. 4:14–17) and even our enemies (Prov. 25:21).

BEN-HADAD. A general title for the kings of Damascus, Syria. Three separate Ben-hadads are mentioned in the Bible:

1. Ben-hadad I (reigned about 950 B.C.). In league with Asa, king of Judah, he invaded the Northern Kingdom (1 Kings 15:18–21).

2. Ben-hadad II (reigned about 900 B.C.). He waged war against King Ahab of Israel. This Ben-hadad is probably the unnamed "king of Syria" whose officer Naaman was healed of leprosy by the prophet Elisha (2 Kings 5:1–19).

3. Ben-hadad III (reigned about 750 B.C.). He was defeated by the Assyrian army, as the prophet Amos predicted (Amos 1:4).

BENJAMIN. The youngest of Jacob's twelve sons and ancestor of the tribe of Benjamin. His mother, Rachel, died at his birth (Gen. 35:16–

SAVING BENJAMIN

At one point in Israel's history, the tribe of Benjamin was almost wiped out. Thousands of Benjaminite men were killed by the other tribes in retaliation for a heinous crime they committed (Judg. 20). To save the tribe from extinction, the other tribes provided women from the clan of Jabesh-gilead to marry the remaining Benjaminite men.

This paid off for the entire nation in future years. Israel's first king, Saul, was from the tribe of Benjamin (1 Sam. 9:1–2). The apostle Paul also traced his lineage through this tribe (Rom. 11:1).

20). Benjamin was greatly loved by his father, Jacob (Gen. 42:2–4), and by his brother Joseph (Gen. 43:29–34). See also *Tribes of Israel.*

BEREA (BEROEA). A city in southern Macedonia visited by Paul. The Bereans searched the Scriptures eagerly, and many became believers (Acts 17:10–12). *Beroea:* NRSV.

BERNICE. The sister of Herod Agrippa II, Roman governor of Palestine before whom Paul appeared. She was present when Paul made his defense (Acts 26).

BERODACH-BALADAN/MERODACH-BALADAN. A king of Babylonia (reigned about 721–704 B.C.) who sent ambassadors to visit King Hezekiah of Judah. Hezekiah showed them his vast wealth—an act condemned by the prophet Isaiah (2 Kings 20:12–19). *Merodach-baladan:* Isa. 39:1. See also *Babylonia.*

BEROEA. See *Berea.*

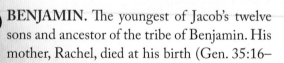

BERYL (CHRYSOLITE). A precious stone, probably similar to emerald, used in the breastplate of the high priest (Exod. 28:20) and in the foundation of New Jerusalem (Rev. 21:20). *Chrysolite:* NIV. See also *Carbuncle; Chrysolite.*

BESEECH. To request or ask earnestly (Rom. 12:1).

BESEECH [ING]

Matt. 8:5 came unto him [Jesus] a centurion, ***b'ing*** him
1 Cor. 4:16 I [Paul] ***b*** you, be ye followers of me
2 Cor. 2:8 I [Paul] ***b*** you...confirm your love toward him
2 Cor. 5:20 ambassadors for Christ...God did ***b*** you by us
Philem. 10 I [Paul] ***b*** thee for my son Onesimus
1 Pet. 2:11 I [Peter] ***b*** you...abstain from fleshly lusts

BESIEGE. To surround with armed forces (Deut. 20:12). This battle tactic was used against walled cities of Bible times to starve the inhabitants into submission. See also *Fenced City; Wall.*

BESTIALITY. Sex relations with an animal. The death penalty was imposed on those who were guilty of this offense (Exod. 22:19).

BESTOW [ED]

1 Cor. 13:3 though I [Paul] ***b*** all my goods to feed the poor
Gal. 4:11 lest I [Paul] have ***b'ed*** upon you labour in vain
1 John 3:1 love the Father hath ***b'ed*** upon us

BETHABARA. A place on the Jordan River where John the Baptist baptized believers (John 1:28). Jesus was also apparently baptized at this place (John 1:29–34).

BETHANY. A village near the Mount of Olives outside Jerusalem (Mark 11:1) and home of Lazarus, Mary, and Martha—friends of Jesus (John 11:1). Jesus ascended to heaven from Bethany (Luke 24:50).

BETHEL/LUZ/EL-BETHEL. A city north of Jerusalem where Jacob had a life-changing vision of angels going up and down a staircase (Gen. 28:10–19). Before it was renamed by Jacob, Bethel was known by its Canaanite name, *Luz* (Gen. 28:19). *El-bethel:* Gen. 35:7.

BETHESDA (BETH-ZATHA). A pool in Jerusalem believed to have miraculous healing powers. Jesus healed a lame man at this pool (John 5:2–8). *Beth-zatha:* NRSV. See also *Pool.*

BETH-HORON. Upper and Lower Bethhoron were twin towns in the territory of Ephraim that served as important military outposts in Bible times. They stood on the main pass through the mountains between the Mediterranean Sea and Jerusalem. Solomon fortified the cities to protect Jerusalem from invading armies (2 Chron. 8:5).

BETHLEHEM/BETHLEHEM-JUDAH/EPHRATH/EPHRATAH. A town in southern Palestine near Jerusalem, also called *Bethlehem-judah* (Judg. 19:18), where Jesus was born in fulfillment of prophecy (Mic. 5:2; Luke 2:4–7). It was called the "City of David" because King David grew up there centuries before (1 Sam. 16:1–13). David's ancestor Ruth gleaned grain in the fields of Boaz nearby (Ruth 2:4–8). Bethlehem was known in O.T. times as *Ephrath* (Gen. 35:19) and *Ephratah* (Ruth 4:11). See also *City of David.*

BETH-MILLO. See *Millo,* No. 1

BETH-PEOR. A town of Moab east of the Jordan River in the territory where Moses was buried (Deut. 34:6).

BETHPHAGE. A village near Bethany and the Mount of Olives just outside Jerusalem

B

mentioned in connection with Jesus' triumphant entry into the city (Matt. 21:1).

5
C
3

BETHSAIDA. A fishing village on the Sea of Galilee; the home of Andrew, Peter, and Philip—apostles of Jesus (John 1:44). Some scholars believe the Bethsaida where the 5,000 were fed (Luke 9:10–17) was a different city with the same name.

2
D
4

BETHSHAN/BETH-SHEAN. A Philistine city where King Saul's corpse was displayed (1 Sam. 31:10–13). In later years, Solomon stationed troops in this city (1 Kings 4:12). *Bethshean:* Josh. 17:11.

2
C
6

BETH-SHEMESH/IR-SHEMESH. A border town between the territories of Judah and Dan taken by the Philistines. Later the ark of the covenant was kept here (1 Sam. 6:1–7:2). *Irshemesh:* Josh. 19:41.

BETH-ZATHA. See *Bethesda*.

2
C
6

BETH-ZUR. A city in the mountains of Judah fortified by King Rehoboam as a defensive outpost along the road leading to Jerusalem (2 Chron. 11:7).

BETRAY [ED, EST, ETH]
Matt. 26:2 Son of man is *b'ed* to be crucified
Matt. 26:16 he [Judas] sought opportunity to *b* him [Jesus]
Mark 14:21 woe to that man by whom the Son of man is *b'ed*
Luke 22:21 hand of him that *b'eth* me [Jesus] is with me on the table
Luke 22:48 Judas, *b'est* thou the Son of man with a kiss?
John 6:64 Jesus knew...who should *b* him
1 Cor. 11:23 Lord Jesus the same night in which he was *b'ed* took bread

BETROTHAL. A marriage agreement, usually made by the groom with the parents of the bride. A betrothed woman was regarded as the lawful wife of her spouse. Joseph and Mary were betrothed before the birth of Jesus

(Matt. 1:18–19; *espoused:* KJV). See also *Dowry; Marriage.*

BETTER
1 Sam. 15:22 to obey is *b* than sacrifice
Ps. 84:10 day in thy [God's] courts is *b* than a thousand
Prov. 8:11 wisdom is *b* than rubies
Prov. 19:22 poor man is *b* than a liar
Prov. 27:5 rebuke is *b* than secret love
Eccles. 7:1 good name is *b* than precious ointment
Matt. 12:12 How much then is a man *b* than a sheep
1 Cor. 7:9 it is *b* to marry than to burn
Phil. 1:23 desire...to be with Christ; which is far *b*
Heb. 1:4 made so much *b* than the angels

BEULAH. A name for Israel after the Babylonian Exile when the nation would be in a fruitful relationship with God (Isa. 62:4).

BEZER. A fortified city in the territory of Reuben designated as one of the six cities of refuge (Josh. 20:8). See also *Cities of Refuge.*

2
E
5

BIBLE. God's written record of His revelation that is accepted by Christians as uniquely inspired and authoritative for faith and practice. The Bible's O.T. books chronicle the expectation of a messiah, while the N.T. books reveal the fulfillment of God's redemptive purpose through Jesus Christ and the church.

The Bible was written under God's inspiration during a period of more than 1,000 years from the time of Moses through the first century A.D. The N.T. was completed within about sixty years of Jesus' resurrection. Much of the N.T., including the Gospels, was recorded by eyewitnesses of the events about which they wrote. The O.T. was written originally in Hebrew and Aramaic, while the N.T. was recorded in the Greek language.

All copies of the Scripture were written by hand until the invention of printing in the fifteenth century A.D. The original writings have been translated into hundreds of languages

BETROTHAL. A Jewish bride and groom in Israel dress in the traditional wedding garments of their former homeland: Yemen, a small nation south of Saudi Arabia. Many Israelis today are Yemenite Jews.

BIBLE. A rabbi touches up fading letters in an old scroll, as scribes in ancient times did to preserve their sacred writings. When scrolls became too worn, scribes made fresh copies from the old ones, carefully preserving the message.

and dialects to make the Bible the world's best-loved and most accessible book. The Geneva Bible, published in 1560, was the first complete English Bible translated from the original languages. The popular King James Version appeared in 1611, and numerous English versions and revisions have followed.

Although written by many people over a long period, the Bible has a remarkable unity, explained only by the inspiration and oversight of the Holy Spirit to bring God's redemptive message to humankind.

BIER. A portable frame for carrying a body to its burial place (2 Sam. 3:31).

BILDAD. One of the three friends who comforted the sorrowing Job (Job 2:11). His speeches expressed the conviction that all suffering is the direct result of sin (Job 8, 18, 25). See also *Job, Book of*.

BILHAH. Rachel's maid and a wife of Jacob. She bore two of Jacob's twelve sons, Dan and Naphtali (Gen. 30:1–8). See also *Jacob*.

BIND [ETH]

Deut. 6:8 shalt *b* them for a sign upon thine hand
Ps. 147:3 He [God]...*b'eth* up their wounds
Prov. 3:3 *b* them [mercy and truth] about thy neck
Isa. 61:1 the Lord...hath sent me to *b* up the brokenhearted
Matt. 16:19 whatsoever...*b* on earth shall be bound in heaven
Mark 5:3 no man could *b* him [demon-possessed man]

BIRD OF PREY. See *Speckled Bird.*

BIRTHRIGHT. The inheritance rights of the firstborn son, who received a double portion of his father's assets (Deut. 21:17) plus the father's blessing and responsibility for family leadership. These inheritance rights could be taken away and conferred on another because of immoral acts or irresponsible behavior by the oldest son (Gen. 25:29–34). Esau sold his birthright to his brother, Jacob, for a bowl of stew (Gen. 25:31; Heb. 12:16). See also *Firstborn; Inheritance.*

BISHOP. An overseer, pastor, or elder who served as leader of a local church in N.T. times (Titus 1:5–9). See also *Deacon; Elder; Pastor.*

BISHOP [S]
Phil. 1:1 saints...at Philippi, with the *b's*
1 Tim. 3:1 man desire the office of a *b*...a good work
1 Tim. 3:2 A *b* then must be blameless...husband of one wife
1 Pet. 2:25 returned unto the Shepherd and *B* of your souls

BITHYNIA. A Roman province of Asia Minor that Paul was prevented from entering through the intervention of the Holy Spirit (Acts 16:7). The gospel did enter this province later (1 Pet. 1:1).

BITTER
Isa. 24:9 strong drink shall be *b* to them that drink it
Jer. 31:15 voice was heard in Ramah...*b* weeping
Hab. 1:6 I [God] raise up the Chaldeans, that *b*...nation
James 3:11 fountain send forth...sweet water and *b*

BITTER HERBS. Herbs eaten by the Hebrew people during their celebration of the Passover to help them remember their bitter affliction during their enslavement in Egypt (Exod. 12:8). See also *Passover.*

BITTER WATER. A test or trial to which a woman was subjected when her husband sus-pected her of being unfaithful (Num. 5:11–31). See also *Water of Jealousy; Water of Separation.*

BITTERN (SCREECH OWL). A bird noted for its melancholy cries and thus symbolic of the loneliness and despair that follow God's judgment (Zeph. 2:14). *Screech owl:* NIV, NRSV. See also *Screech Owl.*

BITTERNESS
Job 9:18 He [God]...filleth me [Job] with *b*
Acts 8:23 thou art in the gall of *b*
Rom. 3:14 mouth is full of cursing and *b*
Eph. 4:31 Let all *b*...be put away from you

BITUMEN. See *Slime.*

BLACK VULTURE. See *Ospray.*

BLAINS (BOILS). Infectious boils on the skin; one of the plagues brought upon the Egyptians for their refusal to release the Hebrew slaves (Exod. 9:8–11). *Boils:* NIV, NRSV.

BLAMELESS
1 Cor. 1:8 ye may be *b* in the day of our Lord
1 Tim. 3:2 bishop...must be *b*, the husband of one wife
1 Tim. 3:10 office of a deacon, being found *b*
Titus 1:7 bishop must be *b*, as the steward of God

BLASPHEME. To revile, curse, or show contempt toward God. This was considered a capital offense by the Jewish people, punishable by death. Jesus was accused of blasphemy by the Jewish leaders. They considered Him only a man, while He claimed to be God's Son (Matt. 9:3).

BLASPHEME [D]
Ps. 74:10 shall the enemy *b* thy [God's] name for ever
Ps. 74:18 foolish people have *b'd* thy [God's] name
Mark 3:29 shall *b* against the Holy Ghost hath never forgiveness

BLASPHEMY [IES]

Matt. 12:31 *b* against the Holy Ghost shall not be forgiven
Matt. 26:65 He [Jesus] hath spoken *b*
Mark 2:7 Why doth this man [Jesus] thus speak *b'ies*?
Col. 3:8 put off all these; anger, wrath, malice, *b*

BLASPHEMY AGAINST THE HOLY SPIRIT.

A sin that consists of attributing Christ's miracles to the work of Satan (Matt. 12:31–32). Jesus declared that such contempt for the work of God was an unforgivable sin (Mark 3:28–29). Paul regarded a person's bitter opposition to the gospel as a form of blasphemy against God (Rom. 2:24). See also *Unpardonable Sin.*

BLESS.

To invoke or declare God's goodness and favor upon others, as Jacob did with his twelve sons (Gen. 49:1–28). God also blesses His people by giving life (Gen. 1:22) and forgiving our sins (Rom. 4:7–8). See also *Benediction.*

BLESS [ED, ING]

Gen. 2:3 God *b'ed* the seventh day, and sanctified it
Gen. 9:1 God *b'ed* Noah and his sons
Gen. 12:2 I [God] will *b* thee [Abraham]
Num. 6:24 LORD *b* thee, and keep thee
Deut. 11:26 set before you...a *b'ing* and a curse
Job 1:21 LORD hath taken away; *b'ed* be the name of the LORD
Job 42:12 LORD *b'ed* the latter end of Job
Ps. 1:1 *B'ed*...walketh not in the counsel of the ungodly
Ps. 32:1 *B'ed*...whose transgression is forgiven
Ps. 41:13 *B'ed* be the LORD God...from everlasting
Ps. 67:1 God...*b* us; and cause his face to shine upon us
Ps. 96:2 Sing unto the LORD, *b* his name
Prov. 31:28 children arise up, and call her *b'ed*
Ezek. 34:26 there shall be showers of *b'ing*
Matt. 5:3 *B'ed* are the poor in spirit
Luke 1:28 *b'ed* art thou [Mary] among women
Luke 11:28 *b'ed*...that hear the word of God, and keep it
Rom. 12:14 *B* them which persecute you: b, and curse not
James 1:12 *B'ed* is the man that endureth temptation

BLIND.

Unable to see, in either a physical (Matt. 9:27) or spiritual (Eph. 4:18) sense. The Hebrews were enjoined to show compassion toward the blind (Deut. 27:18).

Ps. 146:8 The LORD openeth the eyes of the *b*
Isa. 35:5 the eyes of the *b* shall be opened
Matt. 11:5 The *b* receive their sight...lame walk
Matt. 23:24 Ye *b* guides [Pharisees]...strain at a gnat
Mark 10:46 *b* Bartimaeus...sat by the highway
Luke 6:39 Can the *b* lead the *b*?
Luke 7:22 tell John...the *b* see, the lame walk
John 9:2 who did sin...that he was born *b*

BLOOD.

Life-sustaining fluid of the body. In the O.T., the blood of a sacrificial animal represented the essence of life and symbolized repentance and atonement for sin (Lev. 17:11). In the N.T., the phrase "the blood of Christ" refers to the sacrificial death of Jesus on the cross (Heb. 9:12–14).

Jesus' sacrificial blood is the agent of redemption for believers (Heb. 9:12). Christ's shed blood is memorialized in the Lord's Supper (1 Cor. 10:16). Nothing perishable or material can save; only Christ's precious blood has the power to redeem (1 Pet. 1:18–19). See also *Atonement; Redeem.*

Gen. 9:6 sheddeth man's *b*, by man shall his *b* be shed
1 Kings 22:38 dogs licked up his [Ahab's] *b*
1 Chron. 22:8 thou [David] hast shed much *b*
Joel 2:31 sun...turned into darkness...moon into *b*
Matt. 16:17 flesh and *b* hath not revealed it unto thee [Peter]
Matt. 26:28 my [Jesus'] *b* of the new testament
Matt. 27:8 field was called, The field of *b*
Matt. 27:25 answered all the people...His [Jesus'] *b* be on us
Luke 22:44 his [Jesus'] sweat was as...great drops of *b*
Acts 17:26 made of one *b* all nations of men
Eph. 2:13 ye...far off are made nigh by the *b* of Christ
Eph. 6:12 wrestle not against flesh and *b*
Col. 1:14 redemption through his [Jesus'] *b*
Heb. 13:12 he [Jesus] might sanctify...with his own *b*
1 John 1:7 *b* of Jesus Christ...cleanseth us from all sin
Rev. 6:12 sun became black...moon became as *b*

BLOT [TED]
Exod. 32:33 him will I [God] *b* out of my book
Ps. 51:1 *b* out my transgressions
Acts 3:19 Repent...that your sins may be *b'ted* out

BOANERGES.
A name meaning "sons of thunder," given by Jesus to James and John, the sons of Zebedee (Mark 3:17). This was a reference to their fiery zeal. See also *James*, No. 1; *John the Apostle*.

BOAR.
A male wild hog, noted for its vicious nature (Ps. 80:13).

BOAST [ETH, ING]
Ps. 44:8 In God we *b* all the day long
Prov. 27:1 *B* not thyself of to morrow
2 Cor. 9:3 lest our *b'ing* of you should be in vain
Eph. 2:9 Not of works, lest any man should *b*
James 3:5 the tongue is a little member...*b'eth* great things

BOAZ/BOOZ.
The husband of Ruth and an ancestor of Christ. He married Ruth, who gave birth to Obed, grandfather of David (Ruth 4:17). *Booz:* Jesus' ancestry (Matt. 1:5). See also *Ruth*.

BODY
Matt. 26:26 Jesus took bread...Take, eat; this is my *b*
Mark 15:43 Joseph of Arimathaea...craved the *b* of Jesus
Luke 12:22 Take no thought...for the *b*, what ye...put on
Rom. 6:12 sin therefore reign in your mortal *b*
Rom. 7:24 deliver me from the *b* of this death
Rom. 12:5 we, being many, are one *b* in Christ
1 Cor. 6:18 fornication sinneth against his own *b*
1 Cor. 12:12 the *b* is one, and hath many members
1 Cor. 15:44 sown a natural *b*...raised a spiritual *b*
2 Cor. 5:8 absent from the *b*...present with the Lord
Gal. 6:17 I [Paul] bear in my *b* the marks of the Lord Jesus
Col. 1:18 he [Christ] is the head of the *b*, the church
James 3:6 it [the tongue] defileth the whole *b*

BODY OF CHRIST.
A symbolic expression for the church. Paul identified the church as Christ's body (Rom. 7:4; Col. 1:24). The risen Christ dwells in His body and presides over the church (Eph. 1:19–23). Christ assigns spiritual gifts to His body to accomplish His work and bring believers to maturity (Eph. 4:7–13). Members of the body are to care for one another (1 Cor. 12:25–27). See also *Church*.

BODY, SPIRITUAL.
The glorified or redeemed body of believers. Our hope of a glorified body is based on Christ's victory over the grave (Rom. 6:6). Believers will receive a glorified body, free of sin and death, at the return of Christ (1 Cor. 15:50–57). The redeemed body of a believer will be like that of Christ's glorified body (Phil. 3:21), immortal and incorruptible (1 Cor. 15:53–54).

Christians need not fear death, because we are provided a new spiritual body "eternal in the heavens" (2 Cor. 5).

BOILS.
See *Blains*.

BOLDLY
Acts 9:29 he [Paul] spake *b* in the name of the Lord Jesus
Acts 19:8 he [Paul] went into the synagogue, and spake *b*
Heb. 4:16 Let us...come *b* unto the throne of grace

BOLDNESS.
Courage and confidence. Boldness that honors God is aided by earnest prayer (Eph. 6:18–20).

Acts 4:13 they saw the *b* of Peter and John
Eph. 3:12 In whom [Jesus] we have *b*
1 John 4:17 that we may have *b* in the day of judgment

BOND [S]
Ps. 116:16 thou [God] hast loosed my *b's*
Gal. 3:28 neither Jew nor Greek...*b* nor free
Eph. 4:3 unity of the Spirit in the *b* of peace
Eph. 6:20 I [Paul] am an ambassador in *b's*
Col. 3:11 neither...*b* nor free: but Christ is all
Philem. 10 Onesimus, whom I [Paul] have begotten in my *b's*

BONDAGE. Jews once invited to Egypt to escape a drought in their homeland eventually became a slave race, forced to build cities for the king. Moses led them to freedom.

BONDAGE. To be held against one's will by an oppressor. The Israelites were enslaved by the Egyptians for more than 400 years. Sin also holds a person in spiritual bondage (Rom. 8:15). See also *Slave.*

Exod. 6:6 I [God] will rid you [the Israelites] out of their *b*
John 8:33 We be Abraham's seed...never in *b* to any man
Gal. 5:1 not entangled again with the yoke of *b*

BONDSERVANT. A slave; a person who serves another against his will and without wages (1 Kings 9:21). See also *Slave.*

BONE. The skeletal framework of humans. The phrase "bone of my bones" uttered by Adam (Gen. 2:23) showed that he was united to woman in the closest possible relationship.

BOOK. Pieces of animal skin or papyrus written on and then bound together (Job 19:23). See also *Roll; Scroll.*

BOOK OF JASHER. A lost book that apparently described great events in the life of Israel (Josh. 10:13).

BOOK OF LIFE. God's record of the names of the saved and deeds of the righteous (Mal. 3:16–18). This book will be used as the basis for God's final judgment (Rev. 3:5; 20:12–15). Inclusion in the book of life by virtue of one's salvation by God's grace provides reason for joy (Luke 10:20; Phil. 4:3) and hope of heaven (Rev. 21:27).

BOOK OF THE LAW. A term for the Law of Moses or the Pentateuch, the first five books of the O.T. After receiving and recording these instructions from God, Moses delivered the law to the priests for public reading (Deut. 31:9–11). In later years, the Book of the Law became the basis for King Josiah's religious reforms (2 Kings 23:1–25).

BOOK OF THE WARS OF THE LORD. A lost book that may have celebrated Israel's victories in battle under Moses (Num. 21:14).

BOOTH. A temporary shelter made of tree branches. During the Feast of Tabernacles, also called the Feast of Booths, the Israelites lived in such shelters as a reminder of their harsh life in the wilderness after their deliverance from Egyptian slavery (Neh. 8:13–18).

BOOTHS, FEAST OF. See *Tabernacles, Feast of*.

BOOTY. Anything of value taken in war, including livestock, slaves, gold and silver, clothing, and tools (Zeph. 1:13). See also *Spoil*.

BOOZ. See *Boaz*.

BORN
Gen. 17:17 child be *b* unto him [Abraham]...hundred years old
Job 14:1 Man that is *b* of a woman is of few days
Prov. 17:17 brother is *b* for adversity
Eccles. 3:2 time to be *b*, and a time to die
Isa. 9:6 unto us a child is *b*
Matt. 2:1 Jesus was *b* in Bethlehem of Judaea
Luke 1:35 holy thing...*b* of thee [Mary]...called the Son of God
Luke 2:11 unto you is *b* this day...a Saviour
Acts 22:28 Paul said, But I was free *b*
1 John 3:9 Whosoever is *b* of God doth not commit sin
1 John 4:7 every one that loveth is *b* of God

BORN AGAIN. See *New Birth*.

BOSOM. Another word for the human chest, or breast, used symbolically to imply closeness or intimacy (Isa. 40:11). See also *Abraham's Bosom; Breast*.

Prov. 5:20 thou...embrace the *b* of a stranger
Luke 16:22 beggar died...carried...into Abraham's *b*
John 1:18 only begotten Son...in the *b* of the Father
John 13:23 leaning on Jesus' *b* one of his disciples

BOTTLE (WINESKIN). A vessel made of animal skins (Josh. 9:4). Old wineskins became brittle and unable to hold new wine during the fermentation process. Thus, Jesus declared, "No man putteth new wine into old bottles; else the new wine will burst the bottles, and be spilled" (Luke 5:37). *Wineskin:* NIV, NRSV.

BOTTOMLESS PIT. See *Abyss*.

BOUGHT
Jer. 32:9 I [Jeremiah] *b* the field of Hanameel
Matt. 13:46 sold all...he had, and *b* it [pearl]
Mark 11:15 Jesus...cast out them that sold and *b*
1 Cor. 6:20 ye are *b* with a price...glorify God

BOUND
Matt. 18:18 ye shall bind on earth shall be *b* in heaven
John 11:44 he [Lazarus] came forth, *b*...with graveclothes
Acts 20:22 I [Paul] go *b* in the spirit unto Jerusalem
2 Tim. 2:9 but the word of God is not *b*

BOUNDARY MARKER, BOUNDARY STONE. See *Landmark*.

BOW. A weapon used in war and for hunting (Gen. 48:22). Soldiers of the tribe of Benjamin were especially skilled with the bow (1 Chron. 12:2).

BOW, BOWING. To show reverence or submission, performed by kneeling on one knee and bending the head forward. Bowing is considered appropriate for prayer and worship (Ps. 95:6). Jesus knelt or bowed to pray in Gethsemane (Matt. 26:36–39). See also *Kneel*.

BOWED
Ps. 38:6 troubled; I am *b* down greatly
Matt. 27:29 they *b* the knee before him [Jesus]...mocked him
John 19:30 Jesus...*b* his head, and gave up the ghost

BOWELS (INWARD PARTS). The internal digestive system of the human body. The bowels were considered the center of a person's feelings and emotions, expressive of compassion and tenderness (Job 30:27–28). *Inward parts:* NRSV.

BOWL. A vessel for holding food or liquids. Bowls were made of wood, clay, or silver. Large

B

bowls were used by priests in sacrificial rituals (Zech. 9:15). See also *Bason*.

BOX TREE (CYPRESS, PINE). An evergreen that produced a wood ideal for carving. Boxwood was used in the temple in Jerusalem (Isa. 60:13). *Cypress:* NIV; *pine:* NRSV.

3
D
7

BOZRAH. The ancient capital city of Edom. Isaiah spoke of this city in figurative terms to describe the Messiah's victory over the pagan nations (Isa. 63:1). See also *Edom*, No 2.

BRACELET. A piece of jewelry worn on the wrist (Isa. 3:19). The bracelet of King Saul (2 Sam. 1:10) was probably a military armband.

BRAMBLE (THORNBUSH). A bush of thistles. In Jotham's parable, the bramble bush, representing Abimelech, ruled over the trees of the forest, in spite of its lowly position (Judg. 9:7–15). *Thornbush:* NIV. See also *Brier*.

BRASEN SEA (BRONZE SEA). A large brass basin in the temple court that held water for purification rituals (2 Kings 25:13). *Bronze sea:* NIV, NRSV. See also *Molten Sea*.

BRASS. An alloy of copper with some other metal, perhaps zinc or tin (Num. 21:9). The word is also used as a symbol of stubbornness, insensibility, and rebellion toward God (Isa. 48:4).

BRASS SERPENT (BRONZE SNAKE). A serpent cast from metal and raised up by Moses in the wilderness on a pole as an instrument of healing for those who had been bitten by poisonous snakes (Num. 21:9). *Bronze snake:* NIV. See also *Fiery Serpents*.

BREAD. A word often used for food in general. Bread was made from flour or meal and baked in loaves. Jesus described Himself as the "bread of life" (John 6:35). See also *Corn; Wheat*.

BREAD OF THE PRESENCE. See *Shewbread*.

BREAK [ETH, ING]
Job 34:24 He [God] shall *b* in pieces mighty men
Ps. 89:34 My covenant will I [God] not *b*
Eccles. 3:3 a time to *b* down, and a time to build up
Jer. 23:29 my [God's] word like...a hammer that *b'eth* the rock
Hosea 1:5 I [God] will *b* the bow of Israel
Matt. 6:20 treasures...where thieves do not *b* through nor steal
Matt. 12:20 A bruised reed shall he [Jesus] not *b*
Luke 24:35 he [Jesus] was known of them in *b'ing* of bread
1 Cor. 10:16 bread which we *b*...communion of the body of Christ

BREAST. The chest of the human body. To strike or beat one's chest was to signify extreme sorrow (Luke 23:48).

BREASTPLATE (BREASTPIECE). The vestment worn by the Jewish high priest. It contained twelve precious stones and was engraved with the names of the tribes of Israel (Exod. 28:15–30). Paul spoke figuratively of the "breastplate of righteousness" for Christians (Eph. 6:14). *Breastpiece:* NIV.

BREASTS. See *Paps*.

A SAVING SERPENT

Jesus referred to the brass serpent raised up by Moses in the wilderness when He declared, "And I, if I be lifted up from the earth, will draw all men unto me" (John 12:32). He was predicting His atoning death on the cross.

BREATH OF GOD. A symbolic phrase that portrays God as the source of life (Job 33:4). His breath demonstrates His power and creative ability (2 Sam. 22:14–16). In the N.T., God "breathed" the Holy Spirit upon His disciples (John 20:22).

BREECHES (UNDERGARMENTS). Trousers or perhaps an undergarment worn by priests (Exod. 28:42). *Undergarments:* NIV, NRSV.

BRIBERY. The act of giving gifts or favors inappropriately to influence others—a practice condemned often in the Bible (Amos 5:12).

BRICK. A building block made of clay that was mixed with straw then baked in the sun or placed in a kiln for curing. The Israelites made bricks during their enslavement in Egypt (Exod. 1:14). See also *Tile.*

BRICK-KILN. An oven or furnace for curing bricks (2 Sam. 12:31). See also *Furnace.*

BRIDE. A newly married woman. In the N.T., the Church is spoken of figuratively as the bride of Christ (Eph. 5:25–33). See also *Church.*

BRIDEGROOM. A newly married man. The N.T. speaks figuratively of Christ as the Bridegroom (John 3:29) and of the Church as His bride (Eph. 5:25–33).

BRIER. A shrub or plant with thorns and thistles. The word is often used figuratively to describe man's sinful nature (Mic. 7:4).

BRIGANDINE (COAT OF MAIL). Flexible body armor, probably worn by kings and commanders (1 Sam. 17:38; Jer. 46:4). *Coat of mail:* NRSV.

BRIMSTONE (BURNING SULFUR). A bright yellow mineral that burns easily and gives off a strong odor. The cities of Sodom and Gomorrah were destroyed with burning brimstone (Gen. 19:24–25). *Burning sulfur:* NIV.

BRONZE SEA. See *Brasen Sea.*

BRONZE SNAKE. See *Brass Serpent.*

BROOM. See *Juniper.*

BROTHER. A male sibling. The word is also used figuratively for all Christian believers (Matt. 23:8). Christians are counseled not to offend a weak brother (Rom. 14:10–13). See also *Believers.*

BROTHERS OF CHRIST. The four earthly brothers, or half brothers, of Jesus—James, Joses (Joseph), Simon, and Juda (Jude)—who were born by natural conception to Joseph and Mary after the virgin birth of Christ (Mark 6:3). James was leader of the church in Jerusalem (Acts 15:13–21) and likely the author of the epistle of James (James 1:1). Jude wrote the N.T. epistle that bears his name (Jude 1).

BUCKLER (SHIELD). A small piece of protective armor worn on the arm by warriors (Song 4:4). *Shield:* NIV. See also *Shield.*

BUILDER [S]
Mark 12:10 stone which the *b's* rejected...head of the corner
Acts 4:11 This is the stone...set at nought of you *b's*
Heb. 11:10 he [Abraham] looked for a city...whose *b* and maker is God
1 Pet. 2:7 stone which the *b's* disallowed...head of the corner

BUILDING [S]
2 Chron. 3:3 Solomon was instructed for the *b* of the house of God
Mark 13:2 great *b's*? there shall not be left one stone
1 Cor. 3:9 God's husbandry, ye are God's *b*
2 Cor. 5:1 a *b* of God, an house not made with hands

BUL. The eighth month of the Hebrew year, roughly equivalent to parts of our October and November (1 Kings 6:38).

BULL. A general term for the male of the ox or cattle species (Job 21:10).

BULLOCK. A young bull used in animal sacrifices (Num. 15:24).

BULRUSH (PAPYRUS). A reedlike plant that grew in marshy areas of the Nile River and was used for making papyrus, an ancient writing material. The infant Moses was placed in a basket made of this plant (Exod. 2:3). *Papyrus:* NIV, NRSV. See also *Paper; Reed.*

BULWARK (RAMPARTS). A tower in a city's defensive wall that provided a better

BURIAL. *On the Mount of Olives' western slope, stone burial boxes in an ancient cemetery stand guard over Jerusalem. Visitors to grave sites leave small rocks as a witness of their visit.*

position for firing on the enemy below (Ps. 48:13). *Ramparts:* NIV, NRSV.

BURDEN [S]
Ps. 38:4 heavy *b* they [sins] are too heavy for me
Ps. 55:22 Cast thy *b* upon the LORD
Matt. 11:30 my [Jesus'] yoke is easy, and my *b* is light
Matt. 20:12 we have borne the *b* and heat of the day
Matt. 23:4 they [the Pharisees] bind heavy *b's*
Gal. 6:2 Bear ye one another's *b's*
Gal. 6:5 every man shall bear his own *b*

BURIAL. The ceremonial disposal of a body by placement in the ground or a tomb. In Bible times, burial usually took place as soon as possible because of the warm climate and because a body was considered ceremonially unclean (Deut. 21:23). Jesus' body was prepared for burial with aromatic oils and spices and wrapped in a linen cloth (John 19:39–40). See also *Funeral; Sepulchre.*

BURN [ED, ING]
Exod. 3:2 bush *b'ed* with fire...not consumed
Job 30:30 my [Job's] bones are *b'ed* with heat
Ps. 79:5 thy [God's] jealousy *b* like fire
Prov. 6:27 fire in his bosom, and his clothes not be *b'ed*
Dan. 3:17 our God...deliver us from the *b'ing* fiery furnace
Luke 24:32 Did not our heart *b* within us
Rom. 1:27 the men...*b'ed* in their lust one toward another
1 Cor. 7:9 it is better to marry than to *b*
2 Pet. 3:10 earth...shall be *b'ed* up

BURNING AGUE (FEVER). A severe fever, possibly a symptom of a serious illness, such as typhoid or malaria (Lev. 26:16). *Fever:* NIV, NRSV.

BURNING BUSH. The flaming shrub through which God spoke to Moses. As the bush burned, God expressed compassion for His captive people and called Moses to return to Egypt to deliver them from bondage (Exod. 3:9–10).

BURNING SULFUR. See *Brimstone.*

BURNT OFFERING. A meat sacrifice consisting of an unblemished animal that was totally consumed by fire, except for the hide (Lev. 7:8). Burnt sacrifices were made to atone for sin and to restore the broken relationship between man and God (Num. 6:10–11).

BUSHEL. A dry measure of about one peck (Matt. 5:15).

BUSYBODY (MEDDLER, MISCHIEF MAKER). A gossip and troublemaker. This type of behavior is inappropriate for believers (1 Pet. 4:15). *Meddler:* NIV; *mischief maker:* NRSV. See also *Gossip.*

BUTLER. See *Cupbearer.*

BUY [ETH]
Prov. 23:23 *B* the truth, and sell it not
Prov. 31:16 considereth a field, and *b'eth* it
Amos 8:6 *b* the poor for silver...needy for a pair of shoes
Matt. 13:44 man...selleth all...he hath, and *b'eth* that field
John 6:5 Whence shall we *b* bread, that these may eat

BUZZARD. See *Vulture.*

BYWORD. A degrading saying or remark, usually delivered in taunting fashion (1 Kings 9:7).

C

CAB (KAB). The smallest unit of measure for dry material, equal to about three pints (2 Kings 6:25). *Kab:* NRSV.

CAESAR. A formal title for several emperors of the Roman Empire. Four separate Caesars are mentioned in the N.T.:

1. Caesar Augustus (reigned about 27 B.C. to A.D. 14), who issued the taxation or census decree that required Joseph to go to Bethlehem, where Jesus was born (Luke 2:1).

2. Caesar Tiberius (reigned about A.D. 14–37), whose administration paralleled the public ministry of Jesus. Tiberius was known for his strict discipline of subject nations and his intolerance of potential rivals (John 19:12).

3. Caesar Claudius (reigned about A.D. 41–54), who sought to reduce strife throughout his empire. One of his tactics was to expel all the Jewish people living in Rome (Acts 18:2).

4. Caesar Nero (reigned about A.D. 54–68), the first emperor under whom the Christians were persecuted. As a Roman citizen, Paul appealed to him (Acts 25:8–12).

CAESAREA. A Roman coastal city, also known as Caesarea Maritima, named for the Roman

CAESAR. Caesar Augustus was the Roman ruler who ensured that Jesus would be born in Bethlehem. He ordered all Jews to return to their ancestral homes for a census. Joseph and pregnant Mary traveled to Bethlehem, hometown of Joseph's most famous descendant: King David.

emperor Caesar Augustus. As the political capital of Palestine during N.T. times, it was the city of residence for Roman rulers of the district, including Agrippa II, before whom Paul appeared (Acts 26:28–32).

CAESAREA PHILIPPI. A city at the foot of Mount Hermon in northern Palestine where Peter confessed Jesus as the Messiah (Matt. 16:13–16). Named for the Roman tetrarch Philip who rebuilt the city, it was called Caesarea Philippi to distinguish it from the city of Caesarea on the Mediterranean coast in central Palestine.

CAESAR'S HOUSEHOLD. A group of converts probably associated with the palace of the emperor in Rome. Paul sent greetings from this group to the church at Philippi (Phil. 4:22).

CAIAPHAS. The Jewish high priest who presided at the trial of Jesus and advised that He be put to death (Matt. 26:57–66; John 18:12–14). After Jesus' resurrection, the apostles John and Peter also appeared before Caiaphas (Acts 4:6).

CAIN. The oldest son of Adam and Eve who murdered his brother Abel. Exiled by God, he built a city that he named for his son (Gen. 4:1–17).

CAINAN. See *Kenan.*

CALAH. An ancient city of Assyria built by Nimrod (Gen. 10:8–12).

CALAMUS (FRAGRANT CANE, AROMATIC CANE). A reedlike plant known for its sweet fragrance (Song 4:14). It was used in anointing oil (Exod. 30:23). *Fragrant cane:* NIV; *aromatic cane:* NRSV.

CALDRON. A large kettle used by priests for boiling meats for sacrificial purposes (2 Chron. 35:13). See also *Kettle.*

CALEB'S DELAYED REWARD

Caleb must have been more than eighty years old when he was finally rewarded for his faithfulness with a tract of land in the Promised Land (Josh. 14:6–15). He was forty when he served on the scouting expedition into Canaan (Josh. 14:7), and another forty years had passed while the Israelites wandered in the wilderness (Num. 14:33). God's promised reward may be slow in coming, but He always delivers!

CALEB. One of the twelve spies who scouted Canaan. Along with Joshua, he recommended that Israel attack the Canaanites immediately (Num. 13:30). He lived to enter the land forty years later (Josh. 14:6–14). See also *Spies.*

CALF. A young cow prized as a delicacy (Gen. 18:7) and often sacrificed as a burnt offering (Lev. 9:8). See also *Fatling.*

CALF, GOLDEN. An idol built and worshiped by the Israelites in the wilderness as they waited for Moses to come down from Mount Sinai (Exod. 32:1–4). It was probably an image of Apis, a sacred bull worshiped by the Egyptians. In later years, King Jeroboam of Israel set up pagan golden calves at Dan and Bethel (1 Kings 12:26–33). See also *Idol.*

CALL [ED]
Gen. 1:5 God *c'ed* the light Day...the darkness...Night
Gen. 35:10 name shall not be *c'ed*... Jacob
2 Chron. 7:14 my [God's] people...*c'ed* by my name, shall...pray

C

Ps. 18:6 In my distress I *c'ed* upon the LORD
Isa. 9:6 his [Messiah's] name...*c'ed* Wonderful
Isa. 65:24 before they *c*, I [God] will answer
Matt. 1:21 thou [Joseph] shalt *c* his name JESUS
Matt. 9:13 I [Jesus] am not come to *c* the righteous, but sinners
Matt. 20:16 many be *c'ed*, but few chosen
Luke 6:46 why *c* ye me, Lord, Lord
Acts 2:21 shall *c* on...the Lord shall be saved
Acts 11:26 disciples...*c'ed* Christians first in Antioch
Rom. 1:1 Paul, a servant...*c'ed* to be an apostle
Rom. 8:28 work together for good...to them...*c'ed*
Rom. 10:14 *c* on him in whom they have not believed
1 Cor. 1:26 not many mighty...are *c'ed*
Eph. 4:1 walk worthy of the vocation...ye are *c'ed*
Heb. 11:8 Abraham, when he was *c'ed*...obeyed
1 John 3:1 we should be *c'ed* the sons of God

CALLING. The special summons to service that all Christians receive as part of their salvation experience (1 Cor. 7:20). See also *Vocation.*

CALNEH/CALNO. An ancient city built in southern Mesopotamia by Nimrod (Gen. 10:9–10). This may be the same city as *Canneh* (Ezek. 27:23). *Calno:* Isa. 10:9.

CALVARY (THE SKULL). A hill just outside the city walls of Jerusalem where Jesus was crucified (Luke 23:33). The word comes from a Latin word meaning "skull," thus "place of the skull." The Aramaic form of this word is *Golgotha* (Mark 15:22). *The Skull:* NIV, NRSV. See also *Cross.*

CAMEL. A hardy, humpbacked animal ideally suited to the desert climate of Palestine and used as a riding animal and beast of burden (Gen. 24:64).

CAMP. A place where tent dwellers and nomads pitch their tents. The Israelites camped in many different places during their years of wandering in the wilderness (Num. 33:1–49). See also *Wilderness Wanderings.*

CAMPHIRE (HENNA). A plant that produced a valuable red dye, used by women to adorn their lips and fingernails (Song 1:14). *Henna:* NIV, NRSV.

CANA OF GALILEE. A village near Capernaum in the district of Galilee where Jesus performed His first miracle—the transformation of water into wine at a wedding feast (John 2:1–11).

CANAAN
1. A son of Ham whose descendants founded several tribal peoples in and around Palestine (Gen. 10:1, 6, 15–18).
2. The region between the Red Sea and the Jordan River where Canaan's descendants settled and the territory that God promised to Abraham and his descendants (Gen. 15:3–7). *Chanaan:* Greek form (Acts 7:11). See also *Land of Promise.*

CANAANITES
1. The original inhabitants of Canaan who settled the land before Abraham arrived about 2000 B.C. (Gen. 12:5–6). They were eventually forced out of the land by Israel at God's command because of their pagan religious practices. Intermarriage with Canaanites by the Israelites was distinctly prohibited by God (Deut. 7:3).
2. Members of a Jewish sect in N.T. times known for their fanatical opposition to the rule of Rome. Jesus' apostle Simon the Canaanite may have been a member of, or a sympathizer with, this sect (Matt. 10:4). They were also known as the *zelotes* or *zealots.*

CANDACE. A title of the queens of Ethiopia in N.T. times (Acts 8:27).

CANDLE (LAMP). A shallow clay bowl filled with oil and a burning wick, used for illumination (Matt. 5:15). *Lamp:* NIV, NRSV.

CANDLESTICK (LAMPSTAND). A stand that held several small oil-burning lamps (Mark 4:21). *Lampstand:* NIV, NRSV.

CANKER (GANGRENE). A disease that caused rapid deterioration of the flesh (2 Tim. 2:17). *Gangrene:* NIV, NRSV.

CANKERWORM (LOCUST). A locust or grasshopper in the caterpillar stage of its growth (Joel 1:4). *Locust:* NIV, NRSV. See also *Locust; Palmerworm.*

CAPERNAUM. A city on the northwestern shore of the Sea of Galilee that served as the headquarters for Jesus during His Galilean ministry (Matt. 9:1; Mark 2:1). Capernaum was the home of His disciples Matthew (Matt. 9:9), Simon Peter, Andrew, James, and John (Mark 1:21–29).

 CAPHTOR. The original home of the Philistines, probably the island of Crete (Jer. 47:4). See also *Crete; Philistines.*

CAPITALS. See *Pommels.*

CAPPADOCIA. A Roman province of Asia Minor. Christians of Cappadocia were addressed by Peter (1 Pet. 1:1).

CAPTAIN (AUTHOR, PIONEER). A title for a civil or military officer (Judg. 4:7). This is also a title for Christ (Heb. 2:10). *Author:* NIV; *pioneer:* NRSV.

CAPTIVE [S]
Isa. 61:1 anointed me [God's servant]...proclaim liberty to the *c's*
Ezek. 1:1 I [Ezekiel] was among the *c's* by the river
Luke 4:18 he [God] hath anointed me [Jesus]...to preach deliverance to the *c's*
Eph. 4:8 When he [Jesus] ascended...he led captivity *c*

CANDLE. A worshiper lights a candle in Bethlehem's Church of the Nativity, where an ancient tradition says Jesus was born. Candles or lamps have been used in the worship of God for more than three thousand years—since the Exodus, when Jews worshiped at a tent sanctuary.

CENTURION. *Dressed for military success, this Roman soldier is suited in a metal vest and helmet. The figurine is from Roman times.*

CAPTIVITY. The carrying away of the citizens of a country by a conquering nation. The nation of Israel (the Northern Kingdom) was carried into captivity by the Assyrians about 722 B.C. (2 Kings 15:29), while Judah (the Southern Kingdom) suffered the same fate at the hands of the Babylonians in 587 B.C. (2 Chron. 36:6–7). See also *Dispersion.*

CARBUNCLE (BERYL, EMERALD). A precious stone of deep red color in the breastplate of the high priest (Exod. 28:17). *Beryl:* NIV; *emerald:* NRSV. See also *Emerald.*

CARCHEMISH CHARCHEMISH. An ancient city near the Euphrates River in Mesopotamia (Jer. 46:2), where the Assyrian army was victorious over the Egyptians. *Charchemish:* 2 Chron. 35:20–24.

CARE [S, TH]
Mark 4:19 the *c's* of this world...choke the word
John 10:13 hireling, and *c'th* not for the sheep
1 Cor. 7:33 he that is married *c'th* for the things...of
      the world
1 Tim. 3:5 shall he take *c* of the church of God
1 Pet. 5:7 your *c* upon him [Jesus]; for he *c'th* for you

CARMEL, MOUNT. A prominent mountain in northern Palestine where the prophet Elijah demonstrated the power of God in a dramatic encounter with the priests of the pagan god Baal (1 Kings 18:17–39).

CARNAL (WORLDLY). To give in to the desires of the flesh. Following their natural desires led the Christians of Corinth into division and strife (1 Cor. 3:1–5). *Worldly:* NIV.

CARRION VULTURE. See *Gier Eagle.*

CART. A two-wheeled wagon, usually pulled by oxen (1 Sam. 6:7–8). See also *Wagon.*

CASLUHIM (CASLUHITES). An ancient people descended from Mizraim (the Hebrew word for Egypt), son of Ham (Gen. 10:14). *Casluhites:* NIV. See also *Egypt; Mizraim.*

CASSIA. The dried bark of a tree similar to the cinnamon that was prized for its pleasing fragrance. Cassia was used as an ingredient of holy oil (Exod. 30:24).

CAST [ING]

Job 8:20 God will not *c* away a perfect man
Ps. 42:11 Why art thou *c* down, O my soul?
Ps. 51:11 *C* me not away from thy [God's] presence
Ps. 71:9 *C* me not off in the time of old age
Ps. 94:14 the LORD will not *c* off his people
Eccles. 3:5 time to *c* away stones, and a time to gather
Eccles. 11:1 *C* thy bread upon the waters
Jer. 7:15 I [God] will *c* you out of my sight
Matt. 3:10 tree...bringeth not forth good fruit is...*c* into the fire
Matt. 21:12 Jesus...*c* out all them that sold and bought in the temple
Matt. 27:5 he [Judas] *c* down the pieces of silver
Mark 12:43 this poor widow hath *c* more in
John 8:7 without sin...let him first *c* a stone
1 Pet. 5:7 *C'ing* all your care upon him [Jesus]; for he careth for you
Rev. 12:9 great dragon was *c* out, that old serpent

CASTAWAY. A word for "worthlessness" or "rejection." Paul used this word to express the idea of "disqualified" or "rejected" (1 Cor. 9:27).

CASTLE (BARRACKS). A fortress or defense tower. The "castle" into which Paul was taken was the quarters of the Roman soldiers at Jerusalem in the fortress of Antonia near the temple (Acts 21:34). *Barracks:* NIV, NRSV.

CASTOR AND POLLUX (TWIN BROTHERS). The twin sons of Zeus in Greek and Roman mythology who were considered special protectors of sailors. Paul's ship to Rome featured a carving of these two pagan gods (Acts 28:11). *Twin Brothers:* NRSV.

CATHOLIC EPISTLES. See *General Epistles.*

CAVE. A natural passageway or cavern within the earth. Caves were used as residences (Gen. 19:30) and burial places (Gen. 49:29). See also *Sepulchre.*

CEASE [D, ING]

Gen. 8:22 earth remaineth...day and night shall not *c*
Ps. 37:8 *C* from anger, and forsake wrath
Ps. 85:4 God...cause thine anger toward us to *c*
Mark 4:39 wind *c'd*, and there was a great calm
Acts 5:42 they [the apostles] *c'd* not to...preach Jesus Christ
1 Cor. 13:8 whether there be tongues, they shall *c*
1 Thess. 5:17 Pray without *c'ing*

CEDAR. A cone-bearing evergreen tree that produces a reddish, fragrant wood. Lumber from the cedars of Lebanon was used in the temple in Jerusalem (1 Kings 5:1–10).

CEDRON. See *Kidron.*

CENCHREA (CENCHREAE). A harbor of Corinth through which Paul passed during the second missionary journey (Acts 18:18). This was the site of a church mentioned by Paul (Rom. 16:1), perhaps a branch of the church at Corinth. *Cenchreae:* NRSV.

CENSER. A small, portable container in which incense was burned (Num. 16:6–39). See also *Firepan; Incense.*

CENSUS. A count of the population of a country or region (2 Sam. 24:1–9; Luke 2:1–3).

CENTURION. A Roman military officer who commanded a force of one hundred soldiers (Acts 10:1, 22).

CHARIOT. Storming across a field in his chariot, Ramses II, king of Egypt in the 1200s B.C., leads his army to victory over Hittite warriors.

CEPHAS. See *Simon*, No. 1.

CHAFF. The leftover husks of threshed grain, separated when the grain was tossed into the air. The ungodly are compared to chaff (Ps. 1:4). See also *Winnowing*.

CHALCEDONY (AGATE). A precious stone cut from multicolored quartz and used in the foundation of the heavenly city, or New Jerusalem (Rev. 21:19). *Agate:* NRSV. See also *Agate*.

CHALDEA, CHALDEANS. See *Babylonia*.

CHALKSTONE. A soft and easily crushed rock, similar to limestone (Isa. 27:9).

CHAMBER. A word for a room or an enclosed place in a house or public building (2 Kings 23:12).

CHAMBERLAIN (EUNUCH). An officer in charge of the royal chambers or the king's lodgings and wardrobe, and perhaps his harem (Esther 2:3). *Eunuch:* NIV, NRSV. See also *Eunuch*.

CHAMELEON. See *Mole*.

CHAMOIS (MOUNTAIN SHEEP). A word that probably refers to a wild goat or a wild mountain sheep (Deut. 14:5). *Mountain sheep:* NIV, NRSV.

CHANAAN. See *Canaan*.

CHANCELLOR (COMMANDING OFFICER, ROYAL DEPUTY). A high official of the Persian kings whose exact duties are unknown (Ezra 4:8). *Commanding officer:* NIV; *royal deputy:* NRSV.

CHANGE [D, TH]
Jer. 2:11 Hath a nation *c'd* their gods
Jer. 13:23 Can the Ethiopian *c* his skin
Dan. 2:21 he [God] *c'th* the times and the seasons
Rom. 1:23 *c'd* the glory of the uncorruptible God
Rom. 1:26 women did *c* the natural use into that...against nature
1 Cor. 15:51 shall not all sleep, but we shall all be *c'd*
Phil. 3:21 shall *c* our vile body...like...his glorious body

CHARCHEMISH. See *Carchemish.*

CHARGE [D]
Deut. 3:28 *c* Joshua, and encourage him
1 Kings 2:1 David...*c'd* Solomon his son
Ps. 91:11 he [God] shall give his angels *c* over thee
Luke 8:56 he [Jesus] *c'd* them...tell no man what was done
Acts 7:60 Lord, lay not this sin to their *c*

CHARGER (PLATTER). A dish or shallow basin used in sacrificial ceremonies (Num. 7:13, 79). The head of John the Baptist was placed on a charger (Matt. 14:11). *Platter:* NIV, NRSV. See also *Platter.*

CHARIOT. A two-wheeled carriage drawn by horses. High government officials rode in chariots, and chariots were also used as instruments of war (Judg. 4:15).

CHARIOT CITIES. The cities where Solomon stored or headquartered his chariots and chariot forces (1 Kings 9:19).

CHARIOT OF FIRE. The fiery chariot with blazing horses that came between Elijah and Elisha as Elijah was taken into heaven by a whirlwind (2 Kings 2:11). See also *Elijah.*

CHARIOTS OF THE SUN. Chariots dedicated to the sun—a popular custom among the Persians, who worshiped this heavenly body. All chariots devoted to this practice among the Israelites were burned by King Josiah of Judah (2 Kings 23:11). See also *Sun.*

CHARITY. An Old English word for "love" (1 Cor. 13). See *Love.*

Col. 3:14 above all these things put on *c*
1 Tim. 4:12 an example...in conversation, in *c*
1 Pet. 4:8 *c* shall cover the multitude of sins
Rev. 2:19 I [Jesus] know thy works, and, *c*, and service

CHARMERS. Magicians who claimed to be able to commune with the dead (Isa. 19:3). See also *Divination; Magic; Medium; Necromancer.*

CHARRAN. See *Haran.*

CHASTE. A term indicating inward cleanliness, generally referring to sexual purity (2 Cor. 11:2). See also *Clean.*

CHASTEN [ED, EST, ETH, ING]
Ps. 73:14 the day long have I been...*c'ed* every morning
Ps. 94:12 Blessed is the man whom thou *c'est*, O LORD
Prov. 3:11 My son, despise not the *c'ing* of the LORD
Heb. 12:6 whom the Lord loveth he *c'eth*
Rev. 3:19 As many as I love, I rebuke and *c*

CHASTISEMENT (DISCIPLINE). Punishment or discipline inflicted by God for guiding and correcting His children (Heb. 12:8). *Discipline:* NIV, NRSV. See also *Discipline.*

CHEBAR. A river or canal of Babylonia where Jewish captives settled during the Exile. Ezekiel's visions came to him at Chebar (Ezek. 1:3; 10:15, 20).

CHEDORLAOMER. A king of Elam who invaded Canaan in Abraham's time (Gen. 14:1–16).

CHEEK. To strike a person on the cheek was considered a grave insult (Job 16:10). Jesus taught believers to react to such acts with kindness (Luke 6:29).

CHEER
Matt. 9:2 Son [man with palsy], be of good *c*
John 16:33 be of good *c*; I [Jesus] have overcome the world
Acts 23:11 Be of good *c*, Paul...thou bear witness also at Rome

CHEERFUL
Prov. 15:13 merry heart maketh a *c* countenance
Zech. 9:17 corn shall make the young men *c*
2 Cor. 9:7 let him give...for God loveth a *c* giver

CHEMOSH. The chief pagan god of the Moabites and Ammonites to which children were sacrificed (Judg. 11:24; 2 Kings 23:13). See also *Human Sacrifice.*

CHERETHITES/CHERETHIMS. A tribe of the Philistines in southwest Palestine (1 Sam. 30:14). *Cherethims:* Ezek. 25:16.

CHERITH. A brook where the prophet Elijah hid and where he was fed by ravens during a famine (1 Kings 17:3–5).

CHERUBIMS. An order of angelic, winged creatures (Gen. 3:24). Their function was to praise God and glorify His name (Ezek. 10:18–20).

CHIEF. Head of a tribe or family (Num. 3:24, 30, 32, 35). See also *Duke.*

CHIEF SEATS. Places of honor sought by the scribes and Pharisees. Jesus taught His followers that the highest honor is to serve others (Mark 12:38–39).

CHILD
Gen. 17:17 a *c* be born unto him...an hundred years old
Prov. 22:6 Train up a *c* in the way he should go

Isa. 9:6 unto us a *c* is born
Jer. 1:6 behold, I [Jeremiah] cannot speak: for I am a *c*
Hosea 11:1 When Israel was a *c*, then I [God] loved him
Matt. 1:23 a virgin shall be with *c*
Matt. 18:4 humble himself as this little *c*...is greatest
Luke 2:40 the *c* [Jesus] grew, and waxed strong in spirit
1 Cor. 13:11 When I [Paul] was a *c*, I spake as a *c*

CHILD SACRIFICE. See *Human Sacrifice.*

CHILDREN. Children were looked upon as blessings from God (Ps. 127:3), and childlessness was considered a curse (Deut. 7:14). The word is also used symbolically of those who belong to Christ (Rom. 8:16–17). See also *Parents.*

Gen. 3:16 in sorrow thou [Eve] shalt bring forth *c*
Exod. 1:7 *c* of Israel were fruitful, and increased
Exod. 20:5 iniquity of the fathers upon the *c*
Josh. 4:6 your *c*...What mean ye by these stones
Ps. 103:13 father pitieth his *c*, so the LORD pitieth them that fear him
Ps. 127:3 *c* are an heritage of the LORD
Prov. 20:7 *c* are blessed after him [the just man]
Prov. 31:28 *c* arise up, and call her blessed
Jer. 31:15 Rahel weeping for her *c*
Matt. 7:11 give good gifts unto your *c*
Matt. 18:3 become as little *c*, ye shall not enter into the kingdom
Mark 10:13 they brought young *c* to him [Jesus]
John 12:36 that ye may be the *c* of light
Eph. 6:1 *C*, obey your parents in the Lord
Eph. 6:4 fathers, provoke not your *c* to wrath

CHINNEROTH. See *Galilee, Sea of.*

CHISLEU (KISLEV, CHISLEV). The ninth month of the Hebrew year, roughly equivalent to parts of our November and December (Neh. 1:1). *Kislev:* NIV; *Chislev:* NRSV.

CHITTIM. See *Cyprus.*

CHLOE. A Christian disciple at the place from which Paul sent his first epistle to the Corinthians—probably Philippi (1 Cor. 1:11).

CHOOSE [ING]

Deut. 7:7 LORD did not...*c* you, because ye were more in number
Deut. 30:19 *c* life, that both thou and thy seed may live
Josh. 24:15 *c* you this day whom ye will serve
Phil. 1:22 yet what I [Paul] shall *c* I wot not
Heb. 11:25 *C'ing* rather to suffer affliction

CHORAZIN. A city north of the Sea of Galilee where Jesus did many mighty works. He pronounced a woe on this city because of its unbelief (Matt. 11:21).

CHOSEN

Deut. 7:6 God hath *c* thee to be a special people
Prov. 22:1 good name is rather to be *c* than great riches
Isa. 43:10 Ye are...my [God's] servant whom I have *c*
Matt. 12:18 Behold my [God's] servant, whom I have *c*
Matt. 20:16 many be called, but few *c*
Luke 10:42 Mary hath *c* that good part
John 15:16 Ye have not *c* me [Jesus], but I have *c* you
Acts 9:15 he [Paul] is a *c* vessel unto me [Jesus]
1 Cor. 1:27 God hath *c* the foolish things of the world to confound the wise
2 Thess. 2:13 God hath...*c* you to salvation
1 Pet. 2:9 ye are a *c* generation, a royal priesthood

CHOSEN LADY. See *Elect Lady.*

CHRIST. See *Jesus Christ.*

CHRISTIAN. A disciple or follower of Christ. The name apparently was first used of the believers in the church at Antioch (Acts 11:26). Other words that express the same idea are *saint* (Acts 9:13) and *brethren* (Acts 6:3). See also *Way, The.*

CHRONICLES, BOOKS OF FIRST AND SECOND. Two historical books of the O.T. that cover several centuries of history, beginning with a genealogy of Adam and his descendants (1 Chron. 1–9) and ending with the return of Jewish captives to their homeland about 538 B.C. following a period of exile among the Babylonians and Persians (2 Chron. 36).

Major events covered in the books include (1) the death of King Saul (1 Chron. 10); (2) the reign of King David (1 Chron. 10–29); (3) the reign of King Solomon (2 Chron. 1–9); and (4) the reigns of selected kings of Judah after the division of the kingdom into two nations following Solomon's death (2 Chron. 10–36).

CHRYSOLYTE (CHRYSOLITE). A precious stone, possibly yellow topaz, used in the foundation of the heavenly city, or New Jerusalem (Rev. 21:20). *Chrysolite:* NIV, NRSV. See also *Beryl.*

CHRYSOPRASUS (CHRYSOPRASE). A precious stone, green in color and similar to agate, used in the foundation of the heavenly city, or New Jerusalem (Rev. 21:20). *Chrysoprase:* NIV, NRSV. See also *Beryl.*

CHURCH. A local body of believers assembled for Christian worship (Acts 15:4; 1 Cor. 1:22) as well as all the redeemed of the ages who belong to Christ (Gal. 1:13; Eph. 5:27). The word *church* is a translation of a Greek term that means "an assembly."

Christ is head of His body, the Church, and His will is to be preeminent (Col. 1:18) by virtue of His redeeming work and lordship (Col. 1:14; 3:15–17). The Church's mission is to win the lost (Luke 4:18) and minister to others in the world. See also *Assembly; Congregation; People of God; Saint.*

CHURCH [ES]

Matt. 16:18 Peter, and upon this rock I [Jesus] will build my *c*
Matt. 18:17 neglect to hear them, tell it unto the *c*
Acts 2:47 added to the *c* daily such as should be saved
Acts 5:11 fear came upon all the *c*
Acts 8:3 Saul, he made havock of the *c*
Acts 14:23 they [Paul and Barnabas] had ordained them elders in every *c*
Acts 20:28 the Holy Ghost hath made you overseers, to feed the *c* of God

C

Rom. 16:16 The *c'es* of Christ salute you
1 Cor. 14:4 he that prophesieth edifieth the *c*
Gal. 1:13 I [Paul] persecuted the *c* of God
Eph. 3:21 be glory in the *c* by Christ Jesus
Eph. 5:25 Christ also loved the *c*, and gave himself for it
Col. 1:18 he [Christ] is the head of the body, the *c*
1 Tim. 3:5 how shall he take care of the *c* of God
1 Tim. 3:15 *c* of the living God...pillar and ground of...truth
James 5:14 elders of the *c*, and let them pray over him
Rev. 1:4 John to the seven *c'es* which are in Asia

CHUSHAN-RISHATHAIM (CUSHAN-RISHATHAIM).

A king of Mesopotamia who oppressed the Israelites. He was defeated by the first judge, Othniel (Judg. 3:8–10). *Cushan-rishathaim:* NIV, NRSV.

CILICIA.

A province of Asia Minor whose major city was Tarsus, Paul's hometown. Paul visited Cilicia after his conversion (Acts 15:40–41; Gal. 1:21).

CIRCUMCISE [D]

Gen. 17:11 shall *c* the flesh of your foreskin
Gen. 17:24 Abraham was ninety years old and nine, when he was *c'd*
Jer. 4:4 *C* yourselves to the LORD
Acts 15:1 certain men...said, Except ye be *c'd*...cannot be saved
Gal. 5:2 I if ye be *c'd*, Christ shall profit you nothing
Phil. 3:5 *C'd* the eighth day, of the stock of Israel

CIRCUMCISION.

The removal of the foreskin of the male sex organ, a ritual performed generally on the eighth day after birth (Lev. 12:3). This practice, probably initiated with Abraham (Gen. 17:9–14), signified the covenant between God and His people, the Israelites. In the N.T., the word is often used symbolically for the casting off of sin or worldly desires (Col. 2:11).

Acts 10:45 they of the *c* which believed were astonished
Rom. 3:1 or what profit is there of *c*
Rom. 15:8 Christ was a minister of the *c* for the truth of God
1 Cor. 7:19 *C* is nothing, and uncircumcision is nothing
Col. 3:11 neither Greek nor Jew, *c* nor uncircumcision

CIRCUMSPECT.

Prudent and holy. Paul charged the Ephesian Christians to live circumspectly (Eph. 5:15).

CISTERN.

A large pit or hole in the ground that served as a water reservoir (2 Kings 18:31). Empty cisterns were sometimes used as dungeons or prisons (Gen. 37:24). See also *Pit; Prison.*

CITIES OF REFUGE.

Six cities assigned to the Levites and set aside as sanctuaries for those who killed other persons by accident. These cities, scattered throughout Palestine, were Bezer, Golan, Hebron, Kedesh, Ramoth-gilead, and Shechem (Josh. 20:7–9). See also *Avenger of Blood; Manslayer.*

SAFETY IN THE CITIES

In the six cities of refuge (Josh. 20), Jewish citizens were protected from revenge by relatives of the deceased while a system of due process was put into motion. After investigating the matter, city officials issued the final judgment on whether a person was innocent or guilty of murder.

CITIES OF THE PLAIN.

Five cities on the plain of Jordan destroyed in Abraham's time because of the great sin of their inhabitants. These cities were Admah, Bela or Zoar, Gomorrah, Sodom, and Zeboiim (Gen. 14:1–2).

CITRON WOOD.

See *Thyine Wood.*

CITY.

A population center where trade and commerce flourished. Many biblical cities were protected by massive defensive walls. The first city mentioned in the Bible was built by Cain (Gen. 4:17). See also *Fenced City.*

CITY CLERK. See *Town Clerk.*

CITY GATE. A massive wooden door in a city wall, often reinforced with brass or iron for greater strength. Goods were often bought and sold and legal matters were discussed just inside the gate (Ruth 4:11). Gates in the wall of Jerusalem mentioned by name in the Bible include the Beautiful Gate (Acts 3:10), Fish Gate (Neh. 3:3), Horse Gate (2 Chron. 23:15), and Water Gate (Neh. 3:26). See also *Fenced City.*

CITY OF DAVID. A title applied to Bethlehem and Jerusalem because of David's close association with these cities (Neh. 3:15; Luke 2:11). See also *Bethlehem; Jerusalem.*

CITY OF GOD. A name applied to the city of Jerusalem, religious capital of the nation of Israel (Ps. 46:4–5).

CITY OF DAVID. *The City of David rested on a ridge in what is now just a small plug of ground in the urban sprawl of Jerusalem. David's capital sat in the outlined area below the dotted line. His son Solomon later expanded the city above by adding the temple complex.*

CLAUDIUS. See *Caesar,* No. 3.

CLAUDIUS LYSIAS. A Roman military officer who rescued Paul from an angry mob at Jerusalem (Acts 21:30–35; 23:22–30).

CLAY. Fine soil used for making bricks and pottery (Jer. 18:1–6). While still moist, squares of clay were also written on, then baked to produce a hard, permanent tablet.

CLAY TABLET. See *Tile.*

CLEAN. A word used by the Hebrews to describe things that were ceremonially pure (Lev. 11). The word is also used symbolically to signify holiness or righteousness (Ps. 24:4). See also *Purification; Wash.*

CLEANSE [D, TH]
Lev. 16:30 priest make an atonement...to *c* you
Ps. 51:2 Wash me...*c* me from my sin
Matt. 11:5 lepers are *c'd*, and the deaf hear

C

Matt. 23:26 *c* first that which is within the cup
Luke 17:17 not ten *c'd*? but where are the nine
Acts 10:15 God hath *c'd*, that call not thou [Peter] common
2 Cor. 7:1 let us *c* ourselves from all filthiness
1 John 1:7 blood of Jesus Christ...*c'th* us from all sin
1 John 1:9 he [Jesus] is faithful...*c* us from all unrighteousness

CLEAVE. To hold firmly to or to remain faithful. Husbands are instructed to cleave to their wives (Matt. 19:5).

Gen. 2:24 leave his father...mother...*c* unto his wife
Josh. 23:8 But *c* unto the LORD your God
Mark 10:7 leave his father...mother...*c* to his wife
Rom. 12:9 Abhor...evil; *c* to that which is good

CLEOPAS. A Christian believer to whom Christ appeared on the road to Emmaus after His resurrection (Luke 24:18).

CLOKE/CLOAK. A one-piece, sleeveless garment, similar to a short robe, worn by both men and women in Bible times (Matt. 5:40). *Cloak:* NIV, NRSV. See also *Mantle.*

CLOTH. See *Handkerchief; Napkin.*

CLOTHED [ING]
2 Chron. 6:41 LORD God, be *c* with salvation
Ps. 93:1 The LORD...is *c* with majesty
Prov. 31:25 Strength and honour are her *c'ing*

CHRIST'S SUFFICIENCY IN COLOSSIANS

In his epistle to the Colossians, Paul presents Jesus Christ as the all-sufficient Savior. He is the Redeemer (Col. 1:14), the firstborn from the dead (1:18), the mystery of God (2:2), the victor over all principalities and powers (2:10), the exalted and glorified One (3:1), and the guarantee of our eternal inheritance (3:24).

Isa. 61:10 he [God] hath *c* me with the garments of salvation
Matt. 7:15 false prophets...in sheep's *c'ing*
Matt. 25:36 Naked, and ye *c* me
Mark 1:6 John was *c* with camel's hair
Mark 12:38 the scribes...love to go in long *c'ing*
Mark 15:17 they *c* him [Jesus] with purple
Luke 16:19 a certain rich man...*c* in purple

CLOTHES
Josh. 7:6 Joshua rent his *c*, and fell to the earth
Prov. 6:27 take fire in his bosom, and his *c* not be burned
Luke 2:7 wrapped him [Jesus] in swaddling *c*
John 19:40 wound it [Jesus' body] in linen *c*

CLOUD. A mass of water vapor in the sky. Clouds are often associated with God's presence and protection (Exod. 16:10). At His second coming, Christ will come in "the clouds of heaven" (Matt. 24:30). See also *Pillar of Fire and Cloud.*

CLUB. See *Maul.*

COAT OF MAIL. See *Brigandine.*

COCK. A rooster. The crowing of the cock in Mark 13:35 refers to the third watch of the night, just before daybreak.

COCKATRICE (ADDER, VIPER). A poisonous snake (Isa. 11:8). *Adder:* NRSV; *viper:* NIV.

COCKLE (WEED). A weed that grows in fields of grain (Job 31:40). *Weed:* NIV, NRSV.

COLOSSE (COLOSSAE). A city about 100 miles east of Ephesus and the site of a church to which Paul wrote one of his epistles (Col. 1:2). Whether Paul visited this city is uncertain. *Colossae:* NRSV.

8
D
3

COLOSSIANS, EPISTLE TO THE. A short epistle of the apostle Paul on the theme of Christ's glory and majesty and His work of redemption (chaps. 1–2). Paul also challenged the Christians at Colosse to put on the character of Christ and to express His love in their relationships with others (chaps. 3–4).

COLT. A young donkey. Christ rode a colt into Jerusalem (Matt. 21:1–7). See also *Ass.*

COMFORT [ED]
Job 2:11 Job's three friends...came...to *c* him
Ps. 23:4 thy [God's] rod and thy staff they *c* me
Isa. 40:1 *C* ye, *c* ye my people, saith your God
Jer. 31:15 Rahel weeping...refused to be *c'ed* for her children
Matt. 5:4 Blessed are they that mourn...shall be *c'ed*
1 Thess. 4:18 *c* one another with these words

COMFORTER (COUNSELOR, ADVOCATE).
A title for the Holy Spirit that means "to strengthen" or "to bolster" (John 14:16, 26; 15:26; 16:7). *Counselor:* NIV; *Advocate:* NRSV. See also *Advocate; Helper; Holy Spirit; Paraclete.*

COMMAND [ED, ETH]
Gen. 7:5 Noah did...all that the LORD *c'ed* him
Matt. 28:20 observe all things whatsoever I [Jesus] have *c'ed* you
Mark 6:8 [Jesus] *c'ed* them...take nothing for their journey
Luke 4:3 *c* this stone that it be made bread
Luke 8:25 he [Jesus] *c'eth* even the winds and water
John 15:17 These things I [Jesus] *c* you...love one another

COMMANDING OFFICER. See *Chancellor.*

COMMANDMENT. An order imposed by a person of rank or authority (Neh. 11:23). Jesus described the statute to love God and man as the greatest commandment (John 13:34). See also *Statute.*

COMMANDMENT [S]
Exod. 34:28 he [Moses] wrote...the ten *c's*
Ezra 9:10 we have forsaken thy [God's] *c's*
Ps. 111:7 his [God's] *c's* are sure
Prov. 10:8 wise in heart will receive *c's*
Amos 2:4 have...not kept his [God's] *c's*

Matt. 15:3 ye [Pharisees]...transgress the *c* of God
Mark 12:28 Which is the first *c* of all
John 14:15 love me [Jesus], keep my *c's*
John 15:10 keep my [Jesus'] *c's*, ye shall abide in my love
1 John 2:3 we know him [Jesus], if we keep his *c's*
2 John 6 this is love, that we walk after his [God's] *c's*

COMMANDMENTS, TEN. See *Ten Commandments.*

COMMEND [ED, ETH]
Prov. 12:8 man shall be *c'ed* according to his wisdom
Luke 16:8 the lord *c'ed* the unjust steward
Luke 23:46 into thy hands I [Jesus] *c* my spirit
Rom. 5:8 God *c'eth* his love toward us...Christ died for us

COMMISSION. A special assignment from a person of authority (Ezra 8:36). Jesus' Great Commission to all His followers is to make disciples of all people everywhere (Matt. 28:19–20).

COMMIT [TED, TETH]
Exod. 20:14 Thou shalt not *c* adultery
Ps. 31:5 Into thine [God's] hand I [Jesus] *c* my spirit
Prov. 16:3 *C* thy works unto the LORD
Matt. 5:28 looketh on a woman to lust...hath *c'ted* adultery
John 5:22 Father...hath *c'ted* all judgment unto the Son
John 8:34 Whosoever *c'teth* sin is the servant of sin
1 Cor. 6:18 he that *c'teth* fornication sinneth against his own body
2 Cor. 5:19 God...hath *c'ted* unto us the word of reconciliation
1 John 3:9 Whosoever is born of God doth not *c* sin

COMMUNICATION [S]
Matt. 5:37 let your *c* be, Yea, yea; Nay, nay
Luke 24:17 What manner of *c's* are these
Eph. 4:29 Let no corrupt *c* proceed out of your mouth

COMMUNION
1 Cor. 10:16 cup of blessing...*c* of the blood of Christ
2 Cor. 6:14 what *c* hath light with darkness
2 Cor. 13:14 *c* of the Holy Ghost, be with you all

COMPACT. See *League.*

COMPANION. See *Yokefellow.*

COMPASSION. An attitude of mercy and forgiveness. As the compassionate Savior (Matt. 15:32), Jesus expects His followers to show compassion toward others (Matt. 18:33). See also *Mercy.*

Ps. 145:8 The Lord is gracious, and full of *c*
Jer. 12:15 I [God] will return, and have *c* on them
Matt. 14:14 Jesus...was moved with *c* toward them
Mark 9:22 if thou canst do any thing, have *c* on us
Luke 10:33 a certain Samaritan...had *c* on him
Luke 15:20 his father...had *c,* and ran, and fell on his neck
1 Pet. 3:8 be ye all of one mind, having *c* one of another

CONCEIT. Vanity or pride; to have an exaggerated opinion of oneself. Paul warned Christians against such behavior (Rom. 11:25; 12:16). See also *Pride; Vanity.*

CONCEIVE [D]
Gen. 21:2 Sarah *c'd,* and bare Abraham a son
Ps. 51:5 in sin did my mother *c* me
Isa. 7:14 a virgin shall *c,* and bear a son
Matt. 1:20 that...*c'd* in her [Mary] is of the Holy Ghost
Heb. 11:11 Sara herself received strength to *c* seed

CONCUBINE. A female slave or mistress; a secondary or common-law wife. Concubines were common among the patriarchs of the O.T. (Gen. 35:22), but Jesus taught the concept of monogamy—marriage to one person only (Matt. 19:4–9). See also *Paramour.*

CONCUPISCENCE (EVIL DE-SIRES). Sinful desire or sexual lust. Paul warned Christians of the dangers of this sin (Col. 3:5). *Evil desires:* NIV, NRSV.

CONDEMN [ED, ETH]
Job 15:6 Thine own mouth *c'eth* thee
Prov. 12:2 man of wicked devices will he [God] *c*
Matt. 12:37 by thy words thou shalt be *c'ed*
Luke 6:37 *c* not, and ye shall not be *c'ed*
John 3:17 God sent not his Son...to *c* the world
John 8:11 Neither do I [Jesus] *c* thee: go...sin no more

CONDEMNATION. The act of declaring a sinner guilty and deserving of punishment

CONDUIT. Israel's most famous conduit is Hezekiah's Tunnel, chiseled through nearly six hundred yards of solid rock. King Hezekiah built the conduit to bring water from an underground spring outside Jerusalem's protective walls to a pool inside the city.

(Rom. 5:18). Jesus' mission was not to condemn but to save (John 3:17–18).

Rom. 8:1 no *c* to them which are in Christ Jesus
James 3:1 we shall receive the greater *c*
James 5:12 yea be yea...lest ye fall into *c*

CONDUIT. A pipe or aqueduct through which water was channeled. King Hezekiah of Judah cut a conduit through solid rock to pipe water into Jerusalem (2 Kings 20:20). See also *Hezekiah.*

CONEY (BADGER). A small, furry animal that lived among the rocky cliffs of Palestine—probably the rock badger (Prov. 30:26). *Badger:* NRSV.

CONFESS. To admit or acknowledge one's sin (Josh. 7:19) and to proclaim one's faith in a bold and forthright manner (Rom. 10:9–10).

CONFESS [ETH]
Ps. 32:5 I will *c* my transgressions unto the LORD
Luke 12:8 him shall the Son of man also *c*
Rom. 10:9 if thou shalt *c* with thy mouth the Lord Jesus
Phil. 2:11 tongue should *c* that Jesus Christ is Lord
James 5:16 *C* your faults one to another
1 John 1:9 we *c* our sins, he is faithful and just to forgive
1 John 4:2 Every spirit that *c'eth* that Jesus Christ is come in the flesh is of God
Rev. 3:5 I [Jesus] will *c* his name before my Father

CONFIDENCE
Ps. 118:9 better to trust in the LORD...put *c* in princes
Prov. 14:26 In the fear of the LORD is strong *c*
Isa. 30:15 in quietness and in *c* shall be your strength
Eph. 3:12 In whom [Jesus] we have...access with *c*

CONFIDENT
Prov. 14:16 the fool rageth, and is *c*
2 Cor. 5:8 We are *c*...willing...to be absent from the body
Phil. 1:6 Being *c*...he which hath begun a good work...will perform it

CONGREGATION. A gathering of people for worship or religious instruction (Acts 13:43). See also *Assembly.*

CONIAH. See *Jehoiachin.*

CONSCIENCE
John 8:9 they [scribes and Pharisees]...convicted by their own *c*
Acts 23:1 I [Paul] have lived in all good *c* before God
1 Cor. 10:27 eat, asking no question for *c* sake
1 Tim. 3:9 mystery of the faith in a pure *c*

CONSECRATION. To dedicate or set apart for God's exclusive use. Believers are encouraged to consecrate or sanctify themselves to God's service (2 Tim. 2:21). See also *Ordain; Sanctification.*

CONSENT [ING]
Prov. 1:10 if sinners entice thee, *c* thou not
Luke 14:18 all with one *c* began to make excuse
Acts 8:1 Saul was *c'ing* unto his [Stephen's] death
1 Cor. 7:5 Defraud ye not...except it be with *c* for a time

CONSIDER [ING]
1 Sam. 12:24 *c* how great things he [God] hath done
Job 37:14 stand still, and *c* the wondrous works of God
Ps. 8:3 When I *c* thy [God's] heavens, the work of thy fingers
Prov. 6:6 Go to the ant, thou sluggard; *c* her ways
Isa. 43:18 neither *c* the things of old
Hag. 1:5 thus saith the LORD of hosts; *C* your ways
Matt. 6:28 *C* the lilies of the field, how they grow
Gal. 6:1 *c'ing* thyself, lest thou also be tempted

CONSOLATION. A word that expresses the idea of comfort combined with encouragement. Believers find consolation in Jesus Christ and His Holy Spirit (Rom. 15:5).

Luke 2:25 man [Simeon]...waiting for the *c* of Israel
Acts 4:36 Barnabas...being interpreted, The son of *c*
Phil. 2:1 If there be therefore any *c* in Christ

CONTENTION (DISAGREEMENT). Severe disagreement that leads to sharp divisions

C

among people, including Christian believers (Acts 15:39). Christians are encouraged to pursue peace with others (Rom. 12:18–21). *Disagreement:* NIV, NRSV. See also *Discord; Strife.*

CONTENTMENT. Satisfaction; freedom from worry and anxiety. This state of mind was modeled for all believers by Paul (Phil. 4:11; 1 Tim. 6:8).

CONTINUE [D, ING]
Luke 6:12 he [Jesus]...*c'd* all night in prayer
John 8:31 ye *c* in my [Jesus'] word...ye my disciples indeed
Acts 1:14 These all *c'd* with one accord in prayer
Acts 2:46 they [the believers], *c'ing* daily with one accord
Rom. 6:1 Shall we *c* in sin, that grace may abound
1 Tim. 4:16 Take heed...unto the doctrine; *c* in them
Heb. 13:1 Let brotherly love *c*
2 Pet. 3:4 all things *c* as they were from the beginning

CONTRITE. A meek or humble attitude (Ps. 51:17). A contrite person also shows genuine grief or sorrow over his or her sin (2 Cor. 7:10). See also *Humility; Meekness; Repentance.*

CONVERSATION. A word for behavior or lifestyle. Paul urged Christians to live in accordance with the gospel of Christ (Phil. 1:27).

Gal. 1:13 heard of my [Paul's] *c* in time past
1 Tim. 4:12 be thou an example...in *c*, in charity
Heb. 13:5 Let your *c* be without covetousness

CONVERSION. See *New Birth.*

CONVERTED [ING]
Ps. 19:7 The law of the LORD is perfect, *c'ing* the soul
Ps. 51:13 sinners shall be *c* unto thee [God]
Matt. 18:3 Except ye be *c*, and become as little children
Acts 3:19 Repent ye therefore, and be *c*

CONVICTION. An awareness of one's sin and guilt (John 8:9) that leads to confession and repentance. The Holy Spirit is the agent of conviction (Heb. 3:7). See also *Holy Spirit; Repentance.*

CONVOCATION. A sacred assembly of the people of Israel for worship in connection with observance of the Sabbath or one of their major religious festivals, such as Passover or Pentecost (Lev. 23:2–8). See also *Assembly.*

COPPER. See *Brass.*

COR. The largest liquid measure used by the Hebrew people, possibly equivalent to fifty or more gallons (Ezek. 45:14).

CORAL. A precious substance formed in the sea from the bodies of tiny sea creatures (Ezek. 27:16). Coral was apparently used for making beads and other fine jewelry (Job 28:18). See also *Ruby.*

CORBAN. A Hebrew word meaning a sacred gift, or an offering devoted to God. Jesus condemned the Pharisees for encouraging people to make such gifts while neglecting to care for their own parents (Mark 7:11–13).

CORD. See *Line; Rope.*

CORE. See *Korah.*

CORIANDER. A plant whose seeds were used as a medicine and as a seasoning for food (Num. 11:7).

CORINTH. A major port city in Greece on the trade route between Rome and its eastern provinces where Paul lived for eighteen months, establishing a church (Acts 18:1–11). The city was known for its immorality, paganism, and corruption.

8
A
2

THE GOSPEL IN CORINTH

A thriving commercial city, Corinth had a population of about 500,000 people in Paul's time. It was an ideal location for a church, since it could bear a witness to the merchants who visited the city as well as the people in the smaller towns that surrounded the metropolitan area. In spite of its reputation as a pagan and immoral city, Corinth was open to Paul's proclamation of the saving grace of Jesus Christ.

CORINTHIANS, FIRST AND SECOND EPISTLES TO THE. Two letters of the apostle Paul to the church at Corinth, written to believers who were struggling to move beyond their pagan background and lifestyle.

First Corinthians deals mainly with problems in the church, including divisions (chaps. 1–4), sexual immorality (chaps. 5–6), and abuses of the Lord's Supper and spiritual gifts (chaps. 11–12; 14).

The themes of 2 Corinthians include Paul's view of ministry and reconciliation (chaps. 1–6), support of the impoverished Christians at Jerusalem (chaps. 8–9), and Paul's example of suffering and abuse and defense of his credentials as an apostle (chaps. 10–13).

CORMORANT (DESERT OWL, HAWK). A large bird cited by Isaiah as a symbol of desolation and destruction (Isa. 34:11). *Desert owl:* NIV; *hawk:* NRSV. See also *Pelican.*

CORN (GRAIN). A generic term for several different grains, including wheat, barley, and millet (Matt. 12:1). *Grain:* NIV, NRSV. See also *Wheat.*

CORNELIUS. A Roman soldier from Caesarea who sought out the apostle Peter at Joppa and became the first Gentile convert to Christianity (Acts 10). This event showed clearly that the Christian faith was meant for Gentiles as well as Jews (Acts 15:7–11).

CORNER STONE. A stone strategically placed to align two walls and tie the building together. This is also a title for Christ as the keystone of the church (Eph. 2:20). See also *Foundation.*

CORNET (HORN). A musical instrument similar to the horn or trumpet (Dan. 3:5–7). *Horn:* NIV, NRSV.

CORRUPT [ED]
Gen. 6:11 earth also was *c* before God
Job 17:1 My [Job's] breath is *c*
Matt. 6:20 treasures in heaven...moth nor rust doth *c*
Luke 6:43 good tree bringeth not forth *c* fruit
James 5:2 Your riches are *c'ed*...garments are motheaten

CORRUPTION
1 Cor. 15:42 It [the body] is sown in *c*...raised in incorruption
Gal. 6:8 he that soweth to his flesh shall of the flesh reap *c*

COULTER (PLOWSHARE). An agricultural instrument of metal, probably the tip of a plow (1 Sam. 13:21). *Plowshare:* NIV, NRSV. See also *Plowshare.*

COUNCIL/SANHEDRIN. The highest court of the Jewish nation in N.T. times, composed of seventy-one priests, scribes, and elders and presided over by the high priest. The Council accused Jesus of blasphemy against God, but it didn't have the power to put Jesus to death. It brought Him before Pilate, the Roman procurator, for sentencing (Matt. 26:65–66; John 18:31; 19:12). The Council also brought charges against Peter and John and the other

COURT OF THE GENTILES. The expansive Court of the Gentiles outside these walls was as close as non-Jews could get to the Jerusalem temple sanctuary inside. Jews, however, could go to interior courtyards. Only priests were allowed inside the sanctuary.

apostles (Acts 4:1–23; 5:17–41) and Paul (Acts 22–24). *Sanhedrin:* NIV.

COUNSELLOR (COUNSELOR). A person who gives wise counsel or imparts advice. Kings employed counselors (1 Chron. 27:33). This is also one of the messianic titles of Christ (Isa. 9:6). *Counselor:* NIV, NRSV. See also *Comforter; Holy Spirit; Paraclete.*

COUNT [ED, ETH]
Gen. 15:6 and he [God] *c'ed* it [Abraham's faith]...for righteousness
Ps. 44:22 we are *c'ed* as sheep for the slaughter
Luke 14:28 sitteth not down first, and *c'eth* the cost
Rom. 4:3 it was *c'ed* unto him [Abraham] for righteousness
Phil. 3:8 I [Paul] *c* all things but loss
Phil. 3:13 I [Paul] *c* not myself to have apprehended
2 Thess. 1:5 may be *c'ed* worthy of the kingdom of God
James 1:2 *c* it all joy when ye fall into...temptations

COUNTENANCE. A word for the face or the expression on a person's face (Dan. 5:6).

COURAGE. Fearlessness and bravery in the face of danger (Acts 28:15). Moses exhorted Joshua to have courage (Deut. 31:7–8).

COURIER. See *Post.*

COURT. An enclosed yard or patio attached to a house or public building. Both the tabernacle (Exod. 27:9) and the temple in Jerusalem had courts or courtyards (1 Kings 6:36).

COURT OF THE GENTILES. An outer court in the Jewish temple beyond which Gentile worshipers could not go. The splitting of the curtain between this court and the inner court at Jesus' death symbolized the

Gentiles' equal access to God (Matt. 27:51; Eph. 2:11–14). See also *Gentile; Middle Wall of Partition.*

COUSIN. A general term denoting any degree of relationship among blood relatives—cousin, nephew, aunt, uncle, etc. (Luke 1:36).

COVENANT. An agreement between two people or groups, particularly the agreement between God and His people that promised His blessings in return for their obedience and devotion (Gen. 15). Through His sacrificial death, Jesus became the mediator of a new covenant, bringing salvation and eternal life to all who trust in Him (Heb. 10:12–17). See also *Testament.*

COVENANT [S]
Gen. 9:9 I [God] establish my *c* with you [Noah]
Gen. 15:18 the Lord made a *c* with Abram
Deut. 4:23 Take heed...lest ye forget the *c* of the Lord
Deut. 29:9 Keep therefore the words of this *c*
1 Sam. 18:3 Jonathan and David made a *c*
Jer. 11:3 Cursed be the man that obeyeth not...this *c*
Jer. 31:31 I [God] will make a new *c* with...Israel
Eph. 2:12 aliens...and strangers from the *c's* of promise
Heb. 8:6 he [Jesus] is the mediator of a better *c*

COVERED COLONNADE. See *Portico.*

COVET [ED]
Exod. 20:17 Thou shalt not *c* thy neighbour's house
Acts 20:33 I [Paul] have *c'ed* no man's silver
1 Cor. 12:31 But *c* earnestly the best gifts

COVETOUSNESS. Greed, or a burning desire for what belongs to others. This sin is specifically prohibited by the Ten Commandments (Exod. 20:17), and Paul warned against its dangers (Col. 3:5). See also *Greed.*

Ps. 119:36 heart unto thy [God's] testimonies...not to *c*
Luke 12:15 Take heed, and beware of *c*
Heb. 13:5 Let your conversation be without *c*

COW. See *Kine.*

CREATE [D]
Gen. 1:1 God *c'd* the heaven and the earth
Gen. 1:27 God *c'd* man in his own image
Ps. 51:10 *C* in me a clean heart, O God
Jer. 31:22 Lord hath *c'd* a new thing in the earth
1 Cor. 11:9 Neither was the man *c'd* for the woman
Eph. 2:10 we are his workmanship, *c'd* in Christ Jesus
Col. 1:16 all things were *c'd* by him [Jesus]
Rev. 4:11 for thou [God] hast *c'd* all things

CREATION. The actions of God through which He brought man and the physical world into existence. God existed before the world, and He produced the universe from nothing (Gen. 1:1–2). As the sovereign, self-existing God, He also rules over His creation (Ps. 47:7–9). See also *Creature.*

CREATOR. A title for God that emphasizes that He is the maker of all things and the sovereign ruler of His creation (Isa. 40:28; John 1:1–3; Col. 1:15–16). See also *Almighty; Sovereignty of God.*

CREATURE (CREATION). Any being created by God, including humans (Gen. 2:19). Through God's redemption, a believer becomes a new creature (2 Cor. 5:17). *Creation:* NIV, NRSV. See also *Creation.*

CRETE. A large island in the Mediterranean Sea by which Paul sailed during his voyage to Rome (Acts 27:1–13). Titus apparently served as leader of a church on Crete (Titus 1:4–5). See also *Titus.*

CRIMINAL. See *Malefactor.*

CRIMSON. See *Scarlet*.

CRISPING PIN (PURSE, HANDBAG). A purse or bag for carrying money (Isa. 3:22). *Purse:* NIV; *handbag:* NRSV. See also *Purse*.

CRISPUS. Chief ruler of the synagogue at Corinth who became a Christian believer (Acts 18:8) and was baptized by Paul (1 Cor. 1:14).

CROCUS. See *Rose*.

CROOKED
Deut. 32:5 a perverse and *c* generation
Isa. 40:4 the *c* shall be made straight
Phil. 2:15 sons of God...in the midst of a *c*...nation

CROSS. A wooden stake with a cross beam on which Jesus was put to death by the Roman authorities—a common form of capital punishment in N.T. times. Attached to the cross with nails or leather thongs, the victim generally suffered for two or three days before dying from exposure, exhaustion, and the loss of body fluids.

But Jesus died after only six hours on the cross (John 19:30–33). His sacrificial death freed believers from the power of sin (Rom. 6:6–11) and sealed their reconciliation to God (2 Cor. 5:19). See also *Atonement; Redeem; Savior*.

Matt. 27:32 they compelled [Simon] to bear his [Jesus'] *c*
Matt. 27:42 let him [Jesus] now come down from the *c*
Luke 9:23 take up his *c* daily, and follow me [Jesus]
John 19:17 he [Jesus] bearing his *c* went forth into...the place of a skull
1 Cor. 1:18 preaching of the *c* is to them that perish foolishness
Gal. 6:14 forbid that I [Paul] should glory, save in the *c*
Phil. 2:8 he [Jesus]...became obedient unto...death of the *c*
Heb. 12:2 who [Jesus] for the joy that was set before him endured the *c*

CROWN. An ornamental headdress worn by kings and queens as a symbol of power and authority (2 Kings 11:12). The word is also used symbolically for righteous behavior befitting a believer (2 Tim. 4:8) and God's gift of eternal life (James 1:12). See also *Diadem*.

CROWN [ED, EDST]
Ps. 8:5 thou [God]...hast *c'ed* him [man] with...honour
Prov. 17:6 Children's children are the *c* of old men
Mark 15:17 a *c* of thorns, and put it about his [Jesus'] head
Phil. 4:1 joy and *c*, so stand fast in the Lord
2 Tim. 4:8 laid up for me [Paul] a *c* of righteousness
Heb. 2:7 thou *c'edst* him [Jesus] with glory and honour

CROWN OF GLORY/ CROWN OF LIFE
Prov. 16:31 The hoary head is a *c-o-g*
Isa. 62:3 shalt...be a *c-o-g* in the hand of the LORD
James 1:12 he is tried, he shall receive the *c-o-l*
1 Pet. 5:4 chief Shepherd...appear...receive a *c-o-g*
Rev. 2:10 faithful unto death...give thee a *c-o-l*

CRUCIBLE. See *Fining Pot*.

CRUCIFIXION. See *Cross*.

CRUSE (JUG). A small earthen jug or flask for holding liquids (1 Kings 17:14). *Jug:* NIV, NRSV. See also *Pitcher*.

CRYSTAL. A transparent, colorless rock, perhaps a form of quartz (Rev. 22:1).

CUBIT. The standard unit for measurement of length, equivalent to about eighteen inches (Gen. 6:15–16).

CUCKOW (SEA GULL). A bird considered unclean by the Hebrews, probably a type of sea bird (Lev. 11:16). *Sea gull:* NRSV.

CUCUMBER. A climbing vine that produced vegetables probably similar to our cucumbers (Num. 11:5).

CUP. A pair of silver Roman cups from the first Christian century, when Jesus lived on earth.

CUMMIN. A plant that produced seeds used for medicines and for seasoning food (Isa. 28:25, 27). Jesus criticized the Pharisees for their shallow legalism in tithing the seeds from this insignificant plant while ignoring more important matters, such as mercy and faith (Matt. 23:23).

CUP. A drinking utensil (Gen. 44:12). The cup is also symbolic of the blood of the new covenant established by Christ (Matt. 20:22; 1 Cor. 10:16).

CUPBEARER. A royal household servant who tasted wine before it was served to the king to make sure it had not been poisoned (Neh. 1:11). The butler imprisoned with Joseph was probably a cupbearer to the Egyptian pharaoh (Gen. 40:1–13).

CURSE. A call for evil or misfortune against another (Gen. 4:11). Jesus taught that Christians are to return kindness for such actions (Luke 6:28).

CURSE [D, ING, TH]

Gen. 3:14 thou [the serpent] art *c'd* above all cattle

Lev. 20:9 one that *c'th* his father...shall be...put to death

Deut. 27:15 *C'd* be the man that maketh any graven or molten image

Deut. 30:19 I [Moses] have set before you life and death, blessing and *c'ing*

Matt. 5:44 bless them that *c* you

Matt. 15:4 He that *c'th* father...let him die

Mark 14:71 he [Peter] began to *c*...I know not this man [Jesus]

Rom. 12:14 Bless them which persecute you: bless...*c* not

Gal. 3:13 Christ hath redeemed us from the *c* of the law

James 3:10 Out of the same mouth proceedeth blessing and *c'ing*

CURTAIN. See *Veil*, No. 1.

CUSH. Ham's oldest son and a grandson of Noah (1 Chron. 1:8–10).

CUSHAN-RISHATHAIM. See *Chushan-rishathaim.*

CUSTOM
Matt. 9:9 he [Jesus] saw...Matthew...at the receipt of *c*
John 18:39 a *c*, that I [Pilate] should release...one at the passover
Rom. 13:7 Render...to all their dues...*c* to whom *c*

CUTH/CUTHAH. A city or district of Babylonia that provided colonists who settled the Northern Kingdom after it fell to the Assyrians (2 Kings 17:30). *Cuthah:* 2 Kings 17:24.

CYMBALS. Curved metal plates used as musical instruments (1 Cor. 13:1).

CYPRESS. See *Box Tree; Fir; Gopher Wood.*

CYPRUS/CHITTIM/KITTIM. A large island in the Mediterranean Sea about 125 miles off the coast of Palestine that Paul and Barnabas visited during the first missionary journey (Acts 13:2–5). Barnabas was a native of Cyprus (Acts 4:36). *Chittim:* Jer. 2:10; *Kittim:* Gen. 10:4.

CYRENE. A Greek city in North Africa and home of Simon of Cyrene who carried the cross of Jesus (Matt. 27:32).

CYRENIUS (QUIRINIUS). The Roman governor of Syria at the time of Jesus' birth (Luke 2:1–4). *Quirinius:* NIV, NRSV.

CYRUS. The founding king of the Persian empire (reigned about 559–530 B.C.). After defeating the Babylonians, he allowed the Jewish captives to return to their homeland about 536 B.C. (2 Chron. 36:22–23; Ezra 1:1–4). See also *Persia.*

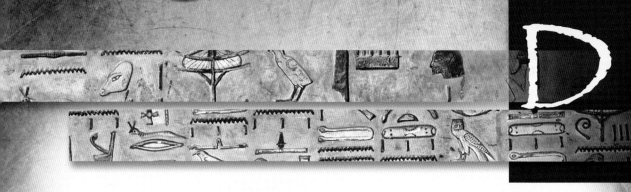

DAGON. The chief pagan god of the Philistines. It apparently had the head of a man and the tail of a fish. This idol fell before the ark of the covenant in the pagan temple at Ashdod (1 Sam. 5:1–5). See also *Philistines*.

DALMANUTHA. A place on the western shore of the Sea of Galilee visited by Jesus (Mark 8:10).

DALMATIA. A province on the eastern coast of the Adriatic Sea visited by Titus (2 Tim. 4:10).

DAMASCUS/SYRIA-DAMASCUS. The capital city of Syria, located north of Mount Hermon in northern Palestine. Paul was traveling to Damascus to persecute Christians when he met the risen Lord in a life-transforming vision (Acts 9:1–8). Damascus is considered the oldest continually inhabited city in the world. *Syria-damascus:* 1 Chron. 18:6. See also *Syria*.

DAMNATION. Judgment and consignment to everlasting punishment; the fate of the wicked or those who reject Christ (Mark 16:16). See also *Hell; Judgment, Last; Perdition*.

Mark 3:29 blaspheme...Holy Ghost...danger of eternal *d*
John 5:29 that have done evil, unto the resurrection of *d*
1 Cor. 11:29 eateth and drinketh *d* to himself

DAMSEL. A word for a young woman (Mark 5:39–42).

DAN/LAISH

1. Jacob's fifth son and ancestor of one of the tribes of Israel (Gen. 30:6; Num. 1:38–39). See also *Tribes of Israel*.

2. A village in the territory allotted to the tribe of Dan. It was located farther north than any other city of Palestine during most of the O.T. era. The phrase "from Dan even to Beersheba" (Judg. 20:1) described the entire territory of the Hebrew nation from north to south. *Laish:* Isa. 10:30.

DANCE. Rhythmic body movements, usually to musical accompaniment, to express joy and gratitude to God (Exod. 15:20–21). King David danced when the ark of the covenant was recovered and brought to Jerusalem (2 Sam. 6:14–16).

DANIEL (BELTESHAZZAR). A prophet of the O.T. known for his faithfulness to the God of Israel among the pagan Babylonians and Persians. Refusing to worship King Darius, he was thrown into a den of lions but was miraculously delivered by the Lord (Dan. 6:1–24). *Belteshazzar:* Babylonian form (Dan. 1:7).

DANIEL, BOOK OF. An apocalyptic book of the O.T. known for its images of horns and beasts that are similar to those described in the Revelation to John in the N.T. The two major sections of Daniel are (1) the trials and tribulations suffered by Daniel and his three friends as captives of the Babylonians and Persians (chaps.

D

1–7) and (2) Daniel's visions and dreams about the future (chaps. 8–12).

The prophet's famous "seventy weeks" prophecy has been interpreted as a period of 490 years (seventy weeks, representing seventy years, multiplied by seven) from Daniel's time until the coming of the Messiah (9:20–27). See also *Apocalypse*.

DARIUS AND DANIEL

King Darius (Darius the Mede) of Persia was a friend and supporter of Daniel, even though the prophet was thrown into a den of lions under an edict that Daniel's enemies had persuaded the king to pass (Dan. 6:1–28). Many scholars believe this king was actually Cyrus, the Persian king who allowed the Jewish exiles to return to their homeland after the Persians defeated the Babylonians (2 Chron. 36:22–23).

DARIC. See *Dram*.

DARIUS. A title for the kings of Persia. Four different kings with this title are mentioned in the O.T.:

1. Darius I or Darius the Great (reigned about 522–485 B.C.). Successor to Cyrus, he continued Cyrus's policy of restoring the Jewish people to their homeland (Ezra 6:1–12).

2. Darius II or Darius the Persian (Neh. 12:22), who reigned about 424–405 B.C.

3. Darius III or Darius Codomannus (reigned about 336–330 B.C.). He is probably the "fourth" king of Persia mentioned by the prophet Daniel (Dan. 11:2).

4. Darius the Mede, who had the prophet Daniel thrown into a den of lions. He eventually

made Daniel a ruler over several provincial leaders (Dan. 6:1–2).

DARKENED
Isa. 24:11 joy is *d*, the mirth of the land is gone
Joel 3:15 sun and the moon shall be *d*
Mark 13:24 tribulation, the sun shall be *d*
Rom. 1:21 they [ungodly]...became vain...heart was *d*

DARKNESS. The absence of light. Darkness ruled the world before God's creation of light (Gen. 1:2). Thus, darkness is symbolic of humankind's sin, rebellion, and ignorance (Job 24:13–17). See also *Light*.

Exod. 10:22 thick *d* in...Egypt three days
2 Sam. 22:29 LORD will lighten my *d*
Job 34:22 no *d*, nor shadow of death
Isa. 5:20 Woe unto them that...put...light for *d*
Isa. 9:2 walked in *d* have seen a great light
Joel 2:31 sun shall be turned into *d*
Matt. 4:16 people...in *d* saw great light
Luke 23:44 a *d* over all the earth until the ninth hour
John 1:5 the *d* comprehended it [the light] not
John 3:19 men loved *d* rather than light
John 12:46 whosoever believeth...not abide in *d*
Acts 2:20 sun shall be turned into *d*
Acts 26:18 open their eyes, to turn them from *d* to light
Eph. 6:12 wrestle...against...*d* of this world
1 John 1:5 God is light, and in him is no *d* at all
1 John 2:11 he that hateth his brother is in *d*

DART (JAVELIN, SPEAR). A javelin or short spear. Absalom was killed by darts (2 Sam. 18:14). *Javelin:* NIV; *spear:* NRSV. See also *Javelin; Spear*.

DATHAN. A leader of the rebellion against Moses in the wilderness. All the rebels were destroyed by an earthquake (Num. 16:1–33).

DAUGHTER. A word for female offspring of parents as well as a distant female relative, such as a granddaughter or niece (Gen. 20:12; 24:48).

DAUGHTER OF ZION. A symbolic expression for the city of Jerusalem and its inhabitants (Ps. 9:14). See also *Jerusalem*.

DAVID. The popular king of Judah described by the Lord as "a man after mine own heart" and an earthly ancestor of the promised Messiah, Jesus Christ (Luke 2:4–7). A descendant of the tribe of Judah (1 Chron. 28:4), he was a native of Bethlehem (1 Sam. 17:12). As a shepherd boy, he defeated the Philistine giant Goliath (1 Sam. 17:44–52).

David served as King Saul's musician and armorbearer (1 Sam. 16:14–21) and was anointed king after Saul's sin and disobedience (1 Sam. 16:11–13). Forced to flee from Saul's jealousy and wrath (1 Sam. 21:10), he was befriended by Saul's son Jonathan (1 Sam. 19:1–3). After he became king, he united the Hebrew tribes into one nation with Jerusalem as the capital city (2 Sam. 5:1–10) and defeated many enemy nations (2 Sam. 8:1–15).

In a moment of weakness, David committed adultery with Bath-sheba (2 Sam. 11:1–4), but he later repented (Pss. 32; 51). He was forgiven and restored, but the consequences of his sin remained (2 Sam. 12:13–14). He suffered family tragedies (2 Sam. 12:15–20; 18:31–33) and wrote many psalms (see Pss. 54; 59; 65). He was succeeded as king by his son Solomon (1 Kings 2:12). In the N.T., Jesus is called the "son of David" (Matt. 1:1; Mark 10:48). See also *Absalom; Bethlehem; Jerusalem*.

DAVID, TOWER OF. A fortress built by David at an unknown location (Song 4:4).

DAY. The twenty-four-hour period during which the earth rotates on its own axis. The Hebrews measured their day from sunset to sunset (Exod. 12:18). The twelve hours of daylight began with the first hour at sunup (about 6:00 A.M.). Midday or noon was the sixth hour, and the twelfth hour ended at sundown, or about 6:00 P.M.

Gen. 1:5 evening...morning were the first *d*
Josh. 24:15 choose you this *d* whom ye will serve
Job 3:3 the *d* perish wherein I [Job] was born
Ps. 1:2 in his [God's] law doth he meditate *d* and night
Ps. 50:15 call upon me [God] in the *d* of trouble
Ps. 84:10 a *d* in thy [God's] courts is better than a thousand
Ps. 118:24 This is the *d* which the LORD hath made
Isa. 60:19 sun shall be no more thy light by *d*
Joel 2:31 before...the terrible *d* of the LORD come
Mal. 3:2 who may abide the *d* of his [God's] coming
Matt. 6:11 Give us this *d* our daily bread
Matt. 25:13 neither the *d* nor the hour...Son of man cometh
Luke 2:11 born this *d* in the city of David a Saviour
Luke 19:9 This *d* is salvation come to this house
John 9:4 I [Jesus] must work...while it is *d*
2 Cor. 6:2 behold, now is the *d* of salvation
Phil. 3:5 Circumcised the eighth *d*...stock of Israel
Heb. 13:8 Jesus Christ the same yesterday, and to *d*
2 Pet. 3:8 one *d* is with the Lord as a thousand years
Rev. 1:10 I [John] was in the Spirit on the Lord's *d*

DAY OF THE LORD. A phrase usually interpreted as a period in the end-time when God will bring His purpose for humans and the world to fulfillment. This will be a day of judgment for the rebellious and sinful (Jer. 46:10) and a time of deliverance for the godly (Joel 2:28–32). Any time—whether now or in the distant future—when the Lord acts, intervening in history for the purpose of deliverance and judgment, may also be described as the "day of the Lord" (Isa. 13:6). See also *Damnation; Judgment, Last; Punishment*.

Joel 1:15 Alas...for the *d-o-t-L* is at hand
Amos 5:20 Shall not the *d-o-t-L* be darkness
Mal. 4:5 Elijah...before the...dreadful *d-o-t-L*
Acts 2:20 darkness...before that great...*d-o-t-L*
1 Thess. 5:2 the *d-o-t-L*...cometh...thief in the night

DAY'S JOURNEY. The distance that could be traveled in one day on foot, probably about twenty-five miles (Jon. 3:3–4).

DAYSMAN (UMPIRE). A word for a mediator, umpire, or judge between contending parties (Job 9:33). *Umpire:* NRSV.

DAYSPRING. A word for dawn or daybreak (Job 38:12).

DAY STAR/LUCIFER (MORNING STAR). A star that appears just before daybreak, signaling the beginning of a new day (2 Pet. 1:19). The word for "day star" is also translated as *Lucifer* (Isa. 14:12) and used as a name for the king of Babylon. *Morning star:* NIV. See also *Morning Star.*

DEACON. An officer or servant of the church. The first "deacons" were probably the seven men of Greek background who were appointed by the church at Jerusalem to coordinate the distribution of food to the needy (Acts 6:1–7). The strict qualifications for deacons (1 Tim. 3:8–13) show this was an important office in the early church. Phoebe, a female believer, is called a "deacon" in the NRSV translation of Rom. 16:1 (*servant:* KJV).

DEAD
Eccles. 9:5 the *d* know not any thing
Matt. 10:8 Heal the sick...raise the *d*
Luke 15:24 son was *d*, and is alive again
Luke 24:46 Christ to suffer...rise from the *d*
John 11:25 though he were *d*, yet shall he live
Acts 17:32 resurrection of the *d*, some mocked
Rom. 6:4 Christ was raised up from the *d*
1 Cor. 15:13 no resurrection of the *d*...Christ not risen
Col. 1:18 who [Jesus] is...firstborn from the *d*
1 Thess. 4:16 the *d* in Christ shall rise first
James 2:17 faith, if it hath not works, is *d*
Rev. 14:13 Blessed are the *d* which die in the Lord

DEAD SEA/SALT SEA/EAST SEA. A body of water (about fifty miles long by ten miles wide) into which the Jordan River empties at the lowest point on earth in southern Palestine.

DEAD SEA. The Dead Sea, photographed from the Space Shuttle. The lowest spot on earth, this super-salty sea is rich in minerals. The southern half is divided into shallow drying pools, making it easier to mine the minerals.

Because of the hot, dry climate, the water evaporates, leaving a high concentration of salt and other minerals. *Salt sea:* Josh. 3:16; *East sea:* Joel 2:20.

DEAD SEA SCROLLS. A group of scrolls or ancient manuscripts discovered since 1947 in caves around the Dead Sea. Written between 250 B.C. and A.D. 68 and placed in clay jars, the scrolls were preserved by the dry climate of the area. Among the scrolls was a complete manuscript of the book of Isaiah, written in Hebrew. See also *Qumran, Khirbet.*

DEAF. Unable to hear. The word is also used symbolically of spiritual coldness or apathy (Isa. 42:18–19).

Isa. 35:5 ears of the *d* shall be unstopped
Mark 7:32 bring unto him [Jesus] one that was *d*
Luke 7:22 tell John...lepers are cleansed...*d* hear

DEATH. The end of physical existence. Death is the price humans pay for their sin and rebellion against God, but God provides salvation and eternal life for believers through the atoning death of Jesus Christ (Rom. 6:23). "Second death" is eternal separation from God—the fate of unbelievers (Rev. 20:6).

Deut. 30:15 I [Moses]...set before thee...*d* and evil
Ps. 23:4 valley of the shadow of *d*
Ps. 116:15 sight of the LORD...*d* of his saints
Mark 14:34 My [Jesus'] soul is...sorrowful unto *d*
John 5:24 believeth...passed from *d* unto life
Acts 8:1 Saul was consenting unto his [Stephen's] *d*
Rom. 5:12 so *d* passed upon all men
Rom. 7:24 shall deliver me [Paul] from the body of...*d*
1 Cor. 11:26 show the Lord's *d* till he come
1 Cor. 15:55 O *d*, where is thy sting
Phil. 2:8 he [Jesus] humbled himself...obedient unto *d*
1 John 3:14 from *d* unto life...we love the brethren
Rev. 21:4 no more *d*, neither sorrow

DEBASED. See *Reprobate.*

DEBAUCHERY. See *Lasciviousness.*

DEBORAH. A prophetess and judge of Israel who, along with Barak, defeated the Canaanite forces of Sisera (Judg. 4:4–14). She celebrated the victory in a triumphant song (Judg. 5). See also *Sisera.*

DEBT. Borrowed property or money that must be repaid. The Hebrews were encouraged not to charge interest to their own countrymen (Lev. 25:35–38), but foreigners could be charged (Deut. 23:20). See also *Usury.*

DEBT [S]
Matt. 6:12 our *d's*, as we forgive our debtors
Matt. 18:27 lord of that servant...forgave him the *d*
Rom. 4:4 to him that worketh is the reward...of *d*

DECALOGUE. See *Ten Commandments.*

DECAPOLIS. A Roman province or district with a large Greek population that was situated mostly on the eastern side of the Jordan River in northern Palestine (Matt. 4:25).

DECEIT. See *Guile.*

DECEIVE [D,ING]
Deut. 11:16 Take heed...your heart be not *d'd*
Prov. 20:1 Wine is a mocker...whosoever is *d'd* thereby is not wise
Luke 21:8 be not *d'd*: for many shall come in my [Jesus'] name
Gal. 6:7 Be not *d'd*; God is not mocked
Eph. 5:6 Let no man *d* you with vain words
James 1:22 doers of the word, and not hearers only, *d'ing* your own selves
1 John 1:8 we say that we have no sin, we *d* ourselves

DECEIVER. A person who misleads another. Deception is one of the evil tricks used by Satan (2 John 7). See also *Satan.*

DECISION, VALLEY OF. See *Jehoshaphat, Valley of.*

DECLARE [D]
1 Chron. 16:24 *D* his [God's] glory among the heathen
Ps. 19:1 heavens *d* the glory of God
Isa. 12:4 Praise the Lᴏʀᴅ...*d* his doings among the people
John 1:18 only begotten Son...he hath *d'd* him [God]
Rom. 1:4 *d'd* to be the Son of God with power
1 Cor. 15:1 I [Paul] *d* unto you the gospel
1 John 1:3 which we have seen...*d* we unto you

DECREE. A command or official order issued by a king. Mary and Joseph were affected by the decree of the Roman emperor Caesar Augustus (Luke 2:1). See also *Statute.*

DEDICATION, FEAST OF. An eight-day festival commemorating the Jewish victories that restored the temple during the era of the Maccabees about 160 B.C. Jesus attended one of these festivals in Jerusalem (John 10:22–23). This feast was also known as the *Feast of Lights* or *Hanukkah.*

DEED [S]
1 Chron. 16:8 known his [God's] *d's* among the people
Luke 23:41 receive the due reward of our *d's*
John 3:19 loved darkness...their *d's* were evil
Rom. 2:6 to every man according to his *d's*
1 John 3:18 not love in word...but in *d* and in truth

DEER. A fleet-footed animal that could be eaten by the Hebrews (Deut. 14:5). See also *Hart; Hind.*

DEFILE [TH]
Ezek. 20:7 *d* not yourselves with the idols of Egypt
Dan. 1:8 Daniel...would not *d* himself
Matt. 15:20 eat with unwashen hands *d'th* not a man
Mark 7:18 from without...it cannot *d* him
1 Cor. 3:17 any man *d* the temple of God
James 3:6 tongue...*d'th* the whole body

DEFILEMENT. Contamination; the act of making something impure by acts of sin and rebellion. The O.T. law emphasized ceremonial cleanliness (Lev. 15:24; Num. 9:13), but Jesus emphasized the need for ethical living and moral purity (Mark 7:1–23).

DEGREES, SONGS OF. A title used in fifteen psalms of the book of Psalms (Pss. 120–134). The Hebrew word for "degrees" means "goings up." These songs of ascent may have been pilgrim psalms, sung by worshipers as they were "going up" to the temple at Jerusalem.

DEHAVITES. An Assyrian tribe that settled in Samaria after the defeat of the Northern Kingdom by the Assyrians. In later years the Dehavites opposed the rebuilding of the Jewish temple at Jerusalem (Ezra 4:9–16). See also *Samaritan.*

DELILAH. A woman, probably a Philistine, who cut off Samson's long hair—the source of his strength—so he could be captured by his Philistine enemies (Judg. 16:13–21). See also *Samson.*

DELIVER [ED]
Job 16:11 God hath *d'ed* me [Job] to the ungodly
Ps. 17:13 Lᴏʀᴅ, *d* my soul from the wicked
Ps. 116:8 thou [God] hast *d'ed* my soul from death
Jer. 1:8 am with thee to *d* thee, saith the Lᴏʀᴅ
Dan. 3:17 God...is able to *d* us from the...furnace
Joel 2:32 call on...the Lᴏʀᴅ shall be *d'ed*
Matt. 6:13 not into temptation...*d* us from evil
Luke 2:6 that she [Mary] should be *d'ed*
Luke 9:44 Son of man...*d'ed* into the hands of men
Rom. 7:24 shall *d* me [Paul] from...this death
2 Tim. 4:18 Lord shall *d* me from every evil work

DEMAS. A fellow believer who deserted Paul (2 Tim. 4:10) after having worked with him on earlier occasions (Col. 4:14; Philem. 24).

DEMETRIUS. A silversmith at Ephesus who made replicas of the temple where the pagan goddess Diana was worshiped. When his livelihood was threatened by Paul's preaching,

DELILAH. A freshly shorn Samson, attacked by Philistine soldiers, finds his superhuman strength gone. Delilah earned a treasure of silver by passing along the secret of Samson's power—that he never cut his hair.

Demetrius incited a riot against the apostle (Acts 19:24–31). See also *Diana*.

DEMON. An evil spirit with destructive power who opposes God. In His healing ministry, Jesus cast demons out of several people (Matt. 12:22–24; Luke 8:27–39).

DEMON POSSESSION. Invasion and control of a person by evil spirits. In N.T. times, these demons often caused disability (Mark 9:17–25), mental anguish (Matt. 8:28), and antisocial behavior (Luke 8:27–39). Jesus cast demons out of several people—an act that showed His power over the demonic forces of Satan (Mark 1:25; 9:29).

DEN OF LIONS. A deep cavern where lions were kept by the Persian kings, probably for the sport of lion hunting. Daniel was thrown into one of these pits, but he was delivered by God's hand (Dan. 6:16–24). See also *Daniel*.

DENARIUS. See *Penny*.

DENY [IED, IETH]
Matt. 10:33 him will I also *d* before my Father
Mark 14:30 thou [Peter] shalt *d* me [Jesus] thrice
Luke 9:23 let him *d* himself, and take up his cross
1 Tim. 5:8 hath *d'ied* the faith...worse than an infidel
2 Tim. 2:12 if we *d* him [Jesus], he also will *d* us
1 John 2:23 Whosoever *d'ieth* the Son...hath not the Father

DEPOSIT. See *Earnest*.

DEPRAVED. See *Reprobate*.

DEPTH [S]
Ps. 106:9 he [God] led them through the *d's*
Ps. 130:1 Out of the *d's* have I cried unto thee, O LORD
Mic. 7:19 thou [God] wilt cast...their sins into...*d's* of the sea
Rom. 8:39 nor *d*...shall...separate us from...God

DEPUTY. A person empowered to act for another (1 Kings 22:47). See also *Proconsul*.

DERBE. A city or village of the province of Lycaonia visited by Paul and Barnabas during the first missionary journey (Acts 14:6, 20).

DESCEND [ED, ING]
Gen. 28:12 angels...ascending and *d'ing* on it [a ladder]
Matt. 7:27 rain *d'ed*, and the floods came
Mark 15:32 Let Christ...*d* now from the cross
Luke 3:22 Holy Ghost *d'ed*...like a dove
John 1:32 I [John] saw the Spirit *d'ing* from heaven like a dove
Rom. 10:7 Who shall *d* into the deep...to bring up Christ
1 Thess. 4:16 Lord himself shall *d* from heaven

DESERT. A dry, barren wilderness place (Isa. 48:21; Luke 1:80). See also *Wilderness.*

DESERT OWL. See *Cormorant; Hawk; Pelican.*

DESIRE [D, TH]
Gen. 3:16 *d* shall be to thy [Eve's] husband
Deut. 5:21 Neither shalt thou *d* thy neighbour's wife
Ps. 38:9 all my *d* is before thee [God]
Ps. 73:25 none...that I *d* beside thee [God]
Song 7:10 my beloved's, and his *d* is toward me
Isa. 26:9 my soul have I *d'd* thee [God]
Hosea 6:6 I [God] *d'd* mercy, and not sacrifice
Mark 9:35 man *d* to be first, the same shall be last
Rom. 10:1 my [Paul's] heart's *d*...for Israel...might be saved
Phil. 1:23 a *d* to depart, and to be with Christ
1 Tim. 3:1 office of a bishop, he *d'th* a good work
1 Pet. 2:2 newborn babes, *d* the sincere milk of the word

DESIRE OF ALL NATIONS (DESIRED OF ALL NATIONS, TREASURE OF ALL NATIONS). A title for the coming Messiah that emphasizes His universal rule and power (Hag. 2:6–7). *Desired of all nations:* NIV; *treasure of all nations:* NRSV.

DESTRUCTION [S]
Job 5:22 At *d* and famine thou shalt laugh
Ps. 90:3 Thou [God] turnest man to *d*
Ps. 107:20 He [God]...delivered them from their *d's*
Prov. 16:18 Pride goeth before *d*...haughty spirit before a fall
Isa. 13:6 day of the LORD...as a *d* from the Almighty
Matt. 7:13 broad is the way, that leadeth to *d*

DEUTERONOMY, BOOK OF. A book of the O.T. containing a series of speeches that Moses delivered to the Hebrew people as they prepared to enter and conquer the land of Canaan. This book repeats many of the laws of God revealed to Moses on Mount Sinai about two generations earlier—thus its name Deuteronomy, which means "second law."

In these speeches (chaps. 1–33), Moses cautioned the people to remain faithful to God in the midst of the pagan Canaanite culture they were about to enter. The final chapter (34) recounts the death of Moses and the succession of Joshua as the leader of the Hebrew people. See also *Moses; Pentateuch.*

DEVIL. A title for Satan which emphasizes his work as a liar and deceiver (Luke 4:3). See also *Satan.*

DEW. Moisture that condenses on the earth during the night (Exod. 16:13–14; Judg. 6:37–40). The heavy dews of Palestine during the dry season from April to September provide moisture for the growing crops (Gen. 27:28).

DIADEM (CROWN). A headpiece decorated with precious stones and worn by a king (Isa. 28:5). *Crown:* NIV. See also *Crown.*

DIAMOND (EMERALD, MOONSTONE). A precious stone in the breastplate of the high priest (Exod. 28:18). *Emerald:* NIV; *moonstone:* NRSV.

DIANA (ARTEMIS). The Roman name for the pagan goddess of hunting and virginity. Paul's preaching at Ephesus, a center of Diana worship, caused an uproar among craftsmen who earned their living by making images of Diana (Acts 19:24–34). *Artemis:* NIV, NRSV. See also *Demetrius; Ephesus.*

DIDYMUS. See *Thomas.*

DIE [D]

Gen. 2:17 eatest thereof [the forbidden tree]...surely **d**
2 Chron. 25:4 every man shall **d** for his own sin
Job 14:14 man **d**, shall he live again
Eccles. 3:2 time to be born...time to **d**
Jon. 4:3 better for me [Jonah] to **d** than to live
John 11:50 expedient...one man should **d** for the people
John 12:24 if it [grain of wheat] **d**, it bringeth forth much fruit
Rom. 5:8 yet sinners, Christ **d'd** for us
Rom. 14:8 live...or **d**, we are the Lord's
1 Cor. 15:22 Adam all **d**...in Christ...all be made alive
2 Cor. 5:14 one **d'd** for all, then were all dead
Phil. 1:21 to me [Paul] to live is Christ, and to **d** is gain
Heb. 9:27 appointed unto men once to **d**
Rev. 14:13 Blessed...dead which **d** in the Lord

DILL. See *Anise.*

DINAH. The daughter of Jacob who was assaulted by Shechem (Gen. 34).

DINAITES. An Assyrian tribe that populated Samaria after the Northern Kingdom fell to the Assyrians (Ezra 4:9). See also *Samaritan.*

DIONYSIUS. A member of the Areopagus of Athens who believed Paul's testimony about Jesus the Messiah (Acts 17:34). See also *Areopagus.*

DIOTREPHES. A church leader condemned by the apostle John for his false teachings (3 John 9–10).

DISAGREEMENT. See *Contention.*

DISCERN [ING]

1 Kings 3:9 I [Solomon] may **d** between good and bad
Matt. 16:3 hypocrites, ye can **d** the face of the sky
1 Cor. 11:29 damnation to himself, not **d'ing** the Lord's body

DISCERNING OF SPIRITS (DISTINGUISHING BETWEEN SPIRITS). A spiritual gift that enables certain believers to tell the difference between true and false teachers and teachings (1 Cor. 12:10). *Distinguishing between spirits:* NIV.

DISCIPLE. A person who follows and learns from another person or group, especially a believer who observes the teachings of Jesus (Acts 6:1–7). See also *Apostle.*

Matt. 10:24 The **d** is not above his master
Luke 14:26 man...hate not his father...cannot be my [Jesus'] **d**
John 19:38 Joseph of Arimathaea, being a **d** of Jesus

DISCIPLINARIAN. See *Schoolmaster.*

DISCIPLINE. To train or teach, as parents impart important truths to a child (Prov. 22:6). A disciplined person also controls his impulses, speech, and actions (1 Pet. 3:10). God disciplines His children through corrective actions (Heb. 12:6). See also *Chastisement.*

DISCORD. Disagreement produced by a contentious spirit (Prov. 6:14). Discord is a sign of worldliness among believers (1 Cor. 3:3). See also *Contention.*

DISGRACE. See *Shame.*

DISH. See *Platter.*

DISOBEDIENT

Acts 26:19 I [Paul] was not **d** unto the heavenly vision
2 Tim. 3:2 boasters, proud...**d** to parents
Titus 1:16 deny him [God], being abominable, and **d**

DISPERSION. A word that refers to the scattering of the Jewish people among other nations. Jeremiah predicted such a scattering (Jer. 25:34), and this happened when the Babylonians overran Judah in 587 B.C. and carried its leading citizens into exile. See also *Captivity.*

D

DISPUTATION. Argument or dissension. Paul cautioned believers against such behavior (Phil. 2:14).

DISTAFF. The staff around which flax or wool was wound for spinning (Prov. 31:19). See also *Spinning; Warp; Weaver.*

DISTINGUISHING BETWEEN SPIR-ITS. See *Discerning of Spirits.*

DISTRESS [ED, ES]
Ps. 18:6 my *d* I called upon the Lord
Ps. 107:13 he [God] saved them out of their *d'es*
Rom. 8:35 separate us...love of Christ? shall tribulation, or *d*
2 Cor. 4:8 troubled on every side, yet not *d'ed*
2 Cor. 12:10 I [Paul] take pleasure...in *d'es* for Christ's sake

DIVIDE [D, ING, TH]
Gen. 1:6 let it [the firmament] *d* the waters
Num. 33:54 shall *d* the land by lot
Judg. 7:16 he [Gideon] *d'd*...men into three companies
Job 26:12 He [God] *d'th* the sea with his power
Dan. 5:28 Thy [Belshazzar's] kingdom is *d'd*
Luke 11:17 kingdom *d'd* against itself is brought to desolation
Luke 12:53 father shall be *d'd* against the son
1 Cor. 1:13 Is Christ *d'd*? was Paul crucified for you?
2 Tim. 2:15 not...ashamed, rightly *d'ing* the word of truth

DIVIDING WALL. See *Middle Wall of Partition.*

DIVINATION. Foretelling the future or determining the unknown through performing acts of magic or reading signs (Jer. 14:14). See also *Magic; Soothsayer.*

DIVINER. See *Soothsayer.*

DIVISION [S]
John 9:16 a *d* among them [Pharisees]
Rom. 16:17 mark them which cause *d's* and offences
1 Cor. 3:3 among you envying, and strife, and *d's*

DIVORCE. A breaking of the ties of marriage. The divine ideal is for permanence in marriage (Matt. 19:3–6), and divorce violates the oneness that God intended (Gen. 2:24). Under the Mosaic Law, divorce was permitted in certain situations (Deut. 24:1–4), but this provision was greatly abused (Matt. 19:8).

Christ regarded adultery as the only permissible reason for divorce (Matt. 5:31–32; 19:9; Mark 10:11; Luke 16:18), and He reprimanded the Jews for their insensitive divorce practices (Matt. 19:3–9). Unfaithfulness to God was regarded as spiritual adultery (Hosea 2:2). See also *Marriage.*

DIVORCE [D]
Lev. 21:14 or a *d'd* woman...these shall he [a priest] not take
Jer. 3:8 I [God] had put her [Israel] away, and given her a bill of *d*

DOCTORS (TEACHERS). Teachers of the Law of Moses who were held in high esteem by the Jewish people. At the age of twelve, Jesus discussed the law with some of these teachers in Jerusalem (Luke 2:46). *Teachers:* NIV, NRSV. See also *Lawyer.*

No Black Magic

The word *divination* may also be translated as "the occult." God made it clear that all forms of the occult are off-limits to His people (Deut. 18:9-14). These practices are "an abomination" (Deut. 18:12) to Him because they are a form of idolatry. Practitioners of black magic attempt to control the so-called "spirit world" to man's advantage, but there is only one supreme power in the universe— and He cannot be manipulated.

DOCTRINE. A system of religious beliefs that followers pass on to others. Paul impressed upon young Timothy the importance of sound doctrinal teachings (1 Tim. 4:6).

Mark 11:18 people was astonished at his [Jesus'] *d*
John 7:16 My [Jesus'] *d* is not mine, but his that sent me
Acts 2:42 continued stedfastly in the apostles' *d*
Eph. 4:14 carried about with every wind of *d*
2 Tim. 3:16 All scripture is...profitable for *d*
2 Tim. 4:3 time will come...not endure sound *d*

DOEG. An overseer of King Saul's herds who betrayed the high priest Ahimelech for assisting David and his soldiers (1 Sam. 22:9–10).

DOER [S]
Prov. 17:4 A wicked *d* giveth heed to false lips
Rom. 2:13 the *d's* of the law shall be justified
James 1:22 be ye *d's* of the word, and not hearers only

DOG. An unclean animal (Deut. 23:18) looked upon with contempt by the Jewish people. Gentiles were called "dogs" (Matt. 15:26). See also *Gentile.*

DOME. See *Firmament.*

DOMINION. Authority to govern or rule. After his creation by God, man was given dominion over God's creation (Gen. 1:26–28).

Job 25:2 *D* and fear are with him [God]
Ps. 8:6 him [man] to have *d* over the works of thy hands
Ps. 72:8 He [God] shall have *d* also from sea to sea
Dan. 4:3 his [God's] *d* is from generation to generation
Rom. 6:9 death hath no more *d* over him [Jesus]
1 Pet. 4:11 to whom [Jesus] be...*d* for ever and ever
Jude 25 To...God our Saviour, be...*d* and power

DOOR (GATE). An opening through which a house or public building is entered. Jesus spoke of Himself as the doorway to salvation and eternal life (John 10:7–10). *Gate:* NIV, NRSV. See also *Gate.*

DOORKEEPER. A person who stood guard at the entrance of a public building (Ps. 84:10). See also *Gate Keeper; Porter.*

DORCAS. See *Tabitha.*

DOTHAN. A city west of the Jordan River near Mount Gilboa. Dothan was the place where Joseph was sold into slavery by his brothers (Gen. 37:17–28).

DOUBT [ED, ING]
Matt. 14:31 thou of little faith, wherefore didst thou *d*
Matt. 28:17 worshiped him [Jesus]: but some *d'ed*
1 Tim. 2:8 lifting up holy hands, without...*d'ing*

DOVE. See *Pigeon; Turtledove.*

DOWRY. Compensation paid by the groom to the bride's family for loss of her services as a daughter (Gen. 24:47–58). See also *Betrothal; Marriage.*

DOXOLOGY. A brief hymn or declaration that proclaims God's power and glory (1 Chron. 29:11; Luke 2:14).

DRAGON. A mythical sea creature or winged lizard. The name is applied to Satan (Rev. 12:9) and the Antichrist (Rev. 12:3). See also *Antichrist.*

DRAM (DRACHMA, DARIC). A Persian coin of small value (Neh. 7:70). *Drachma:* NIV; *daric:* NRSV.

DRAWER OF WATER (WATER CARRIER). A person who carried water from the spring or well back to the household—a menial chore assigned to women, children, or slaves (Josh. 9:27). *Water carrier:* NIV.

D

DREAMS AND VISIONS. Mediums of revelation often used by God to make His will known. Joseph distinguished himself in Egypt by interpreting dreams for the pharaoh and his officers (Gen. 40–41). Daniel interpreted King Nebuchadnezzar's dream that he would fall from power (Dan. 4:18–27). Paul's missionary thrust into Europe began with his vision of a man from Macedonia appealing for help (Acts 16:9–10).

DREGS. Waste that settled to the bottom of the vat in the wine-making process (Ps. 75:8). The word is also used symbolically of God's wrath and judgment (Isa. 51:17). See also *Lees*.

DRINK [ETH]

Ps. 69:21 my thirst they gave me vinegar to *d*
Prov. 5:15 *D* waters out of thine own cistern
Prov. 20:1 Wine is a mocker, strong *d* is raging
Eccles. 9:7 *d* thy wine with a merry heart
Matt. 6:31 shall we eat? or, What shall we *d*
Matt. 25:42 thirsty, and ye gave me no *d*
Mark 2:16 he [Jesus]...*d'eth* with...sinners
Mark 10:38 *d* of the cup that I [Jesus] *d* of
Mark 15:23 gave him [Jesus] to *d* wine...with myrrh
John 6:53 *d* his [Jesus'] blood, ye have no life in you
Rom. 12:20 he [your enemy] thirst, give him *d*
Rom. 14:17 kingdom of God is not meat and *d*
1 Cor. 11:25 oft as ye *d* it, in remembrance of me [Jesus]
1 Cor. 11:29 eateth and *d'eth* damnation to himself

DRINK OFFERING. An offering of fine wine, usually given in connection with

DROMEDARY. Camels were still a main source of transportation in Egypt at the turn of the 1900s, as suggested by this colorized photo taken near the Great Pyramid at Giza.

another sacrifice, such as a burnt offering (Num. 29).

DROMEDARY (YOUNG CAMEL). A distinct species of camel with one hump and known for its swiftness (Jer. 2:23). *Young camel:* NRSV.

DROPSY. A disease that causes fluid buildup in the body. Jesus healed a man with this disease on the Sabbath (Luke 14:2).

DROSS. Impurities separated from ore or metal in the smelting process (Prov. 25:4). The word is used symbolically of God's judgment against the wicked (Ps. 119:119).

DROUGHT. Lack of rainfall for an extended time (Ps. 32:4). The prophet Jeremiah spoke symbolically of a spiritual drought throughout the land (Jer. 14:1–7). See also *Famine.*

DRUNKARD. See *Winebibber.*

DRUNKENNESS. A state of intoxication caused by consuming too much wine or strong drink. This vice is condemned in both the O.T. and the N.T. (Deut. 21:20; 1 Cor. 5:11).

DRUSILLA. The wife of Felix, Roman governor of Judea, who heard Paul's defense (Acts 24:24–25).

DUKE (CHIEF). A leader of a clan (Gen. 36:15–43). *Chief:* NIV. See also *Chief.*

DULCIMER (PIPES). A musical instrument used in Babylonia, probably similar to the bagpipe (Dan. 3:5). *Pipes:* NIV.

DUMB. Unable to speak, or the temporary loss of speech (Ezek. 33:22). The word is also used figuratively of submission (Isa. 53:7).

Mark 7:37 he [Jesus] maketh...the *d* to speak
Luke 1:20 thou [Zacharias] shalt be *d*, and not able to speak
1 Cor. 12:2 Gentiles, carried away unto these *d* idols

DUNG (RUBBISH). Excrement of humans or animals (2 Kings 9:37). Dried dung was used for fuel in Palestine (Ezek. 4:12–15). The word is also used figuratively to express worthlessness (Phil. 3:8). *Rubbish:* NIV, NRSV.

DUNGEON. An underground prison. Some of these were little more than cisterns with the water partially drained. Joseph and Jeremiah were imprisoned in dungeons (Gen. 39:20, 40:15; Jer. 37:15–16). See also *Cistern; Pit; Prison.*

DURA. A plain in Babylonia where the golden image of King Nebuchadnezzar of Babylonia was set up (Dan. 3:1). See also *Adoram.*

DUST. Dried earth in powdered form. Sitting in the dust was a symbol of dejection and humiliation (Lam. 3:29). The word is also used symbolically of man's mortality (Gen. 3:19).

DWELLING. See *Pavilion.*

DYSENTERY. See *Flux.*

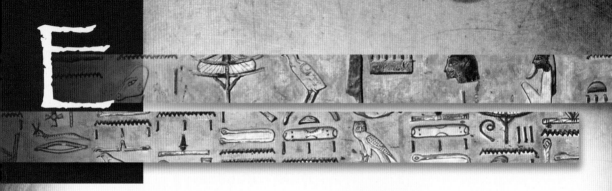

E

EAGLE. A large bird of prey, considered unclean by the Hebrews (Lev. 11:13). Many scholars believe the eagle of the Bible was actually the griffon vulture.

EAR. The ears of the unregenerate are called dull or unhearing (Matt. 13:15). The "ears of the Lord" (1 Sam. 8:21) signify that He hears prayers, in contrast to dumb idols (Ps. 115:6).

EARLY RAIN. See *Former Rain.*

EARNEST (DEPOSIT, FIRST INSTALL-MENT). A down payment given as a pledge toward full payment of the loan. The Holy Spirit is given as a pledge of the believer's inheritance of eternal life (2 Cor. 1:22). *Deposit:* NIV; *first installment:* NRSV.

EARRING. A piece of jewelry worn suspended from the ear lobe (Gen. 35:4).

EARTH
Gen. 1:1 God created the heaven and the *e*
Gen. 9:1 Be fruitful...multiply...replenish the *e*
Ps. 8:1 how excellent is thy [God's] name in all the *e*
Ps. 24:1 The *e* is the Lord's, and the fulness thereof
Ps. 37:11 But the meek shall inherit the *e*
Ps. 96:1 sing unto the Lord, all the *e*
Isa. 6:3 the whole *e* is full of his [God's] glory
Hab. 2:20 all the *e* keep silence before him [God]
Matt. 5:13 Ye are...salt of the *e*
Matt. 16:19 loose on *e* shall be loosed in heaven
Luke 2:14 on *e* peace, good will toward men
John 12:32 if I [Jesus] be lifted up from the *e*
Acts 1:8 ye shall be witnesses...the uttermost part of the *e*
Rev. 21:11 I [John] saw a new heaven and a new *e*

EARTHQUAKE. A violent shaking of the earth (Ps. 77:18). These earth tremors are a token of God's wrath and judgment (Judg. 5:4).

EAST SEA. See *Dead Sea.*

EAST WIND. A violent, scorching desert wind, also known as the sirocco (Job 27:21). See also *Wind.*

EASTER. A word that refers to the Passover festival (Acts 12:4). Easter as a celebration of the resurrection of Jesus developed among Christians many years after the N.T. era.

EAT [ETH]
Gen. 2:17 tree of...good and evil, thou shalt not *e*
Exod. 16:35 children of Israel did *e* manna
Eccles. 2:24 nothing better... he should *e* and drink
Matt. 6:25 thought for your life, what ye shall *e*
Mark 14:18 One...which *e'eth* with me [Jesus] shall betray me
Luke 5:30 Why do ye *e* and drink with...sinners
Luke 15:23 bring...the fatted calf...let us *e*, and be merry
Acts 10:13 came a voice...Rise, Peter; kill, and *e*
1 Cor. 10:31 ye *e*, or drink...do all to the glory of God
2 Thess. 3:10 any would not work, neither should he *e*

EBAL. A rocky mountain in Samaria, or the territory of Ephraim, where Joshua built an altar after destroying the city of Ai (Josh. 8:30).

EBED-MELECH. An Ethiopian eunuch who rescued the prophet Jeremiah from a dungeon (Jer. 38:7–13).

EBENEZER. Site of Israel's defeat by the Philistines (1 Sam. 5:1). Years later, Samuel erected an altar on this site and called it Ebenezer, meaning "the stone of help," to commemorate Israel's eventual victory over the Philistines (1 Sam. 7:10–12).

EBER. A great-grandson of Shem (Gen. 10:21–25) and ancestor of the Hebrew race (Gen. 11:16–26).

EBONY. A hard, durable wood used for decorative carvings and musical instruments (Ezek. 27:15).

ECBATANA. See *Achmetha.*

ECCLESIASTES, BOOK OF. A wisdom book of the O.T., probably written by King Solomon, that declares that life derives joy and meaning not from riches, fame, or work but from reverence for God and obedience to His commandments. One of the book's most memorable passages is the poem on the proper time for all of life's events: "A time to be born, and a time to die...a time to weep, and a time to laugh...a time to keep silence, and a time to speak" (see 3:1–8).

EDEN, GARDEN OF. The fruitful garden created specifically by the Lord as the home for Adam and Eve. The four rivers of Eden, including the Euphrates, suggest that it may have been located in Mesopotamia. Because of their sin and rebellion against God, Adam and Eve were expelled from the garden (Gen. 2:8–3:24). See also *Adam; Eve.*

EDIFICATION. The process by which believers grow in holiness, wisdom, and

EDEN, GARDEN OF. Lush and peaceful—where even predators and prey get along. That's how the Garden of Eden is portrayed in this painting from the 1600s.

righteousness (1 Cor. 14:3; 1 Thess. 5:11). See also *Sanctification.*

EDOM

1. The name given to Esau, Jacob's brother, after he traded away his birthright (Gen. 25:30). See also *Esau.*

2. The land where the descendants of Esau settled. It was in extreme southern Palestine in the barren territory below the Dead Sea. Mount Seir was located in this territory (Gen. 36:8). Edom was referred to by the Greeks and Romans as *Idumaea* (Mark 3:8).

EDOMITES. The descendants of Esau who were enemies of the Israelites. The king of Edom refused to allow the Israelites to pass through his territory after the Exodus (Num. 20:14–21). In later years, David conquered the Edomites (2 Sam. 8:14). But they apparently existed with a distinct territory and culture for several centuries (see Ps. 137:7). See also *Edom; Esau.*

EDREI. A capital city of Bashan. King Og was defeated here by the Israelites (Num. 21:33–35).

EGYPT. The ancient nation along the Nile River that held the Hebrew people in slavery for more than 400 years before their miraculous deliverance by the Lord at the hand of Moses. Egypt had flourished as a highly civilized culture for several centuries before the time of Abraham about 2000 B.C. Soon after entering Canaan in response to God's call, Abraham moved on to Egypt to escape a famine (Gen. 12:10).

This same circumstance led Jacob and his family to settle in Egypt after his son Joseph became a high official of the Egyptian pharaoh (Gen. 45–46). Ham's son Mizraim apparently was the ancestor of the Egyptians (1 Chron. 1:8). See also *Mizraim; Nile River; Pharaoh.*

EHUD. The second judge of Israel who killed Eglon, king of Moab (Judg. 3:15). See also *Judges of Israel.*

EKRON. One of the five chief Philistine cities. It was captured by Judah the judge and allotted to Dan (Judg. 1:18). See also *Philistines.*

ELAH

1. A valley in Judah where David killed the Philistine giant Goliath (1 Sam. 17:2, 49).

2. A king of Israel (reigned about 886–885 B.C.) who was assassinated and succeeded by Zimri (1 Kings 16:6–10).

ELAM. A son of Shem and ancestor of the Elamites (Gen. 10:22).

ELAMITES. Descendants of Elam who lived in Mesopotamia in the area later populated by the Medes and Persians (Jer. 25:25). See also *Persia.*

EL-BETHEL. See *Bethel.*

ELDER

1. In the O.T., an older member of a tribe or clan who was a leader and official representative of the clan (Num. 22:7).

2. In the N.T., a local church leader who served as a pastor and teacher (1 Tim. 5:17).

ELDER [S]

Matt. 15:2 thy [Jesus'] disciples transgress the tradition of the *e's*
Acts 14:23 they [Paul and Barnabas] had ordained them *e's*
Acts 20:17 he [Paul] sent to Ephesus, and called the *e's*
1 Tim. 5:1 Rebuke not an *e*, but entreat him as a father
Rev. 4:10 four and twenty *e's* fall down before him [God]

ELEAZAR. A son of Aaron who succeeded his father as high priest (Num. 20:25–28), serving under Moses and Joshua. He helped divide the land of Canaan among the twelve tribes of Israel (Josh. 14:1).

ELIJAH. On a hilltop in the Mount Carmel range stands this imposing statue of the prophet Elijah. After defeating Queen Jezebel's prophets of Baal in a spiritual battle by calling down fire from heaven to consume a sacrifice, Elijah ordered the false prophets executed.

E

ELECT LADY (CHOSEN LADY). The person, or perhaps a local church, to which the second epistle of John is addressed (2 John 1:1). *Chosen lady:* NIV.

ELECTION, DIVINE. The doctrine that deals with God's choice of persons who will be redeemed. Conflicts between God's electing grace and Christ's invitation that "whosoever will" may come to Him are not easily resolved. God's intentional will is for all to "come to repentance" and be saved (2 Pet. 3:9), but those who reject His Son will be lost (John 5:40).

God's grace is unmerited (Rom. 9:11–16), but it will be lavished on those who are committed to His truth and His will for their lives (2 Thess. 2:13). The elect are characterized by Christlikeness (Rom. 8:29), holiness (Eph. 1:4), good works (Eph. 2:10), and eternal hope (1 Pet. 1:2–5). See also *Foreknowledge; Predestination.*

EL-ELOHE-ISRAEL. A name, meaning "God, the God of Israel," given by Jacob to the altar that he built at Shechem after he was reconciled to his brother, Esau (Gen. 33:20).

ELEVATION OFFERING. See *Wave Offering.*

ELI. A high priest of Israel with whom the prophet Samuel lived during his boyhood years (1 Sam. 1–4). Eli's own two sons, Phinehas and Hophni, were unworthy of the priesthood (1 Sam. 2:12–17, 22–25). They were killed in a battle with the Philistines. Eli fell backward, broke his neck, and died upon learning of their death (1 Sam. 4:1–18).
See also *High Priest.*

ELIADA. See *Beeliada*

ELIAKIM
1. A son of Hilkiah and overseer of the household of King Hezekiah of Judah. Eliakim was praised by the prophet Isaiah for his role in mediating peace with the invading Assyrian army (2 Kings 18:18; Isa. 22:20–25).
2. Another name for Jehoiakim, a king of Judah. See *Jehoiakim.*

ELIAS. See *Elijah.*

ELIHU. A friend who spoke to Job after Eliphaz, Bildad, and Zophar failed to answer Job's questions satisfactorily (Job 32:2–6).

ELIJAH/ELIAS. A courageous prophet who opposed King Ahab and his successor, Ahaziah, because of their encouragement of Baal worship throughout the Northern Kingdom. Because of Ahab's wickedness, Elijah predicted a drought would afflict the land (1 Kings 17). He wiped out the prophets of Baal after a dramatic demonstration of God's power on Mount Carmel (1 Kings 18:17–40).

After selecting Elisha as his successor, Elijah was carried into heaven in a whirlwind (2 Kings 2:1–11). The coming of the Messiah was often associated in Jewish thought with Elijah's return. Some people even thought Jesus was Elijah (Luke 9:8). *Elias:* Greek form (Matt. 17:4). See also *Elisha.*

ELIMELECH. The husband of Naomi and the father-in-law of Ruth. He died in Moab, leaving his family destitute (Ruth 1:1–3).

ELIPHAZ
1. A son of Esau (Gen. 36:2–4).
2. One of Job's friends or "comforters" (Job 2:11). In his speeches, Eliphaz defended the justice, purity, and holiness of God (Job 4; 15; 22; 42:7–9).

EMERALD. *The green emerald was one of twelve precious stones worn on the breastplate of Israel's high priest. The stones symbolized how precious Israel's twelve tribes were to God.*

ELISABETH (ELIZABETH). The mother of John the Baptist and a relative of Mary, earthly mother of Jesus. Elisabeth rejoiced with Mary over the coming birth of the Messiah (Luke 1:36–45). *Elizabeth:* NIV, NRSV. See also *Mary,* No. 1.

ELISHA/ELISEUS. The prophet selected and anointed by Elijah as his successor (1 Kings 19:16–21). He followed Elijah for several years and was present at his ascension into heaven when the mantle of leadership fell upon him (2 Kings 2:9–14).

Elisha served as a counselor and adviser to four kings of the Northern Kingdom—Jehoram, Jehu, Jehoahaz, and Joash—across a period of about fifty years (850–800 B.C.). *Eliseus:* Greek form (Luke 4:27). See also *Elijah.*

ELISHEBA. The wife of Aaron and mother of Abihu, Eleazar, Nadab, and Ithamar (Exod. 6:23).

ELOTH. An Edomite seaport city on the Red Sea captured by David, then later turned into a station for trading ships by King Solomon (1 Kings 9:26).

EL-PARAN. See *Paran.*

ELUL. The sixth month of the Hebrew year, roughly equivalent to our September (Neh. 6:15).

ELYMAS. See *Bar-jesus.*

EMBALM. To prepare a body for burial to protect it from decay. This art was practiced by the Egyptians. Jacob and Joseph were embalmed for burial (Gen. 50:2–3, 26).

EMBROIDERY. The art of fancy needlework (Exod. 28:39).

EMERALD. A precious stone of pure green color used in the high priest's breastplate (Exod. 28:18) and the foundation of New Jerusalem (Rev. 21:19). See also *Diamond.*

EMERODS (TUMORS, ULCERS). A strange disease, exact nature unknown, that struck the Philistines when they placed the stolen ark of the covenant next to their false god Dagon (Deut. 28:27). *Tumors:* NIV; *ulcers:* NRSV.

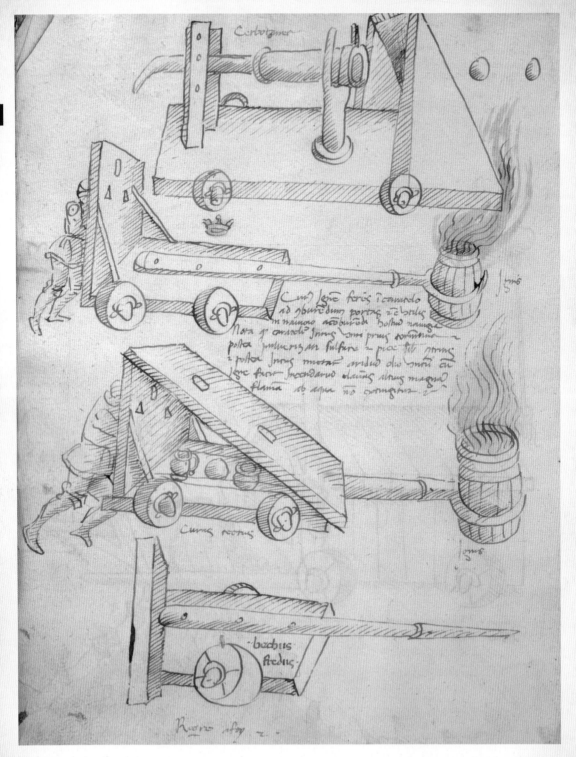

ENGINES. Catapults that could launch fire and stones were used in Bible times to help capture walled cities. This is a partial design for building a fire launcher from the 1400s, not Bible times. Still, it shows the basic workings of a catapult.

E

EMIMS (EMITES, EMIM). A race of giants east of the Dead Sea (Gen. 14:5). They were closely related to another race of giants known as the Anakims (Deut. 2:10–11). *Emites:* NIV; *Emim:* NRSV. See also *Anakims.*

EMMANUEL/IMMANUEL. The name given to the Christ child, meaning "God with us" (Matt. 1:23). The birth of a Savior bearing this name was foretold by the prophet Isaiah (Isa. 7:14; *Immanuel*). As this symbolic name suggests, God incarnate came in the person of Jesus Christ (1 John 4:2). See also *Jesus Christ; Messiah; Son of God; Son of Man.*

EMMAUS. A village near Jerusalem where Jesus revealed Himself to two of His followers shortly after His resurrection (Luke 24:13–31).

EMPTY. See *Void.*

ENCHANTER (MEDIUM, SOOTH-SAYER). A person who used magical chants and rituals to drive away evil spirits (Jer. 27:9). *Medium:* NIV; *soothsayer:* NRSV. See also *Medium; Soothsayer.*

END [ED]
Gen. 2:2 seventh day God *e'ed* his work
Ps. 102:27 thy [God's] years shall have no *e*
Eccles. 7:8 Better...*e* of a thing than the beginning
Eccles. 12:12 making many books there is no *e*
Isa. 9:7 Of...his [the Messiah's]...peace...shall be no *e*
Dan. 12:9 words are...sealed...time of the *e*
Matt. 10:22 endureth to the *e* shall be saved
Matt. 24:6 things must come to pass...*e* is not yet
Matt. 28:20 I [Jesus] am with you always...*e* of the world
Eph. 3:21 glory in the church...world without *e*
1 Pet. 4:7 the *e* of all things is at hand
Rev. 22:13 Alpha and Omega, the beginning and the *e*

ENDOR. A city in the territory of Issachar (Josh. 17:11). King Saul sought advice from a witch in this city (1 Sam. 28:7–10).

ENDURE [D, TH]
Exod. 18:23 thou [Moses] shalt be able to *e*
1 Chron. 16:34 his [God's] mercy *e'th* for ever
Ps. 9:7 LORD shall *e* for ever
Ps. 30:5 his [God's] anger *e'th* but a moment
Ps. 89:36 His [David's] seed shall *e* for ever
Matt. 10:22 that *e'th* to the end shall be saved
1 Cor. 13:7 [charity] hopeth all things, *e'th* all things
2 Tim. 2:3 *e* hardness, as a good soldier of Jesus Christ
2 Tim. 4:5 watch thou in all things, *e* afflictions
Heb. 12:2 who [Jesus] for the joy...set before him *e'd* the cross
James 1:12 Blessed is the man that *e'th* temptation

ENEMY [IES]
Deut. 20:4 LORD...goeth...to fight...against your *e'ies*
Job 19:11 he [God] counteth me...as one of his *e'ies*
Ps. 9:3 *e'ies* are turned back, they shall fall
Ps. 18:17 He [God] delivered me from my strong *e*
Ps. 110:1 I [God] make thine *e'ies* thy footstool
Prov. 25:21 thine *e* be hungry, give him bread
Matt. 5:44 I [Jesus] say unto you, Love your *e'ies*
Rom. 12:20 Therefore if thine *e* hunger, feed him
1 Cor. 15:25 he [Jesus] must reign...put all *e'ies* under his feet
1 Cor. 15:26 last *e*...destroyed is death
Gal. 4:16 I [Paul]...your *e*, because I tell you the truth
2 Thess. 3:15 count him not as an *e*, but admonish him
James 4:4 friend of the world is the *e* of God

EN-GEDI. An oasis on the western shore of the Dead Sea where David hid from King Saul (1 Sam. 23:29–24:1).

ENGINES (MACHINES). A word that refers to the ingenuity of a machine or apparatus. The "engines" in 2 Chron. 26:15 (*machines:* NIV, NRSV) were used to hurl objects from the walls of besieged cities upon the enemy below. See also *Fenced City; Siege; Wall.*

ENGRAVER. A craftsman who engraved metals or carved wood and stone (Exod. 35:35).

ENMITY. Deep animosity toward another (Gen. 3:15). This sin is characteristic of unredeemed persons (Rom. 1:29–30; 8:7). See also *Hate.*

ENOCH/HENOCH

1. The firstborn son of Cain and the name of a city built by Cain and named after Enoch (Gen. 4:17).

2. The father of Methuselah who was taken into God's presence without experiencing physical death (Gen. 5:21–24). *Henoch:* 1 Chron. 1:3.

ENOS (ENOSH). A son of Seth and a grandson of Adam (Gen. 5:6) who is listed in the N.T. ancestry of Jesus (Luke 3:38). *Enosh:* NIV, NRSV.

ENSIGN (BANNER). A symbol on a long pole that identified an army or tribe (Num. 2:2). *Banner:* NIV. See also *Standard*.

ENTER [ED]

Ps. 100:4 *E* into his [God's] gates with thanksgiving
Matt. 6:6 when thou prayest, *e* into thy closet
Mark 14:38 pray, lest ye *e* into temptation
Luke 13:24 Strive to *e* in at the strait gate
Luke 18:25 easier for a camel...rich man to *e* into the kingdom
Luke 22:3 Then *e'ed* Satan into Judas
Rom. 5:12 by one man sin *e'ed* into the world
Heb. 9:12 he [Jesus] *e'ed* in once into the holy place

ENVY. Resentment toward another person's good fortune (Prov. 27:4). Paul cautioned Christians against the dangers of this sin (Rom. 13:13). See also *Jealousy*.

ENVY [IETH, ING]

Prov. 3:31 *E* thou not the oppressor
1 Cor. 13:4 charity *e'ieth* not...vaunteth not itself
Gal. 5:26 not be desirous of...glory,...*e'ing* one another
Phil. 1:15 Some...preach Christ even of *e* and strife
James 3:16 where *e'ing* and strife is, there is confusion

EPAPHRAS. A leader of the Colossian church (Col. 1:7–8) whom Paul called his "fellow prisoner" in Rome (Philem. 23).

EPAPHRODITUS. A believer from Philippi who brought a gift to Paul while he was under house arrest in Rome (Phil. 4:18).

PAUL AND EPAPHRODITUS

Epaphroditus must have stayed in Rome for a while to offer comfort and encouragement to Paul. The apostle informed the Philippian believers that Epaphroditus had been sick but had recovered and would be returning to them soon (Phil. 2:27-28). Paul may have sent his letter to the Philippians by Epaphroditus (Phil. 2:29).

EPHAH. A dry measure equal to about one bushel (Exod. 16:36).

EPHESIANS, EPISTLE TO THE. A letter of the apostle Paul to the church at Ephesus on the theme of the risen Christ as Lord of creation and head of His body, the Church. The first three chapters of the epistle focus on the redemption made possible by the atoning death of Christ and His grace that is appropriated through faith—"not of works, lest any man should boast" (2:9). Chapters 4–6 call on the Ephesian Christians to model their lives after Christ's example and to remain faithful in turbulent times.

EPHESUS. The chief city of Asia Minor and a center of worship of the pagan goddess Diana where Paul spent two to three years, establishing a church (Acts 18:19–21; 19:1–10). Archaeologists have uncovered the remains of the temple of Diana and a Roman theater on this site. See also *Diana*.

8
C
3

EPHOD. A sleeveless linen garment, similar to a vest, worn by the high priest while officiating at the sacrificial altar (2 Sam. 6:14).

EPHPHATHA. An Aramaic word, meaning "be opened," spoken by Jesus to heal a deaf man (Mark 7:34).

EPHRAIM

1. The second son of Joseph who became the founder of one of the twelve tribes of Israel (Gen. 48:8–20). Joshua was a member of this tribe. See also *Tribes of Israel*.

2. A name often used symbolically for the nation of Israel (Hosea 11:12; 12:1).

3. A city in the wilderness to which Jesus and His disciples retreated (John 11:54).

4. A forest where the forces of Absalom were defeated by David's army (2 Sam. 18:6).

EPHRATAH, EPHRATH. See *Bethlehem*.

EPHRON. A Hittite who sold the cave of Machpelah to Abraham as a burial site (Gen. 23:8–20). See also *Machpelah*.

EPICUREANS. Followers of the Greek philosopher Epicurus, who believed the highest goal of life was the pursuit of pleasure, tempered by morality and cultural refinement. Epicureans were among the crowd addressed by Paul in the city of Athens (Acts 17:18). See also *Athens; Stoicks*.

EPISTLE. A type of correspondence best described as a "formal letter." Twenty-two of the twenty-seven N.T. books were written as epistles.

EQUAL
John 5:18 God was his [Jesus'] Father...e with God
Phil. 2:6 Who [Jesus]...thought it not robbery to be e with God
Col. 4:1 give unto your servants...just and e

ERR [ED]
Job 6:24 understand wherein I [Job] have e'ed
Isa. 9:16 leaders of this people cause them to e
Matt. 22:29 Ye do e, not knowing the scriptures
1 Tim. 6:10 they have e'ed from the faith

ERROR
2 Sam. 6:7 God smote him [Uzzah]...for his e
Matt. 27:64 last e...worse than the first
2 Pet. 3:17 led away with the e of the wicked

ESAIAS. See *Isaiah*.

ESAR-HADDON. A son of Sennacherib who succeeded his father as king of Assyria (reigned about 681–669 B.C.; 2 Kings 19:37). Esar-haddon apparently was the king who resettled Samaria with foreigners after the fall of the Northern Kingdom (Ezra 4:1–2). See also *Samaritan*.

ESAU/EDOM. The oldest son of Isaac who sold his birthright to his twin brother, Jacob, for a bowl of stew (Gen. 25:25–34). Esau was the ancestor of the Edomites. *Edom:* Gen. 36:8. See also *Edom; Edomites*.

ESCAPE [D]
1 Sam. 22:1 David...e'd to the cave Adullam
Job 19:20 I [Job] am e'd with the skin of my teeth
Isa. 37:31 remnant that is e'd of the house of Judah
John 10:39 he [Jesus] e'd out of their hand
1 Cor. 10:13 with the temptation also make a way to e
Heb. 2:3 shall we e, if we neglect so great salvation

ESDRAELON. See *Jezreel*, No. 3.

ESEK. A well in the valley of Gerar over which the servants of Isaac and Abimelech quarreled (Gen. 26:20).

ESH-BAAL. See *Ish-bosheth*.

ESPOUSED. See *Betrothal*.

ESAU. In a foolish moment, red-haired Esau—hungry from hunting—trades his inheritance for a bowl of stew. As Isaac's oldest son, Esau would have gotten a double share of the rich inheritance. It's uncertain if he traded everything or just the rights of an elder brother. Either way, the stew was overpriced.

ESSENES. A religious group of N.T. times that practiced strict discipline, withdrawal from society, and communal living. Although they are not mentioned by name in the Bible, many scholars believe they are the group that preserved the Dead Sea Scrolls in caves at Qumran near the Dead Sea. See also *Dead Sea Scrolls; Qumran.*

ESTABLISH [ED]
Gen. 9:9 I [God] *e* my covenant with you [Noah]
Ps. 78:5 he [God] *e'ed* a testimony in Jacob
Ps. 90:17 *e* thou [God] the work of our hands
Ezek. 16:62 I [God] will *e* my covenant with thee
Matt. 18:16 mouth of...witnesses every word...be *e'ed*
Acts 16:5 so were the churches *e'ed* in the faith

ESTHER. A young Jewish woman who became queen under King Ahasuerus of Persia and used her influence to save her countrymen. Her Persian name was *Hadassah.* See also *Ahasuerus; Haman.*

ESTHER, BOOK OF. A historical book of the O.T. named for its major personality, Queen Esther of Persia, who saved her people, the Jews, from annihilation by the evil and scheming Haman—a high official of the Persian king. The book shows clearly that God protects and sustains His people.

ETERNAL
Deut. 33:27 The *e* God is thy refuge
John 17:3 life *e*, that they might know...God

2 Cor. 4:18 things which are not seen are *e*
2 Cor. 5:1 not made with hands, *e* in the heavens
1 Tim. 1:17 unto the King *e*, immortal, invisible
Heb. 5:9 he [Jesus] became the author of *e* salvation
Heb. 9:12 his [Jesus'] own blood...obtained *e* redemption

ETERNAL LIFE. Life without end, or ever-lasting existence. Eternal life was promised to believers at their conversion by Christ (John 11:25–26) and affirmed by the appearance of Moses and Elijah to Jesus and the three disciples (Matt. 17:1–9). Through His resurrection, Christ became the "firstfruits" of eternal life for all believers (1 Cor. 15:12–23). Life everlasting represents God's final victory over sin and death (Rev. 21:4).

Mark 10:17 I do that I may inherit *e-l*
John 3:15 believeth in him [Jesus]...have *e-l*
John 6:54 Whoso eateth my [Jesus'] flesh...hath *e-l*
John 6:68 thou [Jesus] hast the words of *e-l*
John 10:28 I [Jesus] give unto them *e-l*
Rom. 6:23 gift of God is *e-l* through Jesus Christ
1 Tim. 6:12 Fight the good fight...lay hold on *e-l*
1 John 3:15 no murderer hath *e-l* abiding in him
1 John 5:11 God hath given to us *e-l*...in his Son

ETHAN. See *Jeduthun.*

ETHANIM. The seventh month of the Hebrew year, corresponding roughly to our October (1 Kings 8:2).

ETHIOPIA. An ancient nation south of Egypt. Moses married an Ethiopian woman (Num. 12:1). Philip witnessed to a servant of the queen of Ethiopia (Acts 8:27).

EUNICE. The mother of Timothy. She was commended for her great faith by the apostle Paul (2 Tim. 1:5). See also *Timothy.*

EUNUCH. A male household servant of a king. These servants were often emasculated to protect the king's harem (2 Kings 9:32). See also *Chamberlain.*

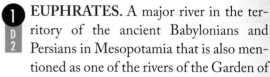

EUPHRATES. A major river in the territory of the ancient Babylonians and Persians in Mesopotamia that is also mentioned as one of the rivers of the Garden of Eden (Gen. 2:14). See also *Tigris.*

EUROCLYDON (NORTHEASTER). A violent wind that struck Paul's ship bound for Rome (Acts 27:14). *Northeaster:* NIV, NRSV.

EUTYCHUS. A young man who went to sleep and fell from a window during Paul's sermon at Troas. He was restored by Paul (Acts 20:9–12).

EVANGELIST. A person who traveled from place to place, preaching the gospel (Eph. 4:11; 2 Tim. 4:5). Philip was one of the zealous evangelists of the early churches (Acts 21:8).

EVE. The name given by Adam to his wife as the mother of the human race (Gen. 3:20). Fashioned from one of Adam's ribs, she was created to serve as his helpmate and companion (Gen. 2:18–23). Because of her sin and rebellion, Eve was to experience pain and sorrow, especially in connection with the birth of children (Gen. 3:16). See also *Adam; Fall of Man.*

EVERLASTING
Deut. 33:27 underneath are the *e* arms
Ps. 24:7 be ye lift up, ye *e* doors
Ps. 90:2 even from *e* to *e*, thou art God
Ps. 100:5 Lord is good; his mercy is *e*
Ps. 119:144 righteousness of thy [God's] testimonies is *e*
Isa. 9:6 his [Jesus'] name shall be called...*e* Father
Isa. 40:28 the *e* God...fainteth not
Isa. 60:19 Lord shall be unto thee an *e* light
Jer. 31:3 I [God] have loved thee with an *e* love
Dan. 7:14 his [God's] dominion is an *e* dominion
Matt. 25:41 Depart from me [Jesus]...into *e* fire

E

EVE. Eve holds unidentified fruit from the Tree of Knowledge, of which God told humanity's first couple not to eat. The fruit is often mistakenly called an apple.

EVERLASTING LIFE. See *Eternal Life*.

EVIL. A force that stands in opposition to God and righteousness. This evil force originates with Satan, the archenemy of good, truth, and honesty (Matt. 13:19). In the end-time, God will triumph over evil, and Satan will be thrown into a lake of fire (Rev. 20:10). See also *Iniquity; Sin; Wickedness.*

1 Sam. 16:14 an *e* spirit...troubled him [Saul]

Ps. 23:4 shadow of death...fear no *e*
Ps. 34:13 tongue from *e*, thy lips from...guile
Prov. 3:7 fear the LORD, and depart from *e*
Prov. 15:3 eyes of the LORD...beholding the *e*
Isa. 5:20 that call *e* good, and good evil
Matt. 6:13 not into temptation...deliver us from *e*
Luke 11:13 being *e*, know how to give good gifts
Rom. 7:19 the *e* which I [Paul] would not, that I do
Rom. 12:9 Abhor that which is *e*; cleave to...good
Eph. 5:16 Redeeming the time...days are *e*
1 Thess. 5:22 Abstain from all appearance of *e*
1 Tim. 6:10 love of money is the root of all *e*
James 3:8 tongue...is an unruly *e*

EVIL DESIRES. See *Concupiscence.*

EVILDOER [S]
Ps. 26:5 I have hated the congregation of *e's*
Ps. 119:115 Depart from me, ye *e's*
1 Pet. 4:15 none of you suffer...as an *e*

EVIL-MERODACH. A successor of Nebuchadnezzar II as king of Babylonia (reigned about 562–560 B.C.). He released King Jehoiachin of Judah from prison (2 Kings 25:27–30). See also *Babylonia.*

EWE LAMB. A female sheep (Gen. 21:30).

EXALT [ED, ETH]
1 Chron. 29:11 thou [God] art *e'ed*...above all
Ps. 57:11 Be thou *e'ed*, O God, above the heavens
Ps. 97:9 thou [God] art *e'ed* far above all gods
Prov. 14:34 Righteousness *e'eth* a nation
Isa. 25:1 LORD, thou art my God; I will *e* thee
Luke 14:11 he that humbleth himself shall be *e'ed*
Phil. 2:9 God also hath highly *e'ed* him [Jesus]

EXAMPLE
Matt. 1:19 Joseph...not willing to make her [Mary] a public *e*
John 13:15 I [Jesus] have given you an *e*
1 Tim. 4:12 be thou an *e* of the believers, in word

EXCEEDING
Matt. 2:10 they [the wise men] rejoiced with *e* great joy
Matt. 5:12 be *e* glad: for great is your reward
Matt. 26:38 My [Jesus'] soul is *e* sorrowful

Eph. 2:7 he [God] might show the *e* riches of his grace
Eph. 3:20 him [Jesus] that is able to do *e* abundantly

EXCELLENT
Ps. 8:9 how *e* is thy [God's] name in all the earth
Ps. 150:2 praise him [God] according to his *e* greatness
Isa. 12:5 he [God] hath done *e* things
1 Cor. 12:31 show I [Paul] unto you a more *e* way
Heb. 8:6 he [Jesus] obtained a more *e* ministry
Heb. 11:4 Abel offered...a more *e* sacrifice than Cain

EXCUSE
Luke 14:18 they all...began to make *e*
Rom. 1:20 they are without *e*

EXHORT [ED, ING]
1 Thess. 2:11 we *e'ed* and comforted...every one of you
2 Tim. 4:2 *e* with all longsuffering and doctrine
Titus 2:9 *E* servants to be obedient unto...masters
Heb. 10:25 Not forsaking the assembling of ourselves...but *e'ing* one another

EXHORTATION. A strong message of encouragement or warning (Heb. 12:5).

EXILE. See *Captivity.*

EXODUS, BOOK OF. A book of the O.T. that recounts the release of the Hebrew people from Egyptian enslavement and the early years of their history as a nation in the wilderness.

Important events covered in the book include (1) God's call of Moses to lead the people out of slavery (chaps. 3–4); (2) the plagues on the Egyptians (chaps. 7–12); (3) the release of the Israelites and the crossing of the Red Sea (chap. 14); (4) God's miraculous provision for His people in the wilderness (16:1–17:7); (5) Moses' reception of the Ten Commandments and other parts of the law (chaps. 20–23); and (6) the building of the tabernacle for worship at God's command (chaps. 36–40). See also *Moses.*

EXPANSE. See *Firmament.*

EXPEDIENT
John 11:50 *e*...one man should die for the people
John 16:7 *e* for you that I [Jesus] go away
1 Cor. 6:12 All things are lawful...all things are not *e*

EYE. An organ of sight (Matt. 6:22). The word is also used symbolically to portray sinful desire (1 John 2:16).

Exod. 21:24 *E* for *e*, tooth for tooth
Job 42:5 now mine [Job's] *e* seeth thee [God]
Ps. 6:7 Mine *e* is consumed because of grief
Ps. 17:8 Keep me as the apple of the *e*
Prov. 28:22 He that hasteth to be rich hath an evil *e*
Mark 9:47 thine *e* offend thee, pluck it out
Luke 6:41 mote that is in thy brother's *e*
1 Cor. 2:9 *E* hath not seen, nor ear heard
1 Cor. 12:21 the *e* cannot say unto the hand
1 Cor. 15:52 twinkling of an *e*, at the last trump
Rev. 1:7 he [Jesus] cometh...every *e* shall see him

EZEKIAS. See *Hezekiah.*

EZEKIEL. A prophet of Judah who was carried into exile by the Babylonians and who prophesied faithfully to his countrymen for more than twenty years. He is the author of the book of Ezekiel in the O.T.

APOCALYPTIC LANGUAGE IN EZEKIEL

Ezekiel is one of the few books in the Bible that contains apocalyptic literature. This was a distinctive type of writing that used visions, numbers, strange creatures, angels, and demons to express religious truths (Ezek. 10:1–17). The best-known example of apocalyptic literature in the Bible is the book of Revelation in the New Testament.

EZEKIEL, BOOK OF. A prophetic book of the O.T. addressed to the Jewish captives in Babylon about 585 B.C. and offering God's promise that His people would be restored to their homeland after their period of suffering and exile was over. This promise from God is exemplified by Ezekiel's vision of a valley of dry bones: "I...shall put my spirit in you, and ye shall live, and I shall place you in your own land" (37:13–14).

EZION-GABER/EZION-GEBER. A place on the coast of the Red Sea where the Israelites camped during their years of wandering in the wilderness (Num. 33:35). This settlement later became a town, serving as a harbor for Solomon's trading ships. *Ezion-geber:* 1 Kings 9:26.

EZRA. A scribe and priest who led an important reform movement among the Jewish people after the Babylonian Exile. He is the author of the book of Ezra. See also *Nehemiah.*

EZRA, BOOK OF. A historical book of the O.T. that describes events in Jerusalem after the Jewish captives began returning to their homeland about 500 B.C. following their period of exile in Babylonia and Persia. After the rebuilding of the temple (Ezra 6:14–15), the people under Ezra's leadership committed themselves to God's law, put away foreign wives (Ezra 10:1–17), and confessed their sins and renewed the covenant (Neh. 9–10).

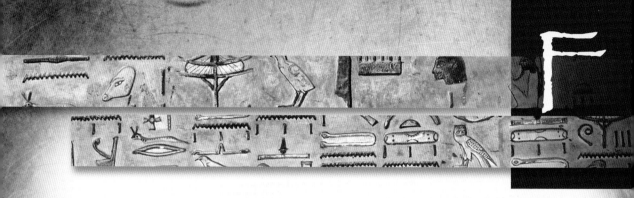

FABLE. A story in which inanimate things are personalized, as in Jotham's narrative of the trees and the bramble (Judg. 9:7–15).

FAIR HAVENS. A harbor on the southern side of the island of Crete where Paul's ship stopped during his voyage to Rome (Acts 27:8).

FAITH. Belief and confidence in the testimony of another, particularly God's promise of salvation and eternal life for all who place their trust in Jesus Christ (John 5:24). A gift of God, faith is essential to salvation (Eph. 2:8). The word also refers to the teachings of Scripture, or the "faith which was once delivered unto the saints" (Jude 3). See also *Trust*.

Hab. 2:4 the just shall live by his *f*
Matt. 17:20 *f* as a grain of mustard seed
Acts 6:8 Stephen, full of *f* and power
Rom. 3:28 justified by *f* without the deeds of the law
Rom. 10:17 So then *f* cometh by hearing
1 Cor. 13:13 abideth *f*, hope, charity
Gal. 2:20 I [Paul] live by the *f* of the Son of God

FAIR HAVENS. Sailing for Rome in a dangerous season, near the start of winter, Paul tried to convince the captain to winter at Crete's harbor in Fair Havens. But the captain sailed for a better harbor at Phoenix. On the short trip, a storm engulfed the ship and drove it some six hundred miles west before running it aground.

Gal. 3:24 unto Christ, that we might be justified by *f*
Gal. 5:22 fruit of the Spirit is love...goodness, *f*
Eph. 2:8 by grace are ye saved through *f*
Eph. 6:16 Above all, taking the shield of *f*
1 Tim. 5:8 denied the *f*, and is worse than an infidel
1 Tim. 6:12 Fight the good fight of *f*
2 Tim. 4:7 finished my course, I [Paul] have kept the *f*
Heb. 10:23 hold fast the profession of our *f*
Heb. 11:1 Now *f* is the substance of things hoped for
Heb. 12:2 Jesus the author and finisher of our *f*
James 2:17 *f*, if it hath not works, is dead
1 John 5:4 victory that overcometh the world, even our *f*

FAITHFUL [NESS]

Ps. 31:23 Lord preserveth the *f*
Ps. 119:90 Thy [God's] *f'ness* is unto all generations
Prov. 27:6 *F* are the wounds of a friend
Lam. 3:23 great is thy [God's] *f'ness*
Matt. 25:21 Well done...good and *f* servant
Luke 16:10 *f* in that which is least is *f* also in much
1 Cor. 4:2 required in stewards...man be found *f*
1 Cor. 10:13 God is *f*...not suffer you to be tempted
2 Thess. 3:3 Lord is *f*, who shall stablish you
1 John 1:9 he [Jesus] is *f*...to forgive us our sins
Rev. 2:10 be thou *f* unto death

FALL [EN, ING]

Ps. 145:14 Lord upholdeth all that *f*
Prov. 16:18 Pride goeth before destruction...haughty spirit before a *f*
Hos. 14:1 thou [Israel] hast *f'en* by thine iniquity
Luke 2:34 child [Jesus] is set for the *f*...of many
1 Cor. 10:12 thinketh he standeth take heed lest he *f*
Heb. 10:31 fearful thing to *f* into the hands of...God
James 1:2 joy when ye *f* into divers temptations
Jude 24 unto him [Jesus]...able to keep you from *f'ing*

FALL OF MAN. A phrase that refers to Adam and Eve's state of sorrow and misery that followed their sin and rebellion against God (Gen. 2–3). Their original sin has afflicted the human race ever since (Rom. 3:23)—a condition cured only by the atoning death of Christ (Rom. 5:6). See also *Adam; Eve; Man; Sin.*

FALLOW DEER. A distinct species of deer, common in Mesopotamia in Bible times, and a clean animal to the Hebrews (Deut. 14:4–5). See also *Deer.*

FALLOW GROUND (UNPLOWED GROUND). A field plowed and left idle for a short time before planting again (Jer. 4:3). *Unplowed ground:* NIV.

FALSE [LY]

Exod. 20:16 not bear *f* witness against thy neighbour
Lev. 19:11 shall not steal, neither deal *f'ly*
Prov. 11:1 A *f* balance is abomination to the Lord
Jer. 29:9 prophesy *f'ly* unto you in my [God's] name
Matt. 5:11 all manner of evil against you *f'ly*, for my [Jesus'] sake

JEREMIAH AND FALSE PROPHETS

False prophets have lived in every age, but the God-called prophet Jeremiah had more than his share of trouble from "yes-men" who told the officials of Judah what they wanted to hear. They denied Jeremiah's message of certain judgment for the nation unless the people changed their ways.

Hananiah was one of the worst of these misleading messengers (Jer. 28:1-17). Jeremiah declared that God would deal severely with Hananiah. He will do the same with anyone who speaks lies in His name and deliberately leads people astray.

FALSE PROPHET. A person who delivers a false or misleading message under the pretense that it comes from God. Believers are warned to beware of false prophets (Matt. 24:11, 24; 2 Pet. 2:1).

FALSE PROPHET [S]

Matt. 7:15 Beware of *f-p's*...in sheep's clothing
Mark 13:22 *f-p's* shall rise...signs and wonders
Acts 13:6 a *f-p*...whose name was Barjesus

1 John 4:1 many **f-p's** are gone out into the world
Rev. 19:20 beast was taken...with him the **f-p**

FALSE WEIGHTS. Deceptive measurements used in weighing merchandise—a practice condemned by the Lord (Deut. 25:13–14).

FALSE WITNESS (FALSE TESTIMONY). A person who gives false testimony or tells lies about others in an attempt to undermine their credibility or slander their character. Such testimony is specifically prohibited by the Ten Commandments (Exod. 20:16). *False testimony:* NIV.

FAMILIAR SPIRIT. The spirit of a dead person that a sorcerer "calls up" in order to communicate with that person (Deut. 18:11). The spirit of Samuel was called up by a witch at Endor (1 Sam. 28:3–20). Such sorcery was considered an abomination by God. See also *Sorcery; Witchcraft.*

FAMILY. A group of persons related to one another by blood kinship and the ties of marriage. The N.T. implies that all Christians are related to one another in a spiritual sense, since we are all members of the "household of faith" (Gal. 6:10). See also *Kindred.*

FAMILY RECORDS. See *Register.*

FAMINE. A time, often an extended period, when food or water is in short supply because of lack of rain and the failure of crops (Gen. 12:10). See also *Drought.*

FAN (FORK). A wooden pitchfork for winnowing grain (Isa. 30:24). The grain was thrown into the wind to separate it from the straw (Matt. 3:12). The fan is also spoken of as a symbol of God's judgment (Jer. 15:7). *Fork:* NIV, NRSV. See also *Winnowing.*

FARMER. See *Husbandman.*

FARTHING (PENNY). A Roman coin of small value (Matt. 10:29). *Penny:* NIV, NRSV. See also *Penny.*

FAST. The practice of giving up eating and drinking for a specified time, generally as part of a religious ritual in times of peril. Elijah and Jesus each fasted for forty days (1 Kings 19:8; Matt. 4:2).

FAST [ING]
Ps. 109:24 knees are weak through **f'ing**
Matt. 17:21 this kind goeth not out but by prayer and **f'ing**
1 Cor. 16:13 Watch ye, stand **f** in the faith
1 Thess. 5:21 Prove all things; hold **f** that which is good
Heb. 10:23 hold **f** the profession of our faith

FAT CALF. See *Fatling.*

FATHER. The male head of a household who was the undisputed authority in the family. This word was also used by Jesus as a title for God (Matt. 11:25).

FATHOM. A nautical measure, equal to about seven feet. The term is mentioned in the account of Paul's shipwreck (Acts 27:28).

FATLING (FAT CALF). A young animal fattened for slaughter (Matt. 22:4). *Fat calf:* NRSV. See also *Calf.*

FAULT [LESS, S]
Luke 23:4 I [Pilate] find no **f** in this man [Jesus]
Gal. 6:1 if a man be overtaken in a **f**
James 5:16 Confess your **f's** one to another
Jude 24 present you **f'less**...presence of his [Jesus'] glory
Rev. 14:5 without **f** before the throne of God

FEAR. An emotion aroused by danger or risk to one's safety (1 Sam. 21:10). The word is also used for respect or reverence toward God (Deut. 10:20).

FEAR [ED, ETH]

Deut. 6:13 *f* the Lord thy God, and serve him
1 Chron. 16:25 he [God]...to be *f'ed* above all gods
Job 1:1 Job...was perfect...*f'ed* God
Job 28:28 the *f* of the Lord, that is wisdom
Ps. 19:9 *f* of the Lord is clean, enduring for ever
Ps. 27:1 Lord is my...salvation; whom shall I *f*
Ps. 111:10 *f* of the Lord is the beginning of wisdom
Ps. 112:1 Blessed is the man that *f'eth* the Lord
Eccles. 12:13 *F* God, and keep his commandments
Phil. 2:12 work out your own salvation with *f*
2 Tim. 1:7 God hath not given us the spirit of *f*
Heb. 13:6 I will not *f* what man shall do unto me
1 John 4:18 perfect love casteth out *f*

FEAR NOT

Gen. 15:1 *F-n*, Abram: I [God] am thy shield
Gen. 21:17 What aileth thee, Hagar? *F-n*
Dan. 10:12 *F-n*, Daniel...words were heard
Joel 2:21 *f-n*, O land; be glad and rejoice
Matt. 1:20 Joseph...*f-n* to take unto thee Mary
Matt. 28:5 *F-n,* ye [women at the tomb]...ye seek Jesus
Luke 1:13 *F-n*, Zacharias...thy prayer is heard
Luke 1:30 *F-n*, Mary...hast found favour with God
Luke 2:10 *F-n*...I [angel] bring you [shepherds] good tidings
Luke 12:32 *F-n*...it is your Father's good pleasure to give you the kingdom
Acts 27:24 Saying, *F-n*, Paul; thou must be brought before Caesar
Rev. 1:17 *F-n*, I [Jesus] am the first and the last

FEARFUL [LY, NESS]

Ps. 55:5 *F'ness* and trembling are come upon me
Ps. 139:14 I am *f'ly* and wonderfully made
Matt. 8:26 Why are ye *f*, O ye of little faith?
Heb. 10:31 a *f* thing to fall into the hands of the living God

FEAST. A festival or a major religious holiday that marked some great event in Jewish history. The Jews celebrated several major festivals.

FEAST OF BOOTHS. See *Tabernacles, Feast of.*

FEAST OF HARVEST. See *Pentecost.*

FEAST OF INGATHERING. See *Tabernacles, Feast of.*

FEAST OF LIGHTS. See *Dedication, Feast of.*

FEAST OF UNLEAVENED BREAD. See *Passover and Feast of Unleavened Bread.*

FEAST OF WEEKS. See *Pentecost.*

FEET. The removal of sandals and the washing of one's feet upon entering a house or a holy place was a token of respect, similar to our custom of taking off the hat (Exod. 3:5).

FELIX. The governor of Judea who heard Paul's defense at Caesarea (Acts 23:24; 24:10–27).

FELLOWSHIP. A mutual sharing or friendly association, particularly that between believers who have a common faith in Jesus Christ (1 Cor. 1:9).

Acts 2:42 continued stedfastly in the apostles' doctrine and *f*
2 Cor. 6:14 what *f* hath righteousness...unrighteousness
Eph. 5:11 no *f* with the...works of darkness
Phil. 3:10 I [Paul] may know him [Jesus]...*f* of his sufferings
1 John 1:7 we have *f* one with another

FENCED CITY (FORTIFIED CITY). A city with a strong defensive wall (2 Sam. 20:6). The wall was erected to provide protection against enemies in times of war. *Fortified city:* NIV, NRSV. See also *City; Siege; Wall.*

FERRET (GECKO). A burrowing animal considered unclean by the Hebrews (Lev. 11:30). *Gecko:* NIV, NRSV.

FESTUS. Successor of Felix as Roman governor of Judea. Paul made his defense before Festus (Acts 24:27).

FETTERS (SHACKLES). Metal bands for binding the wrists or ankles of prisoners (2 Kings 25:7). *Shackles:* NIV. See also *Stocks.*

FEVER. See *Burning Ague.*

FIELD OF BLOOD. See *Aceldama.*

FIERY SERPENTS (VENOMOUS SNAKES, POISONOUS SERPENTS). Snakes that attacked the Israelites in the wilderness. Moses erected a brass serpent on a pole as an antidote for those who were bitten (Num. 21:6–9). *Venomous snakes:* NIV; *poisonous serpents:* NRSV. See also *Brass Serpent.*

FIG. The pear-shaped fruit of the fig tree. The spies sent into Canaan brought back figs to show the bounty of the land (Deut. 8:8). Figs were pressed into cakes and also preserved by drying (1 Sam. 25:18). The fig tree was considered a symbol of prosperity (1 Kings 4:25).

FIGHTING MEN. See *Mighty Men.*

FILTH. See *Offscouring.*

FILTHY
Ps. 14:3 they are all together become *f*
Isa. 64:6 our righteousnesses are as *f* rags
1 Tim. 3:8 deacons be grave...not greedy of *f* lucre

FILTHY LUCRE. A phrase for money (1 Tim. 3:3), which is condemned as an unworthy motive for ministry (1 Pet. 5:2). See also *Money.*

FINER (SILVERSMITH, SMITH). A craftsman who refined or shaped precious metals (Prov. 25:4). *Silversmith:* NIV; *smith:* NRSV. See also *Smith.*

FINGER
    1. A digit of the human hand. The word is also used symbolically of God's power (Exod. 8:19; 31:18; Luke 11:20).
    2. A measure of length equal to about three-fourths of an inch (Jer. 52:21).

FINING POT (CRUCIBLE). A vessel for melting and purifying metal (Prov. 17:3). *Crucible:* NIV, NRSV.

FINISH [ED]
Gen. 2:1 heavens and the earth were *f'ed*
Luke 14:28 counteth the cost...sufficient to *f* it
John 17:4 *f'ed* the work which thou [God] gavest me [Jesus]
John 19:30 is *f'ed*: and he [Jesus]...gave up the ghost
2 Tim. 4:7 I [Paul] have *f'ed* my course

FIR (PINE, CYPRESS). An evergreen tree that grew on Mount Lebanon. Its lumber was used in the construction of Solomon's temple in Jerusalem (1 Kings 6:15, 34). *Pine:* NIV; *cypress:* NRSV.

FIRE. Burning material used for cooking and in religious ceremonies. Fire is often associated with the presence and power of God (Exod. 3:2), as well as the final punishment of the wicked (Matt. 13:49–50). See also *Pillar of Fire and Cloud.*

FIREPAN. A vessel in which incense was burned during worship ceremonies in the tabernacle (Exod. 27:3). See also *Censer.*

FIRKIN. A liquid measure equal to about five or six gallons (John 2:16).

FIRMAMENT (EXPANSE, DOME). A word for the heavens, or the sky above the earth (Gen. 1:6–8). *Expanse:* NIV; *dome:* NRSV.

FIRST DAY OF THE WEEK. Sunday, or the day of Christ's resurrection, which was adopted as the day of worship by the early church (Acts 20:7).

FIRST INSTALLMENT. See *Earnest.*

FIRSTBORN. The first child born into a family (Gen. 49:3). The firstborn son received a double portion of his father's property as his birthright and assumed leadership of the family. See also *Birthright; Inheritance.*

FIRSTFRUITS. The first or best of crops and livestock. According to Mosaic Law, these were to be presented as sacrifices and offerings to the Lord to express thanks for His provision (Exod. 23:19; Prov. 3:9).

JESUS AS THE FIRSTFRUITS

The apostle Paul described Jesus Christ as "the first fruits of them that slept" (1 Cor. 15:20). Just as the firstfruits promised the full harvest to come, the resurrection of Christ guarantees resurrection and eternal life for all who accept Him as Savior and Lord.

FISH GATE. A gate in the wall of Jerusalem, probably so named because fish from the Mediterranean Sea were brought into the city through this gate (Neh. 3:3).

FISHER, FISHERMAN. One who makes his living by fishing. Several of Jesus' disciples were fishermen, and He promised to make them "fishers of men" (Matt. 4:19).

FITCH (SPELT). A plant that produces grain similar to oats or rye (Ezek. 4:9). *Spelt:* NIV, NRSV. See also *Rie.*

FLAG (RUSH). A coarse grass that grows in marshes or wetlands (Isa. 19:6). *Rush:* NIV, NRSV.

FLAGON
1. A cake of dried grapes or raisins served as a delicacy or dessert (Song 2:5).
2. A flask or leather bottle for holding liquids (Isa. 22:24). See also *Spoon; Vial.*

FLASK. See *Vial.*

FLAX. A plant grown in Egypt and Palestine for its fiber, which was woven into linen cloth (Exod. 9:31). See also *Linen.*

FLEA. A tiny insect that sucks the blood of animals or humans. David used this word as a symbol of insignificance (1 Sam. 24:14).

FLEECE. Wool that grows on a sheep. Gideon used a fleece to test God's call (Judg. 6:36–40). See also *Sheep; Wool.*

FLESH. A word for the human body in contrast to the spirit (Matt. 26:41). The word is also used for unredeemed human nature and carnal appetites or desires that can lead to sin (Gal. 5:16–17). See also *Carnal.*

FLESH AND BLOOD
Matt. 16:17 *f-a-b* hath not revealed it unto thee [Peter]
1 Cor. 15:50 *f-a-b* cannot inherit the kingdom of God
Eph. 6:12 wrestle not against *f-a-b*, but...principalities

FLESHHOOK (MEAT FORKS). A large pronged fork used to handle meat for sacrificial purposes (2 Chron. 4:16). *Meat forks:* NIV.

FLINT. A very hard stone, perhaps a variety of quartz (Deut. 8:15). The word is also used symbolically to denote firmness (Ezek. 3:9).

FLOCK. A group of sheep or birds (Gen. 4:4). The word is also used to designate a Christian congregation under a pastor's leadership (1 Pet. 5:2).

FLOGGING. See *Scourging.*

FLOOD, THE. The covering of the earth by water in Noah's time; the instrument of God's judgment against a wicked world. This great deluge came after forty days of continuous rainfall, but Noah and his family and the animals in the ark were saved by the hand of God (Gen. 6–8). See also *Noah; Ark, Noah's.*

FLOUR. Wheat or barley ground into a fine powder and used for baking bread. Flour was often offered as a sin offering (Lev. 5:11). See also *Bread; Wheat.*

FLUTE (PIPE). A musical instrument, played by blowing, similar to the modern flute (Dan. 3:5). Flute players were hired for funerals during N.T. times (Matt. 9:23–24). *Pipe:* NRSV. See also *Organ; Pipe.*

FLUX (DYSENTERY). KJV word for dysentery, a common disease in the Mediterranean world. Paul healed Publius of this ailment (Acts 28:8). *Dysentery:* NIV, NRSV.

FOAL. A colt, or young donkey. Jesus rode a colt on His triumphant entry into Jerusalem (Matt. 21:5), an event foretold in the O.T. (Zech. 9:9). See also *Ass.*

FISHER. Fishermen in the Sea of Galilee at the turn of the 1900s. At least four of Jesus' disciples were fishermen who worked in this freshwater lake in northern Israel.

F

FOOD. *Food served Middle Eastern family style—on the floor—becomes a banquet for a group of men in Saudi Arabia. In Bible times, people often ate food from a blanket or a low table that allowed them to sit on the ground.*

FODDER. See *Provender*.

FOOD. Plants and animals eaten for nourishment. Specific foods mentioned in the Bible include lentils (Gen. 25:34), honey, nuts, and spices (Gen. 43:11). The meats of certain animals were considered unclean and unfit for eating (Lev. 11; Deut. 14).

FOOL. An absurd person; one who reasons wrongly (Prov. 29:11).

FOOLISH. A word characterizing actions that show a lack of wisdom or faulty and shallow reasoning (Prov. 26:11). Jesus described the five virgins who were unprepared for the wedding feast as foolish (Matt. 25:1–13).

FOOLISH [LY, NESS]
Ps. 5:5 The *f* shall not stand in thy [God's] sight
Ps. 69:5 God, thou knowest my *f'ness*

Prov. 12:23 heart of fools proclaimeth *f'ness*
Prov. 14:17 He that is soon angry dealeth *f'ly*
Prov. 15:20 a *f* man despiseth his mother
Matt. 7:26 a *f* man...built his house upon the sand
1 Cor. 1:23 Christ crucified...unto the Greeks *f'ness*
1 Cor. 1:27 chosen the *f* things...to confound the wise
1 Cor. 3:19 wisdom of this world is *f'ness* with God
Gal. 3:1 *f* Galatians, who hath bewitched you
Titus 3:9 avoid *f* questions, and genealogies

FOOT. See *Feet*.

FOOTMAN. A member of the infantry or walking unit of an army (Jer. 12:5); a swift runner who served as a messenger for a king (1 Sam. 22:17). See also *Post*.

FOOTSTOOL. A low stool upon which the feet are rested. The word is also used symbolically to describe the fate of God's enemies (Ps. 110:1).

FOOT-WASHING. An expression of hospitality bestowed upon guests in Bible times. Foot-washing was generally performed by lowly domestic servants, but Jesus washed His disciples' feet to teach them a lesson in humble ministry (John 13:4–15).

FORBEARANCE (TOLERANCE). Restraint and tolerance. God, in His forbearance or patience, gives people opportunity for repentance (Rom. 2:4). *Tolerance:* NIV. See also *Long-suffering; Patience.*

FORD. A crossing through shallow water across a brook or river (Gen. 32:22).

FOREHEAD. The part of the human face above the eyes. God's people were instructed to learn the law so well that it would be as if it were written on their foreheads (Deut. 6:8). See also *Frontlet.*

FOREIGNER (TEMPORARY RESIDENT). A word for an outsider or stranger—a person who was not of the same ethnic stock as the Hebrews and who had no loyalty to Israel's God (Exod. 12:45). *Temporary resident:* NIV. See also *Alien; Sojourner.*

FOREKNOWLEDGE. God's knowledge of events before they happen and His ability to influence the future by actually causing such events (Isa. 41:4). See also *Election, Divine; Predestination.*

FORERUNNER. One who goes before and makes preparations for others to follow (Heb. 6:20). John the Baptist was a forerunner of Christ.

FORESAIL. See *Mainsail.*

FORESKIN. The fold of skin that covers the male sex organ. This foreskin is removed in the rite of circumcision (Gen. 17:11). See also *Circumcision.*

FORGIVE [ING]

Num. 14:18 LORD is longsuffering...*f'ing* iniquity
2 Chron. 7:14 then will I [God] hear...*f* their sin
Ps. 86:5 Lord, art good, and ready to *f*
Matt. 6:14 heavenly Father will also *f* you
Matt. 18:21 oft shall my brother sin...and I [Peter] *f*
Mark 11:26 neither will your Father...*f* your trespasses
Luke 5:21 Who can *f* sins, but God alone
Luke 6:37 *f*, and ye shall be forgiven
Luke 23:34 *f* them; for they know not what they do
Eph. 4:32 be ye kind...*f'ing* one another
1 John 1:9 he [Jesus] is faithful...*f* us our sins

FORGIVEN

Ps. 32:1 Blessed is he whose transgression is *f*
Matt. 12:31 blasphemy against the Holy Ghost shall not be *f*
Luke 6:37 forgive, and ye shall be *f*
Rom. 4:7 Blessed are they whose iniquities are *f*
1 John 2:12 sins are *f*...for his [Jesus']...sake

FORGIVENESS. To pardon or overlook the wrongful acts of another person; God's free pardon of the sin and rebellion of humans. Our sin separates us from God, but He forgives us and reestablishes the broken relationship when we repent and turn to Him in faith (Acts 10:43; Col. 1:14). Just as God forgives believers, He expects us to practice forgiveness in our relationships with others (Matt. 5:43–48). See also *Pardon.*

FORK. See *Fan.*

FORMER RAIN (AUTUMN RAIN, EARLY RAIN). The first rain of the growing season, essential for the germination of seed and the growth of young plants (Joel 2:23). *Autumn rain:* NIV; *early rain:* NRSV.

FORNICATION (SEXUAL IMMORALITY). Sexual relations between two persons who are not married to each other; any form of sexual immorality or unchastity. Paul cited fornication as a sin that believers should scrupulously avoid (1 Cor. 6:18). *Sexual immorality:* NIV. See also *Adultery; Chaste.*

Matt. 19:9 put away his wife, except it be for *f*
1 Cor. 5:1 reported...*f* among you
Gal. 5:19 works of the flesh are...Adultery, *f*
1 Thess. 4:3 will of God...abstain from *f*

FORT. A high wall or fortification built to provide protection against one's enemies in times of war (Isa. 25:12). See also *Fenced City; Wall.*

FORTIFIED CITY. See *Fenced City.*

FORUM OF APPIUS. See *Appii Forum.*

FOUNDATION. The strong base on which a building is erected. The apostle Paul described Christ as the sure foundation for believers (1 Cor. 3:11). See also *Corner Stone.*

FOUNDATION [S]
Matt. 25:34 kingdom prepared for you from the *f* of the world
Eph. 2:20 built upon the *f* of the apostles
Heb. 1:10 Thou, Lord...hast laid the *f* of the earth
Heb. 11:10 city which hath *f's*...builder...is God
Rev. 21:14 wall of the city [New Jerusalem] had twelve *f's*

FOUNTAIN. A source of fresh, flowing water; a spring (Deut. 8:7). The word is also used symbolically of God's blessings upon His people (Jer. 2:13).

FOUNTAIN GATE. A gate in the wall of Jerusalem, perhaps named for the fountain or pool of Siloam (Neh. 12:37).

FOWLER. A person who captures birds by nets, snares, or decoys (Hosea 9:8). The word is also used symbolically of temptations (Ps. 91:3). See also *Hunter.*

FRANKINCENSE. *A block of frankincense recovered from a Red Sea shipwreck. Harvested as sap from a tree, hardened resin was burned as fragrant incense during worship services.*

FOX. An animal of the dog family known for its cunning (Judg. 15:4). See also *Jackal*.

FRAGRANT CANE. See *Calamus*.

FRANKINCENSE (INCENSE). The yellowish gum of a tree, known for its pungent odor when burned as incense during sacrificial ceremonies (Neh. 13:9). Frankincense was one of the gifts presented to the infant Jesus by the wise men (Matt. 2:11). *Incense:* NIV. See also *Incense*.

FREE [LY]
Gen. 2:16 every tree of the garden thou mayest **f'ly** eat
Matt. 10:8 **f'ly** ye have received, **f'ly** give
John 8:32 truth shall make you **f**
Rom. 3:24 justified **f'ly** by his [God's] grace
Rom. 8:2 Jesus hath made me **f** from the law of sin
1 Cor. 9:19 though I [Paul] be **f** from all men
Gal. 3:28 neither bond nor **f**
Gal. 5:1 liberty...Christ hath made us **f**
Col. 3:11 neither Greek nor Jew...bond nor **f**
Rev. 22:17 take the water of life **f'ly**

FREEDMEN. See *Libertines*.

FREEWILL OFFERING. An offering given freely and willingly (Amos 4:5), in contrast to one made to atone for some misdeed (Num. 15:3).

FRINGE (TASSEL). An ornament worn on the edges of one's robe as a profession of piety and commitment to God (Deut. 22:12). *Tassel:* NIV, NRSV. See also *Hem*.

FROG. An amphibious animal sent by the Lord as the second plague upon Egypt (Exod. 8:2–14).

FRONTLET. A small leather case holding passages of Scripture, worn on the forehead as a literal obedience of Deut. 6:6–9. See also *Forehead; Phylactery*.

FRUITFULNESS. Productive; reproducing abundantly. Paul declared that believers should be fruitful in righteousness and goodness toward others (Col. 1:10).

FULLER (LAUNDERER). A laborer who treated or dyed clothes and also did ordinary laundry work (Mal. 3:2). *Launderer:* NIV.

FULLER'S FIELD (WASHERMAN'S FIELD). A place near the wall of Jerusalem where fullers worked and perhaps where they spread their laundry to dry (2 Kings 18:17). *Washerman's field:* NIV.

FUNERAL. A ceremony honoring the dead before burial. These ceremonies were sometimes accompanied by sad music and the loud wailing of friends and professional mourners (Eccles. 12:5; Matt. 9:23). See also *Burial; Minstrel*.

FURLONG. A Greek measure of length equal to about 650 feet or one-eighth of a mile (Luke 24:13).

FURNACE (SMOKING FIREPOT). An enclosed oven for baking (Gen. 15:17; *smoking firepot:* NIV, NRSV), smelting (Gen. 19:28), or drying and firing bricks (Dan. 3:15–17). See also *Brick-kiln*.

F

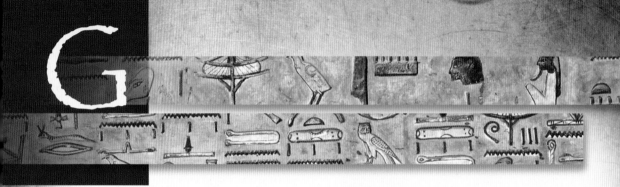

G

GAASH, MOUNT. A mountain in the hill country of Ephraim where Joshua was buried (Josh. 24:30).

GABBATHA. See *Pavement, The.*

GABRIEL. An archangel who appeared to Daniel (Dan. 8:16), Zacharias (Luke 1:18–19), and the Virgin Mary (Luke 1:26–38). See also *Archangel.*

GABRIEL. Gabriel tells the Virgin Mary that she will have a son. His name will be Jesus, "Son of the Most High."

GAD. The seventh son of Jacob, born of Zilpah (Gen. 30:10–11), and ancestor of one of the twelve tribes of Israel. Known as a fierce, warlike people, the Gadites settled east of the Jordan River (Josh. 13:24–28). See also *Tribes of Israel.*

GADARA. A Greek city about six miles southeast of the Sea of Galilee. In N.T. times, Gadara was the capital city of the Roman province of Perea.

GADARENES/GERGESENES. People from the area of Gadara in Perea. Jesus healed a wild, demon-possessed man in this area (Mark 5:1–20). *Gergesenes:* Matt. 8:28.

GAIN
Mark 8:36 profit a man...*g* the whole world
1 Cor. 9:20 I [Paul] became as a Jew...*g* the Jew
Phil. 1:21 me [Paul] to live is Christ...die is *g*
1 Tim. 6:6 godliness with contentment is great *g*

GAIUS
1. A Macedonian and companion of Paul (Acts 19:29).
2. A man of Derbe and companion of Paul (Acts 20:4).
3. A Corinthian baptized under Paul's ministry (1 Cor. 1:14).
4. The person to whom John addressed his third letter (3 John 1).

GALATIA. A territory of central Asia Minor that contained several cities visited by Paul during the first missionary journey—Antioch of Pisidia, Derbe, Iconium, and Lystra (Acts 13–14)—all located in southern Galatia. Paul's letter to the Galatians (Gal. 1:1–2) was apparently addressed to churches in and around these cities.

GALATIANS, EPISTLE TO THE. A short epistle of the apostle Paul to the churches of Galatia on the themes of Christian liberty and justification by faith alone.

The content of the epistle includes (1) a defense of Paul's apostleship and the gospel (chaps. 1–2); (2) his argument that salvation comes by God's grace through faith, not through obeying the law (chaps. 3–4); and (3) the practical dimension of one's faith—living in obedience to God and in harmony with others (chaps. 5–6).

GALBANUM. A gum from a plant used to produce sacred incense, which was burned at the altar (Exod. 30:34).

GALE. See *Whirlwind.*

GALILEAN. A native of the province of Galilee. All of Jesus' disciples except Judas were Galileans. Peter was recognized as a Galilean because of his distinct accent (Mark 14:70).

GALILEE (GALILEE OF THE GENTILES). A Roman province in northern Palestine during N.T. times and the area where Jesus spent most of His earthly ministry (Mark 3:7). Because of its far-north location, Galilee had a mixed population of Jews and Gentiles. The prophet Isaiah referred to it as "Galilee of the nations" (Isa. 9:1). *Galilee of the Gentiles:* NIV.

GALILEE, SEA OF/SEA OF CHINNEROTH/LAKE OF GENNESARET/SEA OF TIBERIAS. A freshwater lake about fourteen miles long and seven miles wide that took its name from the surrounding Roman province. Fed by the Jordan River, it provided the livelihood for many commercial fishermen, including several disciples of

G

GALILEE, SEA OF. The Sea of Galilee, photographed here from a space shuttle, is actually a freshwater lake. It drains into the Jordan River at the south.

Jesus: James, John, Peter, and Andrew (Mark 1:16–20).

Jesus calmed the waters of this lake after He and His disciples were caught in a boat in a sudden storm (Mark 4:35–41). *Sea of Chinneroth:* Josh. 12:3; *Lake of Gennesaret:* Luke 5:1; *Sea of Tiberias:* John 21:1.

GALL. A bitter, poisonous herb used to make a painkilling substance. While on the cross, Jesus was offered a drink containing gall (Matt. 27:34).

GALLIO. The Roman provincial ruler of Achaia who refused to get involved in the dispute between Paul and the Jewish leaders in Corinth (Acts 18:12–17).

GALLOWS. A structure used for executing people by hanging. The wicked Haman was hanged on the gallows that the had prepared for Mordecai (Esther 5:14; 7:10). See also *Haman.*

GAMALIEL. A teacher of the law under whom Paul studied (Acts 22:3). As a member of the Jewish Sanhedrin, he advised against persecution of the apostles and the early church (Acts 5:33–39). See also *Council.*

GAME. See *Venison.*

GANGRENE. See *Canker.*

GARDEN. A fenced plot generally outside the walls of a city where fruit trees or vegetables were grown. The most famous garden in the Bible is the Garden of Eden (Gen. 2:8–10). See also *Orchard.*

GARLAND (WREATH). A ceremonial wreath woven from flowers or leaves and worn on the head (Acts 14:13). *Wreath:* NIV.

GARLICK (GARLIC). A vegetable or herb similar to the onion that was used to flavor food. The Hebrews longed for this vegetable after leaving Egypt (Num. 11:5). *Garlic:* NIV, NRSV.

GASHMU. An influential Samaritan leader who opposed the Jewish people while they were rebuilding Jerusalem's walls under Nehemiah after the Exile (Neh. 6:6).

GATE. An entrance, door, or opening, particularly the strong gate in the walls of a fortified city (Judg. 16:3). The word is also used symbolically of salvation (Matt. 7:13) and heaven (Rev. 21:25). See also *Door.*

GATE KEEPER. A person who guarded the gate in a walled city (1 Chron. 9:19). See also *Doorkeeper; Porter.*

GATH. A royal Philistine city captured by David (1 Chron. 18:1) and home of the giant Goliath, whom David defeated (1 Sam. 17:4). See also *Philistines.*

GATH-HEPHER/GITTAH-HEPHER. A city in the territory of Zebulun and home of the prophet Jonah (2 Kings 14:25). *Gittah-hepher:* Josh. 19:13.

GAZA/AZZAH. A Philistine city where Samson was killed when he destroyed the temple of their pagan god Dagon (Judg. 16:21–30). *Azzah:* Jer. 25:20. See also *Philistines.*

GAZELLE. See *Roe.*

GAZER. See *Gezer.*

GECKO. See *Ferret.*

GEDALIAH. A friend of the prophet Jeremiah (Jer. 39:14; 40:5–6). After the fall of Jerusalem to the Babylonians in 587 B.C., Gedaliah was made supervisor of the vinedressers left in the land (2 Kings 25:22–25).

GEDEON. See *Gideon.*

GEHAZI. A servant of the prophet Elisha who was struck with leprosy because of his dishonesty and greed (2 Kings 5).

GEHENNA. See *Hell; Hinnom, Valley of.*

GENEALOGY. A record of the descendants of a person or family (1 Chron. 1–8). These records were important to the Jewish people because they documented inheritance rights and the right of succession as a clan leader, king, or high priest. See also *Register.*

GENERAL EPISTLES. The epistles of Hebrews; James; 1 and 2 Peter; 1, 2, and 3 John; and Jude—so named because they are addressed to broad, general problems rather than to local, specific issues. They are also referred to as *Catholic Epistles.*

GENERATION. A single step or stage in the line of descent from one's ancestors (Gen. 5:1; Matt. 24:34). The word is used in a more general sense to designate a period or age (Gen. 7:1).

GENERATION [S]
Gen. 2:4 the *g's* of the heavens and of the earth
Ps. 90:1 thou [God]...dwelling place in all *g's*
Ps. 100:5 his [God's] truth endureth to all *g's*
Eccles. 1:4 One *g* passeth...another *g* cometh
Dan. 4:3 his [God's] dominion is from *g* to *g*
Luke 3:7 *g* of vipers, who hath warned you
Luke 16:8 their *g* wiser than the children of light
Col. 1:26 mystery...hath been hid...from *g's*
1 Pet. 2:9 ye are a chosen *g*, a royal priesthood

GENESIS, BOOK OF. The first book of the O.T., often referred to as "the book of beginnings" because of its accounts of the world's creation and the early history of the Hebrew people. Major events and subjects covered in the book include:

1. God's creation of the physical world and Adam and Eve's life in the Garden of Eden; Adam and Eve's sin and introduction of sin to humankind (chaps. 1–3);

2. Adam's descendants and the great flood (chaps. 4–9);

3. The tower of Babel and the scattering of humankind (chap. 11); and

4. The life stories of the Hebrew patriarchs: Abraham and Isaac (chaps. 12–27), Jacob (chaps. 25–35), and Joseph (chaps. 37–50).

GENNESARET. See *Galilee, Sea of.*

GENTILE. A member of any ethnic group other than the Jewish race. The Jews looked down on other races as barbarous and unclean (Jer. 9:26). Jesus, however, abolished this distinction through His atoning death and His acceptance of all people through repentance and faith (Gal. 3:28). See also *Heathen.*

GENTILE [S]

Isa. 60:3 *G's* shall come to thy [God's] light
Jer. 16:19 *G's* shall come unto thee [God]
Mal. 1:11 my [God's] name...great among the *G's*
Matt. 12:18 my [God's] servant...judgment to the *G's*
Acts 9:15 he [Paul] is a chosen vessel...before the *G's*
Acts 13:46 we [Paul and Barnabas] turn to the *G's*
Acts 14:27 he [God]...opened the door of faith unto the *G's*
Acts 18:6 henceforth I [Paul] will go unto the *G's*
Rom. 2:9 Jew first, and also of the *G*
Rom. 3:29 God of the Jews only...also of the *G's*
1 Cor. 12:13 baptized into one body... Jews or *G's*
Eph. 3:6 *G's* should be...partakers of his [God's] promise

GERAH. A coin of small value, equal to one-twentieth of a shekel (Lev. 27:25). See also *Shekel.*

GERAR. An ancient city of southern Canaan, or Philistia, where Abraham was reprimanded by Abimelech for lying about his wife, Sarah's, identity. (Gen. 20).

GERGESENES. See *Gadarenes.*

GERIZIM, MOUNT. A mountain in central Canaan where Joshua pronounced God's blessings for keeping God's laws when the Hebrew people entered the land (Deut. 11:29; 28:1–14). In later years, this mountain was considered a sacred worship place by the Samaritans. See also *Samaritan.*

GESHEM. An Arabian who opposed the rebuilding of Jerusalem's walls under Nehemiah after the Exile (Neh. 2:19; 6:2).

GETHSEMANE. A garden near the Mount of Olives outside Jerusalem where Jesus prayed in great agony of soul on the night before He was betrayed and arrested (Mark 14:32–46). The garden was probably a grove of olive trees, since Gethsemane means "oil press."

GEZER/GAZER. A Canaanite city captured by Joshua (Josh. 10:33) and assigned to the Levites (Josh. 21:21). In later years, Solomon turned Gezer into an important military center (1 Kings 9:15–19). *Gazer:* 2 Sam. 5:25; 1 Chron. 14:16.

GHOST (SPIRIT). An Old English word for "spirit" (Matt. 27:50; 28:19). *Spirit:* NIV, NRSV.

GIANTS. People of unusually large size, such as the Philistine Goliath (2 Sam. 21:22). Races of giants mentioned in the Bible are the *Anakims* (Deut. 2:11), *Emims* (Deut. 2:10),

GETHSEMANE. The Garden of Gethsemane is now a church courtyard on the bottom slopes of the Mount of Olives. Flowers and gnarled old olive trees line the paths.

the judges (Judg. 20:19–36). *Gibeath:* Josh. 18:28.

GIBEON. A royal Canaanite city whose inhabitants surrendered to Joshua to avoid the fate of Jericho and Ai (Josh. 9:3–15).

GIBEONITES. Inhabitants of Gibeon who were made slaves following their surrender to Joshua (Josh. 9:21).

GIDEON/GEDEON/ JERUBBAAL. The famous judge of Israel who delivered the Israelites from oppression by defeating the mighty Midianite army with a force of only 300 warriors. Gideon came from an obscure family of the tribe of Manasseh, but he trusted God at every step of his military campaign and thus was successful (see Judg. 6–8). He is listed in the N.T. as one of the heroes of the faith (Heb. 11:32; *Gedeon*). *Jerubbaal:* Judg. 6:25–32. See also *Midianites.*

Rephaims (Gen. 14:5), and *Zamzummims* (Deut. 2:20).

GIBEAH/GIBEATH. The native city of King Saul and capital of his kingdom (1 Sam. 14:16; 15:34). This was apparently the same city destroyed by the Israelites during the period of

GIER EAGLE (OSPREY, CARRION VULTURE). A bird of prey considered unclean by the Hebrews (Lev. 11:18). *Osprey:* NIV; *carrion vulture:* NRSV. This is probably the same bird as the Egyptian vulture.

G

GIFT [S]

Prov. 19:6 every man is a friend to him that giveth **g's**
Matt. 2:11 they [wise men] presented...him [Jesus] **g's**
1 Cor. 12:4 diversities of **g's**...same Spirit
1 Cor. 12:31 covet earnestly the best **g's**
1 Cor. 13:2 though I [Paul] have the **g** of prophecy
2 Cor. 9:15 Thanks be unto God for his unspeakable **g**
1 Tim. 4:14 Neglect not the **g** that is in thee
James 1:17 good **g** and every perfect **g** is from above

GIFT OF GOD

John 4:10 If thou knewest the **g-o-G**
Rom. 6:23 **g-o-G** is eternal life through Jesus
Eph. 2:8 saved through faith...it is the **g-o-G**
2 Tim. 1:6 stir up the **g-o-G**

GIFTS, SPIRITUAL. See *Spiritual Gifts.*

GIHON

1. One of the four rivers of the Garden of Eden, associated with Ethiopia (Gen. 2:13). Some scholars believe this was either the Nile or the Ganges.

2. A place near Jerusalem where Solomon was anointed and proclaimed king (1 Kings 1:33).

GILBOA, MOUNT. A mountain range in the territory of Issachar where King Saul died after his defeat by the Philistines (1 Chron. 10:1–8).

GILEAD

1. A fertile, flat tableland east of the Jordan River (Judg. 20:1), known in N.T. times as the region of Perea.

2. A mountain or hill overlooking the plain of Jezreel where Gideon divided his army for battle against the Midianites (Josh. 7:2–5).

GILEAD, BALM OF. See *Balm of Gilead.*

GILGAL. A site between the Jordan River and the city of Jericho where the Hebrew people erected memorial stones to commemorate God's faithfulness in leading them into the Promised Land (Josh. 4:19–20). Gilgal apparently served as Joshua's headquarters in his campaign against the Canaanites (Josh. 10). In later years, Saul was crowned as Israel's first king at Gilgal (1 Sam. 11:15).

GIRDLE (BELT). A belt or sash made of cloth or leather and worn by men and women to hold their loose outer garments against the body (2 Kings 1:8). *Belt:* NIV, NRSV.

GIRGASITES/GIRGASHITES. Members of an ancient tribe, descendants of Canaan (Gen. 10:15–16), who inhabited part of the land of Canaan before the arrival of the Hebrew people. *Girgashites:* Deut. 7:1.

GITTAH-HEPHER. See *Gath-hepher.*

GITTITH. A musical instrument or tune associated with the city of Gath. The word is used in the titles of Pss. 8, 81, and 84.

GIVE

1 Chron. 16:34 **g** thanks unto the LORD; for he is good
Ps. 29:11 LORD will **g** strength unto his people
Prov. 25:21 thine enemy be hungry, **g** him bread
Matt. 6:11 **G** us this day our daily bread
Matt. 10:8 freely ye have received, freely **g**
Matt. 11:28 Come unto me [Jesus]...I will **g** you rest
Matt. 20:28 Son of man came...to **g** his life a ransom
Mark 8:37 a man **g** in exchange for his soul
Luke 12:32 Father's good pleasure to **g** you the kingdom
Luke 20:22 lawful for us to **g** tribute unto Caesar
John 14:16 he [God] shall **g** you another Comforter
Rom. 14:12 every one...shall **g** account...to God
2 Cor. 9:7 let him **g**; not grudgingly, or of necessity
1 Pet. 3:15 ready always to **g** an answer
Rev. 2:10 I [Jesus] will **g** thee a crown of life

GLAD [LY, NESS]

1 Chron. 16:31 heavens be **g**...earth rejoice
Ps. 9:2 be **g** and rejoice in thee [God]
Ps. 68:3 let the righteous be **g**

Ps. 100:2 Serve the LORD with *g'ness*
Joel 2:21 be *g* and rejoice...LORD will do great things
Matt. 5:12 be exceeding *g*: for great is your reward
Mark 12:37 common people heard him [Jesus] *g'ly*
John 20:20 disciples *g*, when they saw the Lord
Acts 13:48 Gentiles heard this, they were *g*
Rom. 10:15 beautiful...feet...that...bring *g* tidings

GLASS. A clear liquid mineral used to make utensils, ornaments, and vases. The "sea of glass" in John's vision probably represents God's purity or holiness (Rev. 4:6).

GLEANING. The gathering of grain left behind by the reapers—a courtesy offered to the needy (Lev. 19:9–10). Ruth gleaned in the fields of Boaz (Ruth 2).

GLEDE (RED KITE). A bird of prey, probably the kite or hawk (Deut. 14:13). *Red kite:* NIV.

GLORIFY [IED, ING]
Ps. 86:12 *g* thy [God's] name for evermore
Matt. 5:16 see your good works, and *g* your Father
Luke 2:20 shepherds returned, *g'ing*...God
Luke 23:47 centurion saw what was done, he *g'ied* God
John 12:23 hour is come...Son of man should be *g'ied*
John 17:1 thy Son also may *g* thee [God]
Rom. 8:30 whom he [Jesus] justified, them he also *g'ied*
1 Cor. 6:20 *g* God in your body
2 Thess. 1:12 name of our Lord...*g'ied* in you

GLORY. Splendor, honor, or perfection. The "glory of the Lord" signifies the supreme perfection of His nature (Exod. 16:7). Jesus also partook of the glory of His Father (John 2:11). He shares His divine glory with all believers (John 17:5–6). See also *Transfiguration of Jesus*.

1 Chron. 16:24 Declare his [God's] *g* among the heathen
1 Chron. 29:11 Thine, O LORD, is the greatness...and the *g*
Ps. 24:7 King of *g* shall come in
Ps. 29:2 Give unto the LORD the *g* due unto his name
Ps. 72:19 whole earth be filled with his [God's] *g*
Ps. 96:3 Declare his [God's] *g* among the heathen
Prov. 17:6 the *g* of children are their fathers

Jer. 13:16 Give *g* to the LORD your God
Matt. 6:13 kingdom, and the power, and the *g*
Mark 10:37 sit, one on thy [Jesus'] right hand...in thy *g*
Luke 21:27 Son of man coming...with...great *g*
John 1:14 we beheld his [Jesus'] *g*...full of grace

GLORY OF GOD/GLORY OF THE LORD
Exod. 24:16 the *g-o-t-L* abode upon mount Sinai
Ps. 19:1 The heavens declare the *g-o-G*
Luke 2:9 *g-o-t-L* shone round about them [shepherds]
John 11:4 sickness is not unto death, but for the *g-o-G*
Rom. 3:23 all have sinned...come short of the *g-o-G*
1 Cor. 10:31 whatsoever ye do, do all to the *g-o-G*
Phil. 2:11 Jesus Christ is Lord, to the *g-o-G* the Father

GLUTTONY. The act of eating or drinking to excess—a sin against which believers are warned (Prov. 23:1–8, 21).

GNASH. See *Tooth*.

GNAT. A small, stinging insect considered a great pest in the marshlands of Egypt and Palestine (Matt. 23:24). See also *Lice*.

GNOSTICISM. A heretical movement of N.T. times that taught that salvation came through superior knowledge. While gnosticism is not mentioned by name in the N.T., it was probably what Paul condemned when he declared that true knowledge comes from God and does not consist of idle speculation (Col. 2:8–23).

GOAD. A sharp, pointed stick or rod used in guiding oxen. Shamgar used a goad as a weapon against the Philistines (Judg. 3:31). See also *Ox*.

GOAT. A domesticated animal used for food (Gen. 27:9), clothing (Num. 31:20), and in religious sacrifices (Exod. 12:5). See also *Kid*.

G

G

GOAT DEMON. See *Satyr.*

GOD. The creator and ruler of the universe (Isa. 40:28–31); the first person of the triune Godhead—God the Father, God the Son, God the Spirit (Matt. 28:19; 2 Cor. 13:14)—who reveals Himself through the natural world, the Bible, and His Son, Jesus Christ (Col. 1:19). God is infinite in being and character: omnipresent (Jer. 23:23–24), all-powerful (Rev. 19:6), perfect in holiness (Lev. 11:44), and infinite in mercy (Ps. 136), wisdom (Col. 2:2–3), and truth (Titus 1:2).

God is active in salvation history. He covenanted with Abraham to "make of thee a great nation" and to make the Hebrew people a blessing to the rest of the world (Gen. 12:1–4). He called Moses to deliver the Israelites from Egyptian bondage (Exod. 3:9–10). He promised a Savior to rule Israel (Isa. 9:6–7). This promise was fulfilled in Jesus Christ (Matt. 1:18–21), God's love gift of salvation to the world (John 3:16, 36).

God's Spirit convicts unbelievers of sin and coming judgment (John 16:8–11). Humans can know God through faith in Christ (John 14:1, 6) and obedience to the Father's will (Matt. 7:21; Mark 3:35). God welcomes the worship and fellowship of His adopted children (John 4:23–24; Rom. 8:15–17). See also *I Am; Jehovah; Yahweh.*

THE ALL-KNOWING GOD KNOWS ALL ABOUT US

He knows our weaknesses (Ps. 103:14).
He knows our thoughts (Ps. 44:21).
He knows our words (Ps. 139:4).
He knows our actions (Ps. 139:2).
He knows our needs (Matt. 6:32).

GODDESS. A female deity or idol. Goddesses were prominent in the pagan cultures of Mesopotamia, Egypt, Canaan, Greece, and Rome. For example, Ashtaroth or Asherah was the wife of Baal in Canaanite mythology (1 Kings 11:33; *Ashtoreth:* plural form). Diana (or Artemis) was worshiped in the great temple at Ephesus (Acts 19:24–28). See also *Ashtaroth; Diana.*

GODLINESS. Holy living and righteous behavior that issue from devotion to God. Godliness also leads to love for others (1 Tim. 4:7–9). See also *Righteousness.*

GODLY [INESS]

2 Cor. 7:10 **g** sorrow worketh repentance
1 Tim. 6:6 **g'iness** with contentment is great gain
2 Tim. 3:5 form of **g'iness,** but denying the power
2 Tim. 3:12 live **g** in Christ Jesus...suffer persecution
Titus 2:12 live soberly, righteously, and **g**

GOG, PRINCE OF MAGOG. The leader of a tribal people, enemies of the Israelites, who was condemned by the prophet Ezekiel (Ezek. 38:2; 39:1). In the book of Revelation, Gog and Magog represent the forces of evil that oppose God and His people (Rev. 20:8).

GOLAN. A city in the territory of Manasseh designated as one of the six cities of refuge (Deut. 4:43). See also *Cities of Refuge.*

GOLD. A precious mineral used to make coins, jewelry, and utensils. Used extensively in Solomon's temple (1 Kings 7:48–50), gold also symbolized the splendor of the heavenly city, or New Jerusalem (Rev. 21:18).

GOLD FILIGREE SETTINGS. See *Ouches.*

GOLGOTHA. See *Calvary.*

GOLIATH. *Philistine champion Goliath loses his head in mortal combat with a shepherd boy. Young David takes Goliath's head as a trophy to signal his victory to the Philistine and Israelite armies watching from a distance.*

GOLIATH. A Philistine giant from the city of Gath who defied the entire army of King Saul. He was killed by David the shepherd boy with a single stone from his sling (1 Sam. 17:4–54).

GOMER. The unfaithful wife of the prophet Hosea. After her unfaithfulness, Gomer left Hosea and was sold into slavery, but the prophet restored her as his wife at God's command. His forgiveness of Gomer represented God's unconditional love for His wayward people (Hosea 3). See also *Hosea.*

GOMORRAH/GOMORRHA. A city near the Dead Sea destroyed by God with earthquake and fire because of the sin and wickedness of its inhabitants (Gen. 19:23–29). The city was cited in later years as an example of God's punishment (Isa. 1:9). *Gomorrha:* Matt. 10:15. See also *Cities of the Plain; Sodom.*

GOODMAN (LANDOWNER). A word for the head of a household, head of the house, or "master of the house," as rendered by some translations (Matt. 20:11). *Landowner:* NIV, NRSV.

GOODNESS. Purity and righteousness; a fruit of the Spirit that should characterize followers of Christ (Gal. 5:22). True goodness comes from God, who is holy, righteous, merciful, and loving (Ps. 31:19; Rom. 15:14). See also *Grace; Love; Righteousness.*

Ps. 23:6 Surely *g* and mercy shall follow me
Ps. 33:5 earth is full of the *g* of the LORD
Ps. 107:8 men would praise the Lord for his *g*

GOOD WORKS
Matt. 5:16 see your *g-w*...glorify your Father
Acts 9:36 Dorcas...full of *g-w*
Eph. 2:10 his [God's] workmanship...unto *g-w*
2 Tim. 3:17 man of God...furnished unto all *g-w*

GOPHER WOOD (CYPRESS). The wood used in building Noah's ark, probably cypress (Gen. 6:14). *Cypress:* NIV, NRSV.

GOSHEN. An Egyptian district where the Israelites settled and lived during their years in Egypt (Gen. 45:10).

GOSPEL. The "good news" that God has provided salvation for all people through the atoning death of His Son (Mark 1:1, 15). The word is also used of the teachings of Jesus and the apostles (Col. 1:5).

Matt. 24:14 *g* of the kingdom...preached in all the world
Mark 16:15 preach the *g* to every creature
Luke 4:18 he [God] hath anointed me [Jesus] to preach the *g* to the poor
Rom. 1:16 I [Paul] am not ashamed of the *g*
Rom. 10:15 beautiful...feet...preach the *g* of peace
1 Cor. 9:14 which preach the *g* should live of the *g*
Gal. 1:7 some...would pervert the *g* of Christ
Eph. 6:15 feet shod...*g* of peace
Phil. 1:12 things...fallen out...furtherance of the *g*
2 Tim. 1:8 partaker of the afflictions of the *g*
2 Tim. 2:8 Jesus...raised from the dead according to my [Paul's] *g*

GOSPELS, FOUR. The four books at the beginning of the N.T.—Matthew, Mark, Luke, and John—that describe the life and ministry of Jesus. Each Gospel tells the story from a slightly different perspective, giving us a fuller picture of the Savior than we would get from a single narrative. See also *Synoptic Gospels.*

GOSSIP. Idle talk, rumors, or fruitless tales. This type of speech is associated with the wicked and troublemakers (Prov. 16:28; 1 Tim. 5:13). See also *Busybody; Talebearer.*

GOURD. A poisonous plant that produces fruit similar to the common melon (2 Kings 4:39). Jonah sat under the shade of a gourd vine (Jon. 4:6–10).

GOVERNMENT. A system of power and authority through which stability and order are maintained in society. Governments have a vital function and should be supported by Christians, as long as they do not intrude into the role that belongs to God alone (Mark 12:13–17).

GOVERNOR (RULER). A general term for rulers or officials of differing rank or status (1 Kings 10:15). The chief in command of a Roman province was called a governor (Matt. 27:2; Acts 23:24). This title was applied to Christ (Matt. 2:6). *Ruler:* NIV, NRSV. See also *Lieutenant; Tirshatha.*

GOVERNOR'S HEADQUARTERS. See *Praetorium.*

GOZAN. A town, district, or river of Mesopotamia to which the people of the Northern Kingdom were deported after the fall of Samaria to the Assyrians (2 Kings 18:11).

GRACE. God's unmerited favor and love that lead Him to grant salvation to believers through the exercise of their faith in Jesus Christ (Titus 2:11; Acts 15:11). Salvation cannot be earned; it is a gift of God's grace (Eph. 2:8). See also *Mercy; Salvation.*

Gen. 6:8 Noah found **g** in the eyes of the LORD
Ps. 84:11 LORD will give **g** and glory
John 1:14 his [Jesus'] glory...full of **g** and truth
John 1:17 **g** and truth came by Jesus Christ
Rom. 3:24 justified freely by his [God's] **g**
Rom. 5:20 sin abounded, **g** did much more abound
Rom. 6:1 continue in sin, that **g** may abound
2 Cor. 8:9 ye know the **g** of our Lord Jesus Christ
2 Cor. 9:8 God is able to make all **g** abound
2 Cor. 12:9 My [God's] **g** is sufficient for thee
Eph. 4:7 **g** according to the measure of the gift of Christ
Col. 4:6 speech be alway with **g**, seasoned with salt
1 Tim. 1:14 **g** of our Lord was...abundant

GRAPE. Vineyard workers prune the vines in early spring to improve the harvest in the summer.

Heb. 4:16 come boldly unto the throne of *g*
James 4:6 God...giveth *g* unto the humble
2 Pet. 3:18 grow in *g*...knowledge of...Jesus
Rev. 22:21 *g* of our Lord...be with you all

GRACE OF GOD

Luke 2:40 child [Jesus] grew...*g-o-G* was upon him
1 Cor. 15:10 by the *g-o-G* I [Paul] am what I am
Eph. 3:7 I [Paul]...made a minister...gift of the *g-o-G*
Titus 2:11 the *g-o-G* that bringeth salvation
Heb. 2:9 he [Jesus] by the *g-o-G* should taste death
1 Pet. 4:10 as good stewards of the manifold *g-o-G*

GRACIOUS

Num. 6:25 Lord...be *g* unto thee
Ps. 77:9 Hath God forgotten to be *g*
Ps. 103:8 Lord is merciful and *g*, slow to anger
Isa. 33:2 Lord, be *g* unto us
Amos 5:15 God...will be *g* unto the remnant of Joseph

GRAIN. See *Corn; Wheat.*

GRAIN OFFERING. See *Oblation.*

GRAPE. A fruit used for food and wine-making. It was one of the most important agricultural crops of Palestine (Num. 13:23). See also *Wine.*

GRASS. A word for various types of common plants, such as that which livestock grazed. It is used symbolically for the brevity of life (Ps. 90:5–6). See also *Hay.*

GRASSHOPPER. An insect of the locust species that destroyed vegetation. Also eaten by the Hebrews (Lev. 11:22), the grasshopper was

GRAVE. Graves cover the southern ridge of the Mount of Olives, facing Jerusalem. Since ancient times, thousands of Jews, Christians, and Muslims have chosen to be buried near the Holy City. (Inset) The view from inside a Jerusalem tomb.

seen as a symbol of insignificance (Isa. 40:22). See also *Locust*.

GRATITUDE. See *Thanksgiving*.

GRAVE. A burial place for the dead. In Bible times, bodies were buried in pits (Gen. 35:8), caves (Gen. 25:9), and sepulchres hewn in rocks (Matt. 27:60). See also *Cave; Sepulchre*.

GRAVE [S]
Job 17:1 the **g's** are ready for me [Job]
Job 21:13 moment [the wicked] go down to the **g**
Ps. 30:3 thou [God] hast brought up my soul from the **g**
Ps. 88:3 my life draweth nigh unto the **g**
Eccles. 9:10 no work...nor wisdom, in the **g**
Isa. 53:9 he [God's servant] made his **g** with the wicked
Matt. 27:52 **g's** were opened...bodies of the saints...arose
John 5:28 all that are in the **g's** shall hear his [Jesus'] voice
John 11:17 he [Lazarus] had lain in the **g** four days
1 Cor. 15:55 O **g**, where is thy victory?
1 Tim. 3:8 deacons be **g**, not doubletongued

GRAVEN IMAGE (IDOL). An image of a false god made from wood or stone and set up in a prominent place as an object of worship (Exod. 20:4). The prophets warned God's people against such idolatry (Isa. 44:9–10; Hosea 11:2). *Idol:* NIV, NRSV. See also *Idol*.

GRAVING TOOL. An instrument or tool used for carving or engraving. Aaron used this tool to shape the golden calf (Exod. 32:4).

GREAT [ER]
Gen. 12:2 I [God] will make of thee [Abraham] a **g** nation
Ps. 48:1 **G** is the LORD, and greatly to be praised
Ps. 77:13 who is so **g** a God as our God
Prov. 22:1 good name...to be chosen than **g** riches
Isa. 9:2 people...in darkness have seen a **g** light
Matt. 5:12 Rejoice...for **g** is your reward in heaven
Matt. 20:26 **g** among you...your minister
Mark 12:31 none other commandment **g'er** than these
Luke 10:2 harvest truly is **g**...labourers are few
John 13:16 servant is not **g'er** than his lord

John 15:13 **G'er** love hath no man than this
Heb. 2:3 escape, if we neglect so **g** salvation
Heb. 4:14 Seeing then...we have a **g** high priest [Jesus]

GREAT LIZARD. See *Tortoise*.

GREAT OWL. A species of owl considered unclean by the Hebrews (Deut. 14:16).

GREAT SEA. See *Mediterranean Sea*.

GREAVES. Armor for the legs, covering the area from the knees to the ankles (1 Sam. 17:6).

GRECIAN JEWS, GRECIANS. See *Greeks*.

GREECE/JAVAN. An ancient world power that reached its greatest strength in the time between the testaments, about 400 B.C. to A.D. 1. The O.T. word for Greece was *Javan* (Gen. 10:2). See also *Athens*.

GREED. Excessive desire for material things. The Bible warns that this sin leads to disappointment and destruction (Luke 22:3–6; 1 Tim. 6:9). See also *Covetousness*.

GREEKS (GRECIAN JEWS, HELLENISTS). Natives of Greece or people of Greek heritage or descent. The N.T. often uses the word for people influenced by Greek traditions who were not Jews (John 12:20). The word *Grecians* is used of Greek-speaking Jews (Acts 6:1). *Grecian Jews:* NIV; *Hellenists:* NRSV.

GREYHOUND (STRUTTING ROOSTER). An animal cited as an example of gracefulness (Prov. 30:31). *Strutting rooster:* NIV, NRSV.

GRIDDLE. See *Pan*.

GRIEF

Job 2:13 saw that his [Job's] *g* was very great
Ps. 6:7 eye is consumed because of *g*
Prov. 17:25 foolish son is a *g* to his father
Isa. 53:3 man of sorrows [God's servant], and acquainted with *g*
Jer. 45:3 Lord hath added *g* to my [Jeremiah's] sorrow

GRIEVE [D]

Ps. 78:40 oft did they...*g* him [God] in the desert
Ps. 95:10 Forty years...was I [God] *g'd* with...generation
Mark 3:5 he [Jesus]...*g'd* for the hardness of their hearts
Mark 10:22 he [rich young ruler]...went away *g'd*
Eph. 4:30 *g* not the holy Spirit

GROVE. A wooden pole that represented the Canaanite fertility goddess Ashtoreth (2 Kings 21:7).

GROW

Ps. 104:14 He [God] causeth the grass to *g*
Matt. 6:28 Consider the lilies...how they *g*
1 Pet. 2:2 milk of the word, that ye may *g*
2 Pet. 3:18 *g* in grace, and in...our Lord

GUARANTEE. See *Surety*.

GUARD. A soldier who provided personal protection for a ruler; a bodyguard (2 Chron. 12:11).

GUIDE [S]

Ps. 48:14 God...will be our *g* even unto death
Isa. 58:11 Lord shall *g* thee continually
Matt. 23:24 Ye blind *g's*, which strain at a gnat
John 16:13 he [Holy Spirit] will *g* you into all truth

GUILE (DECEIT). Craftiness, cunning, or deception (Ps. 55:11). Nathanael was commended by Jesus as an Israelite without guile—a model of honesty and truthfulness (John 1:47). *Deceit:* NRSV.

GUILT. Remorse for sin and wrongdoing (Lev. 6:4). The guilt of sin is covered for believers by the sacrificial death of Christ (Rom. 5:1–2). See also *Conviction; Repentance.*

GUILT [Y]

Deut. 19:13 put away the *g* of innocent blood from Israel
Matt. 26:66 They...said, He [Jesus] is *g'y* of death
James 2:10 yet offend in one point, he is *g'y* of all

GUM RESIN. See *Stacte.*

GUTTER (WATERING TROUGH). A drinking trough for animals (Gen. 30:38). *Watering trough:* NIV.

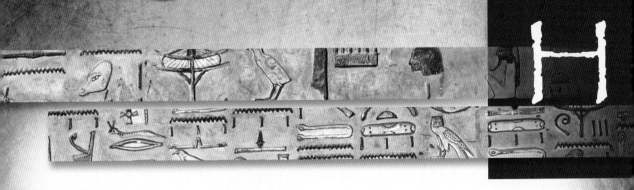

HABAKKUK. A prophet of Judah who was probably a contemporary of Jeremiah; the author of the book that bears his name (Hab. 1:1; 3:1).

HABAKKUK, BOOK OF. A short prophetic book of the O.T. that questions the coming suffering and humiliation of God's people at the hands of the pagan Babylonians (1:1–4; 1:12–2:1). God's response makes it clear that He is using the Babylonians as an instrument of judgment against His wayward people (1:5–11; 2:2–20). The book closes with a psalm of praise to God for His mercy and salvation (chap. 3).

HABERGEON. An Old English word for the priest's breastplate (Exod. 28:32; 39:23). See also *Breastplate.*

HABITATION. A place of residence (Num. 15:2; Acts 17:26).

HADAD. An Edomite prince or ruler who became an enemy of King Solomon (1 Kings 11:14–25).

HADADEZER/HADAREZER. A king of Zobah in Syria. He was defeated by David and Joab (2 Sam. 8:3–13; 10:6–19). *Hadarezer:* 1 Chron. 18:10.

HADASSAH. See *Esther.*

HADES. See *Hell.*

HAGAR/AGAR. Sarah's Egyptian slave who became the mother of Ishmael by Abraham (Gen. 16). She was driven into the wilderness with her son because of conflict with Sarah, but God intervened to save them (Gen. 21:9–21). *Agar:* Gal. 4:24. See also *Ishmael.*

HAGGAI. A prophet after the Babylonian Exile and author of the book that bears his name.

HAGGAI, BOOK OF. A short prophetic book of the O.T. written to encourage the Jewish captives who had returned to their homeland after three generations under the Babylonians and Persians. The people were encouraged to finish the task of rebuilding the temple in Jerusalem (1:1–2:9) and to remain faithful to God in difficult times (2:10–23).

HAGGAI AND THE TEMPLE

The temple in Jerusalem was the central place of worship for the Jewish people, so Haggai declared that it should be rebuilt with all deliberate speed. But the prophet also reminded the people that the physical temple could not serve as a substitute for a living faith. Obeying the Lord was more important than temple sacrifices (Hag. 2:10-19).

HAI. See *Ai.*

HAIL. Frozen rain (Job 38:22). The word is also used as a symbol of God's judgment (Rev. 8:7).

HAIR. Fibers on the human body, especially the head. They are used as a symbol of God's special care of believers (Matt. 10:30).

HAKELDAMA. See *Aceldama.*

HALAH. A region in Assyria where captives from the Northern Kingdom were carried (2 Kings 17:6).

HALF-SHEKEL TAX. A temple tax, also called the two-drachma tax (Exod. 30:13–14; Matt. 17:24–27). See also *Tribute.*

HALF-TRIBE OF MANASSEH. A phrase that refers to the two distinct settlements of the tribe of Manasseh—one in central Palestine and the other east of the Jordan River (Num. 32:33; Josh. 22:10). See also *Manasseh.*

HALLELUJAH. See *Alleluia.*

HALLOW. To set apart for holy use; to make holy (Exod. 20:11; Luke 11:2). See also *Consecration.*

HAM. The youngest son of Noah. Ham's four sons are thought to be the ancestors of the people of several nations: Canaan (Canaanites), Cush and Phut (Africa and Ethiopia), and Mizraim (Egypt). See Gen. 10:6.

HAMAN. An aide to King Ahasuerus of Persia who plotted to kill the Jewish leader Mordecai and all the Jews, only to be hanged himself on the gallows that he had built for Mordecai's execution (Esther 3:1–9:25). See also *Esther; Mordecai.*

HAMATH/HEMATH (LEBO-HAMATH). A Hittite city north of Damascus (Josh. 13:5). *Hemath:* Amos 6:14. *Lebo-Hamath:* NIV, NRSV.

HAMMER. A driving tool (Judg. 4:21). It is used as a symbol of the power of God's Word (Jer. 23:29).

HAMMOTH-DOR/HAMMATH/HAMMON. A city of refuge in the territory of Naphtali (Josh. 21:32). This is probably the same city as *Hammath* (Josh. 19:35) and *Hammon* (1 Chron. 6:76).

HAMMURABI, CODE OF. An ancient and influential law code named for an early king of Babylonia. The code was discovered in 1901–1902 by an archaeologist at Susa.

HANAMEEL (HANAMEL). A cousin of Jeremiah the prophet (Jer. 32:7). Jeremiah bought a field from Hanameel during the siege of Jerusalem by the Babylonians to signify hope for the future for God's people (Jer. 32:8–12). *Hanamel:* NIV, NRSV.

HANANI. Nehemiah's brother, who became governor of Jerusalem (Neh. 7:2). Hanani brought news of the suffering citizens of Jerusalem to Nehemiah in Persia (Neh. 1:2–3).

HANANIAH. See *Shadrach.*

HANDBAG. See *Crisping Pin.*

HANDBREADTH. A measure of length (about four inches) based on the width of the palm of one's hand (Exod. 25:25). It is also symbolic of the frailty and brevity of life (Ps. 39:5).

HANDKERCHIEF (CLOTH). A small cloth for wiping the face or hands (Acts 19:12) and also a burial cloth placed over the face of corpses (John 20:7). *Cloth:* NIV, NRSV. See also *Napkin.*

HANDMAID (MAIDSERVANT). A female servant (Gen. 29:24). This word also signified humility, as in Ruth's conversation with Boaz (Ruth 2:13). *Maidservant:* NIV.

HANDS, LAYING ON OF. See *Laying on of Hands.*

HANGING. A form of capital punishment (2 Sam. 18:10). Haman, the enemy of the Jews, was hanged on the gallows that he had prepared for Mordecai (Esther 7:9–10). See also *Haman.*

HANNAH. The mother of Samuel the prophet. She prayed earnestly for Samuel to be born (1 Sam. 1:5–11), devoted him to God's service (1 Sam. 1:24–28), and offered a beautiful prayer of thanksgiving for God's blessings (1 Sam. 2:1–10). See also *Samuel.*

HANUKKAH. See *Dedication, Feast of.*

HARA. A site in Assyria where some of the captives from the Northern Kingdom were settled after the fall of their nation (1 Chron. 5:26).

HARAN/CHARRAN. A city of Mesopotamia known as a center of pagan worship (2 Kings 19:12). Abraham lived in Haran for a time before he left at God's command to settle in Canaan (Gen. 12:4–5). *Charran:* Acts 7:2, 4.

HARDNESS OF HEART. A symbolic expression for rebellion or a stubborn and unyielding spirit, such as that exemplified by the pharaoh of Egypt in refusing to free the Hebrew slaves (Exod. 9:35).

HARE (RABBIT). A rabbitlike animal with long ears and legs (Deut. 14:7). Hares were considered unclean by the Israelites (Lev. 11:6). *Rabbit:* NIV.

HAREM. A group of women married to one man, especially a king. Esther was a member of the harem of King Ahasuerus of Persia (Esther 2:8–14).

HARLOT (PROSTITUTE). Harlotry was forbidden among God's people (Lev. 19:29). Engaging in prostitution was often compared to the spiritual adultery of God's people (Isa. 57:7–9; Rev. 17). *Prostitute:* NIV.

HARP (LYRE). A stringed musical instrument frequently used in worship (2 Chron. 29:25). David calmed King Saul by playing his harp (1 Sam. 16:16, 23). *Lyre:* NRSV. See also *Psaltery.*

HARPIST. See *Minstrel.*

HARROW. An agricultural tool or implement, probably used to level a plowed field for planting (Job 39:10).

HART (DEER). A male deer. The word is used to illustrate spiritual thirst (Ps. 42:1) and conversion (Isa. 35:6). *Deer:* NIV, NRSV. See also *Deer.*

HARVEST. The gathering of mature crops (Lev. 23:10). This word is used to illustrate the ripe spiritual harvest (Matt. 9:37–38). See also *Reap.*

HARVEST, FEAST OF. See *Pentecost.*

HARLOT. In the city of Jericho, a harlot named Rahab welcomes Israelite scouts sent by Joshua. Because she protected the men, Joshua spared her when the Israelites later destroyed the city.

HATE. Extreme dislike or animosity toward another. Jesus enjoined believers not to hate their enemies but to return love for malice (Luke 6:27). See also *Enmity; Malice.*

HATE [D, TH]
Lev. 19:17 shalt not *h* thy brother in thine heart
Ps. 119:163 I *h*...lying...thy [God's] law do I love
Prov. 8:13 fear of the LORD is to *h* evil
Prov. 14:20 poor is *h'd* even of his own neighbour
Eccles. 3:8 A time to love, and a time to *h*
Amos 5:21 I [God] *h*, I despise your feast days
Matt. 5:44 do good to them that *h* you
Matt. 6:24 will *h* the one, and love the other
Mark 13:13 *h'd* of all men for my [Jesus'] name's sake
Luke 14:26 and *h* not his father, and mother
John 12:25 he that *h'th* his life...shall keep it
John 15:23 He that *h'th* me [Jesus] *h'th* my Father also
1 John 4:20 man say, I love God, and *h'th* his brother, he is a liar

HAUGHTINESS. An arrogant spirit. God's Word indicates that haughty persons will be humbled (Prov. 16:18; Isa. 2:11, 17). See also *Conceit; Pride.*

HAWK. A bird of prey considered unclean by the Israelites (Deut. 14:15). See also *Cormorant.*

HAY (GRASS). A word for grass, which was cut and fed to livestock while fresh and green (Isa. 15:6). *Grass:* NIV, NRSV. See also *Grass.*

HAZAEL. A leader who was anointed king of Syria at God's command by the prophet Elijah (1 Kings 19:15). He murdered Ben-hadad in order to take the throne (2 Kings 8:7–15). Hazael conducted military campaigns against both Judah (2 Kings 12:17–18) and Israel (2 Kings 10:32). See also *Syria.*

HAZEL (ALMOND). A tree from which Jacob cut a rod or switch (Gen. 30:37). *Almond:* NIV, NRSV. See also *Almond.*

HAZOR. A royal Canaanite city destroyed by Joshua (Josh. 11:1–13). The rebuilt fortress city was later ravaged by Deborah and Barak during the period of the judges (Judg. 4:2–24). Hazor was ultimately destroyed by King Tiglath-pileser of Assyria (2 Kings 15:29).

HEAD [S]
Gen. 3:15 it shall bruise thy [the serpent's] *h*
1 Chron. 29:11 thou [God] art exalted as *h* above all
Ps. 23:5 thou [God] anointest my *h* with oil
Matt. 10:30 hairs of your *h* are all numbered
Matt. 21:42 stone...builders rejected...*h* of the corner
Luke 9:58 Son of man hath not where to lay his *h*
Acts 18:6 blood be upon your own *h's*
Rom. 12:20 coals of fire on his [your enemy's] *h*
1 Cor. 11:3 the *h* of the woman is the man
Col. 1:18 he [Jesus] is the *h* of the body, the church

HEAL. To restore a person to good health. Jesus' healing ministry showed His compassion and God's power over sickness and death (Mark 1:34). See also *Balm of Gilead; Medicine.*

HEAL [ING]
2 Chron. 7:14 I [God will] hear...*h* their land
Ps. 41:4 LORD, be merciful...*h* my soul
Eccles. 3:3 A time to kill, and a time to *h*
Jer. 3:22 I [God] will *h* your backslidings
Mal. 4:2 Sun of righteousness...*h'ing* in his wings
Matt. 4:23 Jesus went about...*h'ing*...sickness
Matt. 10:8 *H* the sick... raise the dead
Luke 4:18 he [God] hath sent me [Jesus] to *h* the brokenhearted
Luke 9:2 he [Jesus] sent them [disciples]...to *h* the sick

HEAR [ETH, ING]
Deut. 6:4 *H*, O Israel...LORD our God is one
Job 42:5 heard of thee [God] by the *h'ing* of the ear
Ps. 4:3 LORD will *h* when I call unto him
Prov. 13:1 wise son *h'eth* his father's instruction
Isa. 59:1 neither his [God's] ear heavy, that it cannot *h*
Jer. 22:29 earth...*h* the word of the LORD
Ezek. 37:4 dry bones, *h* the word of the LORD
Matt. 13:9 Who hath ears to *h*, let him *h*
Mark 7:37 he [Jesus] maketh...the deaf to *h*
John 10:27 My [Jesus'] sheep *h* my voice
Acts 2:8 how *h* we every man in our own tongue

Rom. 10:14 how shall they *h* without a preacher
James 1:19 every man be swift to *h*, slow to speak

HEARD

Gen. 3:8 they [Adam and Eve] *h*...the LORD
Exod. 3:7 I [God] have surely...*h* their [Israel's] cry
Ps. 34:4 I sought the LORD, and he *h* me
Ps. 116:1 I love the LORD...he hath *h* my voice
Jer. 31:15 voice was *h* in Ramah...bitter weeping
Matt. 6:7 heathen...think...be *h*...much speaking
Mark 12:37 common people *h* him [Jesus] gladly
Luke 2:20 shepherds...praising God for all...they had *h*
Acts 4:20 speak the things...seen and *h*
Acts 17:32 *h* of the resurrection...some mocked
Rom. 10:14 believe in him [Jesus] of whom they have not *h*
1 Cor. 2:9 Eye hath not seen, nor ear *h*
Phil. 4:9 things, which ye have...*h*, and seen...do
1 John 3:11 message that ye *h* from the beginning

HEART. To the Hebrews, the heart was the center of a person's existence, including emotions (Gen. 42:28), wisdom or skill (Exod. 35:35), and even physical life (Deut. 6:5). A person acts and speaks from the heart, so he or she should guard it carefully (Matt. 15:18–19).

HEART [S]

Deut. 6:5 love the LORD...with all thine *h*
Deut. 10:16 Circumcise...foreskin of your *h*
1 Sam. 12:24 serve him [God]...with all your *h*
Ps. 13:5 my *h* shall rejoice in thy [God's] salvation
Ps. 19:14 meditation of my *h*, be acceptable
Ps. 51:10 Create in me a clean *h*, O God
Ps. 119:11 Thy [God's] word have I hid in mine *h*
Prov. 3:5 Trust in the LORD with all thine *h*
Jer. 17:9 The *h* is deceitful above all things
Matt. 5:8 Blessed are the pure in *h*
Matt. 6:21 your treasure is...your *h* be also
Matt. 11:29 I [Jesus] am meek and lowly in *h*
Mark 12:30 love the Lord...with all thy *h*
John 14:1 Let not your *h* be troubled
2 Cor. 9:7 purposeth in his *h*, so let him give
2 Thess. 3:5 Lord direct your *h's* into the love of God
Heb. 4:12 word of God is...a discerner...of the *h*

HEATH. A dense shrub or bush that grew in the desert regions of Palestine (Jer. 17:6).

HEATHEN (NATIONS, GENTILES). A word for ethnic groups besides the Jews (Ezek. 22:15). It was also used for unbelievers, pagans, or Gentiles (Gal. 1:16). *Nations:* NIV, NRSV. *Gentiles:* NIV, NRSV. See also *Gentile.*

HEAVE OFFERING/PEACE OFFERING. An offering that consisted of the firstfruits of the harvest (Num. 15:17–21) and a tenth of all tithes (Num. 18:21–29). It was presented to God before being given to the priests. This was also known as a *peace offering* (Josh. 22:23).

HEAVEN. A word for (1) the atmosphere or the sky (Ps. 146:6), (2) the place where God dwells (1 Kings 8:45), and (3) the future home of all believers (Col. 1:5), who will dwell with God eternally (Isa. 65:17). See also *Heavenly City; Paradise.*

HEAVEN [S]

Gen. 1:1 God created the *h* and the earth
2 Chron. 7:14 will I [God] hear from *h*...forgive their sin
Ps. 19:1 The *h's* declare the glory of God
Ps. 139:8 ascend up into *h*, thou [God] art there
Eccles. 3:1 time to every purpose under the *h*
Matt. 5:3 poor in spirit...theirs is the kingdom of *h*
Matt. 6:20 lay up for yourselves treasures in *h*
Luke 24:51 he [Jesus] was parted...carried up into *h*
Acts 4:12 none other name under *h*...whereby we must be saved
1 Thess. 4:16 Lord...shall descend from *h* with a shout
2 Pet. 3:13 we...look for new *h's*...new earth
Rev. 21:1 I [John] saw a new *h*...new earth

HEAVENLY

Matt. 6:14 your *h* Father will also forgive you
John 3:12 believe, if I [Jesus] tell you of *h* things
Acts 26:19 I [Paul] was not disobedient...*h* vision

HEAVENLY CITY. The future city built by God as a dwelling place for those who belong to Him (Heb. 11:13–16). It will be known as "New Jerusalem," the place where God dwells eternally among the redeemed (Rev. 21:2–10). See also *Heaven; Paradise.*

HEBREWS, EPISTLE TO THE. An epistle of the N.T., author unknown, written to a group of believers of Jewish background to show that Jesus had replaced the O.T. ceremonial law and sacrificial system. Hebrews declares that Jesus is superior to angels (1:1–2:18) and Moses (3:1–16) and that He is our great High Priest who offered Himself—rather than a sacrificial animal—as an atoning sacrifice for our sins (chaps. 4–10).

The book closes with an appeal to believers to remember the great heroes of the faith (chap. 11) and to remain steadfast and true in their commitment to Christ (chaps. 12–13).

HEBRON/KIRJATH-ARBA. An ancient town in Canaan where Abraham lived and where Sarah died (Gen. 23:2–6). After the conquest of Canaan, it was designated as one of the six cities of refuge. *Kirjath-arba:* Josh. 14:15. See also *Cities of Refuge.*

HEED
Josh. 23:11 Take good *h*...love the LORD
Matt. 6:1 Take *h*...do not your alms before men
Mark 8:15 Take *h*, beware of the...Pharisees
1 Cor. 3:10 take *h* how he buildeth thereupon
1 Cor. 10:12 thinketh he standeth take *h* lest he fall
Heb. 3:12 Take *h*...lest there be in...you an evil heart

HEIFER. A young cow (Gen. 15:9). This word is sometimes used figuratively of contentment or complacency (Jer. 50:11).

HEIR [S]
Mark 12:7 This is the *h*; come, let us kill him
Gal. 3:29 Abraham's seed, and *h's* according to the promise
Gal. 4:7 if a son, then an *h* of God through Christ
Titus 3:7 justified by his [Jesus'] grace...be made *h's*
Heb. 1:2 whom he [God] hath appointed *h* [Jesus] of all things

HELI. Father of Joseph (husband of Mary) in the ancestry of Jesus (Luke 3:23).

HELL. The place of eternal torment reserved for unbelievers. *Sheol*, a Hebrew word rendered as "hell" in the O.T., corresponds to the Greek word *Hades*, which means "unseen underworld" or "place of the dead."

In the N.T. both *Hades* and *Gehenna* are rendered as "hell." *Gehenna* is derived from the Valley of Hinnom, a site for pagan worship that became a dumping ground near Jerusalem where filth and dead animals were burned; hence hell's association with the final state of lost souls in a place of eternal fire (Mark 9:47–48).

Hell is described as a "lake of fire" (Rev. 19:20), "everlasting destruction" (2 Thess. 1:9), and the "second death" (Rev. 20:14). See also *Damnation; Hinnom, Valley of; Lake of Fire.*

Job 26:6 *H* is naked before him, and destruction hath no covering
Ps. 18:5 sorrows of *h* compassed me about
Ps. 139:8 make my bed in *h*, behold, thou [God] art there
Prov. 27:20 *H* and destruction are never full
Jon. 2:2 out of the belly of *h* cried I [Jonah]
Matt. 5:22 say, Thou fool, shall be in danger of *h* fire
Matt. 10:28 fear him...able to destroy...soul and body in *h*
Matt. 16:18 gates of *h* shall not prevail against it [the church]
Luke 10:15 Capernaum...shalt be thrust down to *h*
Rev. 1:18 I [Jesus]...have the keys of *h* and of death

HELLENISTS. Greek-speaking Jews. See *Greeks.*

HELMET. An armored covering for the head to protect soldiers in combat. Paul spoke of the "helmet of salvation" that protects believers in spiritual warfare (Eph. 6:17).

HELPER. One who assists another. This word is used for the Holy Spirit's comfort and intercession on behalf of believers (Rom. 8:26). See also *Advocate; Comforter; Holy Spirit; Paraclete.*

HELL. The word hell *comes from the Valley of Hinnom, which was a dumping ground for ancient Jerusalem. In this painting of Jerusalem in the 1800s, the valley is to the left of the distant ridge where Jerusalem rests. The Kidron Valley and the Mount of Olives are to the right.*

HELP MEET (HELPER). A helper, companion, or mate. God created Eve as a help meet for Adam (Gen. 2:18). *Helper:* NIV, NRSV.

HEM. A decorative border or fringe on a piece of clothing, worn to remind the Jews of God's commandments (Exod. 28:33–34). See also *Fringe.*

HEMAN. A talented musician under David and a grandson of Saul (1 Chron. 6:33; 15:16–17). Heman was regarded as a person of spiritual insight (1 Chron. 25:5).

HEMETH. See *Hamath.*

HEMLOCK (WORMWOOD). A bitter and poisonous plant (Amos 6:12). *Wormwood:* NRSV.

HENNA. See *Camphire.*

HENOCH. See *Enoch*, No. 2.

HEPHZI-BAH. A symbolic name meaning "my delight is in her" that would be used for Jerusalem after her restoration to God's grace and favor (Isa. 62:4).

HERALD. A person sent by a high government official to deliver a formal and public message or to announce good news (Dan. 3:4)

HERB. A plant used to promote healing or to season food (Gen. 1:29). The Israelites used bitter herbs in their bread at the first Passover (Exod. 12:8). See also *Mallows.*

HERD. A group of cattle, sheep, or oxen (1 Sam. 11:5). In O.T. times, a person's wealth was measured by the size of his herd (2 Sam. 12:1–3).

HERDSMAN (SHEPHERD). A tender or keeper of livestock. The prophet Amos was a herdsman and farmer (Amos 7:14). *Shepherd:* NIV. See also *Shepherd.*

HERESY. False teachings that deny essential doctrines of the Christian faith—a serious problem condemned by Paul (1 Cor. 11:19). See also *Doctrine; Gnosticism; Judaizers.*

HERMES. See *Mercurius.*

HERMON, MOUNT/SIRION/ SHENIR/SENIR. The highest mountain in Syria, with an elevation of almost 10,000 feet (Josh. 12:1). It was also called *Sirion* and *Shenir* (Deut. 3:9) and *Senir* (Ezek. 27:5).

HERDSMAN. A herdsman and his son tend sheep in the springtime fields along the Jordan River.

HEROD. The name of several Roman rulers in Palestine during N.T. times:

1. Herod the Great (ruled 37 to 4 B.C.), in power when Jesus was born, who ordered the slaughter of innocent children (Matt. 2:3–16). Herod reconstructed the temple in Jerusalem and completed other ambitious building projects.

2. Herod Archelaus (ruled 4 B.C. to A.D. 6), the son and successor of Herod the Great as Roman ruler in Judea soon after the birth of Jesus (Matt. 2:22).

3. Herod Antipas (ruled 4 B.C. to A.D. 39), who granted his wife's request that John the Baptist be executed. This was the Herod who returned Jesus for sentencing by Pilate (Luke 23:6–12).

4. Herod Philip (ruled 4 B.C. to A.D. 33), ruler in extreme northern Galilee at the time when Jesus began His public ministry (Luke 3:1, 19–20).

5. Herod Agrippa I (ruled A.D. 37–44), who

persecuted the apostles and executed James, leader of the Jerusalem church (Acts 12:1–23).

6. Herod Agrippa II (ruled A.D. 50–100), before whom Paul made his defense at Caesarea (Acts 25:13–26:32).

HERODIANS. An influential Jewish group that favored Greek customs and Roman law in New Testament times. The Herodians joined forces with the Pharisees against Jesus (Mark 3:6).

HERODIAS. The wife or queen of Herod Antipas, the Roman provincial ruler of Palestine, who had John the Baptist executed. Herodias was angry with John because of his criticism of her immorality and illicit marriage (Matt. 14:1–11).

HERON. An unclean bird that lived in the lakes and marshes of Palestine (Deut. 14:18).

HETH. A son of Canaan and ancestor of the Hittites. Abraham dealt with the sons of Heth in securing a burial place for Sarah (Gen. 23:3–20).

HEWER (WOODCUTTER, STONE-CUTTER). A person who cut wood (Josh. 9:21; *woodcutter:* NIV) or stone (2 Kings 12:12; *stonecutter:* NIV, NRSV).

HEZEKIAH/EZEKIAS. The godly king of Judah (ruled about 716–686 B.C.) who implemented religious reforms by abolishing idol worship, restoring and reopening the temple in Jerusalem, and leading in celebration of major religious festivals, such as the Passover (2 Kings 18:4; 2 Chron. 29). Preparing for a siege against Jerusalem by the Assyrians, he cut a tunnel through solid rock to bring water from a spring outside the city wall into the city (2 Kings 20:20). *Ezekias:* Matt. 1:9.

HID
Gen. 3:8 Adam and his wife *h*...from...the LORD
Exod. 3:6 Moses *h* his face...afraid to look upon God
Ps. 38:9 groaning is not *h* from thee [God]
Ps. 119:11 Thy [God's] word have I *h* in mine heart
Matt. 5:14 A city...set on an hill cannot be *h*
Matt. 11:25 thou [God] hast *h* these things from the wise

HIDDEKEL. See *Tigris.*

HIDE [ING, ST]
Job 14:13 thou [God] wouldest *h* me in the grave
Ps. 13:1 how long wilt thou [God] *h* thy face from me
Ps. 17:8 *h* me under the shadow of thy [God's] wings
Ps. 119:114 Thou [God] art my *h'ing* place and my shield
Isa. 45:15 thou art a God that *h'st* thyself

HIEL. A native of Bethel who rebuilt the city of Jericho in King Ahab's time (1 Kings 16:34). This was a fulfillment of Joshua's curse against the city (Josh. 6:26).

HIERAPOLIS. A city of the district of Phrygia in Asia Minor. This city was mentioned by Paul, implying that Christianity had been planted here (Col. 4:13).

HIGGAION. A musical term translated "meditation" in Ps. 19:14, perhaps signifying a soft, quiet sound.

HEZEKIAH AND ISAIAH

King Hezekiah of Judah was fortunate to reign during the time of Isaiah's prophetic ministry. The prophet advised Hezekiah on several matters, assured him of God's mercy when he was sick (Isa. 38:1–8), and even confronted him about his foolish judgment when the king showed off his royal treasures to a Babylonian official (Isa. 39:1–8).

HIGHWAY. The Appian Way was an ancient Italian road that led to Rome. Paul walked on this road when he was taken to Rome for trial.

HIGH PLACE. An elevated place where worship of false gods was conducted (2 Kings 12:3). These shrines of idolatry provoked God's wrath (Ps. 78:58). See also *Altar.*

HIGH PRIEST. The chief priest or head of the priesthood—an office filled by succession of the oldest son of each generation through the lineage of Aaron, Israel's first high priest (Exod. 28). Jesus is called our "great high priest" (Heb. 4:15) because He laid down His life as a "living sacrifice" on our behalf (Heb. 9:26). See also *Priest.*

HIGHWAY. The "highways" of the Bible were little more than paths or crude trails, and they generally connected large cities or major trading centers (Isa. 19:23). See also *Road.*

HILKIAH. A high priest during the reign of King Josiah of Judah who found the lost Book of the Law and used it to bring about religious reforms (2 Kings 22:8–23:4).

HILL. An elevated site. Pagan altars were often built on hills (1 Kings 14:23). See also *High Place.*

HILL COUNTRY (MOUNTAIN REGION). A region of low, rugged mountains in southern Lebanon and northern Judea (Josh. 13:6). *Mountain region:* NIV.

HIN. A unit of measure equal to about one and one-half gallons (Exod. 29:40).

HIND (DEER). A female deer. The word is used symbolically to show spiritual resilience (Hab. 3:19; Ps. 18:33). *Deer:* NIV, NRSV. See also *Deer.*

HINNOM, VALLEY OF. A deep, narrow ravine southwest of Jerusalem where pagan worship involving child sacrifice was conducted (2 Chron. 28:3; Jer. 19:2–4). Some scholars believe this site in N.T. times became a garbage dump for the city of Jerusalem known as *Gehenna*—a word translated "hell" (Matt. 5:22; Mark 9:43). See also *Hell*.

HIRAM/HURAM. The king of Tyre—or perhaps a son and his successor—who assisted David and Solomon with their building projects in Jerusalem by providing materials and skilled workmen (2 Sam. 5:11; 1 Kings 5:1–11). *Huram:* 2 Chron. 2:3–12. See also *Tyre*.

HIRELING (HIRED HAND, LABORER). A common laborer hired for a short time to do farm chores (Job 7:1–2). Unlike a hireling, Jesus as the Good Shepherd takes a personal interest in His sheep (John 10:12–13). *Hired hand:* NIV, NRSV. *Laborer:* NRSV. See also *Laborer*.

HISS. A sound made by forcing air between the tongue and the teeth to show scorn and contempt (Job 27:23; Isa. 5:25–26).

HITTITES. An ancient people who lived in Canaan apparently before Abraham's time, since he bought a burial cave from Ephron, who was probably a Hittite (Gen. 23:7–20). Hittites also served in David's army (2 Sam. 11:6, 15).

HIVITES. Descendants of Canaan (see Gen. 10:6) who lived in the Promised Land before and after the Hebrew people occupied their territory (Deut. 7:1). Some scholars believe these are the same people as the Horites. See also *Horites*.

HOBAB. See *Jethro*.

HOE. See *Mattock*.

HOLD [ING]
Exod. 20:7 Lord will not *h* him guiltless...taketh his name in vain
Ps. 83:1 Keep not thou silence, O God: *h* not thy peace
Jer. 2:13 have...hewed them out...cisterns, that can *h* no water
Phil. 2:16 *H'ing* forth the word of life...I [Paul] may rejoice
1 Tim. 3:9 *H'ing* the mystery of the faith
Heb. 10:23 *h* fast the profession of our faith

HOLINESS. Moral purity; to be set apart and sanctified for service to God. God is holy (Exod. 15:11), and He expects holiness of His people (Rom. 12:1). Since Jesus was the perfect example of holiness, He was called the "Holy One of God" (Mark 1:24). See also *Righteousness*.

HOLY [INESS]
Exod. 3:5 place...thou [Moses] standest is *h* ground
Exod. 20:8 Remember the sabbath day, to keep it *h*
Lev. 11:44 ye shall be *h*; for I [God] am *h*
Lev. 20:7 be ye *h*: for I am the Lord your God
Ps. 11:4 Lord is in his *h* temple
Ps. 24:3 who shall stand in his [God's] *h* place
Ps. 29:2 worship the Lord...beauty of *h'iness*
Ps. 51:11 take not thy [God's] *h* spirit from me
Ps. 103:1 all...within me, bless his [God's] *h* name
Hab. 2:20 Lord is in his *h* temple...earth keep silence
Rom. 16:16 Salute one another with an *h* kiss
1 Cor. 3:17 temple of God is *h*, which temple ye are
Eph. 5:27 it [the church] should be *h*
1 Thess. 4:7 God hath...called us unto...*h'iness*
1 Tim. 2:8 men pray every where, lifting up *h* hands
1 Pet. 2:5 Ye also...are built up...an *h* priesthood
1 Pet. 2:9 ye are a chosen generation...an *h* nation
Rev. 21:2 I John saw the *h* city, new Jerusalem

HOLY GHOST. An Old English phrase for "Holy Spirit" (Acts 5:3). See *Holy Spirit*.

Matt. 1:18 she [Mary] was found with child of the *H-G*
Matt. 3:11 he [Jesus] shall baptize you with the *H-G*
Matt. 12:31 blasphemy against the *H-G*...not be forgiven
Matt. 28:19 baptizing them in the name of the...*H-G*
Luke 1:35 The *H-G* shall come upon thee [Mary]
Luke 1:67 Zacharias was filled with the *H-G*
Luke 2:25 the *H-G* was upon him [Simeon]

Luke 3:22 *H-G* descended...upon him [Jesus]
John 14:26 the *H-G*...shall teach you all things
Acts 1:8 receive power...*H-G* is come upon you
Acts 6:3 look ye out...seven men...full of the *H-G*
Acts 13:2 *H-G* said, Separate me Barnabas and Saul
Rom. 14:17 kingdom of God is...joy in the *H-G*
1 Cor. 12:3 no man can say that Jesus is the Lord, but by the *H-G*
2 Pet. 1:21 holy men of God spake...by the *H-G*

THE HOLY SPIRIT IN ROMANS 8

Romans 8 is one of the greatest chapters in the Bible on the nature and work of the Holy Spirit. A believer can count on God's indwelling presence to guide him or her through every experience of life. God's Spirit frees us from the law of sin and death (Rom. 8:2), gives us life (Rom. 8:10), makes us children of God (Rom. 8:14–15), and intercedes on our behalf with God the Father (Rom. 8:27).

HOLY OF HOLIES (HOLY PLACE). The sacred innermost sanctuary of the temple and tabernacle, containing the ark of the covenant and the mercy seat, which only the high priest could enter. Even he could go in only one day a year on the Day of Atonement, when he made a special sacrifice for the sins of the people (Heb. 9:2–3, 7). *Holy Place:* NRSV. See also *Ark of the Covenant; Atonement, Day of; Mercy Seat.*

HOLY PLACE. A KJV phrase for the section of the tabernacle just outside the Holy of Holies (Exod. 28:29). See also *Holy of Holies.*

HOLY SPIRIT. The third person of the Trinity. The O.T. contains glimpses and promises of the Holy Spirit (Gen. 1:2, 6:3; Zech. 4:6), and the Spirit rested on Jesus from His birth (Luke 1:35), but the full manifestation of the Spirit's power occurred at Pentecost after Jesus' resurrection and ascension to the Father (Acts 2:1–21).

Jesus promised He would send the Holy Spirit as a comforter and advocate in His absence (John 14:16; 1 John 2:1). The Spirit would glorify the Son (John 15:16), empower believers (John 14:12–27), and convict unbelievers of sin and coming judgment (John 16:8–11).

Another function of the Holy Spirit is to inspire the Scriptures, thus providing guidance and direction to believers. See also *Advocate; Comforter; Helper; Paraclete.*

HOMER. The standard unit of dry measure, equal to about six bushels (Ezek. 45:11).

HOMOSEXUALITY. The practice of sexual activity among persons of the same sex—a sin strictly forbidden by the O.T. Law (Lev. 18:22). Paul also condemned this practice (Rom. 1:26–27; 1 Cor. 6:9).

HONEST [LY]

Acts 6:3 seven men of *h* report
Rom. 13:13 Let us walk *h'ly*...not in rioting
Phil. 4:8 things are *h*, whatsoever things are just

HONESTY. Speaking the truth and acting fairly and without deceit in human relationships. This is a virtue that all believers should practice (2 Cor. 13:7).

HONEY. A sweet liquid substance produced naturally by bees and artificially from fruit. It was used to sweeten food (Exod. 16:31). The word is also used symbolically for abundance (Exod. 3:8, 17).

HONEYCOMB. The wax cells built by bees to hold their eggs and honey (1 Sam. 14:27).

HONOR. Respect and esteem toward God and other people. The Ten Commandments enjoins honor toward one's parents (Exod. 20:12). God and His Son, Jesus Christ, are worthy of our highest honor (John 5:23).

HONOUR [ETH]

1 Chron. 16:27 Glory and *h* are in his [God's] presence
Ps. 8:5 thou [God]...hast crowned him [man] with glory and *h*
Prov. 3:9 *H* the LORD with thy substance
Matt. 13:57 prophet...not without *h*...own country
Mark 7:6 *h'eth* me [Jesus] with their lips...heart...far from me
John 12:26 any...serve me [Jesus]...will my Father *h*
Rom. 12:10 in *h* preferring one another
Rev. 4:11 worthy, O Lord, to receive glory and *h*

HOOK. Wire twisted together forms a fishing hook, which was used during Roman times.

HOOK. A metal grasping tool. Different types of hooks mentioned in the Bible include flesh-hooks (Exod. 27:3), fish hooks (Matt. 17:27), pruning hooks (Isa. 18:5), and the hooks that supported the tabernacle curtains (Exod. 26:32).

HOOPOE. See *Lapwing.*

HOPE. A sure and steady faith in God's promises. The believer has hope in God's promise of salvation (1 Thess. 5:8), resurrection (Acts 26:6–7), and eternal life (1 Cor. 15:19–26). See also *Promise.*

HOPE [D]

Job 7:6 My [Job's] days...spent without *h*
Ps. 38:15 in thee, O LORD, do I *h*
Ps. 71:5 thou art my *h*, O Lord
Ps. 146:5 Happy is he...whose *h* is in the LORD
Lam. 3:24 LORD is my portion...I *h* in him
Rom. 12:12 Rejoicing in *h*; patient in tribulation
Rom. 15:13 God of *h* fill you with all joy
1 Cor. 13:13 now abideth faith, *h*, charity
Col. 1:27 Christ in you, the *h* of glory
1 Thess. 4:13 sorrow not...as others which have no *h*
Heb. 11:1 faith is the substance of things *h'd* for

HOPHNI. A sinful and immoral son of Eli the high priest who was not considered worthy of conducting priestly duties (1 Sam. 1:3; 2:22–25). Along with his evil brother Phinehas, he was killed by the Philistines (1 Sam. 4:1–11). See also *Phinehas,* No. 2.

HOPHRA. See *Pharaoh,* No. 5.

HOR, MOUNT. A mountain in the territory of the Edomites where Moses' brother Aaron died and was buried (Num. 20:22–29). A different mountain with the same name was located in northern Palestine (see Num. 34:7–8).

HOREB, MOUNT. See *Sinai.*

HORITES/HORIMS. Inhabitants of Mount Hermon who were driven out by Esau's descendants (Gen. 36:20). These may have been the same people as the Hivites of Joshua's time. *Horims:* Deut. 2:22. See also *Hivites.*

HORN. A bonelike protrusion from an animal's head. The word is also used as a symbol of strength (Hab. 3:4; Rev. 13:1). See also *Cornet.*

HORNET. A wasplike insect with a painful sting, portrayed as a symbol of God's judgment against the enemies of His people (Exod. 23:28).

HORNS OF THE ALTAR. Projections at the four corners of an altar (Exod. 27:1–2). The blood of a sacrificial animal was sprinkled on these four projections (Exod. 29:12). See also *Altar.*

HORSE. An animal used for transportation (Gen. 47:17) as well as in warfare. God warned his people not to "multiply" horses for use in war (Deut. 17:16). But King Solomon's army included numerous horses and chariots (1 Kings 9:17–19).

HORSE GATE. A gate in the old wall of Jerusalem, mentioned by Nehemiah as having been destroyed and then rebuilt under his supervision (Neh. 3:28).

HORSELEACH (LEECH). A parasite that attaches to humans and animals and sucks blood; probably a leech (Prov. 30:15). *Leech:* NIV, NRSV.

HOSANNA. A triumphal shout by the crowds as Jesus entered Jerusalem a few days before His crucifixion (Matt. 21:9, 15). The expression means "save us now."

HOSEA/OSEE. A prophet who delivered God's message of judgment to the Northern Kingdom in the years shortly before this nation fell to the Assyrians in 722 B.C. Author of the book of Hosea, he is best known for his marriage to a prostitute in obedience of God's command (Hosea 1:2–9). *Osee:* Rom. 9:25.

HOSEA, BOOK OF. A prophetic book of the O.T. that compares the spiritual adultery or idolatry of God's people with the physical adultery of the prophet's wife, Gomer (1:2–5; 2:2–5). Just as Hosea redeemed her from slavery and restored her as his mate, God promised that He would eventually restore His people as His own after a period of punishment at the hand of their enemies (chaps. 4–14).

This book is one of the greatest treatises in the Bible on the nature of God, emphasizing His demand for righteousness and impending punishment as well as His steadfast love. See also *Gomer.*

SOWING AND REAPING IN HOSEA

The prophet Hosea's metaphor of sowing the wind and reaping the whirlwind (Hosea 8:7) would have been well understood in the agricultural society of his day. A farmer expects a few planted seeds to grow into an abundant crop. Likewise, sin will yield a crop of wickedness.

The apostle Paul may have had this passage from Hosea in mind when he warned the Galatian believers, "Whatsoever a man soweth, that shall he also reap" (Gal. 6:7).

HOSEN (TROUSERS). An Old English word for trousers, possibly referring to the tunic or inner garment worn during Bible times (Dan. 3:21). *Trousers:* NIV, NRSV.

HOSHEA

1. The original name of Joshua (Deut. 32:44). See *Joshua*.

2. The last king of Israel, or the Northern Kingdom (reigned about 730–722 B.C.), who paid tribute to King Shalmaneser of Assyria. After Hoshea rebelled, Israel was defeated, and Hoshea was taken to Assyria as a captive (2 Kings 17:1–6).

HOSPITALITY. The gracious provision of food and lodging to strangers. Kindness toward travelers and strangers was encouraged in both O.T. and N.T. times (Lev. 19:33–34; 1 Tim. 3:2; 1 Pet. 4:9).

HOST. A hospitable person who entertained guests (Heb. 13:2), or a multitude or crowd of people (Gen. 2:1).

HOST OF HEAVEN. Heavenly beings created by God and associated with His rule of the universe. These beings ("a multitude of the heavenly host") praised God at the angels' announcement of the birth of Jesus (Luke 2:13).

HOUSEHOLD. *A Bedouin household poses for a portrait at the turn of the 1900s. They lived in tents and traveled with their herd from one grazing pasture to another.*

HOSTS, LORD OF (LORD ALMIGHTY). A title of God that emphasizes His sovereignty (Isa. 1:9; 10:23). *Lord Almighty:* NIV.

HOUR [S]
Matt. 24:42 know not what *h* your Lord doth come
Matt. 26:40 ye [Peter] not watch with me [Jesus] one *h*
Mark 13:32 that day and that *h* knoweth no man
Luke 12:40 Son of man cometh at an *h* when ye think not
John 11:9 Are there not twelve *h's* in the day
John 12:23 *h* is come...Son of man...glorified

HOUSE (TENT). A building or residence for a family (1 Sam. 9:18). The word is also used of a clan or all the descendants of a family (1 Sam. 20:16) as well as the believer's final dwelling place in heaven (2 Cor. 5:1). *Tent:* NIV, NRSV. See also *Tent.*

HOUSEHOLD. Members of a family who lived together in the same dwelling or a compound of dwellings, perhaps including several generations (2 Sam. 6:11). Believers are members of God's household (Gal. 6:10; Eph. 2:19).

HOUSEHOLD IDOLS. Images of pagan gods kept in the house in the belief that they protected the family (Gen. 31:19–35). See also *Teraphim.*

HOUSEHOLDER (OWNER). The head of a household or owner of a house (Matt. 13:27). *Owner:* NIV.

HULDAH. The wife of Shallum and a prophetess who foretold the collapse of Jerusalem (2 Kings 22:14–20).

HUMAN SACRIFICE. The practice of sacrificing children to a pagan god (2 Kings 3:26–27). This was common among the pagan religions of Bible times, but the custom was specifically prohibited by God (Lev. 20:2–5; Deut. 18:10). See also *Hinnom, Valley of; Jephthah.*

HUMBLE [D, TH]
Ps. 10:12 God...forget not the *h*
Isa. 5:15 mighty man shall be *h'd*
Matt. 18:4 shall *h* himself..little child...is greatest
Luke 18:14 he that *h'th* himself shall be exalted
Phil. 2:8 he [Jesus] *h'd* himself...obedient unto death
James 4:10 *H* yourselves...he [God] shall lift you up

HUMILITY. The opposite of arrogance and pride; an attitude that grows out of the recognition that all we are and everything we own are gifts from God (Rom. 12:3; 1 Pet. 5:5). See also *Meekness.*

HUNTER. A person who stalks and kills wild animals. Nimrod, a descendant of Noah, was a "mighty hunter" (Gen. 10:9). See also *Fowler.*

HUR. A man who helped Aaron hold up the arms of Moses to give the Israelites victory over the Amalekites (Exod. 24:14).

HURAM. See *Hiram.*

HUSBAND. The male partner in a marriage relationship. Husbands had total authority over their wives in Bible times, but Paul called on male believers to love their wives (Eph. 5:25).

HUSBAND [S]
Gen. 3:16 thy [Eve's] desire shall be to thy *h*
Prov. 12:4 virtuous woman is a crown to her *h*
Matt. 1:19 Joseph her [Mary's] *h*, being a just man
Mark 10:12 put away her *h*...committeth adultery
1 Cor. 7:3 *h* render unto the wife due benevolence
1 Cor. 7:14 unbelieving *h* is sanctified by the wife
Col. 3:19 *H's*, love your wives
1 Tim. 3:2 bishop...must be blameless...*h* of one wife
1 Tim. 3:12 deacons be the *h's* of one wife
1 Pet. 3:1 wives, be in subjection to your own *h's*
Rev. 21:2 new Jerusalem...as a bride adorned for her *h*

HUSBANDMAN (FARMER). A farmer or tiller of the soil (Gen. 9:20). In N.T. times, a husbandman, like a tenant farmer, often took a share of the crops as payment for his labor (2 Tim. 2:6). *Farmer:* NIV, NRSV.

HUSHAI. A friend and adviser of King David (2 Sam. 15:32–37). Hushai remained loyal to David during Absalom's revolt (2 Sam. 17:1–16).

HUSKS (PODS). The fruit of the carob tree, a type of locust. The prodigal son in Jesus' parable was reduced to eating this coarse and unappetizing food in order to survive (Luke 15:16). *Pods:* NIV, NRSV.

HYMENAEUS. An early Christian who denied the faith and was excommunicated by Paul (1 Tim. 1:19–20; 2 Tim. 2:16–17).

HYMN. A song of praise and thanksgiving to God (Eph. 5:19). Jesus and His disciples sang a hymn after they finished the Last Supper (Matt. 26:30).

HYPOCRITE. A person who pretends to be something he or she is not. Jesus called the Pharisees hypocrites because they did good deeds to gain the praise of others and pretended to be godly and righteous but were actually insensitive to God's truth (Matt. 23:13–29; Mark 12:15).

HYPOCRITE [S]

Job 20:5 joy of the *h* but for a moment
Matt. 6:2 do not sound a trumpet...as the *h's* do
Matt. 6:16 be not, as the *h's*, of a sad countenance
Matt. 7:5 *h*, first cast out the beam...thine own eye

HYSSOP. A plant used in purification ceremonies (Exod. 12:22). It was also symbolic of spiritual cleansing (Ps. 51:7). Hyssop was used to relieve Jesus' thirst on the cross (John 19:29).

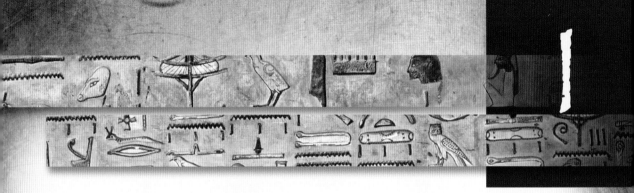

I AM. The name by which God revealed Himself to Moses at the burning bush. It shows His eternity, self-existence, and unsearchableness (Exod. 3:14). In John's Gospel Jesus also used the phrase "I am" several times to reveal His identity as the divine Savior. See also *God; Jehovah; Yahweh.*

"I Am" Statements of Jesus in John's Gospel

1. Bread of life (John 6:35)
2. Light of the world (John 8:12)
3. Door of the sheep (John 10:7)
4. Good shepherd (John 10:11, 14)
5. Resurrection and the life (John 11:25)
6. Way, the truth, and the life (John 14:6)
7. True vine (John 15:1)

IBEX. See *Pygarg.*

IBZAN. A judge of Israel for seven years. A native of Bethlehem, he had thirty sons and thirty daughters (Judg. 12:8–10). See also *Judges of Israel.*

I-CHABOD. The son of Phinehas and grandson of Eli. He was given this symbolic name, meaning "inglorious," by his dying mother when she learned the ark of the covenant had been captured by the Philistines and that Eli and Phinehas were dead (1 Sam. 4:19–22).

ICONIUM. An ancient city in Asia Minor near Lystra and Lycaonia. Paul and Barnabas introduced Christianity here on the first missionary journey (Acts 13:51; 14:1, 21–22). Paul apparently also visited Iconium on the second journey (Acts 16:1–5).

IDLE. Inactive or lazy. This behavior is condemned in the Proverbs (Prov. 24:30–34) and by Paul (2 Thess. 3:10). See also *Sluggard.*

IDLE [NESS]
Prov. 19:15 an *i* soul shall suffer hunger
Prov. 31:27 She...eateth not the bread of *i'ness*
Matt. 12:36 every *i* word that men shall speak...give account
Luke 24:11 words seemed to them [the disciples] as *i* tales

IDOL, IDOLATRY. The worship of false gods or something created rather than the Creator (Rom. 1:25). Idolatry was prohibited by the first two of the Ten Commandments (Exod. 20:3–4). Abraham migrated to Canaan to escape idol worship (Josh. 24:2–3). Prominent idols mentioned in the Bible are the golden calves of Aaron (Exod. 32:4) and King Jeroboam (2 Chron. 11:15) and the grain god of the Philistines known as Dagon (Judg. 16:23).

The prophet Elijah helped overthrow Baal worship in Israel (1 Kings 18:17–40), and the prophet Isaiah described the folly of idolatry (Isa. 44:9–20). In the N.T., idolatry is anything that comes between the believer and God (Col. 3:5). See also *Graven Image.*

IDOL [S]
Lev. 19:4 Turn ye not unto *i's*
1 Chron. 16:26 gods of the people are *i's*
Ps. 135:15 The *i's* of the heathen are silver and gold
Ezek. 14:6 Repent, and turn...from your *i's*
1 Cor. 8:4 an *i* is nothing in the world
2 Cor. 6:16 what agreement hath...temple of God with *i's*
1 John 5:21 Little children, keep yourselves from *i's*

IDUMEA. See *Edom*, No. 2.

IGNORANCE. Lack of knowledge or understanding. While sins of ignorance are less grievous than premeditated sins (Lev. 4; Num. 15:30–31), they are still destructive (Hosea 4:6) and require repentance (Acts 17:30–31). At Pentecost, Peter declared Christ was crucified out of ignorance—a sin that required repentance (Acts 3:17, 19).

IGNORANT [LY]
Acts 4:13 they [the Sanhedrin]...perceived that they [Peter and John] were...*i* men
Acts 17:23 Whom...ye *i'ly* worship, him [Jesus] declare I [Paul] unto you
1 Cor. 12:1 concerning spiritual gifts...I [Paul] would not have you *i*
1 Thess. 4:13 not have you to be *i*...concerning them which are asleep
2 Pet. 3:8 be not *i* of this...one day is with the Lord as a thousand years

ILLYRICUM. A district on the eastern coast of the Adriatic Sea. Paul mentioned Illyricum as the farthermost point to which he had traveled (Rom. 15:19).

IMAGE. An exact likeness or representation of some object of idolatrous worship. God warned Israel to destroy such pagan images (Exod. 34:13, 17).

Exod. 20:4 not make unto thee any graven *i*
Mark 12:16 he [Jesus] saith...Whose is this *i*
Rom. 1:23 glory of...God into an *i*...corruptible man
Rom. 8:29 be conformed to the *i* of his [God's] Son
1 Cor. 15:49 we shall also bear the *i* of the heavenly
Col. 1:15 Who [Jesus] is the *i* of the invisible God

IMAGE OF GOD. Human beings were created to perfectly reflect God's image (Gen. 9:6), marred that image by sinning, but have the potential to be molded back into that image (Rom. 8:28–30). Jesus is the image of the "invisible God" (Col. 1:15), and humans express God's image when they are in right relation with their Creator and faithfully tend God's creation (Gen. 1:26–28). Human's unique attributes of reason, will, and personality are further evidences of divine image.

IMAGINATION [S]
Gen. 6:5 every *i* of the thoughts of his [man's] heart was only evil
Jer. 16:12 ye walk every one after the *i* of his evil heart
Luke 1:51 he [God]...scattered the proud in the *i* of their hearts
Rom. 1:21 they glorified him not as God...but became vain in their *i's*

IMMANUEL. See *Emmanuel*.

IMMORALITY. Behavior that violates established moral principles or laws. This word is used to condemn illicit sexual activity outside of marriage (Prov. 2:16; Rom. 1:26–27) and to describe Israel's worship of pagan gods (Ezek. 23:8, 17). See also *Adultery; Fornication*.

IMMORTALITY. See *Eternal Life*.

IMMUTABILITY. An attribute of God's nature that refers to His unchangeableness (Mal. 3:6). The unchangeable nature of Christ assures us that God's mercy is constant (Heb. 13:8). God, who cannot lie, offers an anchor of hope for all believers, who are the "heirs of promise" (Heb. 6:17–19). See also *God*.

IMPARTIALITY. Justness and fairness. God is impartial in His loving concern for all persons (2 Pet. 3:9) and in His command for repentance (Rom. 3:6). Peter learned that all persons who are cleansed by the Lord are brothers (Acts 10:15, 34–35).

IMPOSSIBLE
Matt. 17:20 nothing shall be *i* unto you
Mark 10:27 With men it is *i*, but not with God
Heb. 11:6 without faith it is *i* to please him [God]

IMPUTATION. To transfer something to another person. Adam's sin was imputed to all persons (Rom. 5:12). Our iniquity was laid on Jesus (Isa. 53:5–6), and He bore our sins (John 1:29). Jesus, the "second Adam," imputed grace and righteousness to all who put their trust in Him (Rom. 5:17–19).

IN CHRIST
Rom. 8:1 no condemnation to them...*i-C*
Rom. 12:5 we...are one body *i-C*
1 Cor. 4:10 fools for Christ's sake...ye are wise *i-C*
1 Cor. 15:19 in this life only we have hope *i-C*
1 Cor. 15:22 in Adam all die...*i-C*...all be made alive
2 Cor. 5:17 any man be *i-C*...a new creature
2 Cor. 5:19 God was *i-C*, reconciling the world
Eph. 1:10 he [God] might gather...all things *i-C*
Phil. 2:5 this mind be in you, which was also *i-C*
Phil. 3:14 prize of the high calling of God *i-C*
1 Thess. 4:16 the dead *i-C* shall rise first

INCARNATION OF CHRIST. The birth and existence of Christ in human form. This was foretold by the O.T. prophets (Isa. 7:14). When Jesus was born into the world, He was described as "the Word...made flesh" (John 1:14). Belief in the incarnation of Christ is a mark of the Christian (1 John 4:2–3). See also *Advent of Christ; Virgin Birth.*

INCENSE. Sweet perfume extracted from spices or gums and used in worship ceremonies. Incense was burned on the altar of incense in the tabernacle by the priests (Exod. 30:7–8). See also *Censer; Frankincense.*

INCEST. Sex relations with members of one's own family. Prohibited by the Levitical law (Lev. 18:6–12), incest was considered such a serious offense that it was punishable by death (Lev. 20:11–17). Lot committed incest with his two daughters (Gen. 19:30–38), and Reuben with his father's concubine (Gen. 35:22).

INCLINE [D]
Ps. 17:6 *i* thine [God's] ear unto me
Ps. 40:1 I waited patiently...and he [God] *i'd* unto me
Prov. 4:20 My son...*i* thine ear unto my sayings

INCREASE [D, TH]
Exod. 1:7 children of Israel...*i'd* abundantly
Lev. 26:4 land shall yield her *i*
Ps. 67:6 Then shall the earth yield her *i*
Prov. 1:5 wise man will hear...*i* learning
Prov. 24:5 man of knowledge *i'th* strength
Eccles. 1:18 he that *i'th* knowledge *i'th* sorrow
Luke 2:52 Jesus *i'd* in wisdom and stature
Luke 17:5 apostles said unto the Lord, *I* our faith
John 3:30 He [Jesus] must *i*, but I [John the Baptist] must decrease
Acts 6:7 word of God *i'd*...disciples multiplied
1 Cor. 3:7 neither is he that planteth any thing...but God that giveth the *i*
1 Thess. 3:12 Lord make you to *i* and abound in love

INDIA. A region near the Indus River that served as the eastern limit of the Persian Empire (Esther 1:1; 8:9). Scholars believe this "India" covered essentially the same region as the modern nations of India and Pakistan.

INDIFFERENCE. Lack of interest and concern—behavior characteristic of unbelievers and backsliders (Rev. 3:15–16). Indifference breeds moral callousness (Matt. 27:3–4; Acts 18:12–16).

INFIDEL (UNBELIEVER). An unbeliever (1 Tim. 5:8). Infidelity is caused by an unregenerate heart (Rom. 2:5) and hatred of the light (John 3:20). An infidel will be punished by eternal separation from God (2 Thess. 1:8–9). *Unbeliever:* NIV, NRSV. See also *Atheism; Unbelief.*

INFIRMITY [IES]

Prov. 18:14 spirit of a man will sustain his *i*
Matt. 8:17 Himself [Jesus] took our *i'ies*
Rom. 8:26 Spirit also helpeth our *i'ies*
Rom. 15:1 strong...bear the *i'ies* of the weak
2 Cor. 12:9 gladly...will I [Paul]...glory in my *i'ies*

INGATHERING, FEAST OF. See *Tabernacles, Feast of.*

INHERIT [ED]

Ps. 37:9 those that wait upon the Lord...*i* the earth
Ps. 37:29 righteous shall *i* the land
Matt. 5:5 Blessed...meek...*i* the earth
Matt. 25:34 Come...*i* the kingdom prepared for you
Luke 18:18 what shall I [rich young ruler] do to *i* eternal life
1 Cor. 6:10 nor extortioners, shall *i* the kingdom of God
Rev. 21:7 He that overcometh shall *i* all things

INHERITANCE. A gift of property or rights passed from one generation to another. In ancient Israel, a father's possessions were passed on to his living sons, with the oldest receiving a double portion (Deut. 21:17). Reuben lost his inheritance because he committed incest with Bilhah (Gen. 35:22; 49:4). Esau traded his birthright as the oldest son to his brother, Jacob, for a bowl of stew (Gen. 25:29–34).

Christians enjoy a spiritual birthright (Eph. 1:13–14). All the redeemed, including Gentiles, become God's adopted children with full inheritance rights (Gal. 4:5–7). See also *Adoption; Birthright; Firstborn.*

Num. 18:23 among...Israel they [Levites] have no *i*
Deut. 32:9 Jacob is the lot of his [God's] *i*
Josh. 11:23 Joshua gave it [Canaan] for an *i* unto Israel
Ps. 2:8 I [God] shall give thee the heathen for thine *i*
Ps. 94:14 neither will he [God] forsake his *i*
Mark 12:7 kill him [the heir], and the *i* shall be ours
Eph. 1:11 In whom [Jesus] also we have obtained an *i*
Eph. 5:5 no...idolater, hath...*i* in the kingdom of Christ

INIQUITY (WICKEDNESS). Sin, wickedness, or evil. Jesus taught that evil or iniquity originates in the heart, or from within (Matt. 23:28). Christ redeems believers from their iniquity, purifies them, and sets them apart for His service (Titus 2:14). *Wickedness:* NIV. See also *Wickedness.*

INIQUITY [IES]

Num. 14:18 Lord is longsuffering...forgiving *i*
Ps. 25:11 Lord, pardon mine *i*; for it is great
Ps. 103:10 He [God] hath not...rewarded us according to our *i'ies*
Isa. 53:6 Lord...laid on him [God's servant]...*i* of us all
Jer. 31:30 every one shall die for his own *i*
Matt. 23:28 ye [Pharisees] are full of...*i*
Rom. 4:7 Blessed are they whose *i'ies* are forgiven
James 3:6 tongue is a fire, a world of *i*

INK. Writing fluid. The earliest ink was probably a mixture of water, charcoal or soot, and gum. The scribe Baruch used ink to write Jeremiah's prophecies (Jer. 36:18). See also *Paper; Writing.*

INKHORN. A carrying case for pens and ink, probably made from the horn of an animal and carried on a belt (Ezek. 9).

INN. A shelter that provided lodging for travelers. Inns were often crude stopping places with no indoor accommodations. Jesus was born in a stable of an inn, which provided shelter for people and their animals (Luke 2:7).

INSANE. See *Mad.*

INSCRIPTION. See *Superscription.*

INSPECTION GATE. See *Miphkad.*

INSPIRATION. Divine influence. God's inspiration is the source of human understanding (Job 32:8). Scripture is inspired by God for our correction and instruction (2 Tim. 3:16). The Holy Spirit moved holy men to prophesy and record God's message (2 Pet. 1:20–21). God has communicated with humans in various ways, including by spoken words (Rev. 1:10–11), dreams (Dan. 7:1), and visions (Ezek. 11:24–25).

INSTRUCT [ED]

Job 40:2 Shall he that contendeth with the Almighty *i* him?

Ps. 32:8 I [God] will *i* thee and teach thee

Prov. 21:11 the wise is *i'ed*, he receiveth knowledge

INTEGRITY

Job 2:9 Dost thou [Job] still retain thine *i*?

Ps. 25:21 Let *i* and uprightness preserve me

Prov. 19:1 Better...poor that walketh in his *i*, than...perverse

Prov. 20:7 just man walketh in his *i*

INTELLIGENT. See *Prudent*.

INTERCESSION. Prayer offered on behalf of others. Christ made intercession for those who were crucifying Him (Luke 23:34) and for His disciples (John 17:6–26). Elders of the early church were instructed to pray for the sick (James 5:14–16).

Paul prayed for Israel to be saved (Rom. 10:1) and for the Colossians to grow spiritually (Col. 1:9–12). Christ, our high priest, lives to make intercession for us (Rom. 8:34; Heb. 7:25–26). The Holy Spirit helps us intercede for others (Rom. 8:26; 1 Tim. 2:1). See also *Petition; Prayer*.

INTERCESSOR. An advocate for others (Isa. 59:16). Abraham interceded for Sodom to be spared (Gen. 18:23–26). Paul encouraged intercession for all people (1 Tim. 2:1–2). Christ is the Christian's advocate or intercessor (Heb. 7:25–26).

INN. The Good Samaritan Inn isn't really a working inn. It's a monument built to look like an ancient inn. It commemorates Jesus' parable of the good Samaritan, and it's located along the route described in the parable—about halfway between Jericho and Jerusalem.

INTEREST. See *Usury.*

INTERMARRIAGE. Marriage between members of different races or religions. Intermarriage of the Israelites with the idolatrous Canaanites was forbidden by God (Josh. 23:12–13). Paul counseled the Corinthian Christians not to marry unbelievers (2 Cor. 6:14–17). See also *Marriage.*

INTERMEDIATE STATE. The condition of believers between death and the resurrection. Paul characterized this state as being "absent from the body" (2 Cor. 5:8) while awaiting the resurrection (1 Thess. 4:13–18) and anticipating a glorified body like that of Jesus (Phil. 3:20–21). This condition is also characterized as a sleeplike state (John 11:11) that is enjoyable (Ps. 17:15) and unchangeable (2 Cor. 5:1).

INVISIBLE
Rom. 1:20 *i* things of him [God]...are clearly seen
Col. 1:15 Who [Jesus] is the image of the *i* God
1 Tim. 1:17 King eternal, immortal, *i*...be honour

INWARD PARTS. See *Bowels.*

IRON

1. A fortified city in the territory of Naphtali (Josh. 19:38), also known as *Beth-shemesh* and *Yiron.*

2. An ancient metal first mentioned in Gen. 4:22. Iron was used to make weapons (Job 20:24) and tools (1 Kings 6:7).

IR-SHEMESH. See *Beth-shemesh.*

ISAAC. The son born to Abraham and Sarah in their old age (Gen. 21:1–3) and thus the person through whom God's chosen people, the Israelites, were descended (Gen. 21:9–13). He married Rebekah (Gen. 24:57–67)—a union to which twin sons Jacob and Esau were born (Gen. 25:19–26). Isaac was considered a man of faith (Heb. 11:9, 20), a patriarch of Israel (Exod. 32:13), and an ancestor of Christ (Luke 3:34). See also *Rebekah.*

ISAIAH/ESAIAS. A major prophet of Judah whose career spanned forty years (about 740–701 B.C.). The son of Amoz, he was married to a "prophetess" (Isa. 8:3). Working in the capital city of Jerusalem, Isaiah was the confidant of King Uzziah (Azariah) and his successors (Isa. 1:1). He warned that the city and nation would be destroyed by Assyria, but a righteous remnant would be saved (Isa. 1:2–9; 11:11). He gave his two sons symbolic names to underscore his message (Isa. 7:3; 8:1–4).

Isaiah encouraged King Hezekiah but foretold the king's death (2 Kings 20:1). He was the author of the book of Isaiah, which prophesied the coming of the Messiah (Isa. 7:14), His rejection (Isa. 53), and the conversion of the Gentiles (Isa. 61:10–11). *Esaias:* Greek form (Matt. 4:14).

ISAIAH, BOOK OF. A major prophetic book of the O.T. noted for its prediction of the coming Messiah (7:14; 9:7) and particularly its emphasis on the Messiah as God's "suffering servant" (42:1–9; 49:1–7; 50:4–9; 52:13–53:12). These messianic passages occur in the midst of the prophet's prediction that God would punish the nation of Judah because of its rebellion and idolatry (1:1–12:6). Other prophecies in the book are directed at the pagan nations surrounding Judah (13:1–23:18).

Many Bible students call Isaiah the "fifth Gospel" because it echoes the N.T. themes of salvation and redemption. Jesus began His public ministry by identifying with this book's promise of comfort and healing for God's people: "The Spirit of the Lord GOD is upon me; because the LORD hath anointed me to preach good tidings unto the meek; he hath sent me to bind up the brokenhearted, to proclaim liberty to the captives" (Isa. 61:1; see also Luke 4:18–19). See also *Messiah*.

ISCARIOT, JUDAS. The disciple who betrayed Jesus (John 13:2, 26; 18:1–8). The word *Iscariot* identifies Judas as a citizen of Kerioth, a city in southern Judah (Josh. 15:25), to distinguish him from Judas (or Jude), brother of James, who was also one of the Twelve (Luke 6:16).

Judas Iscariot apparently served as the treasurer for Jesus and His disciples (John 13:29). After realizing the gravity of his act of betrayal, Judas committed suicide (Matt. 27:3–5). See also *Twelve, The*.

ISH-BOSHETH/ESH-BAAL. The youngest son of Saul who became king of Israel for two years (2 Sam. 2:8–9). He was eventually defeated by David and assassinated in his bed (2 Sam. 4:8–12). *Esh-baal:* 1 Chron. 8:33.

ISHI. A symbolic name meaning "my husband" to be given to God when the Israelites returned to Him (Hosea 2:16–17). Ishi was to be used instead of Baali because the name Baal was associated with a pagan god.

ISHMAEL. Abraham's son born to Sarah's Egyptian maid Hagar (Gen. 16). After conflicts with Sarah, Hagar fled with Ishmael into the desert, where she was assured by angels that Ishmael would have many descendants (Gen. 21:9–

ISCARIOT, JUDAS. Judas betrays Jesus with a kiss—the prearranged code that let the temple officers know who to arrest.

18). Tradition holds that the Arab peoples are descendants of Ishmael. See also *Hagar.*

ISHMAELITES. Descendants of Ishmael, Abraham's son by Hagar (Gen. 16:15). God promised to bless the Ishmaelites, although Ishmael was not Abraham's covenant son (Gen. 21:12–13). Ishmael had twelve sons, whose descendants lived as nomads in the deserts of northern Arabia. Most modern-day Arabs claim descent from Ishmael. See also *Arabia.*

ISH-TOB. See *Tob.*

ISRAEL

1. Another name for Jacob. Jacob was renamed Israel by an angel at Penuel because of his influence with God and man (Gen. 32:28; 35:10). His name was extended to the nation of Israel (Exod. 3:16) and finally narrowed to designate the Northern Kingdom after the nation divided following Solomon's administration. See also *Jacob.*

2. The Northern Kingdom. This nation was formed in 931 B.C. when the ten northern tribes rebelled against the two southern tribes and established their own kingship under Rehoboam (1 Kings 12). Samaria was established as the capital city. After about two centuries, the Northern Kingdom was carried into captivity by Assyria in 722 B.C. and Samaria was populated by foreigners (2 Kings 17:23–24). See also *Samaritan.*

ISRAELITES. Descendants of Israel, or Jacob (Gen. 35:9–12), a nation that was designated by God as His special people. The Israelites were regarded as children of the covenant and heirs of the promises that God made to Abraham (Gen. 12:1–3; Rom. 9:4; 11:1). See also *Jews.*

ISSACHAR. Jacob's fifth son by Leah; father of one of the twelve tribes of Israel (Gen.

30:17–18). The tribe occupied fertile land bounded on the north by Zebulon and Naphtali, on the east by the Jordan River, and on the south and west by Manasseh. The judges Deborah and Barak are assumed to be Issacharites, since they came from this territory (see Judg. 4–5). See also *Tribes of Israel.*

ITALIAN BAND (ITALIAN COHORT, ITALIAN REGIMENT). A unit of the Roman army stationed in Caesarea. Cornelius, one of the first Gentile converts to Christianity, was attached to this unit (Acts 10:1). *Italian Regiment:* NIV; *Italian Cohort:* NRSV.

ITALY. The boot-shaped country between Greece and Spain that juts into the Mediterranean Sea (Acts 18:2). Its capital city, Rome, was the seat of the Roman Empire in N.T. times. Paul sailed to Rome as a prisoner (Acts 27:1–6; 28:14–16).

ITCH. See *Scall.*

ITHAMAR. The youngest son of Aaron who was consecrated as a priest (Exod. 6:23). He oversaw the tabernacle during the wilderness wanderings (Exod. 38:21).

ITUREA. A small province in Palestine at the base of Mount Hermon. This area was ruled by Herod Philip when John the Baptist began his ministry (Luke 3:1).

IVAH, IVVAH. See *Ahava.*

IVORY. Decorative trim from the tusks of elephants that was a symbol of luxury. King Ahab's house was known as the "ivory house" (1 Kings 22:39). See also *Ahab.*

IYYAR. See *Zif.*

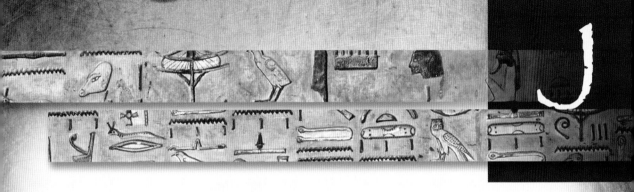

J

JAAZER. See *Jazer.*

JABBOK. A small stream that enters the Jordan River about twenty miles north of the Dead Sea (Num. 21:24). Beside this stream, at a point later called Peniel, Jacob wrestled with an angel (Gen. 32:24–31).

JABESH-GILEAD. A city of Gilead about twenty miles south of the Sea of Galilee. King Saul defended this city against Nahash, king of the Ammonites (1 Sam. 11:1–11).

JABIN

1. The Canaanite king of Hazor who was killed by Joshua at the Merom Brook (Josh. 11:1–14).

2. Another king of Hazor who was defeated by Deborah and Barak at the Kishon River (Judg. 4).

JACHIN (JAKIN) AND BOAZ. Two ornamental bronze pillars, constructed by Hiram of Tyre, that stood in front of Solomon's temple at Jerusalem (1 Kings 7:13–22). *Jakin:* NIV.

JACKAL. A jackal was a wild dog that often traveled in packs. This figurine is from Roman times.

J

JACINTH. A precious stone, perhaps the same as sapphire, used in the foundation of the heavenly city, or New Jerusalem (Rev. 21:20). See also *Ligure.*

JACKAL. A wild dog, or a scavenger that ran in packs. The "foxes" that Samson used to destroy crops of the Philistines may have been jackals (Judg. 15:4). See also *Fox.*

JACOB. The son of Isaac and Rebekah and father of several sons who became the ancestors of the twelve tribes of Israel. Jacob was the twin brother of Esau, who was the firstborn son and thus entitled to the birthright of his father, Isaac. But Jacob bought Esau's birthright for a pot of stew (Gen. 25:29–34). With his mother, Rebekah's, help, he deceived his father and received his blessing as well (Gen. 27:6–29).

While fleeing his brother's wrath, Jacob struggled with an angel and was given the name Israel, meaning "prince with God" (Gen. 32:22–30). His descendants were known as Israelites, or descendants of Israel.

In his later years, after the birth of many children to his wives, Rachel and Leah, and their handmaids, Jacob mourned his favorite son, Joseph, whom he presumed dead. But his joy was restored when Joseph was discovered alive and well in Egypt. Jacob died in Egypt after moving there at Joseph's initiative to escape a famine in Canaan. He was returned to his homeland for burial. See also *Israel; Israelites.*

JACOB'S WELL. The well dug by Jacob and the site where Jesus offered the Samaritan woman "living water" (John 4:1–26). Not mentioned in the O.T., the site today is associated with the ancient city of Shechem (Tell Balatah) near the highway from Jerusalem to Galilee.

JAEL. The wife of Heber the Kenite who killed Sisera, a commander of the forces of King Jabin of Hazor (Judg. 4:17–22). See also *Sisera.*

JAFFA. See *Joppa.*

JAH. See *Jehovah.*

JAIR. The eighth judge of Israel, a member of the tribe of Gilead, who led the nation for twenty-two years (Judg. 10:3–5). See also *Judges of Israel.*

JAIRUS. A ruler of the synagogue near Capernaum whose daughter was raised from the dead by Jesus (Mark 5:22–23).

JAKIN. See *Jachin.*

JAMBRES. A magician of the Egyptian pharaoh who opposed Moses. While he is not mentioned in the O.T., Jambres is cited by Paul as a person who resisted God's truth (2 Tim. 3:8).

JAMES
1. A son of Zebedee and a disciple of Jesus. He and his brother John were called "sons of thunder" by Jesus because of their fiery temperament (Mark 3:17).
2. A son of Alphaeus and a disciple of Jesus (Matt. 10:3).
3. The half brother of Jesus who became a leader in the church at Jerusalem (Acts 21:17–18; Gal. 1:19). He was probably the author of the epistle of James. See also *Brothers of Christ.*

JAMES, EPISTLE OF. A short N.T. epistle—written probably by James, the half brother of Jesus—known for its plain language and practical application of the gospel to the believer's daily life. According to James, the true test of Christianity is in the living and doing of its truth rather than in the speaking, hearing, and even believing of its doctrines (1:22–27).

Authentic faith results in acts of ministry to others, or as James puts it, "Faith, if it hath not works, is dead" (2:17). Other emphases in James are equality of all people before God (2:1–10) and the power of the tongue (3:3–10).

JANNES. A magician of the Egyptian pharaoh who opposed Moses. While he is not mentioned in the O.T., Jannes is cited by Paul as a person who resisted God's truth (2 Tim. 3:8).

JAPHETH. A son of Noah who was saved in the ark (Gen. 5:32). Japheth is considered the father of the Indo-European races (Gen. 9:18–27; 10:2–5).

JAPHO. See *Joppa.*

JAR. See *Cruse; Pitcher.*

JASHER. See *Book of Jasher.*

JASHOBEAM. The chief of David's mighty men, or brave warriors, who helped him become king and kept his kingdom strong (1 Chron. 11:10–11). See also *Mighty Men.*

JASON. A citizen of Thessalonica who was persecuted because he provided lodging for Paul and Silas (Acts 17:5–9). This may be the same Jason whom Paul referred to as "my kinsman" (Rom. 16:21).

JAVELIN. Egyptian warriors carry javelins and shields, used in battle.

JASPER. A precious stone, probably a type of quartz, used in the breastplate of the high priest (Exod. 28:20) and in the foundation of the heavenly city, or New Jerusalem (Rev. 21:19).

JAVAN. A son of Japheth and grandson of Noah. Javan was the father of the Ionians, or Greeks (Gen. 10:2; Isa. 66:19). See also *Greece.*

JAVELIN (SPEAR). A short spear or dart. A javelin was used by King Saul (1 Sam. 19:9–10) and by the high priest Phinehas (Num. 25:7). *Spear:* NIV, NRSV. See also *Dart; Spear.*

JAZER/JAAZER. A fortified Amorite city east of the Jordan River (2 Sam. 24:5) noted for its fertile land (Num. 32:1) and occupied by the conquering Israelites (Josh. 13:24–25). *Jaazer:* Num. 21:32.

JEALOUSY. Ill feelings toward others because of their blessings or favored position. Jacob's sons were jealous of their brother Joseph because he was their father's favorite (Gen. 37:11). Christians are counseled not to participate in such behavior (Rom. 13:13). See also *Envy.*

JEBUS. See *Jerusalem.*

JEBUSITES. Tribal enemies of the Israelites who were descended from Canaan (Gen. 10:15–16). They controlled Jerusalem (known as Jebus at that time) before David conquered the city (2 Sam. 5:6–8) and turned it into his capital. Remnants of the Jebusites became bondservants during Solomon's reign (1 Kings 9:20–21). See also *Jerusalem.*

JECONIAH. See *Jehoiachin.*

JEDIDIAH. A name for Solomon, meaning "beloved of Jehovah," bestowed on him at birth

by Nathan the prophet (2 Sam. 12:25). This name suggested that David's sin of adultery had been forgiven.

JEDUTHUN/ETHAN. A Levite musician and writer of psalms (1 Chron. 9:16) who led in praise services when the ark of the covenant was returned to Jerusalem (1 Chron. 16:41–42). *Ethan:* 1 Chron. 6:44.

JEHOAHAZ/SHALLUM

1. The son and successor of Jehu as king of Israel (reigned 814–798 B.C.; 2 Kings 10:35). A wicked king, he led Israel into sin and idolatry (2 Kings 13:2).

2. The son and successor of Josiah as king of Judah about 610 B.C. A sinful monarch, he reigned only three months before being deposed by Pharaoh Nechoh of Egypt (2 Kings 23:31–34). *Shallum:* 1 Chron. 3:15.

3. Another name for Ahaziah, king of Judah about 850 B.C. See *Ahaziah,* No. 2.

JEHOASH. See *Joash,* No. 1.

JEHOIACHIN/CONIAH/JECONIAH/ JECHONIAS. The son and successor of Jehoiakim as king of Judah (reigned only three months, about 597 B.C.). Evil like his father, Jehoiachin was king when the nation was captured by Nebuchadnezzar and the people were deported to Babylonia (2 Kings 24:8–16). He was released after thirty-seven years in prison (Jer. 52:31–34). Jehoiachin is listed as an ancestor of Christ (Matt. 1:11–12). *Coniah:* Jer. 22:24; *Jeconiah:* 1 Chron. 3:16–17; *Jechonias:* Matt. 1:11–12.

JEHOIADA

1. A military leader at Hebron who apparently recruited 3,700 of his countrymen to serve in David's army (1 Chron. 12:27).

2. A high priest who protected young King Joash from Queen Athaliah until Joash was crowned king of Judah. Jehoiada also led in reducing Baal worship (2 Kings 11:4–21). See also *Joash*, No. 1.

JEHOIAKIM/ELIAKIM.
The son and successor of Josiah as king of Judah (reigned about 609–597 B.C.). An evil ruler who exploited the people and led them into idolatry, Jehoiakim died while Jerusalem was under siege by the Babylonians (2 Chron. 36:6). The prophet Jeremiah foretold his defeat (Jer. 22:18–19). *Eliakim:* 2 Kings 23:34.

JEHORAM/JORAM
1. The wicked king of Judah (rcigncd about 848–841 B.C.) who murdered his own brothers (2 Chron. 21:1–4) in order to succeed his father, Jehoshaphat (1 Kings 22:50). Struck down by God, he died in disgrace, as predicted by the prophet Elijah, from a mysterious disease (2 Chron. 21:12–20). *Joram:* 2 Kings 8:21.

2. Ahab's son and successor as Israel's king (reigned about 852–841 B.C.; 2 Kings 1:17). He died in battle against the Syrians (2 Kings 8:28–29). *Joram:* 2 Kings 8:16.

JEHOSHABEATH/JEHOSHEBA.
The daughter of King Jehoram of Judah who hid her nephew Joash from Queen Athaliah's wrath until Joash was crowned king (2 Chron. 22:11–12). *Jehosheba:* 2 Kings 11:2.

JEHOSHAPHAT/JOSAPHAT.
The son and successor of Asa as king of Judah (reigned about 870–848 B.C.). A reformer like his father, Jehoshaphat attacked idolatry and sent teachers to help people learn about God (2 Chron. 17:3–9). He was rebuked by the prophet Jehu for forming an alliance with King Ahab of Israel (2 Chron. 19:1–3). *Josaphat:* Matt. 1:8.

JEHOSHAPHAT, VALLEY OF.
A place where God will judge the nations in the end-time, according to the prophet Joel (Joel 3:2–14). This site is believed to be part of the Kidron Valley between Jerusalem and the Mount of Olives. The name may refer to a symbolic "valley of decision," where God will judge all nations.

JEHOSHEBA.
See *Jehoshabeath*.

JEHOSHUA.
See *Joshua*.

JEHOVAH/JAH.
A translation of *Yahweh*, a Hebrew word for God in the O.T. that indicated his eternity and self-existence. This word is based on a Hebrew verb meaning "to be"; thus the name "I AM" by which God revealed Himself to Moses at the burning bush (Exod. 3:14).

Yahweh is rendered as "Lord" and printed in small capital letters (Lord) in most English versions of the Bible, although some translations use *Yahweh* or *Jehovah*. *Jah* is an abbreviated form of this name (Ps. 68:4). See also *I Am; Lord; Yahweh*.

JEHOVAH-JIREH.
A name for God meaning "the Lord will provide." It was used by Abraham to commemorate God's provision of a ram in place of Isaac as a sacrifice (Gen. 22:14).

JEHOVAH-NISSI.
A name for God meaning "the Lord is my banner." Moses used this name to show God's victory over the Amalekites (Exod. 17:15–16).

JEHOVAH-SHALOM.
The name of an altar built by Gideon, meaning "the Lord is peace" (Judg. 6:24).

JEHOVAH-SHAMMAH.
The name of a

city of the future envisioned by the prophet Ezekiel, indicating that "the Lord is there" (Ezek. 48:35).

JEHOVAH-TSIDKENNU. The name for the coming Messiah used by the prophet Jeremiah, meaning "the Lord our righteousness" (Jer. 23:6).

JEHU

1. A violent and deceitful king of Israel (reigned about 841–814 B.C.) who gained the throne by killing King Ahab's descendants (2 Kings 9–10).

2. A prophet who delivered a message of doom to King Baasha of Israel (1 Kings 16:1–2) and rebuked King Jehoshaphat of Judah for forming alliances with King Ahab (2 Chron. 19:1–3).

KING JEHU'S MISSION

Jehu was anointed king of Israel by the prophet Elisha (2 Kings 9:1-13) in order to end the dynasty of the wicked king Ahab, who had encouraged Baal worship among his subjects. Jehu seized the throne by assassinating Ahab's son and successor, King Jehoram/Joram. Then he murdered the other sons of Ahab as well as Ahab's wife, Queen Jezebel, to assure that no one connected with Ahab would ever rule over Israel.

JEPHTHAH/JEPHTHAE. A judge of Israel who delivered the nation from the Ammonites. After making a rash and foolish vow, Jephthah sacrificed his only child as an offering to God (Judg. 11). *Jephthae:* Heb. 11:32. See also *Judges of Israel.*

JEREMIAH/JEREMIAS/JEREMY. A major prophet of the O.T. who preached God's message of doom to the nation of Judah for about forty years during the reigns of the last five kings of the nation: Josiah, Jehoahaz, Jehoiakim, Jehoiachin, and Zedekiah (Jer. 1:2–3). Called to his prophetic ministry even before he was born (Jer. 1:4–10), he wept openly over the sins of Judah (Jer. 9:1) and declared that the nation would fall to a foreign enemy as punishment for its sin and idolatry (Jer. 16:1–13).

After Judah was overrun by the Babylonians, Jeremiah remained in Jerusalem while most of his countrymen were deported to Babylonia. Eventually he was taken to Egypt, where he continued to preach to a remnant of Jewish people (Jer. 43:5–13). *Jeremias:* Greek form (Matt. 16:14); *Jeremy:* Matt. 2:17; 27:9.

JEREMIAH, BOOK OF. A major prophetic book of the O.T. noted for its stern warnings to the nation of Judah that it was destined to fall to the Babylonians unless the people repented and turned back to God. After being called and assured of God's guidance and presence (chap. 1), Jeremiah pronounced prophecies of doom against Judah (chaps. 2–45) and then the surrounding pagan nations (chaps. 46–51). The book closes with a description of the destruction of Jerusalem (52:1–23) and the deportation of the influential people of Judah to Babylonia (52:24–30).

The concept of a new covenant (chap. 31) is unique to the book of Jeremiah. This new agreement between God and His people, based on grace and forgiveness, was needed because the old covenant of law had failed to keep the people on the path of righteousness and holiness. See also *Babylonia.*

JERICHO. A fortified Canaanite city near the Jordan River and the Dead Sea (Deut. 32:49)

JERUSALEM. Jerusalem, seen from the Mount of Olives in the east. (Inset) The crowded Damascus Gate serves as a marketplace as well as an entrance into the Old City of Jerusalem.

that was captured by Joshua when the Israelites entered the Promised Land (Josh. 6:1–22).

JEROBOAM

1. Jeroboam I. The first king of Israel (reigned about 931–910 B.C.) after the kingdom of Solomon split into two separate nations following Solomon's death. An official in Solomon's administration, Jeroboam led the ten northern tribes to rebel against the two southern tribes when Rehoboam succeeded his father, Solomon, as king (1 Kings 12:17–20). Jeroboam established idol worship in the cities of Bethel and Dan (1 Kings 12:26–30) and was ultimately defeated by King Abijah of Judah and struck down by the Lord

(2 Chron. 13:19–20).

2. Jeroboam II. A wicked king of Israel (reigned about 782–753 B.C.) who succeeded his father, Jehoash (2 Kings 14:23–29). He was denounced by the prophet Amos for his evil deeds and encouragement of idol worship (Amos 7:7–9).

JERUBBAAL/JERUBBESHETH. A name given to the judge Gideon by his father after he destroyed the altar of Baal at Ophrah (Judg. 6:32). It probably means "let Baal contend." Another name given to Gideon was *Jerubbesheth* (2 Sam. 11:21; *Jerubbaal:* NRSV), probably meaning "contender with the idol." See also *Gideon.*

JERUSALEM/JEBUS/SALEM. The religious and political capital of the Jewish people. Situated forty-eight miles from the

J
D
5

Mediterranean Sea and eighteen miles west of the Jordan River, Jerusalem was known as *Salem* in Abraham's time (Gen. 14:18) and as *Jebus* when the people of Israel entered Canaan, or the Promised Land (Josh. 15:8).

David captured the city from the Jebusites, renamed it, and turned it into his capital (2 Sam. 5:6–9). It was often called the "city of David" (2 Chron. 32:5). Solomon built the magnificent temple in Jerusalem as the center of worship for the Jewish people about 950 B.C. (1 Kings 5:5–8). The city fell to the Babylonians in 587 B.C., and its leading citizens were taken away as captives (Jer. 39:1–8).

After the Persians defeated the Babylonians, King Cyrus of Persia allowed Jewish exiles to return to their homeland and rebuild Jerusalem, including the temple and the city wall (Ezra 1:1–4; Neh. 12:27–47; Zech. 4).

In N.T. times, Christ wept over the city because of its sin and spiritual indifference (Luke 19:41–42). He predicted its destruction (Luke 19:43–44), entered Jerusalem as a conquering spiritual leader (Matt. 21:9–10), and was crucified on a hill just outside the city wall (Luke 23:33). As Jesus predicted, Jerusalem was destroyed in A.D. 70 during a fierce battle between the Roman army and Jewish zealots.

The church was launched in Jerusalem, where it experienced spectacular growth (Acts 2). The apostle John described the future heavenly city as "new Jerusalem" (Rev. 21:2). See also *City of David; Jebusites; Zion.*

JERUSALEM COUNCIL. A conference held during the early days of the Christian movement to determine how Gentile believers would be received into the church. Participants representing the church at Antioch and the church in Jerusalem included Peter, Paul, Barnabas, and James.

The issue was whether Gentile converts first had to identify with Judaism by being circumcised before they could be baptized and received as full members of the church (Acts 15:6).

The council concluded that since Gentile and Jewish believers are saved by grace alone, circumcision was unnecessary (Acts 15:6–19). This solution averted a conflict that would have hampered missionary efforts and could have made Christianity a sect of Judaism. See also *Judaizers.*

JESHANAH GATE. See *Old Gate.*

JESHUA

1. A priest who returned to Jerusalem with Zerubbabel after the Babylonian Exile and helped rebuild the temple and reestablish worship (Ezra 2:2; 3:2–9).

2. Another name for Joshua (Neh. 8:17). See *Joshua.*

JESSE. The father of David and an ancestor of Christ. Jesse presented his eight sons to the prophet Samuel, who anointed David as the future king of Israel (1 Sam. 16:10–13). Jesse is mentioned in Scripture as the root or shoot that would produce the royal line of David (Isa. 11:1, 10; Rom. 15:12) and ultimately the Savior (Matt. 1:5–6).

JESUS CHRIST. The Son of God and Savior of the world. Jesus is the Greek form of the name *Joshua,* meaning "Savior." Christ means "the anointed one," identifying Him as the promised Messiah of O.T. prophecy (Gal. 4:4–5).

Jesus was born during the reign of Herod the Great, Roman ruler over Palestine, sometime before 4 B.C., the date of Herod's death (Matt. 2:1). After a public ministry of perhaps three years, He was crucified about A.D. 30. He

J

JESUS CHRIST. Astonished disciples watch as Jesus meets with Moses and Elijah on the Mount of Transfiguration.

preexisted as the eternal Word of God (John 1:1, 18; 8:58) and participated in the creation of the world (John 1:3). His advent in human form, including his virgin birth in Bethlehem (Isa. 7:14; Mic. 5:2), was foretold in the O.T. (Ps. 2:7–8; Isa. 9:6–7). As the God-man, Jesus was incarnated to reveal God in an understandable way (Matt. 1:23; John 1:14–18) and "to make reconciliation for the sins of the people" (Heb. 2:17–18).

As a boy, Jesus grew physically and advanced in knowledge (Luke 2:51–52). Yet He had a consciousness of His divine mission (Luke 2:49). He was baptized by John the Baptist to "fulfill all righteousness" and to identify with humanity (Matt. 3:15–17). In resisting Satan's temptations at the beginning of His public ministry, the sinless Savior refused to break dependence on the Father and to establish His kingdom in any fashion other than by suffering (Matt. 4:7–10).

Jesus' public ministry was short and revolutionary (John 17:4). He came preaching and healing (Mark 1:38–42), teaching (Luke 6:6), and seeking the lost (Luke 19:10). After an early campaign in Judea in southern Palestine, He began a major campaign in the region of Galilee in northern Palestine with Capernaum as His home base. His hometown synagogue in Nazareth rejected Him, but the common people heard Him gladly (Luke 4:16–32).

Jesus proclaimed a spiritual kingdom that required repentance and faith rather than blind and ritualistic obedience to the law and the legalistic demands of the Pharisees (Matt. 6:10, 33; Luke 13:3). His later ministry was devoted to training His disciples and preparing them for His death and their witness to others in the Holy Spirit's power (Luke 24:46–49).

Jesus' actions such as denouncing the Pharisees (Matt. 23), healing on the Sabbath (Matt. 12:8–14), and cleansing the temple angered the religious leaders among the Jews and disturbed Roman officials (Matt. 21:23). His triumphal entry into Jerusalem on a donkey disappointed His followers who wanted an earthly king (Luke 24:17–21). After observing the Passover with His disciples and instituting the Lord's Supper, He was betrayed into enemy hands (Luke 22:15–21).

In His trial before Pilate, Jesus acknowledged His kingship but declared His kingdom "not of this world" (John 18:36–37). Nevertheless, He was charged with treason and crucified between two thieves (Luke 23:33; John 19:14–16). On the third day He arose from the grave, conquering sin and death for believers (Acts 13:30; 1 Cor. 15:57). Jesus ascended to the Father, where He "ever liveth to make intercession" (Heb. 7:25).

Christ will return for righteous judgment (Acts 17:31), to raise the dead (1 Thess. 4:14–17), and to usher in the time when everyone must confess that "Jesus Christ is Lord" (Phil. 2:9–11; Rev. 11:15). See also *Emmanuel; Messiah; Son of God; Son of Man.*

JETHRO/REUEL/HOBAB. The father-in-law of Moses who was a priest of Midian. Moses married his daughter Zipporah (Exod. 2:16–22; 4:18). Jethro visited Moses in the wilderness and advised him to select leaders to share the responsibility of dispensing justice and settling disputes among the Hebrews (Exod. 18:17–26). *Reuel:* Exod. 2:18; *Hobab:* Judg. 4:11.

JEWELS. Precious stones used as ornaments or jewelry. The breastplate of Aaron the high priest contained twelve jewels symbolizing the twelve tribes of Israel (Exod. 25:7).

JEWS. A word for the Israelites that came into general use during the period after the

Babylonian Exile. In the N.T., it designates Israelites as opposed to Gentiles. See also *Israelites*.

JEZEBEL. The scheming wife of King Ahab who promoted Baal worship in the nation of Israel (Northern Kingdom). She led Ahab to erect pagan altars (1 Kings 16:32–33), killed several prophets of the Lord (1 Kings 18:4–13), and plotted the death of the prophet Elijah (1 Kings 19:1–2), who prophesied her death (1 Kings 21:23). King Jehu had Jezebel assassinated when he came into power, in fulfillment of Elijah's prophecy (2 Kings 9:7–37). See also *Ahab*.

JEZREEL

   1. A symbolic name given by the prophet Hosea to his son to show that King Jehu and his family would be punished for murdering King Ahab's family. The name means "God scatters" or "God sows" (Hosea 1:3–5).

   2. A fortified city where King Ahab's palace was located (1 Kings 21:1) and where his family was assassinated by Jehu's forces (2 Kings 10:1–11).

   3. The name of a valley in O.T. times that separated Samaria from Galilee. Many major battles have occurred here. Some scholars believe the battle of Armageddon in which Satan will be overthrown will be fought in this valley (Rev. 16:16; 20:1–10). The Greek word for this valley is *Esdraelon*.

JOAB. The commander of King David's army during most of David's reign (2 Sam. 8:15–16). He became commander because he was the first to launch an attack against the Jebusites in their fortified city known as Jebus (later called Jerusalem; see 1 Chron. 11:6). His military exploits included victories over the Edomites (1 Kings 11:15) and the Ammonites (2 Sam.

10:6–14). Joab carried out David's plan to have Uriah the Hittite killed in battle (2 Sam. 11:14). He was murdered on orders from the king when Solomon succeeded David as ruler of Judah (1 Kings 2:5–6, 31–34).

JOANNA. A woman who was a faithful follower of Jesus (Luke 8:1–3). She prepared spices for His burial and proclaimed His resurrection (Luke 23:55–56; 24:1–10).

JOASH/JEHOASH

   1. The eighth king of Judah (reigned about 798–782 B.C.) who succeeded his father, Ahaziah (2 Kings 11:20), at age seven. He was hidden by his aunt from wicked Queen Athaliah to prevent his assassination (2 Kings 11:1–3). Jehoiada the priest served as his counselor (2 Kings 11:12, 17). Joash brought needed religious reforms to Judah (2 Kings 12:4–5), but he turned to idol worship after Jehoiada's death (2 Chron. 24:17–19). He was assassinated by his own officers (2 Chron. 24:24–25). *Jehoash:* 2 Kings 11:21.

   2. The son and successor of Jehoahaz as king of Israel (reigned about 798–782 B.C.). He led the nation into sin through his idolatry (2 Kings 13:10–25).

JOATHAM. See *Jotham*.

JOB. A godly man of the O.T. whose faith sustained him through fierce trials and sufferings. Afflicted by Satan with God's permission (Job 1:6–19), Job refused to blame or curse God for his misfortune (1:20–22; 2:10), although he did complain to God, lamenting the day he was born (3:1).

   Job and his three friends had long discussions about his misfortunes and what they meant. He eventually came to a greater understanding of God's ways of dealing with

J

humans (42:3–6), and God restored his family and possessions (42:10–15). Job was praised by James in the N.T. for his patience and faith (James 5:11).

JOB OF UZ

The exact location of the land of Uz where Job lived (Job 1:1) is unknown. The best guess is that it was east of the Jordan River in the Arabian desert. This land is mentioned in only two other places in the Bible (Jer. 25:20; Lam. 4:21).

JOB, BOOK OF. A wisdom book of the O.T. that addresses the issue of human suffering, particularly the question of why the righteous suffer. The book is written in the form of a poetic drama revolving around the discussion of this problem by Job and his three friends: Eliphaz, Bildad, and Zophar.

After Job lost his children and earthly possessions (chaps. 1–2), his three friends arrived to "comfort" him and discuss the reason for Job's suffering (chaps. 3–37). God assured Job that He is the sovereign, almighty God who doesn't have to defend His actions (chaps. 38–41). Armed with a new understanding of God and His nature ("I have heard of thee by the hearing of the ear: but now mine eye seeth thee," 42:5), Job was rewarded by the Lord with the restoration of his family and possessions (42:10–15). See also *Wisdom Literature*.

JOCHEBED. The mother of Moses, Aaron, and Miriam (Exod. 6:20). She is listed as one of the heroes of the faith (Heb. 11:23).

JOEL

1. A prophet of Judah in the days of King Uzziah and author of the O.T. book that bears his name. He predicted the outpouring of God's Spirit at Pentecost (Joel 2:28–32; Acts 2:16–21), proclaimed salvation through Christ (Joel 2:32), sounded the note of God's universal judgment (Joel 3:1–16), and pictured the eternal age with blessings for God's people (3:17–21).

2. The son of Samuel and a corrupt judge of Israel. Joel's dishonesty, along with that of his brother Abiah, led the people to ask Samuel to appoint a king to rule the nation (1 Sam. 8:2–5).

JOEL, BOOK OF. A brief prophetic book of the O.T. that uses a devastating swarm of locusts (chap. 1) as an early warning sign of God's judgment in order to call His people to repentance. The prophet predicted the outpouring of God's Spirit (2:28–32), an event that happened on the day of Pentecost (Acts 2:16–21); proclaimed salvation through Christ (2:32); and pictured the eternal age with blessings for God's people (3:17–21). See also *Pentecost*.

JOHANAN. A supporter of Gedaliah, governor of Judah (2 Kings 25:22–23), who took a remnant of the Jews to Egypt, in spite of the prophet Jeremiah's warning (Jer. 41:16–18; 43:4–6).

JOHN THE APOSTLE. A fisherman from Galilee, the son of Zebedee and brother of James, who became one of the twelve apostles of Jesus (Matt. 4:21–22). He was described as the disciple "whom Jesus loved" and a member of Christ's inner circle of disciples, which included his brother James and Simon Peter (Mark 5:37; 9:2; 14:33). John was ambitious for position and prestige in Christ's kingdom

(Mark 10:35–37), but he showed a willingness to die for Jesus (Mark 10:38–39).

Associated with Peter in bold evangelism in Jerusalem after Jesus' ascension (Acts 4:13; 8:14–15), John left Jerusalem about A.D. 65 for Ephesus, where he wrote the Fourth Gospel and the three epistles of John. He wrote the book of Revelation while exiled as a political prisoner on the island of Patmos (Rev. 1:9–11).

JOHN THE BAPTIST. The prophet of righteousness and preacher of repentance who prepared the way for Christ. John's birth, Nazarite lifestyle, and unique role as the Messiah's forerunner were revealed to his father, Zechariah (Luke 1:13–17), and his mother, Elizabeth, a cousin of Mary—the mother of Jesus (Luke 1:5–7, 39–41).

John preached repentance and baptized converts in the Jordan River (Matt. 3:1–6), reluctantly agreeing to baptize Jesus after proclaiming Him as the "Lamb of God" (Matt. 3:13–17; John 1:29).

John denounced the hypocrisy of the Pharisees and the immorality and adultery of Herod Antipas, a Roman ruler in Palestine (Matt. 3:7–8; 14:4). He was executed by Herod at the request of his wife, Herodias's, dancing daughter (Matt. 14:3–12). John always magnified Jesus rather than himself (John 3:30), and Jesus commended him highly for his faithfulness (Luke 7:24–28).

JOHN, EPISTLES OF. Three short epistles of the N.T. written by John, one of the twelve disciples of Jesus.

First John, the longest of the three, focuses on such themes as the incarnation of Christ (1:1–5), Christian discipleship (1:6–10), false teachings about Christ (2:1–8), and the meaning of love and fellowship (2:15–5:3). Second John calls on believers to abide in the commandments of God (vv. 1–10) and reject false teachers (vv. 7–13). Third John commends the believers Gaius (vv. 1–8) and Demetrius (v. 12), while condemning Diotrephes (vv. 9–11).

The apostle John probably wrote these epistles from Ephesus about A.D. 95. See also *Elect Lady; Gaius*, No. 4; *John the Apostle.*

JOHN THE BAPTIST. As the son of a priest, John the Baptist could have enjoyed the luxury of life in Jerusalem. Instead, he became a traveling prophet who dressed in camel hair clothing and ate locusts and wild honey.

JOHN, GOSPEL OF. One of the four Gospels of the N.T., written by the apostle John to show that "Jesus is the Christ, the Son of God" (20:31). John is unique among the Gospels in that it majors on the theological meaning of the events in Jesus' life rather than the events themselves. Many of the miracles of Jesus are interpreted as "signs" of His divine power and unique relationship to the Father (2:1–11; 5:1–18).

The "I am" sayings of Jesus, in which He reveals selected attributes or characteristics of His divine nature, are also unique to the Gospel of John. See also *John the Apostle; Synoptic Gospels.*

SEVEN SIGNS OF JESUS IN JOHN'S GOSPEL

1. Turning of water into wine (John 2:1-11)
2. Healing of a nobleman's son (John 4:46-54)
3. Healing of a paralyzed man (John 5:1-9)
4. Feeding of the five thousand (John 6:5-14)
5. Walking on the water (John 6:15-21)
6. Healing of a man born blind (John 9:1-7)
7. Raising of Lazarus from the dead (John 11:38-44)

JOKTAN. A son of Eber and descendant of Shem. He was an ancestor of several tribes in the Arabian desert (1 Chron. 1:19–27).

JONAH/JONAS. An O.T. prophet who was swallowed by a "great fish" while fleeing from God's call to preach to the pagan citizens of Nineveh in Assyria (Jon. 1:17). In predicting His death and resurrection, Jesus referred to Jonah's experience (Luke 11:30; *Jonas*). See also *Assyria; Nineveh.*

JONAH, BOOK OF. A short prophetic book of the O.T. that emphasizes God's universal love. Jonah, the "reluctant prophet" (1:1–2:10), finally preached to the citizens of Nineveh in Assyria, a pagan nation noted for its cruelty and opposition to Israel. To his surprise and disappointment, the pagans repented and turned to God (4:1–10). Through this experience, Jonah learned that God is concerned for all people, not just the citizens of his native land (4:1–11). See also *Assyria.*

JONATHAN

1. King Saul's oldest son (1 Sam. 14:49), who was a loyal friend of David, even while his father was trying to kill David (1 Sam. 20). David mourned Jonathan (2 Sam. 1:17–26) after he was killed by the Philistines (1 Sam. 31:2). See also *Mephibosheth.*

2. A supporter of David during Absalom's rebellion. Jonathan hid in a well to warn David of Absalom's plans (2 Sam. 17:17–21).

JONATHAN: A LOYAL FRIEND

The friendship between David and Jonathan is a model of rich and meaningful personal relationships. Jonathan was so committed to David that he risked his life to warn David that Jonathan's father, King Saul, was determined to kill him (1 Sam. 20).

Jonathan was eventually killed by the Philistines, but David never forgot his loyal friend. After David became king, he provided food and lodging for Jonathan's handicapped son, Mephibosheth, at the royal palace in Jerusalem (2 Sam. 9).

JOPPA/JAFFA/JAPHO. A coastal city on the Mediterranean Sea where Peter had his vision of full acceptance of the Gentiles (Acts 10:9–23). This area is known today as *Jaffa*, a part of the city of Tel Aviv. *Japho:* Josh. 19:46.

JORAM. See *Jehoram.*

JORDAN RIVER. The largest and most important river in Palestine. It runs the length of the country, from the Sea of Galilee in the north to the Dead Sea in the south. Jesus was baptized by John in the Jordan (Matt. 3:13).

JOSAPHAT. See *Jehoshaphat.*

JOSEPH

1. The son of Jacob by Rachel who was sold to a band of traders by his jealous brothers. Enslaved and imprisoned in Egypt, Joseph became an important official under the pharaoh. He was eventually reunited with his father and brothers when they came to Egypt to buy grain. A model of faith and forgiveness, Joseph saw God at work in human events (Gen. 37–50; Heb. 11:22). He was called *Zaphnath-paaneah* by the Egyptian pharaoh (Gen. 41:45).

2. The husband of Mary, Jesus' mother. A descendant of King David (Matt. 1:20), he was a carpenter (Matt. 13:55) and a righteous man (Matt. 1:19). Joseph took Mary as his wife after an angel explained Mary's condition (Matt. 1:19–25). He was with Mary when Jesus was born in Bethlehem (Luke 2:16). He took his family to Egypt to escape Herod's wrath, then returned later to Nazareth, where the young Jesus was obedient to His earthly parents (Matt. 2:13–23; Luke 2:51). Since Joseph does not appear later in the Gospels, it is likely that he died before Jesus' public ministry.

3. A devout man from Arimathea (Luke 23:50–51) and secret disciple of Jesus (John 19:38) who prepared Jesus' body for burial and placed Him in his own tomb (Mark 15:43–46; Luke 23:53).

4. A half brother of Jesus. See *Brothers of Christ.*

JORDAN RIVER. Israel's largest river, the Jordan, flows out of the Sea of Galilee and winds its way seventy miles south, emptying into the Dead Sea.

JOSES

1. A half brother of Jesus (Mark 6:3). See *Brothers of Christ*.

2. Another name for Barnabas. See *Barnabas*.

JOSHUA/OSHEA/HOSHEA/JEHOSH-UAH/JESHUA.

Moses' successor who led the Israelites into the Promised Land and rallied the people to victory over the Canaanites. One of two spies who gave Moses a favorable report on Canaan (Num. 13:8), he was the Lord's choice as Moses' successor (Num. 27:18–20).

After his conquest of Canaan (Josh. 10–12), Joshua divided the land among the twelve tribes (Josh. 13–19). Before his death, he led the people to renew their covenant with God (Josh. 24:15–27). *Oshea:* Num. 13:8; *Hoshea:* Deut. 32:44; *Jehoshuah:* 1 Chron. 7:27; *Jeshua:* Neh. 8:17.

JOSHUA, BOOK OF.

A book of the O.T. that details the conquest and settlement of the land of Canaan by the Israelites under the leadership of Joshua.

Major events covered by the book include (1) Joshua's succession of Moses as leader of the people and their spiritual preparation for conquest (chaps. 1–5); (2) battles against the Canaanites and allied tribes (6:1–13:7), (3) division of the land among the tribes of Israel (13:8–19:51); (4) the cities of refuge and Levitical cities (chaps. 20–21); and (5) the farewell address and death of Joshua (chaps. 23–24). See also *Cities of Refuge; Joshua; Levitical Cities*.

JOSIAH/JOSIAS.

The son and successor of Amon as king of Judah (reigned 640–609 B.C.; 2 Kings 21:26). Crowned at age eight, he made a covenant to obey God (2 Kings 23:3) and led an important reform movement to reestablish God's law, repair the temple (2 Kings 22:3–9), and abolish idolatry (2 Kings 23:4–24). *Josias:* Jesus' ancestry (Matt. 1:10–11).

JOTHAM/JOATHAM.

The son and successor of Azariah (Uzziah) as king of Judah (reigned about 750–732 B.C.). A contemporary of the prophets Isaiah, Hosea, and Micah (Isa. 1:1; Mic. 1:1), he was a good king but failed to destroy places of pagan worship (2 Kings 15:34–35). Jotham improved the temple, strengthened the city wall, and fortified buildings throughout Judah (2 Chron. 27:3–4). *Joatham:* Matt. 1:9.

JOY.

Great delight or positive feelings. Joy attended Christ's birth (Luke 2:10) and resurrection (Matt. 28:8). A believer's spiritual joy is produced by the Holy Spirit (Luke 10:21; Phil. 4:4).

Ps. 16:11 in thy [God's] presence is fulness of *j*
Ps. 30:5 *j* cometh in the morning
Ps. 51:12 Restore...the *j* of thy [God's] salvation
Ps. 126:5 They that sow in tears shall reap in *j*
Hab. 3:18 I will *j* in the God of my salvation
Matt. 2:10 they [wise men]...rejoiced with...great *j*
Luke 15:10 *j*...over one sinner that repenteth
John 16:20 your sorrow shall be turned into *j*
Acts 20:24 I [Paul] might finish my course with *j*
Rom. 14:17 kingdom of God is...peace, and *j*
Gal. 5:22 fruit of the Spirit is love, *j*, peace
Heb. 12:2 who [Jesus] for the *j*...set before him
James 1:2 count it all *j* when ye fall into divers temptations
3 John 4 no greater *j*...children walk in truth

JOYFUL [LY]

Ps. 35:9 my soul shall be *j* in the LORD
Ps. 66:1 Make a *j* noise unto God, all ye lands
Ps. 149:5 Let the saints be *j* in glory
Eccles. 9:9 Live *j'ly* with the wife whom thou lovest
Isa. 49:13 Sing, O heavens; and be *j*, O earth

JUBAL.

A son of Lamech, descendant of Cain, and a skilled musician regarded as the ancestor of those who play the harp and the flute (Gen. 4:21).

JUBILE (JUBILEE). A year of celebration devoted to liberty and justice and observed every fifty years by the Israelites. During this year, Israelites serving as indentured servants were released from their debts and set free. All properties that had been given up because of indebtedness since the last Jubilee were returned to the original owners. Cropland was allowed to go unplanted as a conservation measure (Lev. 25:8–55). *Jubilee:* NIV, NRSV.

JUDAH/JUDA

1. A son of Jacob and Leah and ancestor of the tribe of Judah (Gen. 29:35). Judah interceded for his brother Joseph to be sold rather than killed (Gen. 37:26–27). He offered himself as a ransom for his brother Benjamin before Joseph in Egypt (Gen. 43:8–9; 44:32–34). His father, Jacob, predicted that Judah's descendants would become the royal line from which the Messiah would emerge (Gen. 49:10). He is listed as an ancestor of Christ (Matt. 1:2–3) and called *Juda* in Luke's ancestry (Luke 3:33). The tribe Judah is spelled *Juda* in the N.T. (Heb. 7:14). See also *Tribes of Israel.*

2. The Southern Kingdom, or nation of Judah. Founded after Solomon's death, the Southern Kingdom was composed largely of the tribes of Judah and Benjamin, while the rebellious ten northern tribes retained the name of Israel. Solomon's son Rehoboam was the first king of Judah, with the capital at Jerusalem (1 Kings 14:21).

The nation of Judah drifted into paganism and idolatry under a succession of kings, turning a deaf ear to great prophets such as Isaiah and Jeremiah, who tried to bring them back to worship of the one true God. Judah was overrun and taken into exile by the Babylonians about 587 B.C. A remnant returned to rebuild Jerusalem about 530 B.C. (2 Chron. 36:20–23).

JUDAIZERS. An early Christian sect that advocated that Gentiles must be circumcised before they could become Christians (Acts 15:1). They were denounced by Paul, who insisted that believers are justified by faith alone (Acts 15:12; Gal. 6:15). The Judaizers were also opposed by Peter and James at the Jerusalem Council (Acts 15:8–19). See also *Circumcision; Jerusalem Council.*

JUDAS. See *Iscariot, Judas; Jude.*

JUDAS, BROTHER OF JAMES/LEBBAEUS/THADDAEUS. One of the twelve disciples of Jesus, also called *Lebbaeus* (Matt. 10:3) and *Thaddaeus* (Mark 3:18). He was called "brother of James" to set him apart from the Judas who betrayed Jesus (Luke 6:16). See also *Twelve, The.*

JUDE/JUDAS. The half brother of Christ and author of the N.T. epistle that bears his name. He did not believe in Jesus in the beginning (John 7:5), but he apparently became a disciple after His resurrection (Acts 1:14). *Judas:* Matt. 13:55. See also *Brothers of Christ.*

JUDE, EPISTLE OF. A short N.T. letter written like a brief essay or tract and addressed to the problem of false teachings in the early church. Jude called on believers to root their faith in the true doctrine taught by the apostles (v. 17) as well as the love of Christ (v. 21).

JUDEA. A district in southern Palestine in N.T. times. The name was derived from *Jewish,* a word describing Jewish exiles who returned to southern Palestine from the Babylonian Exile about 530 B.C. Judea was a Roman province annexed to Syria when Jesus was born (Matt. 2:1).

J

JUPITER. Jupiter, better known by the Greeks as Zeus, was the chief god in Roman times. After people of one village saw Barnabas and Paul perform miracles, they thought the men were gods Jupiter and Hermes, arriving for a visit.

JUDGE [S]

Gen. 18:25 Shall not the J of all the earth do right?

1 Sam. 2:10 LORD shall *j* the ends of the earth

Ps. 7:8 *j* me, O LORD, according to my righteousness

Ps. 43:1 *J* me, O God, and plead my cause

Ps. 72:2 He [God] shall *j* thy people with righteousness

Prov. 31:9 *j* righteously, and plead the cause of the poor

Matt. 7:1 *J* not, that ye be not judged

John 7:24 *J* not according to the appearance

Rom. 14:10 why dost thou *j* thy brother

2 Tim. 4:1 Jesus Christ, who shall *j* the quick and the dead

James 2:4 ye...are become *j's* of evil thoughts

Rev. 19:11 in righteousness he [Jesus] doth *j*

JUDGES, BOOK OF. A historical book of the O.T. that records the exploits of several different judges, or military deliverers, in Israel's history. The key to understanding Judges is the phrase "The children of Israel again did evil in the sight of the LORD" (see 4:1), which occurs several times throughout the book.

After each period of sin against God, He would send enemy oppressors in judgment. The Israelites would repent and pray for a deliverer, and God would answer their prayer. After their deliverance at the hand of a judge, the cycle of sin/oppression/repentance/deliverance would start all over again. See also *Judges of Israel.*

JUDGES OF ISRAEL. Popular military leaders or deliverers who led Israel between the time of Joshua's death and the beginning of the kingship (about 1380–1050 B.C.). Israel's judges served in times of disunity and spiritual decline among the twelve tribes (Judg. 17:6; 21:25) as well as times when all the tribes were oppressed by their enemies.

While some judges were weak or wicked, noteworthy exploits include Deborah and Barak's defeat of the Canaanite king Jabin (4:4–24), Gideon's 300 warriors who subdued the Midianites (7:1–8:21), and Samson's massacre of the Philistines (15:14–16).

JUDGMENT. Divine retribution against human activities. God's judgment is designed to punish evil (Exod. 20:5), to correct the misguided (2 Sam. 7:14–15), and to deter His people from wrongdoing (Luke 13:3–5). His judgment is an expression of His chastening love for the believer (Heb. 12:5–6). Jesus, God's resurrected Son, has authority to judge all humankind (John 5:27; Acts 17:31). Believers in Jesus will avoid condemnation and enter eternal life (John 9:39). See also *Punishment; Retribution.*

Exod. 12:12 against all the gods of Egypt I [God]...execute *j*
1 Chron. 18:14 David reigned...and executed *j*
Job 8:3 Doth God pervert *j*?
Ps. 72:2 He [God] shall judge...thy poor with *j*
Ps. 119:66 Teach me good *j* and knowledge
Prov. 29:26 every man's *j* cometh from the LORD
Eccles. 12:14 God shall bring every work into *j*
Jer. 9:24 I am the LORD which exercise...*j*
Jer. 33:15 he [Messiah] shall execute *j* and righteousness
Amos 5:24 let *j* run down as waters
John 5:30 as I [Jesus] hear, I judge: and my *j* is just
John 9:39 For *j* I [Jesus] am come into this world
Rom. 14:10 we shall all stand before the *j* seat of Christ
Heb. 9:27 unto men once to die, but after this the *j*
1 Pet. 4:17 *j* must begin at the house of God
1 John 4:17 may have boldness in the day of *j*
Rev. 14:7 Fear God...hour of his *j* is come

JUDGMENT, LAST. Final judgment of unbelievers of all ages. The final judgment is called a day of wrath for unbelievers (Rom. 2:5–8) but a day when believers will enter into eternal life (Rom. 2:7). The Lord will appear suddenly to gather His elect (Matt. 24:32, 42) and to separate unbelievers for judgment (Matt. 25:31–33). We should be prepared for this time (1 Thess. 5:1–11) and avoid self-deception regarding God's final judgment (Matt. 7:21–27). See also *Day of the Lord; Hell; Tribulation, Great.*

JUG. See *Cruse.*

JUNIPER (BROOM). A bush with dense twigs that was used for charcoal (Ps. 120:4). *Broom:* NIV, NRSV.

JUPITER (ZEUS). The chief god of Roman mythology and a name applied to Barnabas by the superstitious citizens of Lystra (Acts 14:12). The Greek name for this god was *Zeus* (NIV, NRSV).

JUST [LY]
Gen. 6:9 Noah was a *j* man
Job 4:17 Shall mortal man be more *j* than God?
Ps. 37:12 wicked plotteth against the *j*
Prov. 11:1 a *j* weight is his [God's] delight
Prov. 20:7 The *j* man walketh in his integrity
Mic. 6:8 doth the LORD require...but to do *j'ly*
Hab. 2:4 the *j* shall live by his faith
Matt. 1:19 Joseph her [Mary's] husband, being a *j* man
1 John 1:9 he [Jesus] is faithful and *j* to forgive us our sins

JUSTICE. Fair and impartial treatment; righteousness. Justice is characteristic of God's nature (Deut. 32:4) and descriptive of Christ (Acts 3:14) and believers (Heb. 12:14). Just dealings with others by God's people were demanded by the O.T. prophets (Mic. 6:8; Amos 5:24). God's justice is fair and merciful (Acts 17:31).

Job 8:3 doth the Almighty pervert *j*
Ps. 82:3 do *j* to the afflicted and needy
Prov. 21:3 To do *j*...is more acceptable...than sacrifice
Jer. 23:5 a King [Jesus] shall...execute...*j*

JUSTIFICATION. The act or event when God both declares and makes a person just or right with Him (Rom. 4:25; 5:9). Justification is not accomplished by personal merit or good works (Gal. 2:16) but by God's grace through personal faith in Christ (Rom. 5:18; Eph. 2:8–9). To be justified is to have peace with God and hope for eternity (Titus 3:5–7). See also *Atonement; Propitiation; Reconciliation.*

JUSTIFIED
Job 25:4 How then can man be *j* with God?
Matt. 12:37 by thy words thou shalt be *j*
Rom. 3:24 *j* freely by his [God's] grace
Rom. 3:28 *j* by faith without the deeds of the law
Rom. 5:1 being *j* by faith, we have peace with God
1 Cor. 6:11 ye are *j* in the name of the Lord
Gal. 2:16 man is not *j* by the works of the law
James 2:21 Was not Abraham our father *j* by works

K

KAB. See *Cab*.

KADESH/KADESH-BARNEA. A wilderness region between Canaan and Egypt that served as the southern boundary of the Promised Land (Num. 34:4). The Israelites camped in this area during the wilderness wandering years before they entered the Promised Land (Num. 32:8; 27:14). *Kadesh-barnea:* Josh. 14:7. See also *Wilderness Wanderings*.

KEDAR. A son of Ishmael, grandson of Abraham, and founder of an Arabic tribe that lived in the desert between Arabia and Babylonia (Gen. 25:12–13).

KEDESH/KEDER/KISHION/KISHON
1. One of the six cities of refuge, situated in the territory of Naphtali in northern Palestine (Josh. 20:1–7). This city is now called *Keder*. See also *Cities of Refuge*.

2. A Canaanite town captured by Joshua

KADESH. Kadesh-barnea, an oasis along the Egyptian–Israeli border, is where Moses and the Israelites probably spent much of their forty years in the wilderness, waiting for God to allow them into the Promised Land.

(Josh. 12:7, 22) and allotted to the tribe of Issachar (1 Chron. 6:72). *Kishion:* Josh. 19:20; *Kishon:* Josh. 21:28.

KEEP [ING]
Exod. 20:8 Remember the sabbath day, to *k* it holy
Ps. 91:11 he [God] shall...*k* thee in all thy ways
Prov. 4:23 *K* thy heart with all diligence
Eccles. 3:7 time to *k* silence...time to speak
Hab. 2:20 earth *k* silence before him [God]
Luke 2:8 shepherds...*k'ing* watch over their flock
John 14:15 love me [Jesus], *k* my commandments
Phil. 4:7 peace of God...*k* your hearts...through Christ
2 Tim. 1:12 he [Jesus] is able to *k* that...I [Paul] have committed
1 John 5:3 this is the love of God...*k* his commandments
Jude 24 unto him [Jesus]...able to *k* you from falling

KENAN/CAINAN. A son of Enoch and grandson of Adam who lived in the days before the great flood (1 Chron. 1:1–2). *Cainan:* Gen. 5:9.

KENITES. A nomadic Midianite tribe associated with the Amalekites (Gen. 15:19). Friendly toward the Israelites, this tribe was likely absorbed into Judah (1 Sam. 27:10).

KENIZZITES. A Canaanite tribe whose land was promised to Abraham's descendants (Gen. 15:18–19).

KENOSIS. Relating to the dual nature of Christ—His divinity and humanity. Citing Phil. 2:7, advocates of this theory claim that God's Son laid aside or "emptied himself" of certain divine attributes when He became human. Most scholars reject the notion that Jesus stopped being God or that He gave up any divine attributes. Rather, the phrase refers to Christ's voluntary servanthood (John 17:5).

KEPT
Ps. 18:21 For I have *k* the ways of the LORD
Ps. 32:3 When I *k* silence, my bones waxed old
Matt. 19:20 these things have I *k* from my youth
Luke 2:19 Mary *k* all these things...in her heart
Gal. 3:23 before faith came, we were *k* under the law
2 Tim. 4:7 I [Paul]...have fought a good fight...*k* the faith
1 Pet. 1:5 *k* by the power of God through faith

KERIOTH. A town in southern Judah (Josh. 15:25). This may have been the hometown of Judas Iscariot, Jesus' disciple and betrayer, since Iscariot means "man of Kerioth."

KETTLE. A vessel used for cooking and in worship rituals (1 Sam. 2:14). The Hebrew word for "kettle" is also translated "basket," "caldron," or "pot" (Jer. 24:2; Job 41:20). See also *Caldron.*

KETURAH. The wife of Abraham after Sarah's death (Gen. 25:1). The six sons born to their union were ancestors of six Arabian tribes in Palestine or Arabia (1 Chron. 1:33).

KEY. A tool used to unlock a door. In Bible times, keys were long rods with metal pins (Judg. 3:25). The word is also used figuratively as a symbol of authority (Isa. 22:22; Rev. 1:18).

KID. A young goat. Kids were used as sacrificial offerings or butchered for special occasions (Luke 15:29). See also *Goat.*

KIDNEY. See *Reins.*

KIDRON/CEDRON. A valley or ravine with a wet-weather stream near Jerusalem. David crossed the Kidron Brook while fleeing from his son Absalom (2 Sam. 15:13–23). Idols from pagan cults were burned in this valley (1 Kings 15:13). Jesus probably crossed this valley on the night of His arrest (John 18:1; *Cedron*).

KILL [ED, EST, ETH]
Exod. 20:13 Thou shalt not *k*
Ps. 44:22 for thy [God's] sake are we *k'ed* all the day long

K

KID. A boy in the Middle East cradles in his arms a kid—a young goat. Kids were among the animals offered as sacrifices in Bible times.

KING. The monarch or supreme ruler of a nation. Beginning with the first king, Saul, who was anointed with God's authority (1 Sam. 10:1), Judah and Israel had a succession of kings across several centuries until both nations were overrun by foreign powers.

The books of 1 and 2 Samuel, 1 and 2 Kings, and 1 and 2 Chronicles report on the reigns of many of these kings. A few were godly and kind rulers who honored God and followed His law, but most were evil and corrupt. They led God's people into sin and idolatry.

The believer should remember that God is our eternal King, worthy of all honor (1 Tim. 1:17). Christ, our ultimate ruler, is Lord of Lords and King of Kings (John 18:37; Rev. 17:14).

Eccles. 3:3 A time to *k*, and a time to heal
Matt. 23:37 Jerusalem...thou that *k'est* the prophets
Mark 8:31 Son of man must suffer...and be *k'ed*
Luke 12:4 Be not afraid of them that *k* the body
Luke 15:23 bring hither the fatted calf, and *k* it
Luke 22:2 sought how they might *k* him [Jesus]
John 16:2 whosoever *k'eth* you...think...doeth God service
Rom. 8:36 For thy sake we are *k'ed* all the day long
2 Cor. 3:6 letter *k'eth*...spirit giveth life

KINDRED. Relatives, or members of one's immediate or extended family. The clan or tribe was the basic family unit in early Hebrew history. Family members considered it their duty to protect one another (Gen. 34). See also *Family; Kinsman-Redeemer.*

KINE (COW). An archaic word for a cow or an ox (Gen. 32:15). The prophet Amos used this word for the oppressive, indulgent leaders of Israel (Amos 4:1–3). *Cow:* NIV, NRSV.

KINGDOM [S]

Exod. 19:6 unto me [God] a *k* of priests
2 Sam. 7:16 thine [David's]...*k*...established for ever
Ps. 68:32 Sing unto God, ye *k's* of the earth
Dan. 4:3 his [God's] *k* is an everlasting *k*
Matt. 6:10 Thy [God's] *k* come. Thy will be done
Matt. 24:7 nation...against nation...*k* against *k*
Mark 3:24 *k*...divided against itself...cannot stand
Luke 1:33 of his [Jesus'] *k* there shall be no end
Luke 12:32 Father's good pleasure to give you the *k*
John 18:36 My [Jesus'] *k* is not of this world
1 Thess. 2:12 God, who hath called you unto his *k*
Rev. 11:15 *k's* of this world are become the *k's* of our Lord

KINGDOM OF GOD. The spiritual reign of God in the hearts of believers (Luke 17:20–21). Partially attained in this life for those who seek God's will, God's kingdom will be fully established in the world to come (John 18:36). Jesus preached the "gospel of the kingdom" (Mark 1:14) and taught His disciples to seek His kingdom (Matt. 6:33) and to pray for its arrival on earth (Matt. 6:10).

Unrepentant sinners cannot inherit this kingdom (Eph. 5:5). It is reserved for those who repent (Matt. 3:2) and experience spiritual rebirth (John 3:3–5). Other phrases for this kingdom are "kingdom of heaven" (Matt. 4:17) and "kingdom of Christ" (Col. 1:13).

Rom. 14:17 **k-o-G** is not meat and drink; but righteousness
1 Cor. 6:9 the unrighteous shall not inherit the **k-o-G**
1 Cor. 15:50 flesh and blood cannot inherit the **k-o-G**

KINGDOM OF HEAVEN

Matt. 5:10 Blessed...[the] persecuted...theirs is the **k-o-h**
Matt. 5:20 shall in no case enter into the **k-o-h**
Matt. 7:21 Not every one...saith...Lord, Lord...enter...**k-o-h**
Matt. 16:19 I [Jesus] will give...thee...keys...**k-o-h**
Matt. 18:4 humble...little child...greatest in the **k-o-h**
Matt. 23:13 ye [scribes and Pharisees] shut up the **k-o-h**

KINGS, BOOKS OF. Two historical books of the O.T. that cover a period of roughly four centuries in Jewish history—from about 970 to 587 B.C. First Kings records the reign of Solomon as successor to David (1 Kings 1–11); the division of the kingdom into two separate nations, Judah and Israel (12–14); and the reigns of selected kings in both these nations until the time of Ahaziah of Israel (about 853–852 B.C.)

Second Kings continues the narrative of Ahaziah's reign (chap. 1) and reports on the reigns of selected kings in both nations up until the time of the fall of the Northern Kingdom under Hoshea (reigned about 730–722 B.C.; chap. 17). Chapters 18 through 25 cover the final years of the surviving nation of Judah, until it fell to the Babylonians in 587 B.C. See also *King.*

KING'S DALE/SHAVEH. The ancient name for a valley east of Jerusalem where Abraham met the king of Sodom and Melchizedek (Gen. 14:17–18). Also called *Shaveh,* this is perhaps

the same place as the Valley of Jehoshaphat (Joel 3:2). See *Jehoshaphat, Valley of.*

KING'S HIGHWAY. An important road linking Damascus and Egypt that ran through Israel. While in the wilderness, the Israelites were denied passage on this road as they traveled toward Canaan (Num. 20:17–21).

3
D
6

KINSMAN-REDEEMER. A close relative who had first option to buy back or redeem personal freedom or property that had been forfeited by impoverished members of the clan (Lev. 25:48–49). Boaz, a near kinsman of Naomi, acted as a redeemer in his marriage to Ruth (Ruth 4). Jesus is our "elder brother" who redeems the believer (Heb. 2:11–17). See also *Kindred.*

K

KIRIOTH/KERIOTH. A fortified city in Moab and possibly its capital in the eighth century B.C., since the prophet Amos predicted its destruction (Amos 2:2). *Kerioth:* Jer. 48:24, 41.

KIRJATH-ARBA. See *Hebron.*

KIRJATH-JEARIM/BAALAH. A fortified city of the Gibeonites where the ark of the covenant was kept for twenty years before being taken to Jerusalem (1 Chron. 13–16). *Baalah:* Josh. 15:9.

2
C
5

KISHION/KISHON. See *Kedesh,* No. 2.

KISHON/KISON. A river in the valley of Jezreel in northern Palestine where Elijah killed the prophets of Baal (1 Kings 18:40). *Kison:* Ps. 83:9.

3
C
3

KISLEV. See *Chisleu.*

KISS. A sign of affection practiced by parents and children (Gen. 27:26). Jesus was betrayed by Judas with a kiss (Matt. 26:49).

KISS [ED]

Gen. 50:1 Joseph...wept upon him [Jacob], and **k'ed** him
Ps. 85:10 righteousness and peace have **k'ed** each other
Luke 15:20 his [prodigal son's] father...**k'ed** him
Luke 22:48 Judas, betrayest thou...with a **k**
2 Cor. 13:12 Greet one another with an holy **k**
1 Pet. 5:14 Greet ye one another with a **k** of charity

KITE.
A bird of prey belonging to the hawk family and regarded as unclean by the Israelites (Deut. 14:12–13).

KITTIM.
See *Cyprus*.

KNEADING TROUGH.
A large bowl used to knead dough to prepare it for baking (Exod. 12:34).

KNEEL.
A symbol of respect (Ps. 95:6) or subjection and surrender (2 Kings 1:13). Kneeling was also a customary stance in prayer, indicating reverence for God (Luke 22:41). See also *Bowing*.

KNIFE.
A sharp-edged weapon or tool made of flint or bronze (Josh. 5:2).

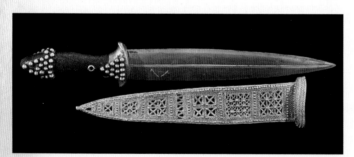

KNIFE. A gold ceremonial knife from Babylon, in what is now Iraq. Most knives in Bible times were made of flint, bronze, or iron.

KNOCK [ED]

Luke 11:9 **k**, and it shall be opened unto you
Acts 12:13 as Peter **k'ed**...a damsel came
Rev. 3:20 I [Jesus] stand at the door, and **k**

KNOP.
An Old English word for the ornamental cap on a column. The word is also used for a decoration on the golden candlesticks in the tabernacle (Exod. 25:31–36).

KNOWLEDGE.
A body of facts or information gained through study and experience. The prophets of the O.T. lamented the Israelites' lack of knowledge (Isa. 5:13). Paul indicated that knowledge of God is to be desired above all else (Phil. 3:8). The verb "to know" was often used in the O.T. for sexual intimacy (Gen. 4:1).

Gen. 2:17 tree of the **k** of good and evil...not eat
1 Sam. 2:3 Lord is a God of **k**
Job 21:22 Shall any teach God **k**?
Job 35:16 he [Job] multiplieth words without **k**
Ps. 144:3 man, that thou [God] takest **k** of him
Prov. 1:7 fear of the Lord...beginning of **k**
Prov. 20:15 lips of **k** are a precious jewel
Prov. 24:5 man of **k** increaseth strength
Eccles. 1:18 he that increaseth **k** increaseth sorrow
Hab. 2:14 earth...filled with the **k** of...the Lord
1 Cor. 13:2 though I [Paul]...understand...all **k**
1 Tim. 2:4 all men...to come unto the **k** of the truth
2 Pet. 1:5 add to your faith virtue...to virtue **k**
2 Pet. 3:18 grow in grace, and in the **k** of our Lord

KOHATH.
The second son of Levi (Gen. 46:8, 11) and founder of the Kohathites, priests who cared for the ark of the covenant and other accessories used in the tabernacle in the wilderness (Num. 3:30–31). Moses and Aaron were Kohathites (Exod. 6:18–20).

KORAH/CORE.
A grandson of Kohath who incited a rebellion against Moses and Aaron in the wilderness. Korah and his followers were swallowed by the earth as punishment for their sin (Num. 16:28–33). *Core:* Greek form (Jude 11).

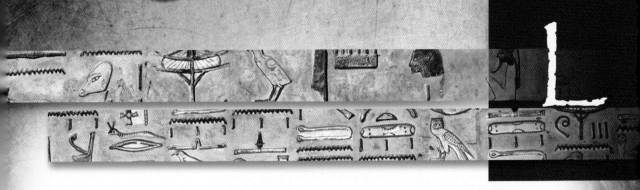

LABAN. A brother of Jacob's mother, Rebekah, and father of Leah and Rachel, who were given in marriage to Jacob. Jacob visited Laban to escape the wrath of his brother, Esau (Gen. 27:43). He worked seven years for Laban for the privilege of marrying Rachel, only to be tricked into marrying Leah instead. Then Jacob worked another seven years for Rachel (Gen. 29:18–30).

LABORER. An unskilled worker who performed such menial tasks as tilling the fields and gathering the crops in Bible times (Ruth 2:2; Ps. 90:10). See also *Hireling.*

LABOUR [ED]
Exod. 20:9 Six days shalt thou *l*, and do all thy work
Ps. 127:1 Except the Lᴏʀᴅ build...they *l* in vain that build it
Eccles. 3:13 man should...enjoy the good of all his *l*
Matt. 11:28 Come unto me [Jesus], all ye that *l*
1 Cor. 15:58 your *l* is not in vain in the Lord
Phil. 2:16 I [Paul] have not...*l'ed* in vain
Heb. 4:11 Let us *l* therefore to enter into that rest

LABOURER [S]
Matt. 9:37 harvest...is plenteous, but the *l's* are few
Luke 10:7 the *l* is worthy of his hire
1 Cor. 3:9 we are *l's* together with God

LACHISH. An Amorite city in southern Judah captured by Joshua (Josh. 10:31–35) and later besieged by King Sennacherib of Assyria (2 Kings 18:13–14). Lachish was reoccupied by the Israelites after the Babylonian Exile (Neh. 11:30).

LACK
Hosea 4:6 people are destroyed for *l* of knowledge
Matt. 19:20 things have I [rich young ruler] kept...what *l I* yet
James 1:5 any of you *l* wisdom, let him ask of God

LAISH. See *Dan*, No. 2.

LAKE OF FIRE. The place of final punishment. Filled with burning brimstone (Rev. 19:20), this place is described as the "second death" (Rev. 20:14). Those consigned to the lake of fire include Satan (Rev. 20:10), persons not named in the Book of Life (Rev. 20:15), and unbelieving sinners (Rev. 21:8). See also *Hell.*

LAKE OF GENNESARET. See *Galilee, Sea of.*

LAMB. A young sheep, used for food (2 Sam. 12:4), clothing (Prov. 27:26), and religious sacrifices (Exod. 12:5, 7). A lamb also symbolized the sufferings of Christ (Isa. 53:7) and the reign of the Messiah (Isa. 11:6). See also *Sheep.*

LAMB OF GOD. A title of Christ that emphasizes the sacrificial nature of His life and His atoning death. This aspect of His ministry was foretold by the prophet Isaiah (Isa. 53:7). John the Baptist greeted Jesus with this title (John 1:29, 36). As the Lamb of God, Jesus is worthy of eternal honor and praise (Rev. 5:12–13). See also *Atonement; Cross.*

LAME. Unable to walk due to an injury (2 Sam. 4:4) or a birth defect (Acts 3:2). Persons with this disability were healed by Jesus (Matt. 11:5) and Peter (Acts 3:2–7).

LAMECH. A son of Methuselah and a man of faith who found "comfort" in the birth of his son Noah (Gen. 5:25–31). Lamech is listed in the ancestry of Jesus (Luke 3:36).

LAMENTATIONS OF JEREMIAH. A short O.T. book that expresses in poetic form the prophet Jeremiah's deep grief and anguish at the destruction of Jerusalem and the Jewish temple by the pagan Babylonians. Chapter 4 paints a bleak picture of life in Jerusalem during the extended siege against the city. See also *Babylonia; Jeremiah.*

IMAGES OF DESPAIR IN LAMENTATIONS

The prophet Jeremiah used numerous images of despair in Lamentations to show his anguish over the fall of Jerusalem. He spoke of throwing dust on one's head (Lam. 2:10), a sign of mourning. He described people as hissing and shaking their heads (Lam. 2:15-16) to show their contempt for the fallen city. The phrase "The crown is fallen from our head" (Lam. 5:16) expresses the loss of Judah's position of honor.

LAMP. See *Candle.*

LAMPSTAND. See *Candlestick.*

LANCE. See *Spear.*

LAND OF PROMISE. Canaan, or the land inhabited by the Israelites. This land was promised by God to Abraham's descendants (Gen. 12:1–7). The promise was fulfilled centuries later when Joshua led the Israelites to take the land from the Canaanites (Josh. 10–12). See also *Canaan,* No. 2; *Palestine.*

LANDMARK (BOUNDARY STONE, MARKER). A marker, usually consisting of a pile of stones, that indicated property lines. Removal of a landmark was forbidden (Deut. 19:14). *Boundary stone:* NIV; *marker:* NRSV.

LANDOWNER. See *Goodman.*

LANTERN. A torch covered with skin or transparent horn for outdoor use. On the night before His crucifixion, Jesus was arrested by armed men with lanterns (John 18:3). See also *Torch.*

LAODICEA. A major city in Asia Minor, located on the Lycus River. One of the seven churches addressed in the book of Revelation was located in Laodicea (1:11). This church was rebuked because of its complacency (Rev. 3:14–18).

LAPIDOTH (LAPPIDOTH). The husband of Deborah the prophetess (Judg. 4:4). *Lappidoth:* NIV, NRSV. See also *Deborah.*

LAPWING (HOOPOE). A small European bird, considered unclean by the Hebrews, that wintered in Palestine (Lev. 11:19; Deut. 14:12, 18). *Hoopoe:* NIV, NRSV.

LASCIVIOUSNESS (DEBAUCHERY, LICENTIOUSNESS). Unbridled lust, a sin characteristic of life apart from Christ (1 Pet. 4:3), which believers are warned to avoid.

According to Paul, victory over lasciviousness requires repentance (2 Cor. 12:21) and living in the spirit of Christ (Gal. 5:19, 22–25). *Debauchery:* NIV; *licentiousness:* NRSV.

LAST
Isa. 44:6 I [God] am the first, and...the *l*
Mark 9:35 desire to be first...shall be *l*
Mark 10:31 many that are first shall be *l*
1 Cor. 15:26 The *l* enemy...destroyed is death
1 Cor. 15:45 the *l* Adam was made a quickening spirit
2 Tim. 3:1 in the *l* days perilous times shall come
Heb. 1:2 in these *l* days spoken...by his [God's] Son
Rev. 1:11 I [Jesus] am Alpha and Omega...first and the *l*

LAST SUPPER. See *Lord's Supper.*

LATCHET (THONGS). A strap that fastened a sandal to the foot (Gen. 14:23). John the Baptist declared he was unworthy to untie the latchet of Christ's sandals (Mark 1:7). *Thongs:* NIV, NRSV. See also *Sandals.*

LATTER RAIN (SPRING RAIN). The rain that fell late in the growing season, allowing crops to reach full maturity before the harvest (Jer. 3:3). *Spring rain:* NIV, NRSV. See also *Former Rain; Rain.*

LATTICE. A screened opening or porch on a house to provide privacy and let in night breezes (Judg. 5:28; 2 Kings 1:2).

LAUNDERER. See *Fuller.*

LAVER (BASIN). A container placed near the altar outside the tabernacle where priests could wash their hands and feet before offering animal sacrifices (Exod. 30:17–21). *Basin:* NIV, NRSV. See also *Bason.*

LAW, LAW OF MOSES. The authoritative rule of conduct spelled out in the Ten Commandments and the Pentateuch—the books of Genesis, Exodus, Leviticus, Numbers, and Deuteronomy. This code was revealed to Moses by the Lord on Mount Sinai (Deut. 5:1–2). While many of the regulations are ceremonial or procedural in nature, the moral law embodied in the Law of Moses is eternal and unchangeable (Rom. 7:7–12). It was fulfilled by the gospel and confirmed by Christ (Matt. 5:17–18). See also *Moses.*

LAWFUL [LY]
Matt. 19:3 Is it *l* for a man to put away his wife
Mark 3:4 Is it *l* to do good on the sabbath...or...to do evil?
Mark 12:14 Is it *l* to give tribute to Caesar
1 Tim. 1:8 law is good, if a man use it *l'ly*

LAWYER/SCRIBE. An interpreter or teacher of the law in the synagogues and schools of N.T. times (Matt. 22:34–40), also called a *scribe* (Luke 11:53). See also *Scribe.*

LAY [ING]
Prov. 10:14 Wise men *l* up knowledge
Matt. 6:20 *l* up...treasures in heaven
Luke 9:58 Son of man hath not where to *l* his head
John 10:15 I [Jesus] *l* down my life for the sheep
John 15:13 man *l* down his life for his friends
1 Tim. 5:22 *L* hands suddenly on no man
Heb. 12:1 *l* aside...sin which doth...beset us
1 Pet. 2:1 *l'ing* aside all malice, and all guile

LAYING ON OF HANDS. A ritual blessing or ordination for service. This ritual was used by the high priest on the Day of Atonement. By placing his hands on the scapegoat, he ritually transferred the sins of the people to the animal (Lev. 16:21).

The patriarchs placed their hands on their descendants to confirm birthright or convey special blessings (Gen. 48:14, 18). The church at Antioch laid hands on Paul and Barnabas to confirm their calling as missionaries and to set them apart for this service (Acts 13:2–3).

LAZARUS. A brother of Mary and Martha whom Jesus raised from the dead. This event impressed the common people (John 11:41–45) but provoked the Jewish leaders to seek the death of both Jesus and Lazarus (John 11:47–57; 12:10–11).

LEAD. A heavy metal cast into weights (Zech. 5:8). It was also a useful agent for refining gold and silver (Num. 31:22–23). The word is used figuratively for the cleansing of Israel (Jer. 6:29).

LEAD [ETH]
Ps. 23:2 he [God] *l'eth* me beside the still waters
Ps. 61:2 *l* me to the rock that is higher than I

Isa. 11:6 a little child shall *l* them
Isa. 40:11 He [God]...gently *l* those...with young
Matt. 6:13 *l* us not into temptation
Matt. 7:14 narrow is the way, which *l'eth* unto life

LEAGUE (COMPACT, TREATY). An alliance of nations for fostering common interests and providing protection against enemies (2 Sam. 5:3). Leagues with the Canaanites and other pagan nations were prohibited (Exod. 23:31–33). *Compact:* NIV (1 Kings 5:12). *Treaty:* NIV, NRSV. See also *Alliance*.

LEAH. Laban's oldest daughter and Jacob's first wife (Gen. 29:16–25). She bore seven children (Gen. 29:32–35; 30:17–21) and remained loyal

LAZARUS. Jesus calls Lazarus back from the dead—four days after Lazarus died.

to Jacob when he had to flee from Laban (Gen. 31:17–20). See also *Jacob*.

LEANNOTH. A musical term of uncertain meaning in the title of Ps. 88.

LEARN [ED, ING]
Prov. 1:5 A wise man...will increase *l'ing*
Matt. 11:29 Take my [Jesus'] yoke...and *l* of me
Phil. 4:11 I [Paul] have *l'ed*...therewith to be content
2 Tim. 3:7 *l'ing*, and never able to come to...truth
Heb. 5:8 he [Jesus] were a Son, yet *l'ed* he obedience

LEAST
Matt. 25:40 ye have done it unto one of the *l* of these
Luke 7:28 *l* in the kingdom...greater than he [John the Baptist]
Luke 9:48 *l* among you all...shall be great
Eph. 3:8 Unto me [Paul]...less than the *l* of all saints

LEATHER. Treated animal skins used for clothing (Lev. 13:48), tent coverings (Exod. 26:14), sandals (Ezek. 16:10), and water and wine containers (Matt. 9:17). See also *Tanner*.

LEAVEN (YEAST). A fermentation agent used in making bread or wine (Hosea 7:4; 1 Cor. 5:6). Jesus used the term to warn against the teachings of the Pharisees and Sadducees (Matt. 16:11–12; Luke 12:1). *Yeast:* NIV, NRSV.

LEBANON. A rugged mountainous region in northern Palestine. Cedar and fir trees from Lebanon were used in the construction of the temple in Jerusalem under Solomon (1 Kings 5:6–10; 7:2).

LEBBAEUS. See *Judas, Brother of James*.

LEBO-HAMATH. See *Hamath*.

LED
Luke 4:1 Jesus...*l* by the Spirit into the wilderness
Luke 24:50 he [Jesus] *l* them out as far as to Bethany
Acts 8:32 He [Jesus] was *l* as a sheep to the slaughter

Rom. 8:14 *l* by the Spirit of God...are the sons of God
Gal. 5:18 if ye be *l* of the Spirit...not under the law

LEECH. See *Horseleach*.

LEEK. An onionlike plant. In the wilderness, the Israelites longed for this vegetable that they had enjoyed in Egypt (Num. 11:5).

LEES (DREGS). The waste that settled to the bottom of the container in the process of wine making (Isa. 25:6). The term is used figuratively for indifference or laziness (Jer. 48:11; Zeph. 1:12). *Dregs:* NIV, NRSV. See also *Dregs*.

LEGION
  1. A Roman military division consisting of several thousand foot soldiers plus cavalrymen (John 18:3–12).
  2. Any large number, such as angels available to Jesus (Matt. 26:53) or demons inhabiting a demoniac (Luke 8:30).

LEMUEL. An unknown king mentioned in the book of Proverbs (Prov. 31:1). Some scholars identify Lemuel as Solomon.

LENTIL. A plant of the pea family used in Jacob's pottage, or stew. Esau sold his birthright to Jacob for a bowl of this stew (Gen. 25:29–34).

LEOPARD. A wild animal of the cat family noted for its speed and fierceness (Jer. 5:6). The reign of the Messiah is pictured as a time when leopards will lie down with goats (Isa. 11:6).

LEPER [S]
2 Kings 5:1 Naaman...a mighty man...but he was a *l*
2 Kings 15:5 king [Azariah]...was a *l* unto...his death
Matt. 8:2 came a *l* and worshiped him [Jesus]
Matt. 11:5 *l's* are cleansed, and the deaf hear
Mark 14:3 house of Simon the *l*...[Jesus] sat at meat
Luke 17:12 met him [Jesus] ten men that were *l's*

LEPROSY. A variety of dreaded skin diseases. The Mosaic Law required a leper to live in isolation from others and to cry, "Unclean," so people could avoid him (Lev. 13:45–46). Jesus healed ten lepers and sent them to the priest for verification and purification (Luke 17:11–14). In the Old Testament, the prophet Elisha miraculously healed Nathan the Syrian of his leprosy (2 Kings 5:1–14).

LEVI

1. The third son of Jacob and Leah (Gen. 29:34) and ancestor of the Levites (Exod. 2:1; Num. 1:49). His three sons were ancestors of the three major branches of the Levitical priesthood: Kohathites, Gershonites, and Merarites (Gen. 46:11). See also *Levites; Tribes of Israel.*

2. Another name for Matthew. See *Matthew.*

A SPECIAL TASK FOR THE LEVITES

The numbering of the Levites in the wilderness (Num. 3:14-20) indicates that God had set these people apart for a special religious function. They were given the responsibility of taking care of the tabernacle and the temple. They also assisted the priests in their sacrificial duties (Num. 3:5-10).

LEVIATHAN. A sea monster, believed by some scholars to be the crocodile (Job 41:1). The word is also used figuratively to describe one of Israel's enemies, probably Egypt (Isa. 27:1).

LEVIRATE MARRIAGE. The marriage of a man to the widow of a deceased relative if she had no male heir. The purpose of this law was to provide an heir and an estate for the deceased relative and to provide for widows (Deut. 25:5–10). The union of Boaz and Ruth was a Levirate marriage (see Ruth 3–4). See also *Widow.*

LEVITES. Members of one of the twelve tribes of Israel who were descendants of Levi, third son of Jacob and Leah (Gen. 29:34). Moses and Aaron were Levites of the family of Kohath, Levi's son. When Canaan was divided, the Levites were assigned forty-eight towns in various tribal territories rather than a specific part of the land (Josh. 21:1–8). See also *Levitical Cities.*

LEVITICAL CITIES. Forty-eight cities assigned to the tribe of Levi instead of one specific territory (Num. 35:2–7). This arrangement gave the priestly class access to the spiritual needs of the other tribes. Six of these cities were designated as cities of refuge to protect those who accidentally killed persons from avenging relatives (Josh. 20:1–6). See also *Cities of Refuge.*

LEVITICUS, BOOK OF. An O.T. book filled with instructions about sanctification of the priests, regulations for worship and ceremonial offerings, and personal purification and dietary laws. The theme of the book is holiness. Because God is a holy God, He demands a holy and separated people who are totally committed to Him. This holiness is obtained through rituals of acceptable sacrifice, the emphasis of the first part of the book (chaps. 1–17); and rituals of sanctification, the theme of the book's second major section (chaps. 18–27).

These instructions in holiness and appropriate worship were revealed by the Lord to Moses during the Israelites' wandering years in the wilderness of Sinai. See also *Clean; Sacrifice; Unclean Animals.*

LIAR. One who tells untruths. Satan is the father of lies (John 8:44), and liars are his agents (Acts 5:3). Lying is associated with idolatry and perversion of truth (Rom. 1:18, 25).

LIAR [S]
Ps. 116:11 I said in my haste, All men are *l's*
Prov. 19:22 a poor man is better than a *l*
Rom. 3:4 let God be true, but every man a *l*
1 John 4:20 say, I love God...hateth his brother...a *l*

LIBERALITY. A generous spirit of helpfulness toward those in need. Ministering in such a spirit validates our faith (Gal. 6:10). Those who are generous will be treated with generosity (Luke 6:38).

LIBERTINES (FREEDMEN). Jews carried to Rome by Pompey as captives (63 B.C.) and later freed. Members of the Jerusalem synagogue who opposed Stephen were Libertines (Acts 6:9). *Freedmen:* NIV, NRSV.

LIBERTY
Lev. 25:10 hallow the fiftieth year, and proclaim *l*
Isa. 61:1 me [God's servant]...proclaim *l*
Luke 4:18 to set at *l* them that are bruised
Acts 26:32 This man [Paul] might have been set at *l*
1 Cor. 8:9 this *l* of yours become a stumblingblock
2 Cor. 3:17 where the Spirit of the Lord is, there is *l*
Gal. 5:1 the *l* wherewith Christ hath made us free

LIBYA/PHUT/LUBIM. The Greek name for the continent of Africa west of Egypt (Acts 2:10). Persons from Libya were in Jerusalem on the day of Pentecost (Acts 2:10). The man who carried Jesus' cross was from Cyrene, Libya's chief city (Matt. 27:32). In the O.T., Libya was also called *Phut* (Ezek. 27:10) and *Lubim* (Nah. 3:9). See also *Phut.*

LICE (GNATS). Small biting insects, perhaps sand ticks, gnats, or mosquitoes. An invasion of lice was the third plague sent by God to persuade the pharaoh to allow the Israelites to leave Egypt (Exod. 8:16–18). *Gnats:* NIV, NRSV. See also *Gnat.*

LICENTIOUSNESS. See *Lasciviousness.*

LIE. See *Liar.*

LIEUTENANT (SATRAP). A military officer (Ezra 8:36). Also a general title for the governor of a Persian province (Esther 3:12). *Satrap:* NIV, NRSV. See also *Satrap.*

LIFE
Ps. 23:6 follow me all the days of my *l*
Ps. 31:10 *l* is spent with grief
Prov. 18:21 Death and *l* are in the...tongue
Jer. 21:8 I [God] set before you...*l*, and...death
Matt. 6:25 thought for your *l*, what ye shall eat
Mark 8:35 will save his *l* shall lose it
John 1:4 him [Jesus] was *l*...light of men
John 3:36 believeth on the Son hath everlasting *l*
John 6:35 I [Jesus] am the bread of *l*
John 10:10 I [Jesus] am come that they might have *l*
John 11:25 I [Jesus] am the resurrection, and the *l*
John 15:13 man lay down his *l* for his friends
Rom. 6:23 gift of God is eternal *l* through Jesus Christ
1 John 5:12 He that hath the Son hath *l*
Rev. 22:17 take the water of *l* freely

LIFE, ETERNAL. See *Eternal Life.*

LIGHT. Illumination. God's first act of creation was to bring light into existence (Gen. 1:3–5). The word is used figuratively in the Bible to represent truth and goodness (Ps. 119:105), which dispel the darkness of ignorance and wickedness (Matt. 4:16; 5:15). See also *Darkness.*

LIGHT [S]
Gen. 1:16 the greater *l* to rule the day
Ps. 27:1 LORD is my *l* and my salvation
Isa. 9:2 people...in darkness have seen a great *l*
Isa. 60:1 Arise, shine; for thy *l* is come

L

LICE. *A woman in the Middle East checks a child for lice in a photo from the turn of the 1900s.*

Isa. 60:3 Gentiles shall come to thy [God's] *l*
Matt. 5:14 Ye are the *l* of the world
Matt. 11:30 my [Jesus'] yoke is easy...burden is *l*
Luke 2:32 A *l* to lighten the Gentiles
John 1:4 In him [Jesus] was life
John 1:9 That was the true *L* [Jesus]
John 8:12 I [Jesus] am the *l* of the world
Acts 13:47 set thee [Paul] to be a *l* of the Gentiles
Acts 26:18 turn them from darkness to *l*
Rom. 13:12 let us put on the armour of *l*
James 1:17 good gift...is...from the Father of *l's*
1 Pet. 2:9 [Jesus] hath called you...into his...*l*
1 John 1:5 God is *l*, and in him is no darkness
1 John 2:10 loveth his brother abideth in the *l*

LIGHTS, FEAST OF. See *Dedication, Feast of.*

LIGN ALOES. A tree from which perfume was made (Num. 24:6).

LIGURE (JACINTH). A precious stone in the breastplate of the high priest (Exod. 28:19). *Jacinth:* NIV, NRSV. See also *Jacinth.*

LILY. A general term for any flower resembling the lily (Song 5:13; Matt. 6:28).

LIME. Powdered limestone used for plaster and cement work (Isa. 33:12).

LINE (CORD). A method of measuring land with a cord (Josh. 2:18). Amos told Amaziah the priest that the Lord's punishment would include division of his land by line (Amos 7:17). *Cord:* NIV, NRSV. See also *Cord; Rope.*

LINEN. Cloth made from flax. The rich wore "fine linen" (1 Chron. 15:27), while the poor wore garments of unbleached flax. Linen was also used for curtains and veils in the tabernacle (Exod. 26:1). See also *Flax.*

LINTEL. A beam of wood over a door (Amos 9:1). In Egypt, the Hebrews were commanded to place blood from a sacrificial lamb over the lintels of their doors to avoid the angel of death (Exod. 12:22–23).

LION. A large catlike animal that preyed on sheep (1 Sam. 17:34–36). Those who offended the king of Persia were thrown into a den of lions (Dan. 6).

LIPS. A part of the human body associated with speaking. Moses described his poor speaking skills as "uncircumcised lips" (Exod. 6:12, 30). Covering the lips was a gesture of shame or mourning (Mic. 3:7). See also *Mouth; Throat; Tongue.*

LIQUOR. A fermented beverage associated with both festive occasions (Luke 15:23, 32) and drunkenness (Rom. 13:13). Paul counseled that believers should be "filled with the spirit" rather than strong drink (Eph. 5:18).

LITTER. A portable chair on poles upon which people were carried. A covering provided protection from the sun and rain (Isa. 66:20).

LIVE [ING, TH]
Gen. 2:7 man became a *l'ing* soul
Job 14:14 man die, shall he *l* again
Hab. 2:4 just shall *l* by his faith
Matt. 4:4 Man shall not *l* by bread alone
Mark 12:27 God of the dead, but...of the *l'ing*
Luke 24:5 Why seek...the *l'ing* among the dead
John 6:51 I [Jesus] am the *l'ing* bread
John 11:26 *l'th*...in me [Jesus] shall never die
Rom. 12:1 your bodies a *l'ing* sacrifice
Rom. 14:8 we *l*...or die, we are the Lord's
Phil. 1:21 to me [Paul] to *l* is Christ...die is gain
1 John 4:9 sent his...Son...we might *l* through him

LIVING GOD
Josh. 3:10 know that the *l-G* is among you
Matt. 16:16 Thou art the Christ...Son of the *l-G*
2 Cor. 6:16 for ye are the temple of the *l-G*
1 Tim. 3:15 church of the *l-G*...ground of the truth
Heb. 10:31 fearful...fall into the hands of the *l-G*

LIZARD. A reptile regarded as unclean by the Mosaic Law (Lev. 11:30). Numerous species of lizards are found in Palestine.

LOAF. See *Bread.*

LO-AMMI. A symbolic name meaning "not my people" given by Hosea to his second son to signify God's rejection of rebellious Israel (Hosea 1:8–9). See also *Hosea.*

LOAN. Borrowed money that had to be repaid with interest. To secure a loan, a debtor often pledged his children or himself (2 Kings 4:1; Amos 8:6). The Mosaic Law specified that loans to the poor were not to accrue interest (Exod. 22:25). See also *Debt; Usury.*

LOCUST. A migratory, plant-eating insect similar to the grasshopper. Swarms of locusts were sent as a plague on the Egyptians to convince the pharaoh to free the Israelite people (Exod. 10:1–4). See also *Cankerworm; Grasshopper; Palmerworm.*

LOD/LYDDA. A town near Joppa built by Shemed, a descendant of Benjamin (1 Chron. 8:12). Peter healed a lame man here (Acts 9:32–35; *Lydda*).

LOFT (UPPER ROOM, UPPER CHAMBER). The small room or upper story built on the flat roof of a house (1 Kings 17–19). *Upper room:* NIV; *upper chamber:* NRSV. See also *Upper Room.*

LOG. A unit of liquid measure equal to about one-twelfth of a hin (Lev. 14:10). See also *Hin.*

LOGOS. A Greek term that means both "the Word" and "reason." Jesus came into the world as the Logos, or the Word of God incarnate—in human form (John 1:1–3; Col. 1:15–17). See also *Word of God.*

LOINS. The midsection of the human body, just below the stomach. The Jewish people wrapped their loose garments around their loins when working or traveling to give greater freedom of movement (2 Kings 4:29). The word is used figuratively by Peter to advise his readers to be ready for Christ's return (1 Pet. 1:13).

LOIS. The grandmother of Timothy who was commended by Paul for her faith (2 Tim. 1:5). See also *Timothy.*

LONGSUFFERING (PATIENT). Forbearance or patience; an attribute of God's nature (Exod. 34:6; Ps. 86:15). His longsuffering is intended to bring people to repentance (2 Pet. 3:9). *Patient:* NIV, NRSV. See also *Forbearance; Patience.*

LORD. A rendering of various Hebrew words that refer to the God of Israel, Jesus, and persons in authority such as kings. The word is also used as a translation of the divine name *Yahweh*, which the Hebrews did not pronounce out of reverence (Gen. 12:8; Exod. 3:15–16). See also *Jehovah; Yahweh.*

LORD ALMIGHTY. See *Hosts, Lord of.*

LORD'S DAY. Sunday, the first day of the week and the Christian day of worship (Rev. 1:10). The Jewish day of rest and worship fell on Saturday, the last day of the week. But after

LORD'S PRAYER. A priest leads tourists through Jerusalem's Church of the Lord's Prayer, which commemorates the prayer Jesus taught His disciples. Sixty-two panels of the prayer decorate the church walls—each panel in a different language.

Christ's resurrection on the first day, Christians adopted this as their normal day of worship (Acts 20:7). The Christian custom of Sunday worship was already well established when the Roman emperor Constantine instituted the day as a Christian holiday in A.D. 321.

LORD'S PRAYER. Jesus' model prayer that He taught to His disciples in response to their request, "Lord, teach us to pray" (Luke 11:1). The prayer teaches us to approach God reverently (Matt. 6:9–10), to ask Him to meet our physical needs, and to seek His forgiveness and protection (Matt. 6:11–13). See also *Prayer; Sermon on the Mount.*

LORD'S SUPPER. Jesus' final meal with His disciples that He observed as a Passover ritual to symbolize His approaching death (Luke 22:15–16). In this act, He established a memorial supper, symbolizing His broken body and shed blood (Matt. 26:26–28), which Christians are enjoined to observe until the Lord's return (1 Cor. 11:26). See also *Love Feast.*

LO-RUHAMAH. A symbolic name for the prophet Hosea's daughter, meaning "unloved." It expressed God's displeasure with rebellious Israel (Hosea 1:6).

LOSE [TH]
Eccles. 3:6 A time to get, and a time to *l*
Matt. 10:39 *l'th* his life for my [Jesus'] sake shall find it
Mark 8:36 gain the whole world...*l* his own soul
Luke 17:33 Whosoever shall...save his life shall *l* it

LOSS

Acts 27:22 no *l* of any man's life...but of the ship
1 Cor. 3:15 man's work shall be burned, he shall suffer *l*
Phil. 3:7 things were gain to me [Paul]...I counted *l*

LOST

Ps. 119:176 I have gone astray like a *l* sheep
Luke 15:6 found my sheep which was *l*
Luke 19:10 Son of man is come to...save...*l*

LOT. Abraham's nephew. He accompanied Abraham to Canaan and traveled with him to Egypt to escape a famine (Gen. 12:5; 13:1). His uncle gave him first choice of Canaan's land on which to settle. He selected the fertile Jordan Valley (Gen. 13:10–11) and settled with his family near the pagan city of Sodom. Lot escaped the destruction of this city, but his wife looked back on their possessions and was turned into a pillar of salt (Gen. 19:15–26).

Lot was an ancestor of the Moabites and the Ammonites, tribes that became bitter enemies of the Israelites in later centuries (Gen. 19:37–38). See also *Ammonites; Lot's Wife; Moabites.*

LOTAN. See *Moab,* No. 2.

LOTS, CASTING OF. The practice of making decisions by casting small stones out of a container, similar to our modern practice of "drawing straws" (Josh. 18:6). It was believed that God made His will known through this method (Prov. 16:33). Matthias was chosen as an apostle to succeed Judas by the casting of lots (Acts 1:26).

LOT'S WIFE. The wife of Abraham's nephew who was turned into a pillar of salt as she looked back on Sodom (Gen. 19:26). Jesus used her experience to warn of the dangers of delay and disobedience (Luke 17:32).

LOVE. Unselfish, benevolent concern for other persons (1 Cor. 13:4–7; *charity:* KJV). To love God supremely and to love others unselfishly are the two most important commands of Jesus (Matt. 22:37–40). Christ's sacrificial death was the supreme expression of love (John 13:1; 15:13). See also *Agape.*

THE TEST OF LOVE

The message that Jesus taught from the very beginning of His ministry was "that we should love one another" (1 John 3:11). This love principle is a simple test for believers. God's love for us empowers our lives and motivates us to love others. Genuine love is an action as well as an emotion: "Let us not love in word, neither in tongue; but in deed and in truth" (1 John 3:18).

LOVE [D, TH]

Lev. 19:18 *l* thy neighbour as thyself
Deut. 6:5 *l* the LORD thy God with all thine heart
Ps. 119:97 how *l l* thy [God's] law
Prov. 17:17 friend *l'th* at all times
Eccles. 3:8 A time to *l,* and a time to hate
Song 8:7 Many waters cannot quench *l*
Hosea 11:4 I [God] drew them with...bands of *l*
Matt. 5:44 *L* your enemies, bless them that curse you
Matt. 22:39 shalt *l* thy neighbour as thyself
John 13:34 *l* one another; as I [Jesus]...*l'd* you
Rom. 5:8 God commendeth his *l* toward us
Rom. 8:37 conquerors through him [Jesus] that *l'd* us
2 Cor. 9:7 God *l'th* a cheerful giver
Eph. 4:15 speaking the truth in *l*
Eph. 5:25 Husbands, *l* your wives
Phil. 1:9 your *l* may abound yet more
1 Tim. 6:10 *l* of money is the root of all evil
2 Tim. 1:7 not given us the spirit of fear; but *l*
Heb. 12:6 whom the Lord *l'th* he chasteneth
1 John 2:10 He that *l'th* his brother abideth in the light
1 John 4:7 every one that *l'th* is born of God
1 John 4:19 We *l* him [Jesus], because he first *l'd* us

LOVE FEAST. A meal observed by the early churches in connection with the Lord's Supper. The purpose of the meal was to promote Christian fellowship and brotherly love (Acts 2:42, 46; 1 Cor. 10:16–17). Paul condemned some of the Corinthian Christians for their sinful behavior and selfish indulgence at such love feasts (1 Cor. 11:20–22). See also *Lord's Supper.*

LOVE ONE ANOTHER
John 13:34 ye *l-o-a*, as I [Jesus] have loved you
Rom. 13:8 Owe no man any thing, but to *l-o-a*
1 John 3:11 message...ye heard...we should *l-o-a*
1 John 4:7 let us *l-o-a*: for love is of God

LOVE THY NEIGHBOUR
Matt. 19:19 Thou shalt *l-t-n* as thyself
Gal. 5:14 law is fulfilled in one word...*l-t-n* as thyself
James 2:8 fulfil the royal law... *l-t-n* as thyself

LOVER. See *Paramour.*

LOVINGKINDNESS. God's gentle and steadfast love and mercy that He extends freely to His people (Pss. 63:3; 69:16; 103:4–12; Jer. 9:24). See also *Mercy.*

LUBIM. See *Libya.*

LUCAS. See *Luke.*

LUCIFER (MORNING STAR, DAY STAR). A name for the pompous king of Babylonia used by the prophet Isaiah (14:12). Some scholars believe this passage describes the fall of Satan (see Luke 10:18). *Morning star:* NIV; *day star:* NRSV. See also *Devil; Satan.*

LUCIUS. A Jewish Christian and kinsman of Paul who greeted believers at Rome (Rom. 16:21). He may be the same person as Lucius of Antioch (Acts 13:1).

LUCRE (GAIN). Material wealth, represented by money or goods (1 Sam. 8:3; Titus 1:7, 11). *Gain:* NIV, NRSV. See also *Filthy Lucre; Money.*

SOLOMON ON WEALTH

Solomon was one of the wealthiest people of his time (1 Kings 4:21–24), but he concluded that great riches were actually a burden because they brought such worries that a rich person couldn't enjoy his possessions (Eccl. 6:1). Jesus taught us not to worry about accumulating earthly riches but to "lay up for yourselves treasures in heaven...where thieves do not break through nor steal" (Matt. 6:20).

LUDIM (LUDITES, LUD). A people descended from Mizraim, a son of Ham (Gen. 10:13, 22). *Ludites:* NIV; *Lud:* NRSV.

LUKE/LUCAS. A Christian of Gentile descent, apparently a physician by vocation (Col. 4:14), who accompanied Paul on some of his missionary journeys (Acts 16:10; 20:5; 28:30). Luke wrote the Gospel that bears his name as well as the book of Acts. Paul commended Luke for his loyalty and friendship (2 Tim. 4:11). *Lucas:* Philem. 24. See also *Acts of the Apostles.*

LUKE, GOSPEL OF. One of the four Gospels of the N.T., written by Luke—a physician of Gentile background—to portray Jesus as the Savior of all people, Gentiles as well as Jews. Luke shows that Jesus associated with all types of people, including sinners (5:30; 15:2), the poor and outcasts (6:20–23; 16:19–31), and the Samaritans (17:11–19).

This theme of Christ as the universal Savior is continued in the book of Acts, which Luke wrote as a sequel to his Gospel. Acts tells how the gospel eventually spread from Jerusalem, the center of Judaism, to Rome, the capital city and nerve center of the Roman Empire. See also *Acts of the Apostles; Luke; Roman Empire.*

LUKEWARM. Neither hot nor cold; a term for indifference or complacency. Members of the church at Laodicea were criticized for their tepid spirituality (Rev. 3:16).

LUST. Evil desire, usually associated with the sex drive. Unbridled lust leads to sin and produces death (Eph. 2:3; James 1:14–15). Believers are warned to flee worldly lust (Titus 2:12) and "follow righteousness" (Gal. 5:16; 2 Tim. 2:22).

LUST [S]
Matt. 5:28 looketh on a woman to *l* after her
Mark 4:19 the *l's*...entering in, choke the word
James 4:3 that ye may consume it upon your *l's*
1 John 2:16 the *l* of the eyes...pride of life

LUZ. See *Bethel.*

LYCAONIA. A Roman province in southern Asia Minor visited by Paul. Cities in this region where he preached included Derbe, Lystra, and Iconium (Acts 14:1–7).

LYCIA. A province of Asia Minor that juts into the Mediterranean Sea. Paul made stops in Patara (Acts 21:1) and Myra, Lycia's major cities.

LYDDA. See *Lod.*

LYDIA. A businesswoman of Thyatira, a dealer in purple cloth, who was apparently converted under Paul's ministry at Philippi. After her conversion, she invited Paul and his friends to spend time in her home (Acts 16:14–15). See also *Philippi.*

LYE. See *Nitre.*

LYRE. See *Harp; Psaltery; Sackbut; Viol.*

LYSANIAS. The governor of Abilene, a region in Syria, when Herod was ruler over Galilee and when John the Baptist began his ministry (Luke 3:1). See also *Abilene.*

LYSIAS, CLAUDIUS. See *Claudius Lysias.*

LYSTRA. A city in the province of Lycaonia in central Asia Minor. Paul preached and healed a lame man here and was stoned by unbelieving Jews (Acts 14:6–20).

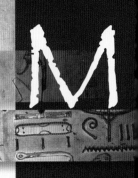

MACCABEES. A family of Jewish patriots who headed a religious revolt against the Syrians in Palestine from 167 to 63 B.C. See also *Antiochus IV Epiphanes.*

MACEDONIA. A mountainous country north of Greece and the first European territory visited by the apostle Paul. He planted churches in the cities of Philippi and Thessalonica (see Acts 16, 17, 20). Paul was beckoned to visit this region through his famous "Macedonian call"—a vision of a man pleading, "Come over into Macedonia, and help us" (Acts 16:9).

MACHINES. See *Engines.*

MACHIR (MAKIR). The oldest son of Manasseh (Josh. 17:1), a grandson of Joseph (Gen. 50:23), and a military hero who became the ancestor of the Macherites (1 Chron. 7:17–18). The Macherites won significant victories over the Amorites during the conquest of Canaan (Num. 32:39). *Makir:* NIV.

MACHPELAH. A field with a cave that Abraham bought as a burial ground (Gen. 23:7–18). Buried here were Abraham and Sarah, Isaac and Rebekah, and Jacob and Leah (Gen. 25:9–10; 49:29–33).

MAD (INSANE). A term for insanity, but it may also refer to anger or confusion (1 Cor. 14:23). David pretended to be insane in order to escape from Achish (1 Sam. 21:13–15). *Insane:* NIV.

MADAI. A son of Japheth and ancestor of the Medes (Gen. 10:2). See also *Medes.*

MADIAN. See *Midian,* No. 2.

MAGDALA. A city of Galilee near Capernaum, and probably the home of Mary Magdalene (Matt. 27:56).

MAGDALENE. See *Mary,* No. 2.

MAGI. See *Wise Men.*

MAGIC. The practice of illusion and sleight of hand to bring benefits or to deceive. The Israelites were forbidden to consult magicians or sorcerers (Lev. 19:31). See also *Sorcery; Witchcraft.*

MAGISTRATE. A civil authority or ruler. Magistrates in Philippi beat and imprisoned Paul and Silas for healing a demented slave girl (Acts 16:16–24).

MAGNIFICAT. The poem or song of the Virgin Mary upon learning she would give birth to the Messiah (Luke 1:46–55). Mary praised God for remembering "the lowliness of his servant" (NRSV) and for keeping His promise to bless Abraham and his descendants. See also *Mary,* No. 1.

MAGNIFY [IED]

Job 7:17 What is man, that thou [God] shouldest *m* him?
Ps. 40:16 The LORD be *m'ied*

MAGIC. In a moment beyond magic, the witch of Endor calls up the spirit of Samuel, at the request of King Saul. Famous as a medium, the woman is shocked and terrified when Samuel actually appears.

Luke 1:46 Mary said, My soul doth *m* the Lord
Phil. 1:20 Christ shall be *m'ied* in my [Paul's] body

MAGOG. See *Gog, Prince of Magog.*

MAHALATH, MAHALATH LEAN-NOTH. A phrase in the titles of Pss. 53 and 88 that probably refers to a musical instrument or a tune to be used in worship.

MAHANAIM. The name that Jacob gave to a site near the Jabbok River where he was visited by angels while waiting for his brother Esau (Gen. 32:1–2). The name means "two armies" or "two camps," perhaps referring to the meeting of his and Esau's forces or to the camps of Jacob and God. A city by the same name was established later on this site (Josh. 21:38).

MAHER-SHALAL-HASH-BAZ. The symbolic name given by the prophet Isaiah to his second son, meaning "hasten the booty" (Isa. 8:1–4). It signified that Assyria would conquer Israel and Syria.

MAHLON. Ruth's first husband and the elder son of Naomi. He died about ten years after his marriage to Ruth (Ruth 1:5).

MAID. A young unmarried woman, often of the servant class (Ruth 2:8). The word may also refer to a virgin or a female slave.

MAIDSERVANT. A female servant or handmaid (Ruth 3:9). Sometimes the word refers to a female slave. See also *Handmaid; Servant.*

MAIL, COAT OF. See *Brigandine.*

MAINSAIL (FORESAIL). The dominant or principal sail of a ship (Acts 27:40). *Foresail:* NIV, NRSV.

MAJESTY. A term referring to the dignity, power, and authority of a king or other high official (1 Chron. 29:24–25).

MAJOR PROPHETS. A term for the prophetic books that appear first in the O.T.—Isaiah, Jeremiah, Ezekiel, and Daniel—because of the longer length of their books. See also *Minor Prophets*.

MAKIR. See *Machir*.

MALACHI. An O.T. prophet and the author of the book that bears his name. His name means "my messenger" (Mal. 1:1). He lived after the Babylonian Exile and was probably a contemporary of the prophet Nehemiah.

MALACHI, BOOK OF. A short prophetic book of the O.T. written about 100 years after the Babylonian Exile and directed against shallow and meaningless worship practices. The prophet condemned the people of Israel for presenting defective animals as sacrifices (1:8) and withholding tithes and offerings (3:8–10). The book closes with a note of hope regarding the future Messiah (chap. 4).

MALCHI-SHUA/MELCHI-SHUA (MALKI-SHUA). A son of King Saul who was killed by the Philistines in the battle at Gilboa (1 Sam. 14:49). *Melchi-shua:* 1 Sam. 31:2; *Malki-shua:* NIV.

MALCHUS. A servant of the high priest whose ear was cut off by Peter. Jesus rebuked Peter and restored the severed ear (John 18:10–11).

MALE SLAVE. See *Manservant*.

MALEFACTOR (CRIMINAL). A rebel or criminal. Christ was crucified between two malefactors (Luke 23:32–33). *Criminal:* NIV, NRSV.

MALICE. A burning desire or intention to hurt others. Christians are urged to renounce malice (Eph. 4:31; 1 Pet. 2:1) and pray for those guilty of this sin (Matt. 5:44). See also *Hate*.

MALKI-SHUA. See *Malchi-shua*.

MALLOWS (HERB). A wild plant or shrub that thrived in the dry, salty regions near the Dead Sea. It was sometimes eaten by the poor (Job 30:3–4). *Herb:* NIV.

MALTA. See *Melita*.

MAMMON (MONEY, WEALTH). Material wealth or possessions. Christ warned that money or physical goods were false gods that should not be worshiped (Matt. 6:24). He urged believers to seek kingdom interests and promised that their material needs would be met (Matt. 6:33). *Money:* NIV; *wealth:* NRSV. See also *Filthy Lucre; Money*.

MAMRE
1. A town or district near Hebron where Abraham lived (Gen. 13:18; 18:1).
2. An Amorite chief and supporter of Abraham who gave his name to the plain where Abraham lived (Gen. 14:13).

MAN. The being created by God in His image and for His glory (Gen. 1:26–27; 9:6; Isa. 43:7). The crown of God's creation, man was given dominion over the natural world (Ps. 8:4–6). Man's sin has separated him from God (Rom. 3:23), but he may be redeemed by God's grace through faith in Christ (Rom. 3:22–24). See also *Fall of Man; Sin*.

MANASSEH/MANASSES
1. Joseph's firstborn son whose descendants became one of the tribes of Israel (Gen. 48:4–6) and occupied both sides of the Jordan

M

River (Josh. 16:4–9). *Manasses:* Rev. 7:6. See also *Tribes of Israel.*

2. The son and successor of Hezekiah as king of Judah (reigned about 687–642 B.C.; 2 Kings 20:21). A wicked ruler who encouraged pagan worship throughout Judah, Manasseh was captured and taken to Babylonia (2 Chron. 33:10–11). He later repented and was allowed to return to Jerusalem (2 Chron. 33:12–13). He was succeeded as king by his son Amon (2 Chron. 33:20).

MANDRAKE. A plant with an aromatic fragrance (Song 7:13). Its fruit was thought to generate fertility (Gen. 30:14–16).

MANEH (MINA). A Hebrew weight equal to fifty shekels, or about two pounds (Ezek. 45:12). *Mina:* NIV, NRSV.

MANGER. A feeding trough for livestock. The infant Jesus was laid in a manger after His birth (Luke 2:7–16).

MANIFEST [ED]

Mark 4:22 nothing hid, which shall not be *m'ed*
John 9:3 works of God...made *m* in him [Jesus]
1 Cor. 3:13 Every man's work shall be made *m*
1 John 3:8 this purpose the Son of God was *m'ed*
1 John 4:9 this [Jesus' death]...*m'ed* the love of God

MANNA. Food miraculously provided by the Lord for the Israelites in the wilderness (Num. 11:7–9). Called "bread from heaven" (Exod. 16:4), manna was provided daily except on the Sabbath for forty years. A different substance by this name drops from various trees, particularly the tamarisk, in the valleys near the Sinai wilderness. See also *Wilderness Wanderings.*

MANSERVANT (MALE SLAVE). A male domestic servant, often a slave (Exod. 21:32). *Male slave:* NIV, NRSV.

MANSLAYER (SLAYER). A person who accidentally killed another. This person could seek asylum from the avenging relatives of the victim in a city of refuge (Num. 35:6–12). *Slayer:* NRSV. See also *Avenger of Blood; Cities of Refuge.*

MANTLE (CLOAK). An outer garment, similar to a robe, made of coarse cloth or sheepskin. Elijah's mantle was placed on Elisha as a symbol of succession and blessing (1 Kings 19:19–21). *Cloak:* NIV. See also *Cloke.*

MARA. A name meaning "bitter" that was assumed by Naomi because it expressed her sorrow at the death of her husband and sons (Ruth 1:3–21).

MARANATHA. An Aramaic phrase meaning "come, O Lord" that expresses hope for the second coming of Jesus (1 Cor. 16:22). See also *Second Coming.*

MARBLE. Crystalline limestone noted for its beauty and durability as a building material. Marble was used in the building of the temple in Jerusalem (1 Chron. 29:2).

MARCUS. See *Mark.*

MARDUK. See *Merodach.*

MARESHAH. A town of Judah (Josh. 15:20, 44) built for defensive purposes by King Rehoboam (2 Chron. 11:5, 8). A battle between King Asa of Judah and King Zerah of Ethiopia was fought here (2 Chron. 14:9–10).

MARINER. A seaman or sailor. Paul reassured the mariners on his ship during a storm (Acts 27:31–36). See also *Ship.*

MARK, GOSPEL OF. One of the four Gospels of the N.T. and probably the first to be written, according to most scholars. A short Gospel of only sixteen chapters, Mark portrays Jesus as a person of action. He uses the words *immediately* (1:12; 2:8) and *straightway* (8:10) to show that Jesus was on an important mission for God and had no time to waste.

While Mark makes it clear that Jesus was the Son of God (15:39), he also emphasizes the humanity of Jesus more than the other Gospel writers, including incidents that reveal His disappointment (8:12), anger (11:15–17), sorrow (14:34), and fatigue (4:38). See also *Mark; Synoptic Gospels.*

MARK, JOHN/MARCUS. A relative of Barnabas who accompanied Paul and Barnabas on the first missionary journey as far as Perga and then returned to Jerusalem (Acts 13:3–5). After Paul's refusal to allow Mark to go with them on the second journey, Barnabas and Paul went their separate ways (Acts 15:36–41). In later years, Paul spoke of Mark with warmth and affection (Col. 4:10–11).

Most scholars believe Mark was the author of the Gospel of Mark, drawing perhaps on the reflections of Peter, who worked closely with Mark (1 Pet. 5:13; *Marcus*).

MARKER. See *Landmark.*

MARKET, MARKETPLACE. A large open area in a city where trade, public trials, and discussions were conducted (Acts 16:19–20). Children often played in this area (Luke 7:32). The Greek word for marketplace is *agora.*

MARRIAGE. The union of a man and a woman in commitment to each other as husband and wife. First instituted by God in the Garden of Eden (Gen. 2:18), marriage was also confirmed by Christ (Matt. 19:5). Love for and submission to one's mate were enjoined by Paul (Eph. 5:22–29). The love of a husband and wife for each other is symbolic of Christ's love for the Church (Eph. 5:23–25). See also *Betrothal; Dowry.*

Matt. 22:2 certain king...made a *m* for his son
Mark 12:25 neither marry, nor are given in *m*
John 2:1 there was a *m* in Cana of Galilee
Heb. 13:4 *M* is honourable in all...the bed undefiled
Rev. 19:9 called unto the *m* supper of the Lamb

MARROW. Tissue in the cavities of the bones. This word is used to illustrate the piercing power of God's Word (Heb. 4:12).

MARRY [IED]
Matt. 5:32 shall *m* her...divorced committeth adultery
Mark 10:11 put away his wife...*m* another, committeth adultery
Luke 14:20 *m'ied* a wife...I cannot come
1 Cor. 7:9 it is better to *m* than to burn
1 Cor. 7:33 that *m'ied* careth for...things...of...world
1 Tim. 5:14 the younger women *m*, bear children

MARS' HILL. See *Areopagus.*

MARTHA. The sister of Mary and Lazarus (John 11:1–2). Jesus rebuked Martha because of her unnecessary worry after she welcomed Him into her home (Luke 10:38–42). She grieved at the death of her brother, Lazarus, and sought Jesus' help (John 11:20–22).

MARVEL [LED]
Matt. 8:10 he [Jesus] *m'led*...not found so great faith
Mark 6:6 he [Jesus] *m'led*...their unbelief
Mark 15:44 Pilate *m'led* if he [Jesus]...already dead
John 3:7 *M* not that I [Jesus] said...Ye [Nicodemus] must be born again

MARVELLOUS
1 Chron. 16:24 Declare...his [God's] *m* works
Ps. 139:14 praise thee [God]...*m* are thy works
1 Pet. 2:9 called you out of darkness...*m* light
Rev. 15:3 Great and *m* are thy works, Lord

M

MARY

1. The earthly mother of Jesus (Matt. 1:16). A descendant of David from Bethlehem, Mary was engaged to Joseph (Luke 1:27). She was informed by an angel that she had been divinely chosen to give birth to the Messiah (Luke 1:28–33). She traveled with Joseph to Bethlehem (Luke 2:4–5) and gave birth to Jesus in fulfillment of prophecy (Isa. 7:14). She was forced to flee to Egypt with Joseph to escape Herod's slaughter of innocent children (Matt. 2:13–18). After she and Joseph returned to Nazareth, she gave birth to other children (Mark 6:3).

Mary visited Jerusalem during the Passover feast with Joseph and Jesus (Luke 2:41–46). She attended a marriage in Cana of Galilee, where Jesus worked His first miracle (John 2:3). She was present at the cross when Jesus commended her to John's care (John 19:25–27). Mary was also present with one of the praying groups in the upper room after the ascension of Jesus (Acts 1:14).

2. Mary Magdalene. A woman who witnessed the crucifixion and visited the tomb of Jesus (Matt. 27:55–61). She told the apostles of Jesus about the empty tomb (John 20:1–2) and was one of the first persons to see the risen Lord (Mark 16:9).

3. The sister of Martha and Lazarus. She was an eager listener at Jesus' feet while Martha performed household duties (Luke 10:38–41). She anointed the feet of Jesus and wiped them with her hair (John 12:1–3). Jesus defended her contemplative temperament (Luke 10:42).

4. The mother of the disciple James. This Mary is probably one of the women who provided food for Jesus and His disciples (Luke 8:2–3). She was also among those who went to the tomb to anoint Jesus' body and discovered He had been raised from the dead (Mark 16:1–8).

5. The mother of John Mark (Acts 12:12). Her house may have been a meeting place for the early Christians of Jerusalem.

6. A fellow believer at Rome greeted and commended by Paul in his letter to the Roman Christians (Rom. 16:6).

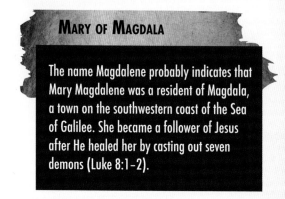

MARY OF MAGDALA

The name Magdalene probably indicates that Mary Magdalene was a resident of Magdala, a town on the southwestern coast of the Sea of Galilee. She became a follower of Jesus after He healed her by casting out seven demons (Luke 8:1-2).

MASCHIL. A Hebrew word that appears in the titles of thirteen psalms, apparently giving directions for the melody to be sung (Pss. 32, 42, 44–45, 52–55, 74, 78, 88–89, 142).

MASHAL. See *Misheal.*

MASON. A bricklayer or stoneworker. Phoenician masons were used by Solomon to build the temple in Jerusalem (1 Kings 5:17–18).

MASSAH AND MERIBAH. A site in the wilderness where the Israelites rebelled against Moses and Aaron (Exod. 17:4–7). Their complaints provoked the wrath of the Lord (Deut. 6:16). See also *Wilderness Wanderings.*

MAST. The rigging or wooden frame that held the sails on a ship (Ezek. 27:5). The word was used figuratively to show the strength of Israel's enemies (Isa. 33:23). See also *Ship.*

MASTER (TEACHER). A word meaning "teacher" that was often applied to Christ

(Matt. 22:16, 24). The word was also used in the O.T. as a term of respect for one's superiors (Gen. 24:48–49). *Teacher:* NIV, NRSV. See also *Teacher.*

MATHUSALA. See *Methuselah.*

MATTANIAH. See *Zedekiah.*

MATTHEW/LEVI. A tax collector who became a disciple of Jesus (Matt. 9:9) and writer of the Gospel that bears his name. He was also known as *Levi* (Mark 2:13–17; Luke 5:27–32). See also *Publican.*

MATTHEW, GOSPEL OF. One of the four Gospels of the N.T., written by a tax collector who became one of the twelve apostles of Jesus. This Gospel apparently was written to show the Jewish people that Jesus was the Messiah promised in the O.T., since many events in His life are interpreted as fulfillment of the Scriptures (1:22; 4:14; 12:17; 21:4; 27:35). In Matthew's genealogies, Jesus' ancestry through Joseph, His earthly father, is traced to two of the greatest personalities in Jewish history—Abraham (1:2) and David (1:6).

Matthew's Gospel also emphasizes the teaching ministry of Jesus, particularly His instructions to His disciples in the Sermon on the Mount (chaps. 5–7). Another prominent

M

MAST. With its sail rolled up and lashed to the mast, this fishing boat in 1938 is rowed ashore to Caesarea, on what is now Israel's Mediterranean coast.

theme of this Gospel is the kingdom of God or the kingdom of heaven (5:3; 6:33; 8:11; 12:28; 13:43–46; 19:23; 21:31; 25:34). See also *Beatitudes; Kingdom of God; Sermon on the Mount.*

MATTHIAS. The person who replaced Judas as an apostle. Matthias was chosen by the other apostles through the casting of lots (Acts 1:15–26). See also *Lots, Casting of; Twelve, The.*

MATTOCK (HOE). An agricultural tool, similar to a crude hoe, used to loosen the soil and remove roots (Isa. 7:25). *Hoe:* NIV, NRSV.

MATURITY. See *Perfection.*

MAUL (CLUB). A heavy club used as a weapon of war. The head was often studded with spikes (Prov. 25:18). *Club:* NIV, NRSV (Jer. 51:20).

MAW (STOMACH). The stomach of an animal that chews the cud. Considered a delicacy by the Hebrews, the maw, shoulders, and cheeks became the priests' portion of sacrificial animals (Deut. 18:3). *Stomach:* NRSV.

MAZZAROTH. A constellation of stars cited by Job as evidence of the power and sovereignty of God (Job 38:31–33).

MEAT FORK. See *Fleshhook.*

MEAT OFFERING. An offering of a sacrificial animal, made to atone for sin (1 Chron. 21:23).

MEDDLER. See *Busybody.*

MEDES, MEDIA. Descendants of Japheth (Gen. 10:2) and an ancient kingdom between the Tigris River and the Caspian Sea to which Sargon of Assyria brought Hebrew captives (2 Kings 17:6; 18:11).

MEDIATOR, CHRIST THE. A title of Christ that describes His work in reconciling us to God. His sacrificial death has made it possible for us to have peace with God and with one another (Eph. 2:13–16; 1 Tim. 2:5). As our mediator, He has made a full and final sacrifice for our salvation (Heb. 7:27; 9:15). See also *Atonement; Propitiation; Reconciliation.*

MEDICINE. A healing substance. In Bible times, medicine was made from herbs, fruits, and minerals. The balm of Gilead was probably made from the gum of an evergreen tree (Jer. 8:22). See also *Balm of Gilead; Healing.*

MEDITATE
Ps. 1:2 in his [God's] law doth he *m* day and night
Ps. 119:15 I will *m* in thy [God's] precepts
Luke 21:14 not to *m* before what ye shall answer

MEDITATION. Contemplation of spiritual truths (Ps. 119:148) that produces understanding (Ps. 49:3) and spiritual satisfaction (Ps. 63:5–6). Meditation on God's commands encourages obedience (Josh. 1:8).

MEDITERRANEAN SEA/GREAT SEA. The sea on Israel's western border that was also called the *Great Sea* (Josh. 9:1). Solomon used the Phoenicians to provide import/export services for Israel across this body of water (1 Kings 9:27). Paul often sailed the Mediterranean during his missionary journeys (Acts 9:30; 18:18; Acts 27).

MEDIUM. A communicator between humans and the spirit world. The Mosaic Law specified that professing mediums or wizards were to be stoned to death (Lev. 20:27). The prophet Isaiah warned against consulting the dead rather than listening to the Lord (Isa. 8:19–20; 19:3). See also *Enchanter; Familiar Spirit; Wizard.*

MEEKNESS. Kind, gentle, and humble. The meek will find spiritual satisfaction (Ps. 22:26) and receive God's instruction (Ps. 25:9). Paul cited meekness as one of the fruits of the spirit (Gal. 5:22–23). Jesus declared that the meek will inherit the earth (Matt. 5:5). See also *Humility*.

MEEK [NESS]
Num. 12:3 Moses was very *m*
Ps. 37:11 the *m* shall inherit the earth
Isa. 61:1 preach good tidings unto the *m*
Matt. 11:29 I [Jesus] am *m*...lowly in heart
Col. 3:12 Put on...kindness...*m'ness*

MEGIDDO/MEGIDDON. A fortified city west of the Jordan River in the plain of Jezreel associated with the great battle in the endtime. This city was the site of Barak's victory over Sisera (Judg. 4:14–16) and King Josiah's death in a battle with Pharaoh Necho of Egypt (2 Chron. 35:22–24). In this area the final battle between God and the forces of evil will occur (Zech. 12:11; Rev. 16:16). *Megiddon:* Zech. 12:11. See also *Armageddon*.

MELCHI-SHUA. See *Malchi-shua*.

MELCHIZEDEK/MELCHISEDEC. The king of Salem who received tithes from Abraham (Gen. 14:18–20) and who is depicted as a type of Christ because of his endless priesthood (Heb. 5:6–10; 7:15–17). The Messiah who is to come was also described as a priest "after the order of Melchizedek" (Ps. 110:4). *Melchisedec:* Heb. 7:11.

MELITA (MALTA). An island south of Sicily in the Mediterranean Sea where Paul was shipwrecked while sailing to Rome (Acts 28:1–8). *Malta:* NIV, NRSV.

MELON. A fruit, apparently grown in Egypt, for which the Israelites longed during their wilderness wanderings (Num. 11:5). Various melons are grown today in Palestine.

MEMBER [S]
Rom. 12:5 one body in Christ...*m's* one of another
1 Cor. 6:15 bodies are the *m's* of Christ
1 Cor. 12:26 one *m* suffer, all the *m's* suffer
James 3:5 tongue is a little *m*...boasteth great things

MEMPHIS. See *Noph*.

MENAHEM. A cruel and idolatrous king of Israel (ruled about 752–742 B.C.) who killed Shallum in order to assume the throne. He paid tribute to Tiglath-pileser III, king of Assyria, in order to maintain his power. He was succeeded by his son Pekahiah (2 Kings 15:16–22).

MEPHIBOSHETH/MERIB-BAAL. The crippled son of David's friend Jonathan and a grandson of King Saul. He was dropped by his nurse and crippled at age five when she received the news that Jonathan and Saul had been killed by the Philistines (2 Sam. 4:4). David sought out Mephibosheth,

MYSTERIOUS MELCHIZEDEK

This mysterious king of Salem (a shorter, older name for Jerusalem) was apparently a priest as well, and he worshiped the Lord just as Abraham did. He appears suddenly out of nowhere and disappears from the biblical record just as quickly (Gen. 14:18–20).

Centuries later, the writer of Hebrews in the New Testament declared that the priesthood of Jesus was far superior to that of Melchizedek, even though this strange priest of Abraham's time seemed supernatural in origin (see Heb. 7:1–17).

M

MERCY SEAT. Golden angelic images sit on the mercy seat, or cover, of the ark of the covenant—a chest containing the Ten Commandments. In this scene the Philistines have captured it and put it on display in their temple. But the statue of their god has toppled over in the presence of the ark.

restored his family's land, and gave him a place at the king's table. *Merib-baal:* 1 Chron. 8:34. See also *Jonathan*, No. 1.

MERARI. The third son of Levi and ancestor of the Merarites (Gen. 46:11; Exod. 6:19).

MERCIFUL
Deut. 21:8 Be *m*, O Lord, unto thy people
Ps. 103:8 Lord is *m*...slow to anger
Matt. 5:7 Blessed are...*m*...shall obtain mercy

MERCURIUS (HERMES). The Roman name for the pagan god Mercury—the god of commerce—and the name applied to Paul by the people of Lystra (Acts 14:12). *Hermes:* NIV, NRSV.

MERCY (COMPASSION). Compassion for others. God's mercies are abundant (1 Pet. 1:3) and fresh every morning (Lam. 3:22–

23). Paul described God as "the father of all mercies" (2 Cor. 1:3). Jesus commended the Samaritan who showed mercy for a wounded traveler (Luke 10:36–37). *Compassion:* NIV. See also *Compassion; Lovingkindness; Pity.*

Ps. 6:2 Have *m* upon me, O Lord; for I am weak
Ps. 23:6 *m* shall follow me all the days of my life
Ps. 103:17 *m* of the Lord is from everlasting
Hosea 6:6 For I [God] desired *m*...not sacrifice
Mic. 6:8 Lord require of thee, but to...love *m*
Eph. 2:4 God, who is rich in *m*...loved us
Titus 3:5 according to his [God's] *m* he saved us
1 Pet. 2:10 but now have obtained *m*

MERCY SEAT (COVER). The gold lid that covered the ark of the covenant. It was called the "mercy seat" because God was believed to be present to hear and answer prayers (Exod. 25:21–22). On the Day of Atonement, the high priest sprinkled blood of the sin offerings on the mercy seat as a propitiation for the people's sins (Lev. 16:11–16). *Cover:* NIV. See also *Ark of the Covenant; Atonement.*

MERIBAH. See *Massah* and *Meribah.*

MERIB-BAAL. See *Mephibosheth.*

MERODACH (MARDUK). The pagan Babylonian god of war whose overthrow was predicted by the prophet Jeremiah (Jer. 50:2). *Marduk:* NIV.

MERODACH-BALADAN. See *Berodach-baladan.*

MERRY
Prov. 15:13 A *m* heart maketh a cheerful countenance
Luke 15:23 bring...the fatted calf...eat, and be *m*
James 5:13 Is any *m*? let him sing psalms

MESHA. A king of Moab who led an unsuccessful invasion of Judah (2 Chron. 20). He offered his oldest son as a sacrifice to the pagan god Chemosh (2 Kings 3:4, 26–27).

MESHACH/MISHAEL. The Babylonian name for Daniel's friend who was thrown into the fiery furnace for refusing to worship an idol (Dan. 1:7). He was saved through God's miraculous intervention. His Hebrew name was *Mishael* (Dan. 1:6). See also *Daniel.*

MESOPOTAMIA/PADAN-ARAM. The territory between the Tigris and Euphrates rivers also known as *Padan-aram* (Gen. 25:20). Abraham and his family migrated from the city of Ur in this region (Gen. 11:31–32; Acts 7:2). The Babylonian Empire flourished in this general vicinity during O.T. times. Citizens of Mesopotamia were present in Jerusalem on the day of Pentecost (Acts 2:9). See also *Ur of the Chaldees.*

MESS. A portion of food served at a meal (2 Sam. 11:8). To receive a larger-than-usual mess or portion was considered an honor (Gen. 43:34).

MESSENGER. A person sent to deliver a special message. Jewish kings sent couriers to distant cities to proclaim laws and edicts (2 Chron. 36:22–23). John the Baptist was a messenger who prepared the people for the coming of Jesus (Matt. 11:10).

Prov. 13:17 A wicked *m* falleth into mischief
Mal. 3:1 I [God] will send my *m*
Luke 7:27 I send my [God's] *m* before thy face

MESSIAH/MESSIAS (ANOINTED ONE). The title given by the Jewish people to a future leader whom they expected to restore their honor and glory after delivering them from their oppressors (Dan. 9:25–26). Jesus fulfilled their longing but in an unexpected way by becoming a spiritual Savior who delivered believers from sin (Rom. 6:1–9). *Messias:* Greek form (John 1:41; 4:25). *Anointed one:* NIV. See also *Emmanuel; Jesus Christ; Son of God.*

METHUSELAH/MATHUSALA. A son of Enoch (Gen. 5:21) and the grandfather of Noah. Methuselah lived to the age of 969, the oldest recorded age in the Bible. *Mathusala:* Luke 3:37.

MICAH. A prophet of the O.T., a contemporary of Isaiah, whose ministry paralleled the reigns of kings Jotham, Ahaz, and Hezekiah from about 750 to 687 B.C. (Mic. 1:1). A stern prophet of judgment, he denounced the social injustices of his time (Mic. 2:1–3).

MICAH, BOOK OF. A short prophetic book of the O.T. known for its prediction

M

that the Messiah would be born in Bethlehem (5:2). The prophet also condemned the rich for oppressing the poor (2:1–2; 6:7–13) and announced that God's judgment against the nations of Judah and Israel would be wrought by the conquering Assyrians (chaps. 1; 3; 7:10–13).

THE REMNANT IN MICAH

The prophet Micah declared that God would make a new beginning with "the remnant of Israel" (Mic. 2:12). The remnant was a small group of people who remained faithful to the Lord, even though the rest of the nation was rebellious and disobedient. This theme of the faithful few occurs throughout the Bible.

MICAIAH. An O.T. prophet who predicted that King Ahab of Israel would be killed in a battle at Ramoth-gilead, in contrast to false prophets who assured the king he would be victorious (1 Kings 22:8–28). Micaiah was imprisoned for his stinging message, but his prediction was correct (1 Kings 22:29–39).

MICHAEL

1. A son of Jehoshaphat, king of Judah. Michael was killed by his brother Jehoram, who became king (2 Chron. 21:2–4).

2. An archangel who was thought to serve as a prince and guardian over the nation of Israel (Dan.10:21; 12:1). See also *Archangel.*

MICHAL. A daughter of King Saul presented to David as a wife after David killed 200 Philistine warriors (1 Sam. 14:49; 18:25–27). She died without children (2 Sam. 6:21–23).

MICHMAS/MICHMASH (MICMASH). A town near Jerusalem occupied by Saul's army (1 Sam. 13:2–4) and the site of Jonathan's victory over the Philistines (1 Sam. 14:6–18). Some Jewish citizens returned to this city after the Babylonian Exile (Ezra 2:27). *Michmash:* Isa. 10:28; *Micmash:* NIV.

MICHTAM. A word in the titles of Ps. 16 and Pss. 56–60, perhaps designating a particular type of psalm.

MIDDLE WALL OF PARTITION (BARRIER, DIVIDING WALL). The curtain or barrier in the Jewish temple at Jerusalem that separated Jews and Gentiles. Christ's atonement removed this partition and brought reconciliation and peace to people of all races and nationalities (Eph. 2:14–18). *Barrier:* NIV; *Dividing wall:* NRSV. See also *Court of the Gentiles.*

MIDIAN/MADIAN

1. A son of Abraham by Keturah and founder of the Midianites (Gen. 25:1–4; 1 Chron. 1:32–33).

2. A region in the Arabian desert east of the Jordan River, including Edom and the Sinai Peninsula, that was occupied by the Midianites (Exod. 2:15). *Madian:* Acts 7:29.

MIDIANITES. Nomadic traders who occupied the land of Midian. A band of Midianites probably bought Joseph and sold him as a slave in Egypt (Gen. 37:28). This tribe joined the Moabites in attacking Israel but failed (Num. 22). The Midianites were probably absorbed into the Moabites and the Arabs. See also *Gideon.*

MIDWIFE. A Hebrew woman who assisted other women in the process of childbirth. Many midwives refused the Egyptian pharaoh's orders to kill male children (Exod. 1:15–17).

MIGDOL. A place in northeastern Egypt where some citizens of Judah fled after their nation fell to the Babylonians about 587 B.C. (Jer. 44:1; 46:14).

MIGHT

Deut. 6:5 love the LORD...with all thy *m*
2 Sam. 6:14 David danced...all his *m*
Zech. 4:6 Not by *m*...but by my [God's] spirit
John 3:17 world through him [Jesus] *m* be saved
John 10:10 I [Jesus] am come that they *m* have life
John 20:31 ye *m* believe that Jesus is the Christ
Gal. 4:5 we *m* receive the adoption of sons
Eph. 6:10 be strong in the Lord...power of his *m*

MIGHTY

Exod. 1:7 children of Israel...waxed...*m*
2 Sam. 1:27 How are the *m* fallen
Job 12:19 He [God]...overthroweth the *m*
Job 36:5 Behold, God...is *m* in strength
Ps. 50:1 The *m* God...hath spoken
Isa. 9:6 his [Jesus'] name...called...*m* God
Acts 2:2 sound from heaven...rushing *m* wind
1 Cor. 1:26 not many *m*...are called
1 Cor. 1:27 weak things...confound the...*m*
1 Pet. 5:6 Humble yourselves...under the *m* hand of God

MIGHTY MEN (FIGHTING MEN, WARRIORS). The brave and loyal warriors who risked their lives for David before and after he became king (2 Sam. 23:8–39). Joshua also had the support of courageous warriors known as "mighty men of valor" (Josh. 1:14; 10:7). *Fighting men:* NIV; *warriors:* NRSV. See also *Jashobeam.*

MILCOM/MOLECH/MOLOCH. The supreme god of the Ammonites (1 Kings 11:5). Solomon built a sanctuary for worship of this pagan god, but it was destroyed during King Josiah's reforms (2 Kings 23:12–13). *Molech:* Lev. 20:2; *Molech:* NIV; *Moloch:* Acts 7:43. See also *Ammonites.*

MILE. A Roman unit for measuring distance that equaled 1,000 paces, or 1,616 yards. Jesus used this term to teach His followers forgiveness and forbearance (Matt. 5:41).

MILETUS/MILETUM. A coastal city of Asia Minor about forty miles south of Ephesus. Paul met the leaders of the Ephesian church here and gave a moving farewell address (Acts 20:15–38). *Miletum:* 2 Tim. 4:20.

MILK. A liquid for drinking and cheese making taken from cows, goats, sheep, and camels (Gen. 32:14–15). The word is also used figuratively to indicate abundance (Exod. 3:8) and the diet of immature Christians (1 Cor. 3:1–2).

MILL. A device for grinding grain into flour, consisting of two stones that pulverized the grain between them (Exod. 11:5; Matt. 24:41).

MILLENNIUM. A term for the period of 1,000 years described in Rev. 20:1–8. Opinions vary on how to interpret this period. Premillennialists expect a literal reign of 1,000 years by Christ on earth after His return. Postmillennialists believe that 1,000 years of peace will precede Christ's second coming, during which time much of the world will be converted. While believing in the Lord's return, amillennialists view Christ's millennial reign in a spiritual sense.

MILLET. A plant that produced small heads of grain, used for making bread (Ezek. 4:9).

MILLO/BETH-MILLO

1. A stronghold or fortress at Shechem whose occupants proclaimed Abimelech as

MILK. A Middle Eastern herder milks a camel. The milk is used as a drink and to make cheese, as is milk from goats and cows.

their king (Judg. 9:6, 20). *Beth-millo:* NIV, NRSV.

2. A defensive fortress tower built by David near Jerusalem (2 Sam. 5:9) and improved by Solomon in anticipation of an Assyrian siege (1 Kings 9:15).

MINA. See *Maneh; Pound.*

MIND. The reasoning faculty of human beings. In the Bible, the word *heart* often means "mind" (see Ps. 19:14). Those who reject God have corrupt minds (Rom. 1:28), and the carnally minded are enemies of God (Rom. 8:5–7). Jesus urged His followers to love God with all their minds and hearts (Matt. 22:37). Paul encouraged the Christians at Rome to have their minds renewed so they would know and follow the will of God (Rom. 12:2).

MIND [S]
Neh. 4:6 people had a *m* to work
Prov. 29:11 fool uttereth all his *m*
Mark 12:30 love the Lord...with all thy *m*
Rom. 11:34 hath known the *m* of the Lord
Phil. 2:2 being of one accord, of one *m*
Phil. 2:5 this *m* be in you...also in Christ
Phil. 4:7 peace of God...keep your hearts and *m's*
2 Tim. 1:7 not given us the spirit of fear; but...of a sound *m*

MINE. A place where metals were extracted from the earth. Iron and copper were mined in the area around the Dead Sea, especially during Solomon's reign (1 Kings 9:26–28).

MINISTER. A term for a person who serves others, often used interchangeably with the word *servant.* In addition to the religious meaning of the word, it is also applied to court attendants (1 Kings 10:5) and civil rulers (Rom. 13:4–6). All Christians are instructed to "preach the word" and perform duty as God's servants (2 Tim. 4:2–5). See also *Deacon; Pastor; Priest; Shepherd.*

MINISTER [ED, S]
Ps. 9:8 he [God] shall *m* judgment to the people
Matt. 20:28 Son of man came not to be *m'ed* unto
Mark 10:43 great among you, shall be your *m*
Rom. 15:16 I [Paul] should be...*m* of Jesus
2 Cor. 11:23 Are they *m's*...I [Paul] am more
Eph. 3:7 I [Paul] was made a *m*

MINISTRY. Service in the name of God. Such service demands a spirit of sacrificial service after the example of Christ (Matt. 20:26–28). All Christians are called to be ambassadors for Christ in the work of reconciliation (2 Cor. 5:18–20), to be fishers of men (Mark 1:17), and to perfect believers (Eph. 4:11–12).

Acts 6:4 give ourselves...to the *m* of the word
2 Tim. 4:5 make full proof of thy *m*
Heb. 8:6 he [Jesus] obtained a more excellent *m*

MINOR PROPHETS. The twelve prophets of the O.T. whose books were placed last in the prophetic writings because of their shorter length—Hosea, Joel, Amos, Obadiah, Jonah, Micah, Nahum, Habakkuk, Zephaniah, Haggai, Zechariah, and Malachi. See also *Major Prophets.*

MINSTREL (HARPIST, MUSICIAN). A singer or musician (2 Kings 3:15); often employed at funerals or wakes, as in the case of the daughter of Jairus (Matt. 9:23). *Harpist:* NIV; *musician:* NRSV.

MINT. A common, inexpensive herb used in medicine and for seasoning foods. Jesus mentioned mint as an object scrupulously tithed by the scribes and Pharisees (Matt. 23:23).

MIPHKAD (INSPECTION GATE, MUSTER GATE). A gate in the walls of Jerusalem or the temple rebuilt by Nehemiah (Neh. 3:31). *Inspection Gate:* NIV; *Muster Gate:* NRSV.

MIRACLE. God's intervention or suspension of the natural laws of the universe. Miracles are described in the N.T. as signs, wonders, mighty works, and powers. Most miracles in the Bible occurred during (1) the period of the Exodus (Exod. 7, 9, 10, 14), (2) Elijah's and Elisha's ministry (2 Kings 4:2–7), (3) the period of the Exile (Dan. 3:9–27), (4) the ministry of Jesus, when miracles attested to His divine power (Matt. 15:33–39), and (5) the ministry of the apostles, signifying their apostleship (Acts 3:6).

Jesus worked miracles to relieve suffering (Matt. 8:14–17), to raise the dead (Matt. 9:23–25), to calm nature (Luke 8:22–25), or to give an object lesson (Mark 11:12–14). See also *Sign.*

MIRACLES
John 2:11 beginning of *m* did Jesus in Cana
John 9:16 How can a man that is a sinner do such *m*?
Acts 6:8 Stephen...did great wonders and *m*
1 Cor. 12:10 To another the working of *m*

MIRIAM. The sister of Aaron and Moses (1 Chron. 6:3). Miriam protected her baby brother Moses by arranging for their mother, Jochebed, to care for him (Exod. 2:4–10). She led a triumphant song of praise and thanksgiving to God after the Israelites were delivered from the pursuing Egyptian army at the Red Sea (Exod. 15:2–21). She died and was buried in the wilderness at Kadesh (Num. 20:1). See also *Aaron; Jochebed; Moses.*

MISCHIEF MAKER. See *Busybody.*

MISHAEL. See *Meshach.*

MISHEAL (MISHAL). A city in the territory of Asher assigned to the Levites and designated

M

as a city of refuge (Josh. 19:26). *Mishal:* NIV, NRSV. See also *Cities of Refuge.*

MISSIONS. The process of carrying out Jesus' Great Commission to disciple and teach all peoples. Even in the O.T., Abraham was called to be a blessing to all nations (Gen. 12:1–3), and Jonah was sent by the Lord to preach to the pagan citizens of Nineveh (Jon. 1:2). Missions is prompted by God's love (John 3:16) and humankind's lost condition (Rom. 3:9–31).

Believers are equipped for the task of missions by the Holy Spirit's presence (Acts 1:8), the Word of God (Rom. 10:14–15), and the power of prayer (Acts 13:1–4). Christ's followers are to evangelize all nations, baptize believers, and teach His commands (Matt. 28:19–20). See also *Commission.*

MIST. A vapor or fog. The earth was watered by a mist before the first rainfall (Gen. 2:6). Mist and darkness are used figuratively to describe spiritual blindness (Acts 13:11).

MISTRESS. A woman with power or authority (Gen. 16:4–9). The Queen of Sheba (1 Kings 10:1–3) and Queen Jezebel (1 Kings 21:7–11) were women of authority.

MITE. The coin of smallest value in N.T. times, worth less than a penny. Jesus commended a poor widow's sacrificial gift of two mites (Mark 12:42).

MITRE (TURBAN). A headdress worn by the high priest (Lev. 8:9). A gold plate inscribed with "holiness to the Lord" was attached to the mitre (Exod. 39:28–31). *Turban:* NIV, NRSV.

MIZPAH. A place where Jacob and his father-in-law, Laban, made a covenant and agreed to a friendly separation. They marked the site with a pile of stones (Gen. 31:44–53).

MIZRAIM
1. The second son of Ham and father of Ludim (Gen. 10:6–13). His descendants settled in Egypt (Gen. 45:20; 50:11).
2. The Hebrew name for Egypt (Gen. 50:11). See *Egypt.*

MNASON. A Christian from the island of Cyprus who accompanied Paul on his last visit to Jerusalem (Acts 21:16).

MOAB
1. A son of Lot and an ancestor of the Moabites (Gen. 19:33–37).
2. The country of the Moabites, lying east of the Jordan River and the Dead Sea and south of the Arnon River (Deut. 1:5–7). Its earliest name was *Lotan* or *Lot,* since the inhabitants were descended from Lot (Gen. 19:37).

MOABITE STONE. A black memorial stone that confirms a significant event of the O.T.— the rebellion of King Mesha of Moab against King Ahaziah of Israel (2 Kings 3:4–27).

MOABITES. Pagan inhabitants of Moab, worshipers of Chemosh (Num. 21:29), and enemies of the Israelites. The strength of the Moabites varied across several centuries of Israel's history. The tribes of Reuben and Gad settled in northern Moab before the conquest of Canaan (Num. 32:1–37). Ehud won a significant victory over their forces during the period of the judges (Judg. 3:15–30). David also fought and conquered the Moabites (2 Sam. 8:2). Ruth was a native of Moab (Ruth 1:22).

MOCK [ED, ETH]
Prov. 17:5 Whoso *m'eth* the poor reproacheth his Maker
Jer. 20:7 I am in derision daily, every one *m'eth* me
Mark 10:34 they shall *m* him [Jesus]...scourge him

MOLE (CHAMELEON). A KJV word that probably refers to a chameleon or lizard since no true moles are found in Palestine (Lev. 11:30). *Chameleon:* NIV, NRSV.

MOLECH, MOLOCH. See *Milcom.*

MOLTEN SEA. A large bronze vessel made by King Hiram of Tyre for ceremonial use by the priests in Solomon's temple at Jerusalem (1 Kings 7:23). See also *Brasen Sea.*

MONEY. A medium of exchange. In O.T. times before the Babylonian Exile, money was a specific weight of precious metal, such as silver or gold. The coins of N.T. times were issued by the Romans or Greeks (Matt. 17:27; Mark 12:42). The earliest coins used in Palestine before the N.T. era were Persian in origin. See also *Filthy Lucre; Mammon.*

MONEYCHANGERS. Independent agents, much like cashiers, who converted money into "shekels of the sanctuary," which could be used in the temple at Jerusalem. These "bankers" provided worshipers with the required temple tax, the half-shekel (Exod. 30:13–15). Jesus denounced these moneychangers who were charging excess fees for their services. He overturned their tables and drove them out of the temple (Matt. 21:12).

MONOGAMY. The marriage of a man to one woman only—the pattern established by God in the Garden of Eden (Gen. 2:18–24). Many

MOABITE STONE. The Moabite Stone confirms the Bible's report that King Mesha of Moab drove off the Israelite army. The stone was apparently engraved at Mesha's command.

Luke 23:36 soldiers also *m'ed* him [Jesus]

Gal. 6:7 Be not deceived; God is not *m'ed*

MODERATION. Temperance and forbearance. Paul described moderation as a quality of gentleness to be practiced before others (Phil. 4:5). Christians are counseled to be moderate in all things (1 Cor. 9:25). See also *Temperance.*

M

M

of the O.T. patriarchs, such as Jacob, had more than one wife (Gen. 29:16–35). See also *Marriage; Polygamy.*

MONOTHEISM. The belief in one—and only one—supreme God, in contrast to polytheism, or the worship of several gods. The one true God is to be loved supremely and His commands taught to others (Deut. 6:4–7). God demands absolute loyalty, and He will not tolerate the worship of any other god by His people (Exod. 20:3–5). See also *Polytheism.*

MONTH. One of the twelve divisions of the year. The length of the Hebrew month was calculated from one new moon to the next (Num. 10:10; 28:11–14).

MOON. The heavenly body or satellite that revolves around the earth, referred to as the "lesser light" in the account of creation (Gen. 1:16). Each new moon marked the beginning of another Jewish month, and its arrival was celebrated with special sacrifices (Num. 28:11–15). The moon was worshiped under various names by pagan peoples, but God forbade this practice by the Hebrews (Deut. 4:19).

MOONSTONE. See *Diamond.*

MORDECAI. A Jewish exile in Persia who befriended Esther, helping her to become the king's favorite and assume the queenship (Esther 2:5–11). With Esther's help, Mordecai thwarted the plot of Haman to destroy the Jews (Esther 2:19–23). He was honored by the king and promoted (Esther 6:10–11; 8:1–2). See also *Ahasuerus; Esther; Haman.*

MORESHETH-GATH. The birthplace of Micah the prophet in the lowland plain of Judah (Mic. 1:14).

MORIAH. The mountainous area in Jerusalem where Abraham was commanded by God to sacrifice his son Isaac (Gen. 22:1–13). After God provided a sacrifice other than Isaac, Abraham renamed the site Jehovah-jireh, meaning "the Lord will provide" (Gen. 22:14).

MORNING STAR. The planet Venus as it appears at dawn and a figurative title for Christ (Rev. 22:16). Christ is described as the morning star, which outshines the light of prophetic witness (2 Pet. 1:19). See also *Day Star.*

MORTALITY. The human condition that leads eventually to physical death. Mortality is the common lot of all human beings, but it serves as the entrance to eternal life for believers (2 Cor. 5:4–6). For the Christian, bodily resurrection and eternal life are as certain as physical death (1 Cor. 15:21–23). See also *Eternal Life.*

MORTAR. A mixture of lime and sand used to build the tower of Babel (Gen. 11:3). The Israelites in Egypt worked with bricks and mortar (Exod. 1:14). See also *Untempered Mortar.*

MOSERA/MOSEROTH. A place in the wilderness where the Israelites camped on their way to Canaan. Aaron died and was buried here (Deut. 10:6). *Moseroth:* Num. 33:30–31.

MOSES. The great lawgiver and prophet of Israel who led the Hebrew people out of Egypt. His life is best understood in three forty-year periods.

Forty years in Egypt. Moses was born into slavery and hidden by his mother to escape the pharaoh's order that all male Hebrew babies should be killed (Exod. 1:22; 2:1–10). Discovered and "adopted" by the pharaoh's daughter, he was raised and schooled as an

MOSES. *Michelangelo's famous statue of Moses rests on display in Rome's Church of Saint Peter in Chains. The statue covers the tomb of Pope Julius II, a lover of art who lived at the time of Michelangelo. Julius died in 1513.*

M

Egyptian (Exod. 2:10). After killing an Egyptian who was abusing an Israelite slave, he became a fugitive in the desert (Exod. 2:14–15).

Forty years in Midian. Moses became a shepherd (Exod. 3:1) and married Zipporah, the daughter of a priest, and she bore two sons, Gershom and Eliezer (Exod. 18:3–4). Moses reluctantly answered God's call to lead His people out of slavery (Exod. 3:11–4:9) and returned to Egypt, where he enlisted his brother, Aaron, as his helper and spokesman (Exod. 4:27–31). After ten plagues sent by the Lord upon the Egyptians, the pharaoh finally released the Hebrews, who entered the wilderness area in the Sinai Peninsula under Moses' leadership.

Forty years in the wilderness. In the wilderness Moses received the Ten Commandments (Exod. 20:1–24) and other parts of the Mosaic Law, exhorted the people to remain faithful to God, built the tabernacle at God's command (Exod. 36–40), and sent spies to investigate Canaan (Num. 13). He impatiently struck a rock for water at Kadesh (Num. 20:1–13), a sin that led God to deny his entrance into the Promised Land. He died in Moab at Canaan's border at the age of 120 (Deut. 34:1–8). See also *Aaron; Law.*

MOST HIGH. A name for God signifying His majesty (Acts 7:48–49). The title was used by nonbelievers in both the O.T. (Num. 24:16) and the N.T. (Acts 16:17). See also *I AM; Jehovah; Yahweh.*

MOTE (SPECK). A small particle of anything. Jesus used this word to indicate the hypocrisy of those who found small flaws in others while ignoring major defects of their own (Matt. 7:3–5). *Speck:* NIV, NRSV.

MOTH. A destructive insect. Since wealthy Jews stored clothes that could be destroyed by moths, Jesus used the word to indicate the fleeting nature of earthly riches (Matt. 6:19–20).

MOTHER. A term for a female parent as well as a grandmother and other female relatives. Eve is regarded as the "mother of all living" (Gen. 3:20). Mothers are worthy of honor and obedience by those who desire long life (Exod. 20:12; Eph. 6:1–3). The prophets alluded to Israel as "mother" in denouncing the nation's shameful sins (Jer. 50:12–13; Ezek. 19).

MOUNT OLIVET. See *Olives, Mount of.*

MOUNT PARAN. See *Paran, Mount.*

MOUNTAIN REGION. See *Hill Country.*

MOUNTAIN SHEEP. See *Chamois.*

MOURN. To express grief or sorrow. The usual mourning period was seven days, but this was extended to thirty days for Moses and Aaron (Num. 20:29). Jesus mourned at the death of his friend Lazarus (John 11:33–36). See also *Sackcloth; Sorrow.*

MOURN [ETH, ING]
Job 2:11 Job's...friends...came...to *m* with him
Ps. 38:6 I am troubled...*m'ing* all the day long
Ps. 88:9 Mine eye *m'eth* by reason of affliction
Eccles. 3:4 a time to *m*, and a time to dance
Isa. 61:2 to comfort all that *m*
Matt. 5:4 Blessed are they that *m*...shall be comforted

MOUSE. A rodent (1 Sam. 6:5). Many species of these destructive animals are found in Palestine. They were "unclean" according to Mosaic Law (Lev. 11:29; Isa. 66:17).

MOUTH. The mouth has potential for good or evil. It may be used for praise and prayer (Ps.

34:1; 1 Sam. 1:12) or as an instrument of idolatry (1 Kings 19:18) and lying (1 Kings 22:13, 22). See also *Lips; Throat; Tongue.*

MOVE [D]
Gen. 1:2 Spirit of God *m'd* upon the...waters
Ps. 96:10 LORD reigneth...world...shall not be *m'd*
Mark 6:34 Jesus...was *m'd* with compassion
Acts 17:28 in him [God] we live...*m*...have our being
Heb. 12:28 kingdom which cannot be *m'd*

MUFFLER (VEIL, SCARF).
A veil or a long scarf worn about the head or chest (Isa. 3:19). *Veil:* NIV; *scarf:* NRSV.

MULBERRY (BALSAM).
A common tree of Palestine, probably the aspen, baca, or balsam (2 Sam. 5:23). *Balsam:* NIV, NRSV. See also *Sycamine.*

MULE.
A beast of burden of the horse family used extensively by the Hebrews. A runaway mule carried Absalom to his death (2 Sam. 18:9–15).

MULTITUDE [S]
Gen. 32:12 thy [Jacob's] seed...cannot be numbered for *m*
Matt. 5:1 seeing...*m's*, he [Jesus] went up into a mountain
Matt. 22:33 *m* heard this, they were astonished
Luke 2:13 with the angel a *m* of the heavenly host
John 6:2 great *m* followed him [Jesus]
Rev. 7:9 great *m*...no man could number

MURDER.
The unlawful killing of a human being, an act that was prohibited by Mosaic Law (Exod. 20:13). The Israelites exacted the death penalty for willful murder (Exod. 21:12; Lev. 24:17) but provided cities of refuge for persons guilty of manslaughter, or accidental

MUSIC. Listening to music from a small harp, called a lyre, was a popular form of relaxation in Bible times. David played a lyre to calm King Saul. This silver lyre is from Abraham's era and his hometown of Ur, in modern-day Iraq.

killing (Num. 35:11). Jesus warned of intense anger that could lead to murder (Matt. 5:20–25). See also *Avenger of Blood; Manslayer.*

MURMUR [ED, ING, INGS]
Exod. 15:24 people *m'ed* against Moses
Num. 14:27 I [God] have heard the *m'ings* of...Israel
Luke 5:30 Pharisees *m'ed* against his [Jesus'] disciples
John 7:12 much *m'ing*...concerning him [Jesus]

MURRAIN.
A mysterious disease and the fifth plague that God brought against the Egyptians, attacking their animals (Exod. 9:1–6). It may have been anthrax.

MUSIC. Vocal and instrumental music were prominent in temple choirs (2 Sam. 6:5). Musical instruments were invented by Jubal, son of Lamech (Gen. 4:21). The Hebrews used cymbals, harps, organs, pipes, psalteries, and trumpets in their worship (1 Chron. 15:16–22).

MUSICIAN. See *Minstrel*.

MUSTARD SEED. The tiny, almost microscopic seed from a common herb of Palestine. Jesus used this small seed to illustrate the power of faith in the believer's life (Luke 17:6). See also *Faith*.

MUSTER GATE. See *Miphkad*.

MUTH-LABBEN. A musical term in the title of Ps. 9, perhaps referring to the tune for the psalm.

MYRRH (RESIN). An aromatic gum resin found chiefly in Arabia (Gen. 37:25). It was one of the gifts presented to the infant Jesus (Matt. 2:11). Myrrh was used in incense perfume, anointing oil, embalming fluid, and medicine (Exod. 30:23; John 19:39). *Resin:* NRSV.

MYRTLE. A common evergreen shrub of Palestine. Its branches were used at the Feast of Tabernacles (Neh. 8:15). A myrtle tree in the desert was symbolic of God's provision for His people (Isa. 41:19; 55:13).

MYSTERY (SECRET). Something unknown except through divine revelation (Rom. 16:25–26). The gospel is called a mystery (Eph. 3:8–9). Jesus taught in parables to reveal the mysteries of God's kingdom to His disciples (Luke 8:10). Paul reveals that Christ within us inspires our hope to share in His glory (1 Cor. 15:51; Col. 1:26–27). *Secret:* NIV, NRSV.

MYSTERY [IES]

Mark 4:11 you [the disciples]...know the *m* of the kingdom
1 Cor. 2:7 we speak the wisdom of God in a *m*
1 Cor. 4:1 stewards of the *m'ies* of God
1 Cor. 13:2 though I [Paul]...understand all *m'ies*
1 Tim. 3:9 the *m* of the faith in a pure conscience

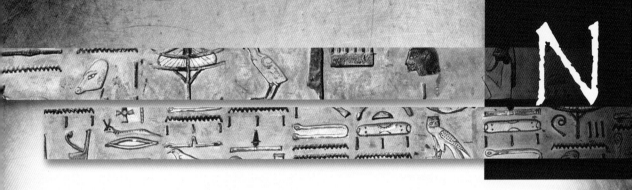

NAAMAN. A captain in the Syrian army who was healed of leprosy by the prophet Elisha. At first Naaman was reluctant to bathe in the Jordan River for healing, as commanded by Elisha. But he finally obeyed, received healing, and praised the God of Israel (2 Kings 5:1–15). Naaman was mentioned by Jesus (Luke 4:27).

NABAL. A wealthy herdsman who refused to provide food for the desperate David and his army in the wilderness. His wife, Abigail, secretly offered hospitality, and Nabal died ten days later (1 Sam. 25). See also *Abigail.*

NABOTH. An Israelite who was framed and killed by Jezebel so Ahab could take possession of Naboth's vineyard. God pronounced judgment against them for this despicable act (1 Kings 21:1–23).

NACHOR. See *Nahor.*

NADAB

1. The oldest son of Aaron who was destroyed, along with his brother Abihu, for offering "strange fire" to God (Lev. 10:1–2). See also *Abihu.*

2. A king of Israel (reigned about 910–909 B.C.), the son of Jeroboam I. Nadab was assassinated by Baasha, who succeeded him (1 Kings 15:25–31).

NAHASH. A king of Ammon who befriended David. David tried to return the favor to his son Hanun but was rejected (2 Sam. 10:1–4).

NAHOR/NACHOR. The grandfather of Abraham and father of Terah (Gen. 11:22–25). *Nachor:* Luke 3:34.

NAHUM. A prophet of Judah from Elkosh who prophesied against Nineveh before 612 B.C., probably during the reign of King Hezekiah (Nah. 1:1, 8, 13); author of the book of Nahum.

NAHUM, BOOK OF. A short prophetic book of the O.T. that predicted the downfall of the pagan nation of Assyria (3:7–19) because of the atrocities that it committed against God's people. The prophet portrays God as the sovereign Lord of history who has the final word in the conflict between good and evil (chap. 1). See also *Assyria.*

NAIN. A village south of Nazareth near the Sea of Galilee where Jesus raised a widow's son from the dead (Luke 7:11–17).

NAIOTH. A place in Ramah where David fled from King Saul and where Samuel lived and conducted his school for prophets (1 Sam. 19:18–20).

NAME. The word or title by which someone or something is known. Adam gave names to the animals (Gen. 2:20). Persons and places in the Bible often bore symbolic names, such as the children of the prophets Isaiah (Isa. 8:3) and Hosea (Hosea 1:4).

NAOMI. The mother-in-law of Ruth. After marrying Elimelech, Naomi moved to Moab to escape a famine. Her husband and two sons died, leaving Naomi and her two daughters-in-law alone. She returned to Bethlehem with Ruth and helped arrange Ruth's marriage to Boaz (see Ruth 1–4).

NAPHTALI

1. A son of Jacob by Bilhah, Rachel's maid (Gen. 30:1, 8). He received Jacob's blessing (Gen. 49:21–28), and his descendants became one of the twelve tribes of Israel.

2. The tribe consisting of Naphtali's descendants (Num. 1:42), who were assigned the fertile, mountainous territory in northern Palestine, including the cities of Hazor, Kedesh, and Ramah (Josh. 19:36–38; 20:7). Isaiah prophesied that Naphtali in "Galilee of the nations" would see a great light (Isa. 9:1–7). This was fulfilled in Jesus' Galilean ministry (Matt. 4:12–16). See also *Tribes of Israel.*

NAPHTUHIM (NAPTUHITES). The inhabitants of central Egypt who were descendants of Mizraim, son of Ham (Gen. 10:13). *Naptuhites:* NIV in 1 Chron. 1:11.

NAPKIN (CLOTH). A handkerchief or small piece of cloth (Luke 19:20) used for wiping perspiration and for other purposes (Acts 19:12). A similar cloth was used for binding the face and head of the dead for burial (John 11:44; 20:7). *Cloth:* NIV, NRSV. See also *Handkerchief.*

NARD. See *Spikenard.*

NATHAN

1. A son of David by Bath-sheba, born after David became king (1 Chron. 3:5). A brother of Solomon (2 Sam. 5:14), he is listed as an ancestor of Jesus (Luke 3:31).

2. The brave prophet who used an allegory to rebuke King David for his sin with Bath-sheba and his plot to kill Bath-sheba's husband, Uriah (2 Sam. 12:1–15). Nathan also assisted David when Adonijah attempted to seize the throne (1 Kings 1:8–45) and wrote histories of David's and Solomon's administrations (1 Chron. 29:29; 2 Chron. 9:29).

NATHAN THE BRAVE

The prophet Nathan dared to stand toe to toe with King David and tell him the unvarnished truth about his sin of adultery with Bath-sheba (2 Sam. 12:1-9). The prophets of the Old Testament were often called on by the Lord to deliver unpopular messages to those in authority (Jer. 36:27-32; Dan. 5:17-28).

NATHANAEL. See *Bartholomew.*

NATION. A word used in various ways in the Bible: (1) to describe all the inhabitants of a country or the country itself (Deut. 4:34); (2) to refer to natives of the same stock (Acts 26:4); (3) to denote the father or head of a tribe or clan; and (4) to refer to pagans or Gentiles (Isa. 9:2).

NATION [S]

Gen. 12:2 make of thee [Abraham] a great *n*
Exod. 19:6 ye [Israel] shall be...an holy *n*
Ps. 33:12 Blessed is the *n* whose God is the LORD
Ps. 72:11 all *n's* shall serve him [God]
Ps. 113:4 LORD is high above all *n's*
Prov. 14:34 Righteousness exalteth a *n*
Isa. 2:4 not lift up sword against *n*
Hag. 2:7 desire of all *n's* shall come
Matt. 25:32 before him [Jesus]...gathered all *n's*
Matt. 28:19 teach all *n's*, baptizing them
Luke 24:47 repentance...preached...among all *n's*
Acts 2:5 devout men, out of every *n*

NAZARETH. Jesus' hometown of Nazareth sits on a hilltop above the Galilean plains. Today, it's home to Jews, Christians, and Muslims.

Acts 17:26 [God] hath made of one blood all **n's**
1 Pet. 2:9 ye are a chosen generation...an holy **n**

NATURE. A word that refers to the physical universe as well as the essence or disposition of humans. God created the natural world and gave humans dominion over it (Gen. 1:1, 26–31). Adam and Eve's disobedience in the garden introduced sin and corrupted nature (Gen. 3:12–19).

The natural world is intended to draw humankind to the Creator (Ps. 8; Rom. 1:20), but the carnal nature of humans has worshiped the creature instead of the Creator (Rom. 1:25–26). Fallen humanity's faith in Christ appropriates God's divine nature (2 Pet. 1:3–4).

NAVE (RIM). The hub or rim of a wheel into which spokes were fitted (1 Kings 7:33). *Rim:* NIV, NRSV.

NAVEL. The umbilical connection of a newborn child with its mother. Ezekiel compared Jerusalem's unfaithfulness and neglect to an untended newborn child whose navel cord had not been cut (Ezek. 16:1–4).

NAZARENE (NAZOREAN). A native or inhabitant of the city of Nazareth. Since this was His hometown, Jesus was referred to as a "Nazarene" (Matt. 2:23). *Nazorean:* NRSV in Mark 1:23–24.

NAZARETH. An obscure town in Galilee that was the boyhood home of Jesus (Mark 1:24). Mary, Joseph, and Jesus returned to Nazareth after their flight into Egypt (Matt. 2:20–23). The town was located in the district of Galilee beside the plain of Esdraelon, fifteen miles southeast of Mount Carmel. Jesus was rejected by the townspeople of Nazareth at the beginning of His public ministry (Luke 4:16–30).

NAZARITE (NAZIRITE). A man or woman especially consecrated to God according to the law of the Nazarites (Num. 6:2). Voluntarily or because of a devout parent's promise, a Nazarite assumed strict

N

NAZARETH. A priest performs Mass in Nazareth's Church of the Annunciation. The church was built to commemorate the announcement that Gabriel made to the Virgin Mary—that Mary would have a son named Jesus.

religious vows, including abstaining from strong drink and not cutting his hair. The vow might be for life or a fixed period. Samson (Judg. 13:4–7), Samuel (1 Sam. 1:11, 28), and John the Baptist (Luke 1:15) were Nazarites. *Nazirite:* NIV, NRSV.

NEAPOLIS. A seaport at Philippi where Paul landed on the second missionary journey (Acts 16:11).

NEBO

1. The highest point of Mount Pisgah in Moab near Jericho where Moses died after viewing the Promised Land and where he was buried (Deut. 32:49; 34:5–6). See also *Pisgah, Mount.*

2. The Babylonian god of science and knowledge. Mount Nebo was possibly a center of Nebo worship. Isaiah declared the vanity of such idols (Isa. 46:1).

NEBUCHADNEZZAR/NEBU-CHADREZZAR. The king of Babylonia (reigned about 605–561 B.C.) who captured Jerusalem and carried Judah into exile about 587 B.C. (see Dan. 1–4). The only strong Babylonian king, he was the son of Nabopolassar, founder of the empire. After a revolt by King Zedekiah of Judah, Nebuchadnezzar destroyed Jerusalem, burned the temple, and carried the nation's leading citizens into exile (2 Kings 25:1–26). *Nebuchadrezzar:* Jer. 51:34. See also *Babylonia.*

NEBUZAR-ADAN. An officer in Nebuchadnezzar's army during the the Babylonian siege of Jerusalem (2 Kings 25:8–20). He looked after the prophet Jeremiah, who remained in Jerusalem after the siege (Jer. 39:11–14; 40:1–5).

NECHO. See *Pharaoh,* No. 4.

NECK. A word used figuratively for stubbornness ("stiffnecked," Deut. 9:6). It was also used to express the coming siege of Judah by Assyria (Isa. 8:8) and to represent the burden which circumcision would place on Gentile Christians (Acts 15:10).

NECKLACE. An ornament or jewelry worn around the neck. The pharaoh placed a gold chain around Joseph's neck, symbolizing his appointment as governor of Egypt (Gen. 41:41–43).

NECROMANCER. A person who communicated with the dead in an effort to foretell the future (1 Sam. 28:7–20). This practice was forbidden by the Mosaic Law (Deut. 18:11). See also *Familiar Spirit; Medium; Wizard.*

NEED [ETH]
Matt. 6:8 Father knoweth what...ye have **n** of
Luke 5:31 They that are whole **n** not a physician
1 Cor. 12:21 eye cannot say unto the hand...no **n** of thee
Phil. 4:19 my God shall supply all your **n**
2 Tim. 2:15 workman that **n'eth** not to be ashamed
Heb. 4:16 grace to help in time of **n**

NEEDLE. A tool for sewing. Jesus compared the difficulty of the wealthy reaching heaven with a camel passing through the eye of a needle (Matt. 19:24).

NEEDLEWORK. Embroidery or delicate sewing. Embroidered robes and curtains were used in the tabernacle (Exod. 28:39; 36:37).

NEEDY. See *Poor.*

NEGEV. See *South Country.*

NEGINAH/NEGINOTH. Phrases in the titles of several psalms that may refer to stringed instruments (Pss. 4, 6, 54, 55, 61, 67, 76).

N

NEHEMIAH. The governor of Jerusalem (445–433 B.C.) who helped rebuild the city wall after the Babylonian Exile; author of the book of Nehemiah. The son of Hathaliah, he was cupbearer to King Artaxerxes of Persia (Neh. 1:11; 2:1). He received permission from the king to return to Jerusalem to assist the returned exiles in their rebuilding efforts (Neh. 2:3–6).

In addition to rallying the people to rebuild the city wall, Nehemiah led a religious reform with the assistance of Ezra the priest (Neh. 8:1–13; 12:36). See also *Ezra*.

NEHEMIAH THE CUPBEARER

While they were in exile among the Babylonians and Persians, many of the Jewish citizens rose to responsible positions among their captors. For example, Nehemiah served as a cupbearer for King Artaxerxes of Persia (Neh. 1:11; 2:1). A cupbearer tasted the king's wine before he drank it to make sure it had not been poisoned by his enemies.

NEHEMIAH, BOOK OF. A historical book of the O.T. that records the rebuilding of Jerusalem's defensive wall after the Babylonian Exile under the leadership of Nehemiah (chaps. 1–7). The book also recounts the religious reforms undertaken by Nehemiah and Ezra. They led the people to renew the covenant and recommit themselves to God's law (chaps. 8–13). See also *Ezra*.

NEHILOTH. A musical term in the title of Ps. 5, probably denoting a wind instrument such as the flute.

NEIGHBOR. A fellow human being. Paul declared that Christians should love and speak truth to their neighbors (Rom. 13:9–10; Eph. 4:25). The Pharisees restricted the meaning of "neighbor" to people of their own nation, but Jesus' parable of the good Samaritan indicates that all people are neighbors and should help one another (Luke 10:25–37).

NEIGHBOUR
Exod. 20:16 not bear false witness against thy *n*
Lev. 19:18 thou shalt love thy *n* as thyself
Prov. 11:12 He that is void of wisdom despiseth his *n*
Prov. 24:28 Be not a witness against thy *n* without cause
Jer. 31:34 teach no more every man his *n*
Matt. 22:39 Thou shalt love thy *n* as thyself
James 2:8 fulfil the royal law...love thy *n* as thyself

NEPHEW. A term for a grandson (Judg. 12:14) or other male relative (Job 18:19). Lot, however, was a true nephew of Abraham (Gen. 11:27).

NERGAL. The Babylonian god of war that was worshiped by the men of Cuth (2 Kings 17:30). Images of Nergal were placed throughout Israel by King Shalmaneser of Assyria (2 Kings 17:24, 30).

NERGAL-SHAREZER. A Babylonian prince of King Nebuchadnezzar's court during the capture of Jerusalem (Jer. 39:1–3). He helped release Jeremiah from prison (Jer. 39:13–14).

NERO. The fifth emperor of Rome (reigned A.D. 54–68) who severely persecuted Christians. Although he is not named in the Bible, he is probably the emperor under whom Paul and Peter were martyred. Secular history confirms that Nero placed blame for Rome's great fire (A.D. 64) on the Christians and had many put to death during his administration. See also *Roman Empire*.

NERO. Roman Emperor Nero started the officially sanctioned persecution of Christians in A.D. 64, after accusing them of setting the fire that destroyed most of Rome. He committed suicide four years later.

NEST. The dwelling place of birds. The loftiness of the eagle's nest demonstrated the foolishness of man's pride (Jer. 49:16; Obad. 4).

NET. A meshed fabric used to capture birds or fish. The word is also used figuratively for entrapment of the innocent and for winning others to Christ (Matt. 4:18).

NETHANEEL (NETHANEL). A priest who helped transport the ark of the covenant to Jerusalem (1 Chron. 15:24). *Nethanel:* NIV, NRSV.

NETHER, NETHERMOST. The lower or lowest part. The children of Israel assembled on the nether part of Mount Sinai to receive a message from God (Exod. 19:17).

NETHINIM (TEMPLE SERVANTS). Persons assigned to do menial work as assistants to the priests in temple service. Many of the Nethinim were slaves or captives of war assigned to the Levites (Ezra 8:17–20). *Temple servants:* NIV, NRSV.

NETTLE. A shrub with prickly briars (Prov. 24:31), possibly a variety of acanthus that grew near the Mediterranean Sea (Isa. 34:13).

NEW

Exod. 1:8 arose a *n* king...knew not Joseph
Ps. 96:1 sing unto the LORD a *n* song
Eccles. 1:9 no *n* thing under the sun
Isa. 65:17 I [God] create *n* heavens...new earth
Lam. 3:23 they [God's mercies] are *n* every morning
Ezek. 36:26 a *n* spirit will I [God] put within you
Mark 2:22 no man putteth *n* wine into old bottles
Luke 22:20 cup is the *n* testament in my [Jesus'] blood
John 13:34 A *n* commandment I [Jesus] give unto you
2 Cor. 3:6 ministers of the *n* testament...of the spirit
2 Cor. 5:17 any man be in Christ, he is a *n* creature
2 Pet. 3:13 we...look for *n* heavens...new earth
Rev. 21:5 Behold, I [Jesus] make all things *n*

NEW BIRTH. A state of regeneration or resurrection from spiritual death (Rom. 6:4–8). The Holy Spirit brings regeneration (John 3:5–8) and produces a changed person. This comes about by God's grace through faith in Christ rather than through one's own efforts or good works (Eph. 2:8–9).

Regeneration helps the believer overcome the world and lead a victorious life (1 John 5:4–5). The new birth is required before a person can enter the kingdom of God (John 3:3–7). See also *Regeneration; Salvation.*

NEW COVENANT. God's final covenant with His people through which His grace is expressed to all believers. Prophesied by the prophet Jeremiah (Jer. 31:31–34), the new covenant was symbolized by Jesus at the Passover meal with His disciples. He called the cup the "new covenant in my blood" (Luke 22:20 NIV, NRSV). Christ, mediator of a new and better covenant, assures our eternal inheritance (Heb. 8:6–8, 13; 9:11–15; 12:24). See also *Covenant; Jeremiah, Book of; Testament.*

NEW JERUSALEM. See *Jerusalem.*

NEW MOON. See *Month; Moon.*

NEW TESTAMENT. The second major division of the Bible, composed of twenty-seven books, also known as the "new covenant" to magnify the coming of the Messiah and His redemptive ministry of grace (Jer. 31:31–34; Heb. 9:15). The complete N.T. in its current form was formally adopted by the Synod of Carthage in A.D. 397.

NIBHAZ. An idol of the Avites, a displaced Assyrian tribe that settled in Samaria (2 Kings 17:31). The name means "barker"; this pagan god was in the form of a dog-headed man.

NILE RIVER. The Nile River cuts a fertile swath through the desert nation of Egypt. (Inset) A space shuttle photo shows the Nile flowing north into the Mediterranean Sea. Above and to the right is the Red Sea with its two rabbit ears, the Gulf of Suez and the Gulf of Aqaba. Between the two gulfs is the rugged Sinai Peninsula, where Moses led the Israelites.

NICODEMUS. An influential Pharisee who talked with Jesus about the new birth. Jesus impressed upon him the necessity of being born of the Spirit (John 3:1–7). Later, Nicodemus cautioned the Jewish officials not to prejudge Jesus (John 7:50–51). He helped prepare Jesus' body for burial (John 19:39).

NICOLAITANES (NICOLAITANS). An early Christian sect whose origin is unknown. Their idolatrous practices were abhorrent to God, being compared to those of Balaam (Rev. 2:14). The church at Ephesus was commended for not tolerating the Nicolaitanes (Rev. 2:6), while the church at Pergamos was rebuked for its openness to their teachings (Rev. 2:15). *Nicolaitans:* NIV, NRSV.

NIGER. See *Simeon*, No. 3.

NIGHT. The period of the day when darkness prevails. The Creator established night along with the daylight hours (Gen. 1:5). The word is used figuratively to denote death (John 9:4) or sin (1 Thess. 5:5).

NIGHT HAWK (SCREECH OWL). An unclean bird, probably an owl or other night creature (Lev. 11:13–16; Deut. 14:15). *Screech owl:* NIV.

NILE RIVER. The great river of Egypt that begins in Africa and runs for more than 4,000 miles across Africa and Egypt, emptying finally into the Mediterranean Sea. In Bible times, Egypt's fertility depended on the annual overflow of the Nile (Isa. 23:10). God's judgment on Egypt was often depicted as a drying up of the Nile (Zech. 10:11). The baby Moses was hidden in the tall grass at the edge of the river (Exod. 2:3). See also *Egypt*.

NIMROD. Ham's grandson and son of Cush. A skilled hunter and warrior, he became a powerful king and empire builder in Babylonia, or Shinar (Gen. 10:8–12; 1 Chron. 1:8–10).

NINEVEH/NINEVE. The capital of Assyria on the Tigris River where the prophet Jonah preached God's message of judgment. Founded by Asshur, a son of Shem, Nineveh reached the height of wealth and splendor during Jonah's time (Jon. 3:3). It was taken by the Medes about 750 B.C. and destroyed by the Medes and Babylonians about 606 B.C. *Nineve:* Luke 11:32. See also *Assyria*.

NISAN. See *Abib*.

NISROCH. An Assyrian god with a temple at Nineveh where King Sennacherib was killed about 698 B.C. It was believed to have a human body with an eagle's head (2 Kings 19:36–37).

NITRE (SODA, LYE). A mineral used as a cleaning agent; probably lye or sodium carbonate (Jer. 2:22). *Soda:* NIV; *lye:* NRSV.

NO (THEBES). A thriving Egyptian city on both sides of the Nile River that served as the capital of upper Egypt (Nah. 3:8). No was destroyed in 81 B.C., as predicted by the prophet Jeremiah (Jer. 46:25). *Thebes:* NIV, NRSV.

NOADIAH. A prophetess who tried to frighten Nehemiah and hinder his efforts to rebuild the wall of Jerusalem (Neh. 6:14).

NOAH/NOE. The person chosen by the Lord to preserve life on earth by building an ark to escape the great flood. Noah was the son of Lamech and the father of Shem, Ham, and Japheth. He "found grace in the eyes of the Lord" (Gen. 6:8) and was described in the N.T. as a preacher of righteousness (2 Pet. 2:5). After building the ark, he entered with his family and selected animals (Gen. 7:1–24). Upon leaving the ark after the flood ended, he built an altar for worship (Gen. 8:18–22).

God covenanted with Noah not to destroy the earth with water again (Gen. 9:1–19). After pronouncing blessings and curses on his sons, he died at the age of 950 (Gen. 9:29). *Noe:* Greek form (Luke 17:26). See also *Ark, Noah's*.

NOAH'S FAITHFULNESS

The account of Noah and the flood (Gen. 6:9–8:22) shows that God has never given up hope for the salvation of humankind. The world may be filled with sin, but He always preserves a remnant, or a tiny minority, who remain faithful to Him and His commandments. This concept of the faithful remnant appears throughout the Bible, particularly the prophets of the Old Testament.

NOSE JEWELS. Nose rings, popular in Bible times, are still among the jewelry favored by various tribal groups throughout the Middle East.

NOB. A Levitical city near Jerusalem (Isa. 10:32) where David fled to escape King Saul's wrath (1 Sam. 21:1–6). Saul ordered the slaughter of eighty-five priests here in retaliation for their kindness to David (1 Sam. 22:13–19).

NOBLEMAN (ROYAL OFFICIAL). A person of high rank or privileged position. A nobleman sought Jesus to heal his son who was seriously ill (John 4:46–54). *Royal official:* NIV, NRSV.

NOD. An unknown region east of Eden where Cain lived after murdering his brother Abel (Gen. 4:16–17). It may have been China, according to some scholars.

NOE. See *Noah.*

NOMADS. Tent dwellers or herdsmen who moved from one grazing ground to another with their flocks (Gen. 13:5–7). The children of Israel led a nomadic life in the wilderness for forty years (Num. 14:2). See also *Wilderness Wanderings.*

NOOSE. See *Snare.*

NOPH (MEMPHIS). An ancient royal city of the Egyptians (Jer. 46:19). Noph flourished about 3000 to 2200 B.C. on the west bank of the Nile River about thirteen miles south of modern Cairo. Many of the royal pyramids and the famous Spinx are located near the site of this ancient city. *Memphis:* NIV, NRSV.

NORTHEASTER. See *Euroclydon.*

NOSE JEWELS. Jeweled rings worn in the nose as ornaments (2 Kings 19:28).

NOSE, NOSTRILS. God created man and breathed life into his nostrils (Gen. 2:7). The word is figurative of God's power in parting the Red Sea for the Israelites (Exod. 15:8).

NOTHING

Isa. 40:17 nations before him [God] are as *n*
Jer. 32:17 there is *n* too hard for thee [God]
Matt. 5:13 salt...good for *n*, but to be cast out
Matt. 17:20 *n* shall be impossible unto you
Mark 7:15 *n* from without a man...can defile him
John 3:27 receive *n*, except...given...from heaven
John 5:19 The Son [Jesus] can do *n* of himself
John 15:5 without me [Jesus] ye can do *n*
1 Cor. 7:19 Circumcision is *n*...uncircumcision is *n*
1 Tim. 6:7 For we brought *n* into this world
Heb. 7:19 For the law made *n* perfect

NOVICE (RECENT CONVERT). An inexperienced or recent Christian convert. Paul instructed Timothy that a novice in the faith lacked the maturity to serve as a pastor or bishop (1 Tim. 3:1, 6). *Recent convert:* NIV, NRSV.

NUMBERS, BOOK OF. An O.T. book that focuses on the Israelites in the wilderness of Sinai—a period of more than forty years between their departure from Egypt and their occupation of Canaan. The book describes the "numbering" of the people in two separate censuses (chaps. 1, 26); their failure to trust God and fear of the Canaanites (chap. 13); their numerous rebellions and complaints in the wilderness (chaps. 15–25); and their final preparation for entering the Land of Promise (chaps. 26–36). See also *Wilderness Wanderings.*

NUN. The father of Joshua and an Ephraimite servant of Moses who helped lead the Israelites across the Jordan River into the Promised Land (Josh. 1:1–2).

NURSE. A woman servant who breast-fed an infant or helped rear the child. Deborah, Rebecca's nurse, accompanied the family to Canaan (Gen. 24:59; 35:8).

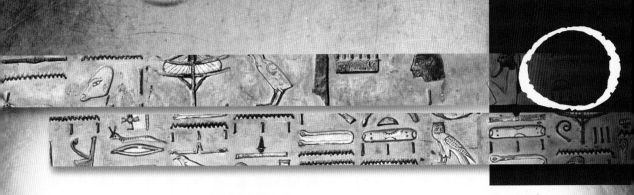

OAK. Several species of oak grew in Palestine. This word was often used to describe any strong tree or grove of trees (Gen. 35:8). Oak was used for carving idols (Isa. 44:9–15).

OAR. A paddle for pulling a ship through the water. Even large sailing vessels used oars when there was not enough wind to fill the sails (Isa. 33:21–23).

OATH. A solemn promise, often used to appeal to God to attest that a statement was true or to affirm a covenant (2 Sam. 21:7). The taking of an oath was accompanied by raising the hand or placing the hand under the thigh (Gen. 24:2–3). Jesus warned against careless oaths (Matt. 5:34–36).

Matt. 26:72 he [Peter] denied with an *o*
Heb. 7:20 not without an *o* he [Jesus] was made priest
James 5:12 neither by any other *o*: but let your yea be yea

OBADIAH

1. A prophet of Judah and author of the O.T. book that bears his name (Obad. 1). He probably lived after the destruction of Jerusalem in 587 B.C. Nothing more is known about him.

2. A godly servant of King Ahab who hid 100 prophets in a cave so they could escape Jezebel's wrath (1 Kings 18:3–16).

OBADIAH, BOOK OF. A prophetic book of only twenty-one verses—the shortest book in the O.T.—that pronounces judgment against the Edomites, the descendants of Esau (vv. 1,

6), because of their mistreatment of God's people, the Israelites (vv. 10–14). See also *Edomites; Esau.*

OBED-EDOM. A Philistine from the city of Gath. The ark of the covenant was left at his house for three months before its removal to Jerusalem (1 Chron. 13:13–14).

OBEDIENCE

Rom. 5:19 the *o* of one [Jesus]...many be made righteous
2 Cor. 10:5 captivity every thought to the *o* of Christ
Heb. 5:8 he [Jesus] were a Son, yet learned he *o*

OBEDIENT

Acts 6:7 company of the priests were *o* to the faith
Phil. 2:8 he [Jesus] humbled himself...*o* unto death
1 Pet. 1:14 As *o* children, not...according to the former lusts

OBEY. To submit to authority. Children are commanded to obey their parents (Exod. 20:12; Eph. 6:1–3). Jesus was obedient to Joseph and Mary (Luke 2:51). Jesus was perfectly obedient to the Father, and He requires obedience of His followers (Heb. 5:8–9).

OBEY [ED, ETH]

Gen. 22:18 thou [Abraham] hast *o'ed* my [God's] voice
Deut. 27:10 Thou shalt...*o* the voice of the LORD
1 Sam. 15:22 to *o* is better than sacrifice
Jer. 11:3 Cursed be the man...*o'eth* not...this covenant
Mark 4:41 the wind and the sea *o* him [Jesus]
Acts 5:29 We [the apostles]...*o* God rather than men
Col. 3:20 Children, *o* your parents
Heb. 11:8 he [Abraham]...*o'ed*...not knowing whither he went

OBLATION (GRAIN OFFERING). An offering sanctified to God, consisting usually of meat, meal, firstfruits of the harvest, or land (Lev. 2). *Grain offering:* NIV, NRSV.

OBSERVER OF TIMES. A person who was thought to be able to foretell the future through reading signs (Deut. 18:10–14). See also *Omen; Witchcraft.*

OFFENSE. A charge or accusation against another. Reconciling with an offended brother should take priority over making an offering (Matt. 5:24).

OFFER [ED, ING, INGS]
Gen. 4:4 LORD had respect unto Abel...his *o'ing*
Lev. 10:1 Nadab and Abihu...*o'ed* strange fire
Ps. 51:16 thou [God] delightest not in burnt *o'ing*
Ps. 96:8 bring an *o'ing*, and come into his [God's] courts
Mal. 3:8 have we robbed thee [God]? In tithes and *o'ings*
Matt. 5:24 be reconciled to thy brother...*o* thy gift
Eph. 5:2 Christ...hath given himself for us an *o'ing*
2 Tim. 4:6 I [Paul] am now ready to be *o'ed*
Heb. 7:27 he [Jesus] did once...*o'ed* up himself
Heb. 13:15 let us *o* the sacrifice of praise to God

OFFERING. Something given to God as a confession, consecration, expiation, or thanksgiving, generally as a part of worship. Because of his sinfulness and frailty, man recognizes he cannot covenant with God without obedience and faith. Jesus offered Himself as a full and final sacrifice for sin (Heb. 7:25–27). See also *Sacrifice.*

OFFSCOURING (SCUM, FILTH). Refuse; something vile or despised (Lam. 3:45). Paul indicated that faithful Christians may be regarded as "the scum of the earth" by the world (1 Cor. 4:13). *Scum:* NIV; *filth:* NRSV.

OFFSPRING. Children or descendants (Job 5:25). The risen Lord declared He was the "offspring of David" (Rev. 22:16). All people are regarded as offspring of the Creator (Acts 17:28–29). See also *Posterity; Seed.*

OG. An Amorite king of Bashan who was defeated by the Israelites at Edrei (Num. 21:33–35). His territory was assigned to the tribe of Manasseh (Deut. 3:1–13).

OIL. A liquid extracted from olives that was burned in lamps (Matt. 25:3) and used for anointing (Ps. 23:5), food preparation (1 Kings 17:12), and medicine (Luke 10:34). Olive groves were numerous throughout Palestine. See also *Anointing; Olive.*

OIL TREE (OLIVE). The olive tree or the oleaster shrub (Isa. 41:19). The oleaster shrub resembled the wild olive, with its yellow flowers and olivelike fruit. *Olive:* NIV, NRSV.

OINTMENT (PERFUME). A salve or perfumed oil made of olive oil and spices and used in anointing ceremonies. Jesus was anointed by devoted followers (Mark 14:3). *Perfume:* NIV in John 12:3. See also *Perfume.*

OLD GATE (JESHANAH GATE). A gate in the walls of Jerusalem rebuilt by Nehemiah (Neh. 3:6; 12:39). *Jeshanah Gate:* NIV.

OLD TESTAMENT. The first major section of the Bible, containing thirty-nine books, also known as the "old covenant" because it points to the coming of the new covenant in Jesus Christ. The O.T. begins with God's creation of the world, contains the books of the law and wisdom, and ends with prophecies that point to the Messiah's coming (Isa. 53; Jer. 31:31–34).

OLIVE. Black and green olives along with a jar of pickled lemons—each a delicious fruit of the tree—decorate a dinner table.

OLIVE. The fruit of the olive tree that was used for food and olive oil. The branch of an olive tree was a symbol of peace (Gen. 8:11). See also *Oil.*

OLIVES, MOUNT OF/MOUNT OLIVET. A hill in eastern Jerusalem where Jesus was betrayed by Judas on the night before His crucifixion (Matt. 26:30, 47). The branches of olive trees from the Mount of Olives were used to make booths for the Feast of Tabernacles (Neh. 8:15). *Mount Olivet:* Acts 1:12.

OMEGA. See *Alpha and Omega.*

OMEN. A sign used to predict future events. Witchcraft and divination were forbidden by the Mosaic Law (Deut. 18:10). The Lord frustrates the efforts of fortune-tellers and astrologers (Isa. 44:25). See also *Observer of Times; Witchcraft.*

OMER. A dry measure of two to three quarts (Exod. 16:16).

OMNIPOTENCE. The unlimited and infinite power that belongs to God. This characteristic of God's nature is expressed by His names *almighty* (Gen. 17:1) and *omnipotent* (Rev. 19:6). God controls nature (Amos 4:13) and the destiny of nations (Amos 1–2). God's omnipotence is also expressed by the Holy Spirit's power to convict and save (Rom. 15:19). See also *God; Sovereignty of God.*

OMNIPRESENCE. The universal presence of God. No person can hide from God (Jer. 23:23–24). Christ is present with the multitudes or with two or three believers (Matt. 18:20). God's Spirit is our companion in all circumstances (John 14:3, 18). See also *God*.

OMNISCIENCE. The infinite knowledge of God. The all-wise and all-knowing God requires no counselor (Isa. 40:13–14). Christ is the key who opens all the hidden treasures of God's wisdom and knowledge (Col. 2:2–3). God's Spirit reveals the "deep things of God" to those who are spiritually receptive (1 Cor. 2:10–14). See also *God*.

OMRI. The king of Israel who built Samaria as the capital city of the Northern Kingdom (reigned about 885–874 B.C.; 1 Kings 16:23–28). He was a wicked king who led the nation into idolatry (1 Kings 16:26). Omri was the father of the wicked king Ahab, who succeeded him (1 Kings 16:29), and grandfather of the ruthless queen Athaliah of Judah (2 Kings 11:1–3). See also *Samaria*.

ON

1. A Reubenite leader who joined Korah and others in the rebellion against Moses and Aaron in the wilderness (Num. 16:1–14).

2. A city of lower Egypt noted for its learning and its prominence as a center of sun worship. Joseph's wife, Asenath, was from this city (Gen. 41:45). *Aven:* Amos 1:5.

ONAN. The second son of Judah who was killed because of his failure to consummate a marriage union with Tamar, wife of his slain brother (Gen. 38:8–10).

ONESIMUS. A slave who was converted under Paul. Onesimus escaped and fled to Rome, where he came under Paul's influence. After his conversion, he returned to his master Philemon with an epistle from Paul, who

ONESIMUS THE SLAVE

Slavery was a common practice in New Testament times. Slaves were used as agricultural workers and as household servants. Onesimus was probably a household slave (Philem. 16). Paul did not condemn the practice of slavery, but he did commend the principle of Christian love to Philemon, the owner of Onesimus. Christian love and brotherhood were two factors that eventually led to the decline of slavery throughout the world.

appealed for Onesimus to be treated with mercy (Col. 4:9; Philem. 10). See also *Philemon*.

ONESIPHORUS. A Christian from Ephesus who befriended Paul when he was a prisoner in Rome. Paul commended him for his service (2 Tim. 1:16–18; 4:19).

ONION. A popular vegetable in Egypt and Palestine (Num. 11:5).

ONYCHA. An ingredient in sacred incense that Moses was instructed to prepare (Exod. 30:34). It may have come from the mollusk shell. See also *Incense*.

ONYX. A precious stone in the breastplate of the high priest (Exod. 28:20). David collected onyx to decorate the temple in Jerusalem (1 Chron. 29:2). See also *Sardonyx*.

OPHEL. The southern side of ancient Jerusalem's eastern hill, perhaps a tower or other fortification. The Nethinims lived here after the Babylonian Exile (Neh. 3:26).

OPHIR

1. A son of Joktan and grandson of Eber (Gen. 10:26–29).

2. The territory, probably in Arabia, populated by Ophir's descendants (Gen. 10:29–30). A famous gold-producing region, Ophir was visited by the ships of Solomon and the Phoenicians (1 Kings 9:26–28).

OPHRAH. Gideon's hometown in Manasseh where an angel assured him of the Lord's guidance and protection (Judg. 6:11–14).

OPPRESSOR. One who defrauds and mistreats others. The Egyptians oppressed the Hebrews by making them slaves (Exod. 3:9). See also *Taskmasters.*

ORACLE. A revelation or wise saying given to a person for his or her guidance (Rom. 3:2). Ministers are charged to preach God's message (1 Pet. 4:11).

ORCHARD. A garden planted with trees (Eccles. 2:5), particularly fruit-bearing trees (Song 4:13). See also *Garden.*

ORDAIN. To set a person apart for special service. Paul and Silas ordained elders for the churches they established (Acts 14:23). Paul instructed Titus to ordain elders to serve as leaders in the churches he served (Titus 1:5). Christ ordained His disciples to bear enduring fruit (John 15:16). See also *Consecration.*

ORDAIN [ED]

1 Chron. 17:9 I [God] will *o* a place for my people
Mark 3:14 he [Jesus] *o'ed* twelve...they should be with him
Rom. 13:1 powers that be are *o'ed* of God

ORDINANCES. Baptism and the Lord's Supper, rituals or procedures intended to commemorate the great events of redemption.

The Lord's Supper memorializes the shed blood and broken body of Christ (1 Cor. 11:23–26). Baptism symbolizes the death, burial, and resurrection of Jesus and the believer's victory over sin and death (Rom. 6:3–6). See also *Baptism; Lord's Supper.*

ORGAN (FLUTE, PIPE). A wind instrument made of reeds of various lengths and played by blowing across their open ends (Gen. 4:21). *Flute:* NIV; *pipe:* NRSV. See also *Pipe.*

ORION. A constellation of stars cited as evidence of God's power (Job 9:9).

ORNAMENTS. Items of jewelry, such as rings on the fingers, ears, and nose (Isa. 3:18–23). Bracelets and earrings were presented to Rebekah by Abraham's servant (Gen. 24:22).

ORNAN. See *Araunah.*

ORONTES. The major river of Syria. The important cities of Kadesh, Riblah (2 Kings 23:33), and Hamath (1 Kings 8:65) were situated on the Orontes.

ORPAH. A Moabite woman who married Chilion, son of Naomi and Elimelech. She returned to her own people after the death of her husband (Ruth 1:4–15).

ORPHANS. Children whose parents have died. Kindness toward orphans was commanded by the Mosaic Law (Deut. 24:17). Visiting orphans and widows was considered a mark of true religion, or godliness (James 1:27). Jesus promised that believers would not be treated as orphans (John 14:18).

OSEE. See *Hosea.*

OSHEA. See *Joshua*.

OSNAPPAR. See *Asnapper*.

OSPRAY (BLACK VULTURE). An unclean bird, perhaps similar to the eagle or hawk (Lev. 11:13). *Black vulture:* NIV. See also *Gier Eagle*.

OSSIFRAGE (VULTURE). An unclean bird, probably similar to the eagle, or perhaps the vulture (Deut. 14:12). *Vulture:* NIV, NRSV. See also *Vulture*.

OSTRICH. A large, flightless bird noted for its speed (Job 39:13–18) and its mournful cry (Mic. 1:8, NRSV). It was listed as "unclean" in the Mosaic Law (Lev. 11:16, NRSV).

OTHNIEL. The first judge of Israel who defeated the king of Mesopotamia (Judg. 3:9–11). See also *Judges of Israel*.

OUCHES (GOLD FILIGREE SETTINGS). Sockets or mountings in which precious stones were set in the ephod of the high priest (Exod. 28:11–14). *Gold filigree settings:* NIV, NRSV.

OUGHT

Luke 18:1 men *o* always to pray, and not to faint
John 13:14 ye also *o* to wash one another's feet
Acts 5:29 We [the apostles]...*o* to obey God rather than men
Rom. 12:3 think of himself more highly...he *o* to think
Eph. 5:28 So *o* men to love...wives as their own bodies
Col. 4:6 ye may know how ye *o* to answer every man
1 John 4:11 Beloved...we *o* also to love one another

OVEN. Replica of a clay oven and stove used in Bible times. Hot coals burned inside, while food cooked on top. Bread was baked inside the oven, on top of the coals.

OUTCASTS. Dispossessed people. This word was used by the prophets to describe the Jews scattered among foreign nations (Isa. 11:12; Jer. 30:17). Jesus had compassion on lepers who were social outcasts (Luke 17:11–19). See also *Remnant.*

OVEN. A large earthenware container filled with hot coals and ashes. Utensils with food were placed over the opening for cooking (Hosea 7:7).

OVERCOME [TH]
Num. 13:30 we are well able to *o* it [Canaan]
John 16:33 I [Jesus] have *o* the world
Rom. 12:21 Be not *o* of evil, but *o* evil with good
1 John 5:4 the victory that *o'th* the world
Rev. 21:7 He that *o'th* shall inherit all things

OVERSEER. An elder, bishop, presbyter, or supervisor in charge of a congregation (Acts 20:28).

OWL. A bird of prey with large eyes and strong claws that hunts at night (Ps. 102:6). It was considered unclean by the Israelites (Lev. 11:13–17).

OWNER. See *Householder.*

OX. An animal of the cow family used for plowing (Deut. 22:10), for threshing grain (Deut. 25:4), and as a beast of burden (1 Chron. 12:40). Oxen also supplied milk and meat and were used as sacrifices (Lev. 17:3–4). See also *Bull; Bullock.*

OX GOAD. A spike used to drive oxen. Shamgar, judge and deliverer of Israel, killed 600 Philistines with an ox goad (Judg. 3:31).

OZIAS. See *Uzziah.*

0

P

PACE (STEP). A measure of length, based on the step of a man (2 Sam. 6:13). *Step:* NIV.

PADAN-ARAM. See *Mesopotamia.*

PADDLE. A spadelike tool at the butt end of a spear for digging a hole in the ground to cover waste (Deut. 23:13).

PAINT. A cosmetic cover. Hebrew women painted around their eyes, but the practice was condemned (Jer. 4:30). Paint was also used to color walls and adorn pagan temples (Ezek. 23:14).

PALACE. A residence for a king or other high official. Solomon's palace on Mount Zion near the temple featured an ivory throne (1 Kings 7:1–12; 10:18). Jesus was tried in the hall of Herod's palace by Pilate (Mark 15:16) and in the palace of Caiaphas the high priest (Matt. 26:57–58).

PALESTINE/PALESTINA. The territory of the Canaanites that became known as the land of the people of Israel. The name *Palestine* referred originally to the territory of the Philistines, especially the coastal plain south of Mount Carmel. The name was extended during the Christian era to include all of the Holy Land, including both sides of the Jordan River and the Dead Sea region south to Egypt.

After the Canaanites were displaced, the country was called the land of Israel (1 Sam. 13:19) and the "land of promise" (Heb. 11:9). Three great world religions—Judaism, Christianity, and Islam—originated here. *Palestina:* Exod. 15:14. See also *Canaan,* No. 2; *Land of Promise.*

PALM. A tropical tree (Exod. 15:27), so named because its leaf resembles a human hand. Most biblical references are to the date palm, which grows sixty to eighty feet tall.

PALMERWORM (LOCUST). A caterpillar or a distinct species of locust that ate vegetation (Joel 1:4). This insect or worm was sent as a plague upon rebellious Israel (Amos 4:9–10). *Locust:* NIV, NRSV. See also *Locust.*

PALSY. A disease that caused paralysis and possible loss of feeling (Acts 8:7). Although it was regarded as incurable, Jesus healed many people with palsy (Matt. 4:24).

PAMPHYLIA. A coastal region in southern Asia Minor visited by Paul (Acts 13:13; 14:24). Perga was its capital and Attalia its main seaport (Acts 14:25). Residents of Pamphylia were present in Jerusalem on the day of Pentecost (Acts 2:1–10).

PAN (GRIDDLE). A utensil or cooking container (Lev. 6:21). *Griddle:* NIV, NRSV.

PANTHEISM. A doctrine that teaches that God and His universe are identical, or that

P

PALACE. This is a model of the Jerusalem palace of Herod the Great—one of many elegant residences for this vicious king of the Jews appointed by Rome.

physical things are merely attributes of an all-encompassing God. Jews and Christians reject this doctrine because God created the universe separate and apart from Himself (Gen. 1:1). He exists apart from, in addition to, and above the world (see Ps. 8). See also *Creation*.

PAPER. Papyrus, or an ancient writing material made from reeds that grew on the banks of the Nile River in Egypt (2 John 12). See also *Bulrush; Ink; Reed; Writing*.

PAPHOS. A city on the island of Cyprus where Paul blinded Elymas the magician. This led to the conversion of the Roman governor, Sergius Paulus (Acts 13:6–13).

PAPS (BREASTS). An Old English word for "breasts" (Luke 11:27). *Breasts:* NRSV.

PAPYRUS. See *Bulrush*.

PARABLE. A short story drawn from daily life that is used to convey an important truth; a favorite teaching device used by Jesus (Matt. 13:3). In the O.T., Nathan told a parable to convict King David of his sin of adultery (2 Sam. 12:1–7). Jesus used parables to present truth to His receptive hearers and to conceal the lesson from those who were critical or unreceptive (Matt. 13:10–16, 35). Drawn from daily life, His parables revealed lessons about salvation, the kingdom, and the future life (Luke 15).

PARACLETE (COUNSELOR, ADVOCATE). A Greek word for the Holy Spirit that expresses the idea of a helper called to one's side. It is translated as "Comforter" in the Gospels (John 14:16). *Counselor:* NIV; *Advocate:* NRSV. Also *advocate* in 1 John 2:1. See also *Advocate; Comforter; Helper; Holy Spirit*.

PARADISE. A word that describes the heavenly home of the redeemed (2 Cor. 12:4). Jesus used the term to comfort the repentant dying thief (Luke 23:43). See also *Heaven; Heavenly City*.

PARADOX. A contradictory statement that expresses a great truth; a favorite teaching device of Jesus. He declared that a person can find his or her life by losing it (Matt. 10:39) and that a person becomes great by serving others (Mark 10:43).

PARALYSIS. See *Palsy*.

PARALYTIC. A paralyzed person. Jesus honored the faith of a paralytic by offering forgiveness and healing (Matt. 9:1–7).

PARAMOUR (LOVER). A slave or concubine who provided sexual favors (Ezek. 23:20). *Lover:* NIV. See also *Concubine*.

PARAN/MOUNT PARAN/EL-PARAN. A mountainous wilderness region in the Sinai Peninsula, sometimes called *Mount Paran* (Hab. 3:3) or *El-paran* (Gen. 14:6). The Israelites camped here during their years in the wilderness (Num. 10:12; 12:16).

PARAPET. See *Battlement*.

PARCHED CORN (ROASTED GRAIN, PARCHED GRAIN). Roasted grains of wheat, barley, or millet (1 Sam. 25:18). *Roasted grain:* NIV; *parched grain:* NRSV.

PARCHMENT. Writing material made from the skin of sheep or goats. Paul asked Timothy to bring parchments to him in prison (2 Tim. 4:13).

PARDON. Forgiveness. God will pardon those who repent and turn to the Lord (Isa. 55:7). The loving father in Jesus' parable had compassion on his repentant son, extended pardon, and celebrated his return (Luke 15:18–24). God promised to pardon the iniquity of Judah and Israel that led to their captivity and exile (Jer. 33:8–9). See also *Forgiveness; Remission.*

PARDON [ED, ETH]
Neh. 9:17 a God ready to *p*, gracious and merciful
Ps. 25:11 O Lord, *p* mine iniquity; for it is great
Isa. 40:2 her [Jerusalem's] iniquity is *p'ed*
Jer. 33:8 I [God] will *p* all their iniquities
Mic. 7:18 Who is a God like unto thee, that *p'eth* iniquity

PARENTS. People who bear and rear children. The duty of parents is to train (Deut. 4:9; 6:6–7) and correct (Deut. 21:18–21) their children. They should avoid favoritism (Gen. 25:28) and anger (Eph. 6:4). God promised to bless parents who bring up their children in the nurture of the Lord (Prov. 22:6; Eph. 6:4). See also *Children.*

PARLOUR. A room in a house for entertaining guests (1 Sam. 9:22), a secret chamber for retreat (1 Chron. 28:11), or a room on the roof for enjoying cool breezes (Judg. 3:20–25).

PAROUSIA. A Greek word that refers to the second coming of Christ. See also *Second Coming.*

PARTHIANS. Inhabitants of Parthia, a country north of Media and Persia. Parthians were in Jerusalem on the day of Pentecost (Acts 2:1, 9).

PARTIALITY. To show favoritism or preference toward some people over others.

P

PARCHMENT. Before paper came along, Jews wrote on scrolls of parchment—made from the leather of animals, usually sheep or goats. The leather was cut into strips, stitched together, and rolled into scrolls.

God's wisdom is available to all and free of favoritism or hypocrisy (James 3:17).

PARTITION. See *Middle Wall of Partition*.

PARTRIDGE. A wild bird in Palestine prized for its meat and eggs. Jeremiah compared ill-gotten wealth to a partridge sitting on eggs that will not hatch (Jer. 17:11).

PARVAIM. An unidentified place that provided gold for Solomon's temple (2 Chron. 3:6). Some scholars believe this was the same place as Ophir (1 Kings 9:28).

PASCHAL LAMB. See *Passover*.

PASHUR. A priest who struck Jeremiah and had him imprisoned. Jeremiah predicted that Pashur and his household would die as captives in Babylonia (Jer. 20:1–6).

PASSOVER AND FEAST OF UNLEAVENED BREAD. A Jewish festival that commemorated the Exodus from Egypt (Josh. 5:10). The Passover celebrated how God "passed over" the Hebrew houses in Egypt that were sprinkled with blood while killing the firstborn of the Egyptians on the eve of the Exodus (Exod. 12). The seven-day Feast of Unleavened Bread recalled the haste with which the slaves left Egypt (Exod. 12:33–34).

PASTOR. One who leads and instructs a congregation. Jeremiah predicted the coming of faithful pastors who would lead Israel back to God (Jer. 3:15). Pastors are called of God to perfect the saints and build up the body of Christ (Eph. 4:11–13). See also *Bishop; Elder; Minister; Shepherd*.

PASTORAL EPISTLES. The three letters of Paul—1 and 2 Timothy and Titus—that deal with pastoral concerns, or practical matters involving the operation and government of a local church.

PASTURE. Grazing lands for livestock. The word is also used figuratively for the protection of God's people under the Good Shepherd (Ps. 23:1–2; Ezek. 45:15).

PASTURE LANDS. See *Suburbs*.

PATH. A crude road. The word is also used figuratively for the route of one's life. The righteous are warned not to walk the paths of darkness (Prov. 2:13–15).

PATHROS (UPPER EGYPT). A name for upper Egypt where Egyptian civilization likely began. Jewish people lived here during the Babylonian Exile (Jer. 44:1, 15). *Upper Egypt:* NIV.

A PERMANENT PASSOVER

Of all the Jewish religious holidays and holy days specified in the Old Testament (Lev. 23), perhaps the annual Passover was the most important in terms of its significance for modern believers.

Centuries after the first Passover, Jesus was crucified when the Jewish people gathered in Jerusalem to celebrate this religious holiday. The apostle Paul declared that Christ is "our passover," or sacrificial lamb, who has been "sacrificed for us" (1 Cor. 5:7).

PAUL, THE APOSTLE. Paul is beheaded—punishment for preaching about Jesus. The Bible doesn't say how Paul died, but church leaders later said he was beheaded in Rome.

PATIENCE. Forbearance or restraint. God is the author of patience (Rom. 15:5), and Christ is its perfect model (2 Thess. 3:5). Believers are urged to labor with patience in the service of Christ (1 Thess. 5:14). See also *Forbearance; Longsuffering; Steadfastness.*

Rom. 5:3 tribulation worketh **p**
1 Tim. 6:11 follow after...faith, love, **p**, meekness
Heb. 12:1 run with **p** the race...set before us
James 1:3 the trying of your faith worketh **p**

PATIENT [LY]
Ps. 40:1 I waited **p'ly** for the LORD
Eccles. 7:8 the **p** in spirit is better than the proud in spirit
Rom. 12:12 Rejoicing in hope; **p** in tribulation
James 5:7 **p** therefore, brethren, unto the coming of the Lord

8 C 3 PATMOS. A desolate island in the Aegean Sea, used as a prison by the Romans, where the apostle John was exiled and where he wrote the book of Revelation. Christ revealed Himself to John and told him to send messages to the seven churches of Asia Minor (Rev. 1:9–20). See also *John the Apostle.*

PATRIARCH. The head of a tribe or clan in O.T. times who ruled by authority passed down from father to oldest son. Abraham, Isaac, and Jacob, along with the sons of Jacob and David, are notable examples of patriarchal rule (Acts 2:29; 7:8–9).

PAUL THE APOSTLE. The great apostle to the Gentiles; defender and advocate of the Christian faith in its early years through his thirteen N.T. letters. A complex personality, Paul demonstrated both toughness and tenderness in his devotion to Christ. His teachings are both profound and practical (Phil. 3:7–10).

Paul's Hebrew name as a Jew of Benjamite ancestry was Saul, but his Roman name was Paul (Acts 13:9). A Roman citizen born at Tarsus in Cilicia (Acts 22:3), he was a tentmaker by trade—a vocation by which he often supported himself as a minister to the churches that he established (Acts 18:3).

A strict Pharisee and member of the Jewish Sanhedrin, Paul opposed Christianity in its early years in Jerusalem. He consented to the death of Stephen, the first martyr of the church (Acts 7:58–8:1). He was on his way to persecute Christians at Damascus when he was converted to Christianity in his famous "Damascus road" experience (Acts 9:1–19). From that point on, Paul was zealous for the cause of Christ.

Under the sponsorship of the church at Antioch in Syria, Paul undertook three great missionary journeys to the Roman world, extending westward through Cyprus and Asia Minor into Europe (Acts 13–21). His traveling companions on these tours included Barnabas, John Mark, Timothy, Silas, Titus, and Luke. Along with his successes in making disciples, healing, and planting churches, he suffered a "thorn in the flesh" (2 Cor. 12:7), was frequently arrested, was stoned, and was imprisoned (Acts 16:22–23).

Falsely accused by his enemies, he appealed to the Roman emperor for justice (Acts 25:10–12). After an arduous voyage by ship, he spent two years in Rome under house arrest. While guarded by Roman soldiers, he received friends and preached the gospel (Acts 28:16–31; Phil. 1:12–14).

Four of Paul's epistles—Ephesians, Colossians, Philippians, and Philemon—were written from Rome. Most scholars believe he was beheaded in Rome about A.D. 67 during Nero's reign (Phil. 2:17; 2 Tim. 4:6–8).

PAULUS, SERGIUS. The Roman proconsul of Cyprus who was converted under Paul's ministry (Acts 13:4–12). See also *Cyprus; Paphos.*

PAVEMENT, THE/GABBATHA. An area in Pilate's courtroom paved with stones where Jesus was judged, sentenced to crucifixion, and turned over to the mob (John 19:13–16). Its Aramaic name was *Gabbatha*.

PAVILION (DWELLING, SHELTER). A tent or booth for kings or other members of the royal family. The word is also used figuratively for the dwelling place of God (Ps. 27:5). *Dwelling:* NIV; *shelter:* NRSV.

PAY [ETH]
Ps. 37:21 wicked borroweth, and *p'eth* not again
Ps. 66:13 I will *p* thee [God] my vows
Matt. 18:34 delivered...tormentors, till he should *p* all

PEACE. Harmony and accord brought about by cordial relationships. Peace has its source in God (Phil. 4:7) through Christ (John 14:27) and the Holy Spirit (Gal. 5:22). Christians are urged to pursue peace and to live peaceably with all people (2 Cor. 13:11; 2 Tim. 2:22).

Ps. 4:8 lay me down in *p*, and sleep
Ps. 55:18 He [God] hath delivered my soul in *p*
Prov. 17:28 a fool...holdeth his *p*, is counted wise
Eccles. 3:8 a time of war, and a time of *p*
Isa. 9:6 his [Messiah's] name...Prince of *P*
Isa. 53:5 chastisement of our *p*...upon him [God's servant]
Matt. 10:34 I [Jesus] came not to send *p*, but a sword
Luke 2:14 on earth *p*, good will toward men
John 16:33 in me [Jesus] ye might have *p*
Rom. 5:1 we have *p* with God through...Jesus Christ
1 Cor. 14:33 God is not the author of confusion, but of *p*
Eph. 2:14 he [Jesus] is our *p*...made both one
Col. 3:15 the *p* of God rule in your hearts

PEACE OFFERING. See *Heave Offering; Wave Offering.*

PEACOCK (BABOON). An exotic animal imported by King Solomon, probably from Spain (2 Chron. 9:21). *Baboon:* NIV.

PEARL. A precious stone found in the shells of oysters. Jesus compared the kingdom of heaven to a merchant seeking valuable pearls (Matt. 13:45–46).

PEG. See *Pin.*

PEKAH. A king of Israel (reigned about 740–732 B.C.) who assassinated Pekahiah to gain the throne. He was killed by Hoshea in a conspiracy (2 Kings 15:23–31).

PEKAHIAH. An evil king of Israel (reigned about 742–740 B.C.) who was murdered and succeeded by Pekah, one of his military officers (2 Kings 15:23–26).

PELEG/PHALEC. A descendant of Shem (Gen. 10:25, 31). *Phalec:* Luke 3:35.

PELETHITES. A unit or division of David's soldiers who remained loyal to him during the rebellions of Absalom and Sheba (2 Sam. 15:14–18; 20:7).

PELICAN (DESERT OWL). A large bird, considered unclean by the Israelites (Lev. 11:13, 18), that was cited as a symbol of loneliness and desolation (Ps. 102:6). This may be the same bird as the *cormorant* (Isa. 34:11). *Desert owl:* NIV. See also *Cormorant.*

PEN. A word for various writing instruments, including those that wrote on scrolls (Jer. 8:8), skin or parchment, and stones (Job 19:24). See also *Ink; Writing.*

PENKNIFE (SCRIBE'S KNIFE). A small knife used for sharpening the writing pen, or reed pen (Jer. 36:23). *Scribe's knife:* NIV.

PENCE. See *Penny.*

P

2 D 4

PENIEL/PENUEL. A place east of the Jordan River near the Jabbok River where Jacob wrestled with an angel (Gen. 32:24–32). *Penuel:* Judg. 8:8. See also *Jacob.*

PENITENCE. See *Repentance.*

PENNY/PENCE (DENARIUS). A silver coin of small value (Matt. 20:1–13). It varied in value, but it generally equaled the daily wage of an unskilled worker. *Pence:* plural form (Luke 10:35). *Denarius:* NIV. See also *Farthing.*

PENTATEUCH. The Greek name for the first five books of the O.T.: Genesis, Exodus, Leviticus, Numbers, and Deuteronomy. It was called the Torah or the Law of Moses by the Hebrews (Ezra 7:6). Jesus recognized the value of the law and came to fulfill its spiritual requirements (Matt. 5:17–18; 12:5). See also *Law.*

P

PENTECOST/FEAST OF WEEKS/ FEAST OF HARVEST. An annual Jewish feast or holy period, commemorating the end of the harvest, that fell on the fiftieth day after the Passover. This was the holiday being observed in Jerusalem when the Holy Spirit came in power upon the early Christian believers (Acts 2). This feast was also known as the *Feast of Weeks* and the *Feast of Harvest* (Exod. 34:22).

PENUEL. See *Peniel.*

PEOPLE OF GOD. A phrase for the nation of Israel as well as the people of the new covenant, or the Church. The Israelites were called by God as His special people (Deut. 8:6–9), but all who have accepted Christ as Lord and Savior, including Gentiles, are also His people—members of God's "chosen generation, a royal priesthood" (1 Pet. 2:9–10). God's people

include every kindred, tongue, and nation (Rev. 5:9; 7:9). See also *Church; Congregation; Saints.*

PEOR. A mountain of Moab across the Jordan River from Jericho. From Peor, Balak and Balaam observed the camp of the Israelites with the intention to curse them (Num. 23:28; 24:1–2).

PERAZIM. See *Baal-perazim.*

PERCEIVE [D, ING]
Job 38:18 Hast thou [Job] *p'd* the breadth of the earth?
Isa. 6:9 see ye indeed, but *p* not
Luke 8:46 I [Jesus] *p* that virtue is gone out of me
Luke 9:47 Jesus, *p'ing*...their heart, took a child
Acts 10:34 I [Peter] *p* that God is no respecter of persons

PERDITION. The state of the damned, or those who have rejected Christ. Jesus called Judas the "son of perdition" because of his betrayal of Christ (John 17:12). Perdition is the final destiny of the ungodly (2 Pet. 3:7) as well as the final abode of the Antichrist (Rev. 17:8, 11). See also *Damnation; Hell; Judgment, Last.*

PEREA. A word used by some translations of the Bible for the territory east of the Jordan River across from Judea and Samaria. Jews often traveled from Galilee to Judea through Perea to avoid going through the territory of the despised Samaritans (Matt. 4:15; 19:1). This region is called the land "beyond Jordan" in the KJV.

5 C 4

PEREZ. See *Pharez.*

PERFECT [ING]
Gen. 6:9 Noah was...just...*p* in his generations
Job 1:1 that man [Job] was *p* and upright
Ps. 19:7 law of the LORD is *p*, converting the soul
Matt. 5:48 Father which is in heaven is *p*
Rom. 12:2 prove what is that...*p*, will of God
2 Cor. 12:9 strength is made *p* in weakness

Eph. 4:12 **p'ing** of the saints...work of the ministry
2 Tim. 3:17 the man of God may be **p**
Heb. 5:9 made **p**, he [Jesus]...author of...salvation
James 1:17 good gift and every **p** gift is from above
1 John 4:18 but **p** love casteth out fear

PERFECTION (MATURITY). A state of completion or fulfillment. Believers are urged to advance to mature teachings and "perfection" or fulfillment in good works (Heb. 6:1). While disclaiming perfection, Paul urged believers to keep striving for perfection by being like Christ (Phil. 3:12–15). *Maturity:* NIV.

Ps. 50:2 Out of Zion, the **p** of beauty, God hath shined
2 Cor. 13:9 this also we wish, even your **p**
Heb. 7:11 If...**p** were by the Levitical priesthood

PERFUME. A sweet-smelling fragrance, usually an extract of spices used in ointments, incense, and oils (Prov. 27:9). See also *Oil; Ointment.*

PERFUMER. See *Apothecary.*

PERGA. The capital of Pamphylia and a city visited by Paul. John Mark left Paul and Barnabas at Perga (Acts 13:13–14), and Paul preached here on the return to Antioch after the first missionary journey (Acts 14:25).

8 D 3

PERGAMOS (PERGAMUM). A city where one of the seven churches of Asia Minor addressed by John in Revelation was located. The church was rebuked for its toleration of sexual immorality and false teachings. The phrase "where Satan's seat is" is probably a reference to a pagan temple in the city (Rev. 2:12–17). *Pergamum:* NIV, NRSV.

8 C 2

P

PERFUME. As Egyptian perfumers have done for thousands of years, they continue to gather a delicate harvest of scents from flowers and herbs that grow along the Nile River.

PERISH [ETH]

Ps. 1:6 way of the ungodly shall *p*
Ps. 68:2 wicked *p* at the presence of God
Prov. 19:9 he that speaketh lies shall *p*
Prov. 29:18 Where there is no vision, the people *p*
Mark 4:38 carest thou not that we [the disciples] *p*
John 3:16 whosoever believeth in him [Jesus] should not *p*
John 6:27 Labour not for the meat which *p'eth*
1 Cor. 1:18 preaching of the cross is to them that *p* foolishness

PERIZZITES. Descendants of Perez who were subdued by Joshua's forces. Natives of the hill country, they were associated with the Canaanites (Josh. 3:10).

PERSECUTE [D, ST]

Ps. 31:15 deliver me...from them that *p* me
Matt. 5:11 Blessed are ye when men shall...*p* you
Matt. 5:44 Love your enemies...pray for them...*p* you
Acts 9:4 Saul, Saul, why *p'st* thou me [Jesus]?
Rom. 12:14 Bless them which *p* you...curse not
2 Cor. 4:9 *P'd*, but not forsaken; cast down, but not destroyed

PERSECUTION. Oppression in matters of conscience or religious practice, or punishment because of one's convictions. Believers who are not well grounded in the faith cannot endure persecution (Matt. 13:21). Jesus declared that those who are persecuted because of their commitment to Him will inherit the kingdom of God (Matt. 5:10–12). See also *Affliction; Suffering; Tribulation.*

Lam. 5:5 necks are under *p*: we...have no rest
Acts 8:1 great *p* against the church...at Jerusalem
Rom. 8:35 separate us...love of Christ? shall...distress, or *p*

PERSEVERANCE. Persistence, or the ability to endure through difficult circumstances. Paul counseled steadfastness in the Lord's work because labor for Him is never in vain (1 Cor. 15:58). Endurance of God's chastening or discipline is a mark of God's sonship (Heb. 12:7–8). See also *Patience; Steadfastness.*

PERSIA. A great empire whose territory covered what is now western Asia and parts of Europe and Africa, reaching the height of its greatness around 486 B.C. under Cyrus. The Persians conquered Babylonia in 539 B.C. and allowed the Israelites to return to their native land (2 Chron. 36:20–23). The Persian king Artaxerxes allowed Nehemiah to return to Jerusalem to rebuild the city wall (Neh. 2:1–8). The Persians were defeated by the Greek military conqueror Alexander the Great in 330 B.C. (Ezek. 38:5). See also *Elam; Elamites.*

PERSUADE [D, ST]

Luke 16:31 be *p'd*, though one rose from the dead
Acts 26:28 thou [Paul] *p'st* me [Agrippa] to be a Christian
Rom. 8:38 I [Paul] am *p'd*...neither death, nor life
2 Tim. 1:12 I [Paul] have believed...am *p'd*...he [Jesus] is able

PESTILENCE. A plague or widespread fatal disease (Hab. 3:5), usually coming as a result of God's judgment against sin (Exod. 5:3; Ezek. 33:27). See also *Plague.*

PESTLE. A short, blunt tool used for grinding grain or crushing other material in a container known as a mortar (Prov. 27:22).

PETER. See *Simon,* No. 1.

PETER, EPISTLES OF. Two short N.T. epistles, probably from the apostle Peter, written to encourage Christians experiencing persecution and discouragement (1 Peter) and to warn them against false teachers (2 Peter).

In response to scoffers who doubted the second coming of Christ—since He had not yet returned—Peter declared, "The Lord is not slack concerning his promise, as some men count slackness; but is longsuffering to us-ward, not willing that any should perish, but that all should come to repentance" (2 Pet. 3:9).

PETRA. Petra was once a thriving rock city south of the Dead Sea, carved into cliffs. This temple-looking building, however, is just a façade. It's chiseled just a few yards deep.

PETHOR. A town in northern Mesopotamia near the Euphrates River; home of Balaam, who was sent to curse the Israelites (Num. 22:5–7).

PETITION. An earnest request. King Ahasuerus granted Esther's petition to save her people (Esther 7:2–5). Believers are confident their petitions will be answered (1 John 5:14–15). See also *Intercession; Prayer.*

PETRA. An ancient city located south of the Dead Sea. Named for its rocky terrain, Petra was once the capital of Edom and later of Nabatea. Some scholars believe it was the same city as *Selah* (2 Kings 14:7).

PHALEC. See *Peleg.*

PHARAOH. The title of the king of Egypt. The pharaoh of Egypt, who is unnamed (Exod. 1:8–11), refused to release the Israelites from slavery until God killed the Egyptian firstborn throughout the land. The named pharaohs of the Bible are:

1. Shishak, who attacked Jerusalem and plundered the temple (1 Kings 14:25–26).

2. So, who made an alliance with King Hoshea of Israel (2 Kings 17:4).

3. Tirhakah, who aided King Hezekiah of Judah against Sennacherib of Assyria (2 Kings 19:9).

4. Necoh, whose archers mortally wounded King Josiah of Judah at Megiddo (2 Kings 23:29). *Necho:* Jer. 46:2.

5. Hophra, whom God declared would fall to his enemies (Jer. 44:30).

PHAREZ/PEREZ/PHARES. One of Judah's twin sons by Tamar (Gen. 38:24–30) and founder of the family or clan of Pharzites (Num. 26:20–21). *Perez:* Neh. 11:4; *Phares:* Matt. 1:3.

PHARISEES. Members of a Jewish sect pledged to uphold the oldest traditions of Israel. In Jesus' time the Pharisees were the most powerful party—political or religious— among the Jews. Jesus exposed the hypocrisy of the Pharisees, who emphasized minute details of the law while neglecting more important issues such as justice, mercy, and love (Matt. 23:1–7). Pharisees in the N.T. who were known for their generosity and noble spirit were the apostle Paul, Nicodemus, Gamaliel, and Joseph of Arimathea. See also *Sadducees.*

PHARPAR. One of two rivers of Damascus mentioned by the Assyrian commander Naaman. He was offended when told by Elisha to bathe in the Jordan River rather than the rivers of Damascus (2 Kings 5:9–12). See also *Abana River.*

PHEBE (PHOEBE). A believer at Cenchrae near Corinth who was commended by Paul for her support of him and others (Rom. 16:1–2). *Phoebe:* NIV, NRSV.

PHENICE/PHENICIA (PHOENICIA). A Mediterranean coastal region, including the cities of Ptolemais, Tyre, and Sidon. The inhabitants of Phoenicia, descended from the Canaanites, became a seafaring and colonizing people. King Hiram of Tyre furnished cedar timber and craftsmen for the construction of Solomon's temple in Jerusalem (2 Sam. 5:11; 1 Kings 5:1–10). Jesus ministered in this region (Matt. 15:21), and Christians fled here to escape persecution after Stephen's death (Acts 11:19). *Phenicia:* Acts 21:2. *Phoenicia:* NIV, NRSV. See also *Hiram; Tyre.*

PHILADELPHIA. A city of Lycia in Asia Minor and site of one of the seven churches of Asia Minor addressed in the book of Revelation (Rev. 1:11). This church was commended for its faithfulness (Rev. 3:7–9).

PHILEMON. A Christian at Colossae to whom Paul wrote on behalf of Philemon's slave Onesimus (Philem. 1). See also *Onesimus.*

PHILEMON, EPISTLE TO. A short N.T. book written by Paul to help a runaway slave Onesimus—a convert under Paul's ministry. Philemon, the owner of Onesimus and a fellow believer, was encouraged to welcome his slave back as a Christian brother (v. 16). Paul also hinted that Onesimus be given his freedom in the spirit of Christian love (v. 21).

PHILIP
1. One of the twelve apostles of Jesus. He responded to Jesus' invitation to discipleship and brought another disciple, Nathanael, to Jesus (John 1:43–51). He also brought a group of Greeks, or Gentiles, to see Jesus in Jerusalem (John 12:21). See also *Twelve, The.*

2. One of the seven men of Greek background chosen as "deacons" in the church at Jerusalem (Acts 6:5–6) and an evangelist in the early church. Philip preached extensively in Samaria and responded to God's call to the Gaza desert (Acts 8:25–27), where he led a eunuch to Christ and baptized him (Acts 8:28–38). He entertained Paul's group of missionaries (Acts 21:8) and was the father of four daughters who prophesied (Acts 21:9).

3. A Roman ruler in northern Palestine. See *Herod,* No. 4.

PHILIPPI. A city of Macedonia where Paul and Silas were imprisoned but miraculously rescued by God. This was the first city in Greece to receive the gospel, and Lydia became the first convert (Acts 16:12–15). While imprisoned in Rome, Paul wrote a letter to the Christians in the church at Philippi (Phil. 1:1). See also *Lydia.*

PHILIPPIANS, EPISTLE TO THE. A short N.T. epistle written by Paul to the church at Philippi—a group for whom the apostle expressed great appreciation, thanksgiving, and admiration (1:1–11). Paul appealed to these fellow believers to follow Christ's example of humility (chap. 2), to continue to grow toward maturity in Christian service (chap. 3), and to experience the peace and joy that Christ promises to all believers (chap. 4).

Philippians has been called Paul's "epistle of joy" because of his exhortation, "Rejoice in the Lord alway: and again I say, Rejoice" (4:4). See also *Kenosis; Philippi.*

PHILISTIA. A coastal region about forty miles long beside the Mediterranean Sea that served as the land of the Philistines in O.T. times (Gen. 21:32–34). The name *Palestine* was derived from *Philistia*. The chief cities of Philistia were Ashdod, Askelon, Ekron, Gath, and Gaza (Josh. 13:3). See also *Palestine.*

PHILISTINES/PHILISTIM. The people of Philistia who were enemies of the Israelites, especially during the days of Saul and David. After settling in Canaan, the Philistines often battled the Israelites (2 Sam. 5:17–25). Their chief pagan gods were Dagon (Judg.16:23) and Baalzebub (2 Kings 1:2–3). Their kingdom disappeared after the Babylonian Exile. *Philistim:* Gen. 10:14. See also *Caphtor.*

PHILOSOPHY. The study of truths regarding ultimate reality. The early Christians encountered Greek dualism and the teachings of the Stoics and Epicureans (Acts 17:18; Col. 2:8–10).

PHINEHAS

1. Aaron's grandson who became Israel's high priest and chief of the Korahite branch of the Levites (1 Chron. 9:19–20). He killed Zimri and Cozbi at God's command for allowing Israel to be corrupted with idolatry (Num. 25:6–15).

2. A priest who corrupted his office by immorality and corrupt leadership (1 Sam. 1:3; 2:22–24). Phinehas and his brother Hophni died in battle with the Philistines, as foretold by a prophet (1 Sam. 2:27, 34; 4:10–11). Phinehas's wife also died in childbirth (1 Sam. 4:19–20). See also *Hophni.*

PHOEBE. See *Phebe.*

PHOENICIA. See *Phenice.*

PHRYGIA. A region of central Asia Minor visited by Paul (Acts 16:6). Jews from Phrygia were in Jerusalem on the day of Pentecost (Acts 2:1–10).

PHUT/PUT. A son of Ham (Gen. 10:6). This reference may be to people related to the Egyptians, or possibly to the Libyans. *Put:* 1 Chron. 1:8. See also *Libya.*

PHYGELLUS (PHYGELUS). A believer condemned by Paul because he deserted the apostle Paul in the Roman province of Asia (2 Tim. 1:15). *Phygelus:* NIV, NRSV.

PHYLACTERY. A verse of Scripture worn on the forehead or near the heart (Exod. 13:11–16; Deut. 6:4–8). Jesus denounced the conspicuous wearing of phylacteries (Matt. 23:5). See also *Forehead; Frontlet.*

PHYSICIAN. A healer or person who practiced medicine. Medical studies were prominent in Egypt (Gen. 50:2), with midwives and physicians practicing among the Israelites (2 Chron. 16:12). Luke was described as a "beloved physician" (Col. 4:14).

PHYSICIAN [S]
Jer. 8:22 Is there no balm in Gilead...no **p** there?
Mark 5:26 [a certain woman]...suffered...of many **p's**
Luke 5:31 They that are whole need not a **p**

PIERCE [D]
Zech. 12:10 me [the Messiah] whom they have **p'd**
Luke 2:35 sword shall **p** through thy [Mary's]...soul
John 19:34 one of the soldiers...**p'd** his [Jesus'] side

PIG. See *Swine.*

PIGEON. A bird used for sacrifices, particularly by the poor. The word is used interchangeably with *dove* in most Bible passages. Mary and Joseph offered bird sacrifices when Jesus was dedicated to God in the temple (Luke 2:24). See also *Turtledove.*

PILATE. The procurator or Roman governor of Judea (ruled about A.D. 26–36) who presided at Jesus' trial. An opportunist, Pilate was unwilling to condemn Jesus as a criminal (John 18:28–38), so he sought to have him tried by Herod at the next judicial level (Luke 23:11). Then he proposed that Jesus be the prisoner customarily dismissed at Passover, but this move also failed (John 18:39–40). Finally he released Jesus to be crucified but tried to dodge responsibility for the decision (Matt. 27:24–25).

PILGRIMAGE. A stay in a foreign country (Exod. 6:4). The term is applied figuratively to the earthly life span (Heb. 11:13). See also *Alien; Foreigner.*

PILLAR OF FIRE AND CLOUD. Supernatural signs that guided the Israelites in the wilderness (Exod. 13:21). Given to protect the Hebrews, the signs represented God's presence with His people (Num. 14:13–14). These signs

PILGRIMAGE. Jews from around the world make a pilgrimage to Jerusalem to celebrate the springtime festival of Passover. This holiday commemorates Moses' leading the Israelites to freedom, out of Egypt. Jews not able to make the trip often add this phrase to their observance: "Next year in Jerusalem."

were repeated in the transfiguration of Christ (Matt. 17:5). See also *Cloud; Fire.*

PILLOW. A headrest for sleeping. The Hebrews used quilts, stones (Gen. 28:18), netting of goat hair (1 Sam. 19:13), or leather cushions (Mark 4:38).

PIN (PEG). A peg or stake. Copper or brass tent pins were used to hold the cords of the tabernacle (Exod. 27:19). The Hebrew word for "pin" is also rendered as *nail* (Judg. 4:21). *Peg:* NIV, NRSV.

PINE. See *Fir; Box Tree.*

PINNACLE (HIGHEST POINT). A wing of the temple, perhaps an elevated area over Solomon's porch. Satan tempted Jesus to impress the crowds with a spectacular leap from this high place (Matt. 4:5–7). *Highest point:* NIV.

PINT. See *Pound.*

PIPE (FLUTE). A musical instrument probably blown like a flute (Isa. 30:29). This may have been similar to the instrument called an organ in some passages. *Flute:* NIV, NRSV. See also *Flute; Organ.*

PIPES. See *Dulcimer.*

PISGAH, MOUNT. A mountain peak in Moab from which Moses viewed Canaan before his death (Deut. 34:1–6). Balaam built altars and offered sacrifices on this mountain. The highest point of Pisgah was called *Nebo.* See also *Nebo,* No. 1.

PISHON. See *Pison.*

PISIDIA. A large mountainous district in Asia Minor visited by Paul, who preached in the city of Antioch (Acts 13:14–50). See also *Antioch of Pisidia.*

PISON (PISHON). One of four rivers that flowed out of the Garden of Eden (Gen. 2:10–14). *Pishon:* NIV, NRSV.

PIT (CISTERN). A hole in the ground. This word may refer to a deep hole lightly covered to trap animals (Jer. 18:22) as well as to an empty cistern like that into which Joseph was thrown (Gen. 37:24). Sometimes Sheol is referred to as a pit (Num. 16:30). *Cistern:* NIV. See also *Cistern; Prison.*

PITCH. A tarlike substance used on Noah's ark, probably asphalt or bitumen found in the Dead Sea area (Gen. 6:14). It was used like mortar and caulk. See also *Slime.*

PITCHER (JAR). An earthenware vessel used to carry water (Gen. 24:14). The word is also used symbolically of the human life span (Eccles. 12:6). *Jar:* NIV, NRSV. See also *Cruse.*

PITHOM. An Egyptian city built by Hebrew slaves (Exod. 1:11). It was located in Goshen east of the Nile River.

PITY. Compassion toward others. James described God as "very pitiful, and of tender mercy" (James 5:11). God showed pity on the pagan peoples of Nineveh (Jon. 4:10–11) as well as His people, the Israelites (Isa. 63:9). See also *Mercy.*

PLAGUE. A disastrous affliction or epidemic. Plagues were often interpreted as signs of God's judgment (Exod. 9:14). Ten plagues were sent upon the Egyptians for their failure to release the Hebrew slaves (Exod. 7–12). The children of Israel were plagued for their complaining in the wilderness (Num. 11:1, 31–33). See also *Pestilence.*

TEN PLAGUES AGAINST EGYPT

1. Water turned into blood (Exod. 7:15-25)
2. Frogs (Exod. 8:1-15)
3. Lice (Exod. 8:16-19)
4. Flies (Exod. 8:20-32)
5. Diseased livestock (Exod. 9:1-7)
6. Boils, or sores (Exod. 9:8-12)
7. Hail (Exod. 9:13-35)
8. Locusts (Exod. 10:1-20)
9. Darkness (Exod. 10:21-29)
10. Death of Egyptian firstborn
    (Exod. 12:29-36)

PLAIN. A meadow or rolling expanse of land (Judg. 11:33). Given a choice by Abraham, Lot chose the fertile plain near Sodom rather than Canaan's hill country (Gen. 13:10–12).

PLASTER. A thick paste used as a coating for walls and stones (Lev. 14:42).

PLATTER (DISH, PLATE). A dish or utensil for food. Jesus used the word figuratively to condemn the scribes and Pharisees for their hypocrisy (Matt. 23:25–26). *Dish:* NIV; *plate:* NRSV. See also *Charger.*

PLEASURE [S]
Ps. 147:11 LORD taketh *p* in them that fear him
Ezek. 33:11 I [God] have no *p*...death of the wicked
Luke 12:32 Father's good *p* to give you the kingdom
2 Tim. 3:4 lovers of *p's* more than lovers of God

PLEDGE. A vow or something given for security of a debt. Under the Mosaic Law, an outer garment pledged by a poor man had to be returned at sunset for his use as a bed covering (Exod. 22:26–27). A creditor was forbidden to enter his neighbor's house to take a pledged item (Deut. 24:10–11). See also *Surety.*

PLEIADES. A constellation of stars cited as evidence of God's sovereignty (Job 9:9). See also *Seven Stars.*

PLOWSHARE. A piece of iron at the end of a plow shaft, used to till the soil. The word is also used figuratively for a coming age of peace (Isa. 2:4). See also *Coulter.*

PLUMBLINE. A tool used by carpenters to determine precise uprightness of a wall. The word is also used figuratively for God's test for the uprightness of His people (Amos 7:7–9).

PLUNDER. See *Spoil.*

PODS. See *Husks.*

POETIC WRITINGS. The five books of the O.T. that are written almost entirely in poetic form—Job, Psalms, Proverbs, the Song of Solomon, and Lamentations—as well as those sections of other books that use this form. Sections of several of the prophetic books, for example, appear in poetry.

POETRY, HEBREW. A unique form of Hebrew writing that uses a repetition technique known as parallelism rather than rhyming or alliteration to express ideas. In parallelism, one line of poetry is advanced, contrasted, or repeated by the next line to convey thought. For example, "Have mercy upon me, O LORD; for I am weak: / O LORD, heal me; for my bones are vexed" (Ps. 6:2).

POISON. A deadly substance when swallowed or introduced into the bloodstream. Dipping

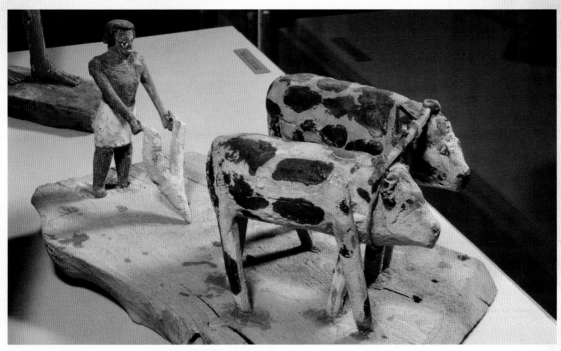

PLOWSHARE. In this ancient model, an Egyptian farmer breaks ground with a wooden plow pulled by oxen. The tips of such plows were often plated with metal and were called plowshares.

the tips of arrows into poison is probably referred to in Job 6:4. The word is also used figuratively for destructive speech (James 3:8). See also *Venom*.

POISONOUS SERPENTS. See *Fiery Serpents*.

POLLUX. See *Castor and Pollux*.

POLYGAMY. A family system under which a man is allowed to have more than one wife at the same time. The O.T. patriarchs practiced polygamy (for example, Abraham; Gen. 16:1–4), but it was contrary to God's original plan (Gen. 2:24) and divine ideal of marriage (Matt. 19:5). See also *Monogamy*.

POLYTHEISM. The practice of worshiping many gods, in contrast to monotheism, which emphasizes devotion to the one and only true God. The nations surrounding Israel worshiped multiple gods, a practice that led to immorality (Num. 25:1–9), prostitution (2 Kings 23:7), and child sacrifice (Jer. 7:29–34).

The first two of the Ten Commandments make it clear that devotion to the one and only supreme God was not to be mixed with worship of any other false or pagan god (Exod. 20:3–5). See also *Monotheism*.

POMEGRANATE. A small tree that bore apple-shaped fruit that was popular in Palestine. The spies who explored Canaan discovered this tree (Deut. 8:7–8).

POMMELS (CAPITALS). Round ornaments at the top of pillars or columns; an architectural feature used in Solomon's temple at Jerusalem (2 Chron. 4:11–13). *Capitals:* NIV, NRSV.

PONTIUS PILATE. See *Pilate*.

PONTUS. A coastal region along the Black Sea in northern Asia Minor where Priscilla and Aquila settled (Acts 18:2; 1 Pet. 1:1).

POOL. A water reservoir that supplied water for cities (John 5:2). King Hezekiah of Judah built a pool with an aqueduct to pipe water into Jerusalem (2 Kings 20:20). See also *Bethesda; Siloam; Solomon, Pools of*.

POOR. Needy or impoverished people. The Hebrews were instructed by the Lord to show compassion for the poor (Luke 14:13–14). Gleanings of the harvest were left for the poor (Lev. 19:9–10; Ruth 2). Jesus showed compassion for widows and other poor persons (Mark 12:42–44). The early church appointed "deacons" to serve the neglected poor (Acts 6:1–4). See also *Alms; Beggar*.

Deut. 15:11 the **p** shall never cease out of the land
Job 36:6 he [God]...giveth right to the **p**
Ps. 72:13 He [God] shall spare the **p** and needy
Prov. 22:2 rich and **p**...Lord...maker of them all
Isa. 25:4 thou [God] hast been a strength to the **p**
Amos 2:6 they [Israel] sold...**p** for a pair of shoes
Matt. 5:3 Blessed are the **p** in spirit
Mark 14:7 ye have the **p** with you always
Luke 4:18 anointed me [Jesus] to preach...to the **p**
Luke 19:8 half of my [Zacchaeus's] goods I give to the **p**
2 Cor. 8:9 he [Jesus] was rich, yet...became **p**
James 2:5 God chosen the **p** of this world rich in faith

POOL. A young resident of Jerusalem washes in Siloam Pool. King Hezekiah built the pool inside the walled city of Jerusalem. Then he connected it to an underground spring outside the city—by chiseling through almost 600 yards of solid rock. The passageway became known as Hezekiah's Tunnel.

POPLAR. A tree of the willow family. Jacob used poplar branches to produce speckled flocks (Gen. 30:37–39). See also *Willow*.

PORCH (PORTICO, VESTIBULE). A veranda or covered deck around a building. Solomon's porch was along the east side of the temple in Jerusalem (1 Kings 6:3). *Portico:* NIV; *vestibule:* NRSV. See also *Portico*.

PORCIUS FESTUS. See *Festus*.

PORK. The flesh of pigs, an unclean meat to the Jews (Lev. 11:7–8).

PORTER (GATEKEEPER, DOOR-KEEPER). A doorkeeper or watchman stationed at a city gate (2 Sam. 18:26) or private house (Mark 13:34). Porters were also assigned to guard duty in the temple at Jerusalem (1 Chron. 23:5). *Gatekeeper:* NIV; *doorkeeper:* NRSV. See also *Doorkeeper; Gatekeeper*.

PORTICO (COVERED COLONNADE). A porch. Jesus healed a paralytic lying on one of the porches of the Pool of Bethesda (John 5:2–9). *Covered colonnade:* NIV. See also *Porch*.

PORTION. See *Mess*.

POSSESSION [S]

Gen. 17:8 I [God] will give...Canaan, for an everlasting *p*
Mark 10:22 he [rich young ruler]...grieved...had great *p's*
Acts 5:1 Ananias, with Sapphira his wife, sold a *p*

POSSIBLE

Matt. 19:26 with God all things are *p*
Matt. 26:39 if it be *p*, let this cup pass from me [Jesus]
Mark 9:23 all things are *p* to him that believeth
Luke 18:27 things...impossible with men are *p* with God
Rom. 12:18 If it be *p*...live peaceably with all men

POST (COURIER). A person who relayed messages for a king or other high official. King Hezekiah used posts to order the Israelites to keep the Passover (2 Chron. 30:6–10). *Courier:* NIV, NRSV. See also *Footman*.

POSTERITY. One's children and grandchildren. The prophet Jehu told King Baasha of Israel that his sinful leadership would destroy him and his family (1 Kings 16:1–4). See also *Seed*.

POT. A kitchen vessel usually made of clay (Isa. 29:16), but brass pots were used in the sanctuary (1 Kings 7:45).

POTENTATE (SOVEREIGN). A person of great power or authority. Jesus Christ will be recognized as the only true Potentate (1 Tim. 6:15). *Sovereign:* NRSV.

POTIPHAR. A high Egyptian officer who had Joseph imprisoned because his wife accused Joseph of trying to seduce her (Gen. 39:1–20).

POTSHERD. A fragment of pottery, often used by the poor as a drinking vessel or for carrying coals (Ps. 22:15). See also *Pottery*.

POTTAGE (STEW). A thick vegetable soup (Hag. 2:12); the price paid by Jacob for his brother, Esau's, birthright (Gen. 25:29–34). *Stew:* NIV, NRSV.

POTTER. A craftsman who made vessels from clay on a revolving wheel (Jer. 18:3). To Isaiah, the power of the potter over the clay was symbolic of the Creator's sovereignty (Isa. 45:9).

POTTER'S FIELD. A burial place for poor people outside Jerusalem. This field was bought with the betrayal silver returned by Judas to Jewish officials (Matt. 27:6–8).

POTTERY. Vessels made from clay. The broken piece of pottery cited by Jeremiah was a symbol of Judah's coming destruction (Jer. 19:1–11). See also *Potsherd.*

POUND (PINT, MINA). A dry measure of uncertain volume. Mary of Bethany anointed Jesus with a pound of costly ointment (John 12:3). *Pint:* NIV. This term was also used of money (Luke 19:13). *Mina:* NIV.

POWER
Job 37:23 he [God] is excellent in **p**
Prov. 18:21 Death and life are in the **p** of the tongue
Nah. 1:3 Lord is slow to anger, and great in **p**
Zech. 4:6 might, nor by **p**, but by my [God's] spirit
Matt. 6:13 thine [God's] is the kingdom, and the **p**
Matt. 28:18 All **p** is given unto me [Jesus]
John 1:12 gave he [Jesus] **p** to become the sons of God
Acts 6:8 Stephen, full of faith and **p**, did great wonders
1 Cor. 4:20 kingdom of God is not in word, but in **p**
Eph. 6:10 be strong in the Lord...**p** of his might
2 Tim. 1:7 God hath not given...spirit of fear; but of **p**

POWER OF GOD
Matt. 22:29 not knowing...scriptures, nor...**p-o-G**
Luke 22:69 Son of man sit...right hand of...**p-o-G**
Rom. 1:16 it [the gospel]...**p-o-G** unto salvation
1 Cor. 1:18 preaching of the cross...is the **p-o-G**
1 Cor. 2:5 faith should...stand...in the **p-o-G**

PRAETORIUM (GOVERNOR'S HEADQUARTERS). The Roman governor's official residence at Jerusalem. After being scourged by Pilate, Jesus was taken to Pilate's residence, where he was mocked by the soldiers (Mark 15:16). *Governor's headquarters:* NRSV.

PRAISE. Worship of God with honor and thanksgiving (Ps. 42:4). God is pleased and glorified with our praise (Ps. 50:23). Our praise of the Father is commanded in Jesus' model prayer (Matt. 6:9–13). See also *Thanksgiving.*

PRAISE [D, ING, S]
1 Chron. 16:25 great is the Lord...greatly to be **p'd**
Ps. 18:3 call upon the Lord...worthy to be **p'd**
Ps. 67:3 Let the people **p** thee, O God
Ps. 79:13 show forth thy [God's] **p** to all generations
Luke 2:20 shepherds returned, glorifying and **p'ing** God
Acts 16:25 Paul and Silas...sang **p's** unto God
Rev. 19:5 **P** our God, all...ye that fear him

PRAY [EST, ING]
2 Chron. 7:14 my [God's] people...humble...and **p**
Matt. 6:6 thou **p'est**, enter into thy closet
Mark 6:46 he [Jesus] departed into a mountain to **p**
Mark 11:25 when ye stand **p'ing**, forgive
Luke 6:28 **p** for them which despitefully use you
Luke 11:1 Lord, teach us [disciples] to **p**
John 14:16 I [Jesus] will **p**...Father...give...Comforter
Rom. 8:26 know not what we should **p** for as we ought
1 Thess. 5:17 **P** without ceasing
James 5:13 any among you afflicted? let him **p**

PRAYER. Communion with God. Elements of sincere prayer are adoration (Matt. 6:9–10), confession (1 John 1:9), supplication (1 Tim. 2:1–3), intercession (James 5:15), and thanksgiving (Phil. 4:6).

Jesus was a model for His followers in the practice of prayer. He arose early in the morning to pray (Mark 1:35), prayed all night before choosing the Twelve (Luke 6:12), prayed in Gethsemane on the night of His betrayal (Luke 22:44), and prayed on the cross for His enemies (Luke 23:34). He also gave His disciples a model prayer to follow in their communion with the Father (Matt. 6:9–13). See also *Intercession; Petition.*

2 Chron. 7:12 I [God] have heard thy [Solomon's] **p**
Ps. 66:20 God...hath not turned away my **p**
Matt. 21:22 ye...ask in **p**, believing, ye shall receive
Luke 19:46 My [God's] house is the house of **p**
Acts 6:4 we [the apostles] will give ourselves...to **p**
James 5:15 the **p** of faith shall save the sick
James 5:16 fervent **p** of a righteous man availeth much

P

PRAYER. An Orthodox Jew prays at Jerusalem's famous Western Wall, the most sacred place on earth for Jews. This wall is all that's left of their temple, destroyed by Romans 2,000 years ago. The wall once held up dirt for the mound on which the temple was built.

PREACH

PREACH. To proclaim the truths of the gospel. Paul's preaching was motivated by the lost condition of His hearers (Rom. 10:1–3). The prophets were anointed by God to preach good tidings of His deliverance (Isa. 61:1–2). Jesus urged His disciples to preach the gospel to everyone (Mark 16:15).

PREACH [ED, ING]

Matt. 3:1 John the Baptist, *p'ing* in the wilderness
Matt. 4:17 Jesus began to *p*...to say, Repent
Matt. 24:14 gospel...shall be *p'ed* in all the world
Acts 5:42 they [the apostles] ceased not to...*p* Jesus Christ
Acts 8:4 they [believers]...went...*p'ing* the word
1 Cor. 1:18 the *p'ing* of the cross is...foolishness
1 Cor. 15:14 if Christ be not risen...our *p'ing* vain
2 Cor. 4:5 we *p* not ourselves, but Christ Jesus
Eph. 3:8 I [Paul] should *p* among the Gentiles
2 Tim. 4:2 *P* the word; be instant in season
1 Pet. 3:19 he [Jesus]...*p'ed*...spirits in prison

PREACHER

Eccles. 1:2 Vanity of vanities, saith the *P*...all is vanity
Rom. 10:14 how shall they hear without a *p*
2 Tim. 1:11 I [Paul] am appointed a *p*...of the Gentiles

PREACH THE GOSPEL

Mark 16:15 Go ye...and *p-t-g* to every creature
Luke 4:18 he [God]...anointed me [Jesus]...*p-t-g* to...poor
Rom. 1:15 I [Paul]...ready to *p-t-g* to you...at Rome
Rom. 10:15 beautiful...feet of them that *p-t-g*
1 Cor. 1:17 Christ sent me [Paul] not to baptize...*p-t-g*
1 Cor. 9:14 they which *p-t-g* should live of the gospel

PRECEPT. A command or directive. Vain worship results when human precepts rather than God's commands are given priority (Matt. 15:9).

PRECIOUS

Ps. 116:15 *P* in the sight of the Lord is the death of his saints
Eccles. 7:1 A good name is better than *p* ointment
1 Cor. 3:12 build upon this foundation gold, silver, *p* stones

PREDESTINATE [D]

Rom. 8:29 whom he [God] did foreknow, he also did *p*

Eph. 1:5 Having *p'd* us unto the adoption of children
Eph. 1:11 *p'd* according to the purpose of him [God]

PREDESTINATION. God's plan for the eternal salvation of those who choose Him. God has ordained good for those who love Him and are called within His purpose (Rom. 8:28). Those called to salvation will be justified and will share God's glory (Rom. 8:30). Those chosen before the foundation of the world will be adopted by God, redeemed, and given an eternal inheritance (Eph.1:4–11). See also *Election, Divine; Foreknowledge.*

PREPARATION DAY. The day before the Jewish Sabbath or the celebration of a religious festival (Matt. 27:62). Preparation for the Passover celebration involved cooking the Passover meal, baking unleavened bread, and choosing appropriate clothing for the occasion.

PRICE

Job 28:18 the *p* of wisdom is above rubies
Isa. 55:1 buy wine...without money and without *p*
Matt. 13:46 when he had found one pearl of great *p*
1 Cor. 6:20 ye are bought with a *p*: glorify God

PRIDE. Arrogance, vanity, or conceit. This sin results in self-righteousness (Luke 18:11–12) and self-deception (Jer. 49:16). Paul, however, expressed justifiable pride in his fellowship with the Philippians (Phil. 1:3–6). See also *Conceit; Haughtiness; Vanity.*

Lev. 26:19 I [God] will break the *p* of your power
Ps. 10:2 wicked in his *p* doth persecute the poor
Prov. 16:18 *P* goeth before destruction
1 John 2:16 the lust of the eyes...*p* of life

PRIEST. A religious leader who made sacrificial offerings. The priesthood originated with Aaron, and his descendants were sanctified to the office (Exod. 29:9, 44). Jesus, our faultless high priest, paid for our sins once and for all by sacrificing Himself (Heb. 7:26–28). See also *High Priest*.

PRIESTHOOD OF BELIEVERS. The doctrine that each believer has direct access to God. This was symbolized by the torn veil in the temple at Jerusalem when Jesus died on the cross, providing access to the Holy of Holies for all believers (Matt. 27:50–51). Christ is the only authorized mediator between God and man (Eph. 3:11–12). Therefore, we can come boldly and directly to Him (Heb. 4:15–16). As priests of God, believers should minister to others in a spirit of love (Gal. 5:13).

PRIESTHOOD OF CHRIST. One of Christ's offices as the Son of God, emphasizing His offering of Himself on our behalf. Christ obtained eternal redemption for believers by making a perfect sacrifice "by his own blood" (Heb. 9:11–12).

PRINCE (RULER). A leader or ruler; a title for tribal officials (Exod. 2:14). Also a title for Jesus, who is called the "Prince of life" (Acts 3:15) and the "prince of the kings of earth" (Rev. 1:5). The word is also applied to Satan as the ruler of evil (John 12:31). *Ruler:* NIV, NRSV.

PRINCESS. The daughter of a king. King Solomon had princesses among his hundreds of wives (1 Kings 11:3). Athaliah, daughter of King Ahab, killed all the royal descendants and usurped Judah's throne (2 Kings 11:1–3).

PRINCIPALITY. A powerful class of angels and demons. Christ is "far above" all earthly or cosmic powers (Rom. 8:38; Eph. 1:21; 3:10). Believers will share His victory over hostile principalities (Col. 2:10, 15).

PRISCILLA, PRISCA. See *Aquila*.

PRISON. A place of confinement for prisoners, often consisting of little more than a crude dungeon, cistern, or hole in the ground,

P

PRISON. This dungeon in Rome's Mamertinum Prison is where Peter and Paul were imprisoned, according to an ancient tradition. Prisoners were dropped in through the hole at the top and sealed in utter darkness.

particularly in O.T. times (Jer. 52:11). Paul wrote several epistles from prison and regarded his confinement as an opportunity to advance the gospel (2 Cor. 6:3–5; Phil. 1:12–14). See also *Cistern; Pit.*

PRIVY. Something kept private or secret. Solomon said Shimei's heart was privy to the wickedness plotted against King David (1 Kings 2:44).

PROCLAMATION. A reading or announcement of an official decree. King Cyrus of Persia proclaimed that the Jewish exiles could return to Jerusalem to rebuild the temple (Ezra 1:1–3).

PROCONSUL. An official of a Roman province, perhaps the second in command. Paul was brought before the proconsul Gallio at Corinth (Acts 18:12). See also *Deputy.*

PRODIGAL SON. The main character in Jesus' parable who spent his inheritance foolishly, fell into poverty, and finally returned to his father to ask forgiveness and reinstatement as a servant. His father, representing the love and forgiveness of God, welcomed him back as a son (Luke 15:11–32).

PROFANE [D]
Ezek. 23:38 they have...*p'd* my [God's] sabbaths
Mal. 2:11 Judah hath *p'd* the holiness of the Lord
1 Tim. 4:7 refuse *p* and old wives' fables
2 Tim. 2:16 shun *p* and vain babblings

PROFESS [ING]
Matt. 7:23 will I [Jesus] *p*...I never knew you
Rom. 1:22 *P'ing* themselves...wise...became fools
Titus 1:16 *p* that they know God; but...deny him

PROFESSION
1 Tim. 6:12 thou...hast professed a good *p*
Heb. 3:1 consider the High Priest of our *p*, Christ Jesus
Heb. 10:23 Let us hold fast the *p* of our faith

PROFIT [ETH]
Eccles. 1:3 what *p* hath a man of all his labour
Mark 8:36 *p* a man...gain the...world...lose his...soul
Rom. 3:1 what *p* is there of circumcision
1 Cor. 13:3 have not charity, it *p'eth* me nothing

PROGNOSTICATOR. A fortune-teller, or one who foretold the future by consulting the stars. The Lord promised to judge Babylonia, in spite of the power of these astrologers (Isa. 47:12–14). See also *Astrologer.*

PROMISE. A pledge or guarantee, particularly of some blessing from God. Israel's history included significant promises from God: (1) the promise of a son to Abraham (Gen. 18:10); (2) the land of Canaan promised to Israel (Exod. 6:4); and (3) a Savior promised from the house of David (Isa. 7:13–14; Matt. 1:20–23). See also *Hope.*

PROMISE [D]
Jer. 33:14 I [God] will perform...which I have *p'd*
Luke 24:49 I [Jesus] send the *p* of my Father
Gal. 3:29 Abraham's seed...heirs...to the *p*
Gal. 4:28 we, brethren...are the children of *p*
Eph. 3:6 Gentiles should be...partakers of his [God's] *p*
Heb. 11:9 he [Abraham] sojourned in the land of *p*
James 1:12 crown of life...Lord hath *p'd*
2 Pet. 3:4 Where is the *p* of his [Jesus'] coming

PROPHECY [IES]
1 Cor. 12:10 another *p*...another discerning of spirits
1 Cor. 13:2 though I [Paul] have the gift of *p*
1 Cor. 13:8 there be *p'ies*, they shall fail

PROPHESY [IED]
Joel 2:28 sons and your daughters shall *p*
Matt. 7:22 we not *p'ied* in thy [Jesus'] name
1 Cor. 13:9 know in part, and we *p* in part

PROPHET. An inspired messenger called by God to declare His will (Ezra 5:2). Prophets were described as God's servants (Zech. 1:6), watchmen (Ezek. 3:17), and holy men (2 Pet. 1:21). In the N.T., the prophets were cited as a noble example of patient suffering (James 5:10). Another word for prophet is *seer*.

SYMBOLIC ACTIONS OF THE PROPHETS

The prophet Isaiah walked around without his outer robe at the Lord's command (Isa. 20:2). This was a symbolic action designed to get the attention of the people and warn them to turn from their sinful ways, or they would be stripped by their enemies. The prophet also gave his sons symbolic names that predicted God's judgment (Isa. 7:3; 8:1-4).

The prophets Jeremiah and Ezekiel also declared God's message in dramatic fashion through symbolic actions (Jer. 13:1-11; Ezek. 4).

PROPHETESS. A female prophet or the wife of a prophet. Noted prophetesses include Miriam (Exod. 15:20), Deborah (Judg. 4:4), Hulda (2 Kings 22:14), and Anna (Luke 2:36). Four daughters of Philip were said to prophesy (Acts 21:8–9).

PROPITIATION. Atonement or expiation. Christ was appointed to be a propitiation for our sins "through faith in his blood" (Rom. 3:24–25). His sacrificial death is the supreme demonstration of love (1 John 2:2; 4:10). See also *Atonement; Mediator, Christ the; Reconciliation.*

PROSELYTE (CONVERT). A Gentile who converted to Judaism. Some of these converts renounced their pagan lifestyle but refused to accept such Jewish practices as circumcision. Well-known proselytes of the Bible include Cornelius, Lydia, and Nicolas of Antioch (Acts 6:5). *Convert:* NIV.

PROSTITUTE. See *Harlot.*

PROUD
Ps. 119:69 The *p* have forged a lie against me
Prov. 6:17 A *p* look, a lying tongue
Prov. 16:5 one that is *p* in heart...abomination
Eccles. 7:8 patient in spirit...better than...*p* in spirit
2 Tim. 3:2 men shall be...covetous, boasters, *p*
James 4:6 God resisteth the *p*...giveth grace unto the humble

PROVE
Ps. 26:2 Examine me, O LORD, and *p* me
Mal. 3:10 *p* me now...saith the LORD of hosts
Rom. 12:2 *p* what is that good, and...perfect, will of God
Gal. 6:4 let every man *p* his own work
1 Thess. 5:21 *P* all things; hold fast that which is good

PROVENDER (FODDER). Food for livestock, consisting of chopped straw mixed with barley, beans, or dates (Gen. 24:32). *Fodder:* NIV, NRSV.

PROVERBS, BOOK OF. A book of wisdom in the O.T. filled with short, pithy sayings on how to live with maturity and integrity under the watchful eye of God—the source of all wisdom. These wise sayings, written by Solomon as well as other sages of Israel, deal with such practical matters as strong drink (23:20–21), pride (16:18), work (6:6–11), child rearing (22:6), friendship (17:17), anger (19:11), speech (15:1–4), sexual temptation (chap. 5), and honesty in business (11:1–4). See also *Solomon; Wisdom Literature.*

PROVIDENCE. Divine guidance of human events (Neh. 9:6). This doctrine affirms God's absolute lordship over His creation and the activities by which He preserves and governs. God is constantly working in accord with His purpose (Eph. 1:11). He sustains the moral universe by operating within spiritual principles (Gal. 6:7–9).

PROVINCE. A district or section of a nation, often the outlying area of an extended world power such as the Persian and the Roman empires (Esther 3:12). In the N.T., this word refers to districts conquered and controlled by the Romans (Acts 25:1).

PROVISION. A supply or ration of some substance, such as food. Solomon's court required a large provision of food (1 Kings 4:22–23).

PROVOKE [D]
Deut. 32:16 They *p'd* him [God]...with strange gods
1 Cor. 10:22 Do we *p* the Lord to jealousy?
1 Cor. 13:5 [charity] is not easily *p'd*, thinketh no evil
Eph. 6:4 fathers, *p* not your children to wrath

PRUDENT (LEARNED, INTELLIGENT). To have discernment or understanding (Matt. 11:25). The prudent person foresees evil (Prov. 22:3) and is crowned with knowledge (Prov. 14:18). *Learned:* NIV; *intelligent:* NRSV.

PRUNINGHOOK. A tool for cutting shrubs and vines. To beat pruninghooks into spears was a sign of war (Joel 3:10). To do the opposite was a sign of peace (Isa. 2:4).

PSALMS, BOOK OF. A poetic book of the O.T. filled with hymns of praise and prayers of thanksgiving to God as well as laments against one's enemies and misfortune. Its title is derived from a Greek word that implies that these psalms were to be sung to the accompaniment of a musical instrument. King David of Judah wrote many of these psalms (see 54, 59, 65). But many other unknown writers contributed to this book, which was probably compiled across many centuries of Jewish history.

Generations of believers have found the psalms to be a rich source of devotional inspiration, with their emphasis on the goodness, stability, power, and faithfulness of God. See also *David; Poetic Writings; Poetry, Hebrew.*

MUSICAL TERMS IN THE PSALMS

Several musical terms appear throughout the Psalms, particularly in the titles of individual psalms. For example, the word *michtam* in the title of Psalm 16 probably indicated that this psalm was to be sung to a particular cadence or tune. The word *selah* (Ps. 44:8) may have marked the place for a pause in the singing. *Sheminith* (Ps. 12 title) probably indicated the instrument to be used when this particular hymn was sung.

PSALTERY (LYRE, HARP). A stringed musical instrument that was probably similar to the harp (1 Sam. 10:5). *Lyre:* NIV; *harp:* NRSV. See also *Harp.*

PTOLEMAIS. See *Accho.*

PTOLEMY. The title of Greek kings who ruled throughout Egypt and Palestine from about 323 to 30 B.C. These kings are possibly referred to in Daniel's visions (see Dan. 11:5–30). Their kingdom eventually fell to the Romans.

PUBLICAN (TAX COLLECTOR). A Jewish citizen who purchased the right to collect taxes in a specific area of his country for the Roman government. Publicans were hated and looked upon as traitors by their fellow citizens (Matt. 5:46). Matthew (Matt. 9:9–11) and Zacchaeus (Luke 19:1–10) were prominent publicans who followed Jesus. *Tax collector:* NIV, NRSV. See also *Matthew.*

PUBLIUS. A Roman official who entertained Paul on the island of Miletus after a shipwreck. Paul healed his father of a fever (Acts 28:7–8).

PUL. See *Tiglath-pileser.*

PULSE (VEGETABLES). Food made of vegetables, such as peas or beans; the food eaten by Daniel and his friends instead of the king's provisions (Dan. 1:12–16). *Vegetables:* NIV, NRSV.

PUNISHMENT. A penalty for wrongdoing. Cain reacted to God's penalties for murdering Abel by saying, "My punishment is greater than I can bear" (Gen. 4:13). Jesus urged forgiveness of offenders rather than the Mosaic tradition of "an eye for an eye" (Matt. 5:38–39). See also *Judgment; Retribution; Wrath.*

PURIFICATION. Ceremonial or spiritual cleansing. The Mosaic Law prescribed purification rites for those ceremonially defiled by touching a corpse, by contact with bodily discharges, by childbirth, and by leprosy (see Lev. 14–15). The mother of Jesus offered turtledoves and pigeons as a sacrifice in her ceremonial cleansing (Luke 2:21–24). See also *Clean; Wash.*

PURIFY [IED, IETH]
James 4:8 and *p* your hearts, ye double minded
1 Pet. 1:22 *p'ied* your souls in obeying the truth
1 John 3:3 man that hath this hope...*p'ieth* himself

PURIM, FEAST OF. A Jewish festival that celebrated the rescue of the Jews from Haman's oppression in Esther's time (Esther 9:20–32).

PURPLE. The color preferred by kings and other royal officials; a bright dye made from shellfish. Lydia was a businesswoman who sold purple cloth (Acts 16:14).

PURPOSE [TH]
Eccles. 3:1 a time to every *p* under the heaven
Rom. 8:28 to them...called according to his *p*
2 Cor. 9:7 as he *p'th* in his heart, so let him give

PURSE. A bag for carrying items (Luke 10:4), generally placed in the folds of the sash around the waist. The purse in Jesus' instructions to His disciples was probably a money bag (Mark 6:8). See also *Crisping Pin.*

PUT. See *Phut.*

PYGARG (IBEX). An animal of the deer family, perhaps the antelope or the addax. It was considered unclean by the Jews (Deut. 14:5). *Ibex:* NIV, NRSV.

QUAILS. Small game birds provided miraculously by the Lord as food for the Israelites in the wilderness (Exod. 16:12–13).

QUATERNION. A company of four soldiers who guarded prisoners during a night-watch assignment consisting of three hours (Acts 12:4).

QUEEN. A woman who exercised royal power, or the wife or mother of a king. Esther exercised great power as the wife of King Ahasuerus of Persia (Esther 5:2). Solomon provided a seat at his right hand for his mother, Bath-sheba (1 Kings 2:19).

QUEEN OF HEAVEN. A fertility goddess worshiped by the citizens of Jerusalem during the idolatrous days before the fall of the nation of Judah (Jer. 7:18; 44:17). This may have been the goddess Ashtaroth, or Asherah. See also *Ashtaroth*.

QUEEN OF SHEBA. See *Sabeans*.

QUAILS. Quail like these migrate between Africa and Europe each year. Not strong fliers, they sometimes stop to rest, too exhausted to move. These may have been the kinds of quail God provided for the Israelites during the Exodus.

QUENCH [ED]
Song 8:7 Many waters cannot **q** love
Jer. 7:20 mine [God's] anger...not be **q'ed**
Mark 9:44 worm dieth not...fire is not **q'ed**
Eph. 6:16 shall...**q**...fiery darts of the wicked
1 Thess. 5:19 **Q** not the Spirit

QUICKEN.
To preserve or give life. The psalmist praised God who will "quicken me again" (Ps. 71:20). The Father and Son have authority to raise the dead and give eternal life (John 5:21).

QUICK [EN, ENED, ENING]
Ps. 143:11 **Q'en** me, O LORD, for thy name's sake
1 Cor. 15:45 last Adam was made a **q'ening** spirit
Eph. 2:1 hath he **q'ened**...dead in trespasses and sins
2 Tim. 4:1 Jesus Christ...judge the **q** and the dead
Heb. 4:12 the word of God is **q**, and powerful

QUICKSANDS (SYRTIS).
Sandbars and shifting sands off the African coast in the Mediterranean Sea that posed a hazard for ships (Acts 27:17). *Syrtis:* NRSV.

QUIRINIUS.
See *Cyrenius.*

QUIVER.
A sheath for arrows carried by foot soldiers or hung on the sides of chariots (Lam. 3:13). The word is also used figuratively for God's protection (Isa. 49:2) and the blessing of children (Ps. 127:5).

QUMRAN, KHIRBET.
A site near the Dead Sea where the Dead Sea Scrolls were discovered. See also *Dead Sea Scrolls; Essenes.*

Q

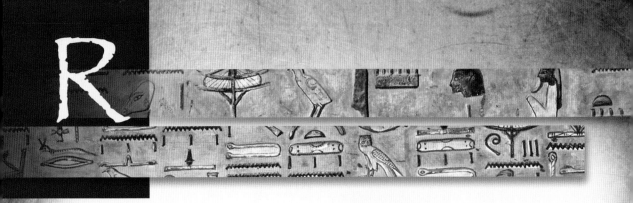

R

RAAMSES. See *Rameses*.

RABBAH/RABBATH. The capital city of the Ammonites (Deut. 3:11) captured by David's army under Joab. The city's destruction was prophesied by Amos (Amos 1:14). *Rabbath:* Ezek. 21:20.

RABBI/RABBONI (RABBOUNI). A title of great respect, meaning "master" or "teacher," used by Nicodemus in addressing Jesus (John 3:2). Its Aramaic form is *rabboni* (John 20:16). *Rabbouni:* NRSV.

RABBIT. See *Hare*.

RAB-SHAKEH. The chief cupbearer or aide for King Sennacherib of Assyria who demanded the surrender of Jerusalem from King Hezekiah (2 Kings 18:17; Isa. 36:13–22).

RACA. A term of insult, meaning "worthless" or "good for nothing," that was forbidden by Christ. Expressing such contempt for a fellow human being will lead to God's judgment and condemnation (Matt. 5:21–22).

RACE. This word in the N.T. refers to popular Grecian contests, such as races by foot, horseback, or chariot (1 Cor. 9:24). It is also used figuratively of the Christian's call to pursue the goal of Christlikeness (Heb. 12:1).

RACHAB. See *Rahab*.

RACHEL/RAHEL. Jacob's favorite wife (Gen. 29:28–30) and the mother of his sons Joseph and Benjamin (Gen. 30:22–24; 35:16–18). She died giving birth to Benjamin and was buried near Bethlehem (Gen. 35:16–20). Jeremiah referred to Rachel weeping for her children carried into the Babylonian Exile (Jer. 31:15; *Rahel*). See also *Jacob*.

RAHAB/RACHAB. A harlot in Jericho who hid the spies sent by Joshua to scout the city (Josh. 2:1–6). Later she and her family were spared when Jericho fell to the invading Israelites (Josh. 6:22–25). In the N.T., Rahab was commended for her faith (Heb. 11:31). *Rachab:* Jesus' ancestry (Matt. 1:5).

RAHEL. See *Rachel*.

RAID. See *Road*.

RAIN. God's life-giving moisture from the sky was sometimes withheld because of the sin of His people (Deut. 11:17). Excessive rain produced the great flood in Noah's time as an instrument of God's judgment (Gen. 7:4). See also *Former Rain; Latter Rain*.

RAINBOW. A colored arch in the clouds after the great flood, given by God as a promise that He would never again destroy the world with water (Gen. 9:9–17).

RAISE [D, TH]

Ps. 113:7 He [God] *r'th* up the poor

Matt. 10:8 Heal the sick...*r* the dead

Matt. 16:21 he [Jesus] must...be killed...be *r'd* again

Acts 10:40 Him [Jesus] God *r'd* up the third day

Rom. 6:4 Christ was *r'd*...we...walk in newness of life

Rom. 10:9 believe...God hath *r'd* him [Jesus] from the dead

1 Cor. 6:14 God...will also *r* up us by his...power

1 Cor. 15:16 dead rise not, then is not Christ *r'd*

2 Tim. 2:8 Christ...was *r'd* from the dead

Heb. 11:19 God was able to *r* him [Jesus] up

RAISINS. Dried grapes that were preserved in clusters (1 Sam. 25:18) and used in cakes known as flagons (Song 2:5). See also *Flagon*, No. 1.

RAM

1. A long beam used to batter down the gates of walled cities (Ezek. 4:2).

2. A male sheep used for food (Gen. 31:38) and favored as a sacrificial animal (Num. 15:6).

RAMA (RAMAH). A Benjamite city near Jerusalem and the probable site of Rachel's tomb (Matt. 2:18). *Ramah:* NIV, NRSV.

RAMAH. See *Ramoth-gilead.*

RAMESES/RAAMSES. A fertile district of Egypt where Jacob and his descendants settled (Gen. 47:11). This name may have been given later to a royal treasure city built by the Hebrew slaves (Exod. 1:11; *Raamses*).

RAMOTH-GILEAD/RAMAH/RAMOTH. An ancient Amorite stronghold east of the Jordan River that became one of the six cities of refuge after its conquest by the

RAM. *This gold statue of a ram eating from a bush is reminiscent of the ram that got caught in a bush for Abraham. The statue is from Abraham's era and from his hometown, Ur, in what is now Iraq. God provided a ram for Abraham as a substitute sacrifice for Isaac.*

Israelites (Deut. 4:43). *Ramah:* 2 Kings 8:29; *Ramoth:* 1 Kings 22:3. See also *Cities of Refuge.*

RAMPART. A low wall around a military trench or embankment that served as the first line of defense for a walled city (Lam. 2:8; Nah. 3:8). See also *Bulwark.*

RAM'S HORN. The curved horn of a ram that was blown like a trumpet as a signal to worshipers and warriors (Josh. 6:4–13). See also *Trumpet.*

RANSOM. To redeem or buy by making a payment. Because of His atoning death, Christ is described as a "ransom for all" (1 Tim. 2:6).

Prov. 13:8 The *r* of a man's life are his riches
Hosea 13:14 I [God] will *r* them from...the grave
Mark 10:45 Son of man came...to give his life a *r*

RAPTURE, THE. A doctrine held by some that deals with the transformation of the redeemed into a glorified state at Christ's return (Phil. 3:20–21). The dead in Christ will be raised at Christ's return and given an incorruptible body (1 Cor. 15:51–53). They will be caught up into the air, along with living saints, to meet the Lord (1 Thess. 4:16–17). See also *Second Coming.*

RAVEN. A bird of prey considered unclean under the Mosaic Law (Lev. 11:15). God used ravens to sustain the prophet Elijah (1 Kings 17:4–6).

RAZOR. A sharp instrument made of flint, bronze, or steel and used for cutting hair (Ezek. 5:1).

READY
Exod. 17:4 they be almost *r* to stone me [Moses]
Ps. 86:5 thou, Lord, art good, and *r* to forgive
Mark 14:38 spirit truly is *r*...flesh is weak

Luke 22:33 Lord, I [Peter] am *r* to go with thee
Rom. 1:15 I [Paul] am *r* to preach...at Rome also
2 Tim. 4:6 I [Paul] am now *r* to be offered
1 Pet. 3:15 be *r* always to give an answer to every man

REAP. To harvest grain (Ruth 2:3, 14). The spiritual law of the harvest declares that we reap what we sow (Gal. 6:7–8). See also *Harvest.*

REAP [ETH]
Lev. 19:9 not wholly *r* the corners of thy field
Ps. 126:5 They that sow in tears shall *r* in joy
Hosea 8:7 they have sown the wind...*r* the whirlwind
Luke 12:24 they [ravens] neither sow nor *r*
John 4:37 One soweth, and another *r'eth*
Gal. 6:9 shall *r*, if we faint not

REASON
Ps. 90:10 by *r* of strength they [days of our years] be fourscore years
Isa. 1:18 let us *r* together, saith the Lord
1 Pet. 3:15 asketh you a *r* of the hope that is in you

REBEKAH/REBECCA. The wife of Isaac and the mother of his twin sons, Jacob and Esau. She encouraged her favorite son, Jacob, to obtain Esau's birthright by deceiving the aging Isaac. Then she encouraged Jacob to flee to her relatives in Mesopotamia to escape Esau's wrath (Gen. 27). *Rebecca:* Greek form (Rom. 9:10). See also *Isaac.*

REBUKE [D]
Ps. 6:1 Lord, *r* me not in thine anger
Eccles. 7:5 It is better to hear the *r* of the wise
Matt. 16:22 Peter took him [Jesus], and began to *r* him
Mark 8:33 he [Jesus] *r'd* Peter...behind me, Satan
Luke 8:24 he [Jesus] arose, and *r'd* the wind
Rev. 3:19 As many as I [Jesus] love, I *r*

RECEIVE [D, TH]
Mal. 3:10 not be room enough to *r* it [God's blessing]
Matt. 7:8 every one that asketh *r'th*
Matt. 10:8 freely ye have *r'd*, freely give
Matt. 21:22 ask in prayer, believing, ye shall *r*
Acts 1:8 ye [the apostles] shall *r* power

Acts 20:35 It is more blessed to give than to *r*
Rom. 8:15 ye have *r'd* the Spirit of adoption
1 Cor. 3:14 any man's work abide...*r* a reward
James 4:3 ask, and *r* not, because ye ask amiss
1 Pet. 5:4 shall *r* a crown of glory that fadeth not
Rev. 4:11 Thou art worthy, O Lord, to *r* glory

RECENT CONVERT. See *Novice.*

RECHAB. The father of Jehonadab and founder of the Rechabites, a tribe committed to abstain from wine and to live in tents. Because of their faithfulness, the prophet Jeremiah promised they would not cease to exist (Jer. 35:8–19). The descendants of this tribe still live in Iraq and Yemen.

RECOMPENSE. To pay back in kind (Prov. 12:14). Believers are assured their courage and faith will be rewarded (Heb. 10:35–36). See also *Reward.*

RECONCILIATION. The process of bringing opposing parties or people together (Matt. 5:24). Believers, who are justified by faith and reconciled to God by Christ's victory over sin and death (Rom. 5:1, 10; 2 Cor. 5:20), are to be ambassadors of reconciliation for others (2 Cor. 5:18–20). See also *Atonement; Mediator, Christ the; Propitiation.*

RECORD (TESTIMONY). A witness or testimony to one's faithfulness. Jesus told His enemies, "My record is true" (John 8:14). Paul defended his record of faithfulness to God (Acts 20:26–27). *Testimony:* NIV, NRSV. See also *Testimony; Witness.*

RECORDER. An aide to a king who kept official records and served as a counselor or adviser (2 Kings 18:18, 37).

RED DRAGON. A name for Satan. After being cast out of heaven, Satan turned his fury on God's people (Rev. 12:3–17). See also *Satan.*

RED HEIFER. An unblemished cow or ox that had never been yoked. It was used as a sacrifice in a sin offering (Num. 19:1–9).

RED KITE. See *Glede; Vulture.*

RED SEA. The sea between Egypt and Arabia that the Israelites crossed miraculously through God's intervention when fleeing from the Egyptian army (Exod. 14:16; 15:4, 22). This body of water is also called the Sea of Reeds because of its reed-filled marshes at the head of the Gulf of Suez.

RED SEA. The Red Sea is alive with coral the color of the sea's name. Moses and the Israelites miraculously crossed the sea while fleeing from an Egyptian chariot unit.

REDEEM. To buy back property that had been forfeited because of indebtedness or to buy back a person who had been sold into slavery (Exod. 6:6). This idea describes perfectly the work of Christ, who "bought us back" from sin and death through His atonement on the cross as our Redeemer (Matt. 20:28). See also *Atonement; Lamb of God.*

REDEEM [ED, ETH, ING]

Ps. 34:22 Lord *r'eth* the soul of his servants
Ps. 107:2 Let the *r'ed* of the Lord say so
Isa. 43:1 I [God] have *r'ed* thee [Israel]
Isa. 52:9 Lord...hath *r'ed* Jerusalem
Luke 1:68 Lord...hath visited and *r'ed* his people
Gal. 3:13 Christ hath *r'ed* us...curse of the law
Gal. 4:5 To *r* them that were under the law
Eph. 5:16 *R'ing* the time...the days are evil
Col. 4:5 Walk in wisdom...*r'ing* the time

REDEMPTION

Ps. 130:7 with the Lord there is...*r*
Rom. 3:24 justified...through the *r*...in Christ
Eph. 1:7 we have *r* through his [Jesus'] blood
Heb. 9:12 by his [Jesus'] own blood he...obtained...*r*

REED. A tall grass, common in marshes and swamps, used to make paper, musical instruments, and writing pens. The word is also used figuratively for weakness and fragility (Matt. 11:7). See also *Bulrush; Paper.*

REFINER. A craftsman who removed impurities from precious metals by melting the ore (Jer. 6:29)—an apt description of God, who purifies His people through affliction and chastisement (Isa. 48:10). See also *Finer.*

REFUGE, CITIES OF. See *Cities of Refuge.*

REFUSE (RUBBISH). Waste or worthless matter (Amos 8:6). Paul declared his accomplishments were as garbage compared to the riches of knowing Christ (Phil. 3:8). *Rubbish:* NIV, NRSV. See also *Dung.*

REGENERATION. New birth; spiritual change brought about by the Holy Spirit in those who trust in Christ (2 Cor. 5:17–21). See also *New Birth; Salvation.*

REGISTER (FAMILY RECORDS, GENEALOGICAL RECORDS). A tablet on which census records or genealogical lists were inscribed, with the names of the living on one side and the dead on the other (Ezra 2:62). *Family records:* NIV; *genealogical records:* NRSV. See also *Genealogy.*

REHOBOAM/ROBOAM. The son and successor of Solomon as king of Judah (reigned about 931–913 B.C.). He refused to implement the reform measures called for by northern leaders after Solomon's death—a foolish act that resulted in the split of the ten northern tribes into the Northern Kingdom (1 Kings 12:1–24). *Roboam:* Jesus' ancestry (Matt. 1:7).

REIGN [ED]

Gen. 37:8 Shalt thou [Joseph] indeed *r* over us
Judg. 9:8 trees...said unto the olive tree, *R*...over us
2 Sam. 5:4 David was thirty years old...began to *r*
Ps. 146:10 Lord shall *r* for ever
Luke 1:33 he [Jesus] shall *r* over the house of Jacob
Rom. 5:14 death *r'ed* from Adam to Moses
Rom. 6:12 Let not sin...*r* in your mortal body
Rev. 11:15 Christ...shall *r* for ever and ever

REINS. KJV word for the kidneys, a vital body organ in humans and animals. The reins of an animal were considered a special ceremonial sacrifice (Lev. 3:4–5). In humans, the kidneys were regarded as the seat of conscience and affection (Prov. 23:16).

REJECT [ED]

1 Sam. 15:26 thou [Saul] hast *r'ed* the...Lord
Isa. 53:3 he [God's servant] is despised...*r'ed* of men
Mark 7:9 ye [Pharisees] *r* the commandment of God
Mark 12:10 The stone which the builders *r'ed*
Luke 17:25 must he [Jesus] suffer...be *r'ed* of this generation

REJOICE. To be glad or to express one's joy. Joy may result from God's blessings (Exod. 18:9) or assurance of salvation (Acts 8:39). See also *Joy*.

REJOICE [D]

Ps. 97:1 Lᴏʀᴅ reigneth; let the earth *r*
Ps. 118:24 the day...Lᴏʀᴅ hath made; we will *r*
Joel 2:21 glad and *r*...Lᴏʀᴅ will do great things
Matt. 2:10 they [the wise men] *r'd* with...great joy
Matt. 5:12 *R*...great is your reward
Luke 15:6 *R* with me; for I have found my sheep
Rom. 12:15 *R* with them that do *r*

REMEMBER [ED]

Exod. 2:24 God heard their [Israel's] groaning...*r'ed* his covenant
Exod. 20:8 *R* the sabbath day, to keep it holy
Deut. 8:18 thou shalt *r* the Lᴏʀᴅ thy God
Ps. 20:7 we will *r* the name of the Lᴏʀᴅ
Ps. 137:1 we [Israelites] wept, when we *r'ed* Zion
Eccles. 12:1 *R* now thy Creator in...thy youth
Jer. 31:34 I [God] will *r* their sin no more

Luke 22:61 Peter *r'ed* the word of the Lord
Luke 24:8 they [the disciples] *r'ed* his [Jesus'] words
2 Tim. 2:8 *R* that Jesus Christ...raised from the dead
Heb. 10:17 their sins...will I [God] *r* no more

REMEMBRANCE

Ps. 30:4 give thanks at the *r* of his [God's] holiness
Luke 22:19 this is my [Jesus'] body...this do in *r* of me
John 14:26 Comforter...bring all things to your *r*

REMISSION. God's forgiveness or pardon of our sins. This forgiveness is based on Christ's atoning death (Matt. 26:28; Heb. 9:22) and our repentance (Mark 1:4; Acts 2:38) and faith in Christ (Acts 10:43). See also *Forgiveness; Pardon.*

REMNANT (SURVIVORS). A small group of God's people who remained loyal to Him in the midst of widespread sin and idolatry. The prophet Isaiah declared that Israel would be

REMNANT. Jewish prisoners are marched into exile as their nation falls to invaders. But God promised he would save a remnant of his people and bring them back to rebuild their country.

punished for its unfaithfulness (Isa. 1:9). However, a righteous remnant of His people would be preserved (Isa. 10:20–22). God continues to work through His righteous remnant, the Church (Rom. 11:5). *Survivors:* NIV, NRSV. See also *Outcasts.*

REMPHAN (REPHAN). A star god of the Babylonians worshiped secretly by the Israelites—an act for which they were taken into exile by the Babylonians (Acts 7:41–43). *Rephan:* NIV, NRSV.

REND (TEAR). To tear apart by force. Rending one's clothes was a sign of great sorrow or repentance (Esther 4:1). *Tear:* NIV, NRSV.

RENDER [ED]
Ps. 116:12 *r* unto the LORD for all his benefits
1 Cor. 7:3 husband *r* unto the wife due benevolence
1 Thess. 5:15 See that none *r* evil for evil

RENEW [ED, ING]
Ps. 51:10 *r* a right spirit within me
Isa. 40:31 they that wait upon the LORD...*r* their strength
Rom. 12:2 transformed by the *r'ing* of your mind
2 Cor. 4:16 inward man is *r'ed* day by day

REPENTANCE. The act of turning from sin and changing one's orientation from rebellion against God to acceptance of God's will and lordship. A patient God commands all persons to repent (Matt. 9:13; Acts 17:30). Christ came to call sinners to repentance (Luke 5:32), and He also counsels believers to forgive a brother who repents (Luke 17:3). See also *Contrite; Conviction.*

REPENT [ED, ETH]
Gen. 6:6 it *r'ed* the LORD that he had made man
Job 42:6 I [Job] abhor myself...*r* in dust and ashes
Matt. 4:17 Jesus began to preach, and to say, *R*
Luke 15:7 joy...in heaven over one sinner that *r'eth*
Acts 2:38 Peter said...*R*, and be baptized

REPHAIM
1. A race of giants in Palestine defeated by Chedorlaomer, a king of Elam, and allied kings (Gen. 14:5). *Rephaites:* NIV.
2. A fertile valley near Jerusalem where David defeated the Philistines (2 Sam. 5:18–25).

REPHAN. See *Remphan.*

REPHIDIM. A camping site of the Israelites between the wilderness of Sin and Mount Sinai where Moses struck the rock and where Amalek was defeated (Exod. 17:1).

REPROACH. Shame, blame, or scorn. Jesus the Messiah suffered reproach for our sake (Isa. 53:3–6; Rom. 15:3).

REPROACH [ED]
Ps. 31:11 I was a *r* among all mine enemies
Prov. 14:34 sin is a *r* to any people
Heb. 11:26 *r* of Christ greater riches than...treasures in Egypt
Heb. 13:13 go...unto him [Jesus]...bearing his *r*
1 Pet. 4:14 ye be *r'ed* for the name of Christ, happy are ye

REPROBATE (DEPRAVED, DEBASED). A person who is depraved, corrupt, or worthless—a term applied to those who reject God (Rom. 1:28; 2 Tim. 3:8). *Depraved:* NIV; *debased:* NRSV.

REPROOF. A sharp rebuke for misconduct. John the Baptist reproved Herod for his incestuous marriage (Luke 3:19–20).

REPROVE
Ps. 50:8 I [God] will not *r* thee for thy sacrifices
John 16:8 he [the Holy Spirit] will *r* the world of sin
2 Tim. 4:2 *r*, rebuke, exhort with all longsuffering

RESIN. See *Myrrh.*

RESIST [ED]

Matt. 5:39 I [Jesus] say...That ye *r* not evil
Acts 7:51 ye do always *r* the Holy Ghost
Heb. 12:4 Ye have not yet *r'ed* unto blood
James 4:7 *R* the devil, and he will flee from you

RESPECT [ETH]

Gen. 4:4 Lord had *r* unto Abel and to his offering
Ps. 40:4 Blessed is that man that...*r'eth* not the proud
Ps. 119:15 I will...have *r* unto thy [God's] ways

RESTITUTION. To make a fair settlement with a person for property lost or wrong done. Restitution was strictly required by the Mosaic Law (Exod. 22:1). Zacchaeus promised to make fourfold restitution of what he had taken unlawfully as a tax collector (Luke 19:8).

RESTORE [TH]

Ps. 23:3 He [God] *r'th* my soul
Ps. 51:12 *R*...the joy of thy [God's] salvation
Acts 1:6 Lord, wilt thou...*r*...the kingdom to Israel?
Gal. 6:1 *r* such an one in the spirit of meekness

RESURRECTION. A raising to life beyond physical death that leads to eternal life for believers. This truth was taught by Jesus (John 6:40, 44) and demonstrated by His miracles (Matt. 9:24–25) as well as His own resurrection (Acts 2:32). Paul taught that Christians will have a glorified body like that of Christ (Phil. 3:20–21) and that it will last through eternity (Rom. 2:7).

Matt. 27:53 [the saints] came out of the graves after his [Jesus'] *r*
Luke 20:33 in the *r* whose wife of them is she
John 11:25 I [Jesus] am the *r*, and the life
Acts 4:33 gave the apostles witness of the *r* of...Jesus
Acts 17:32 they [philosophers] heard of the *r*...mocked
1 Cor. 15:13 no *r* of the dead, then is Christ not risen
1 Pet. 1:3 a lively hope by the *r* of Jesus Christ
Rev. 20:6 Blessed...is he that hath part in the first *r*

RESURRECTION OF CHRIST. The return of Jesus to physical life following His death. His resurrection was foretold in the Psalms (Ps. 16:10–11) and prophecy (Isa. 53:10–12), announced by Christ Himself (Mark 9:9–10), and proclaimed by the apostles (Acts 2:32; 3:15). It validates our faith and witness (1 Cor. 15:14–15), assures believers of resurrection (1 Cor. 15:19–20), emphasizes our final victory over sin and death (1 Cor. 15:17, 26, 54, 57), and inspires faithfulness in Christian service (1 Cor. 15:58).

APPEARANCES OF JESUS AFTER HIS RESURRECTION

1. To Mary Magdalene at the empty tomb (Mark 16:9; John 20:11–18)
2. To other women at the empty tomb (Matt. 28:1–10)
3. To two followers on their way to Emmaus (Mark 16:12–13; Luke 24:13–32)
4. To Peter, apparently in Jerusalem (Luke 24:33–35)
5. To ten of His disciples in Jerusalem, Thomas absent (Luke 24:36–43; John 20:19–25)
6. To the eleven disciples in Jerusalem, Thomas present (John 20:26–29)
7. To His disciples at the Sea of Galilee (John 21:1–14)
8. To His disciples at His ascension near Jerusalem (Mark 16:19–20; Luke 24:44–53)
9. To 500 followers (1 Cor. 15:6)
10. To James and all the apostles (1 Cor. 15:7)
11. To the apostle Paul (1 Cor. 15:8)

RETRIBUTION. A repayment for wrong done; God's wrath and punishment against man's rebellion and unbelief (Rom. 1:18). Only

R

trust in Jesus and His atoning death can deliver us from God's retribution (1 Thess. 1:10). See also *Judgment, Last; Punishment; Tribulation, Great.*

REUBEN. The oldest son of Jacob and Leah and founder of one of the twelve tribes of Israel (Gen. 29:32). He lost his birthright by committing adultery with his father's concubines (Gen. 35:22; 49:3–4). Reuben likely saved Joseph's life when his brothers proposed to kill him (Gen. 37:21–22). The tribe of Reuben settled east of the Jordan River, along with Gad and Manasseh (Num. 32:1–25). See also *Tribes of Israel.*

REUEL. See *Jethro.*

REVEAL [ED]
Job 20:27 heaven shall *r* his [man's] iniquity
Isa. 40:5 glory of the LORD shall be *r'ed*
Matt. 16:17 flesh and blood...not *r'ed* it unto thee [Peter]
Luke 10:21 hid...from the wise...*r'ed* them unto babes
Rom. 1:17 righteousness of God *r'ed*...faith to faith
1 Cor. 3:13 it [man's work] shall be *r'ed* by fire
1 Pet. 4:13 when his [Jesus'] glory shall be *r'ed*

REVELATION. The uncovering or presentation of truth at God's initiative (2 Cor. 12:1–7). Christ, the only begotten Son, reveals the Father (John 1:18). God's searching Spirit (1 Cor. 2:10) interprets the divine purpose through the prophets (1 Pet. 1:10–12) and the apostles (Gal. 1:16).

Gal. 1:12 was I [Paul] taught it...by the *r* of Jesus Christ
Eph. 3:3 by *r* he [God] made known...the mystery
Rev. 1:1 *R* of Jesus Christ, which God gave

REVELATION OF JOHN. The last book of the N.T. consisting of a series of seven visions revealed directly by the Lord to the apostle John. Through symbols such as angels, horsemen, and plagues, these visions are considered by some to portray the end of the present age and the coming of God's kingdom.

The seven visions serve as a convenient outline of the book: (1) Christ encouraging His church against attacks (1:9–3:22); (2) Christ the Lamb with a sealed scroll (chaps. 4–7); (3) seven angels blowing trumpets (chaps. 8–11); (4) Satan and the beast persecuting the church (chaps. 12–14); (5) seven bowls pouring out the wrath of Christ (chaps. 15–16); (6) the judgment of Babylonia, or Rome (17:1–19:10); and (7) the final victory of God and His final judgment (19:11–21).

The book ends on a triumphant note with God's promise of a new heaven and a new earth (chaps. 21–22). See also *Apocalypse; John the Apostle; Seven Churches of Asia.*

REVENGE. Retaliation against another, or "getting even." Jesus rebuked His disciples for a vengeful spirit (Luke 9:54–56) and commanded forbearance (Matt. 5:38–44). He commanded us to love our enemies and show mercy toward others (Luke 6:35–38). The Bible declares that vengeance should be exacted only by God (Prov. 20:22; Heb. 10:30).

REVERENCE. A feeling of deep respect and awe that believers are to show toward God and the sanctuary devoted to worship (Lev. 19:30; Ps. 89:7). Reverence should also be shown to kings (1 Kings 1:31), parents (Heb. 12:9), and family members (Eph. 5:33).

REVILE [D]
Matt. 5:11 Blessed are ye, when men shall *r* you
Mark 15:32 [two thieves]...crucified with him [Jesus] *r'd* him
1 Pet. 2:23 Who [Jesus], when he was *r'd*, *r'd* not

REVILER (SLANDERER). A mocker. Revilers will not inherit God's kingdom (1 Cor. 6:10). Those reviled for Christ's sake will be blessed and rewarded (Matt. 5:11–12). *Slanderer:* NIV.

REWARD. A return or payment for service. God rewards those who diligently seek Him (Heb. 11:6). See also *Recompense.*

REWARD [ED]
Gen. 15:1 I [God] am thy [Abraham's]...great *r*
Ps. 18:20 Lord *r'ed* me according to my righteousness
Ps. 103:10 He [God]...not...*r'ed* us...our iniquities
Matt. 5:12 great is your *r*...so persecuted they the prophets
Matt. 5:46 love them which love you, what *r* have ye
Luke 23:41 we [two thieves] receive...due *r* of our deeds
1 Cor. 3:8 every man shall receive his own *r*
Col. 3:24 ye shall receive the *r* of the inheritance
1 Tim. 5:18 labourer is worthy of his *r*

RHODA. A servant girl in the home of Mary, mother of John Mark, who answered the door for Peter after his miraculous release from prison (Acts 12:13–16).

RHODES. A Greek island in the Aegean Sea that Paul's ship passed when sailing from Assos to Palestine (Acts 21:1). This was the site of the ancient lighthouse known as the Colossus of Rhodes, one of the seven wonders of the ancient world.

RICHES. Material goods and earthly treasures, which are portrayed as deceitful (Matt. 13:22), fleeting (Prov. 23:5), and uncertain (1 Tim. 6:17). Jesus urged believers to lay up spiritual treasures in heaven rather than earthly possessions (Matt. 6:19–20).

RICH ROBE. See *Stomacher.*

RIDDLE. A story with a hidden meaning. Samson posed a riddle to the Philistines (Judg. 14:12–19).

RIE (SPELT). A common Egyptian grain plant that thrived in poor soil under hot, dry conditions (Exod. 9:32). *Spelt:* NIV, NRSV. See also *Fitch.*

RIGHT HAND. A symbol of power and strength (Ps. 77:10). Jesus is exalted in power at God's right hand (Eph. 1:20). See also *Anthropomorphisms.*

RIGHTEOUS, RIGHTEOUSNESS. An attribute of God that signifies His holiness, sinlessness, and justice (Ps. 35:24). Through faith in Christ, God's righteousness is imputed or granted to believers (Titus 3:5). Christians are encouraged to pursue the interests of God's righteous kingdom (Matt. 6:33). See also *Godliness; Goodness.*

RIGHTEOUS [NESS]
Gen. 15:6 Lord...counted it [Abraham's faith]...for *r'ness*
Ps. 1:6 Lord knoweth the way of the *r*
Ps. 19:9 judgments of the Lord are true and *r*
Ps. 97:6 heavens declare his [God's] *r'ness*
Prov. 15:29 Lord...heareth the prayer of the *r*
Amos 5:24 judgment run down...*r'ness* as a mighty stream
Matt. 5:6 Blessed are they...thirst after *r'ness*
Matt. 6:33 seek...first...kingdom of God...his *r'ness*
Rom. 3:10 There is none *r*, no, not one
Rom. 4:3 Abraham believed God...counted...for *r'ness*
Rom. 10:10 with the heart man believeth unto *r'ness*
Eph. 6:14 having on the breastplate of *r'ness*
2 Tim. 4:8 laid up for me [Paul] a crown of *r'ness*
James 5:16 fervent prayer of a *r* man availeth much

RIM. See *Nave.*

RIMMON. A Syrian god worshiped by Naaman the leper (2 Kings 5:18), possibly a god of the sun or rain.

RING. A circular band worn as an ornament on fingers, wrists, ankles, and in ears and nostrils. The pharaoh of Egypt presented a ring to Joseph as a symbol of authority as his aide or adviser (Gen. 41:42).

RIVER. A freshwater stream. The largest rivers mentioned in the Bible are the Abana (2 Kings 5:12), Euphrates (Gen. 2:14), Jordan

R

(Matt. 3:6), Pharpar (2 Kings 5:12), and Tigris, or Hiddekel (Gen. 2:14). The river mentioned in Exod. 7:21 is probably the Nile.

RIVER OF EGYPT (WADI OF EGYPT). A small stream flowing into the Mediterranean Sea that marked the old boundary between Egypt and Palestine (Num. 34:5). *Wadi of Egypt:* NIV, NRSV.

RIZPAH. The concubine of King Saul who was taken by Abner after Saul's death (2 Sam. 3:6–8). Her two sons were hanged by the Gibeonites during David's reign (2 Sam. 21:8–11).

ROAD (RAID). A path or trail for public travel, also called a highway or way (Mark 10:46). The word is also used as a figure of speech for a raid by robbers or invaders (1 Sam. 27:10). *Raid:* NRSV. See also *Highway.*

ROBE. A long outer garment similar to a tunic or mantle. The soldiers mocked Jesus at His crucifixion by dressing him in a scarlet robe (Matt. 27:28). See also *Mantle.*

ROBOAM. See *Rehoboam.*

ROCK. A stone. The word is used metaphorically for God to show His strength and stability (Ps. 18:31). Jesus changed Peter's name to "rock" or "rocklike" (Greek: *petras*) when He called him as His disciple (John 1:42).

ROCK BADGER. See *Coney.*

ROD (SHOOT). A staff or stick (Ps. 23:4). The word is used figuratively for a branch or offshoot of a tribe or family; for example, in reference to Christ (Isa. 11:1). *Shoot:* NIV, NRSV.

ROE/ROEBUCK (GAZELLE). A graceful deer noted for its swiftness (2 Sam. 2:18).

It was considered a clean animal by the Jews (Deut. 12:15, 22). *Roebuck:* 1 Kings 4:23. *Gazelle:* NIV, NRSV. See also *Deer; Hart; Hind.*

ROLL (SCROLL). A strip of parchment that was written on, then rolled on a stick (Jer. 36:2). It was unrolled for reading, just as a modern reader turns the pages of a book. *Scroll:* NIV, NRSV. See also *Scroll.*

ROMAN EMPIRE. The powerful pagan empire that dominated the known world during N.T. times (Rom. 1:7). Founded on the Tiber River in 735 B.C. by Romulus, the nation was governed by kings until 509 B.C., when it became a republic. Rome extended its borders greatly during the republic period, eventually annexing Palestine and Syria in 63 B.C.

Augustus Caesar became emperor of the far-reaching empire in 27 B.C. and was reigning at Jesus' birth (Luke 2:1–7). Jesus was crucified by Roman soldiers under sentence from Pilate, the Roman governor of Judea (Matt. 27:24–26).

ROMANS, EPISTLE TO THE. An epistle of the N.T. on the themes of righteousness and salvation, written by the apostle Paul to the Christians at Rome. The most systematic and theological of all of Paul's epistles, Romans expresses his conviction that the gospel is the power of salvation to all who believe (1:16–17).

Other themes discussed in the epistle include (1) the truth that all people, both Jews and Gentiles, are unworthy of God's grace (1:18–3:20); (2) God's imputed righteousness, through which He justifies and sanctifies believers (3:21–8:39); (3) Israel in God's plan of redemption (chaps. 9–11); and (4) the practical application of faith in the life of believers (12:1–15:13). See also *Righteousness; Salvation.*

THE GOSPEL IN ROME

Rome was a prosperous city of more than a million people when Paul wrote his letter to the Roman Christians about A.D. 57 (Rom. 1:7). A thoroughly pagan city, it contained scores of temples dedicated to the worship of many different gods.

Yet even in this pagan atmosphere, Christianity had gained a foothold. Two early believers from Rome, Priscilla and Aquila (Rom. 16:3), were associated with Paul in his work at Corinth (Acts 18:2) and Ephesus (Acts 18:24-26).

ROME. The capital city of the Roman Empire (Rom. 1:7) and the place where Paul was imprisoned during his final days and where he likely died as a martyr (Phil. 1:12–13; 4:22; 2 Tim. 4:6–8). His epistle to the Romans was addressed to the Christians in this city (Rom. 1:1–7). In the N.T., Rome is figuratively portrayed as Babylon (1 Pet. 5:13).

ROOT. The life-sustaining part of a plant. The word is also used figuratively to describe Christ's humiliation (Isa. 53:2) and exaltation (Isa. 11:10) and the believer's foundation in Christ (Col. 2:7).

ROPE/CORD. A heavy cord. Ropes on the head or neck signified distress (1 Kings 20:31–32) and perhaps submission, since cords were used to bind prisoners. *Cord:* Judg. 15:13. See also *Line.*

ROSE (CROCUS). A flowering plant, perhaps the narcissus—a fragrant flower that grew in the plain of Sharon (Isa. 35:1). *Crocus:* NIV, NRSV.

ROYAL DEPUTY. See *Chancellor.*

ROYAL OFFICIAL. See *Nobleman.*

RUBBISH. See *Dung; Refuse.*

RUBY (CORAL). A precious stone, perhaps coral or pearl (Prov. 3:15; Lam. 4:7). *Coral:* NRSV. See also *Coral.*

RUDDY. Having a reddish or fair complexion, in contrast to the dark skin of most people of the Middle East (1 Sam. 16:12).

RUE. An herb with a strong odor and bitter taste. Jesus denounced the Pharisees who were careful to tithe this insignificant plant while neglecting more important matters (Luke 11:42).

RUFUS. A fellow believer at Rome greeted and commended by Paul (Rom. 16:13). He was perhaps the son of Simon of Cyrene, who carried the cross of Jesus (Mark 15:21).

RUHAMAH. A symbolic name for Israel, meaning "having obtained favor," given by Hosea to his daughter to show that Israel would be forgiven after their repentance (Hosea 2:1).

RULE [ING, TH]
Gen. 1:16 the greater light to *r* the day
2 Sam. 23:3 He that *r'th* over men must be just
Matt. 2:6 a Governor...shall *r* my people Israel
Col. 3:15 let the peace of God *r* in your hearts
1 Tim. 3:5 a man know not how to *r* his own house
1 Tim. 3:12 deacons...*r'ing*...their own houses well

RULER. See *Governor; Prince.*

RUN [NETH]
Ps. 23:5 my cup *r'neth* over
Isa. 40:31 they shall *r*, and not be weary
Amos 5:24 let judgment *r* down as waters

R

Hab. 2:2 Write the vision...may *r* that readeth it
1 Cor. 9:24 *r* all, but one receiveth the prize
Gal. 5:7 Ye did *r* well; who did hinder you
Heb. 12:1 us *r* with patience the race...before us

RUSH. A plant that grew in marshes, perhaps the same as the bulrush (Job 8:11). See also *Bulrush; Flag.*

RUST. A substance that corrodes metal. Jesus used this word to warn against the instability and uncertainty of earthly treasures (Matt. 6:19–20).

RUTH. A Moabite woman who remained loyal to her Jewish mother-in-law, Naomi, after the death of their husbands. Ruth moved with Naomi to Bethlehem (Ruth 1:16–19), where she gleaned grain in the fields of Boaz. She eventually married Boaz and became an ancestor of David and Christ (Ruth 4:9–22). See also *Boaz; Naomi.*

RUTH, BOOK OF. A short book of the O.T. that reads almost like a short story on the power of love in dismal circumstances. Love bound Ruth and her mother-in-law, Naomi, together in spite of the death of their husbands (chaps. 1–2). And Ruth found happiness and security again through her marriage to Boaz, a kinsman of Naomi's family (chaps. 3–4). See also *Levirate Marriage.*

R

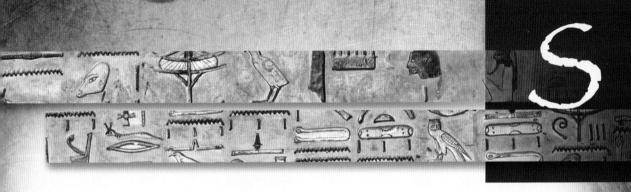

SABAOTH. A Hebrew word for "hosts." See *Hosts, Lord of.*

SABBATH. The Jewish day of worship and rest, established when God rested after the six days of creation (Gen. 2:1–3). The fourth of the Ten Commandments calls for the Sabbath to be observed and "kept holy" (Exod. 20:8). The Pharisees placed restrictions on Sabbath observance that prohibited acts of mercy or necessity (Mark 2:23–24). But Jesus declared that "the sabbath was made for man and not man for the sabbath" (Mark 2:27).

The O.T. Sabbath fell on the seventh day of the week, or our Saturday. Most Christian groups observe Sunday as the day of worship because of Christ's resurrection on the first day of the week (1 Cor. 16:2).

SABBATH DAY'S JOURNEY. The distance under law by which a person was permitted to travel on the Sabbath—2,000 paces outside the city wall, or about 3,000 feet (Exod. 16:29–30; Acts 1:12).

SABBATICAL YEAR. Every seventh year—or a Sabbath year—considered sacred to the Lord, when the land went uncultivated and debtors were released from their obligations (Lev. 25:20–21).

SABEANS. Natives or inhabitants of ancient Sheba in southwest Arabia, a country now known as Yemen. Job's livestock was stolen by Sabeans (Job 1:13–15). The wealthy queen of Sheba visited King Solomon (1 Kings 10).

SACKBUT (LYRE, TRIGON). A triangular-shaped stringed musical instrument similar to a harp (Dan. 3:5). *Lyre:* NIV; *trigon:* NRSV.

SACKCLOTH. A coarse fabric made of goat hair that was worn to express grief, sorrow, and repentance (Joel 1:8, 13). Jacob wore sackcloth in anguish when he thought his son Joseph was dead (Gen. 37:34). See also *Mourn.*

SACRAMENT. A ritual or religious act that serves as a channel of God's grace. While Roman Catholics and most orthodox churches observe seven sacraments, most Protestants admit only two—baptism and the Lord's Supper—and even these are called "ordinances" by most evangelical groups.

SACRIFICE. An offering made to God or to false gods for the purpose of gaining favor or showing respect. In O.T. times, animals were sacrificed on the altar to atone for transgression against God and His law (Deut. 18:3). Christ offered Himself as the final and perfect sacrifice for our sins (Heb. 9:11–14). See also *Atonement; Burnt Offering; Redeem.*

SACRIFICE [S]

1 Sam. 15:22 to obey is better than *s*
Hosea 6:6 I [God] desired mercy...not *s*
Jon. 2:9 I will *s* unto thee [God] with...thanksgiving
Rom. 12:1 present your bodies a living *s*

Heb. 7:27 Who [Jesus] needeth not daily...to offer up **s**
Heb. 11:4 Abel offered...more excellent **s** than Cain
Heb. 13:15 offer the **s** of praise to God
1 Pet. 2:5 offer up spiritual **s's**, acceptable to God

SACRILEGE. See *Blaspheme.*

SADDUCEES. A priestly aristocratic party of N.T. times that—in contrast to the Pharisees—rejected the oral traditions of the Jewish faith and accepted only the original teachings of Moses as authoritative. They did not believe in a bodily resurrection (Matt. 22:23) or angels and spirits (Acts 23:8). They often opposed Jesus and His teachings (Matt. 16:6, 12). See also *Pharisees.*

SAFFRON. A plant used in perfume, dyes, and medicines and for flavoring food and drinks (Song 4:13–14).

SAINT. A N.T. word for a Christian believer set apart for God's service (Rom. 1:7; Heb. 6:10). In the O.T., the word refers to a pious Jew (Ps. 16:3). Spiritual blessings are reserved for the saints of God's kingdom (Col. 1:12). See also *Church; Congregation; People of God.*

SAINTS
2 Chron. 6:41 let thy [God's] **s** rejoice in goodness
Ps. 30:4 Sing unto the LORD, O ye **s**
Ps. 116:15 Precious in the sight of the LORD is the death of his **s**
Matt. 27:52 bodies of the **s** which slept arose
Rom. 12:13 Distributing to the necessity of **s**
1 Cor. 1:2 sanctified in Christ Jesus, called to be **s**
Eph. 3:8 Unto me [Paul]...less than the least of all **s**
Eph. 4:12 perfecting of the **s**...work of the ministry

SAKE [S]
Ps. 23:3 paths of righteousness for his [God's] name's **s**
Matt. 5:10 Blessed...those...persecuted for righteousness' **s**
Luke 21:17 ye shall be hated...for my [Jesus'] name's **s**
Acts 9:16 he [Paul] must suffer for my [Jesus'] name's **s**
1 Cor. 4:10 We are fools for Christ's **s**
2 Cor. 8:9 for your **s's** he [Jesus] became poor
1 Pet. 3:14 suffer for righteousness' **s**, happy are ye

SALAMIS. A town on the island of Cyprus where Paul and Barnabas preached during the first missionary journey (Acts 13:4–5).

SALEM. See *Jerusalem.*

SALIM. A place near Aenon west of the Jordan River where John the Baptist baptized (John 3:23).

SALOME. A woman who witnessed the Crucifixion and visited Jesus' tomb after His resurrection (Mark 15:40; 16:1). She may have been the mother of Jesus' disciples James and John.

SALT. A mineral used to season and preserve food. Jesus called His followers the "salt of the earth" but warned that compromise would diminish their witness (Matt. 5:13; Luke 14:34–35).

SALT, CITY OF. A city in the wilderness of Judah near the Dead Sea, or "Salt Sea" (Josh. 15:62).

SALT SEA. See *Dead Sea.*

SALT, VALLEY OF. A valley with heavy salt deposits near the Dead Sea where King David and King Amaziah were victorious in battle (2 Sam. 8:13; 2 Kings 14:7–8).

SALUTATION. An elaborate greeting, usually involving repeated bowing and embracing (Luke 15:20). Perhaps because of the urgency of their message, Jesus advised His disciples whom He sent out to "salute no man by the way" (Luke 10:4).

SALVATION. The total work of God in delivering us from sin and reconciling us to Himself. The apostle Peter declared that salvation is found in Christ alone (Acts 4:12). See also *New Birth; Regeneration.*

SAMARIA. The capital city of Israel, or the Northern Kingdom, and a name often applied to the surrounding region. The city was built by Omri, king of Israel, about 900 B.C. It was destroyed about 722 B.C. when the Assyrians overran the Northern Kingdom (2 Kings 17:3–24). See also *Omri.*

SAMARITAN. An inhabitant of the district of Samaria between Judea and Galilee. These people were considered inferior by the Jews because of their mixed-blood ancestry going back to their intermarriage with foreign colonists placed there by the Assyrians (2 Kings 17:3–24). Jesus, however, associated with Samaritans (Luke 9:51–52; John 4:4–30) and even used a

kindhearted Samaritan as an example of a good neighbor (Luke 10:29–37).

SAMGAR-NEBO. A prince of the family of Nebuchadnezzar of Babylonia who sat in the middle gate of Jerusalem while the city was being captured (Jer. 39:3).

SAMOS. An island of Greece off the coast of Lydia visited by the apostle Paul (Acts 20:15).

SAMOTHRACIA (SAMOTHRACE). An island in the Aegean Sea visited by Paul on his way to Macedonia (Acts 16:11). *Samothrace:* NIV, NRSV.

SAMSON. A judge of Israel set apart as a Nazarite before his birth. Samson had great physical strength, which he used effectively

SAMARITAN. Samaritans in the early 1900s gather to celebrate Passover on Mount Gerizim, a mountain sacred to them. It was from this hilltop that Joshua ordered the blessings of God read to the Israelites after they conquered the Promised Land.

against the Philistines, as long as he was faithful to his vows. But his strength failed when he revealed his secret to Delilah, who cut his hair and turned him over to his enemies. Samson died, along with his captors, when he destroyed the pagan Philistine temple at Gaza (see Judg. 14–16). See also *Nazarite*.

SAMSON THE NAZARITE

A Nazarite was a person who made a vow to dedicate himself exclusively to God for some special service (Num. 6:1-21). While under such a vow, he was not to shave, cut his hair, drink wine, or defile himself by touching a dead body.

Most people made such a vow for a limited time, but it was also possible to become a Nazarite for life. Samson was a lifelong Nazarite (Judg. 13:5).

SAMUEL/SHEMUEL. A prophet and the last judge of Israel who anointed the first two kings of Judah—Saul (1 Sam. 10:1) and David (1 Sam. 16:1–13). Samuel was dedicated to God's service by his mother, Hannah, even before his birth (1 Sam. 1:11–22), and he grew up under the tutelage of Eli the priest to prepare for priestly service (1 Sam. 3:1–20). A popular leader, he was mourned by the entire nation at his death (1 Sam. 25:1). *Shemuel:* 1 Chron. 6:33. See also *Hannah*.

SAMUEL, BOOKS OF. Two historical books of the O.T. named for the prophet Samuel, who anointed Saul and David as the first two kings of Israel. Their anointing marked the transition of the nation from a loose confederacy of tribes to a united kingdom under the leadership of a king.

Major events covered by these books include (1) Samuel's rule as the last judge of Israel (1 Sam. 1–7); (2) King Saul's reign (1 Sam. 8:1–15:9); (3) the rivalry between Saul and David (1 Sam. 15:10–31:13); and (4) the accession of David to the throne and his military triumphs, shortcomings, and troubles (2 Samuel). Some of the information about David's administration in 2 Samuel is repeated in the book of 1 Chronicles. See also *Chronicles, Books of; David; Samuel; Saul*, No. 1.

SANBALLAT. An influential Samaritan who plotted to kill Nehemiah to stop his rebuilding projects and reform projects in Jerusalem (Neh. 4:7–8; 6:1–4). See also *Tobiah*.

SANCTIFICATION. The process of consecrating or setting something apart for holy purposes. In the O.T., priests, Levites, and each family's firstborn child were consecrated to the Lord. In the N.T., sanctification was regarded as a work of grace following conversion (Phil. 1:6). God calls all believers to holiness and sanctification (1 Thess. 4:3, 7; 2 Thess. 2:13). Those sanctified are committed to God's truth and serve as witnesses to His power and grace in the world (Rom. 6:11–13). See also *Consecration*.

SANCTIFY [IED]
Gen. 2:3 God blessed the seventh day...*s'ied* it
Lev. 20:7 *S* yourselves...and be ye holy
Josh. 3:5 Joshua said unto the people, *S* yourselves
1 Cor. 6:11 ye are *s'ied*...ye are justified
1 Tim. 4:5 it is *s'ied* by the word of God and prayer
1 Pet. 3:15 But *s* the Lord God in your hearts

SANCTUARY. A holy place (Lev. 4:6), a place of public worship (Ps. 73:17), or a place of refuge where a person is safe under God's protection (Ezek. 11:16).

SAND. Fine, granular soil that is seldom found in Palestine except along the seashore. The word is used figuratively for countless numbers or multitudes (Gen. 32:12).

SANDALS. Footwear consisting of leather or wood bound to the feet with straps (Acts 12:8). They were removed before entering a house or holy place (Josh. 5:15). See also *Latchet.*

SANHEDRIN. See *Council.*

SAPPHIRA. An early believer at Jerusalem who was struck dead for lying and withholding money she had pledged to the church's common treasury (Acts 5:1–11). See also *Ananias.*

SAPPHIRE. A light blue gem or precious stone used in the breastplate of the high priest (Exod. 28:18) and in the foundation of New Jerusalem (Rev. 21:19).

SARAH/SARA/SARAI. A wife of Abraham and the mother of Isaac (Gen. 11:29; Rom. 9:9), also called *Sarai.* Although she was barren for many years, Sarah received God's promise that she would be "a mother of nations" (Gen. 17:15–16), and she bore Isaac past the age of ninety (Gen. 17:17–21; 21:2–3). She is commended in the N.T. for her faith and obedience (Heb. 11:11; *Sara:* Greek form). See also *Abraham.*

SARDINE (CARNELIAN). A precious stone (Rev. 4:3). Probably the same as the sardius. *Carnelian:* NIV, NRSV. See *Sardius.*

SARDIUS (CARNELIAN). A precious stone of blood-red color used in the high priest's breastplate (Exod. 28:17) and in the foundation of New Jerusalem (Rev. 21:20). *Carnelian:* NIV, NRSV.

SARDONYX (ONYX). A precious stone that combines the qualities of sardius and onyx, thus its name *sardonyx.* It is used in the foundation of New Jerusalem (Rev. 21:20). *Onyx:* NRSV. See also *Onyx; Sardius.*

SARDIS. The chief city of Lydia in Asia Minor and site of one of the seven churches of Asia Minor. This church was characterized as "dead" (Rev. 3:1–5).

SAREPTA. See *Zarephath.*

SARGON. The king of Assyria (reigned about 722–705 B.C.) who completed the siege of Samaria and carried the Northern Kingdom into captivity (Isa. 20:1). See also *Assyria.*

SARON. See *Sharon.*

SATAN. An evil being who opposes God; the devil. In the Garden of Eden, Satan was represented as a serpent who tempted Eve (Gen. 3:1–6). He falsely accused and harassed Job (Job 1:6–12). Jesus regarded Satan as a person (Matt. 4:1–10) whom He described as a murderer and the father of lies (John 8:44). While he is called "the prince of this world" (John 16:11), Satan is subject to God's greater power (1 John 4:4) and will be cast into the bottomless pit (Rev. 20:1–3). See also *Belial; Lucifer.*

SATRAP. NIV, NRSV word for the governor of a province in the ancient Persian Empire (Dan. 6:1). *Prince:* KJV. See also *Governor; Lieutenant.*

SATYR (GOAT-DEMON). A word used by Isaiah for a wild animal that would dance among the ruins of Babylon (Isa. 13:21). *Goat-demon:* NRSV. A satyr was a mythological creature with the features of a man and a goat.

SAUL AND THE PHILISTINES

Saul had the misfortune of serving as king of Israel when the Philistines were the nation's most formidable enemy. Their monopoly on making and sharpening iron weapons put Saul and his army at a distinct disadvantage (1 Sam. 13:15–23). His sons were eventually killed in a battle with the Philistines, and he was mortally wounded (1 Sam. 31:1–13). Not until the time of David, Israel's popular warrior-king, were the Philistines finally defeated.

SAUL

1. The first king of Israel who displeased God by his disobedience and his insane jealousy against David. Anointed privately by Samuel (1 Sam. 10:1) and publicly proclaimed king at Gilgal (1 Sam. 11:15), he waged war against the Philistines during his administration (1 Sam. 17–18). He kept the spoils of war from at least one battle, assumed duties of the priestly office, and murdered Ahimelech and eighty-four other priests (1 Sam. 22:11–19)—acts that brought God's judgment. After his sons were killed, Saul committed suicide rather than be captured by the Philistines (1 Sam. 31:1–6).

2. The original name of Paul the apostle. See *Paul*.

SAVE [D]

Isa. 45:22 be ye *s'd*, all the ends of the earth
Matt. 1:21 he [Jesus] shall *s* his people from their sins
Matt. 10:22 he that endureth to the end shall be *s'd*
Mark 8:35 will *s* his life shall lose it
Luke 19:10 Son of man...seek and to *s* that which was lost
John 3:17 world through him [Jesus] might be *s'd*
John 12:47 I [Jesus] came not to judge...but to *s* the world
Acts 4:12 none other name...whereby we must be *s'd*
Rom. 5:10 we shall be *s'd* by his [Jesus'] life

1 Cor. 1:21 foolishness of preaching to *s* them that believe
Eph. 2:8 by grace are ye *s'd* through faith
1 Tim. 1:15 Christ Jesus came into the world to *s* sinners
James 2:14 though a man...have not works? can faith *s* him

SAVIOR. A title for Christ that emphasizes His work of salvation (Matt. 1:21)—a ministry foretold by the prophet Isaiah (Isa. 61:1–3).

SAVIOUR

Isa. 43:11 beside me [God] there is no *s*
Luke 2:11 unto you is born...a *S*
1 John 4:14 Father sent the Son...*S* of the world

SAW. A tool with sharp teeth used in building the temple in Jerusalem and sometimes used to execute prisoners of war (2 Sam. 12:31).

SCAB. A sore on the skin or a hardened, scaly spot left by a skin disease (Lev. 13:2, 6–8).

SCABBARD. See *Sheath*.

SCALES. See *Balance, Balances*.

SCALL (ITCH). An inflammation of the scalp (Lev. 13:30–37). *Itch:* NIV, NRSV.

SCAPEGOAT (AZAZEL). A goat symbolically bearing the sins of the people and sent into the wilderness by the high priest on the Day of Atonement (Lev. 16:8–22). This goat is a symbol of Christ, our sin bearer (see Isa. 53:6). *Azazel:* NRSV.

SCARF. See *Muffler*.

SCARLET (CRIMSON). A red color highly prized as a symbol of wealth and position (2 Sam. 1:24). Its brilliance symbolized Israel's glaring sin against God (Isa. 1:18). *Crimson:* NRSV.

SCENTED WOOD. See *Thyine Wood.*

SCEPTRE. A staff or baton carried by a king or other high official as an emblem of authority (Esther 4:11).

SCEVA. A Jewish priest at Ephesus whose sons tried in vain to cast out evil spirits in imitation of Paul (Acts 19:11–16).

SCHOOLMASTER(DISCIPLINARIAN). A household servant who accompanied children to school but did not function as a teacher. Paul used the word to show the shortcomings of the law. It could make a person aware of sin, but it fell short of providing salvation (Gal. 3:24–25). *Disciplinarian:* NRSV.

SCORPION. An eight-legged insect with a poisonous tail (Deut. 8:15). The word is also used symbolically of a whip for scourging (2 Chron. 10:11). See also *Scourging.*

SCOURGING (FLOGGING). A severe beating with a leather strap containing bits of sharp metal. This punishment was limited to forty lashes (Deut. 25:3). Jesus was scourged before His crucifixion (Matt. 27:26). *Flogging:* NIV, NRSV.

SCREECH OWL. A bird noted for its strange cries at night (Isa. 34:14). See also *Bittern; Night Hawk.*

SCRIBE (TEACHER OF THE LAW). A public secretary who specialized in copying the law, in the days when documents had to be laboriously reproduced by hand. Many scribes became interpreters and teachers, and in N.T. times they were committed to preserving the law. Their burdensome technicalities brought Jesus' condemnation (Matt. 5:20). *Teacher of the law:* NIV. See also *Lawyer.*

SCRIBE'S KNIFE. See *Penknife.*

SCRIP (BAG). A small bag or satchel (Matt. 10:10) used for carrying food or other provisions on a journey (Luke 9:3). *Bag:* NIV, NRSV.

SCRIPTURE. See *Bible.*

SCROLL. A piece of papyrus or leather written on and then rolled on a stick. It was unrolled for reading (Rev. 6:14). See also *Roll.*

SCUM. See *Offscouring.*

SCURVY. A skin disease caused by extended exposure and an unbalanced diet, characterized by dry, scaly skin with bright spots (Lev. 21:20; 22:22).

SCYTHIANS. Members of the nomadic tribes north of the Black Sea and the Caspian Sea. Paul used the word as a general term for barbaric persons (Col. 3:11).

SEA. A large body of salt water. In the O.T., the word is used for any large expanse of water, including rivers and lakes (Gen. 1:10; Isa. 19:5).

SEA GULL. See *Cuckow.*

SEA MONSTER. A giant sea creature of uncertain identity, perhaps a whale or large fish (Lam. 4:3).

SEA OF CHINNEROTH. See *Galilee, Sea of.*

SEA OF GLASS. A clear, crystal sea or lake that appeared to John in a vision, indicating

S

S

SCOURGING. *A Louisiana slave in 1863 shows the lingering effects of a scourging. (Inset) Romans often beat prisoners with a whip made of several loose strips of leather, sometimes lashed with sharp bits of metal.*

God's purity and holiness and the victory of His redeemed people (Rev. 4:6).

SEA OF THE PLAIN. See *Dead Sea.*

SEA OF TIBERIAS. See *Galilee, Sea of.*

SEAL. See *Signet.*

SEBA. A son of Cush and grandson of Ham (Gen. 10:6–7); the nation made up of Seba's descendants (Ps. 72:10; Isa. 43:3).

SEBAT (SHEBAT). The eleventh month of the Hebrew year (Zech. 1:7). *Shebat:* NIV, NRSV.

SECOND COMING. Christ's return to earth to punish the wicked and unbelieving and to receive glory from believers (2 Thess. 1:7–10). This event will happen suddenly, and Jesus will be "revealed from heaven with his mighty angels" (2 Thess. 1:7). He will raise the dead (1 Thess. 4:13–17), destroy death (1 Cor. 15:25–26), gather the redeemed (Matt. 24:31), judge the world (Matt. 25:32), and reward God's people (Matt. 16:27).

Christians should be prepared for the Lord's coming (Matt. 24:42) and remain faithful in Christian service (1 Cor. 15:58). See also *Maranatha; Rapture.*

SECRET. See *Mystery.*

SECT. A religious movement in Judaism (Pharisees, Sadducees, Essenes) as well as a political party (Herodians, zealots). Early Christians were regarded as "the sect of the Nazarenes" (Acts 24:5). The word also relates to early perversions of Christian truth (Gal. 5:20).

SECUNDUS. A Christian who accompanied Paul on his third missionary journey (Acts 20:4).

SEED (OFFSPRING). A person's descendants and thus the means of transmitting life from one generation to another (Gen. 21:12). Believers in Christ were said to be born of "incorruptible seed" (1 Pet. 1:23) and true heirs of the promise made by God to Abraham (Gal. 3:29). *Offspring:* NIV, NRSV. See also *Offspring; Posterity.*

SEEK [ETH]

2 Chron. 7:14 If my [God's] people...pray...*s* my face
Ps. 63:1 thou art my God; early will I *s* thee
Ps. 105:4 *S* the LORD, and his strength
Isa. 55:6 *S* ye the LORD while he may be found
Matt. 7:7 *s*, and ye shall find
Mark 8:12 doth this generation *s* after a sign
Luke 12:31 rather *s* ye the kingdom of God
Luke 17:33 shall *s* to save his life shall lose it
Luke 19:10 Son of man is come to *s* and to save...lost
Rom. 3:11 none that *s'eth* after God
1 Cor. 1:22 Greeks *s* after wisdom
Col. 3:1 *s* those things...above

SEER. See *Prophet.*

SEIR, MOUNT. See *Edom,* No. 2.

SELA. See *Petra.*

SELAH. A musical term in the Psalms, possibly calling for a pause or a sudden outburst of voices or instruments (Ps. 44:8).

SELEUCIA. A seaport in Syria from which Paul and Barnabas set sail on the first missionary journey (Acts 13:4).

SELF-CONTROL. See *Sober; Temperance.*

SEPULCHRE. The Garden Tomb in Jerusalem is one of the most famous sepulchers, or tombs, on earth. Though most experts agree it probably wasn't the tomb in which Jesus was buried, the garden setting helps Christian worshipers visualize the kind of place where Jesus was buried.

SELF-DENIAL. Voluntary limitation of one's desires, a requirement of Jesus for His followers (Matt. 16:24). Paul also urged Christians to make an offering of themselves to God (Rom. 12:1). Sacrifices for Christ's sake will be rewarded (Luke 18:29–30).

SEM. See *Shem.*

SENIR. See *Hermon, Mount.*

SENNACHERIB. The king of Assyria (reigned about 705–681 B.C.) who captured all fortified cities of Judah except Jerusalem and then demanded tribute from King Hezekiah (2 Kings 18:13–16). Sennacherib was eventually assassinated by his own sons as he worshiped a pagan god (2 Kings 19:36–37). See also *Assyria.*

SENSIBLE. See *Sober.*

SENTINEL. See *Watchman.*

SEPARATE [D]
Isa. 59:2 iniquities have **s'd** between you and…God
Matt. 25:32 he [Jesus] shall **s** them one from another
Acts 13:2 **S** me Barnabas and Saul for the work
Rom. 8:39 Nor height…shall…**s** us from the love of God
2 Cor. 6:17 come out…and be ye **s**, saith the Lord

SEPHARVAIM. A city whose residents, the Sepharvaites, were sent to colonize the Northern Kingdom after Samaria was captured by the Assyrians (2 Kings 17:24–31). See also *Samaritan.*

SEPTUAGINT. The translation of the O.T. from Hebrew into the Greek language about 250 to 150 B.C.—a work accomplished by Jewish scholars who were brought to Alexandria, Egypt, especially for this purpose.

Seven

SEPULCHRE (TOMB). A natural cave or a place carved out of rock where bodies were buried (Gen. 23:6–9). Some sepulchers were whitened for easy visibility (Matt. 23:27), since contact with a body made a person ceremonially unclean (Num. 19:16). Jesus was buried in a sepulcher or tomb prepared by Joseph of Arimathea (Matt. 27:57–60). *Tomb:* NIV. See also *Cave; Grave.*

SERAIAH

1. David's secretary or recorder who served also in Solomon's administration (2 Sam. 8:17). Also called *Sheva* (2 Sam. 20:25), *Shisha* (1 Kings 4:3), and *Shavsha* (1 Chron. 18:16).

2. A prince of Judah who carried Jeremiah's prophecy of doom to the city of Babylon (Jer. 51:59–64).

SERAPHIM (SERAPHS). Six-winged creatures that sang God's praises and also purified Isaiah's lips in his vision in the temple (Isa. 6:1–7). *Seraphs:* NIV, NRSV.

SERGIUS. See *Paulus, Sergius.*

SERMON ON THE MOUNT. Jesus' ethical teachings in Matt. 5–7, delivered to His followers on a hillside near Capernaum. Subjects covered include true happiness (5:3–12); Christian influence (5:13–16); relation of the law and Christian conduct (5:17–48); the practice of charity, prayer, and fasting (6:1–18); God and possessions (6:19–24); freedom from anxiety (6:25–34); judging others (7:1–6); the key to God's blessings (7:7–12); warnings about deception (7:13–23); and building life on a secure foundation (7:24–27). See also *Beatitudes.*

SERPENT. A snake. Satan in the form of a serpent tempted Adam and Eve to sin (Gen. 3:1–5). Poisonous serpents were sent to punish the Israelites for complaining in the wilderness (Num. 21:6). Moses' upraised serpent symbolized Jesus' future sacrificial death (John 3:14).

SERVANT. One who serves others; any person under the authority of another (Matt. 8:9). Isaiah depicted the coming Messiah as a Suffering Servant (Isa. 53:3–12). Jesus declared His mission was to serve and save (Matt. 20:28; Luke 22:27). See also *Maidservant; Manservant.*

SERVANT [S]
Ps. 34:22 Lord redeemeth the soul of his *s's*
Ps. 119:125 I am thy [God's] *s*; give me understanding
Prov. 14:35 king's favour is toward a wise *s*
Isa. 42:1 Behold my [God's] *s*, whom I uphold
Mal. 1:6 son honoureth his father, and a *s* his master
Matt. 23:11 he that is greatest...shall be your *s*
Matt. 25:21 Well done...good and faithful *s*
Mark 9:35 same shall be last of all, and *s* of all
Luke 15:19 make me [the prodigal son] as one of thy hired *s's*
John 8:34 Whosoever committeth sin is the *s* of sin
1 Cor. 9:19 I [Paul] made myself *s* unto all
Gal. 4:7 Wherefore thou art no more a *s*, but a son
Phil. 2:7 took upon him [Jesus] the form of a *s*

SERVANT GIRL. See *Handmaid.*

SERVE [ING]
Gen. 27:29 Let people *s* thee [God]...nations bow down
Deut. 6:13 fear the Lord thy God, and *s* him
Ps. 72:11 all nations shall *s* him [God]
Matt. 4:10 worship the Lord...him only shalt thou *s*
Luke 16:13 No servant can *s* two masters
John 12:26 any man *s* me [Jesus], let him follow me
Rom. 12:11 fervent in spirit; *s'ing* the Lord
Gal. 5:13 by love *s* one another

SETH/SHETH. The third son of Adam and the father of Enoch (Gen. 4:25–26). *Sheth:* 1 Chron. 1:1.

SEVEN. A number often used symbolically because it was considered a round or perfect number. God's creation established an order of seven days (Gen. 2:2). Seven times or sevenfold suggested abundance (Matt. 18:21–22).

S

SEVEN CHURCHES OF ASIA. The seven churches in Asia Minor addressed by John in Revelation. The messages to these churches ranged from warnings and rebukes to commendations for their faithfulness (see Rev. 2–3).

MESSAGE TO THE SEVEN CHURCHES

1. To Ephesus: Recover your lost love (Rev. 2:1-7).
2. To Smyrna: Hold steady under persecution (Rev. 2:8-11).
3. To Pergamos: Shun idolatry and immorality (Rev. 2:12-17).
4. To Thyatira: Watch out for false teachings (Rev. 2:18-29).
5. To Sardis: Renew your dead faith (Rev. 3:1-6).
6. To Philadelphia: Keep on being loyal to Christ (Rev. 3:7-13).
7. To Laodicea: Move beyond spiritual apathy (Rev. 3:14-22).

SEVEN SAYINGS FROM THE CROSS. The seven separate utterances that Jesus made as He suffered on the cross: (1) "Father, forgive them" (Luke 23:34); (2) "To day shalt thou be with me in paradise" (Luke 23:43); (3) "Woman, behold thy son!" (John 19:26); (4) "My God, my God, why hast thou forsaken me?" (Matt. 27:46); (5) "I thirst" (John 19:28); (6) "It is finished" (John 19:30); and (7) "Father, into thy hands I commend my spirit" (Luke 23:46).

SEVEN STARS (PLEIADES). A brilliant cluster of stars named for the seven daughters of Atlas and Pleione in Greek mythology (Amos 5:8). *Pleiades:* NIV, NRSV. See also *Pleiades.*

SEVENTH MONTH FESTIVAL. See *Trumpets, Feast of.*

SEVENTY WEEKS. See *Daniel, Book of.*

SEXUAL IMMORALITY. See *Fornication.*

SHACKLES. See *Fetters; Stocks.*

SHADRACH. The Babylonian name of Hananiah, one of Daniel's friends, who was cast into the fiery furnace but miraculously delivered at God's hand (Dan. 3). See also *Daniel.*

SHALLUM. See *Jehoahaz,* No. 2.

SHALMANESER. An Assyrian king (reigned about 730–720 B.C.) who defeated Israel, or the Northern Kingdom, and carried its leading citizens into captivity (2 Kings 17:3–6.) See also *Assyria.*

SHAME. Disgrace or disrepute that produces a feeling of guilt. It may be caused by idleness (Prov. 10:5), excessive pride (Prov. 11:2), or evil companions (Prov. 28:7).

SHAME [D]

Ps. 4:2 will ye turn my [God's] glory into **s**
Ps. 14:6 Ye have **s'd** the counsel of the poor
Ps. 119:31 O Lord, put me not to **s**
Prov. 19:26 wasteth his father...is a son that causeth **s**
Prov. 29:15 a child left to himself bringeth his mother to **s**
Acts 5:6 they [apostles]...suffer **s** for his [Jesus'] name
1 Cor. 14:35 a **s** for women to speak in the church
Phil. 3:19 glory is in their **s**, who mind earthly things
Heb. 12:2 Jesus...endured the cross, despising the **s**

SHAMGAR. A judge who delivered Israel from oppression by killing 600 Philistines with an ox goad (Judg. 3:31). See also *Judges of Israel.*

SHAPHAN. A scribe who helped King Josiah carry out his religious reforms by recording temple contributions and proclaiming the law (2 Kings 22:3–13).

SHARON/SARON. A fertile coastal plain between Joppa and Mount Carmel along the Mediterranean Sea (1 Chron. 27:29). *Saron:* Acts 9:35.

SHAVEH. See *King's Dale.*

SHAVSHA. See *Seraiah,* No. 1.

SHEARING HOUSE. A place between Jezreel and Samaria where Jehu assassinated the family of King Ahaziah of Judah in order to become king (2 Kings 10:12–14).

SHEAR-JASHUB. A symbolic name meaning "a remnant shall return" given by Isaiah to his son to show God's promise to His people after their period of exile (Isa. 7:3).

SHEATH (SCABBARD). A carrying case for a dagger or sword (1 Sam. 17:51). *Scabbard:* NIV (John 18:11).

SHEBA. See *Sabeans.*

SHEBAT. See *Sebat.*

SHEBNA. A treasurer under King Hezekiah who made a sepulchre for himself. Isaiah predicted Shebna would die in exile (Isa. 22:15–19).

SHECHEM

1. A tribal prince who was killed by Simeon and Levi for seducing their sister, Dinah (Gen. 34).

2. A city of refuge on a trade route in the territory of Ephraim (Josh. 20:7). *Sichem:* Gen. 12:6. *Sychem:* Acts 7:16. See also *Cities of Refuge.*

SHECHINAH. See *Shekinah.*

SHEEP. A domesticated animal prized for the food and fleece that it provided, and also used as a sacrificial offering (Lev. 9:2–4; 12:6). Large flocks of sheep were a sign of wealth (Job 1:3). Jesus spoke of straying sheep as a symbol of lost or sinful persons (Luke 15:4–6). See also *Fleece; Lamb; Wool.*

Ps. 44:22 we are counted as **s** for the slaughter
Ps. 119:176 I have gone astray like a lost **s**
Isa. 53:6 All we like **s** have gone astray
Matt. 10:16 send you forth as **s** in the midst of wolves
Matt. 15:24 I [Jesus] am...sent...unto the lost **s** of...Israel
Mark 6:34 Jesus...saw...people...as **s** not having a shepherd
John 10:7 I [Jesus] am the door of the **s**
John 10:11 good shepherd [Jesus] giveth his life for the **s**
John 21:16 He [Jesus] saith to him [Peter]...Feed my **s**
1 Pet. 2:25 ye were as **s** going astray

SHEEP GATE. A gate in the wall of Jerusalem repaired under Nehemiah's leadership (Neh. 3:1, 32).

SHEEPFOLD. A strong enclosure that provided protection for sheep. Jesus is the Good Shepherd who protects His sheep (John 10:1–11).

SHEKEL. A Jewish coin or unit of measure. The silver shekel was worth about sixty cents; the gold shekel about eight dollars (Gen. 23:15; Neh. 10:32; Jer. 32:9).

SHEKELS OF SILVER. See *Silverlings.*

SHEKINAH. A visible manifestation of God's glory, usually as a bright light, fire, or cloud (Exod. 13:21; Matt. 17:5).

SHELTER. See *Pavilion.*

S

SHEPHERD. A young shepherd keeps an eye on his family's sheep near Jericho.

SHEM/SEM. The oldest son of Noah who was preserved in the ark (Gen. 5:32). Shem was the father of Elam, Asshur, Arphaxad, Lud, and Aram—ancestors of the Semitic nations known as the Jews, Arameans, Persians, Assyrians, and Arabians (Gen. 10:22). *Sem:* Greek form (Luke 3:36).

SHEMA, THE. The noted confession of faith quoted by faithful Jews each day: "Hear, O Israel: The LORD our God is one LORD" (Deut. 6:4–9). The complete Shema also includes Num. 15:37–41 and Deut. 11:13–21.

SHEMAIAH. A prophet of Judah who warned King Rehoboam not to attack Israel (1 Kings 12:22–24). He revealed that Pharaoh Shishak of Egypt was being used by the Lord to punish Judah for its sins (2 Chron. 12:5–9).

SHEMER. The landowner who sold King Omri of the Northern Kingdom a hill on which the capital city of Samaria was built (1 Kings 16:24). His name is reflected in the city's name.

SHEMINITH. A musical term appearing in the titles of Pss. 6 and 12 and in 1 Chron. 15:21. It may designate the manner of singing or the instrument to be used.

SHEMUEL. See *Samuel.*

SHENIR. See *Hermon, Mount.*

SHEOL. See *Hell.*

SHEPHERD. A person who tends sheep, an honorable but dangerous vocation among the Jews (Gen. 31:38–40). The word is also used of ministers and of Christ, who referred to Himself as the "good shepherd" (John 10:11, 14). See also *Minister; Pastor.*

SHEPHERD [S]
Gen. 47:3 Thy servants [the Hebrews] are **s's**
Ps. 23:1 LORD is my **s**; I shall not want
Isa. 40:11 He [God] shall feed his flock like a **s**
Matt. 9:36 were scattered abroad, as sheep having no **s**
Luke 2:8 in the same country **s's** abiding in the field
Heb. 13:20 that great **s** [Jesus] of the sheep
1 Pet. 5:4 when the chief **S** [Jesus] shall appear

SHESHACH. See *Babylonia.*

SHESH-BAZZAR. See *Zerubbabel.*

SHETH. See *Seth.*

SHEVA. See *Seraiah*, No. 1.

SHEWBREAD (BREAD OF THE PRESENCE). Unleavened bread kept in the temple or tabernacle for ceremonial purposes. Its name indicated it was exhibited in the presence of the Lord (Num. 4:7). *Bread of the Presence:* NRSV.

SHIBBOLETH. A password used to distinguish Ephraimites from Gileadites in battle. Unable to pronounce the first *h* in *shibboleth*, 42,000 Ephraimites were killed by the Gileadites (Judg. 12:5–6).

SHIELD. A piece of armor made of wood and covered with hide or metal and carried in battle for protection (1 Chron. 18:7). See also *Buckler.*

Gen. 15:1 Fear not, Abram: I [God] am thy **s**
2 Sam. 22:3 in him will I trust: he [God] is my **s**
Ps. 33:20 the LORD...is...our **s**
Ps. 84:11 the LORD God is a sun and **s**
Eph. 6:16 Above all, taking the **s** of faith

SHIGGAION. A musical term in the title of Ps. 7, possibly referring to an increased tempo for singing.

SHILOAH. See *Siloam.*

SHILOH

1. A town in the territory of Ephraim where the Philistines defeated the Israelites and captured the ark of the covenant (1 Sam. 4:3–11).

2. A title of the coming Messiah that identified Him as a descendant of Judah (Gen. 49:10).

SHIMEI. A Benjamite who insulted David when he was fleeing from Absalom (2 Sam. 16:5–13). Pardoned by David, he was later executed by Solomon (1 Kings 2:36–46).

SHINAR. See *Babylonia.*

SHINE [D, ING, TH]

Num. 6:25 Lord make his face **s** upon thee
Prov. 4:18 path of the just is as the **s'ing** light
Eccles. 8:1 man's wisdom maketh his face to **s**
Isa. 9:2 upon them [people in darkness] hath the light **s'd**
Isa. 60:1 Arise, **s**; for thy light is come
Matt. 5:16 Let your light so **s** before men
Matt. 17:2 his [Jesus'] face did **s** as the sun
John 1:5 light **s'th** in darkness
2 Cor. 4:6 God...hath **s'd** in our hearts
Rev. 21:23 city had no need of the sun...to **s**

SHIP. A seagoing vessel propelled by oars or sails (Jon. 1:4–5). The Jews were not mariners,

SHIP. Model of an ancient Greek warship. The Jews weren't famous as seafaring people because other coastal nations controlled the Mediterranean Sea. Jews were better known for their skills as herders and farmers.

S

since most of the Mediterranean coast was controlled by the Phoenicians and Philistines. Solomon's fleet was manned by Phoenicians (1 Kings 9:26–28). See also *Mariner.*

SHISHA. See *Seraiah,* No. 1.

SHISHAK. See *Pharaoh,* No. 1.

SHITTAH (ACACIA). A tree that produced lumber used in building the ark of the covenant and furnishing the tabernacle (Exod. 25:10–16; 30:1; Isa. 41:19). *Acacia:* NIV, NRSV.

SHITTIM
   1. The last campsite of the Israelites before they entered the land of Canaan. It was located across from Jericho in Moab on the eastern side of the Jordan River (Num. 25:1).
   2. The wood or lumber produced from the shittah tree. See *Shittah.*

SHOA. A tribal enemy of the Jews. The prophet Ezekiel predicted these people would invade Judah (Ezek. 23:23–25).

SHOBI. An Ammonite who brought provisions to David at Mahanaim when he fled from Absalom (2 Sam. 17:27–29).

SHOE. See *Sandals.*

SHOOT. See *Rod.*

SHOSHANNIM. A musical term meaning "lilies" in the titles of Pss. 45, 69, and 80, possibly indicating the pitch or tune to which these psalms were to be sung.

SHOULDER. To drop the shoulder signified servitude (Gen. 49:15); to withdraw it denoted rebellion (Neh. 9:29); to put a responsibility on a person's shoulder was to entrust it to his or her keeping (Isa. 9:6).

SHOVEL. A tool used by priests to remove ashes from the altar (Exod. 27:3). The word sometimes refers to a winnowing fork or fan (Isa. 30:24). See also *Fan.*

SHRINE. A miniature replica of the temple where the pagan goddess Diana was worshiped, placed in homes as an object of devotion. The silversmiths of Ephesus earned their livelihood by making and selling these trinkets (Acts 19:24). See also *Demetrius.*

SHUHITE. A member of an Arabic tribe that descended from Shuah, son of Abraham and Keturah. Job's friend Bildad was a Shuhite (Job 2:11).

SHULAMITE (SHULAMMITE). A native of Shulam; the beloved or cherished one in Solomon's song (Song 6:13). *Shulammite:* NIV, NRSV.

SHUNAMMITE. A native of Shunem; a woman from Shunem who provided food and lodging for Elisha. The prophet restored her son to life (2 Kings 4:8–37).

SHUR. A wilderness in southern Palestine (Gen. 16:7) where the Hebrew people wandered for three days after passing through the Red Sea (Exod. 15:22).

SHUSHAN/SUSA. A wealthy and powerful city where Persian kings lived and where Esther interceded for her people (Esther 1:2). *Susa:* NIV, NRSV.

SHUTTLE. A weaving device that shoots the thread rapidly from one side of the cloth to the other between threads of the warp. The word is used as a symbol of fleeting time (Job 7:6). See also *Warp; Weaver.*

SIBBOLETH. See *Shibboleth.*

SICHEM. See *Shechem,* No. 2.

SICKLE. A tool for cutting or harvesting grain (Deut. 16:9). The word is also used as a symbol of God's coming judgment (Rev. 14:14–19).

6 D 1 SIDON/ZIDON. A Canaanite city about twenty miles north of Tyre founded by Sidon, the oldest son of Canaan (Gen. 10:15). Noted for its shipbuilding (Ezek. 27:8), silverware, and dyed fabrics, the city was often rebuked by the prophets for its idolatry (Isa. 23:4; Ezek. 28:21). Jesus ministered in this city (Matt. 15:21). *Zidon:* Josh. 11:8.

SICKLE. Restored bronze tools from the time of King David include a sickle, far right, used to cut grain in the field.

SIEGE. An extended military assault and blockade against a walled city. King Sennacherib of Assyria besieged Jerusalem and other fortified cities of Judah (Isa. 36:1). See also *City; Fenced City.*

SIEVE. A cooking utensil for sifting flour or meal. Early sieves were made of bulrushes, horsehair, or papyrus (Amos 9:9).

SIGN. An event foretelling future happenings or a miracle confirming a person's faith (John 4:48). Jesus warned the wicked to heed the sign of Jonah's deliverance from the stomach of the great fish (Matt. 16:1–4). Jesus foretold signs of His return (Matt. 24:3, 29–31). See also *Miracle; Token.*

SIGN [S]
Gen. 1:14 let them [lights] be for *s's*
Deut. 6:8 bind them [Scriptures] for a *s* upon thine hand
Isa. 7:14 Lord himself shall give you a *s*

Dan. 4:3 How great are his [God's] **s's**
Matt. 12:39 evil...generation seeketh after a **s**
Luke 2:12 this shall be a **s** unto you
1 Cor. 1:22 the Jews require a **s**

SIGNS AND WONDERS

Deut. 6:22 LORD showed **s-a-w**...upon Egypt
Mark 13:22 false prophets shall rise...show **s-a-w**
John 4:48 Except ye see **s-a-w**, ye will not believe
Acts 5:12 by the...apostles were many **s-a-w** wrought

SIGNET. An official or royal seal, used like a signature to legalize documents (Jer. 22:24).

SIHON. An Amorite king who refused to allow the Israelites to pass through his territory on their way to Canaan. He was defeated by Moses (Num. 21:21–30).

SILAS/SILVANUS. A leader in the Jerusalem church who accompanied Paul on the second missionary journey and who was imprisoned with him at Philippi (Acts 15:40–41; 16:19–23). He was also with Paul at Corinth and Thessalonica (2 Cor. 1:19). *Silvanus:* 2 Thess. 1:1.

SILENCE

Ps. 39:2 I was dumb with **s**, I held my peace
Eccles. 3:7 a time to keep **s**...a time to speak
Hab. 2:20 all the earth keep **s** before him [God]
1 Cor. 14:28 no interpreter, let him keep **s**
1 Cor. 14:34 your women keep **s** in the churches

SILK. A cloth derived from the silkworm (Rev. 18:12).

SILOAM/SHILOAH/SILOAH. A reservoir in Jerusalem supplied with water through King Hezekiah's underground tunnel from a spring outside the city (2 Kings 20:20). Jesus commanded a blind man to wash in the Pool of Siloam for healing (John 9:6–7). *Shiloah:* Isa. 8:6; *Siloah:* Neh. 3:15. See also *Hezekiah; Pool.*

SILVER. A precious metal used in utensils and jewelry (Gen. 44:2). First mentioned in the days of Abraham (Gen. 13:2), silver was used as a medium of exchange and was valued by weight (Ezek. 27:12).

SILVERLINGS (SILVER SHEKELS, SHEKELS OF SILVER). Bits of silver used like money as a medium of exchange (Isa. 7:23). *Silver shekels:* NIV; *shekels of silver:* NRSV.

SILVERSMITH. A craftsman who formed silver into valuable objects. The Ephesian silversmiths made models of the temple of Diana (Acts 19:24–29). See also *Finer.*

SIMEON

1. A son of Jacob by Leah (Gen. 29:33) and ancestor of one of the twelve tribes of Israel (Gen. 46:10). He was held hostage by Joseph to assure Benjamin's safe arrival in Egypt (Gen. 42:24, 36). See also *Tribes of Israel.*

2. A righteous man who blessed the child Jesus in the temple at Jerusalem (Luke 2:25–35).

3. A Christian prophet at Antioch associated with Paul and Barnabas (Acts 13:1). He was also called *Niger.*

SIMON

1. Simon Peter, one of the twelve apostles or disciples of Christ and the leader of the church in Jerusalem after the resurrection and ascension of Jesus. A fisherman from Galilee, Peter followed Jesus after he was encouraged to do so by his brother Andrew (John 1:40–41). He was called *Cephas* by Jesus, a name meaning "stone" (John 1:42), perhaps indicating the promise that Jesus saw in him in spite of his reckless temperament and impetuous personality.

Peter swore he would never forsake Christ,

but he denied Him three times on the night before His crucifixion (Matt. 26:69–75). He went on to become a bold spokesman for Christ in the early years of the Christian movement (Acts 2:14–40). Peter's surname was *Bar-jona* (Matt. 16:17). *Son of Jonah:* NIV, NRSV. See also *Twelve, The.*

2. Another of the twelve apostles or disciples of Jesus, called Simon Zelotes (Luke 6:15) or Simon the Canaanite (Matt. 10:4) to distinguish him from Simon Peter. He may have been a zealot, a Jew fanatically opposed to Roman rule. See also *Canaanites,* No. 2; *Twelve, The; Zelotes.*

3. A magician or sorcerer condemned by the apostle Peter because he tried to buy the power of the Holy Spirit (Acts 8:18–24).

4. A tanner at Joppa and apparently a friend with whom the apostle Peter lodged (Acts 9:43; 10:6, 17, 32).

SIN. Rebellion against God. Adam and Eve's disobedience in the Garden of Eden resulted in the introduction of sin into the human race (Rom. 5:12–14). Sin is committed against three parties: ourselves (Prov. 8:36), others (Rom. 5:12), and God (Ps. 51:4; 1 Cor. 8:12). Sin is described as transgression (Matt. 15:3), perversion of the right (1 John 5:17), disobedience (Rom. 5:19), rebellion (Isa. 1:2), and lawlessness (1 John 3:4).

The consequence of unforgiven sin is spiritual death, but God's gift to the believer is eternal life through Jesus Christ (Rom. 6:23). See also *Evil; Iniquity; Transgression.*

SIN [NED, S]

Ps. 32:1 Blessed is he...whose *s* is covered
Prov. 14:34 but *s* is a reproach to any people
Isa. 1:18 though your *s's* be as scarlet...white as snow
Jer. 31:34 I [God] will remember their *s* no more
Matt. 1:21 he [Jesus] shall save his people from their *s's*
Matt. 18:21 how oft shall my brother *s* against me

John 1:29 Lamb of God...taketh away the *s* of the world
John 8:7 without *s*...let him first cast a stone
John 9:2 who did *s*, this man, or his parents
Rom. 3:23 all...*s'ned*...come short of the glory of God
Rom. 6:1 continue in *s*, that grace may abound
2 Cor. 5:21 he [God] hath made him [Jesus]...*s* for us
Heb. 9:28 Christ was...offered to bear the *s's* of many
1 John 1:7 blood of Jesus...cleanseth us from all *s*
1 John 1:8 say that we have no *s*, we deceive ourselves
1 John 1:9 he [Jesus] is faithful...to forgive us our *s's*
1 John 2:2 he [Jesus] is the propitiation for our *s's*

SIN OFFERING. An offering of a sacrificial animal presented to God to gain forgiveness for sins, particularly those committed unintentionally or in ignorance (Lev. 4:2–3). A sin offering for all the people was made once a year by the high priest on the Day of Atonement (Lev. 16:6, 15). See also *Atonement, Day of; Sacrifice.*

SIN AND SUFFERING

In Bible times, many of the Jewish people believed that suffering was a direct result of sin in one's life. While Jesus was on earth, His disciples asked about a blind man, "Master, who did sin, this man, or his parents, that he was born blind?" (John 9:2).

Jesus replied that this man's suffering could not be explained by such a neat theory. Then He healed the man in a demonstration of His power and compassion.

SIN, WILDERNESS OF. A wilderness region between the Red Sea and Sinai where manna and quail were miraculously provided by the Lord for the Israelites (Exod. 16).

SINAI/SINA (HOREB). A mountain peak more than one mile high in the wilderness of

SISERA. Sisera, a Canaanite commander on the run from a lost battle, stops for a little rest in the tent of a stranger. What he gets is a tent peg hammered into his head while he's sleeping.

Sinai where Moses tended sheep and saw the burning bush with God's call to deliver His people (Exod. 3:1–10). *Sina:* Greek form (Acts 7:30). *Horeb:* KJV, NIV, NRSV.

SINEW. A muscle along the thigh by which muscles are attached to bones (Job 10:11). Because of Jacob's thigh injury, Israelites avoided eating the sinew of the thigh (Gen. 32:24–32). See also *Thigh*.

SING [ING]

Exod. 15:21 *S* ye to the LORD...he hath triumphed
Ps. 67:4 let the nations be glad and *s* for joy
Ps. 100:2 come before his [God's] presence with *s'ing*
Ps. 137:4 How shall we *s* the Lord's song in a strange land?
Isa. 49:13 break forth into *s'ing*, O mountains

Col. 3:16 *s'ing* with grace in your hearts to the Lord
James 5:13 Is any merry? let him *s* psalms

SINIM (ASWAN, SYENE). An unidentified country or region—perhaps China, Egypt, or the wilderness of Sin—from which Jewish exiles would return (Isa. 49:12). *Aswan:* NIV; *Syene:* NRSV.

SINITES. Members of a tribe descended from Canaan who settled in northern Phoenicia (Gen. 10:17; 1 Chron. 1:15). They were perhaps inhabitants of Sin, a city near Mount Lebanon.

SINNER [S]

Ps. 1:1 Blessed is the man that walketh not...way of *s's*
Eccles. 9:18 one *s* destroyeth much good

S

Mark 2:17 I [Jesus] came...to call...*s's* to repentance
Luke 5:30 Why do ye [Jesus] eat...with...*s's*
Luke 15:10 joy...over one *s* that repenteth
Luke 18:13 God be merciful to me [publican] a *s*
Rom. 5:8 we were yet *s's*, Christ died for us
1 Tim. 1:15 Christ...came into the world to save *s's*

SION. See *Zion.*

SIPHMOTH. A place in southern Judah where David hid from King Saul during his days as a fugitive (1 Sam. 30:26–28).

SIRION. See *Hermon, Mount.*

SISERA. A Canaanite commander killed by Jael, who drove a tent peg through his head while he slept (Judg. 4:2–22). See also *Deborah; Jael.*

SISTER. A general term for any near female relative, including a stepsister or half sister (2 Sam. 13:2; Matt. 13:56). The word is also used to denote members of the same spiritual family (Rom. 16:1).

SIVAN. The third month of the Hebrew year (Esther 8:9), corresponding closely to our June.

SKULL, THE. See *Calvary.*

SLANDER. A deceitful and destructive statement against another (Ps. 52:2). Such statements are uttered by the wicked against the righteous (Job 1:9–11) and believers (1 Pet. 2:12).

SLANDERER. See *Reviler.*

SLAVE. A person bought as a piece of property and pressed into service by his or her owners. Slavery was common in Bible times, but Christian teachings brought some moderation of the practice (Eph. 6:5–9). Paul appealed to Philemon to receive his runaway slave Onesimus as a brother in the faith (Philem. 10–18).

SLAVEMASTER. See *Taskmaster.*

SLAYER. See *Manslayer.*

SLEEP [ETH, ING]
Ps. 13:3 lighten mine eyes, lest I *s* the *s* of death
Prov. 6:9 How long wilt thou *s*, O sluggard?
Mark 5:39 damsel is not dead, but *s'eth*
Mark 13:36 suddenly he [Jesus] find you *s'ing*
Mark 14:41 *S* on...take your [the disciples'] rest
John 11:11 he [Jesus] saith...Lazarus *s'eth*
1 Cor. 15:51 shall not all *s*...shall all be changed

SLIME (TAR, BITUMEN). A tarlike substance, possibly bitumen or mortar, used in building the tower of Babel (Gen. 11:3). It was used as mortar for bricks and waterproofing (Exod. 2:3). *Tar:* NIV; *bitumen:* NRSV. See also *Pitch.*

SLING. A weapon made of leather thongs and used to throw stones (Judg. 20:16). The shepherd boy David killed Goliath with a sling (1 Sam. 17:50).

SLUG. See *Snail.*

SLUGGARD. A lazy, inactive person. Habitual idleness leads to poverty (Prov. 13:4; 20:4). Paul declared that those who won't work shouldn't eat (2 Thess. 3:10). See also *Idleness.*

SMITH. A metalworker who fabricated tools, weapons, and ornamental objects. Tubal-cain is the first smith mentioned in the Bible (Gen. 4:22). See also *Finer.*

SMYRNA. A city of Ionia about sixty miles north of Ephesus where one of the

S

S

SNOW. Snow rarely accumulates in Israel and is mentioned only once in the Bible. Here, a blanket of snow shrouds the cold tombs overlooking Jerusalem from the Mount of Olives.

seven churches of Asia Minor was located (Rev. 1:11). The Lord encouraged this church, which was being persecuted by the "synagogue of Satan" (Rev. 2:8–11).

SNAIL (SLUG). A creature with a spiral shell that leaves a trail of slime. The psalmist expressed hope that his enemies would "melt away" even as a snail shrinks after depositing its slime (Ps. 58:7–8). *Slug:* NIV.

SNARE (NOOSE). A trap or net for catching animals. The word is used figuratively for the pitfalls of the wicked (Job 18:10). It also represents calamity or death (2 Sam. 22:6). *Noose:* NIV.

SNOW. Frozen precipitation. One snowfall is recorded in the Bible (2 Sam. 23:20). The word is used figuratively of winter (Prov. 31:21) and moral purity (Matt. 28:3).

SNUFFER, SNUFF DISH. Two separate tools for ceremonial use, one for trimming the wicks of lamps in the tabernacle and the other for carrying away the trimmings (Exod. 25:38). See also *Tongs.*

SO. See *Pharaoh,* No. 2.

SOAP. See *Sope.*

SOBER (SENSIBLE, TEMPERATE, SELF-CONTROLLED). Moderation or seriousness, a quality desired in church leaders (1 Tim. 3:2). This is an appropriate attitude for believers as we await the Lord's return (1 Thess. 5:5–6). *Sensible:* NRSV (1 Tim. 3:11). *Temperate:* NIV, NRSV. *Self-controlled:* NIV.

SOBER [LY, NESS]
Acts 26:25 I [Paul]...speak...words of *s'ness*
1 Thess. 5:6 let us not sleep...watch and be *s*

1 Tim. 3:2 bishop...must be blameless...vigilant, *s*
Titus 2:12 should live *s'ly*, righteously, and godly

SODA. See *Nitre.*

SODOM/SODOMA. One of five cities destroyed by God because of its wickedness (Gen. 19:1–28). It is often mentioned in the Bible as a symbol of evil and as a warning to sinners (Isa. 1:9; Rev. 11:8). *Sodoma:* Greek form (Rom. 9:29). See also *Cities of the Plain; Gomorrah.*

SODOMITE (TEMPLE PROSTITUTE). A man who engaged in sexual activities with other men—a perversion condemned by God (Deut. 23:17–18). *Temple prostitute:* NRSV.

SOJOURNER. A person who lived temporarily in a foreign country (Heb. 11:9). Abraham sojourned in Egypt (Gen. 12:10) as did the Jews in captivity and exile (Ezra 1:4). The word is also used symbolically of Christians in the world (1 Pet. 1:17). See also *Alien; Foreigner.*

SOLDIER. A person engaged in military service (Num. 1:3). The word is also used figuratively of Christian workers (Eph. 6:11–18).

SOLEMN ASSEMBLY. A religious gathering, usually occurring during a major Jewish festival, that was devoted to repentance, confession, and prayer (Lev. 23:36; Deut. 16:8).

SOLOMON. David's son and successor as king of Israel (reigned about 970–930 B.C.). Solomon got off to a good start by praying for divine wisdom and insight (1 Kings 3), and he developed fame as a wise and efficient king of great wealth (1 Kings 4).

At God's command, Solomon completed the building of the temple in Jerusalem (1 Kings 5–8). But he drifted away from commitment to the one true God through his marriages with pagan wives (1 Kings 11:1–8). He also oppressed his people with burdensome taxes to support his ambitious kingdom-building projects (1 Kings 12:4).

After Solomon's death, the ten northern tribes rebelled under Jeroboam and formed their own nation known as Israel, or the Northern Kingdom (1 Kings 12:1–19).

SOLOMON, POOLS OF. Water reservoirs built by King Solomon near Bethlehem to supply water for Jerusalem through a system of underground passages (Eccles. 2:6).

SOLOMON'S PORCH (SOLOMON'S COLONNADE, SOLOMON'S PORTICO). A porch on the eastern side of the temple in Jerusalem that featured a double row of elaborate columns about forty feet high (Acts 3:11). Jesus entered the temple by Solomon's porch (John 10:23). *Solomon's Colonnade:* NIV; *Solomon's Portico:* NRSV).

SOLOMON'S SERVANTS. Canaanites enslaved by Solomon and forced to work on the temple and other building projects (1 Kings 5:17–18).

SON. A male descendant. The birth of a son brought joy and celebration, since a family's heritage and traditions were passed on through its sons (Gen. 21:2).

SON OF GOD. A title of Christ that emphasizes His deity. An angel revealed to Mary that she would give birth to the "Son of God" (Luke 1:35). After Jesus was baptized, a voice from heaven declared, "This is my beloved Son" (Matt. 3:17). John's Gospel was written specifically to encourage belief in the Son of God (John 20:31). See also *Emmanuel; Jesus Christ; Messiah.*

SON OF MAN. A title of Christ, used often by Jesus Himself, that emphasized His humanity and messiahship. This title was probably inspired by Daniel's prophecy of God's messenger who would come on a mission of redemption (Dan. 7:13–14). See also *Messiah.*

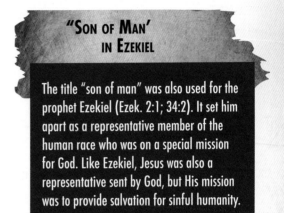

"SON OF MAN"
IN EZEKIEL

The title "son of man" was also used for the prophet Ezekiel (Ezek. 2:1; 34:2). It set him apart as a representative member of the human race who was on a special mission for God. Like Ezekiel, Jesus was also a representative sent by God, but His mission was to provide salvation for sinful humanity.

SONG OF SOLOMON. A short book of the O.T. filled with expressions of affection between two lovers (see 1:13; 4:1–11; 7:1–10). These words have been interpreted both symbolically and literally. Some insist the song symbolizes God's love for His people Israel, while others believe the book is a healthy affirmation of the joys of physical love between husband and wife. Most scholars believe Solomon wrote the book, since he is mentioned several times in the poems (1:1, 5; 3:7, 9, 11; 8:11–12). See also *Solomon.*

SOOTHSAYER (DIVINER). A fortuneteller who claimed to have the power to foretell future events (Josh. 13:22), reveal secrets (Dan. 2:27), and interpret dreams (Dan. 4:7). Paul and Silas healed a soothsayer in Philippi who was being exploited. *Diviner:* NIV, NRSV. See also *Enchanter; Medium.*

S

SOP. A small portion of food or bread held in the hand in accordance with Palestinian dining customs and used to soak up liquid foods, such as soup (John 13:26–30).

SOPATER. A Christian who accompanied Paul on the third missionary journey (Acts 20:4). This may be the same person as Sosipater (Rom. 16:21). See *Sosipater.*

SOPE (SOAP). An alkaline substance used for bathing and for purifying metals. Jeremiah indicated soap would clean externally but could not remove sin or iniquity (Jer. 2:22). *Soap:* NIV, NRSV.

SORCERY (MAGIC). The exercise of power received from evil or departed spirits to gain hidden knowledge (Exod. 7:11; Acts 8:9–24). The practice of sorcery and witchcraft was specifically prohibited by God (Lev. 19:31). *Magic:* NRSV. See also *Magic; Witchcraft.*

SORROW. Grief or sadness, which may be caused by sin (Gen. 3:16–17), the death of a loved one (John 11:33–35), or persecution (Esther 9:22). The Christian's eternal hope is a source of comfort in times of sorrow (1 Thess. 4:13, 18). See also *Mourn.*

SORROW [FUL, S]
Ps. 38:17 my **s** is continually before me
Isa. 53:3 man of **s's**...acquainted with grief
Jer. 45:3 LORD hath added grief to my **s**
Matt. 19:22 he [rich young ruler] went away **s'ful**
Matt. 24:8 these are the beginning of **s's**
Matt. 26:38 My [Jesus'] soul is exceeding **s'ful**
John 16:20 your **s** shall be turned into joy

SOSIPATER. A kinsman of Paul whose greetings were sent to the church at Rome (Rom. 16:21). This may be the same person as Sopater (Acts 20:4). See *Sopater.*

SOSTHENES. A ruler of the synagogue at Corinth who was beaten by a mob when Paul was arrested for preaching there (Acts 18:17). This may be the same person as the believer greeted by Paul in 1 Cor. 1:1.

SOUL. The part of humans' inner nature that is the seat of our appetites, passions, and sensations. Sometimes the word *soul* means "person" (Rom. 13:1). See also *Spirit.*

SOUL [S]
Gen. 2:7 man became a living **s**
Deut. 6:5 love the LORD...with all thy **s**
Ps. 25:1 Unto thee, O LORD, do I lift up my **s**
Ps. 35:9 my **s** shall be joyful in the LORD
Ps. 84:2 My **s**...fainteth...courts of the LORD
Prov. 11:30 he that winneth **s's** is wise
Ezek. 18:20 The **s** that sinneth, it shall die
Matt. 11:29 find rest unto your **s's**
Matt. 16:26 man give in exchange for his **s**
Mark 14:34 My [Jesus'] **s** is...sorrowful unto death

SOUND [ING]
John 3:8 wind bloweth...hearest the **s**
Acts 2:2 **s** from heaven...mighty wind
1 Cor. 13:1 I [Paul] am become as **s'ing** brass
1 Cor. 14:8 the trumpet give an uncertain **s**
1 Cor. 15:52 trumpet shall **s**, and the dead...raised
2 Tim. 4:3 they will not endure **s** doctrine

SOUR WINE. See *Vinegar.*

SOUTH COUNTRY (NEGEV, NEGEB). A hilly, wilderness region in southern Palestine around the Dead Sea. This region is also called "the South" and "the land of the South" (Judg. 1:16). *Negev:* NIV; *Negeb:* NRSV.

SOUTH RAMOTH. A place bordering the desert in southern Judah where David hid when fleeing from King Saul (1 Sam. 30:26–27).

SOVEREIGN. See *Potentate.*

SOVEREIGNTY OF GOD. A theological phrase that expresses the truth that God is in control of the universe. God's creation of humans and the world implies His continuing rule and sovereignty (Gen. 1:1; Ps. 8:1–5). His supreme authority is also expressed by the title "Almighty" (Rev. 1:8). In His holy character, the Sovereign must punish sin, but He has graciously provided salvation for all who trust Christ (Rom. 9:22–24). See also *Almighty; Omnipotence.*

SOW [ED, ETH]
Prov. 22:8 He that *s'eth* iniquity shall reap vanity
Luke 8:5 he [a sower] *s'ed*, some fell by the way side
Luke 12:24 Consider the ravens...neither *s* nor reap
John 4:37 One *s'eth*, and another reapeth
2 Cor. 9:6 *s'eth* bountifully...reap also bountifully
Gal. 6:7 a man *s'eth*, that shall he also reap

SOWER. One who plants seeds, as in Jesus' parable of the sower (Matt. 13:3–23). Sowing was done mostly by hand.

SOWN
Hosea 8:7 have *s* the wind...reap the whirlwind
Hag. 1:6 Ye have *s* much, and bring in little
1 Cor. 15:42 It [the body]...*s* in corruption...raised in incorruption

SPAIN. A country in southwestern Europe that Paul expressed a desire to visit (Rom. 15:24, 28). It was known to ancient Greeks as Iberia and to Romans as Hispania. Jonah's ship was headed for Tarshish, Spain, when he was thrown overboard by the superstitious sailors (Jon. 1:3, 15).

SPAN. A measure of length equal to about nine inches (Exod. 28:16). The word was also used to indicate a small amount of space or time (1 Sam. 17:4; Isa. 40:12).

SOWER. Egyptian farmers sow their seed, in a collection of paintings that portrays the cycle of planting and harvest.

SPARROW. A small bird, common in Palestine, that was sold as food for the poor (Matt. 10:29, 31).

SPEAR. A weapon of war (2 Sam. 2:23) consisting of a metal point on the end of a long shaft (1 Sam. 13:22). It was similar to but bigger than a dart or javelin. See also *Dart; Javelin.*

SPEARMEN. Soldiers with light arms, such as spears (Acts 23:23).

SPECK. See *Mote.*

SPECKLED BIRD (BIRD OF PREY). A phrase of uncertain meaning. Jeremiah compared the nation of Israel to a speckled bird (Jer. 12:9). *Bird of prey:* NRSV.

SPEECH
Gen. 11:1 the whole earth was...of one **s**
Exod. 4:10 I [Moses] am slow of **s**
1 Cor. 2:1 I [Paul]...came not with excellency of **s**
Col. 4:6 Let your **s** be...seasoned with salt

SPELT. See *Fitch; Rie.*

SPICE. An aromatic vegetable compound used in perfumes and ointments (Exod. 30:22–38) and also used to prepare bodies for burial (Mark 16:1).

SPIDER. An insect whose frail web provided a lesson on the fleeting schemes of the wicked (Job 8:14; Isa. 59:5).

SPIES. The twelve scouts, one from each of the twelve tribes of Israel, sent to investigate Canaan and report on their findings (Num.13:1–3, 30–33).

SPIKENARD (NARD). An expensive and highly prized perfume or ointment (Song 4:13–14) that was used to anoint Jesus' hands and feet (John 12:3). *Nard:* NIV, NRSV.

SPINNING. The process of making yarn into cloth by hand on a rotating loom or wheel (Prov. 31:19). See also *Warp; Weaver.*

SPIRIT. A word that denotes our reason, conscience, and nobler affections (2 Cor. 7:1; Eph. 4:23)—in contrast to the soul—our appetites, passions, and sensations. The root meaning of the word is "wind" (John 3:8). See also *Ghost; Soul.*

Ps. 31:5 Into thine hand I [Jesus] commit my **s**
Ps. 51:10 O God...renew a right **s** within me
Ezek. 11:19 I [God] will put a new **s** within you
Dan. 6:3 an excellent **s** was in him [Daniel]
Joel 2:28 I [God] will pour out my **s** upon all flesh
Matt. 5:3 Blessed are the poor in **s**
Matt. 26:41 the **s**...is willing...flesh is weak
John 3:5 a man be born of water and of the **S**
John 4:23 worship the Father in **s** and in truth
John 16:13 the **S** of truth [Holy Spirit], is come
Gal. 5:22 fruit of the **S** is love, joy, peace
Eph. 4:3 unity of the **S** in the bond of peace
Eph. 6:17 sword of the **S**...the word of God
Rev. 2:7 hear what the **S** saith unto the churches

SPIRIT OF GOD/SPIRIT OF THE LORD
Gen. 1:2 **S-o-G** moved upon the face of the waters
Judg. 6:34 the **s-o-t-L** came upon Gideon
1 Sam. 11:6 And the **S-o-G** came upon Saul
1 Sam. 16:13 the **s-o-t-L** came upon David
Job 33:4 The **S-o-G** hath made me [Job]
Isa. 11:2 the **s-o-t-L** shall rest upon him [God's servant]
Isa. 61:1 The **s-o-t-L** GOD is upon me [God's servant]
Matt. 3:16 Jesus...saw the **S-o-G** descending like a dove
Luke 4:18 The **S-o-t-L** is upon me [Jesus]
Acts 8:39 the **S-o-t-L** caught away Philip
Rom. 8:14 led by the **S-o-G**, they are the sons of God
1 Cor. 3:16 Know ye not...the **S-o-G** dwelleth in you?
2 Cor. 3:17 where the **S-o-t-L** is, there is liberty
Eph. 4:30 And grieve not the holy **S-o-G**

SPIRITIST. See *Wizard.*

SPIRITS IN PRISON. A much-debated phrase from 1 Pet. 3:18–20 that seems to indicate that Christ, in His spiritual existence, preached to the "spirits in prison" who disobeyed God during the days of Noah. Some scholars claim that Christ did not descend into hell but that His eternal spirit (which later was made alive in His resurrection) preached to the spirits at the time of their disobedience.

SPIRITUAL [LY]
Rom. 8:6 to be *s'ly* minded is life and peace
1 Cor. 14:1 Follow after charity...desire *s* gifts
1 Cor. 15:44 sown a natural body...raised a *s* body
Eph. 6:12 we wrestle...against *s* wickedness

SPIRITUAL GIFTS. Gifts bestowed freely by the Holy Spirit upon believers (James 1:17) for the edification of fellow believers and the church (Rom. 1:11; 1 Cor. 12:28). Gifts listed in Romans are preaching, serving, teaching, encouraging, giving, leading, and helping others (Rom. 12:6–8). Gifts listed in 1 Corinthians are wisdom, knowledge, faith, healing, miracles, prophecy, discernment of spirits, tongues, and interpretation of tongues (1 Cor. 12:8–11). Love is the supreme spiritual gift (1 Cor. 12:31; 13:13).

SPIT. To spit was a gesture of extreme contempt (Num. 12:14), but Jesus used saliva to cure a man's blindness (Mark 8:23).

SPOIL (PLUNDER, BOOTY). Plunder taken in war or seized by bandits (Num. 31:9). David established strict regulations for division of the spoils of war among his soldiers (1 Sam. 30:20–25). *Plunder:* NIV; *booty:* NRSV. See also *Booty.*

SPOON (PITCHER, FLAGON). A shallow dish or pan used as a censer for burning incense in the tabernacle and temple (Exod. 25:29). *Pitcher:* NIV; *flagon:* NRSV. See also *Pitcher; Flagon,* No. 2.

SPRING RAIN. See *Latter Rain.*

STABLE. A shelter for animals. Ezekiel denounced the Ammonites by prophesying the city of Rabbah would become a stable for livestock (Ezek. 25:2, 5).

STACTE (GUM RESIN). An ingredient used in the sacred incense burned in temple ceremonies, possibly a gum or spice from the styrax tree (Exod. 30:34). *Gum resin:* NIV.

STAFF. A long stick or rod used to goad animals, to remove fruit from trees (Isa. 28:27), and as support or defense for the old and infirm (Exod. 21:19).

STALL. A stable and storage area. King Solomon had at least 4,000 stalls "for horses and chariots" (2 Chron. 9:25).

STAND [ETH]
Exod. 14:13 *s* still...see...salvation of the LORD
Ps. 24:3 who shall *s* in his [God's] holy place
Isa. 40:8 word of our God shall *s* for ever
Matt. 12:25 house divided...shall not *s*
Rom. 14:10 all *s* before the judgment seat of Christ
1 Cor. 10:12 thinketh he *s'eth* take heed lest he fall
1 Cor. 16:13 Watch ye, *s* fast in the faith
Gal. 5:1 *S* fast...in the liberty...Christ hath made us free
Eph. 6:11 able to *s* against the wiles of the devil
2 Thess. 2:15 Therefore, brethren, *s* fast
Rev. 3:20 I [Jesus] *s* at the door, and knock

STANDARD (ENSIGN). A banner, flag, or streamer to identify groups of troops or warriors. In the wilderness, each tribe of Israel marched under its own unique banner (Num. 2:2, 34). *Ensign:* NRSV. See also *Ensign.*

S

STANDARD BEARER. A person who carried the flag or standard of his army or his people—a highly regarded position (Isa. 10:18).

STAR. A luminous body visible in the sky at night. The Hebrews regarded all heavenly bodies as stars, except the sun and moon (Gen. 1:16). The stars were considered a noble mark of God's creative power (Ps. 19:1). Stars were used symbolically for rulers, princes, angels, and ministers (Job 38:7; Dan. 8:10; Rev. 1:16–20). Christ was called "the bright and morning star" (Rev. 22:16).

STARGAZERS. Astrologers; persons who predicted the future by the movement of the stars. The Babylonians were noted for their reliance on astrology (Isa. 47:1, 13). See also *Astrologer; Wise Men.*

STATUTE (DECREE). A law, commandment, or official pronouncement that regulates behavior and conduct (Exod. 18:16). *Decree:* NIV. See also *Commandment; Decree.*

STATUTE [S]
Exod. 27:21 a *s* for ever unto their generations
Lev. 16:34 this shall be an everlasting *s*
Ps. 19:8 The *s's* of the LORD are right
Ps. 119:12 O LORD: teach me thy *s's*

STEADFASTNESS. Persistence and patience in one's faith and activities (Heb. 3:6, 14). Believers are encouraged to endure chastening (Heb. 12:7) and persecution (Rom. 8:35–37). See also *Patience; Perseverance.*

STEDFAST [LY, NESS]
Luke 9:51 he [Jesus] *s'ly* set his face to go to Jerusalem
1 Cor. 15:58 Therefore...be ye *s*, unmoveable
Col. 2:5 the *s'ness* of your faith in Christ

STAR. Pleiades star cluster, known since ancient times as the Seven Sisters. The books of Job and Amos each mention this cluster.

STEEL. KJV word for copper or brass (Jer. 15:12). See also *Brass*.

STEP. See *Pace*.

STEPHEN. A zealous believer who became the first martyr of the Christian cause. A Jewish believer of Greek background, Stephen was among the seven "deacons" selected by the early church to provide relief for other Greek-speaking Christians (Acts 6:5–8). His criticism of O.T. laws and traditions brought him into conflict with Jewish leaders, and he was stoned to death on a charge of blasphemy (Acts 7:55–60).

STEW. See *Pottage*.

STEWARD. A person employed as a custodian, manager, or administrator, usually of a large household (Gen. 43:19). Christians are urged to be faithful stewards of God's gifts (1 Cor. 4:1–2). See also *Treasurer*.

Matt. 20:8 said unto his **s**...give them their hire
Luke 16:8 lord commended the unjust **s**
Titus 1:7 bishop must be blameless, as the **s** of God

STEWARDSHIP. Wise and responsible use of one's God-given resources. Christian stewardship is based on God's ownership of all things (Gen. 1:1; Ps. 24:1–2) and man's assigned dominion of God's creation (Gen. 1:26; 2:15). Good stewardship involves faithfulness in use of one's time (Eph. 5:16), talents (2 Tim. 1:6; 2:15), and money (Mal. 3:10). See also *Tithe*.

STIFFNECKED. See *Neck*.

STOCKS (SHACKLES). A wooden frame for public punishment of offenders, containing holes for confining hands, feet, and sometimes the neck (Job 33:11). *Shackles:* NIV (Job 13:27). See also *Fetters*.

STOICKS (STOICS). A group of philosophers encountered by Paul in his visit to Athens (Acts 17:18). Highly independent moralists, the Stoics were fatalistic in their outlook on life. *Stoics:* NIV, NRSV. See also *Epicureans*.

STOMACH. See *Maw*.

STOMACHER (RICH ROBE). An expensive, festive robe worn by women (Isa. 3:24). *Rich robe:* NRSV.

STONE. See *Rock*.

STONECUTTER. See *Hewer*.

STONING. The Jewish mode of capital punishment, specified in the law for these offenses: sacrificing of children to idols (Lev. 20:2–5), breaking of the Sabbath (Num. 15:32–36), idolatry (Deut. 17:2–7), rebellion of children against parents (Deut. 21:18–21), and adultery (Deut. 22:23–24). Godly men who were stoned for their faith included the prophets (Heb. 11:37), Stephen (Acts 7:59), and Paul, who was presumed dead from stoning (Acts 14:19–20).

STORE CITY (STORAGE TOWN). A city or a supply depot in a city for the storage of food, equipment, and weapons of war (2 Chron. 8:4). *Storage town:* NRSV. See also *Treasure City*.

STOREHOUSE. A building for storing food. Joseph built grain storehouses in Egypt to get ready for the years of famine (Gen. 41:48–49).

STORK. A long-necked migratory bird similar to the crane (Ps. 104:17); an unclean animal to the Jews (Lev. 11:19).

STORM. See *Tempest; Whirlwind*.

S

S

STRAIGHT
Isa. 40:3 make *s*...a highway for our God
Luke 3:4 Prepare ye the way of the Lord, make his paths *s*
Acts 9:11 go into the street which is called **S**

STRANGER. See *Foreigner.*

STRAW. A food for livestock. Straw was also used as a strengthening and binding ingredient in bricks (Exod. 5:7, 16).

STREET. A traffic lane in a city. Streets of Bible times were mostly crude, crooked, and narrow, much like a dirty alley (Jer. 37:21). The street in Damascus called Straight was exceptionally wide (Acts 9:11).

STRENGTH
Exod. 15:2 LORD is my *s* and song
Job 12:13 With him [God] is wisdom and *s*
Ps. 27:1 the LORD is the *s* of my life
Ps. 46:1 God is our refuge and *s*
Ps. 71:9 forsake me not when my *s* faileth
Isa. 12:2 LORD...is my *s* and my song
Isa. 30:15 quietness and in confidence shall be your *s*
Isa. 40:31 that wait upon the LORD...renew their *s*
Mark 12:30 love the Lord thy God...with all thy *s*

STRENGTHEN [ETH, ING]
Ps. 27:14 he [God] shall *s* thine heart
Luke 22:43 appeared an angel...*s'ing* him [Jesus]
Phil. 4:13 all things through Christ which *s'eth* me [Paul]

STRIFE. Bitter conflict caused by self-seeking (Luke 22:24) or a worldly spirit (1 Cor. 3:3). Strife may be avoided by unselfishness and a brotherly spirit (Gen. 13:7–8; Phil. 2:3). See also *Contention.*

STRIPES
Isa. 53:5 with his [God's servant's] *s* we are healed
2 Cor. 11:24 five times received I [Paul] forty *s*
1 Pet. 2:24 by whose [Jesus'] *s* ye were healed

STRIVE [D, ING]
Luke 13:24 **S** to enter in at the strait gate
Rom. 15:20 so have I [Paul] *s'd* to preach the gospel
Phil. 1:27 one mind *s'ing* together for...the gospel

STRONG [ER]
Deut. 31:6 Be *s* and of a good courage
Ps. 24:8 The LORD *s* and mighty
Ps. 71:7 thou [God] art my *s* refuge
Prov. 18:10 name of the LORD is a *s* tower
Eccles. 9:11 race is not to the swift, nor the battle to the *s*
Luke 2:40 child [Jesus] grew, and waxed *s* in spirit
Rom. 15:1 *s* ought to bear the infirmities of the weak
1 Cor. 1:25 weakness of God is *s'er* than men
2 Cor. 12:10 when I [Paul] am weak, then am I *s*

STRONG DRINK. See *Wine.*

STRUTTING ROOSTER. See *Greyhound.*

STUBBLE. The short stumps of grain stalks left in the ground after harvesting (Exod. 5:12). Regarded as worthless, stubble symbolized instability and impermanence (Isa. 33:11).

STUMBLINGBLOCK. A hindrance to belief or understanding. Israel's iniquity and idolatry were a stumblingblock (Jer. 6:21; 18:15). Paul urged Christians not to offend or serve as a hindrance to a weak brother (Rom. 14:13; 1 Cor. 8:9). The preaching of "Christ crucified" was a stumblingblock to the Jews (1 Cor. 1:23).

SUBMIT [TING]
Eph. 5:21 *S'ting* yourselves one to another...fear of God
Eph. 5:22 Wives, *s* yourselves unto your own husbands
James 4:7 **S** yourselves therefore to God
1 Pet. 5:5 younger, *s* yourselves unto the elder

SUBURBS (PASTURE LANDS). The open country around a city used for grazing livestock or other purposes (Josh. 21:11). *Pasture lands:* NIV, NRSV.

SUPPER. At a supper in the village of Emmaus, after His resurrection, Jesus blesses the bread. Only then do those with Him recognize who He is. Then suddenly He disappears.

SUCCOTH-BENOTH. An idol set up in Samaria by the pagan peoples who colonized the area after Israel (Northern Kingdom) fell to the Assyrians (2 Kings 17:29–30).

SUCKLING. An infant or young animal not yet weaned from its mother's milk. As judge, Samuel offered a suckling lamb as a burnt offering to the Lord (1 Sam. 7:9).

SUFFER [ED, ETH, INGS]
Ps. 55:22 he [God]...never *s* the righteous to be moved
Matt. 16:21 Jesus...must go...*s* many things
Matt. 19:14 *S* little children...forbid them not
Luke 24:26 Ought not Christ to have *s'ed* these things
Luke 24:46 thus it behoved Christ to *s*

Acts 9:16 he [Paul] must *s* for my [Jesus'] name's sake
1 Cor. 10:13 not *s* you to be tempted above that ye are able
1 Cor. 13:4 Charity *s'eth* long, and is kind
2 Tim. 2:12 we *s*, we shall also reign with him [Jesus]
Heb. 5:8 learned he [Jesus] obedience by the things...he *s'ed*
1 Pet. 4:13 ye are partakers of Christ's *s'ings*

SUFFERING. Pain or distress. Suffering for Jesus' sake may be regarded as fellowship with Christ (Phil. 3:10) and as a stewardship (Phil. 1:29).See also *Affliction; Anguish.*

SUICIDE. To take one's own life. Suicide may be brought on by hopelessness (Judg. 16:28–30), sin (1 Kings 16:18–19), disappointment (2 Sam. 17:23), and betrayal (Matt. 27:3–5).

This act violates the principles of life's sacredness (Gen. 9:5–6; 1 Cor. 6:19) and God's sovereign rule (Rom. 9:20–21).

SUKKIIM (SUKKITES). An African or Ethiopian tribe allied with Pharaoh Shishak of Egypt when he invaded Judah (2 Chron. 12:3). *Sukkites:* NIV.

SULFUR. See *Brimstone.*

SUMER. The southern division of ancient Babylonia (now southern Iraq), consisting largely of the fertile plain between the Tigris and Euphrates rivers. In the O.T., it was called Shinar (Gen. 10:10) or Chaldea (Jer. 50:10). See also *Babylonia.*

SUN. The luminous solar body that provides light and heat to Earth. Some of the ancient civilizations surrounding Israel worshiped the sun, and even the Israelites burned incense to the sun on occasion (2 Kings 23:5). God is spoken of figuratively as a sun and shield (Ps. 84:11).

SUPERSCRIPTION (INSCRIPTION). Words engraved on coins or other surfaces. The superscription "King of the Jews" was placed above Jesus on the cross (Mark 15:26). *Inscription:* NRSV.

SUPPER. The main daily meal of ancient times, usually the evening meal (Luke 14:6) as observed by Jews, Greeks, and Romans. In the N.T. the word is used of the Passover (John 13:1–2) and the Lord's Supper (1 Cor. 11:20).

SUPPLICATION (PETITION). An earnest prayer or request. Paul urged supplication with thanksgiving as an antidote to anxiety (Phil. 4:6). *Petition:* NIV. See also *Petition.*

SUPPLY CITY. See *Store City; Treasure City.*

SUPREME COMMANDER. See *Tartan.*

SURETY (GUARANTEE). One who guarantees payment of another person's debt or obligation. Jesus' perfect priesthood was a surety or guarantee of a better covenant (Heb. 7:22). *Guarantee:* NIV, NRSV.

SURVIVORS. See *Remnant.*

SUSA. See *Shushan.*

SUSANNA. A female follower of Jesus who apparently provided food and lodging for Him and perhaps His disciples (Luke 8:2–3).

SWADDLING CLOTHES, SWADDLING BANDS. A square cloth like a quilt or a blanket that was wrapped around a newborn baby (Luke 2:7, 12). This cloth was held in place by swaddling bands—narrow strips of cloth (Job 38:9).

SWALLOW. A swift bird that nests in buildings and makes a mournful sound (Ps. 84:3; Prov. 26:2).

SWAN (WHITE OWL, WATER HEN). An unclean water bird, perhaps the ibis or water hen (Lev. 11:18). *White owl:* NIV; *water hen:* NRSV.

SWEAR
Lev. 19:12 not *s* by my [God's] name falsely
Matt. 5:34 I [Jesus] say unto you, **S** not at all
Mark 14:71 he [Peter] began to curse and to *s*

SWEARING. See *Oath.*

SWINE (PIGS). Pigs or hogs. The flesh of swine was forbidden as food (Lev. 11:7). Swine were regarded as offensive to the Lord (Isa. 65:2–4). *Pigs:* NIV, NRSV.

SWORD. A sharp blade carried by soldiers as a weapon of war. Simeon and Levi used swords in the massacre at Shechem (Gen. 34:25).

SYCAMINE (MULBERRY). A tree or shrub that bore a fruit similar to blackberries (Luke 17:6). *Mulberry:* NIV, NRSV. See also *Mulberry.*

SYCHAR. A city of Samaria where Jesus talked to the woman at Jacob's well (John 4:5–40).

SYCHEM. See *Shechem,* No. 2.

SYCOMORE (SYCAMORE). A fig-bearing tree valued for its fruit and soft, durable wood (Luke 19:4). *Sycamore:* NIV, NRSV.

SYENE. See *Sinim.*

SYMBOL. A word, action, or object that stands for truths or spiritual realities. Circumcision was a symbol of God's covenant with Israel (Rom. 4:11). The rainbow signified God's promise not to destroy the world by water again (Gen. 9:12–13). The tearing of the temple curtain at Christ's death represented the believer's direct access to God through Christ (Matt. 27:50–51).

SYNAGOGUE. A house of worship for the Jews that developed during their period of exile in Babylonia and Persia. Synagogues shifted the emphasis of the Jews from animal sacrifices to worship and teaching of the law. Paul regularly proclaimed the message of Christ in Jewish synagogues on his missionary journeys outside Palestine (Acts 18:4).

SYNOPTIC GOSPELS. A phrase used for the Gospels of Matthew, Mark, and Luke to set them apart from the Gospel of John. The Synoptic Gospels are similar in their straightforward and factual treatment of the life of Jesus, while John gives the theological meaning of these facts and events.

SYRIA/ARAM. A nation northeast of Israel that was a persistent enemy of the Jews across several centuries (1 Kings 15:18–20), particularly from David's administration until Syria fell to the Assyrians about 700 B.C. This nation was allied with Babylonia and Assyria at one point in its history; thus its name *Syria.* When Jesus was born, Syria was a province under Roman control (Luke 2:2). This nation was also known as *Aram* (Num. 23:7). See also *Damascus.*

DAMASCUS, SYRIA

Syria's capital was Damascus, a city that still exists today. It is one of the oldest continually inhabited cities in the world. The apostle Paul was converted to Christianity while traveling to Damascus to persecute Christian believers in that city (Acts 9:1–9).

SYRIA-DAMASCUS. See *Damascus.*

SYRO-PHOENICIAN. An inhabitant of Phoenicia during the time when Phoenicia was part of the Roman province of Syria. Jesus ministered in this area (Mark 7:25–31).

SYRTIS. See *Quicksands.*

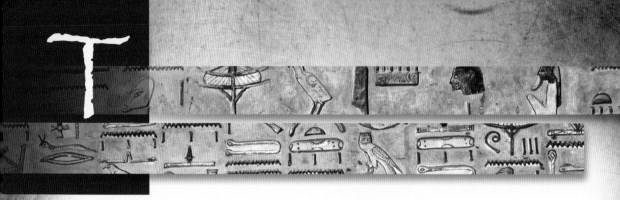

TAANACH/TANACH. A Canaanite city west of the Jordan River conquered by Joshua and assigned to the Levites (Josh. 12:21). *Tanach:* Josh. 21:25.

TABERNACLE/TENT OF MEETING. A tent or portable sanctuary built in the wilderness at God's command as a place of worship for the Israelites (Exod. 40:1–8). It was also called the *Tent of Meeting* because it was considered a place of encounter between God and His people. The tabernacle foreshadowed Christ's incarnation when "the Word was made flesh, and dwelt among us" (John 1:14). See also *Holy Place; Holy of Holies.*

TABERNACLES, FEAST OF/FEAST OF BOOTHS. A festival, also known as the Feast of Booths and the Feast of Ingathering (Exod. 23:16; Num. 29:12), observed annually during the harvest season to commemorate Israel's wilderness wandering experience. The people lived in tents or booths in remembrance of their days as tent dwellers while waiting to enter Canaan (Lev. 23:39–43).

TABERNACLE. The Tabernacle—a tent worship center—is where Israelites offered sacrifices to God during the Exodus. Priests carried the animal remains to the horned altar, in the foreground, and burned them as fragrant offerings to God.

TABITHA/DORCAS. A Christian widow at Joppa whom Peter restored to life (Acts 9:36–40). Her Greek name was *Dorcas.*

TABLET. A flat piece of stone on which the Ten Commandments were engraved by the finger of God (Exod. 24:12).

TABOR, MOUNT. A mountain on the border of the territories of Zebulun and Issachar about six miles from Nazareth in Galilee. From this mountain the judge Deborah sent Barak to defeat Sisera and the Canaanites (Judg. 4:6–14).

TABRET (TAMBOURINE). A musical instrument that was probably similar to the tambourine (Gen. 31:27). *Tambourine:* NIV, NRSV.

TADMOR (TAMAR). A trading center between the city of Damascus in Syria and the Euphrates River that was rebuilt by King Solomon about 1000 B.C. (1 Kings 9:17–18). *Tamar:* NRSV.

TAHPANHES/TAHAPANES/TEHAPH-NEHES. An Egyptian city on the Nile River to which citizens of Judah fled after the fall of Jerusalem to the Babylonians (Jer. 43:7–10). *Tahapanes:* Jer. 2:16; *Tehaphnehes:* Ezek. 30:18.

TALEBEARER (GOSSIP). A person who gossips about or slanders another with destructive words (Prov. 18:8). *Gossip:* NIV. See also *Busybody; Gossip.*

TALENT. A common unit of weight or measure of monetary value used by the Hebrews, Greeks, and Romans (Matt. 25:14–30).

TAMAR

1. The widow of Er and Onan, sons of Judah, who eventually bore Judah's twin sons, Perez and Zerah (Gen. 38:6–30). *Thamar:* Jesus' ancestry (Matt. 1:3).

2. Absalom's sister who was sexually assaulted by her half brother Amnon. Absalom avenged the crime by killing Amnon (2 Sam. 13:1–32).

3. NRSV word for Tadmor (1 Kings 9:17–18). See *Tadmor.*

TAMARISK. A small tree or shrub. King Saul and his sons were buried under a tamarisk (1 Sam. 22:6).

TAMBOURINE. See *Tabret; Timbrel.*

TANNER. A person who cured animal skins. This probably was not a reputable vocation among the Jews because of the problem of defilement by touching unclean animals. Peter lodged with a tanner at Joppa (Acts 10:5–6). See also *Leather.*

TAPESTRY. An expensive curtain or cloth embroidered with artwork and owned generally by the wealthy (Prov. 7:16; 31:22).

TAR. See *Slime.*

TARE. A weed, now known as the darnel plant, that resembles wheat. In Jesus' parable, tares represent wicked seed sown by Satan that will ultimately be separated and destroyed (Matt. 13:25–30, 36–43).

TARPELITES. A tribe that colonized Samaria after the citizens of the Northern Kingdom were carried to Assyria as captives about 722 B.C. (Ezra 4:9). See also *Samaritan.*

TARSHISH/THARSHISH. A coastal city, probably in Spain, that was the destination of the ship boarded by the prophet Jonah (Jon. 1:3). *Tharshish:* 1 Kings 10:22.

TARSUS. Capital city of the Roman province of Silicia and the place where Paul was born (Acts 9:11). Once an important center of learning, Tarsus was on the Cydnus River about ten miles north of the Mediterranean Sea.

TARTAK. A false god worshiped by the Avites, a people who colonized Samaria after the Northern Kingdom fell to the Assyrians (2 Kings 17:31).

TARTAN (SUPREME COMMANDER). The title of the commander of the Assyrian army who demanded the surrender of Jerusalem from King Hezekiah (2 Kings 18:17). *Supreme commander:* NIV.

TASKMASTERS (SLAVEMASTERS). Egyptian overseers or supervisors who forced the Hebrew slaves to do hard labor at the command of the pharaoh (Exod. 1:11–14). *Slavemasters:* NIV.

TASSEL. See *Fringe.*

TATNAI (TATTENAI). A Persian official who appealed to King Darius of Persia to stop the Jews from rebuilding the temple in Jerusalem (Ezra 5:3–9). *Tattenai:* NIV, NRSV.

TAUGHT
Isa. 54:13 thy children shall be *t* of the LORD
Mark 1:22 he [Jesus] *t* them as one...authority
2 Thess. 2:15 hold the traditions...ye have been *t*

TAVERNS, THE THREE. A station on the Roman road known as the Appian Way about thirty miles south of Rome where believers met the apostle Paul (Acts 28:15).

TAX COLLECTOR. See *Publican.*

TAXES. Money, goods, or labor paid by citizens to a government. The Hebrews originally paid taxes known as tithes or firstfruits to support priests and Levites. The tax burden grew heavier under kings, particularly Solomon, and rebellion against his son and successor Rehoboam eventually split the kingdom (1 Kings 12:4, 8). The Romans sold the privilege of collecting taxes to independent contractors, resulting in great extortion (Luke 19:2, 8). See also *Toll.*

TEACH [ING]
Job 21:22 Shall any *t* God knowledge?
Ps. 25:4 Show me thy [Lord's] ways...*t* me thy paths
Ps. 90:12 So *t* us to number our days
Jer. 31:34 shall *t* no more every man his neighbour
Matt. 28:20 *T'ing* them to observe all things
Mark 8:31 he [Jesus] began to *t*...Son of man must suffer
Luke 11:1 Lord, *t* us [the disciples] to pray
Luke 12:12 Holy Ghost shall *t* you...what ye ought to say
John 14:26 the Comforter...shall *t* you all things
1 Tim. 3:2 A bishop...given to hospitality, apt to *t*

TEACHER. A person who communicates knowledge or religious truth to others. Teachers are mentioned along with pastors as persons whose skill and ministry are needed in the church (Eph. 4:11–12). See also *Master.*

TEACHER OF THE LAW. See *Scribe.*

TEAR. See *Rend.*

TEARS. Visible signs of sorrow. Jesus shed tears over the unbelief of Jerusalem (Luke 13:34) and wept at the grave of his friend Lazarus (John 11:35).

TEMPLE. The Jewish temple dominated the Jerusalem landscape, as seen in this model of the city in Jesus' time. The large building is the sanctuary, which only priests could enter.

T

Ps. 126:5 They that sow in *t* shall reap in joy
Jer. 9:1 my [Jeremiah's]...eyes [were] a fountain of *t*
Rev. 21:4 God shall wipe away all *t* from their eyes

TEBETH. The tenth month of the Hebrew year (Esther 2:16).

TEETH. See *Tooth*.

TEHAPHNEHES. See *Tahpanhes*.

TEIL (TEREBINTH). A common tree in Palestine that resembled the elm or oak (Isa. 6:13). *Terebinth:* NIV, NRSV.

TEKOA/TEKOAH. A fortress city of Judah near Bethlehem; home of Amos the prophet (Amos 1:1). *Tekoah:* 2 Sam. 14:4.

TEL, TELL. An Arabic word for "mound," or a hill marking the site of an ancient city that has been built up over centuries of occupation. See also *Archaeology of the Bible.*

TEL-ABIB. A Babylonian city on the Chebar River where Ezekiel lived with the other Jewish captives (Ezek. 3:15).

TEMPERANCE (SELF-CONTROL). Moderation, restraint, or self-discipline— behavior that should characterize believers (Gal 5:23; 2 Pet. 1:6). *Self-control:* NIV, NRSV.

See also *Moderation; Sober.*

TEMPEST (STORM). A furious storm. Jesus calmed a tempest on the Sea of Galilee to save His disciples (Matt. 8:24–26). *Storm:* NIV.

TEMPLE. The central place of worship for the Jewish people. Three separate temples were built on the same site in Jerusalem.

The first was Solomon's temple, built about 961–954 B.C. A partition divided the Holy Place from the Holy of Holies (1 Kings 6:2; 20, 31). Ten golden candlesticks, the table of shewbread, and the ark of the covenant were housed in this temple. Solomon's temple was destroyed by the Babylonian army in 587 B.C.

Zerubbabel's temple was completed in 515 B.C. by Jews who returned to Jerusalem after a period of exile among the Babylonians and Persians. The partition was replaced by a veil or curtain. The ark, which had been destroyed by the Babylonians, was not replaced.

About 10 B.C. Herod the Great began reconstruction of Zerubbabel's temple. The third temple was more ornate and larger than its predecessors, with outer courts added. The infant Jesus was brought to this temple for dedication, and here Jesus taught and drove out the moneychangers (Mark 11:15; John 2:14–15). This temple was destroyed by the Romans in A.D. 70. A Moslem mosque known as the Dome of the Rock stands on the site today. See also *Herod,* No. 1; *Zerubbabel.*

TEMPLE PROSTITUTE. See *Sodomite.*

TEMPLE SERVANTS. See *Nethinim.*

TEMPORARY RESIDENT. See *Foreigner.*

TEMPT [ED, ING]
Deut. 6:16 Ye shall not *t* the Lord your God
Ps. 78:41 they [Israelites] turned back and *t'ed* God
Matt. 4:1 was Jesus led into the wilderness to be *t'ed*
Matt. 4:7 Thou shalt not *t* the Lord thy God
John 8:6 *t'ing* him [Jesus]...to accuse him
1 Cor. 10:13 not suffer you to be *t'ed* above that ye are able
Heb. 4:15 high priest [Jesus]...was...*t'ed* like as we are
James 1:13 Let no man say...I am *t'ed* of God

TEMPTATION. Testing, or enticement to sin (Matt. 4:1–10). Jesus' temptation experiences provide a guide to help believers resist Satan the tempter (Matt. 4:10; Heb. 2:18). God promises a means of escape for every temptation (1 Cor. 10:13).

TEMPTATION [S]
Matt. 6:13 lead us not into *t*
James 1:2 count it all joy...fall into divers *t's*
James 1:12 Blessed is the man that endureth *t*
2 Pet. 2:9 Lord knoweth how to deliver...out of *t's*

TEN COMMANDMENTS. The ethical commands given by God to Moses on Mount Sinai. Also called the Decalogue, the Ten Commandments summarize the basic moral laws of the O.T. Four of these commandments enjoin duties to God (Exod. 20:1–11), while six deal with obligations to other people (Exod. 20:12–17). Jesus summed up these commandments in two great principles—loving God above all else and loving our neighbors as ourselves (Matt. 22:37–40).

TENT. The house or dwelling place of nomadic peoples (Gen. 12:8). Tents were made of goat hair and supported by poles and ropes tied to stakes. See also *House.*

TENT OF MEETING. See *Tabernacle.*

TENTH DEAL. A dry measure equaling one-tenth of an ephah (Exod. 29:40). See also *Ephah.*

TENTMAKER. A skilled workman who

TENT. *A Bedouin couple at the turn of the 1900s poses in front of their mobile home, a tent they take with them as they follow their herds from one pasture to the next.*

T

made tents, a lucrative trade in Bible times. Paul supported himself as a tentmaker (Acts 18:3).

TERAH/THARA. The father of Abraham and a native of Ur in Chaldea or ancient Babylonia. Through his sons Abraham, Nahor, and Haran, he was an ancestor of the Israelites, Ishmaelites, Midianites, Moabites, and Ammonites (Gen. 11:26–32). *Thara:* Jesus' ancestry (Luke 3:34).

TERAPHIM. Small images representing human figures that were venerated in households as guardians of good fortune (Judg. 17:5). Rachel stole her father's teraphim when Jacob left for Canaan (Gen. 31:19, 35). See also *Household Idols.*

TEREBINTH. See *Teil.*

TERTULLUS. A lawyer who accused Paul of desecrating the temple in a hearing before Felix at Caesarea (Acts 24:1–8).

TESTAMENT. A covenant or agreement with legal standing. The Old and New Testaments are covenants ratified first by the blood of sacrificial animals and then by the blood of Christ (Exod. 24:8; Matt. 26:28). See also *Covenant.*

TESTIFY [IED]
Isa. 59:12 our sins *t* against us
Acts 23:11 Paul...hast *t'ied* of me [Jesus] in Jerusalem
1 John 4:14 we...do *t* that the Father sent the Son

TESTIMONY. A declaration of truth based on personal experience (Acts 4:20). The testimony of Paul and Barnabas at Iconium was confirmed by their performance of miracles (Acts 14:3). See also *Record; Witness.*

TESTIMONY [IES]
Ps. 19:7 *t* of...LORD is sure, making wise the simple
Ps. 119:24 Thy [God's] *t'ies* also are my delight
Mark 6:11 shake off the dust...for a *t* against them
John 21:24 we know that his [God's] *t* is true

TETRARCH. The governor or ruler of a Roman province (Luke 3:1). See also *Governor.*

THADDAEUS. See *Judas, Brother of James.*

THAMAR. See *Tamar,* No. 1.

THANK OFFERING. A sacrificial animal presented to God as an expression of thanks for an unexpected special blessing (2 Chron. 29:31). See also *Sacrifice.*

THANKS
1 Chron. 16:34 give *t* unto the LORD; for he is good
Ps. 92:1 good thing to give *t* unto the LORD
Luke 22:19 he [Jesus] took bread, and gave *t*
1 Cor. 15:57 *t* be to God, which giveth us the victory
1 Thess. 5:18 in every thing give *t*...this is the will of God

THANKSGIVING. The act of expressing one's gratitude. The psalmist praised the Lord for His goodness and blessings (Ps. 116:12–19). Our Christian inheritance of salvation and eternal life should inspire our thanksgiving to God (Col. 1:12). See also *Praise.*

THARA. See *Terah.*

THARSHISH. See *Tarshish.*

THEATER. An outdoor meeting place, similar to a stadium, where dramatic performances and sporting events were held. The theater at Ephesus was an impressive Roman structure made of stone and marble that seated thousands (Acts 19:29–31).

THEBES. See *No.*

THEOCRACY. A government in which God is the ruler. Israel was an imperfect example of this form of rule, beginning with their deliverance from Egypt (Exod. 15:13) and the giving of the law at Mount Sinai (Exod. 19:5–8), until Samuel agreed to the people's demand for a king (1 Sam. 8:5).

THEOPHANY. A visible appearance of God. Examples are the burning bush (Exod. 3:1–6), the pillar of cloud and fire (Exod. 13:21–22), and the cloud and fire at Mount Sinai (Exod. 24:16–18). Some scholars believe theophanies before the incarnation of Jesus were visible manifestations of the preincarnate Son of God (John 1:1, 18).

THEOPIIILUS. A friend of Luke to whom he addressed his writings—the Gospel of Luke and the book of Acts (Luke 1:3; Acts 1:1). See also *Luke.*

THESSALONIANS, EPISTLES TO THE. Two N.T. epistles written by the apostle Paul to the believers in the church at Thessalonica. The theme of both letters is the second coming of Christ, although Paul also included instructions on sexual morality (1 Thess. 4:1–8) and the need for diligent labor rather than idle speculation (1 Thess. 4:9–12; 2 Thess. 3:6–15).

Paul declared that believers' assurance of Christ's return should motivate them to righteous living (1 Thess. 3:13; 5:23) but that uncertainty about the exact time of His return should make them watchful and alert (1 Thess. 5:1–11).

THESSALONICA. A city on the Macedonian coast where Paul preached and founded a church. It was also the scene of a riot incited by Jews who opposed the preaching of Paul and Silas (Acts 17:1–9).

THEUDAS. The leader of an unsuccessful revolt mentioned by Gamaliel before the Sanhedrin. Gamaliel probably named this person to discourage premature action that might result in bloodshed (Acts 5:34–36).

THIEF [VES]
Matt. 6:20 where *t'ves* do not break through nor steal
Mark 15:27 with him [Jesus] they crucify two *t'ves*
Luke 10:30 A certain man...fell among *t'ves*
Luke 19:46 ye have made it [God's house] a den of *t'ves*
John 12:6 This he [Judas] said...because he was a *t*
2 Pet. 3:10 day of the Lord will come as a *t* in the night

THIGH. The part of the leg between the hip and the knee. Placing the hand under the thigh signified obedience or subjection. Abraham's servant swore by this method that a Canaanite wife would not be chosen for Abraham's son Isaac (Gen. 24:2–9). See also *Sinew.*

THINK [ETH]
Prov. 23:7 as he *t'eth* in his heart, so is he
Jer. 29:11 I [God] know the thoughts...I *t* toward you
John 16:2 killeth you will *t*...doeth God service
Rom. 12:3 *t* of himself...highly than he ought to *t*
1 Cor. 10:12 *t'eth* he standeth take heed lest he fall
1 Cor. 13:5 [charity]...*t'eth* no evil
Gal. 6:3 man *t* himself to be something, when he is nothing
Eph. 3:20 [Jesus]...able to do...above all that we ask or *t*

THIRTY PIECES OF SILVER. The blood money given to Judas to betray Christ—the usual price for a slave. A remorseful Judas threw his silver on the temple floor and hanged himself (Matt. 27:3–8).

THISTLE. A briar or thorn that was used for hedges and burned for fuel (Isa. 33:12; Hosea 2:6). The word was also used figuratively of neglect and desolation (Prov. 24:30–31).

THOMAS. One of the twelve apostles or disciples of Jesus, also called *Didymus* or "twin"

(Luke 6:15), who refused to believe that Christ was alive until he could actually see and feel the wounds on Christ's resurrected body (John 20:25–28). See also *Twelve, The.*

THONG. A strip of leather. Paul was bound with thongs at Jerusalem (Acts 22:25–29). See also *Latchet.*

THORN. A plant with heavy briars or thistles. A crown of thorns was placed on Jesus' head in mockery as He hung on the cross (Matt. 27:29).

THORN IN THE FLESH. An unknown affliction from which the apostle Paul prayed to be delivered (2 Cor. 12:7–8). Some scholars believe it was an eye ailment, since he normally dictated his epistles and apologized for his own large handwriting (Gal. 6:11).

THORNBUSH. See *Bramble.*

THOUGHT [S]

Job 21:27 I [God] know your *t's*
Ps. 92:5 O Lᴏʀᴅ...thy *t's* are very deep
Isa. 55:8 my [God's] *t's* are not your *t's*
Matt. 6:27 you by taking *t* can add one cubit
Mark 7:21 out of the heart of men, proceed evil *t's*
1 Cor. 3:20 Lord knoweth the *t's* of the wise
1 Cor. 13:11 I [Paul]...*t* as a child

THRESHINGFLOOR. A place where grain was threshed, or separated from the stalk and husk after harvesting (2 Sam. 6:6). See also *Fan; Winnowing.*

THROAT. The throat was compared to an "open sepulchre" because of the deadly falsehoods that it could utter through the mouth (Ps. 5:9; Rom. 3:13). See also *Lips; Mouth; Tongue.*

THRONE. An ornate chair occupied by kings (1 Kings 2:9) and sometimes priests and judges (1 Sam. 1:9; Jer. 1:15) as a symbol of their power and authority. The word is also used to designate the Lord's supreme authority (Isa. 6:1).

Ps. 45:6 Thy *t*, O God, is for ever
Isa. 66:1 The heaven is my [God's] *t*
Lam. 5:19 thy [God's] *t* from generation to generation
Matt. 19:28 Son of man shall sit...*t* of his glory
Luke 1:32 God shall give unto him [Jesus] the *t* of...David
Heb. 4:16 Let us...come boldly unto the *t* of grace
Rev. 4:2 one [Jesus] sat on the *t*

THUMB. The thumb was involved in the ceremony consecrating Aaron and his sons to the priesthood. The blood of rams was smeared on their thumbs as well as their ears and feet (Exod. 29:19–20).

THUMMIN. See *Urim* and *Thummin.*

THUNDER. Since thunder was rare in Palestine, it was considered a form of speaking by the Lord (Job 40:9) and often regarded as a sign of His displeasure (Exod. 9:23; 1 Sam. 12:7).

THYATIRA. A city in the Roman province of Asia and home of Lydia, a convert under Paul's ministry (Acts 16:14). Noted for its dye industry, Thyatira was also the site of one of the seven churches of Asia Minor addressed by the apostle John. This church was commended for its faith and good works but condemned for its tolerance toward the false prophetess Jezebel and her heretical teachings (Rev. 2:18–29).

THYINE WOOD (CITRON WOOD, SCENTED WOOD). A valuable wood resembling cedar used for fine cabinet work (Rev. 18:12). It was also burned as incense because of its fragrance. *Citron wood:* ɴɪᴠ; *scented wood:* ɴʀsᴠ.

TIBERIAS. Tiberias, a village along the Sea of Galilee, as painted in 1839 by David Roberts.

TIBERIAS. A city on the western shore of the Sea of Galilee (John 6:1, 23) built by Herod Antipas and named for the Roman emperor Tiberius. It was shunned by many Jews because it was built on a cemetery site. Tiberias became a center of learning after the fall of Jerusalem in A.D. 70.

TIBERIUS. See *Caesar,* No. 2.

TIBNI. A king of Israel (reigned about 885–880 B.C.) who ruled at the same time as Omri. Upon Tibni's death, Omri became the sole claimant to the throne (1 Kings 16:21–22).

TIGLATH-PILESER III/TILGATH PILNESER III/PUL. A powerful Assyrian king (reigned about 745–727 B.C.) who defeated the Northern Kingdom and carried Jewish captives to Assyria (2 Kings 15:29). *Tilgath-pilneser:* 2 Chron. 28:20. *Pul:* 1 Chron. 5:26.

TIGRIS. A major river of southwest Asia that is possibly the same as the *Hiddekel* of the Garden of Eden (Gen. 2:14). Beginning in the Armenian mountains, the Tigris flows southeastward for more than 1,100 miles until it joins the Euphrates River. Mesopotamia, or "the land between the rivers," lies between these two streams. See also *Euphrates.*

TILE (CLAY TABLET, BRICK). A slab of baked clay used as roofing on houses (Ezek. 4:1). The tiles were removed from a roof to give a paralyzed man access to Jesus for healing (Luke 5:18–19). *Clay tablet:* NIV; *brick:* NRSV. See also *Brick.*

TIGRIS. Photographed from a space shuttle, the Tigris and Euphrates rivers merge just north of the Persian Gulf, where they empty into the sea. The fertile land in the center was once called Mesopotamia, meaning "land between the rivers." The Tigris flows on the east side of that land, with the Euphrates on the west.

TILGATH-PILNESER. See *Tiglath-pileser.*

TIMBREL (TAMBOURINE). A small hand drum or percussion instrument believed to resemble the tambourine (Exod. 15:20). *Tambourine:* NIV, NRSV. See also *Tabret.*

TIMNATH-SERAH/TIMNATH-HERES. A town in the territory of Ephraim given to Joshua as an inheritance and the place where he was buried (Josh. 24:29–30). *Timnath-heres:* Judg. 2:9.

TIMOTHY/TIMO-THEUS. A young missionary friend of Paul, also called *Timotheus* (see Rom. 16:21), who accompanied the apostle on some of his travels and briefly shared his imprisonment at Rome (Heb. 13:23). Born to a Greek father and a Jewish mother (Acts 16:1), Timothy was reared by his mother, Eunice, and grandmother, Lois, in a godly home (2 Tim. 1:5). He was converted during Paul's first visit to Lystra (Acts 16:1) and served for a time as leader of the church at Ephesus (1 Tim. 1:3; 4:12). Paul addressed two of his pastoral epistles to Timothy. See also *Eunice.*

TIMOTHY, EPISTLES TO. Two short epistles of the apostle Paul to his young friend and fellow missionary, Timothy. The first epistle is practical in scope, instructing Timothy to teach sound doctrine (chap. 1), organize the church appropriately (chaps. 2–3), beware of false teachers (chap. 4), administer church discipline (chap. 5), and exercise his pastoral gifts with love and restraint (chap. 6).

Second Timothy is perhaps Paul's most personal epistle, in which he expresses tender affection for the young minister (chaps. 1–2) and speaks of approaching days of persecution for the church (3:1–4:5) as well as the possibility of his own execution (4:6–22). See also *Pastoral Epistles; Timothy.*

TIN. A well-known and malleable metal (Num. 31:22) brought by ship from Tarshish and used in making bronze (Ezek. 27:12).

TINDER. See *Tow.*

TIRE. A headdress, such as a turban, or an ornament worn in the hair by a high priest, a bridegroom, or women (2 Kings 9:30; Isa. 3:18).

TIRHAKAH. See *Pharaoh,* No. 3.

TIRSHATHA (GOVERNOR). The title of the governor of Judea under Persian rule. Both Zerubbabel and Nehemiah were appointed by Persian kings to this position (Ezra 2:63; Neh. 7:65). *Governor:* NIV, NRSV. See also *Governor; Lieutenant.*

TIRZAH. A Canaanite town captured by Joshua (Josh. 12:24). In later years it served as a capital of the Northern Kingdom until Samaria was built (1 Kings 14:17).

TISHBITE. An inhabitant of Tishbeh, a city of Gilead. The prophet Elijah was called a Tishbite (1 Kings 17:1).

TITHE. One-tenth of a person's income presented as an offering to God. Abraham paid tithes to Melchizedek (Gen. 14:18–20), and Jacob vowed to give tithes in accordance with God's blessings (Gen. 28:20–22). In N.T. times, the Pharisees were scrupulous tithers (Matt. 23:23). Jesus encouraged generosity and promised to bless sacrificial giving (Luke 6:38). Paul endorsed the principle of proportionate giving (1 Cor. 16:2). See also *Stewardship.*

TITHE [S]
Lev. 27:30 the *t* of the land...is the LORD's
Deut. 14:22 shalt...*t* all the increase of thy seed
Neh. 13:12 brought all Judah the *t* of the corn
Mal. 3:8 robbed thee [God]? In *t's* and offerings
Mal. 3:10 Bring ye all the *t's* into the storehouse
Luke 11:42 ye [Pharisees] *t* mint...and...herbs
Heb. 7:6 he [Melchisedec]...received *t's* of Abraham

TITTLE. A dot or other small mark that distinguished similar letters of the alphabet. Jesus used the word to emphasize the enduring quality of the law's most minute requirement (Matt. 5:18).

TITUS. A Greek Christian and traveling companion of Paul who was sent by the apostle to correct problems in the church at Corinth

TITUS THE DEPENDABLE

Titus was one of Paul's most dedicated and dependable missionary associates. The apostle sent messages to the Corinthian church by Titus (2 Cor. 7:5-16). He also assigned Titus the task of collecting an offering for the impoverished believers of Jerusalem (2 Cor. 8:6, 16-24; 12:18).

(2 Cor. 7:6; 8:6, 23). Titus also served as a church leader in Crete (Titus 1:4–5). See also *Crete.*

TITUS, EPISTLE TO. A short epistle written by the apostle Paul to his helper and companion Titus, who apparently was serving as a leader of the church on the island of Crete (1:5). Paul dealt with several practical church matters, including the qualifications of elders (1:5–9), ways to deal with false teachers (1:10–16), and the behavior of Christians in an immoral world

(3:1–11). See also *Pastoral Epistles.*

TOB/ISH-TOB. A place in Syria east of the Jordan River where the judge Jephthah took refuge (Judg. 11:3, 5). The soldiers of Tob sided with the Ammonites against David (2 Sam. 10:6, 8). *Ish-tob:* 2 Sam. 10:8.

TOBIAH. An Ammonite servant of Sanballat who ridiculed the Jews and opposed Nehemiah's reconstruction of Jerusalem's wall (Neh. 2:10, 19; 4:3, 7). See also *Sanballat.*

TOKEN (SIGN). A sign or signal. Circumcision was a token of God's covenant with Abraham (Gen. 17:11). The blood on the Israelites' doorposts was a sign for the death angel to "pass over" these houses (Exod. 12:13). *Sign:* NIV, NRSV. See also *Miracle; Sign.*

TOLA. A minor judge of Israel who succeeded Abimelech and ruled for twenty-three years (Judg. 10:1–2). See also *Judges of Israel.*

TOLERANCE. See *Forbearance.*

TOLL (TAX). A tax or fee levied against the citizens of a conquered nation (Ezra 4:13). *Tax:* NIV. See also *Taxes; Tribute.*

TOMB. See *Sepulchre.*

TONGS. A tool for handling hot coals or trimming burning lamps (Exod. 25:38; Num. 4:9); probably the same as a *snuffer.* See also *Snuffer.*

TONGUE. The organ of the body associated with speech. The tongue may be used as an instrument of punishment (Gen. 11:1–9) or blessing (Acts 2:1–12) and for good or evil (James 3:5–10). See also *Lips; Mouth; Throat.*

TONGUES, SPEAKING IN. Glossolalia or ecstatic utterances; a spiritual gift exercised by some believers in the N.T. church. This gift apparently first occurred on the day of Pentecost with the outpouring of God's Spirit on believers (Acts 2:1–13). Paul also mentioned this gift in 1 Cor. 14:2–28, although it is unclear whether this is the same as the phenomenon described in Acts.

TOOTH. The gnashing or grinding of one's teeth symbolized frustration or despair (Matt. 8:12).

TOPAZ (CHRYSOLITE). A precious stone, thought to resemble modern chrysolite, used in the high priest's breastplate (Exod. 28:17). It is also used in the foundation of New Jerusalem (Rev. 21:20). *Chrysolite:* NRSV. See also *Chrysolyte.*

TOPHET (TOPHETH). A place of human sacrifice in the Valley of Hinnom near Jerusalem (Jer. 7:31–32). *Topheth:* NIV, NRSV. See also *Hell; Hinnom, Valley of.*

TAMING THE TONGUE

James compared the tongue to a fire that rages out of control, leaving destruction in its wake (James 3:6). All of us have learned through personal experience that careless, thoughtless words can cause great damage—to ourselves as well as others. The book of Proverbs also has some wise words on this subject: "Whoso keepeth his mouth and his tongue keepeth his soul from troubles" (Prov. 21:23).

TORAH. A Hebrew word meaning "teaching" or "instruction" and used for the Pentateuch or the Law, the first five books of the O.T. See also *Law, Law of Moses; Pentateuch.*

TORCH. A burning brand made of resinous wood or twisted flax and used to light one's path at night (John 18:3). See also *Lantern.*

TORTOISE (GREAT LIZARD). A reptile regarded as unclean by the Jews (Lev. 11:29). *Great lizard:* NIV, NRSV.

TOW (TINDER). The waste or refuse produced from flax when spinning thread. Isaiah used the word figuratively of the weakness of sinful people when facing God's punishment (Isa. 1:31). *Tinder:* NIV, NRSV.

TOWER (STRONGHOLD). A defensive turret in a city wall or a tall structure used as a watchtower. The word is also used figuratively of God's protection (2 Sam. 22:3). *Stronghold:* NIV, NRSV.

TOWNCLERK (CITY CLERK). An official of the city of Ephesus who restored order after a riot against Paul (Acts 19:29–41). *City clerk:* NIV.

TRADITION. An unwritten code or interpretation of the law that the Pharisees considered as binding as the written law itself (Matt. 15:2, 6; Mark 7:5).

TRANCE. A state of semiconsciousness, often accompanied by visions. Peter's trance at Joppa prepared him for a ministry to Cornelius the Gentile. See also *Dreams and Visions.*

TRANSFIGURATION OF JESUS. A radical transformation in the Savior's appearance through which God was glorified. Accompanied by His disciples Peter, James, and John, Jesus went to a mountain at night to pray. Moses and Elijah appeared and discussed Jesus' death, emphasizing Jesus as the fulfillment of the Law and the Prophets (Matt. 17:1–8). This experience attested Christ's divinity and mission and helped prepare Jesus and His disciples for the events leading to His death.

TRANSGRESS [ED, ETH]
Deut. 26:13 I have not *t'ed* thy [God's] commandments
Jer. 2:29 all have *t'ed* against me, saith the LORD
1 John 3:4 Whosoever committeth sin *t'eth* also the law

TRANSGRESSION. A violation of God's law that may be personal (1 Tim. 2:14), public (Rom. 5:14), or premeditated (Josh. 7:19–25). Transgression produces death (1 Chron. 10:13) and destruction (Ps. 37:38), but it may be forgiven by confession (Ps. 32:1, 5) through the atoning death of Christ (Isa. 53:5–6). See also *Sin.*

TRANSGRESSION [S]
Job 13:23 make me [Job] to know my *t*
Ps. 32:1 Blessed is he whose *t* is forgiven
Ps. 51:3 I acknowledge my *t's*
Prov. 12:13 wicked is snared by the *t* of his lips
Prov. 29:6 In the *t* of an evil man there is a snare
Isa. 53:5 he [God's servant] was wounded for our *t's*

TRANSGRESSOR [S]
Ps. 51:13 Then will I teach *t's* thy [God's] ways
Prov. 22:12 he [God] overthroweth the words of the *t*
Mark 15:28 he [Jesus] was numbered with the *t's*

TRANSJORDAN. A large mountainous plateau or tableland east of the Jordan River, generally referred to in the KJV as the land "beyond Jordan" (Gen. 50:10; Matt. 4:15). This is the area from which Moses viewed the Promised Land (Deut. 34:1–4). After the conquest of Canaan, it was occupied by the tribes of Reuben, Gad, and East Manasseh.

TRAVAIL. The labor pains associated with childbirth (Gen. 38:27). The word is also used figuratively of the birth of God's new creation (Rom. 8:22–23).

TREASURE [S]

Ps. 135:4 Lord hath chosen...Israel for his peculiar *t*

Matt. 2:11 they [the wise men] opened their *t's*

Matt. 6:20 lay up for yourselves *t's* in heaven

Matt. 13:44 kingdom of heaven is like unto *t* hid in a field

Luke 12:34 where your *t* is...will your heart be also

2 Cor. 4:7 we have this *t* in earthen vessels

TREASURE CITY (STORE CITY, SUPPLY CITY). A fortified city in which a king stored his valuables. The Hebrew slaves built treasure cities at Pithom and Raamses for the Egyptian pharaoh (Exod. 1:11). *Store city:* NIV; *supply city:* NRSV. See also *Store City.*

TREASURE OF ALL NATIONS. See *Desire of All Nations.*

TREASURER (STEWARD). An important financial officer in a king's court, charged with accounting for receipts and disbursements (Isa. 22:15). *Steward:* NIV, NRSV. See also *Steward.*

TREASURY. The place in the temple where offerings were received (Mark 12:41–44). Thirteen trumpet-shaped receptacles for offerings were placed in the outer court.

TREATY. See *League.*

TREE OF KNOWLEDGE OF GOOD AND EVIL. A specific tree placed in the Garden of Eden to test the obedience of Adam and Eve. Eating of the fruit of this tree was specifically prohibited by the Lord (Gen. 2:9, 17). After they ate the forbidden fruit, Adam and Eve were banished from the garden and became subject to hard labor and death (Gen. 3).

TREE OF LIFE. A tree in the Garden of Eden with fruit that would bring eternal life if eaten (Gen. 3:22). In the heavenly Jerusalem, there will also be a tree of life, with leaves for the healing of the nations (Rev. 22:2).

TRESPASS [ES]

Ezra 9:15 we are before thee [God] in our *t'es*

Mark 11:25 your Father...may forgive you your *t'es*

Luke 17:3 thy brother *t* against thee, rebuke him

2 Cor. 5:19 God was...not imputing their *t'es* unto them

TRESPASS OFFERING. A sacrificial animal offering presented for lesser sins or offenses after full restitution to persons wronged had been made (Lev. 5:6–7, 15–19). See also *Sacrifice.*

TRIALS OF JESUS. A series of trials or appearances of Jesus before Jewish and Roman authorities that ended with His death. Jesus appeared before Annas, the former high priest (John 18:12–23); Caiphas, the current high priest, and the full Jewish Sanhedrin (Matt. 26:57–68); Pilate, the Roman governor (John 18:28–38); and Herod Antipas, ruler of Galilee (Luke 23:6–12) before finally being sentenced to death by Pilate (Mark 15:6–15).

TRIBES OF ISRAEL. The tribes that descended from the sons of Jacob—Asher, Benjamin, Dan, Gad, Issachar, Judah, Levi, Naphtali, Reuben, Simeon, and Zebulon (Gen. 49:1–28)—plus the two sons of Joseph (Ephraim and Manasseh; Gen. 48:5). After the conquest of Canaan, these tribes were assigned specific territories in the land, with the exception of Levi, the priestly tribe. The Levites were assigned to forty-eight different towns and scattered among all the other tribal territories to perform ceremonial duties. See also *Levites.*

TRIBULATION. Affliction and trouble caused by persecution (1 Thess. 3:4) and severe testing (Rev. 2:10, 22). The tribulation of believers may be overcome by patience (Rom. 8:35–37; 12:12) and a joyful spirit (2 Cor. 7:4). See also *Affliction; Persecution.*

TRIBULATION
Matt. 24:21 then shall be great *t*
John 16:33 In the world ye shall have *t*
Rom. 5:3 *t* worketh patience
2 Cor. 1:4 Who [Jesus] comforteth us in all our *t*

TRIBULATION, GREAT. A time of great suffering and affliction in the end-time, sent upon the earth by the Lord to accomplish His purposes (Dan. 12:1; Rev. 7:14). Students of the Bible disagree on whether this event will precede or follow Christ's millennial reign or come before the ushering in of the new heavens and new earth. See also *Millennium; Persecution.*

TRIBUTE. A toll or tax imposed on citizens by a government. Every Hebrew male over age twenty paid an annual tribute of a half-shekel to support temple services (Exod. 30:13; Matt. 17:24–27). See also *Half-Shekel Tax; Taxes; Toll.*

TRIGON. See *Sackbut.*

TRINITY, THE. God as expressed through the Father, the Son, and the Holy Spirit. The word *Trinity* does not appear in the Bible, but the reality of the triune God was revealed in the O.T. at the creation of the world (Gen. 1:1–3, 26). In the N.T., the Trinity was revealed at Christ's baptism (Matt. 3:16–17) and in His teachings (John 14:26; 15:26) as well as His Great Commission (Matt. 28:19).

The Holy Spirit, whom Christ sent, convicts of sin, inspires believers, and empowers them for service (John 16:8, 13). The Father gives converts to Christ, and they hear His voice and follow Him (John 10:27, 29).

TRIUMPHAL ENTRY OF JESUS. Jesus' entry into Jerusalem on the Sunday before His crucifixion the following Friday. He was greeted by shouts of joy from the crowds, who were looking for an earthly king. With His entry, Jesus acknowledged He was the promised Messiah—but a spiritual deliverer rather than a conquering military hero (Matt. 21:1–11).

TROAS. An important city on the coast of Mysia where Paul received a vision. A man across from Troas in Macedonia pleaded, "Come . . .and help us" (Acts 16:8–10).

TROPHIMUS. A Christian who accompanied Paul on the third missionary journey (Acts 20:4).

TROUBLE [D]
Job 14:1 Man...is of few days, and full of *t*
Ps. 9:9 The Lord...a refuge...in times of *t*
Ps. 46:1 God is...a very present help in *t*
Ps. 90:7 by thy [God's] wrath are we *t'd*
Luke 1:29 she [Mary] was *t'd* at his [the angel's] saying
John 12:27 Now is my [Jesus'] soul *t'd*
John 14:1 Let not your heart be *t'd*...believe...in me [Jesus]
2 Cor. 4:8 We are *t'd* on every side
Gal. 1:7 some that *t* you, and would pervert the gospel

TROUSERS. See *Hosen.*

TRUE
Ps. 19:9 judgments of the Lord are *t*
John 1:9 the *t* Light [Jesus]...lighteth every man
John 6:32 my [Jesus'] Father giveth you the *t* bread
John 15:1 I [Jesus] am the *t* vine
John 21:24 his [John's] testimony is *t*
Rom. 3:4 let God be *t*, but every man a liar

TRUMPET. A wind musical instrument made

TRUMPET. Blowing a shofar, a trumpet made from a ram's horn, an Orthodox Jew calls worshipers to the synagogue for Sabbath.

of animal horn or metal. Trumpets were used in temple ceremonies (1 Chron. 16:6). See also *Ram's Horn.*

TRUMPETS, FEAST OF. A Jewish religious festival, also called the *Seventh Month Festival* (Lev. 16:29). It was ushered in by the blowing of trumpets and observed by reading the law and presenting burnt offerings (Lev. 23:24–25; Neh. 8:2–3, 8–12). The exact reason for its observance is not clear.

TRUST. To put one's confidence in a person or thing. God's name and His Word are worthy of our trust (Ps. 33:21; 119:42). Christ warned that humans may deceive and be unworthy of trust (Matt. 10:17–21), but we may place ultimate trust and confidence in Him (John 6:35–37). See also *Faith.*

TRUST [ED, ETH]
Deut. 32:37 Where are their gods...in whom they *t'ed*
2 Sam. 22:3 God of my rock; in him will I *t*
Job 13:15 he [God] slay me [Job]...I *t* in him
Ps. 56:3 What time I am afraid, I will *t* in a thee [God]
Prov. 3:5 *T* in the Lord with all thine heart
Prov. 11:28 He that *t'eth* in his riches shall fall
Mark 10:24 hard...for them...*t* in riches to enter...the kingdom

TRUTH. That which is reliable and consistent with God's revelation. Truth is established by God's law (Ps. 119:142–144) and personified by Jesus Christ (John 14:6). Believers are purified by obedience to the truth (1 Pet. 1:22) and worshiping God in spirit and truth (John 4:23–24).

Ps. 100:5 his [God's] *t* endureth to all generations
Ps. 119:30 I have chosen the way of *t*
John 1:17 grace and *t* came by Jesus Christ
John 8:32 the *t* shall make you free
John 16:13 Spirit of *t*...will guide you into all *t*
John 18:38 Pilate saith unto him [Jesus], What is *t* ?
1 Cor. 13:6 [charity] rejoiceth in the *t*
Eph. 4:15 speaking the *t* in love
2 Tim. 2:15 rightly dividing the word of *t*
1 John 1:8 say that we have no sin...*t* is not in us

TUBAL. The fifth son of Japheth (Gen. 10:2) and ancestor of a tribe descended from Tubal and Japheth. Isaiah mentioned Tubal as a

KING HIRAM OF TYRE

King Hiram, also known as Huram, entered a trade agreement with Solomon (1 Kings 5:1–18). He was the king of Tyre, a city on the coast of the Mediterranean Sea about 100 miles north of Jerusalem. The Tyrians were known for their ambitious trade ventures, especially by sea.

Judah was not a seafaring nation. When Solomon established a port on the Red Sea for trading with other countries, he used ships and sailors from Hiram's fleet (2 Chron. 8:17–18).

people who would declare God's glory among the Gentiles (Isa. 66:19).

TUMORS. See *Emerods.*

TURBAN. See *Mitre.*

TURTLEDOVE (DOVE). A migratory bird noted for its plaintive cooing and affection for its mate (Song 2:12). A turtledove was an acceptable sacrificial offering for the poor (Lev. 12:6–8). *Dove:* NIV. See also *Pigeon.*

TWELVE, THE. The twelve apostles or disciples chosen by Jesus. They were Andrew; Bartholomew (Nathanael); James, son of Alphaeus; James, son of Zebedee; John; Judas; Lebbaeus (Thaddaeus); Matthew; Philip; Simon the Canaanite; Simon Peter; and Thomas (Matt. 10:1–4; Mark 3:13–19; Luke 6:12–16).

TWIN BROTHERS. See *Castor and Pollux.*

TYCHICUS. A Christian who accompanied Paul on his third missionary journey (Acts 20:4).

TYPE. A person or thing that foreshadows something else. For example, the brass serpent placed upon a pole by Moses in the wilderness (Num. 21:4–9) pointed to the atoning death of Jesus on the cross (John 3:14–15).

TYRANNUS. A man of Ephesus who allowed Paul to use his lecture hall. Paul taught here for two years after he was banned from the local synagogue (Acts 19:8–10).

TYRE/TYRUS. An ancient coastal city of Phoenicia north of Palestine. Hiram, Tyre's ruler, helped David and Solomon with their building projects (1 Kings 5:1–10). In the prophet Ezekiel's day, the city was a thriving trade center. He predicted Tyre's destruction because of its sin and idolatry (Ezek. 28:1–10). Jesus visited the city (Mark 7:24), and Paul landed here (Acts 21:3, 7). *Tyrus:* Amos 1:10.

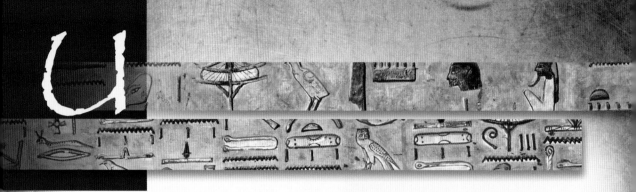

UCAL. An unknown person to whom proverbs in the book of Proverbs are addressed (Prov. 30:1).

ULAI. A river of Persia beside which Daniel was standing when he saw the vision of the ram and goat (Dan. 8:2–16).

ULCERS. See *Emerods.*

UMPIRE. See *Daysman.*

UNBELIEF. Refusal to believe in God and to acknowledge His works (John 16:9). Unbelief is caused by Satan's power (John 8:43–47), an evil heart (Heb. 3:12), and self-glorification and pride (John 5:44). Those who refuse to believe and reject the gospel are in turn rejected by God (John 3:18–20; 8:24). See also *Atheism; Infidel.*

Mark 9:24 Lord, I believe; help thou mine *u*
Heb. 3:12 lest there be in...you an evil heart of *u*
Heb. 4:11 lest any man fall after the...example of *u*

UNBELIEVER. See *Infidel.*

UNBELIEVING

Acts 14:2 the *u* Jews stirred up the Gentiles
1 Cor. 7:14 the *u* husband is sanctified by the wife
Titus 1:15 unto them that are...*u* is nothing pure

UNCIRCUMCISED. A Jewish term for impurity or wickedness of any kind (Jer. 6:10) as well as a general reference to Gentiles (Rom. 2:25–29). See also *Circumcision.*

1 Sam. 17:26 this *u* Philistine [Goliath]
Ezek. 44:9 No stranger, *u* in heart...shall enter...[God's] sanctuary
Acts 7:51 stiffnecked and *u* in heart and ears

UNCIRCUMCISION

1 Cor. 7:19 Circumcision is nothing...*u* is nothing
Gal. 5:6 neither circumcision availeth any thing, nor *u*
Col. 3:11 neither Greek nor Jew, circumcision nor *u*

UNCLEAN. A term for physical, spiritual, or ritual impurity—a condition for which rituals of purification were prescribed (Lev. 11–15). See also *Clean.*

UNCLEAN [NESS]

Isa. 6:5 I [Isaiah] am a man of *u* lips
Isa. 64:6 we are all as an *u* thing
Mark 6:7 he [Jesus]...gave them [the disciples] power over *u* spirits
Acts 10:14 I [Peter] have never eaten any thing...*u*
Rom. 1:24 God also gave them up to *u'ness*
Gal. 5:19 works of the flesh...Adultery...*u'ness*
1 Thess. 4:7 God hath not called us unto *u'ness*

UNCLEAN ANIMALS. Under Mosaic Law, only animals that chewed the cud and were cloven-footed were considered "clean" and suitable for eating (Lev. 11:2–3). Even touching the flesh of an "unclean" animal made a person unclean (Lev. 11:8).

UNDEFILED

Ps. 119:1 Blessed are the *u*...walk in the law of the LORD
Heb. 7:26 high priest [Jesus]...who is holy...*u*
James 1:27 Pure religion and *u* before God and the Father

UNDERGARMENT. See *Breeches.*
UNDERSTAND [ETH, ING]

1 Kings 4:29 God gave Solomon wisdom and *u'ing*
Job 28:28 to depart from evil is *u'ing*
Ps. 119:27 to *u* the way of thy [God's] precepts
Prov. 2:2 apply thine heart to *u'ing*
Prov. 3:5 lean not unto thine own *u'ing*
Mark 8:21 How is it that ye [the disciples] do not *u*?
Rom. 3:11 none that *u'eth*...that seeketh after God
1 Cor. 13:2 though I [Paul]...*u* all mysteries
Phil. 4:7 peace of God, which passeth all *u'ing*

UNDERSTANDING. See *Knowledge; Wisdom.*

UNDERSTOOD

Job 13:1 mine [Job's] ear hath heard and *u* it
Job 42:3 I [Job] uttered that I *u* not
John 12:16 These things *u* not his [Jesus'] disciples
1 Cor. 13:11 When I [Paul] was a child...I *u* as a child

UNGODLY [INESS]

Ps. 1:1 man that walketh not in the counsel of the *u*
Prov. 16:27 An *u* man diggeth up evil
Rom. 1:18 wrath of God is revealed...against all *u'iness*
Rom. 5:6 in due time Christ died for the *u*
Titus 2:12 denying *u'iness*...we should live soberly
Jude 18 mockers...walk after their own *u* lusts

UNICORN (WILD OX). A large animal of great strength, probably the wild ox (Num. 23:22). Yoking it and harnessing its power was considered impossible (Job 39:9–11). *Wild ox:* NIV, NRSV.

UNJUST

Matt. 5:45 he [God]...sendeth rain on the just and...*u*
Luke 16:8 the lord commended the *u* steward
1 Pet. 3:18 Christ...suffered for sins...just for the *u*

UNKNOWN

Acts 17:23 altar with this inscription, TO THE *U* GOD
1 Cor. 14:4 speaketh in an *u* tongue edifieth himself
1 Cor. 14:19 rather speak...with...understanding...than...in an *u* tongue

UNLEAVENED BREAD, FEAST OF. See *Passover and Feast of Unleavened Bread.*
UNPARDONABLE SIN. Blasphemy against the Holy Spirit, or attributing the work of Christ to Satan, as the critics of Jesus did (Mark 3:22–30). Many interpreters believe this sin consists of rejecting the testimony of the Holy Spirit about Christ's person and work.

UNPLOWED GROUND. See *Fallow Ground.*

UNRIGHTEOUS [NESS]

Ps. 92:15 there is no *u'ness* in him [God]
Isa. 55:7 Let the wicked forsake his way...*u* man his thoughts
Rom. 1:18 wrath of God is revealed...against all...*u'ness*
1 Cor. 6:9 the *u* shall not inherit the kingdom of God
2 Cor. 6:14 what fellowship...righteousness with *u'ness*
1 John 1:9 he [Jesus] is faithful...to cleanse us from all *u'ness*

UNSEARCHABLE

Ps. 145:3 Great is the LORD...his greatness is *u*
Rom. 11:33 how *u* are his [God's] judgments
Eph. 3:8 I [Paul] should preach...the *u* riches of Christ

UNTEMPERED MORTER (WHITE-WASH). A thin layer of clay used as a protective coating on the exterior walls of buildings. The term is used figuratively of the futile promises of false prophets (Ezek. 13:10–15; 22:28). *Whitewash:* NIV, NRSV.

UPHAZ. A place in Arabia where gold was obtained, perhaps the same place as Ophir (Jer. 10:9).

UPPER EGYPT. See *Pathros.*

U

UPPER ROOM. A chamber or room usually built on the roof of a house and used in the summer because it was cooler than the regular living quarters (Mark 14:15). Such a room was the site of Jesus' last meal with His disciples (Luke 22:12). See also *Loft*.

UR OF THE CHALDEES (UR OF THE CHALDEANS). A city in Mesopotamia where Abraham spent his early life with his father, Terah, and his wife, Sarah, before he was called by the Lord to go to Canaan (Gen. 11:28, 31). Excavation has revealed that Ur was a thriving city and center of moon worship. *Ur of the Chaldeans:* NIV, NRSV. See also *Mesopotamia*.

URIAH

1. A Hittite warrior in David's army whose wife, Bath-sheba, was taken by David after the king plotted to have Uriah killed in battle (2 Sam. 11:15, 24–27). *Urias:* Greek form (Matt. 1:6).

2. NIV, NRSV name for the prophet Urijah. See *Urijah*.

URIJAH (URIAH). A faithful prophet in Jeremiah's time who was killed by King Jehoiakim for predicting God's judgment on Judah (Jer. 26:20). *Uriah:* NIV, NRSV.

URIM AND THUMMIN. Two objects in the breastplate of the high priest (Exod. 28:30), possibly colored stones cast as lots to help determine God's will (Num. 27:21). See also *Lots, Casting of.*

USURY (INTEREST). Interest on money loaned. Under the Mosaic Law, Jews could exact interest only from non-Jews, not from their own countrymen (Lev. 25:36–37). Nehemiah denounced those who were breaking this law (Neh. 5:7, 10). *Interest:* NIV, NRSV. See also *Debt; Loan.*

UZ. A place in southern Edom west of the Arabian desert where Job lived (Job 1:1; Jer. 25:20).

UZZA (UZZAH). An Israelite who was struck dead for touching the ark of the covenant while carting it to Jerusalem (1 Chron. 13:7–11). *Uzzah:* NIV, NRSV.

UZZIAH/AZARIAH/OZIAS. The son and successor of Amaziah as king of Judah (reigned about 767–740 B.C.). A godly king, excellent general, and noted city builder (2 Chron. 26:1–15), he contracted leprosy as a divine punishment for assuming duties that belonged to the priesthood (2 Chron. 26:16–21). *Azariah:* 2 Kings 14:21; *Ozias:* Jesus' ancestry (Matt. 1:8).

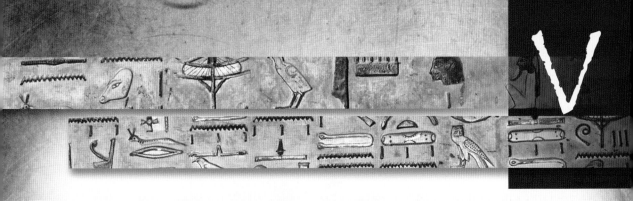

VAGABOND (WANDERER). A wanderer or fugitive. Life as a fugitive was part of the curse against Cain for murdering his brother Abel (Gen. 4:12). *Wanderer:* NIV, NRSV. The "vagabond Jews" of Acts 19:13 were professional exorcists.

VAIN
Exod. 20:7 not take the name of the LORD...in **v**
Ps. 2:1 Why do...the people imagine a **v** thing?
Prov. 31:30 Favour is deceitful...beauty is **v**
Matt. 6:7 when ye pray, use not **v** repetitions
1 Cor. 3:20 Lord knoweth...thoughts of the wise...**v**
1 Cor. 15:14 if Christ be not risen...our preaching **v**
2 Tim. 2:16 shun profane and **v** babblings

VALE OF SIDDIM. A valley of tar pits near the Dead Sea where Sodom and Gomorrah were located (Gen. 14:1–10).

VALLEY OF DRY BONES. A vision of the prophet Ezekiel. When Ezekiel addressed the bones, representing Israel's exile in a foreign land, they came to life by God's Spirit. This served as God's assurance that His people would return one day to their native land (Ezek. 37:1–14). See also *Ezekiel, Book of.*

VANITY. Emptiness and futility. Life is vain and empty unless it is lived in obedience to God and His will (Eccles. 12:13).

VANITY [IES]
Job 35:13 God will not hear **v**
Ps. 39:5 every man...is altogether **v**
Eccles. 1:2 **v** of **v'ies**; all is **v**
Isa. 41:29 they are all **v**; their works are nothing
Eph. 4:17 walk not...in the **v** of their mind

VASHTI. The queen of Ahasuerus of Persia who refused the king's command to appear with the royal court and was replaced by Esther (Esther 1:10–12; 2:2, 15–17).

VEGETABLES. See *Pulse.*

VEIL
1. A screen or curtain that separated the Holy Place and the Holy of Holies in the tabernacle and temple. This veil was torn at Christ's death to symbolize direct access of all people to God's salvation through Jesus Christ (Matt. 27:51). *Curtain:* NIV, NRSV (Heb. 4:14–16). See also *Court of the Gentiles; Middle Wall of Partition.*
2. NIV word for *muffler.* See *Muffler.*

VENGEANCE. See *Revenge.*

VENISON (GAME). The flesh of any wild animal used for food. Isaac loved his son Esau because he was a "cunning hunter" who cooked venison (Gen. 25:27–28). *Game:* NIV, NRSV. See also *Hunter.*

VENOM (POISON). A poisonous fluid secreted by animals such as snakes and scorpions. The word is used figuratively of the destructive power of wine (Deut. 32:33). *Poison:* NRSV. See also *Poison.*

VENOMOUS SNAKES. See *Fiery Serpents.*

VERMILION. A bright red substance used for ornamentation and painting of houses and images (Ezek. 23:14).

VESTIBULE. See *Porch.*

VIA DOLOROSA. The name, meaning "way of sorrow," for the traditional route that Jesus took from Pilate's judgment hall to Calvary for His crucifixion. It is impossible to determine the precise route, since Jerusalem was destroyed by the Romans in A.D. 70 and then rebuilt. This name does not appear in the Bible.

VIAL (FLASK). A bottle or flask that held oil or other liquids (1 Sam. 10:1). *Flask:* NIV.

VICTORY
Isa. 25:8 He [God] will swallow up death in **v**
1 Cor. 15:55 O grave, where is thy **v**?
1 Cor. 15:57 God...giveth us the **v** through...Jesus Christ
1 John 5:4 the **v** that overcometh the world

VILLAGE. A collection of houses or a small town not protected by a defensive wall (Ezek. 38:11).

VINE. A plant that bore grapes. Jesus referred to Himself as the "true vine" (John 15:1).

VINE [S]
Judg. 9:12 said the trees unto the **v**...reign over us
Song 2:15 little foxes, that spoil the **v's**
Mic. 4:4 sit every man under his **v** and...fig tree
Luke 22:18 I [Jesus] will not drink...fruit of the **v**
John 15:5 I [Jesus] am the **v**, ye are the branches

VINE OF SODOM. A plant that grew near the Dead Sea and produced a beautiful fruit that was unfit to eat—a fitting description of Israel's idolatry (Deut. 32:32).

VINEGAR (SOUR WINE). A beverage consisting of wine or strong drink that was excessively fermented until it turned sour. This drink was offered to Jesus on the cross (Matt. 27:34, 48). *Sour wine:* NRSV.

VINEYARD. A field or orchard of grapevines. The word is used symbolically for Israel (Ps. 80:8, 15–16).

VINTAGE. The time of year for making wine. Grapes were gathered with shouts of joy (Jer. 25:30), then put in baskets and carried to the winepress (Jer. 6:9). See also *Wine.*

VIOL (LYRE). A stringed musical instrument probably similar to the psaltery (Isa. 5:12). *Lyre:* NIV. See also *Harp; Psaltery.*

VIPER. See *Asp.*

VIRGIN. A general term for a young unmarried woman (Gen. 24:16).

VIRGIN BIRTH. The miraculous conception of Jesus by the Holy Spirit and His birth to the Virgin Mary. This event was foretold by the

ISRAEL AS A VINE

The image of the nation of Israel as a vine (Ps. 80:8-11) appears throughout the Bible. The prophet Isaiah declared that the nation yielded the "wild grapes" of idolatry (Isa. 5:1-7). Hosea the prophet called Israel an "empty vine" (Hosea 10:1).

Perhaps Jesus had this image in mind when He identified Himself as the "true vine" (John 15:1). As the perfectly obedient Son, He fulfilled the purpose to which God the Father had called His chosen people.

prophet Isaiah (Isa. 7:14) and revealed to Mary by an angel (Luke 1:26–33). The Messiah's supernatural conception in a human mother corresponds to His unique role as God-man. See also *Advent of Christ, The First; Incarnation of Christ.*

VIRTUE.
Moral excellence in association with power and ability—a characteristic of Jesus (Luke 6:19).

Mark 5:30 Jesus...knowing that **v** had gone out of him
Phil. 4:8 if there be any **v**...think on these things
2 Pet. 1:5 add to your faith **v**; and to virtue knowledge

VIRTUOUS
Ruth 3:11 all the city...doth know...thou art a **v** woman
Prov. 12:4 A **v** woman is a crown to her husband
Prov. 31:10 Who can find a **v** woman?...price...above rubies

VISION [S]
Prov. 29:18 Where there is no **v**, the people perish
Joel 2:28 your young men shall see **v's**
Hab. 2:2 Write the **v**...make it plain upon tables
Luke 1:22 he [Zacharias] had seen a **v** in the temple
Acts 16:9 a **v** appeared to Paul in the night
Acts 26:19 I [Paul] was not disobedient...heavenly **v**

VOCATION (CALLING).
A calling based on God's purpose and grace (2 Tim. 1:9). Paul urged believers to "walk worthy" of their Christian vocation (Eph. 4:1). *Calling:* NIV, NRSV. See also *Calling.*

VOICE [S]
Gen. 22:18 thou [Abraham] hast obeyed my [God's] **v**
Exod. 5:2 is the LORD, that I [Pharaoh]...obey his **v**
1 Kings 19:12 and after the fire a still small **v**
Isa. 40:3 The **v** of him that crieth in the wilderness
Matt. 3:3 The **v** of one crying in the wilderness
Matt. 3:17 a **v** from heaven...my [God's] beloved Son
John 10:27 My [Jesus'] sheep hear my **v**
Acts 9:4 a **v**...Saul, why persecutest...me [Jesus]
1 Cor. 14:10 There are...many...**v's** in the world
Heb. 3:15 To day if ye will hear his [God's] **v**
Rev. 1:10 I [John]...heard behind me a great **v**

VULTURE. Figurines of a vulture and a hawk, from ancient Egypt. Scavengers, vultures feed mostly on abandoned carcasses.

VOID (EMPTY).
Containing nothing; empty. The earth was formless and void before God shaped it and filled it with life through His creative power (Gen. 1:2). *Empty:* NIV.

VOW.
A pledge or agreement to perform a service for God in return for some expected benefit (Gen. 28:20–22).

VOW [ED, EST, S]
Ps. 50:14 pay thy **v's** unto the most High
Eccles. 5:4 **v'est** a **v** unto God, defer not to pay it
Jon. 2:9 I will pay that that I have **v'ed**

VOW OFFERING.
A gift or freewill offering that accompanied a vow to the Lord (Deut. 23:23).

VULTURE (RED KITE, BUZZARD).
A large bird that fed mostly on dead animals or other wastes and was thus considered unclean (Lev. 11:14). *Red kite:* NIV; *buzzard:* NRSV. See also *Ossifrage.*

V

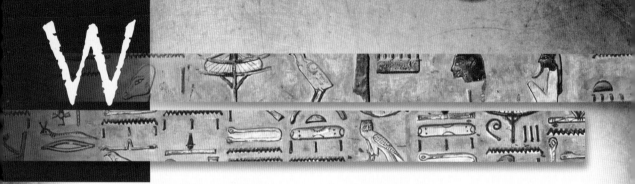

WADI. A bed of a stream that is dry except during the rainy season (Gen. 26:19). This word does not occur in the Bible, but Palestine has hundreds of these wadis.

WADI OF EGYPT. See *River of Egypt.*

WAFER. A thin cake made of fine, unleavened flour and anointed with oil for meal offerings (Exod. 29:2). Wafers were sometimes sweetened with honey (Exod. 16:31).

WAGES. Payment for work rendered by field hands or common laborers. Wages were paid daily, at the end of the workday (Lev. 19:13). Paul declared that the wages, or payoff, of sin is death (Rom. 6:23).

WAR. In a war with the Jews, Roman General Titus leads his troops in the battle for Jerusalem. Rome overran and destroyed Jerusalem and the temple in A.D. 70.

WAGON. A crude wooden cart pulled by oxen (Gen. 45:19). See also *Cart*.

WALL. A massive fence of stone or brick around a city for protection against enemy attack (2 Sam. 18:24). Defense towers and even houses were often built on these walls (Isa. 2:15). See also *Fenced City; Siege*.

WALL OF PARTITION. See *Middle Wall of Partition*.

WANDERER. See *Vagabond*.

WAR. Armed conflict between nations or tribes. The Hebrews considered their conflicts with enemy nations as the Lord's battles (Num. 10:9). Early skirmishes were fought by spearmen, archers, and slingers; horses and chariots were a later development in Israel's history. The prophets envisioned an age without war (Mic. 4:3).

WARD. A prison cell or lockup room. This word is also used for a detachment of soldiers on guard duty (Acts 12:10). See also *Prison*.

WARDROBE. A place where royal robes or priestly vestments were kept (2 Kings 22:14).

WARP. The long threads in hand-spun cloth. These threads are extended lengthwise in the loom and crossed by the *woof*, or threads running in the opposite direction. See also *Weaver*.

WARRIORS. See *Mighty Men*.

WASH. To cleanse (Matt. 27:24). The Hebrews emphasized cleanliness and ceremonial purity. Washing the hands before meals or the feet after a journey was considered a religious duty (Matt. 15:2). See also *Clean; Purification*.

WASHERMAN'S FIELD. See *Fuller's Field*.

WATCH
Job 14:16 dost thou [God] not *w* over my sin
Matt. 24:42 *W* therefore...ye know not what hour
Mark 14:37 couldest not thou [Peter] *w* one hour
Luke 2:8 shepherds...keeping *w* over their flock
1 Pet. 4:7 be ye...sober, and *w* unto prayer

WATCHMAN (SENTINEL). A guard or sentry stationed at a city gate. These watchmen also patrolled the streets and called out the hours of the night (2 Sam. 18:24–27). *Sentinel:* NRSV.

WATCHTOWER. A tall guard station or lookout post that provided early warning of approaching dangers (Isa. 21:5).

WATER. In Palestine's arid climate, water was a precious commodity. People were dependent on wells or cisterns during the dry summer and fall. Public wells or reservoirs were provided for travelers (Gen. 26:19). Jesus promised the "water of life" to a sinful Samaritan woman (John 4:10–14). See also *Well*.

WATER [S]
Gen. 1:2 Spirit of God moved upon...*w's*
Num. 20:11 Moses...smote the rock...*w* came out
Ps. 1:3 tree planted by the rivers of *w*
Prov. 5:15 Drink *w's* out of thine own cistern
Eccles. 11:1 Cast thy bread upon the *w's*
Song 8:7 Many *w's* cannot quench love
Isa. 55:1 every one that thirsteth, come ye to the *w's*
Jer. 2:13 forsaken me [God] the fountain of living *w's*
Amos 5:24 let judgment run down as *w's*
Mark 1:8 I [John the Baptist]...have baptized you with *w*
John 3:5 Except a man be born of *w* and of the Spirit
Acts 1:5 John...baptized with *w*; but ye...with the Holy Ghost
Rev. 22:17 let him take the *w* of life freely

WATER CARRIER. See *Drawer of Water*.

WATER HEN. See *Swan*.

W

WATER OF JEALOUSY. A mixture of water with dust prescribed as a test for a woman accused of adultery by her husband (Num. 5:11–31).

WATER OF SEPARATION (WATER OF CLEANSING). Water mixed with ashes to purify a person after defilement through contact with the dead (Num. 19:13–22). *Water of cleansing:* NIV. See also *Bitter Water.*

WATERING TROUGH. See *Gutter.*

WATERPOT. A large clay vessel in which water for the household was stored (John 2:6–7).

WATERS OF MEROM. A lake ten miles north of the Sea of Galilee through which the Jordan River flows on its southward passage (Josh. 11:5–7).

WAVE OFFERING (ELEVATION OFFERING). A sacrificial animal presented to God to celebrate restoration of a right relationship with God. The sacrifice was "waved" before the Lord to gain acceptance (Exod. 29:24). *Elevation offering:* NRSV. See also *Sacrifice.*

WAX. A substance formed by bees while making honey. The word is also used figuratively for the punishment of the wicked in God's presence (Ps. 68:2).

WAY OF THE SEA. A road that ran from Sidon in Phoenicia to Egypt, passing through Palestine (Isa. 9:1). See also *Highway; Road.*

WAY, THE. A term of contempt for the Christian faith used by the enemies of the early church (Acts 9:2; 24:14, 22).

WAYS
1 Sam. 18:14 David behaved...wisely in all his **w**
2 Chron. 7:14 If my [God's] people...turn from their wicked **w**
Ps. 25:4 Show me thy **w**, O LORD
Prov. 3:6 In all thy **w** acknowledge him [God]
Prov. 14:12 the end thereof are the **w** of death
Prov. 28:18 he that is perverse in his **w** shall fall
Isa. 55:8 neither are your **w** my **w**, saith the LORD
James 1:8 A double minded man is unstable in all his **w**

WEAK [NESS]
Ps. 6:2 Have mercy upon me, O LORD; for I am **w**
Matt. 26:41 spirit...is willing...flesh is **w**
Acts 20:35 ye ought to support the **w**
1 Cor. 1:27 **w** things of the world to confound the...mighty
1 Cor. 9:22 became...**w**, that I [Paul] might gain the **w**
1 Cor. 15:43 it [the body] is sown in **w'ness**...raised in power
2 Cor. 12:9 my [Jesus'] strength is made perfect in **w'ness**

WEALTH. See *Mammon; Money.*

WEASEL. An unclean animal, possibly the mole or polecat (Lev. 11:29).

WEAVER. A craftsman who made cloth from several different raw materials, including wool and camel hair (Exod. 35:35; Lev. 13:47). The Hebrews may have learned the art of weaving in Egypt.

WEDDING. A marriage ceremony. A Jewish wedding was a festive occasion with the entire community participating. The bride wore jewels and an ornamented white robe with a veil. The bridegroom, accompanied by friends and musicians, proceeded to the bride's home to conduct her to the wedding hall. Festivities continued for seven days (Matt. 25:6–10; Luke 12:36; 14:8). See also *Betrothal; Dowry; Marriage.*

WEED. See *Cockle.*

WEEKS, FEAST OF. See *Pentecost.*

WELL. A deep hole dug in the ground to reach groundwater. Wells were usually covered with stone slabs or surrounded by low stone walls (John 4:6). The word is also used figuratively of salvation (Isa. 12:3) and wisdom (Prov. 16:22). The phrase "wells without water" shows the futility of wickedness (2 Pet. 2:17). See also *Water.*

WHALE. A large sea-dwelling fish (Gen. 1:21). The "great fish" that swallowed Jonah is thought to be an enormous white shark, common in the Mediterranean Sea (Jon. 1:17).

WHEAT. A grain that was ground and baked into bread (1 Kings 5:11). The wheat harvest was observed as a festival and time of celebration (Exod. 34:22). See also *Corn.*

WHIRLWIND (GALE, STORM). A great storm or tempest (Job 37:9). Elijah was transported to heaven by a whirlwind (2 Kings 2:1, 11). The word was also used figuratively for swift and sudden destruction (Isa. 17:13). *Gale:* NIV; *storm:* NRSV. See also *Tempest.*

WHITE OWL. See *Swan.*

WHITED SEPULCHRE. See *Sepulchre.*

WHITEWASH. See *Untempered Mortar.*

WICKED [NESS]
Gen. 6:5 God saw that the *w'ness* of man was great
Job 4:8 they that...sow *w'ness*, reap the same
Ps. 10:2 *w* in his pride doth persecute the poor
Ps. 71:4 Deliver me...out of the hand of the *w*
Ps. 94:3 LORD...how long shall the *w* triumph?
Prov. 4:17 they [evil men] eat the bread of *w'ness*
Prov. 15:29 The LORD is far from the *w*
Isa. 53:9 he [God's servant] made his grave with the *w*
Jer. 4:14 O Jerusalem, wash thine heart from *w'ness*
Jer. 17:9 The heart is...desperately *w*
Matt. 16:4 A *w*...generation seeketh after a sign

Eph. 6:12 we wrestle...against spiritual *w'ness*
Eph. 6:16 quench all the fiery darts of the *w*

WICKEDNESS. Evil, malice, and wrongdoing. See *Evil; Iniquity; Sin.*

WICKED ONE
Matt. 13:19 the *w-o*...catcheth...which was sown
Matt. 13:38 tares are the children of the *w-o*
1 John 2:14 and ye have overcome the *w-o*
1 John 3:12 Cain...was of that *w-o*...slew his brother

WIDOW. A woman whose husband has died. Fair and just treatment of widows was enjoined under Mosaic Law (Exod. 22:22). In the N.T., visiting the fatherless and widows was cited as evidence of true religion (James 1:27). See also *Levirate Marriage.*

MINISTRY TO WIDOWS

Paul's admonition to his missionary associate, Timothy, was that the church should "relieve them that are widows indeed" (1 Tim. 5:16)—those without any means of support who were in dire financial need. In Bible times, women whose husbands died did not have public assistance or life insurance to fall back on. The early church provided a measure of support for widows within its fellowship (Acts 6:1).

WIFE. A married woman. Wives are urged to love and respect their husbands and to be faithful to them (Eph. 5:33; Prov. 31:11–12). Husbands and wives are to be mutually committed to each other and to fulfill each other's needs (1 Cor. 7:2–5). See also *Family; Husband.*

WILD OX. See *Unicorn.*

WILDERNESS. A dry, desolate, uncultivated region where little vegetation grew. John the Baptist preached in the Judean wilderness (Matt. 3:1). See also *Desert*.

WILDERNESS WANDERINGS. The aimless course taken by the Hebrew people in the Sinai Peninsula for forty years after they left Egypt—God's punishment for their sin of disobedience (Deut. 1:1; Josh. 5:6). God provided food and guidance through Moses until they arrived in Canaan (Exod. 16:35; Neh. 9:24).

WILL OF GOD. God's desire and wish for His people. The Father's will is that those who believe on the Son will have eternal life and that none will be lost (John 6:39–40). The disciples of Jesus were taught to pray for God's will to be done on earth as it is in heaven (Matt. 6:10). Paul urged the Christians at Rome to allow God to transform their minds to know the perfect will of God (Rom. 12:2).

Mark 3:35 do the *w-o-G*...same is my brother
1 Thess. 4:3 the *w-o-G*...abstain from fornication
1 Thess. 5:18 give thanks...the *w-o-G* in Christ Jesus
1 John 2:17 doeth the *w-o-G* abideth for ever

WILLOW (POPLAR). A tree that grew by streams; perhaps the weeping willow (Ps. 137:1–2). Its branches were used for booths at the Feast of Tabernacles (Lev. 23:40). *Poplar:* NIV. See also *Poplar*.

WIMPLE (CLOAK). A mantle, scarf, or shawl worn around the neck by women (Isa. 3:22). *Cloak:* NIV, NRSV.

WIND. The movement of the air. The Bible speaks of the "four winds" (Jer. 49:36): the north wind (Job 37:22), the warm south wind (Luke 12:55), the cool west wind bringing rain (Luke 12:54), and the scorching east wind from the desert (Job 27:21). Jesus illustrated the freedom of the Holy Spirit with the mysteries of the wind (John 3:8).

WINDOW. A small opening in a house or public building that let in light and cool breezes (1 Chron. 15:29). These openings were probably covered with shutters or latticework.

WINE/STRONG DRINK. The juice of grapes, fermented to produce a strong beverage that was very popular among the Jews (Gen. 40:11). Commonly referred to as *strong drink* (Prov. 31:6), wine was prohibited to Nazarites (Num. 6:3) as well as to priests before they officiated at the altar (Lev. 10:9). Excessive consumption of wine was denounced (Prov. 20:1; Eph. 5:18). See also *Grape*.

WINE

Prov. 4:17 they...drink the *w* of violence
Isa. 5:22 Woe unto them that are mighty to drink *w*
Mark 2:22 no man putteth new *w* into old bottles
John 2:3 mother of Jesus saith...They have no *w*
Acts 2:13 men [believers at Pentecost] are full of new *w*
1 Tim. 3:8 deacons be grave...not given to much *w*
1 Tim. 5:23 use a little *w* for thy stomach's sake

WINEBIBBER (DRUNKARD). A person addicted to wine (Prov. 23:20–21). Jesus was accused of being a winebibber because He befriended sinners (Matt. 11:19). *Drunkard:* NIV, NRSV.

WINEPRESS. A vat or tank where juice was squeezed from grapes in the wine-making process. Usually hewn out of rock, the winepress had an upper vat where the grapes were crushed and a lower vat that received the juice (Judg. 6:11; Isa. 63:2–3). See also *Grape*.

WINESKIN. See *Bottle*.

WINEPRESS. In this ancient mosaic, Roman vineyard workers walk on grapes to squeeze out the juice for wine. The juice flows out of the stone vat and into small containers below.

valuable than riches (Prov. 8:11), and it produces good fruit (James 3:17). Christ is the key that opens the hidden treasures of God's wisdom (Col. 2:3).

Job 28:28 the fear of the Lord, that is **w**
Job 34:35 his [Job's] words were without **w**
Ps. 90:12 number our days...apply our hearts unto **w**
Prov. 4:7 **W** is the principal thing; therefore get **w**
Eccles. 1:18 in much **w** is much grief
Jer. 9:23 Let not the wise man glory in his **w**
Luke 2:52 Jesus increased in **w** and stature
Acts 6:3 seven men...full of the Holy Ghost and **w**
1 Cor. 1:20 God made foolish the **w** of this world
1 Cor. 1:22 Jews require a sign...Greeks seek after **w**
1 Cor. 3:19 **w** of this world is foolishness with God
Col. 3:16 word of Christ dwell in you...in all **w**
James 1:5 any of you lack **w**, let him ask of God

WISDOM LITERATURE. A distinct category of literature in the Bible, including Job, Proverbs, Ecclesiastes, and some of the psalms, so named because they deal with some of the most important ethical and philosophical issues of life—the meaning of suffering, the nature and purpose of God, human relationships, and so on.

WING. A symbolic expression for God's protection. He delivers His people on the wings of eagles (Exod. 19:4).

WINNOWING. The process of separating chaff or straw from the grains of wheat by beating the stalks and throwing them into the air; symbolically, to rid oneself of sin or worldly desire (Matt. 3:12). See also *Fan; Threshingfloor.*

WINTERHOUSE (WINTER APARTMENT). A dwelling used by kings in the winter months (Jer. 36:22). *Winter apartment:* NIV, NRSV.

WISDOM. Knowledge guided by insight and understanding. Reverence for God is the source of wisdom (Prov. 9:10). Wisdom is more

WISE
Prov. 6:6 consider her [the ant's] ways...be **w**
Isa. 5:21 Woe unto them that are **w** in their own eyes
Jer. 9:23 Let not the **w** man glory in his wisdom
Matt. 2:1 when Jesus was born...came **w** men from the east
Matt. 7:24 a **w** man...built his house upon a rock
Matt. 10:16 **w** as serpents...harmless as doves
Matt. 11:25 thou [God] hast hid these things from the **w**
Matt. 25:8 foolish said unto the **w**, Give us of your oil
Rom. 12:16 Be not **w** in your own conceits
1 Cor. 1:26 not many **w** men after the flesh...are called

WISE MEN. Astrologers from Mesopotamia or Persia, often referred to as the *magi,* who brought gifts to the young child Jesus in Bethlehem (Matt. 2:10–11). See also *Astrologer.*

W

WITCHCRAFT. The practice of sorcery or black magic by witches and wizards—an activity denounced by God (Deut. 18:10; Mic. 5:12). King Saul displeased God by asking the witch of Endor to summon the spirit of Samuel from the dead (1 Sam. 28:3–25). See also *Magic; Sorcery.*

WITNESS. One who gives testimony about an event or another person's character. Under Mosaic Law, the testimony of at least two persons was required to convict a person of a capital offense (Deut. 17:6). False witnesses were punished severely (Deut. 19:18–19). Believers are empowered to serve as witnesses for Christ (Acts 1:8). See also *Record; Testimony.*

WITNESS [ES]
Exod. 20:16 not bear false *w* against thy neighbour
Ps. 35:11 False *w's* did rise up
Prov. 19:9 false *w* shall not be unpunished
Mark 14:56 many bare false *w* against him [Jesus]
Rom. 8:16 Spirit itself beareth *w* with our spirit
Heb. 12:1 compassed about with...a cloud of *w's*

WIVES
Matt. 19:8 Moses...suffered you to put away your *w*
Eph. 5:22 *W*, submit...unto your own husbands
Eph. 5:25 Husbands, love your *w*...as Christ...loved the church
Col. 3:18 *W*, submit...unto your own husbands
Col. 3:19 Husbands, love your *w*...be not bitter
1 Tim. 4:7 But refuse profane and old *w'* fables
1 Pet. 3:1 *w*, be in subjection to your own husbands

WIZARD (SPIRITIST). A male witch, or practitioner of black magic, who claimed to have secret knowledge given by a spirit from the dead (2 Kings 21:6). Under Mosaic Law, wizards were to be put to death by stoning (Lev. 20:27). *Spiritist:* NIV. See also *Familiar Spirit.*

WOE. An expression of extreme grief or distress (Matt. 24:19). The word also expressed the threat of future punishment (Jer. 48:46).

WOLF. A fierce wild animal of the dog family that posed a threat to sheep (Isa. 11:6). Jesus also used the word figuratively of false prophets (Matt. 7:15).

WOMB. Barren women regarded themselves as cursed by the Lord (1 Sam. 1:5–10). Children were described as "fruit of the womb" and a blessing from God (Ps. 127:3–5). See also *Barren; Children.*

WONDERS
Ps. 77:14 Thou art the God that doest *w*
Ps. 96:3 declare his [God's]...*w* among all people
John 4:48 Except ye see signs and *w*, ye will not believe
Acts 2:43 *w* and signs were done by the apostles
Acts 6:8 Stephen, full of faith...did great *w*

WOODCUTTER. See *Hewer.*

WOOF. See *Warp.*

WOOL. The furlike coat of sheep that was highly prized by the Jews for making clothes (Prov. 31:13). Its vulnerability to moths was a problem (Matt. 6:19). See also *Fleece; Sheep.*

WORD [S]
Ps. 12:6 The *w's* of the LORD are pure *w's*
Ps. 19:14 *w's*...be acceptable in thy [God's] sight
Ps. 119:11 Thy [God's] *w* have I hid in mine heart
Ps. 119:105 Thy [God's] *w* is a lamp unto my feet
Isa. 40:8 the *w* of our God shall stand for ever
Mal. 2:17 have wearied the LORD with your *w's*
Luke 4:32 his [Jesus'] *w* was with power
John 1:1 In the beginning was the *W*
John 6:68 thou [Jesus] hast the *w's* of eternal life
Acts 8:4 they...went every where preaching the *w*
2 Cor. 5:19 committed unto us the *w* of reconciliation
2 Tim. 2:15 workman...rightly dividing the *w* of truth
James 1:22 doers of the *w*...not hearers only
1 John 3:18 let us not love in *w*...but in deed

WORD OF GOD. God's revelation of Himself to humans, especially through Jesus and the

W

Bible (Heb. 4:12). The written Scriptures, which Christians accept as the Word of God, testify to Jesus as the eternal and living Word of God (John 1:1; 5:39). See also *Bible; Logos.*

Prov. 30:5 Every **w-o-G** is pure
Luke 4:4 not live by bread alone but by every **w-o-G**
Rom. 10:17 faith...by hearing...hearing by the **w-o-G**
Eph. 6:17 sword of the Spirit, which is the **w-o-G**
Heb. 11:3 the worlds were framed by the **w-o-G**

WORK.
Labor in a worthwhile cause; fruitful activity. A Christian's work should be performed as service to the Lord (Eph. 6:6–8).

WORK [ETH]
Exod. 23:12 Six days thou shalt do thy **w**
Neh. 4:6 people had a mind to **w**
Ps. 115:4 idols are...the **w** of men's hands
John 4:34 My [Jesus'] meat is...to finish his [God's] **w**
John 9:4 night cometh, when no man can **w**
Acts 13:2 Separate...Barnabas and Saul for the **w**
Rom. 8:28 all things **w** together for good
Rom. 13:10 Love **w'eth** no ill to his neighbour
Eph. 4:12 perfecting of the saints...**w** of the ministry
1 Tim. 3:1 office of a bishop, he desireth a good **w**

WORKERS
Ps. 6:8 Depart from me...ye **w** of iniquity
1 Cor. 12:29 are all teachers? are all **w** of miracles?
Phil. 3:2 Beware of dogs, beware of evil **w**

WORKS.
Good deeds performed as an expression of a believer's commitment to Christ. Works cannot save or justify (Eph. 2:9), but they do fulfill God's purpose for His people. We are created in Jesus Christ in order to perform good works for the building of God's kingdom (Eph. 2:10).

1 Chron. 16:9 talk ye of all his [God's] wondrous **w**
Job 37:14 consider the wondrous **w** of God
Ps. 40:5 Many, O Lord...are thy wonderful **w**
Matt. 5:16 see your good **w**, and glorify your Father
Matt. 13:58 he [Jesus] did not many mighty **w** there
John 6:28 that we might work the **w** of God
John 14:12 greater **w** than these shall he do

Gal. 2:16 man is not justified by the **w** of the law
Titus 3:5 Not by **w** of righteousness...we have done
James 2:17 faith, if it hath not **w**, is dead

WORK [S] OF GOD/WORK [S] OF THE LORD
Ps. 64:9 all men...shall declare the **w-o-G**
Ps. 66:5 Come and see the **w's-o-G**
Ps. 77:11 I will remember the **w's-o-t-L**
Ps. 78:7 not forget the **w's-o-G**
Ps. 118:17 I shall...declare the **w's-o-t-L**
Eccles. 7:13 Consider the **w-o-G**
Eccles. 8:17 Then I beheld all the **w-o-G**
Jer. 51:10 declare in Zion the **w-o-t-L** our God
John 6:28 that we might work the **w's-o-G**
Acts 2:11 hear them speak...wonderful **w's-o-G**
1 Cor. 15:58 stedfast...abounding in the **w-o-t-L**

WORK. Working his way up a Jerusalem street, a broom vendor sells his wares to anyone willing to buy. The Bible praises hard work and condemns laziness.

W

WORLDLY. See *Carnal.*

WORM. An insect that destroyed plants and consumed dead flesh (Job 7:5). The word is also used symbolically of human helplessness or insignificance (Isa. 41:14) and frailty (Ps. 22:6).

WORMWOOD. A plant noted for its bitter taste (Jer. 9:15). The phrase "gall and wormwood" describes something offensive or sorrowful (Deut. 29:18). See also *Hemlock.*

WORSHIP. The praise and adoration of God expressed both publicly and privately (Deut. 6; 1 Chron. 16:29). The Jews worshiped in the tabernacle until the temple became their worship center. After their period of exile among the Babylonians and Persians, they worshiped in neighborhood synagogues. The book known as Psalms contains many spiritual songs and hymns chanted or sung in public worship. See also *Hymn; Praise; Psalms, Book of.*

WORSHIP [PED]
Ps. 95:6 *w* and bow down [before God]
Ps. 99:5 *w* at his [God's] footstool...he is holy
Jer. 25:6 go not after other gods...to *w* them
Matt. 2:2 we [the wise men]...are come to *w* him [Jesus]
John 4:24 they...must *w* him [God] in spirit and in truth
Acts 17:25 Neither is [God] *w'ped* with men's hands
Rev. 7:11 angels...fell...on their faces...*w'ped* God

WORTHY. Of value or merit. The Lamb of God is worthy of praise because He redeemed us, made us kings and priests, and will share His reign with us (Rev. 5:9–14).

WRATH. Strong anger or indignation. Human wrath may be kindled by false accusation (Gen. 31:36) or disobedience (Num. 31:14–18), but God's wrath is exercised against ungodliness (Rom. 1:18), idolatry (Ps. 78:58–59), and unbelief (John 3:36). See also *Judgment; Punishment.*

Exod. 32:11 why doth thy [God's] *w* wax hot
Ps. 21:9 LORD shall swallow them up in his *w*
Ps. 90:7 by thy [God's] *w* are we troubled
Matt. 3:7 warned you [Pharisee] to flee from the *w*
Eph. 4:26 let not the sun go down upon your *w*
Eph. 6:4 fathers, provoke not your children to *w*
Rev. 6:17 great day of his [God's] *w* is come

WRATH OF GOD
Ps. 78:31 The *w-o-G*...slew the fattest of them
John 3:36 believeth not the Son...*w-o-G* abideth on him
Rom. 1:18 *w-o-G* is revealed...against all ungodliness
Rev. 16:1 pour out the vials of the *w-o-G* upon the earth

WREATH. See *Garland.*

WRITING. The Hebrews probably learned writing from the Egyptians. Earliest writing was done on stone, clay tablets, papyrus, and animal skins. See also *Ink; Paper.*

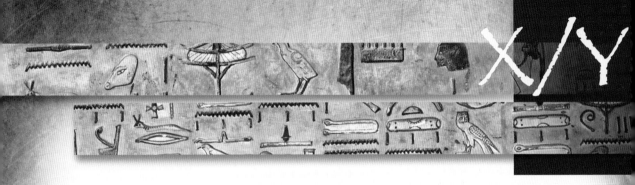

XERXES. See *Ahasuerus.*

YAHWEH. The Hebrew spelling of the major name for God in the O.T., translated in most English Bibles as "Lord" or "Jehovah." See *Jehovah.*

YARN. Thread used in weaving cloth. Yarn was produced from linen and wool fiber as well as the hair of camels and goats (Exod. 35:25–26). See also *Warp; Weaver.*

YEAR OF JUBILEE. See *Jubile.*

YEAST. See *Leaven.*

YIELD [ED, ING]
Gen. 1:11 earth bring forth grass, the herb *y'ing* seed
Ps. 67:6 Then shall the earth *y* her increase
Matt. 27:50 Jesus...*y'ed* up the ghost
Rom. 6:13 but *y* yourselves unto God

YIRON. See *Iron,* No. 1.

YOKE. A wooden collar or harness placed on the neck of draft animals and attached to plows and other agricultural tools (Jer. 31:18). The word was also used to denote servitude or oppression (1 Kings 12:1–4). Jesus declared His yoke is not burdensome (Matt. 11:29–30).

YOKEFELLOW (COMPANION). A fellow worker or comrade in a common cause. Paul appealed to an unknown "yokefellow" in Philippi to help two women resolve their differences (Phil. 4:3). *Companion:* NRSV.

YOUTH
Ps. 25:7 Remember not the sins of my *y*
Prov. 5:18 rejoice with the wife of thy *y*
Eccles. 12:1 Remember now thy Creator in the days of thy *y*
Matt. 19:20 All these things have I kept from my *y* up
1 Tim. 4:12 Let no man despise thy *y*

Z

ZABULON. See *Zebulun*.

ZACCHAEUS. A wealthy tax collector who, after a conversation with Jesus at Jericho, vowed to give half of his wealth to the poor and make fourfold restitution to those whom he had cheated. Jesus declared that salvation had come to Zacchaeus (Luke 19:1–10). See also *Publican*.

ZACHARIAH. The son and successor of Jeroboam II as king of Israel. Zachariah ruled only about three months (about 753–752 B.C.) before being assassinated by Shallum (2 Kings 14:29; 15:8–12).

ZACHARIAS (ZECHARIAH). A godly priest and the father of John the Baptist. Zacharias was stricken speechless for his reluctance to believe a son would be born to him in his old age (Luke 1:18–22). *Zechariah:* NIV, NRSV.

ZADOK. The priest who anointed Solomon king. He served as high priest for a time under both David and Solomon (2 Sam. 8:17; 1 Kings 1:39; 2:35).

ZAMZUMMIMS (ZANZUMMITES, ZAMZUMMIM). A race of giants who lived in the region later occupied by the Ammonites (Deut. 2:20–21). *Zanzummites:* NIV; *Zamzummin:* NRSV. See also *Zuzim*.

ZAPHNATH-PAANEAH. See *Joseph*, No. 1.

ZAREPHATH/SAREPTA. A coastal town of Phoenicia where Elijah restored a widow's son to life. Elijah lodged with her during a drought (1 Kings 17:10–24). *Sarepta:* Luke 4:26.

ZEAL. Ardent desire and determination (Ps. 69:9; Phil. 3:6). Isaiah predicted the "zeal of the Lord" would establish the Messiah's kingdom (Isa. 9:7).

ZEALOTS. See *Zelotes*.

ZEALOUS

Acts 21:20 Jews...which believe...*z* of the law
Acts 22:3 I [Paul]...was *z* toward God
Titus 2:14 a peculiar people, *z* of good works

ZEBEDEE. A Galilean fisherman and father of two of Jesus' disciples, James and John (Matt. 4:21–22).

ZEBOIM/ZEBOIIM. One of the five cities near the Dead Sea destroyed along with Sodom and Gomorrah because of its sin (Deut. 29:23). *Zeboiim:* Gen. 14:8. See also *Cities of the Plain*.

ZEBULUN/ZABULON. The sixth son of Jacob and Leah (Gen. 30:19–20) and the tribe descended from Zebulun's three sons (Num. 26:26). This tribe settled in the fertile hill country of Galilee (Josh. 19:10–16). *Zabulon:* Greek form (Matt. 4:13). See also *Tribes of Israel*.

ZECHARIAH'S VISIONS

God revealed His messages for the people to the prophet Zechariah in a series of visions, including the vision of four chariots in Zechariah 6:1–8. Other prophets who had visionary experiences were Jeremiah (Jer. 1:4–19), Ezekiel (Ezek. 1), and Daniel (Dan. 7). Visions left no doubt that the message of these prophets came directly from the Lord.

ZECHARIAH

1. A prophet after the Babylonian conquest of Judah who probably helped rebuild the temple in Jerusalem (Ezra 5:1), and author of the O.T. book that bears his name.

2. NIV, NRSV name for *Zacharias*. See *Zacharias*.

ZECHARIAH, BOOK OF. A prophetic book of the O.T. written to encourage the Jewish people during the difficult years back in their homeland following their period of exile among the Babylonians and Persians. Zechariah, through a series of eight visions (1:7–6:8) and four specific messages from God (7:4–8:23), encouraged the people to complete the task of rebuilding the temple in Jerusalem.

The prophet also presented God's promises for the future, including the coming of the Messiah (9:9–10:12), the restoration of the nation of Israel (chap. 10), and the universal reign of God (chap. 14). See also *Messiah*.

ZEDEKIAH/MATTANIAH. The last king of Judah (reigned about 597–587 B.C.), who was renamed and placed on the throne as a puppet ruler by King Nebuchadnezzar of Babylonia (2 Kings 24:15, 17). Ignoring Jeremiah's advice, he rebelled against the Babylonians, only to be blinded and taken to Babylon in chains after seeing his sons put to death (2 Kings 25:6–7). His original name was *Mattaniah* (2 Kings 24:17).

ZELAH (ZELA). The place where King Saul and his son Jonathan were buried in the territory of Benjamin (2 Sam. 21:14). *Zela:* NIV, NRSV.

ZELOPHEHAD. A member of the tribe of Manasseh whose five daughters petitioned for the right to inherit his property because he had no sons. Their request was granted on the condition that they not marry outside the tribe (Num. 26:33; 27:1–8).

ZELOTES (ZEALOT). A member of a political-religious party of zealous Jews in N.T. times whose aim was to overthrow Roman rule and establish a Jewish theocracy. Jesus' disciple known as Simon the Canaanite may have been a member of this party or sympathetic with its views (Luke 6:15). *Zealot:* NIV, NRSV. See also *Canaanites*, No. 2.

ZEPHANIAH. A priest and friend of Jeremiah and author of the O.T. book that bears his name. Zephaniah often served as a messenger between Jeremiah and King Zedekiah of Judah (Jer. 21:1–2). After Jerusalem fell, Zephaniah was killed by the Babylonians (Jer. 52:24–27).

ZEPHANIAH, BOOK OF. A short prophetic book of the O.T. known for its vivid portrayal of the certainty of God's judgment against the nation of Judah (chaps. 1–2). The prophet also declared that God would spare a faithful remnant (3:13), through which His promise of a future Messiah would be accomplished.

Z

ZERUBBABEL/ZOROBABEL/SHESH-BAZZAR. A leader of the second group of Jews who returned to Jerusalem about 520 B.C. after their period of exile in Babylonia and Persia (Ezra 2:2). He supervised the rebuilding of the temple and helped restore religious practices among his people (Zech. 4; Ezra 5:2). He apparently was appointed governor of Judah by King Cyrus of Persia (Hag. 2:21). *Zorobabel:* Jesus' ancestry (Matt. 1:12). *Sheshbazzar:* Ezra 5:14.

ZEUS. See *Jupiter.*

ZIBA. A former servant of King Saul who helped David locate Jonathan's son Mephibosheth. He became Mephibosheth's servant on the land restored by the king (2 Sam. 9:2–11).

ZIDON. See *Sidon.*

ZIF (ZIV). The second month of the Hebrew year, corresponding to *Iyyar* in the later Jewish calendar (1 Kings 6:1, 37). *Ziv:* NIV, NRSV.

ZIGGURAT. A tall Mesopotamian temple tower, built like a pyramid with staircases outside and a shrine for pagan worship on top. The tower of Babel was a ziggurat (Gen. 11:1–9). See also *Babel, Tower of.*

ZIKLAG. A city on the border of Judah assigned to David by King Achish of Gath as a place of refuge from King Saul (1 Sam. 27:5–6).

ZILPAH. Leah's maid who became a concubine of Jacob and bore two of his twelve sons, Gad and Asher (Gen. 30:9–13). See also *Jacob; Leah.*

ZIMRI. A chariot commander under King Elah of Israel who killed the king and assumed the throne (about 885 B.C.), only to commit suicide seven days later to escape the wrath of Omri's army (1 Kings 16:8–18).

ZIN. A desert wilderness near the Dead Sea through which the Hebrews passed. Moses' sister, Miriam, died and was buried here (Num. 20:1).

ZION/SION. One of the hills on which Jerusalem was built and the site of an ancient Jebusite fortress before the city was captured by David. In Solomon's time this section of Jerusalem was extended to include the temple area. Sometimes all of Jerusalem is referred to as "Zion" (1 Kings 8:1). *Sion:* Rev. 14:1. See also *Jerusalem.*

ZIPPORAH. A daughter of Jethro the Midianite priest, the wife of Moses, and mother of Moses' sons Gershom and Eliezer (Exod. 2:21–22).

ZIV. See *Zif.*

ZOAR/BELA. An ancient city of Canaan destroyed, along with Sodom and Gomorrah, because of its sin (Gen. 19:20–25). This city was also known as *Bela* (Gen. 14:2). See also *Cities of the Plain.*

ZOPHAR. One of Job's friends or "comforters" (Job 2:11).

ZOROBABEL. See *Zerubbabel.*

ZUZIM (ZUZITES). A race of giants in the land east of the Jordan River (Gen. 14:5). This is probably the same tribe as the *Zamzummins. Zuzites:* NIV. See also *Zamzummins.*

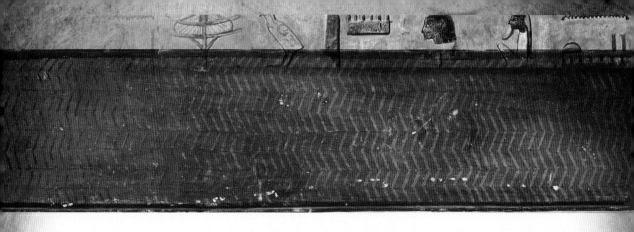

Bible Handbook

with

Notes on Bible
Customs and Curiosities

A Note on the Notes

This section of *The Barbour Bible Reference Companion* consists of two distinct elements: (1) a Bible Handbook and (2) Notes on Bible Customs and Curiosities.

The Bible Handbook gives an overview of the entire Bible by following a book-by-book format. Each of the sixty-six books of the Bible is introduced and summarized in thumbnail fashion to help you gain a "big picture" understanding of God's Word.

Notes on Bible Customs and Curiosities are scattered as sidebars throughout the Bible Handbook text. These notes are designed to help you dig deeper into the customs and practices of Bible times that are puzzling and strange to many modern readers.

For example, the Israelites were commanded by the Lord not to move "thy neighbour's landmark" (Deut. 19:14). These landmarks were actually boundary stones that marked property lines, much as fences do today. The Israelites were not to move these markers over by a few feet to increase their own land holdings. This was a form of stealing from their neighbors. When we understand these facts, we realize why the Lord would issue such a command.

This Customs and Curiosities note, entitled "Boundary Stones," appears as a sidebar close to the summary of the passage that it clarifies—Deuteronomy 19:14–21—in the Handbook (see p. 395). This is how you will find these illuminating notes scattered throughout the Handbook text.

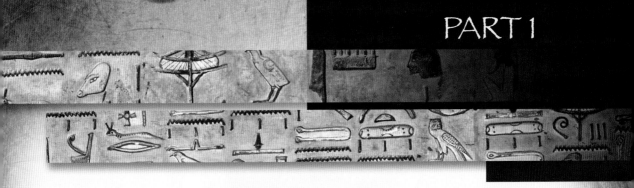

THE OLD TESTAMENT

The Bible has two grand divisions—the Old Testament and the New Testament. The Old Testament is the larger of these two divisions, containing more than twice as much material as the New Testament. The thirty-nine individual Old Testament books were written under the inspiration of the Lord across a period of many centuries by several different authors. The Old Testament also contains many different types of literature: law, history, poetry, prophecy, and wisdom writings.

The word *testament* means "covenant." The Old Testament tells how God called a people, the nation of Israel, to live in covenant with Him.

The five major divisions of the Old Testament are (1) books of the Law—Genesis through Deuteronomy; (2) historical books—Joshua through Esther; (3) books of poetry and wisdom—Job through the Song of Solomon; (4) books of the major prophets—Isaiah through Daniel; and (5) books of the minor prophets—Hosea through Malachi. These divisions of the Old Testament are discussed in the following chapters.

CHAPTER 1
BOOKS OF THE LAW

The first five books of the Old Testament are known as the "Books of the Law." This title is appropriate because the laws and commands of God are the central theme of this section of the Old Testament. God revealed to Moses His expectation of the nation of Israel. Moses recorded these commands as laws in the books of Exodus, Leviticus, Numbers, and Deuteronomy. Genesis contains no specific laws, but it does describe the covenant relationship that God established with His people, the Israelites. This covenant relationship demanded loyalty and obedience from God's chosen people.

These first five books of the Old Testament are also known as the Pentateuch, a Greek term meaning "five-volumed." These five books together take us from the creation of the physical world through the formation of the nation of Israel under the leadership of Moses.

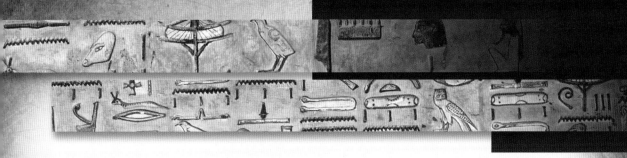

OVERVIEW: Creation of humans, animals, and the physical universe and establishment of the covenant relationship between God and His people.

Introduction to Genesis

The word *Genesis* means "creation, origin, source, or the coming into being of something." Thus, Genesis is the Bible's book of beginnings. As the first book in God's Word, it recounts (1) the beginning of the physical world, (2) the beginning of God's plan of salvation for the human race, and (3) the beginning of the nation of Israel.

Creation. Genesis gives us a picture of a sovereign, all-powerful God who brought the physical world into being through the power of His spoken word. The words "and God said" appear as an introduction before each of the six days of creation.

The six days of creation also show that God brought the world into existence in an orderly fashion in accordance with His divine plan. The crowning achievement of His creation was man, whom He created in His image.

As the all-powerful Creator, God had the right to set limits and boundaries beyond which man could not go. But man chose to disobey God in the Garden of Eden. This brought about the need for the second major theme of Genesis.

Sin and Salvation. Before his sin, man enjoyed unlimited fellowship with God. But this relationship was marred and broken when Adam and Eve ate the forbidden fruit. They were banished from the garden and from God's presence.

2:1–25. God creates Adam from the dust of the earth. A snake coils around Adam, a visual foreshadowing of humanity's fall from grace at the enticement of a serpent.

But in an act of mercy, God killed an animal and made clothes from its hide to cover their nakedness (3:21). This symbolized His commitment to provide salvation for man, to restore the broken relationship between Himself and humankind.

Throughout the Old Testament, the restoration of this relationship depended on man's keeping the law and obeying God's commandments. But in the New Testament, He sent Christ—His own Son—to do away with law keeping as the basis of salvation. Through His death on the cross, Christ paid the penalty for humankind's sin.

Nation of Israel. From the beginning, God was concerned for the salvation of all humanity. But He chose to channel this concern to the world through a people who would belong to Him in a special sense—the nation of Israel.

God began to build this nation when He called Abraham to leave his pagan surroundings and to go to a new land "that I will shew thee" (12:1)—the land of Canaan. God made a covenant with Abraham in which He promised, "I will make of thee a great nation, and I will bless thee, and make thy name great; and thou shalt be a blessing" (12:2).

The book of Genesis shows how this covenant was renewed across several generations with the descendants of Abraham: Isaac, Jacob, and Jacob's twelve sons, particularly Joseph. It was several hundred years before the tribal descendants of Jacob claimed the land of Canaan as their own, but the promise was planted and nourished in the book of Genesis.

Summary of Genesis

1:1–31. God creates the world in six days (Heb. 1:10).

2:1–25. God creates Adam and Eve, the first man and woman.

3:1–24. Adam and Eve disobey God by eating the forbidden fruit and are cast out of the Garden of Eden.

4:1–2. Two sons, Cain and Abel, are born to Adam and Eve.

4:3–15. Cain murders his brother Abel. God punishes Cain by driving him out of his homeland but protects him by placing a mark on him.

4:16–24. Cain's descendants are listed.

[4:16–24] **THE TERM** *FATHER. Jubal...was the father of all such as handle the harp and organ* (Gen. 4:21).

In the ancient Middle East, the originator of any custom was frequently spoken of as the "father" of that custom. Thus, Jubal was called "the father of all such as handle the harp and organ" because he invented those instruments.

In Isaiah 9:6 the Messiah is called "the everlasting Father," meaning He is the giver of eternal life. In 2 Corinthians 1:3, God is called "the Father of mercies," and in Ephesians 1:17, "the Father of glory."

4:25–5:32. Adam's descendants are listed.

6:1–8. Wickedness spreads throughout the earth, and God determines to destroy the world. But Noah is looked upon with favor by the Lord because of his righteousness (see Exod. 33:12).

6:9–22. The Lord tells Noah to build a huge ark, or boat, in which he and his family will be safe from the catastrophe that He plans to send on the earth. Noah does exactly as God commands.

7:1–16. Noah and his family enter the ark, along with pairs of different animals. Rain pounds the earth for forty days and forty nights.

7:17–24. The earth is struck with a great flood, which lasts for 150 days. But Noah and his family and the animals are safe in the ark (2 Pet. 2:5).

6:9–22. Noah and his sons build the ark, a floating warehouse longer than a football field and half as wide.

8:1–22. The floodwaters recede, and Noah and his family leave the ark. Noah builds an altar and offers sacrifices to the Lord.

9:1–19. God makes a covenant with Noah and causes a rainbow to appear in the sky as a token of His promise.

9:20–27. Noah falls into a drunken stupor and pronounces a curse on Canaan, a descendant of Noah's son Ham.

9:28–29. Noah dies after living for 950 years.

10:1–32. Noah's descendants are listed.

11:1–9. God confuses human languages at the Tower of Babel because of man's pride and arrogance.

11:10–32. Descendants of Noah's son Shem—the ancestors of Abram/Abraham—are listed.

12:1–20. God calls Abram/Abraham to leave his homeland and settle in a new country, Canaan, where He will give him many descendants and make them into a great nation (Heb. 11:8).

13:1–18. Abram/Abraham and his nephew Lot go their separate ways after a disagreement over grazing lands for their livestock.

14:1–24. Abram/Abraham rescues Lot and pays tithes to Melchizedek, a priest and king.

15:1–21. God makes a covenant with Abram/Abraham and renews His promise to give him a land and many descendants (Gen. 12:1–2).

16:1–16. Abram/Abraham fathers a son, Ishmael, by the Egyptian servant of his wife, Sarah.

17:1–27. God renews His covenant with Abram, renames him Abraham, and promises that Sarah will bear a son. All males in Abraham's household are circumcised as a sign and seal of the divine covenant.

18:1–33. Abraham pleads with God to spare the wicked cities of Sodom and Gomorrah.

19:1–29. Lot escapes when Sodom and Gomorrah are destroyed by the Lord (2 Pet. 2:6).

[11:1–9] BABYLONION BRICKS. *They [builders of the tower of Babel] said…, Let us make brick, and burn them throughly. And they had brick for stone, and slime [tar, NIV] had they for mortar (Gen. 11:3).*

Many of the bricks used in Babylonia, where the Tower of Babel was built, were sun-dried, but others were cured by burning, just like those used in this tower. Fire-cured bricks were stronger, so they were sometimes laid next to a wall of sun-dried brick to give it strength and stability.

[15:1–21] A STARTLING SIGN. *And it came to pass, that, when the sun went down, and it was dark, behold a smoking furnace, and a burning lamp that passed between those pieces* (Gen. 15:17).

A few hours before this event, the Lord had made a covenant with Abraham. He promised to bless Abraham with many descendants and make them into a nation devoted to Him.

To seal the covenant, Abraham cut several animals into two pieces and walked between the two sections. This was a solemn declaration of his intention to keep the covenant. Just as the two separate pieces belonged to one animal, so the two people making this agreement were of one mind about the terms of the covenant.

When darkness fell, God caused a burning lamp, signifying His divine presence, to pass between the two sections of the slaughtered animals. This was a bold and startling sign to Abraham that God would keep His promise.

19:30–38. Lot fathers two sons, who become the ancestors of the Moabites and the Ammonites.

20:1–18. Abraham tries to pass off Sarah as his sister in the territory of Abimelech, a Philistine king.

21:1–21. A son, Isaac, is born to Abraham and Sarah; Hagar and Ishmael are banished to the wilderness.

21:22–34. Abraham and Abimelech reach an agreement about a well at Beersheba.

22:1–14. God tests Abraham's faithfulness, but Abraham is prevented from sacrificing his son Isaac.

22:15–19. God renews His promise to make Abraham's descendants into a great nation (Gen. 12:1–2).

22:20–24. Abraham's relatives are listed.

23:1–20. Abraham's wife, Sarah, dies; Abraham buys a cave at Machpelah as a burial site.

[23:1–20] MONEY BY WEIGHT. *Abraham weighed to Ephron the silver…four hundred shekels of silver, current money with the merchant* (Gen. 23:16).

Abraham paid Ephron the Hittite four hundred shekels of silver for a plot of ground as a burial site for his family.

Coins and paper money did not exist in Bible times, so Abraham paid Ephron in silver bullion. This bullion weighed four hundred shekels—the agreed-upon price. Money had to be weighed rather than counted by bills and coins, as we do today.

The exact weight of a shekel is not known. The word *shekel* (from the Hebrew *shukal*, "to weigh") indicated this method of figuring money by weight rather than by number or coins or bills.

The weighing of money is also referred to in Jeremiah 32:9–10 and Zechariah 11:12.

[19:1–29] SITTING AT THE CITY GATE. *And there came two angels to Sodom at even; and Lot sat in the gate of Sodom* (Gen. 19:1).

Cities of the ancient world were surrounded by massive defensive walls made of stone. People gathered at the gateway through the city wall to conduct business, pass the time with friends, catch up on the latest news, or just to watch the passing crowds.

Lot happened to be sitting in the gateway of the city of Sodom, just as evening was falling, when these two angels entered the city.

The Bible refers several times to the city gate as a gathering place (Gen. 23:10; 1 Sam. 4:18; Ps. 127:5; Prov. 1:21).

24:1–67. Abraham's son Isaac is married to Rebekah.

25:1–11. Abraham dies and is buried.

25:12–18. Descendants of Ishmael, Abraham's son by Hagar, are listed.

25:19–26. Twin sons, Jacob and Esau, are born to Isaac and Rebekah.

[26:1–35] CONTROVERSY OVER WELLS. *All the wells which his [Isaac's] father's servants had digged in the days of Abraham his father, the Philistines had stopped them, and filled them with earth (Gen. 26:15).*

Springs and streams are scarce in the hot, dry climate of the ancient Middle East. Shepherds had to dig wells to provide water for their flocks and herds.

The wells that Abraham had dug for his animals years before in the unoccupied territory of southern Canaan had given him and his heirs the right to graze their flocks in this region. But after Abraham died, the Philistines had filled these wells with dirt, denying Isaac the right as Abraham's heir to continue using these pasturelands.

Isaac and the Philistines eventually reached a compromise that allowed him access to the grazing lands around a productive well that he named Sheba ("productive well"). The ancient city of Beersheba ("well of Sheba") took its name from this well (Gen. 26:17–23).

25:27–34. Esau, the older brother, trades his birthright to Jacob for a bowl of stew (1 Chron. 5:1–2).

26:1–35. Isaac digs several wells in the territory of the Philistines; God promises Isaac that the covenant He has made with His father, Abraham, will be continued through him and his descendants.

27:1–46. Jacob tricks his father into blessing him rather than his older son, Esau.

28:1–22. Jacob travels to Haran in search of a wife; God assures him in a dream that His promise to Abraham will be realized through Jacob's descendants (Gen. 15:1–21).

29:1–30. In Haran, Jacob works seven years for the hand of Leah and seven years for Rachel, daughters of Laban.

29:31–30:24. Jacob fathers many sons by several different wives.

30:25–43. Jacob prospers while raising livestock in the household of his father-in-law, Laban.

31:1–32:23. With Laban's blessing, Jacob returns to Canaan with his family, along with presents for his estranged brother, Esau (Gen. 27:41).

32:24–32. Jacob wrestles with an angel; he is renamed Israel and assured of God's blessings.

33:1–20. Jacob is greeted and forgiven by his brother, Esau (Gen. 27:41).

34:1–31. Jacob and his sons avenge the sexual assault of Jacob's daughter Dinah by Shechem.

35:1–15. God renews His covenant with Jacob at Bethel and assures him that his descendants will receive the land promised to Abraham (Gen. 15:1–21).

35:16–20. Rachel dies while giving birth to Jacob's twelfth son, Benjamin.

35:21–26. The twelve sons of Jacob by four different wives are listed.

35:27–29. Jacob's father, Isaac, dies.

[29:1–30] MARRIAGE AMONG RELATIVES. *It is better that I [Laban] give her [Rachel] to thee [Jacob], than that I should give her to another man (Gen. 29:19).*

Laban was the brother of Jacob's mother, Rebekah (Gen. 29:10). This relationship would have made Laban's daughter Rachel—the woman whom Jacob wanted to marry—Jacob's first cousin.

Sometimes the term *brother* was used loosely in Bible times to refer to any male relative such as a nephew or an uncle. So Rachel may have been a distant relative of Jacob.

Marriage among distant relatives from the same tribe or bloodline was common in Old Testament times. Abraham sought a wife for his son Isaac from among his kinsmen in Mesopotamia (Gen. 24:2–4).

[33:1–20] GIFTS FOR AN ENEMY. *Jacob said, Nay, I pray thee [Esau], if now I have found grace in thy sight, then receive my present at my hand (Gen. 33:10).*

In Bible times people presented gifts to others for many reasons: to secure a bride through a dowry, or bride price; to seal a friendship, or to show love. In this instance Jacob presented gifts to his estranged brother, Esau, because he had wronged him in the past. He hoped his gifts would appease Esau's anger.

The giving of gifts is mentioned many times in the Bible (Judg. 3:18; 1 Sam. 10:27; Ps. 72:10; Prov. 18:16; Matt. 2:11).

36:1–43. Descendants of Esau, Jacob's brother, are listed.

37:1–36. Jacob's son Joseph is sold into slavery by his brothers and taken into Egypt.

38:1–30. Judah, a son of Jacob, fathers twin sons by his daughter-in-law Tamar.

39:1–23. Joseph is imprisoned in Egypt on a false charge.

40:1–23. Imprisoned with the pharaoh's chief butler and baker, Joseph explains the meaning of their dreams and develops a reputation as an interpreter of dreams.

41:1–43. Joseph is appointed a high official in the Egyptian pharaoh's administration after foretelling a severe famine by interpreting the pharaoh's dream.

41:44–52. Joseph fathers two sons, Manasseh and Ephraim, through his Egyptian wife, Asenath.

41:53–57. The famine that Joseph has foretold strikes Egypt.

42:1–6. Because of the famine, ten of Joseph's brothers come to Egypt to buy grain. Benjamin, Joseph's full brother and youngest son of Jacob (Gen. 35:16–20), does not make the trip. The ten brothers appear before Joseph, now one of Egypt's high officials.

42:7–17. Joseph recognizes his brothers, but they do not recognize him. He has them imprisoned for several days after accusing them of being spies.

42:18–38. Joseph holds his brother Simeon as a hostage. He sends the others back to Jacob with the charge to bring their youngest brother, Benjamin, to him in Egypt. This will prove that they are not spies and result in the release of their brother Simeon.

43:1–34. Joseph's brothers, including Benjamin, return to Egypt to buy grain. Joseph

41:1–43. Sun-bleached bones of a dead animal warn of the harsh Middle Eastern heat. It was during a seven-year drought that the Israelites moved to Egypt for relief. What they found was slavery.

[37:1–36] JOSEPH'S UNUSUAL COAT. *Israel [Jacob] loved Joseph more than all his children, because he was the son of his old age: and he made him a coat of many colours* (Gen. 37:3).

Joseph's "coat of many colours" has been translated in various ways by modern translations ("richly ornamented robe," NIV; "long robe with sleeves," RSV). The precise meaning of the Hebrew word behind this phrase is uncertain.

This "coat" may have been the long outer robe that was worn by both men and women in Bible times. It was different than the robes worn by Joseph's brothers, thus setting him apart as his father's favorite son.

releases Simeon and invites all of them to a feast at his house. Again, they do not recognize Joseph.

44:1–13. Joseph sends all his brothers back to Jacob with their sacks of grain. But he plants one of his silver cups in Benjamin's sack. Then he sends his soldiers after them to search for stolen merchandise. All the brothers are arrested and returned to Joseph after the soldiers find the silver cup.

[43:1–34] SUPER-FRESH MEAT. *Joseph…said to the ruler of his house, Bring these men [Joseph's brothers] home, and slay, and make ready; for these men shall dine with me at noon* (Gen. 43:16).

The meat that Joseph served his brothers came from a freshly slaughtered animal. In Old Testament times, there was no way to preserve meat. An animal was slaughtered immediately before the meal at which meat was to be served (Gen. 18:7–8; 1 Sam. 28:24).

44:14–34. Judah pleads with Joseph on behalf of his brother Benjamin. He offers to become a slave of Joseph if he will let Benjamin return to his father.

45:1–28. Overcome with emotion, Joseph finally reveals himself to his brothers. He sends them back to their homeland to tell Jacob that his son Joseph is alive and doing well in Egypt.

46:1–47:31. With the help of Joseph, Jacob and his sons and their families move to Egypt to escape the famine (Acts 7:14–15).

48:1–22. Jacob blesses the two sons of Joseph—Ephraim and Manasseh.

49:1–33. After predicting the future for each of his sons, Jacob dies in Egypt.

[49:1–33] A HAND OF VICTORY. *Judah, thou art he whom thy brethren shall praise: thy hand shall be in the neck of thine enemies* (Gen. 49:8).

Before he died Jacob called his twelve sons together and predicted their future. He foretold the importance of Judah and his descendants—the tribe of Judah—by using the image of Judah's hand on the neck of his enemies. To place one's hand on the neck of another was a symbol of superiority and victory in battle (2 Sam. 22:41; Lam. 5:5).

Judah did become the central tribe in Israel's history. King David was born into this tribe, and it was through David's lineage that the Messiah emerged (Matt. 1:1–17; Judah is spelled *Judas* in the KJV; see Matt. 1:2).

50:1–13. Joseph and his brothers return Jacob's body to Canaan for burial (Acts 7:16).

50:14–21. Joseph assures his brothers of his unconditional forgiveness.

50:22–26. Joseph dies in Egypt.

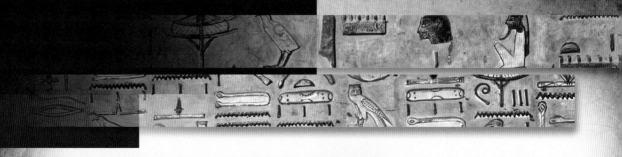

EXODUS

3:1–22. At the base of Mount Sinai, a monastery marks the spot where an ancient tradition says God talked to Moses from a burning bush, sending him to free the Israelites. Tradition also says that this mountain is where God later gave Moses the Ten Commandments.

OVERVIEW: The Lord delivers His people from enslavement by the Egyptians.

Introduction to Exodus

The book of Exodus begins where the book of Genesis ends—with the descendants of Jacob who settled in Egypt to escape a severe famine in their territory (Gen. 46:1–47:31). This move to Egypt was possible because of the favored status of Joseph—one of Jacob's sons—who rose to a high position in the Egyptian government. For many years the Hebrew people multiplied and prospered with the blessings of the Egyptian pharaoh.

But then the political climate changed: "There arose up a new king over Egypt, which knew not Joseph" (Exod. 1:8). Jacob's descendants were reduced to the status of slaves and forced to work on various Egyptian building projects.

But God did not forget His people. He called Moses to lead His people out of Egypt. With his brother, Aaron, as his helper, Moses confronted the pharaoh of Egypt and insisted that he let the Hebrew people go. God worked many miracles on behalf of His people to win their freedom.

The book of Exodus also tells how God took care of His people while they wandered in the wilderness area around Mount Sinai. Through Moses, God also delivered the Ten Commandments and other laws to guide their lives as His special people.

At God's command through Moses, the people also built a tabernacle in the wilderness. This sacred tent, a central place for sacrifice and worship, traveled with the Hebrew people when they moved from place to place in the wilderness. It symbolized God's presence in the midst of His people.

The dominant personality of the book of Exodus is Moses. God often spoke directly to him and gave him a message to pass on to the people. Moses was responsible for leading the people in their quest for the Promised Land—the territory of the Canaanites that God had promised to Abraham and his descendants many centuries before (Gen. 12:1–5).

Moses continues his leadership of the Hebrew people up through the book of Deuteronomy. Many scholars believe he wrote these four Old Testament books, as well as the book of Genesis. His important role in God's plan for His people makes him one of the central figures of biblical history.

Summary of Exodus

1:1–7. The descendants of Jacob/Israel multiply at an astonishing rate in Egypt.

1:8–14. The pharaoh of Egypt enslaves the Israelites.

1:15–22. The pharaoh orders all male Israelite infants killed to control their population growth.

2:1–4. A baby boy named Moses is hidden in a basket on the Nile River to escape the pharaoh's decree (Heb. 11:23).

1:8–14. Bricks molded of mud and straw bake in the Egyptian sun. As a race of slave laborers, the Israelites did much the same work in Egypt some three thousand years ago, building cities for the pharaoh.

[2:1–4] MOSES' PAPER ARK. *She [Moses' mother] took for him an ark of bulrushes [papyrus basket, NIV], and daubed it with slime [tar, NIV] and with pitch and put the child therein (Exod. 2:3).*

Moses was hidden by his mother to protect him from the death order issued by Pharaoh against all male children of the Israelites (Exod. 1:15–16).

The "ark" in which he was hidden was probably a basket woven from leaves of the papyrus plant. This reedlike plant grew in abundance along the banks of the Nile River. The Egyptians used papyrus for making paper, as well as shoes and clothes.

2:5–10. The pharaoh's daughter discovers Moses and adopts him as her son.

2:11–15. After he reaches adulthood, Moses kills an Egyptian official who is abusing an Israelite slave. Moses flees to Midian to escape the pharaoh's wrath.

2:16–25. Moses becomes a shepherd in the household of a Midianite named Reuel (also known as Jethro) and marries his daughter Zipporah.

3:1–22. God appears to Moses in a burning bush and calls him to deliver His people, the Israelites, from enslavement by the Egyptians (Acts 7:30).

4:1–13. God assures Moses through miraculous signs that He will stand with him before the pharaoh.

4:14–31. God deals with Moses' excuses by appointing his brother, Aaron, to serve as Moses' spokesman. Moses returns to Egypt to confront the pharaoh.

[5:1–23] **EGYPTIAN BRICKS WITH STRAW.** *Ye [Egyptian slave supervisors] shall no more give the people [Israelite slaves] straw to make brick, as heretofore: let them go and gather straw for themselves* (Exod. 5:7).

The bricks used in the building projects of ancient Egypt were molded from mud, then placed in the sun to dry. Over time sun-dried bricks would crumble from exposure to the wind and rain.

To give these bricks greater strength and stability, chopped straw from wheat or barley stalks was sometimes added. Pharaoh added to the hard labor of the Israelite slaves by forcing them to forage for straw to be used in the manufacturing process.

Apparently the Israelites were under a quota system. They were expected to produce so many bricks per day—no excuses accepted (Exod. 5:13–14).

5:1–23. The pharaoh responds to Moses' demands by forcing the Israelite slaves to make bricks without straw.

6:1–13. God assures Moses and the Israelites that the covenant He had made with Abraham over 400 years before (Gen. 15:1–21) is still in force; God will bring the Israelites out of slavery into their own land.

6:14–15. The descendants of Jacob's sons Reuben and Simeon are listed (Num. 26:5–14).

6:16–30. The descendants of Jacob's son Levi (Gen. 29:34), who include Moses and Aaron, are listed.

7:1–13. Aaron's rod turns into a snake, but this miraculous sign fails to impress the Egyptian pharaoh and his court magicians.

7:14–10:29. God sends nine plagues upon the Egyptians to convince the pharaoh to release the Israelite slaves, but he remains stubborn and unmoved.

11:1–10. God announces through Moses the tenth and final plague—the death of all the Egyptian firstborn.

12:1–30. All the Egyptian firstborn are killed. The Israelites are spared because they obey God's command to mark the doorposts of their houses with the blood of sacrificial lambs (Ezek. 9:6).

12:31–51. Crushed by the widespread death of his people, the pharaoh releases the Israelites, who travel into the desert territory east of Egypt.

13:1–20. God directs that the firstborn of both animals and people among the Israelites are to be dedicated to Him.

13:21–22. God leads the Israelites with a cloud by day and a fire by night.

14:1–31. God swallows the pursuing Egyptian army in the Red Sea after the Israelites pass over on dry land (Heb. 11:29).

15:1–22. Through the "Song of Moses," the Israelites celebrate God's miraculous deliverance (Deut. 31:30–32:47).

15:23–27. At Marah, God miraculously turns bad water into good water for the Israelites.

[12:1–30] **ALL THE GODS OF EGYPT.** *Against all the gods of Egypt I will execute judgment: I am the LORD* (Exod. 12:12).

To be superior to "all the gods of Egypt" was quite a claim, since the Egyptians are known to have worshiped more than thirty pagan deities. These included the bull god Apis, who ensured fertility; Hathor, the goddess of love; and Thoth, the god of wisdom and books.

But God proved, through the death of all the Egyptian firstborn (Exod. 12:29), that He held the power of life and death over the Egyptians and their religious system. Months later, after Moses had led the Israelites out of slavery in Egypt, God declared to him, "I am the LORD thy God, which have brought thee…out of the house of bondage. Thou shalt have no other gods before me" (Exod. 20:2–3).

[16:1–36] EGYPT AND THE GOOD OLD DAYS. *Would to God we [Israelites] had died...in the land of Egypt, when we sat by the flesh pots [pots of meat, NIV], and when we did eat bread to the full* (Exod. 16:3).

Soon after leaving Egypt, the Israelites began to whine for the "good old days." They began to think their existence as slaves was preferable to the harsh life of the wilderness.

Flesh pots were three-legged metal containers in which the Egyptians cooked meat over an open fire. But it is likely that meat was a delicacy enjoyed only by the elite of Egyptian society. The Israelites exaggerated when they claimed they had eaten meat regularly from these cooking pots.

That's the problem with nostalgia: Looking back, things always seem better than they actually were.

16:1–36. God miraculously provides manna, a bread substitute, to feed the complaining Israelites in the wilderness.

17:1–7. The Lord produces water from a rock to sustain His people.

17:8–16. God gives the Israelites a victory over the Amalekites.

18:1–27. Taking the advice of his father-in-law, Jethro, Moses delegates some of his burdensome duties on behalf of the people to other Israelite leaders (Deut. 1:1–18).

19:1–25. God reveals Himself in smoke and fire to Moses and the Israelites at Mount Sinai; He promises to make them "a kingdom of priests, and an holy nation" (v. 6).

20:1–17. God reveals the Ten Commandments to Moses (Deut. 5:1–22).

20:18–26. God cautions the Israelites against worshiping false gods.

21:1–23:33. Various laws governing human relationships, property rights, slavery, and treatment of the poor are listed (Deut. 22:1–25:4).

24:1–18. Moses enters the cloud of God's glory and communes with Him for forty days on Mount Sinai.

25:1–27:21. God tells Moses to rally the Israelites to build the tabernacle as a place of worship; He gives Moses a detailed blueprint of the tent and its furnishings.

28:1–29:46. The Lord instructs Moses to appoint and consecrate his brother, Aaron, and Aaron's descendants as the official priesthood for the Israelites (Num. 3:32).

30:1–10. God gives Moses instructions about the altar in the tabernacle on which incense is to be burned as an act of worship.

30:11–16. The Lord directs Moses to collect a half-shekel tax from every male Israelite to support the tabernacle and its services (Matt. 17:24–27).

30:17–38. God specifies that a special anointing oil is to be used by the priests to consecrate the tabernacle's altar and its vessels and furnishings.

31:1–11. God reveals to Moses that He has selected two craftsmen, Bezaleel and Aholiab, to perform the skilled stonecutting, metalwork, and woodworking required for the tabernacle.

[19:1–25] CLEAN BEFORE THE LORD. *The LORD said unto Moses, Go unto the people, and sanctify them to day and to morrow, and let them wash their clothes* (Exod. 19:10).

About three months after leaving Egypt, Moses led the Israelites to the base of Mount Sinai in the wilderness (Exod. 19:1–2). Here they would have a dramatic encounter with the living Lord, who had led them out of slavery.

In order to prepare the people for this special revelation of Himself, God commanded that the people be both spiritually ("sanctify them") and physically ("wash their clothes") clean. Such cleanliness was essential for those who would stand in the presence of the holy God.

32:1–35. A gold-plated calf recovered from what is now Lebanon. Calves were among many idols worshiped in the time of Moses, when Israelites molded a gold calf and worshiped it during the Exodus.

33:1–34:35. Moses pleads for God to forgive the sinful Israelites; the Lord renews His pledge to guide and protect them.

35:1–35. At the urging of Moses, the Israelites contribute the materials needed for the building of the tabernacle.

36:1–38:31. The tabernacle is built according to the specifications issued by the Lord (Exod. 25:1–27:21).

39:1–31. The distinctive styles of dress required for Aaron as the high priest and the other priests of Israel are described.

39:32–43. The features and furnishings of the completed tabernacle are reviewed as they are presented to Moses.

40:1–38. Moses and the Israelites dedicate the tabernacle as they assemble its furnishings; God shows His pleasure by filling the sacred tent with His glory (Neh. 9:12).

[32:1–35] A GOLD-PLATED CALF. *All the people brake off the golden earrings which were in their ears…and he [Aaron] received them at their hand, and fashioned it with a graving tool, after he had made it a molten calf* (Exod. 32:3–4).

The word *molten* implies that the calf idol that Aaron created in the wilderness was cast from gold. But thousands of melted-down earrings would have been required to produce such an idol.

It is more likely that the calf image was first carved from wood. Then it was plated with a thin layer of gold to produce the final idol worshiped by the people. This method of producing pagan images was described by the prophet Isaiah (Isa. 40:19–20).

[40:1–38] INCENSE ALTAR. *Thou [Moses] shalt set the altar of gold for the incense before the ark of the testimony* (Exod. 40:5).

Incense was a sweet-smelling substance burned in the tabernacle as an offering to God. It was offered by a priest on this special altar made of gold. The pleasant aroma symbolized the prayers of the Israelites before the Lord.

Only incense made by using a formula specified by God (Exod. 30:34–38) was to be burned on the incense altar. Two sons of Aaron were destroyed for burning incense by "strange fire" (Lev. 10:1–3). They may have been offering incense not produced by this divine formula.

31:12–18. God reminds Moses that the Israelites are to observe the seventh day of the week as the Sabbath; they are not to do any work on this day (Exod. 20:8–11).

32:1–35. Aaron and the Israelites sin against God during Moses' absence on Mount Sinai by fashioning a golden calf as an object of worship.

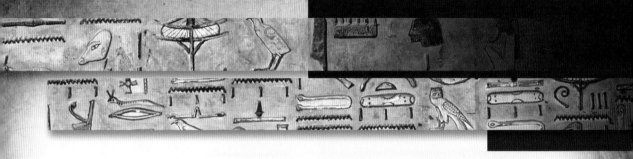

OVERVIEW: God institutes the ceremonial law to govern the life of His people.

Introduction to Leviticus

In the book of Exodus, God gave His people the moral law—instructions for moral and ethical behavior. The book of Leviticus contains His ceremonial law—how to observe the rituals that were considered important acts of worship for the people of ancient Israel.

Leviticus describes the formal establishment of the priesthood, at God's command, through Aaron, his sons, and their successors. The priests were to preside at the altar in the tabernacle—later the temple—when people presented their offerings to God. Various types of offerings are described in Leviticus—burnt offerings, grain offerings, peace offerings, sin offerings, and guilt or trespass offerings.

But perhaps the most significant offering in terms of its symbolism for modern believers was the blood offering—presenting the blood of a sacrificial animal to God. New Testament believers taught that Jesus was the ultimate blood sacrifice. He gave His life by shedding His own blood to make atonement for our sins.

1:1–7:38. Noah and his sons offer animal sacrifices. Though godly people had been offering sacrifices since the time of Abel, it wasn't until Moses' day that God gave detailed instructions on how to worship him through sacrificial rituals. Leviticus preserves those instructions, along with other laws.

In addition to sacrifice, another important theme of Leviticus is holiness. The concept of holiness involves difference or separation. God's people were to be different than, and separate from, the pagan peoples of the surrounding nations. Thus, they were not to eat certain foods that were considered unclean. They were to avoid contact with anything that was considered unclean. Even a house could be made unclean if touched by a person with an infectious skin disease. God was concerned that His people should remain clean and undefiled in the midst of a depraved and corrupt world.

[1:1–7:38] NO YEAST OR HONEY. *Ye [Israelites] shall burn no leaven, nor any honey, in any offering of the LORD made by fire (Lev. 2:11).*

Leaven, or yeast, was mixed with dough to cause bread to rise. Any bread brought to the Lord as an offering was to be baked without leaven. Neither was honey, used as a sweetening agent, to be used in any food items presented to the Lord.

The reason for these prohibitions is that both yeast and honey were associated with offerings presented to pagan gods.

12:1–8. God prescribes the ritual by which a woman may be declared clean after giving birth to a child.

13:1–14:57. God issues regulations for dealing with leprosy—or an infectious skin disease. Even a house or tent that has been exposed to this disease is to be cleansed in accordance with a prescribed ritual.

15:1–33. Procedures are established by which a person who experiences a bodily discharge may be rendered clean again.

16:1–34. God specifies how Aaron, the high priest, is to make atonement for himself and

Summary of Leviticus

1:1–7:38. God prescribes the procedures to be followed by the Israelites and the priests in making various offerings to the Lord (Num. 15:1–31).

8:1–36. Moses consecrates Aaron and his sons as priests in holy service to the Lord and His people.

9:1–24. Aaron and his sons present a sin offering, a burnt offering, and a peace offering on behalf of the people.

10:1–3. Nadab and Abihu, sons of Aaron, are destroyed by fire for using an unauthorized procedure in burning incense at the altar (Num. 16:35).

10:4–20. Moses reminds Aaron and his remaining sons of the responsibility of priests to show reverence and respect toward God and His requirements.

11:1–47. God lists the clean animals that may be eaten by the Israelites, but those considered unclean are not to be eaten or even touched (Deut. 14:1–21).

23:1–44. An Orthodox Jew walks down a street in Old Jerusalem, a part of the city still protected by stone walls. Many Jews, including those in the conservative Orthodox branch, still carefully observe the laws God gave Moses.

[13:1–14:57] **REPLASTERING WITH MORTAR.** *They [Israelites] shall take other stones, and put them in the place of those stones; and he shall take other morter [clay, NIV], and shall plaister the house* (Lev. 14:42).

These instructions were intended for the Israelites after they had settled in permanent homes in the land of Canaan. If a plague of mildew or fungus broke out in a house, the owner was to replace the infected stones and replaster the entire dwelling with "morter," or clay.

The mortar of Bible times was made by mixing clay with finely chopped straw. Sometimes sand, ashes, or lime was added to give this substance more body and to make it last longer.

If this renovation of the house with new stones and new mortar did not eliminate the plague, the dwelling was to be torn down. The debris was to be carried outside the city to "an unclean place" (Lev. 14:45)—perhaps a garbage dump designated for this purpose.

all the people on one specific day each year known as the Day of Atonement (Num. 29:7).

17:1–9. God prohibits the Israelites from presenting offerings at any place other than the tabernacle.

17:10–16. God cautions the people not to eat the meat of a slaughtered animal unless the blood has first been drained from the flesh.

18:1–30. God warns the people not to participate in the depraved sexual practices of the surrounding pagan nations.

19:1–21:15. God calls His people to a high moral standard. They are to honor the Lord with their behavior and to treat other people with fairness and justice.

21:16–22:16. God establishes strict physical and moral requirements for Aaron and his descendants who serve as priests among the people.

22:17–33. Animals offered to God as sacrifices are to be healthy and free of physical defects (Mal. 1:8–9).

23:1–44. God cites the special days and religious holidays or festivals that are to be observed by the Israelites: the weekly Sabbath (v. 3), the yearly Passover and Feast of Unleavened Bread (vv. 5–8), the offering of firstfruits (vv. 9–14), the Feast of Pentecost (vv. 15–21), the Feast of Trumpets (vv.

23–25), the Day of Atonement (vv. 27–30), and the Feast of Tabernacles (vv. 33–36) (Deut. 16:1–17).

[23:1–44] **THE DRINK OFFERING.** *They [sacrificial animals] shall be for a burnt offering unto the LORD, with their meat offering, and their drink offerings* (Lev. 23:18).

A drink offering to God was usually given along with other offerings, such as the burnt offering, the sin offering, and the trespass offering. The drink offering was a quantity of wine. It was presented by the worshiper to a priest, who poured it out at the base of the altar of burnt offering.

24:1–4. God directs that the oil-burning lamps before the altar in the tabernacle are to be kept burning continuously.

24:5–9. Twelve loaves of fresh-baked bread, representing the twelve tribes of Israel, are to be placed on a table near the altar in the tabernacle each week to replace the old loaves; the old loaves are then to be eaten by the priests (2 Chron. 2:4).

24:10–23. The people stone a man for blasphemy, or disrespect toward God, at Moses' command.

25:1–7. God directs that the farmland of the Israelites, once they possess it, is to be given a Sabbath of its own; after six consecutive

[26:1–46] **PAGAN HIGH PLACES.** *I [God] will destroy your [pagan worshipers'] high places* (Lev. 26:30).

A "high place" was generally a mountaintop or a hilltop on which pagan worshipers bowed down before images of their false gods. They believed these elevated sites would put them closer to their gods and increase their chance of being heard.

God made it clear that He would judge the Israelites if they adopted the worship practices of their pagan neighbors.

years of production, it is to remain idle during the seventh year.

25:8–55. God decrees that every fiftieth year (following seven "Sabbaths" of seven years each) is to be a liberating year known as the "jubile." During this year, Israelites who were forced to sell themselves into slavery to pay off a debt are to be set free. Tracts of land that were sold because Israelite families fell upon hard times are to be returned to the original owners.

26:1–46. God declares that His covenant with Israel is conditional. If they obey and worship Him after they possess the land, He will bless and prosper His people. But if they rebel against Him and worship other gods, He will withdraw His presence and visit them with disaster.

27:1–34. If a person has made a voluntary vow to give himself or his property to God, he is allowed to pay a redemption price to the priest in order to "buy back" himself or the property. God establishes guidelines for determining the redemption price to be paid under various circumstances.

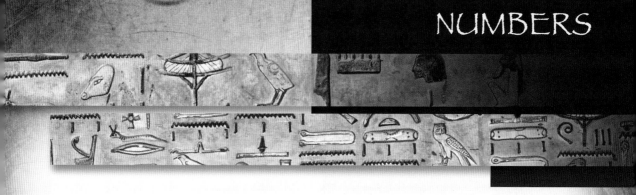

OVERVIEW: The Israelites wander for many years in the wilderness of Sinai.

Introduction to Numbers

The book of Numbers is so named because of the two "numberings" (censuses) of the Israelites that were commanded by the Lord in chapters 1 and 26. The book traces the aimless wanderings of the Israelites in the wilderness during a period of more than forty years as God was preparing them to enter the Promised Land.

Why this long delay? Why didn't the Israelites proceed immediately to conquer the land of Canaan? The first census counted more than 600,000 able-bodied men above twenty years of age who were ready for military duty (1:18–46). Surely this would have been a potent fighting force against any enemy.

The problem was the people's lack of faith in God and His promises. In preparation for military action, Moses chose twelve scouts—one from each of the tribes—and sent them on a fact-finding mission into Canaan. They returned with good news and bad news. The land was rich and fertile and able to support the Israelites. But it would not be easy to conquer the warlike Canaanites, who seemed invincible behind their walled cities.

Only two of the twelve spies—Joshua and Caleb—recommended that the Israelites proceed immediately to take the land. They believed God's promise that He would lead them to victory. But the majority of the people, paralyzed by fear, refused to move by faith against the enemy. So the Lord sentenced them to forty years of wandering in the wilderness before they could enter the land of promise (14:1–38).

During these years the people also showed their rebellious, faithless spirit in other ways. They complained about Moses and his leadership and about their food and water supply. They grumbled against God and accused Him of abandoning them in the wilderness, even though He provided miraculously for their needs time after time. Some of the Israelite men even worshiped the false gods of the Moabites (25:1–18).

Finally, even Moses lost his patience with the people. At God's command, he struck a rock to provide a miraculous flow of water for the people—but he did so in a fit of anger. God punished Moses by declaring that he would not be allowed to enter the Promised Land (20:1–13).

The book of Numbers shows that the Lord does not hesitate to punish His people for their sin. But He is also a God who keeps His promises. He would ultimately bless His people by bringing them into a land of their own.

Summary of Numbers

1:1–3. God directs Moses to take a census of all able-bodied Israelite men, twenty years old and above, who are able to go to war (2 Sam. 24:2).

[2:1–2] STANDARDS AND BANNERS. *Every man of the children of Israel shall pitch by his own standard, with the ensign [banners, NIV] of their father's house* (Num. 2:2).

God directed the twelve tribes of Israel to camp in three-tribe units on the northern, southern, eastern, and western sides of the tabernacle (Num. 2:3–31). Each of these three-tribe units had a distinct sign on a pole, known as a standard, around which they gathered to make sure they followed the camping arrangement specified by the Lord.

These standards may have been similar to those used by the Egyptians as military symbols for different units of their army. Many of these Egyptian standards featured images of their pagan gods. The Bible does not say what symbols were used on the Israelite standards.

The phrase "ensign of their father's house" probably refers to a small flag or banner that was carried by each tribe or even the separate clans that made up each tribe.

1:4–17. Representatives of each tribe are appointed to assist with the census.

1:18–46. Male descendants of twelve Israelite tribes—Reuben, Simeon, Gad, Judah, Issachar, Zebulun, Ephraim, Manasseh, Benjamin, Dan, Asher, and Naphtali —are counted in the census. The total number of males twenty years old and above is 603,550.

1:47–54. The Levites, descendants of the tribe of Levi, are not included in the census because they do not have a military role in the life of Israel. Their function is to take care of the tabernacle and preside over its religious ceremonies (Num. 3:5–10).

2:1–2. God specifies that the tribes of Israel are to camp at a distance all around the tabernacle.

2:3–9. The tribes of Judah, Issachar, and Zebulun will camp east of the tabernacle.

2:10–17. The tribes of Reuben, Simeon, and Gad will camp south of the tabernacle.

2:18–24. The tribes of Ephraim, Manasseh, and Benjamin will camp west of the tabernacle.

2:25–31. The tribes of Dan, Asher, and Naphtali will camp north of the tabernacle.

2:32–34. The tribal census and the camping order of the tribes around the tabernacle are summarized.

3:1–4. Descendants of Aaron are listed (Exod. 28:41).

3:5–13. The Levites, descendants of the tribe of Levi, are set apart and consecrated for their religious duties on behalf of the other tribes of Israel.

3:14–20. God directs Moses to take a census of the tribe of Levi. All male Levites one month old and above are to be counted. Separate counts are to be made for the three divisions of Levi—Gershonites, Kohathites, and Merarites—that sprang from Levi's three sons.

3:21–26. The Gershonites, 7,500 in number, are assigned specific tabernacle duties from their position west of the tabernacle.

3:27–32. The Kohathites, 8,600 in number, are assigned specific tabernacle duties from their position south of the tabernacle.

3:33–37. The Merarites, 6,200 in number, are assigned specific tabernacle duties from their position north of the tabernacle.

3:38–39. Moses, Aaron, and Aaron's sons are to be positioned to the east and directly in front of the tabernacle for its general oversight and protection.

3:40–51. God directs Moses to take a census of all the firstborn males among the Israelites who are one month old and above. God accepts the Levites as a substitute for these firstborn, who are considered the Lord's own. But the census reveals that the number of firstborn Israelite males exceeds the number of Levites by 273. The redemption price paid by the parents of these 273 sons is to be given to Aaron and his sons, the priests.

4:1–49. God gives a more detailed description of

[3:5–13] DUTIES OF THE LEVITES. *Bring the tribe of Levi near, and present them before Aaron the priest, that they may minister unto him* (Num. 3:6).

Since Levi was a son of Jacob (Gen. 29:34), Levi's descendants evolved into one of the twelve tribes of Israel. It was designated as the tribe that would minister on behalf of all the other Israelites.

Aaron was a member of the tribe of Levi. Aaron's direct descendants became the priests who officiated at the altar (Num. 3:2–3), offering sacrifices for the people. All the other members of the tribe of Levi were designated as Levites. Their duty was to assist the priests in these sacrificial functions.

The three separate divisions of the Levites were named for Levi's three sons: Gershon, Kohath, and Merari (Num. 3:17). During the days when the Israelites wandered in the wilderness, these three units had specific responsibilities for setting up and taking down the tabernacle, transporting it, and caring for its sacred objects and furnishings (Num. 3:23–37).

The Levites assisted the priests by slaughtering sacrificial animals, baking the showbread for the Most Holy Place in the tabernacle, and serving as doorkeepers and musicians in the tabernacle and temple.

the tabernacle duties required of the three branches of the Levites—Kohathites, Gershonites, and Merarites.

5:1–4. People with an infectious skin disease and other unclean people are to be banished outside the camp (Lev. 13:45–46).

5:5–10. God makes provision for the atonement of sin through the trespass offering.

5:11–31. A woman accused of adultery is to be proven innocent or guilty through an ordeal known as the water of jealousy, or bitter water.

6:1–21. God establishes regulations and procedures to be observed by any person who vows to be especially consecrated to God as a Nazarite (Judg. 13:5).

6:22–27. God issues a benediction with which the Israelites are to be blessed by the priests.

7:1–89. At the dedication of the altar of the tabernacle, representatives of the twelve tribes of Israel present offerings to support the Levites and their priestly service.

8:1–4. The seven-branched candlestick, or menorah, is placed to illuminate the altar of the tabernacle (Exod. 40:25).

8:5–26. The Levites are purified and dedicated to serve at the tabernacle under the direction of Aaron and the priests (Num. 1:47–54).

9:1–14. The Passover is to be observed annually by the Israelites to memorialize their deliverance by the Lord from enslavement by the Egyptians.

9:15–23. God assures Israel of His presence with a cloud over the tabernacle during the daytime and a fire over the tabernacle at night (Exod. 13:21–22). The cloud signals when the people are to camp and when they are to break camp and move on.

10:1–10. Moses makes two silver trumpets to alert the people when to assemble for battle and when it is time to move the camp.

10:11–36. The twelve tribes of Israel move out in orderly fashion when the cloud tells them to leave the wilderness of Sinai and camp in the wilderness of Paran.

11:1–35. The Israelites complain about Moses' leadership and the food they are forced to eat. God sustains them with manna and quail meat (Exod. 16:12–15).

12:1–16. Miriam and Aaron complain about the leadership of their brother, Moses. God punishes Miriam by striking her with leprosy, then heals her at Moses' request.

13:1–16. Moses selects one representative

[11:1–35] **FULL TO THE NOSE.** *Ye [Israelites] shall not eat one day...nor twenty days; but even a whole month, until it come out at your nostrils* (Num. 11:19–20).

The Israelites complained to Moses that they had no meat to eat—only the bread substitute known as manna, which had been miraculously provided by the Lord (Exod. 16:15, 31). This complaining angered God, and He promised to send them so much meat to eat that it would make them sick. Being filled "to the nose" is a common expression for overeating still heard in many cultures today.

The Lord kept His promise by sending "quails from the sea" (Num. 11:31) to provide meat for the people, accompanied by a plague to punish the complainers.

from each of the twelve tribes of Israel to go into Canaan on a spying and exploration mission.

13:17–33. The scouts explore Canaan and return with good news and bad news: The land is fertile and productive, but it is inhabited and well defended by several strong tribal groups.

14:1–4. The Israelites moan over this bad news, rebel against God, and declare that they should have stayed in Egypt (Deut. 17:16).

14:5–10. Joshua and Caleb, two of the twelve spies, encourage the people to remain faithful to God. They declare that the Israelites can take the land if they follow His guidance.

14:11–19. God declares that He will wipe out the Israelites because of their lack of faith. Moses pleads for God to show them mercy.

14:20–35. God responds by sentencing the Israelites to forty years of wandering in the wilderness before they will be allowed to enter the Promised Land. During this time the older generation of rebellious Israelites will die in the wilderness.

14:36–45. Some of the Israelites attack the residents of Canaan, but they are turned back in defeat.

15:1–31. God establishes regulations and procedures for the various offerings to be presented by the Israelites after they enter the Promised Land (Lev. 1:1–7:38).

15:32–36. A man is stoned to death for desecrating the Sabbath by doing work on this sacred day (Exod. 20:8–11).

15:37–41. God directs the Israelites to put tassels on their clothes to remind them to obey His commandments (Deut. 22:12).

16:1–40. God destroys Korah and a group of his followers, including Dathan and Abiram, because they rebelled against the leadership of Moses and Aaron.

16:41–50. God threatens to destroy all the Israelites by sending a plague upon them because they sympathized with Korah. But Aaron turns back the plague by burning incense among the people to atone for their sin.

17:1–13. God causes Aaron's rod to bloom and produce almonds to demonstrate Aaron's spiritual authority over all the tribes of Israel (Heb. 9:4).

[17:1–13] **AARON'S PRIESTHOOD CONFIRMED.** *On the morrow Moses went into the tabernacle of witness; and behold, the rod of Aaron for the house of Levi was budded* (Num. 17:8).

Some Israelites questioned Aaron's right to serve as priest and for his descendants to continue his priestly work among the nation (Num. 16:1–3). So Moses conducted a test to determine who should serve in this leadership position.

Moses placed twelve staffs or sticks, representing the twelve tribes of Israel, in the tabernacle overnight. The next morning Aaron's staff had budded and produced almonds. This was undeniable proof that Aaron of the tribe of Levi and his descendants had been selected by the Lord for this ministry.

[20:23–29] ELEAZAR SUCCEEDS AARON. *Moses stripped Aaron of his garments, and put them upon Eleazar his son; and Aaron died there in the top of the mount* (Num. 20:28).

At Aaron's death the special clothes that he wore as high priest of Israel (Exod. 40:13) were transferred to his son Eleazar. This showed that Eleazar was the legitimate successor to his father in this role.

Eleazar served as high priest for the rest of Moses' life and also for a time after Joshua succeeded Moses as leader of the Israelites. Eleazar assisted in the division of the land of Canaan among the twelve tribes (Josh. 14:1).

18:1–19. Through the offerings of the people, God provides for the material needs of Aaron and his sons and the priests who will come after them.

18:20–32. Through the tithes of the people, God provides for the material needs of the Levites (Deut. 18:1–8).

19:1–22. Moses and Aaron are instructed to use the ashes of a red heifer to make a solution called the water of separation. People who have been made ritually unclean are to be cleansed when sprinkled by a priest with this special solution.

20:1–13. In anger, Moses strikes a rock at Meribah to produce water for the Israelites. God punishes him and Aaron for disobeying His directions, refusing to let them enter the Promised Land (Num. 27:12–14).

20:14–22. The king of Edom refuses to allow the Israelites to pass through his territory (Deut. 2:8).

20:23–29. Aaron dies on Mount Hor.

21:1–9. God punishes the Israelites for their rebellion by sending poisonous snakes to bite them. Then God delivers the people by means of a brass serpent on a pole erected by Moses (John 12:32).

21:10–20. Several camping sites of the Israelites are listed.

21:21–32. The Israelites defeat Sihon, king of the Amorites.

21:33–35. The Israelites defeat Og, king of Bashan.

22:1–21. Balak, king of Moab, sends messengers to hire Balaam the soothsayer to curse the Israelites.

22:22–35. On his way to meet Balak, Balaam encounters the angel of the Lord, who gets Balaam's attention through his stubborn donkey. The angel tells Balaam to meet Balak but to speak only the words that God will direct him to speak.

22:36–41. Balaam meets Balak and prepares to curse the Israelites.

23:1–24:25. On three separate attempts, Balaam fails to curse the Israelites, blessing them instead.

25:1–18. Some of the Israelites commit idolatry because of the temptations of Moabite women.

26:1–56. All able-bodied Israelite males twenty years old and above are counted again at the end of the forty years of wandering in the wilderness. This census is to be used as the basis for assigning land to the tribes after they conquer the territory of the Canaanites (Num. 1:1–3).

26:57–65. A separate count is made of the tribe of Levi, or the Levites.

27:1–11. The five daughters of Zelophehad are allowed to inherit his property, since he died with no male heirs; principles of inheritance are established.

27:12–14. God reminds Moses that he will not be allowed to enter the Promised Land with the other Israelites (Num. 20:1–13).

27:15–23. Joshua is selected by the Lord as Moses' successor (Deut. 34:9).

28:1–29:40. Regulations and procedures for various types of offerings are prescribed by the Lord.

32:1–42. Livestock graze the green pastures of Jordan, east of Israel. When Israelites of the Exodus arrived in Jordan, the tribes of Reuben and Gad and half the tribe of Manasseh decided to settle there because of the fertile pastures.

30:1–16. Vows made to the Lord are a serious matter, but people may be excused from their vows in special circumstances (Gen. 28:20–22).

31:1–54. Israel defeats the Midianites, and all the people share in the spoils of war.

32:1–42. Moses allows the tribes of Reuben and Gad and half the tribe of Manasseh to settle on the fertile pasturelands east of the Jordan River across from Canaan (Josh. 12:1–6). In return, these three tribes promise to help the other tribes in their campaign against the Canaanites.

33:1–49. The places where the Israelites camped in the wilderness for forty years after they left Egypt are listed.

33:50–56. God repeats His promise to give the land of Canaan to the Israelites. He urges them to drive out all the pagan Canaanites, lest they become a stumbling block to His people.

34:1–15. God establishes the boundaries of the territory in which the Israelite tribes will settle.

34:16–29. Tribal representatives are selected to serve with Joshua and Eleazar the priest to divide the land among the various tribes.

35:1–34. The tribe of Levi will not receive a specific land inheritance like the other tribes because of their religious function. Rather, Levites are to live among all the other tribes in forty-eight designated cities. Six of these cities are to be known as cities of refuge— places to which a person can go after killing another person to keep from being killed by an avenging relative. In these refuge cities, guilt or innocence of the person accused of murder will be determined through due process (Deut. 19:1–13).

36:1–13. Once the land is divided among the tribes, each tribal allotment is to remain intact. The daughters of Zelophehad (Num. 27:1–11) are to marry within their tribe to ensure that the land they inherited from their father does not pass to another tribe.

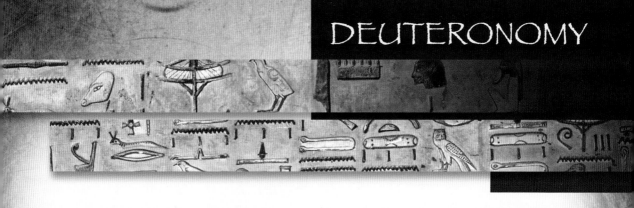

DEUTERONOMY

OVERVIEW: Moses restates God's law for the Israelites before they enter the Promised Land.

Introduction to Deuteronomy

This book takes its name from the Greek word *Deuteronomion*, which means "second law." It consists of a series of speeches to the people from Moses. This great leader realized that he was approaching the time of his death, so he repeated many of the laws that God had revealed to His people at Mount Sinai more than forty years before. Moses wanted to make sure that the people remained loyal to the Lord and His commands as they prepared to enter the land of promise.

Moses especially warned the Israelites of the perils of idolatry. He knew they would be settling a land where the Canaanites worshiped many false gods, especially the fertility god Baal. He called upon the people to remain faithful to the one true God, who demanded their exclusive loyalty and total commitment: "Thou shalt love the LORD thy God with all thine heart, and with all thy soul, and with all thy might" (6:5; see Matt. 22:37).

The final chapter of Deuteronomy departs from its speech format to report on the death of Moses. He died on Mount Nebo after God allowed him to look across the Jordan River to view the Promised Land. His greatness as a leader of God's people is acknowledged in these words: "There arose not a prophet since in Israel like unto Moses, whom the Lord knew face to face" (34:10).

Deuteronomy's significance was recognized by the New Testament writers, who quoted from this book more than eighty times. At the beginning of His public ministry, Jesus cited several passages from Deuteronomy to turn aside the temptations of Satan (Matt. 4:4, quoting Deut. 8:3; Matt. 4:7, quoting Deut. 6:16; Matt. 4:10, quoting Deut. 6:13).

Summary of Deuteronomy

1:1–18. Moses recalls the experiences of the Israelites after they first came out of Egypt, including his appointment of officials to help him lead the people (Exod. 18:1–27).

1:19–46. Moses reminds the people of their rebellion and refusal to enter Canaan after spies were sent to investigate the land (Num. 13:17–33).

2:1–23. Moses recounts the marching orders given the Israelites by the Lord after their

---

[2:1–23] CAMPING GROUNDS. *The Avims which dwelt in Hazerim* (Deut. 2:23).

This verse is part of an extended review by Moses of the different tribes and ethnic groups encountered by the Israelites during their years of wandering in the wilderness.

The Hebrew word *Hazerim* is not the name of a specific place. In this context it should be translated as "camping grounds." The Avims were probably a nomadic people who moved from place to place with their grazing livestock.

forty years of wandering in the wilderness came to an end.

2:24–37. Moses recalls the victory of the Israelites over King Sihon of Heshbon (Num. 21:21–32).

3:1–22. Moses reminisces about the victory of the Israelites over King Og of Bashan and the settlement of the tribes of Reuben, Gad, and one-half of the tribe of Manasseh in Og's territory (Num. 21:33–35; 32:1–42).

3:23–29. Moses reminds the people of God's decision that he—Moses—would not be allowed to enter the Promised Land (Num. 20:1–13).

4:1–49. Moses challenges the Israelites to remain faithful to the covenant that God established with His people and to follow the teachings of the law that God handed down through Moses at Mount Sinai.

5:1–22. Moses restates the Ten Commandments, which God delivered to him at Mount Sinai (Exod. 20:1–17).

5:23–33. Moses reminds the people that the awesome, unapproachable God of the universe has chosen to reveal Himself to the nation of Israel.

6:1–25. Moses reminds the people of their responsibility to teach the laws and commandments of God to their children.

7:1–26. God promises to give the Israelites victory over the pagan peoples who inhabit Canaan and bring prosperity to His people when they are settled in the land.

[6:1–25] WRITING ON THE DOOR. *Thou [Israelites] shalt write them upon the posts [doorframes, NIV] of thy house, and on thy gates* (Deut. 6:9).

The Israelites were commanded by the Lord to write passages from His law on the doorframes of their houses after they settled permanently in the land of Canaan. Every time they entered or left their dwellings, they would be reminded of God's Word and their promise to obey His commands.

[11:1–32] IRRIGATION OF EGYPTIAN CROPS. *The land, whither thou [Israelites] goest in to possess it, is not as the land of Egypt, from whence ye came out, where thou sowedst thy seed, and wateredst it with thy foot* (Deut. 11:10).

This verse contrasts the land of Egypt, where the Israelites had been enslaved, with the land of Canaan, which God had promised to His people. Egyptian crops grew in the fertile flood plain along the Nile River. But Canaan was a land of hills and valleys. Here the crops of the Israelites would flourish from the "waters of the rain of heaven" (Deut. 11:11).

Watering crops "with thy foot" in Egypt probably refers to the small waterwheels that were turned by foot to pump water from the Nile River into irrigation canals. This artificial watering system was essential for crop production in Egypt's hot, dry climate.

8:1–20. The Lord warns the people of the perils of prosperity. They must not forget Him after they have become comfortable and affluent in the land He is giving them.

9:1–29. Moses warns the people not to become overconfident after they settle in Canaan. They are capable of ignoring and rejecting God and turning to false gods, just as they did at Mount Sinai and during their years of wandering in the wilderness.

10:1–5. Moses recalls how God wrote the Ten Commandments a second time on two tablets of stone, which Moses placed in the ark of the covenant (Exod. 34:1).

10:6–22. Moses reminds the Israelites of the awesome God whom they serve and the signs and wonders He has performed on behalf of His people.

11:1–32. God places two choices before the Israelites. If they remain faithful to Him, He will bless them. But if they turn to false gods, He will curse them (Josh. 24:1–15).

12:1–32. After the Israelites settle in the land,

[19:14–21] BOUNDARY STONES. *Thou [Israelites] shalt not remove thy neighbour's landmark [boundary stone, NIV], which they of old time have set in thine inheritance* (Deut. 19:14).

After the Israelites settled in Canaan and received their land allotments, they marked their property by placing small stones around the edges of their plots.

Unlike permanent fences, these stones could be moved easily. A dishonest person on an adjoining plot could move these markers and encroach on his neighbor's property. The Lord specifically prohibited this practice because it was a form of stealing (Exod. 20:15).

Moving boundary stones is also forbidden in Proverbs 22:28; 23:10.

God promises to give the nation a central place of worship, where they will present various offerings and sacrifices.

13:1–18. A false prophet or any other Israelite who causes people to worship pagan gods is to be put to death.

14:1–21. The Lord reminds the Israelites of the animals that may be eaten and those that are prohibited as food (Lev. 11).

14:22–29. A tithe, or one-tenth of one's crops or livestock, is to be presented as an offering to the Lord (Num. 18:20–32).

15:1–18. God establishes guidelines for fair and just treatment of the poor.

15:19–23. Firstborn animals from herds of livestock are to be presented as offerings to God.

16:1–17. God reminds the people of the regulations for observing three major festivals or religious holidays: Passover and Feast of Unleavened Bread (vv. 1–8), Feast of Weeks (vv. 9–12), and Feast of Tabernacles (vv. 13–15) (Lev. 23).

16:18–20. Judges are expected to be fair and just in their decisions.

16:21–22. The making of idols or images of false gods is prohibited (Exod. 20:3–4).

17:1–7. A person found guilty of idolatry—on the testimony of at least two witnesses—is to be put to death.

17:8–13. A sentence handed down by judges and priests through due process is considered a binding judgment. Refusal to abide by the verdict will result in the death penalty.

17:14–20. If a king is ever appointed to rule over Israel, he must not trust in military might or marry many wives. He is expected to rule with justice and to fear God and obey His commandments.

18:1–8. Since the Levites will not receive an inheritance of land in Canaan, they are to be supported by tithes and offerings from the people (Num. 18:20–32).

18:9–14. All forms of "black magic"—witchcraft, fortune-telling, and communing with the dead—are prohibited for God's people.

18:15–22. God promises to send prophets—particularly a special Prophet after the pattern of Moses—to declare His will to His people. True prophets are those whose predictions come true.

19:1–13. God repeats His instructions that

[16:21–22] NO TREES AROUND ALTARS. *Thou [Israelites] shalt not plant thee a grove of any trees near unto the altar of the LORD thy God* (Deut. 16:21).

Shrines devoted to worship of false gods were surrounded by thick groves of trees, perhaps to hide the immoral acts that occurred around these altars. The Lord prohibited the planting of trees around His altars to avoid any hint of idol worship among His people.

cities of refuge are to be established throughout the land after the Israelites have settled in Canaan. These cities are to serve as safe harbors for innocent people who are accused of murder (Num. 35).

19:14–21. Bearing false witness is a serious matter. Any person who wrongly accuses another of a crime is to bear the penalty the innocent person would have received if convicted (Exod. 20:16).

20:1–8. Any man who has just built a house, planted a new vineyard, or married a wife may be excused from military duty (Luke 14:16–20).

20:9–20. Israelite armies are expected to observe specific "rules of war" when engaging their enemies in battle.

21:1–9. The elders of a city are given a handwashing ritual by which they can proclaim their innocence when the body of a person is found near their city.

21:10–14. An Israelite man may marry a woman who is captured from their enemies in times of war, but specific guidelines are prescribed by the Lord for such a marriage.

21:15–17. If a man is married to more than one wife, he cannot play favorites by transferring inheritance rights from his firstborn son to a son born later to a favorite wife. The father's true firstborn son should receive a double portion when his property is divided at his death.

21:18–21. A son who is stubborn and rebellious toward his parents may be stoned to death if they bring charges against him before the elders of the city.

21:22–23. To avoid defiling the land, a person executed by hanging must be taken down and buried before nightfall.

22:1–25:4. The Lord issues regulations for the conduct of Israelites in various situations: the provision of a protective railing on the

---

[22:1–25:4] GUARDRAILS ON THE ROOF. *When thou [Israelites] buildest a new house, then thou shalt make a battlement [parapet, NIV] for thy roof, that thou bring not blood upon thine house, if any man fall from thence* (Deut. 22:8).

This verse is something of an ancient "building code." A house was to be built with a guardrail around the edge of the roof to protect people from accidental falls.

In Bible times the roofs of houses were flat. A stairway on the outside of the house allowed the residents to use the roof much like a patio or deck is used today. Particularly at night, the roof was a good place to relax and catch a cooling breeze. Sometimes a family would even sleep on the roof to escape the oppressive heat (2 Sam. 11:2).

Perhaps the most famous "rooftop incident" in the Bible was King David's chance encounter with Bathsheba. The king was tempted to commit adultery with her when he looked down from the roof of his palace and saw her taking a bath (2 Sam. 11:2).

---

roof of a house, the treatment of borrowed property, physical disabilities that prevent a person from entering the sanctuary, the restoration of an unclean person to cleanliness, the lending of money, and fair and just treatment of the poor (Exod. 21–23).

25:5–10. If an Israelite man should die without children, his brother is encouraged to marry his widow to produce children so the dead man's family name will continue. A brother who dodges this responsibility will be ridiculed and humiliated by the elders of the city.

25:11–19. Israelites are charged to be honest in all their business dealings, not using one pair of scales for buying and another for selling (Lev. 19:35–36).

26:1–19. The people are to present the firstfruits of their harvest as a special offering to God (Exod. 23:19).

27:1–10. Moses instructs the people to build

an altar of stones after they cross the Jordan River to enter the Promised Land (Josh. 4:1–9). On this altar, sacrifices of thanksgiving are to be offered to God.

27:11–26. The Levites are instructed to issue a series of warnings to the Israelites after they enter the Promised Land. These warnings will remind the people to obey God's commands.

32:48–52. Standing on Mount Nebo, where Moses surveyed the Promised Land before dying, the late Pope John Paul II looks toward Israel.

28:1–30:20. If God's people obey Him, they will live long and prosper in their new land. But if they turn away from Him and worship other gods, they will be afflicted with pain and disaster.

31:1–13. Moses calls upon the Israelites to be brave and courageous, since the time for them to do battle with the Canaanites is drawing near. He charges them to be diligent in obedience to God's laws.

31:14–30. Moses recalls how the Lord directed him to write a song for the Israelites to remind them to remain loyal to the powerful God who brought them out of slavery and sustained them in the wilderness.

32:1–47. Moses reminisces about how he delivered a song he wrote to the people of Israel. He praised the Lord for His faithfulness and graciousness to His chosen people, in spite of their rebellion and worship of false gods (Exod. 15:1–22).

32:48–52. God commands Moses to climb to the top of Mount Nebo, the highest peak in the Abarim Mountains, and look across the Jordan River to view the land He has promised to Israel.

33:1–29. Moses blesses the people of Israel tribe by tribe, just as Jacob had spoken hundreds of years before to each of his sons (Gen. 49). The descendants of Jacob's sons have grown into the twelve tribes of Israel.

34:1–12. Moses dies in Moab after viewing the Promised Land and is succeeded by Joshua.

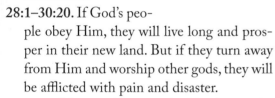

[33:1–29] CRUSHING OLIVES. *Of Asher he [Moses] said…let him be acceptable to his brethren, and let him dip his foot in oil* (Deut. 33:24).

Before his death, Moses predicted the future for each of the tribes of Israel after they settled in the land of Canaan (Deut. 32:1–25). The tribe of Asher would be known for its olive oil production. "Dip his foot in oil" refers to the ancient practice of crushing olives by foot to expel the oil.

Olive oil was used as fuel in oil-burning lamps (Exod. 27:20) and as an anointing agent (Lev. 2:1).

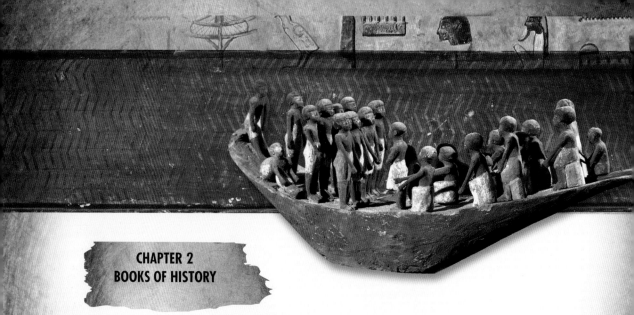

CHAPTER 2
BOOKS OF HISTORY

The second major section of the Old Testament contains twelve books classified as historical writings: Joshua, Judges, Ruth, 1 and 2 Samuel, 1 and 2 Kings, 1 and 2 Chronicles, Ezra, Nehemiah, and Esther.

These books trace the history of the nation of Israel across a period of more than 800 years—from the conquest of Canaan under Joshua about 1400 B.C. to their return from capivity by the Babylonians and Persians about 530 B.C. In between these two pivotal events were such happenings as rule by charismatic judges after the death of Joshua, the establishment of a central kingship form of government, the glory days of the Israelites under King David and his son Solomon, the division of the nation into northern and southern factions, the destruction of the Northern Kingdom by Assyria, and the fall of the Southern Kingdom to Babylonia.

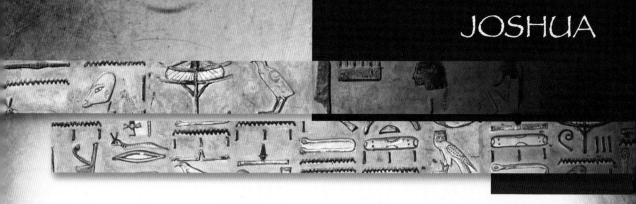

OVERVIEW: Moses' successor, Joshua, leads the people to capture and settle the Promised Land.

Introduction to Joshua

The book of Joshua takes its name from its major personality, Joshua, who became the new leader of the Israelites upon the death of Moses (Deut. 34:9).

God charged Moses with the responsibility of leading the Israelites out of slavery and bringing them to the border of Canaan, the land that He had promised to Abraham and his descendants many centuries before (Gen. 12:1–5). Joshua would pick up where Moses left off, leading the people to conquer the territory and getting them settled in their new land.

Joshua was ideally suited for the task that he inherited. He had been trained and groomed for leadership by Moses himself (Num. 13:8; 14:6–9; 27:18–23). A stalwart follower of the Lord, Joshua realized that Israel could not overcome the Canaanites without God's help. He kept the people focused on following the Lord's leadership.

Joshua was also a good organizer and military commander. In a period of about twenty-five years, he led the people to victory over the Canaanites. Then he supervised the process of dividing the land among the twelve tribes and getting them settled in their new territory.

One of Joshua's legacies is his recognition that the worship of God is not to be mixed with the worship of false gods. The Lord will not tolerate such practices. He demands exclusive loyalty from His people. Joshua set the example for all Israel near the end of his life when he gathered the people and declared: "Choose you this day whom ye will serve; whether the gods which your fathers served that were on the other side of the flood, or the gods of the Amorites, in whose land ye dwell: but as for me and my house, we will serve the LORD" (24:15).

Joshua himself probably wrote most of the book that bears his name (see a description of his writing efforts in 24:26). The one exception to this is the final section that reports his death (24:29–33). These verses were probably added, under God's inspiration, by an unknown editor after Joshua died. They serve as a tribute to Joshua and his contribution to the nation of Israel.

Summary of Joshua

1:1–10. God orders Joshua, Moses' successor, to lead the people across the Jordan River and into the land of Canaan.

1:11–18. Joshua spreads the word for the people to get ready to move out. He reminds the tribes of Reuben and Gad and one-half of the tribe of Manasseh of their promise to help the other tribes when the time comes for them to conquer the Canaanites (Num. 32).

2:1–24. Joshua sends two spies to investigate

[2:1–24] **A HOUSE ON A WALL.** *She [Rahab] let them [Israelite spies] down by a cord through the window: for her house was upon the town wall, and she dwelt upon the wall* (Josh. 2:15).

Some walled cities of Bible times had an inner wall and an outer wall for maximum protection. To strengthen these walls, the space between them was filled with dirt and rubble at selected points. Houses were sometimes built right into the city wall by placing them on top of these piles of rubble.

Since Rahab "dwelt upon the wall" of Jericho, she must have lived in one of these "wall houses." She helped the Israelite spies escape over the city wall by lowering them with ropes from her window.

Another similar escape was made in New Testament times by the apostle Paul. Believers in the city of Damascus delivered him from his enemies, who were watching the city gates "day and night to kill him" (Acts 9:24). They placed Paul in a basket and lowered him over the city wall.

the Canaanite city of Jericho. Rahab the prostitute hides them in her house and helps them escape over the city wall. They report to Joshua that conditions are right for conquest of the land.

3:1–17. Led by the priests carrying the ark of the covenant, the people cross the flooded Jordan River on dry land as God miraculously stops the flow of water (Exod. 14).

4:1–24. Twelve stones are taken from the Jordan River and set up as a memorial in Gilgal to remind the Israelites of God's presence and protection (Deut. 27:1–10).

5:1. The Canaanites are frightened when they learn about the miraculous crossing of the Jordan River by the Israelites.

5:2–12. Joshua performs the rite of circumcision on all male Israelites who have not been circumcised (Gen. 17:9–14).

5:13–15. At Jericho, the mysterious captain of the host of the Lord meets and encourages Joshua.

6:1–27. God miraculously delivers the city of Jericho to Joshua and his warriors by causing the walls to collapse. Rahab the prostitute and her family are spared because she helped the two Israelite spies when they investigated the city (Josh. 2).

7:1–26. The Israelites fail to conquer the city of Ai because one of their own warriors, Achan, disobeyed the Lord by keeping some of the spoils of war for himself. The people stone Achan to death when they discover his sin.

8:1–29. After dealing with Achan, Joshua and his warriors capture the city of Ai by pretending to retreat, then ambushing Ai's pursuing army.

8:30–35. Joshua builds an altar on which sacrifices are offered. He reads to all the Israelites the book of the law that God delivered to Moses.

9:1–27. The Gibeonites trick Joshua into making a peace treaty with them. Joshua makes good on his promise not to harm them, but they become menial servants of the Israelites (2 Sam. 21:1–9).

10:1–11:23. Joshua and his army defeat the united forces of several Canaanite kings and occupy their territories.

[7:1–26] **MONUMENT TO A CRIME.** *They [Joshua and the Israelites] raised over him [Achan] a great heap of stones* (Josh. 7:26).

Achan was executed because he kept some of the spoils of war taken in battles against the Canaanites for himself (Josh. 7:20–21). This was a violation of the Lord's command (Josh. 6:19).

To commemorate Achan's crime, Joshua and other Israelite leaders piled stones on his grave. This makeshift monument served as a constant reminder to others of the seriousness of disobeying God.

Throughout Israel's history, stones were also heaped up to serve as memorials of positive events in the life of the nation (Exod. 24:4; Josh. 4:3–9; 24:26; 1 Sam. 7:12).

6:1–27. Walls tumble at the border town of Jericho as the Israelites begin their conquest of the Promised Land.

12:1–6. The territories east of the Jordan River—those captured by the Israelites under Moses' leadership—are listed. This area had already been settled by the tribes of Reuben and Gad and one-half of the tribe of Manasseh (Num. 32).

12:7–24. The kings and their territories west of the Jordan River in Canaan—those captured under Joshua's leadership—are listed.

13:1–7. The Lord reminds Joshua in his old age that the Canaanites still occupy parts of the land that He has promised to the Israelites.

13:8–14. God gives a general description of the territories east of the Jordan River that have already been settled by the tribes of Reuben and Gad and one-half of the tribe of Manasseh.

13:15–23. The territory east of the Jordan River assigned to the tribe of Reuben is listed.

13:24–28. The territory east of the Jordan River assigned to the tribe of Gad is listed.

13:29–31. The territory east of the Jordan River assigned to one-half of the tribe of Manasseh is listed (1 Chron. 5:23).

13:32–33. A summary statement about the territories east of the Jordan River assigned to the Israelites and a reminder that the Levites received no land inheritance.

14:1–5. A general statement about the division of the land of Canaan among the Israelite tribes.

14:6–15. Caleb receives a special inheritance of land, which includes the city of Hebron. Moses had made this promise of land to Caleb forty years before. Caleb was one of the twelve spies who investigated the land. Only he and Joshua had trusted God and recommended that the Israelites move forward immediately to conquer the land (Num. 14:5–10).

15:1–63. The territory, including cities, assigned to the tribe of Judah is listed.

16:1–4. A general statement about the territories assigned to the two tribes that sprang from Joseph's two sons, Ephraim and Manasseh.

16:5–10. The territory assigned to the tribe of Ephraim is listed.

17:1–13. The territory, including cities, assigned to the tribe of Manasseh is listed.

17:14–18. The tribes of Ephraim and Manasseh ask for additional land, and Joshua grants their request.

18:1–10. Joshua sends representatives from each tribe to survey the remaining land so it can be divided among the tribes that have not yet received an inheritance.

18:11–28. The territory, including cities, assigned to the tribe of Benjamin is listed.

19:1–9. The territory, including cities, assigned to the tribe of Simeon is listed.

19:10–16. The territory, including cities, assigned to the tribe of Zebulun is listed.

19:17–23. The territory, including cities, assigned to the tribe of Issachar is listed.

19:24–31. The territory, including cities, assigned to the tribe of Asher is listed.

19:32–39. The territory, including cities, assigned to the tribe of Naphtali is listed.

19:40–48. The territory, including cities, assigned to the tribe of Dan is listed.

19:49–51. The tribes of Israel grant Joshua a city as a reward for his faithful leadership.

20:1–9. Six cities throughout the territory of the tribes are designated as cities of refuge (Num. 35; Deut. 19:1–13). Three of these are to be on the western side and three on the eastern side of the Jordan River.

21:1–45. The Levites receive no land inheritance, so they are given forty-eight cities throughout the territory of the tribes. These cities are assigned to the three branches of the Levites: Kohathites (vv. 10–26), Gershonites (vv. 27–33), and Merarites (vv. 34–40) (see Num. 35).

22:1–9. Now that the war with the Canaanites is over, Joshua allows the warriors from the tribes of Reuben and Gad and one-half of the tribe of Manasseh to return to their homes on the eastern side of the Jordan River. They have made good on their promise to help the other tribes conquer the land (Num. 32).

22:10–34. The tribes of Reuben and Gad and one-half of the tribe of Manasseh build a huge altar on their side of the Jordan River. The tribes on the other side of the river fear this is an altar for pagan worship. But they are assured it has been built as a gesture of praise and thanksgiving to God.

23:1–16. In his old age, Joshua gathers the people and reminds them that God has fulfilled His promise to give them a land of their own. He challenges them to love the Lord and to keep His commandments.

24:1–28. In his farewell speech to Israel, Joshua gives the people a history lesson to show how gracious God has been to His people. He challenges them to remain faithful to God and to put away the worship of false gods; then he leads them to renew the covenant with the Lord.

24:29–33. Joshua dies and his accomplishments are summarized.

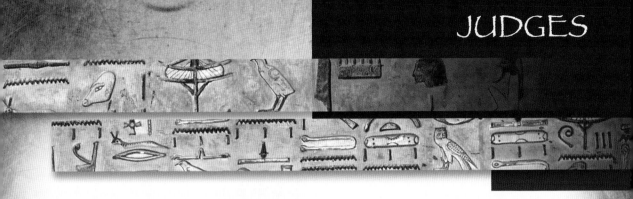

OVERVIEW: A series of judges, or military leaders, deliver the Israelites from their enemies.

Introduction to Judges

The book of Judges, written by an unknown author, covers a dark period of about 300 years in the history of the Israelites. This was the time between the conquest and settlement of Canaan by the tribes of Israel and the establishment of a centralized government under a human king about 1000 B.C.

These were chaotic years for Israel because the people turned away from the Lord and worshiped false gods. The writer of Judges tells us that it was a time when "every man did that which was right in his own eyes" (17:6; 21:25) rather than following the Lord.

God would punish His people by sending oppressors against them. These included tribal groups such as the Canaanites, Midianites, Moabites, and Philistines. The Israelites would repent and cry out to God for deliverance. Then the Lord would send a judge, or a military leader, to raise an army among the Israelite tribes to throw off the yoke of oppression.

After God's intervention on their behalf, the people would follow the Lord for a while, only to fall back again into the same old pattern of idolatry. Then the cycle of oppression-repentance-deliverance would begin all over again (see summary of 2:6–23 below). The onset of the cycle is introduced by the phrase, "The children of Israel did evil in the sight of the LORD," which occurs seven times throughout the book (2:11; 3:7,12; 4:1; 6:1; 10:6; 13:1).

One of the subtle messages of the book of Judges is that God is no respecter of persons when He is looking for people to carry out His will. One of the judges whom He raised up to deliver His people was a woman named Deborah (4:1–24). This must have been surprising to the people, since ancient Israel was a male-dominated society.

1:1–36. A Canaanite man's face, found in what is now Israel and painted onto pottery in about 1300 B.C. This is when many experts say the Israelites were settling in the land.

Deborah did enlist a male warrior named Barak to help her raise an army to defeat the Canaanites, but she was clearly the leader of the campaign (4:8).

Summary of Judges

1:1–36. When Joshua dies, pockets of Canaanites still live in the territory settled by the tribes of Israel. Battles with the Canaanites and other enemies continue.

2:1–5. An angel of the Lord reveals that God is not pleased because the Israelites have not driven all the Canaanites out of the land. They have allowed the pagan worship practices of the Canaanites to continue.

2:6–23. After Joshua's death, a new generation of Israelites that does not obey the Lord comes on the scene. They are corrupted by worshiping the false gods of their enemies. As punishment, God raises up a group to oppress them. The people then repent of their idolatry and cry out to God for deliverance. Then God empowers a judge, or military leader, to lead the Israelites to defeat the enemy.

3:1–6. Some of the nations or tribal groups that oppressed the Israelites during the period of the judges are listed.

3:7–11. The Lord empowers the judge Othniel, Caleb's brother (Josh. 14:6–15), to deliver the Israelites from oppression by King Chushan-rishathaim of Mesopotamia.

[1:1–36] MUTILATION OF CAPTIVES. *They [tribe of Judah] pursued after him [King Adoni-bezek], and caught him, and cut off his thumbs and his great [big, NIV] toes* (Judg. 1:6).

Adoni-bezek, a Canaanite king, was defeated by warriors from the tribe of Judah. In ancient warfare captive soldiers were sometimes mutilated like Adoni-bezek was to take away their fighting abilities. With both thumbs and both big toes missing, the king would not be able to move quickly or handle a bow or spear.

The ancient Assyrians were known to mutilate captives just for sport, cutting off body parts that had nothing to do with waging war. One monument left by an Assyrian king testifies to their military cruelty: "Their men, young and old, I took prisoners. Of some I cut off the feet and hands; of others I cut off the noses, ears, and lips; of the young men's ears I made a heap."

3:12–15. The Lord empowers the judge Ehud to deliver the Israelites from oppression by the Moabites (2 Sam. 8:2).

3:16–26. Ehud, pretending to bring a gift, assassinates King Eglon of Moab in his own house.

3:27–30. Ehud leads the Israelite army to victory over the Moabites.

3:31. The judge Shamgar leads Israel to defeat the Philistines (2 Sam. 5:17–25).

4:1–5. The Lord empowers the judge Deborah, a prophetess, to deliver the Israelites from oppression by the Canaanites.

[3:31] AN OX GOAD AS A WEAPON. *After him [Ehud] was Shamgar the son of Anath, which slew of the Philistines six hundred men with an ox goad* (Judg. 3:31).

As one of the judges, or military deliverers, of Israel, Shamgar used an ox goad as an efficient weapon against the Philistines. An ox goad was a pole about eight feet long and two inches in diameter. It was sharpened to a point on one end. A farmer used this end when plowing an ox to prod him into a faster gait. The other end had a metal blade that he used to clean roots or clay from the tip of the plow.

Jesus referred to an ox goad when He appeared to the apostle Paul on the road to Damascus: "Saul, Saul, why persecutest thou me? It is hard for thee to kick against the pricks [goads, NIV]" (Acts 26:14).

4:6–9. Deborah enlists Barak (Heb. 11:32) to lead the army of Israel against the Canaanites.

4:10–17. Barak gathers an army from the tribes of Zebulun and Naphtali. They defeat the Canaanites, whose commander, Sisera, escapes on foot.

4:18–24. Victory over the Canaanites is sealed by the assassination of Sisera. A woman named Jael drives a tent stake through his skull while he is in a deep sleep from exhaustion.

5:1–31. Deborah and Barak celebrate the defeat of the Canaanites with a song of praise to the Lord, "The Song of Deborah."

6:1–6. The combined forces of the Midianites and the Amalekites oppress Israel, destroying their crops and stealing their livestock.

6:7–10. A prophet arrives in Israel to remind the people that they are suffering because they have disobeyed the Lord.

6:11–16. The judge Gideon (Heb. 11:32) learns from an angel of the Lord that he has been selected to deliver Israel from oppression by the Midianites.

7:1–8. Tourists drink water from a hillside stream fed by Harod Spring. It was at a spring in this area where Gideon cut the size of his army by keeping only the men who scooped up water with their hands.

[7:16–25] GIDEON'S SECRET WEAPONS. *He [Gideon] divided the three hundred men into three companies, and he put a trumpet in every man's hand, with empty pitchers, and lamps within the pitchers* (Judg. 7:16).

Gideon relied on the Lord, as well as shock and surprise, to defeat the huge Midianite army with a force of only three hundred warriors. He and his men advanced on the enemy camp at night while most of the Midianites were still asleep. Then, at Gideon's signal, they blew their trumpets and broke their pitchers with torches inside, suddenly bathing the camp in light.

All the noise and light convinced the Midianites that they were being attacked by a huge army. In the shock and confusion, they "set every man's sword against his fellow" (Judg. 7:22) and fled into the night. Their disorganization made them easy prey for the pursuing Israelites.

6:17–24. The angel disappears after proving to Gideon through a miracle that he is God's messenger. Gideon builds an altar to the Lord to show he accepts God's call.

6:25–32. Obeying God's orders, Gideon tears down an altar devoted to the pagan god Baal. He builds in its place an altar dedicated to the Lord.

6:33–35. The combined forces of the Midianites and the Amalekites gather at the valley of Jezreel. Gideon raises an army from the tribes of Manasseh, Asher, Zebulun, and Naphtali.

6:36–40. Gideon asks God for two miraculous signs involving a fleece, or a piece of wool, to prove that He will use Gideon to deliver Israel.

7:1–8. The Lord trims Gideon's army—from 32,000 to 22,000 to 10,000 and finally to just 300—to show that the battle will not be won through military might but by dependence on the Lord to deliver on His promise.

7:9–15. Gideon hears two enemy soldiers discussing a dream about a battle in which the Midianites are defeated. This is another sign from the Lord that victory over the Midianites is assured.

7:16–25. Using torches, pitchers, and trumpets, Gideon and his 300 warriors launch a surprise attack on the Midianite army at night. The resulting chaos causes the warriors to attack and kill one another. Gideon seals the victory by capturing and executing two Midianite princes.

8:1–3. Warriors from the tribe of Ephraim complain because they were not summoned to join the battle against the Midianites. Gideon uses diplomacy to soothe their wounded pride.

8:4–21. Gideon captures and executes two kings of Midian, Zebah and Zalmunna, to break the power of the Midianite kingdom.

8:22–23. The Israelites ask Gideon to become their king, but he refuses.

8:24–27. Gideon makes a golden ephod, or apron, which apparently becomes an object of worship in the city where he lives.

8:28–35. After Gideon dies, the Israelites again turn away from God and begin to worship the pagan Canaanite god Baal.

9:1–6. Abimelech, a son of Gideon, is appointed king by the people of the city of Shechem. He kills the other sons of Gideon to eliminate any challengers for the throne. Only Gideon's youngest son, Jotham, escapes the slaughter.

9:7–21. Jotham ridicules Abimelech by telling a parable about the bramble, or thornbush, and the trees. Abimelech, just like the

[13:1–25] SAMSON THE NAZARITE. *Thou [Manoah's wife] shalt conceive, and bear a son; and no razor shall come on his head: for the child shall be a Nazarite unto God from the womb* (Judg. 13:5).

A Nazirite was a person who took an oath known as the Nazirite vow. He promised to avoid worldly things and to devote himself totally to the Lord. As evidence of this commitment, a Nazirite was not to drink wine or any intoxicating beverages and he was not to cut his hair (Num. 6:5).

The Nazirite vow was voluntary, and it was generally taken for a limited time, perhaps thirty or sixty days. But Samson was designated as a Nazirite for life; this choice was made for him by the Lord and his parents even before he was born.

Samson failed to live up to the vow that others had made for him. He indulged in worldly pleasures and sinned against the Lord. When Delilah succeeded in cutting his hair, the spirit of the Lord left him and his great strength was taken away (Judg. 16:19).

thornbush, isn't worthy of the kingship.

9:22–57. The people of Shechem turn against Abimelech. He is eventually killed by a woman who drops a piece of millstone on his head while he is leading a siege against a walled city.

10:1–5. Tola and Jair serve as judges to deliver Israel from their enemies.

10:6–18. The people of Israel turn to idol worship; God punishes them by raising up the Philistines and the Ammonites as their oppressors.

11:1–33. The judge Jephthah leads Israel to victory over the Ammonites (Deut. 23:3).

11:34–40. Jephthah is obligated to offer his own daughter as a sacrifice because of his rash vow to give God the first thing that came out to meet him when he returned from battle (see v. 31).

12:1–6. Jephthah leads his forces in a civil war against the tribe of Ephraim.

12:7. Jephthah dies and is buried in Gilead.

12:8–15. Three different men—Ibzan, Elon, and Abdon—serve for a brief time as judges over Israel.

13:1–25. The judge Samson (Heb. 11:32) is born to godly parents in the tribe of Dan. Consecrated as a Nazarite (Num. 6:1–21), his mission is to deliver Israel from oppression by the Philistines.

14:1–20. Samson selects a Philistine woman as his wife. He taunts his friends by giving them a riddle to solve.

15:1–20. Samson burns the crops of the Philistines and slaughters 1,000 men with the jawbone of a donkey.

16:1–3. Samson escapes from a Philistine trap by tearing a city gate out of the wall and carrying it off to Hebron.

16:4–21. Samson reveals to Delilah, a Philistine woman, that the source of his superhuman strength is his long hair that has never been cut. Delilah shaves his head while he is asleep. Samson is captured, blinded, and sentenced to a life of hard labor as a prisoner of the Philistines.

16:22–31. Samson dies, along with thousands of the Philistines, when he pushes down the support columns of a building where he was being taunted by his captors.

13:1–25. Etched into stone is this image of a Philistine warrior, like those Samson once fought.

17:1–13. Micah fashions several objects of idol worship and hires a Levite as his household priest.

18:1–6. The tribe of Dan sends out scouts to find a territory or city they can claim as their own. Micah's household priest assures them that God will bless their efforts.

18:7–31. The Danite scouts recommend that Laish, a city of the Zidonians, be taken. Danite warriors stop at Micah's house on their way to Laish, stealing Micah's objects of idol worship and taking away his

[16:22–31] **DAGON OF THE PHILISTINES.** *The lords of the Philistines gathered them [the Philistines] together for to offer a great sacrifice unto Dagon their god, and to rejoice: for they said, Our god hath delivered Samson our enemy into our hand* (Judg. 16:23).

This pagan god to whom the Philistines attributed such power was their primary, national god. They must have gathered often in ceremonies such as this—probably in a temple devoted to Dagon—to worship and pay tribute to him.

Stone carvings of Dagon portray him with the head, hands, and upper body of a man and the lower part of his body as a fish. The Hebrew word for Dagon actually means "little fish." This pagan god represented the reproductive powers of nature. The fish was an appropriate image because of its ability to reproduce rapidly and in great numbers.

The Philistines boasted that Dagon had delivered their enemy Samson into their hands. But when he pushed down the pillars that held up Dagon's temple (Judg. 16:29–30), he proved that Israel's God was superior to this pagan idol.

household priest. These become part of the worship system of the Danites after they occupy Laish.

19:1–30. A Levite's concubine is violated and killed by perverted residents of the city of Gibeah in the territory of the tribe of Benjamin. The Levite informs the other Israelite tribes of this outrage and urges them to take action against the city of Gibeah and the Benjaminites.

20:1–48. The tribes of Israel raise an army and attack the Benjaminites at Gibeah. They wipe out most of the tribe, including the women.

21:1–25. Because of its great losses, the tribe of Benjamin is in danger of going extinct, especially since the other tribes made a vow not to give their daughters in marriage to the few remaining Benjaminite men. But the tribes find a way to produce wives for Benjamin so this tribe will not be "cut off from Israel" (v. 6).

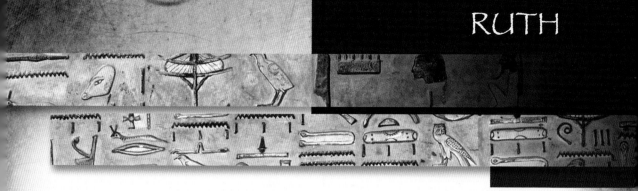

OVERVIEW: Ruth's commitment to her mother-in-law exemplifies God's love and care.

Introduction to Ruth

The book of Ruth is only four chapters long, but it is one of the most inspiring books of the Bible. It takes its name from a Moabite (Gentile) woman who married into an Israelite family. When all the men of the family died, Ruth remained steadfastly loyal to her mother-in-law, Naomi. The name Ruth means "friendship," and she modeled love and friendship at their best.

Modern Christian wedding ceremonies often include the words of devotion spoken by Ruth to Naomi: "Intreat me not to leave thee... for whither thou goest, I will go; and where thou lodgest, I will lodge: thy people shall be my people, and thy God my God" (1:16).

The author of Ruth is unknown. What we do know is that the events of the book happened during "the days when the judges ruled" (1:1). This was a dark period in Israel's history (see the introduction to Judges on p. 403). Ruth shows us that even in the worst of times, God is at work in His world.

Summary of Ruth

1:1–5. Elimelech and his wife and two sons move to Moab from Judah to escape a famine in their homeland. Then Elimelech and his two sons die, leaving three widows in distress: his wife, Naomi, and the two Moabite women whom his sons had married.

1:6–22. Naomi decides to return to her homeland. One of her widowed daughters-in-law, Ruth, insists on going with her.

2:1–23. Ruth goes into the barley fields to gather left-behind stalks of grain to make bread for herself and Naomi. By chance, this field belongs to Boaz, a distant relative of Naomi's late husband, Elimelech. Ruth meets Boaz, who arranges with his harvesters to leave many stalks in the field for her to glean. Naomi is pleased when she learns that Ruth has met Boaz.

[2:1–23] GLEANING IN THE FIELDS OF BOAZ. *She [Ruth] went, and came, and gleaned in the field after the reapers* (Ruth 2:3).

Ruth's gathering of grain in the fields of Boaz is the best example in the Bible of the practice of gleaning. After crops had been harvested, poor people were allowed in the fields and orchards to pick up any grain or fruit that had been left behind.

Old Testament law specified that the corners of fields were not to be harvested by landowners. Grain in these spots was to be left for the poor (Lev. 23:22). Likewise, a sheaf of grain left accidentally in the field was to remain there as provision for the poor (Deut. 24:19).

Some generous landowners went beyond the letter of the law and deliberately left part of the harvest in the fields for the poor. For example, when Boaz learned about Ruth gleaning on his property, he instructed his workers, "Pull out some stalks for her from the bundles [of grain] and leave them for her to pick up" (Ruth 2:16 NIV).

[4:1–12] SIGN OF THE SHOE. *Now this was the manner in former time in Israel concerning redeeming and concerning changing, for to confirm all things; a man plucked off his shoe, and gave it to his neighbour: and this was a testimony in Israel* (Ruth 4:7).

Naomi's deceased husband, Elimelech, had some land in Bethlehem that she had been forced to sell because of her poverty conditions (Ruth 4:3). Elimelech had a relative who, as his next of kin, had the right to buy back or redeem this property to keep it in the family.

But this unnamed relative gave up that right by removing his sandal. Only the owner of a plot of land had the right to walk on it. Removal of his sandal symbolized that he was giving up his ownership rights and transferring them to Boaz, who could then proceed to buy back the property from the current owner.

males who had no children to marry their widows in order to produce children to carry on the family name (Deut. 25:5–10). Boaz, as a distant relative of Naomi's late husband, Elimelech, is willing to marry Ruth but indicates there is a relative closer to Elimelech who has first choice in the matter.

4:1–12. With the elders of the city looking on as witnesses, Boaz sits down with this relative at the city gate. The man gives up the right to marry Ruth, leaving Boaz free to take her as his wife.

4:13–22. Boaz marries Ruth, who gives birth to a son named Obed. Obed becomes the father of Jesse and the grandfather of the great King David of Judah (Matt. 1:5).

3:1–18. Naomi sends Ruth to lie at the feet of Boaz at night, a custom that indicates she is willing to marry Boaz. The law of levirate marriage encouraged relatives of deceased

2:1–23. After the harvest, the widowed Ruth collects leftover grain—as Jewish law allowed the poor to do. Ruth later marries the Bethlehem farm owner, Boaz, and they become great-grandparents of King David.

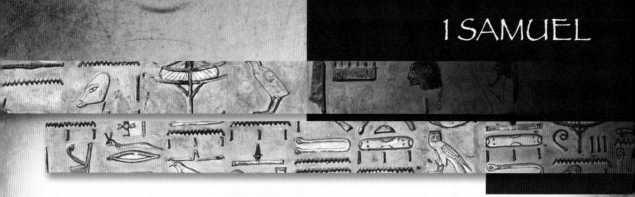

OVERVIEW: The Israelite tribes unite under a kingship form of government. Saul fails as the first king.

2:11. From the time Samuel was able to eat solid food, he was raised in the Jewish worship center. This was to honor a promise his previously infertile mother had made to God.

Introduction to 1 Samuel

The book of 1 Samuel is a pivotal book in the history of Israel. Up to this point, about 1050 to 1000 B.C., the nation had no centralized form of government. It existed as a loose tribal society, with each of the twelve tribes living to itself and minding its own affairs. This changed when Saul was anointed the first king of Israel by the prophet Samuel (10:1). For the rest of their history during Old Testament times, God's people would be ruled by an earthly king.

First Samuel is named for the prophet Samuel, the author and one of the central personalities of the book. As the last of the judges and the first of the prophets, he served as the moral conscience of the nation during this critical period in its history.

As the first king of Israel, Saul got off to a good start. He showed humility, patience, and courageous leadership and was able to win some decisive victories over Israel's number one enemy, the Philistines. But over time he degenerated into a sullen, impatient, and rebellious leader who refused to follow the clear commands of the Lord. Samuel was finally commanded by the Lord to anoint the young shepherd boy David as Saul's successor (16:1–13).

David knew he was destined to become king someday. But in the meantime he showed loyalty to Saul by serving as his aide and becoming a heroic warrior in his army. Saul eventually became consumed by a jealous rage, and David was forced to flee for his life into Philistine territory.

The book of 1 Samuel ends tragically— with the death of Saul and his three sons at the hands of the Philistines (chap. 31). This paved the way for David to succeed to the kingship.

Summary of 1 Samuel

1:1–8. Hannah expresses her sorrow over her childlessness by weeping and refusing to eat.

1:9–18. Hannah prays for a son and promises to devote him to the Lord.

[1:9–18] ELI'S SEAT OF JUDGMENT. *Eli the priest sat upon a seat by a post of the temple of the LORD* (1 Sam. 1:9).

Since Eli was the high priest of Israel, the seat on which he sat was probably a "seat of judgment" from which he advised the people. As the final judge in religious matters, he helped people solve their problems by subjecting themselves to the Lord's will. Hannah, a godly woman who had been unable to have children, brought this problem before Eli for his advice and counsel.

Eli told Hannah, "Go in peace: and the God of Israel grant thee thy petition" (1 Sam. 1:17). She eventually did give birth to a son—the prophet Samuel.

1:19–28. Samuel is born as an answer to Hannah's prayer. She follows through on her promise to devote him to the Lord by presenting him to the priest Eli at Shiloh.

2:1–10. Hannah prays and sings a song of thanksgiving to God for the birth of Samuel and His continuing faithfulness to Israel.

2:11. The boy Samuel lives with the priest Eli at Shiloh and helps him with his ceremonial religious duties.

2:12–17. The dishonest sons of Eli cheat people when they offer sacrifices to the Lord at Shiloh.

2:18–21. The boy Samuel continues his work with Eli at Shiloh. Samuel's mother and father are blessed with other children.

2:22–36. A prophet warns Eli that he and his household will be judged by the Lord because of the wicked behavior of his two sons, Hophni and Phinehas.

3:1–9. The Lord speaks to the boy Samuel three times; he assumes he is being called by the priest Eli.

3:10–21. God speaks to Samuel for the fourth time, revealing that He will punish Eli and his descendants because he has failed to deal with his wicked sons. Samuel is recognized throughout the land as a true prophet of the Lord.

4:1–11. Eli's sons, Hophni and Phinehas, are killed in a battle with the Philistines. The Philistines carry away the Israelites' sacred chest known as the ark of the covenant (Exod. 37:1–9).

4:12–18. The aged priest Eli dies at the news that his sons have been killed and the ark of the covenant has been captured by the Philistines.

4:19–22. Eli's daughter-in-law names her newborn child Ichabod, symbolizing that God's glory has left Israel.

5:1–12. God punishes the Philistines for capturing the ark. He works miracles and sends plagues upon them in three different cities where it is being kept.

6:1–21. After keeping the ark for seven months, the Philistines return it to Israel, along with gifts of gold as a trespass offering.

7:1–2. The ark is kept at the Israelite city of Kirjath-jearim for twenty years.

7:3–6. Samuel calls on the Israelites to turn from their idolatry back to God and offers sacrifices to the Lord at Mizpeh.

7:7–14. Israel wins a victory over the Philistines after Samuel prays and makes a special offering to the Lord.

7:15–17. Samuel serves as a priest and judge for all Israel from his home at Ramah.

[6:1–21] PAGAN CHARMS. *Ye [Philistines] shall make images [models, NIV] of your emerods [tumors, NIV], and images of your mice that mar the land* (1 Sam. 6:5).

The Philistines captured the ark of the covenant from the Israelites and carried it to the city of Ashdod (1 Sam. 5:1). God punished the Philistines by sending swarms of mice throughout their land. These mice apparently carried a disease that caused the Philistines to break out in sores, or tumors.

Pagan priests among the Philistines recommended that they send the ark back to the Israelites, along with images of the mice and tumors that were causing their suffering. They thought these images would serve as magic charms to cure their sores and ward off evil spirits.

8:1–3. In his old age, Samuel appoints his two sons as judges over Israel, but they become dishonest and corrupt.

8:4–9. The elders of Israel ask Samuel to appoint a king to rule over all the tribes (Hosea 13:10).

8:10–22. At God's command, Samuel informs the people about the suffering they will experience under a human king. But his warnings fall on deaf ears. God tells Samuel to proceed to select a king to rule over Israel.

9:1–27. Saul, a handsome young man from the tribe of Benjamin, encounters Samuel while searching for his father's lost donkeys. The Lord informs Samuel that Saul is the person who should be anointed as Israel's king.

10:1. Samuel pours oil on Saul's head to anoint him as king over the Israelites.

10:2–16. Samuel tells Saul to look for several miraculous signs to show that he is the Lord's anointed to rule over Israel.

10:17–27. Samuel calls the tribes of Israel together for a public presentation of Saul as their new king. The reluctant Saul is summoned from his hiding place to begin his duties.

11:1–15. Saul gathers an army from among all the tribes and defeats the Ammonites at Jabesh-gilead. This quiets minority opposition to his kingship, and he is acclaimed king by all Israel at Gilgal.

12:1–25. Samuel reminds the people of how God has blessed them in past years; he challenges them to remain faithful to Him during this new era of their history under a human king (Josh. 24:1–28).

13:1–14. Preparing for battle with the Philistines, Saul offers a sacrifice to God on his own rather than waiting for Samuel the priest to present the offering with the prescribed ritual. Samuel informs him that this act of impatience and obedience will cost him the kingship.

13:15–23. Saul's warriors have only a few iron weapons to fight with. Their Philistine enemies have developed a monopoly on making and sharpening iron weapons throughout the entire territory of Israel (2 Kings 24:14).

14:1–19. Saul's son Jonathan, accompanied by his armorbearer, leads a secret mission against a company of Philistines, causing panic throughout the enemy camp.

14:20–23. Saul and his army join the battle and chase the Philistine garrison from the area.

14:24–42. Saul warns all Israelite warriors against partaking of food during the day when a great battle rages against the Philistines. His own son Jonathan violates the command.

14:43–46. Saul prepares to execute Jonathan for his disobedience, but other Israelite warriors intervene to save Jonathan's life.

14:47–52. Saul's victories over Israel's enemies are listed, along with the members of his family (1 Chron. 8:33).

15:1–9. The prophet Samuel directs Saul to destroy the Amalekites and all their livestock (Exod. 17:8–16). But Saul spares the life of

[17:40–51] DAVID'S SLING. *His [David's] sling was in his hand* (1 Sam. 17:40).

The sling that David carried was a simple but effective weapon used by shepherds, farmers, and even soldiers in Bible times. It was similar to the slingshot in its design and how it was used.

Like a slingshot, the sling had a pocket in which a small stone was placed. Attached to this pocket were two leather straps. The slinger grasped the ends of the straps, twirled the stone around several times in a circular motion, then released one of the straps at just the right time to hurl the stone toward its target.

In skilled hands, the sling was a formidable weapon. The force of the stone was strong enough to kill wild animals and—in Goliath's case—even a giant of a man (1 Sam. 17:49).

During the time of the judges, the tribe of Benjamin had a unit of seven hundred soldiers who specialized in use of the sling. All the slingers in this elite corps were left-handed, and they "could sling a stone at a hair and not miss" (Judg. 20:16 NIV).

King Agag and keeps some of the choice spoils of war.

15:10–35. Samuel reprimands Saul for his disobedience. He declares that the kingship has been taken away from him by the Lord and will be given to another.

16:1–13. At the Lord's command, Samuel anoints the shepherd boy David—the youngest son of Jesse—as Saul's replacement as king of Israel.

16:14–23. Saul selects David to serve as his armorbearer and to play the harp to soothe his troubled mind.

17:1–22. Saul's army is stationed for battle against the Philistines, but they are bullied into inaction by the taunts of a Philistine giant named Goliath.

17:23–39. The shepherd boy David arrives on the scene and prepares to fight Goliath, since no Israelite warrior will accept his challenge. David refuses to wear the armor of Saul for the battle.

17:40–51. David fells Goliath with a single stone from his sling, then executes the giant with his own sword.

17:52–58. At the death of their champion, the Philistine army flees in panic and suffers a

17:40–51. Whirling a rock to take advantage of centrifugal force, a teenager in Israel wields the kind of slingshot that the shepherd boy David probably used to bring down the Philistine champion Goliath.

humiliating defeat by the army of Israel.

18:1–4. David and Saul's son Jonathan make a pact of everlasting friendship.

18:5–16. David becomes a commander in Saul's army and is praised by the Israelites for his bravery. In a fit of jealousy, Saul tries to kill David.

18:17–30. David takes Saul's daughter Michal as his wife after leading a successful campaign against the Philistines.

19:1–7. Jonathan intercedes with his father, Saul, on behalf of David, receiving Saul's assurance that he will not harm David.

19:8–18. Saul breaks his promise and attempts to kill David again. David seeks sanctuary with the prophet Samuel.

19:19–24. Saul sends soldiers to capture David, but they are moved by God's Spirit to prophesy instead. The same thing happens to Saul when he comes looking for David in Samuel's household.

20:1–42. Jonathan warns David that Saul intends to kill him and that he should flee for his life. Then David and Jonathan bid each other a sorrowful farewell.

21:1–9. David visits the priest Ahimelech at Nob. Ahimelech gives him food and the sword of the Philistine giant Goliath to use as his own weapon.

21:10–15. David pretends to be insane in order to find sanctuary with Achish, king of Gath, in Philistine territory.

22:1–5. David gathers an army of 400 warriors while hiding from Saul.

22:6–23. Saul slaughters Ahimelech and scores of other priests at Nob for providing assistance to David.

23:1–5. David and his fighting men defeat a Philistine force to save the city of Keilah.

23:6–29. David eludes Saul and his army by hiding in various places in the wilderness.

24:1–15. David gets close enough to Saul in a dark cave to cut off a piece of his robe, but he refuses to kill him. From a distance, David condemns Saul for wasting his time by chasing him and trying to kill him.

24:16–22. Saul admits that David is a righteous man and that he is destined to become the new king of Israel. He secures David's promise that he will not murder all of Saul's descendants after he is anointed king.

25:1. Samuel dies and is buried at Ramah.

25:2–13. David asks a wealthy livestock owner named Nabal for food supplies for his hungry army, but Nabal insults David and refuses his request. David prepares to take the needed supplies by force.

25:14–35. Nabal's wife, Abigail, gathers food supplies and presents them to David to appease his anger.

25:36–44. Nabal dies, and David takes Abigail as one of his wives.

26:1–16. David and one of his warriors slip into Saul's camp at night. David gets close enough to Saul to kill him, but he refuses—once again (1 Sam. 24:1–15)—to do so.

[19:19–24] NOT QUITE NAKED. *He [Saul] stripped off his clothes also, and prophesied before Samuel in like manner, and lay down naked all that day and all that night* (1 Sam. 19:24).

The basic dress for both men and women of Bible times was a full-length outer garment, or robe, as well as a full-length undergarment of lighter material. Thus, the term *naked* as rendered by the KJV in this verse does not mean totally nude. A person who took off his outer robe was considered "naked," although he might still be wearing his undergarment.

This is the sense in which the prophet Isaiah went around "naked" (Isa. 20:2) at the Lord's command to symbolize the fate of the people of Judah unless they turned from their idolatry. The NIV says that Isaiah went around "stripped"—without his outer robe.

[25:1] SAMUEL'S TOMB. *Samuel died; and all the Israelites were gathered together, and lamented him, and buried him in his house at Ramah* (1 Sam. 25:1).

Some interpreters believe this verse means that Samuel was buried in a tomb in the house he lived in at Ramah. But it is likely that the term *house* was just a poetic way of referring to a tomb. Job spoke of the grave as a "house appointed for all living" (Job 30:23).

26:17–20. From a distance, David again condemns Saul for trying to kill him (1 Sam. 24:9–15).

26:21–25. Saul again admits his wrongdoing (1 Sam. 24:16–22) and predicts that David will be victorious and successful as king of Israel.

27:1–4. David and his army of 600 warriors again seek sanctuary with Achish, king of Gath, in Philistine territory (1 Sam. 21:10–15).

27:5–12. David lives among the Philistines for sixteen months. From his headquarters at the city of Ziklag, he conducts raids against several tribal enemies of the Israelites, including the Geshurites, Gezrites, and Amalekites.

28:1–4. A coalition of several Philistine armies assembles against Saul's forces at Gilboa.

28:5–25. Saul asks for the Lord's direction but gets no response. He hires a medium to conjure up the spirit of Samuel, who predicts that Saul's army will be defeated by the Philistines.

29:1–11. The commanders of the allied Philistine forces do not trust David. They insist that he and his fighting men not be allowed to go into battle against Saul, lest they turn against the Philistines. David is dismissed by his Philistine friend Achish, king of Gath.

30:1–21. David and his army defeat the Amalekites, who had raided his headquarters city of Ziklag and carried away captives and spoils of war.

30:22–31. David shows his kindness and fairness by sharing the spoils of war with 200 of his warriors who were too weak to pursue the battle with the Amalekites to the end. He shows his political astuteness by sharing the spoils with his fellow Israelites in several selected cities.

31:1–13. The Philistines defeat Saul's forces at Mount Gilboa (1 Chron. 10:1–4). Among the dead are Saul and his three sons, whose corpses are displayed on the wall of a Philistine city. Some brave Israelite warriors take the bodies down under the cover of darkness and give them a decent burial.

28:5–25. Dead Samuel's spirit appears to King Saul, conjured up by a medium. Samuel warns that Saul and his three sons will join him the following day, after a doomed battle with the Philistines.

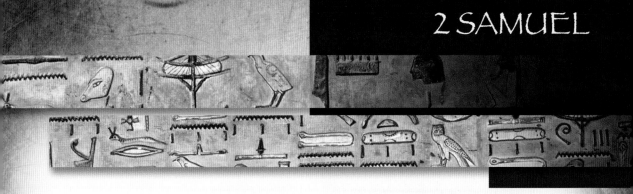

OVERVIEW: David succeeds Saul as king and leads Israel to victory over its enemies.

Introduction to 2 Samuel

The book of 2 Samuel picks up where 1 Samuel leaves off—with the death of King Saul and the succession of David to the kingship. At first David was recognized by the people as king over only a part of Israel. But David eventually won out over other challengers and reigned over the entire territory of Israel. Second Samuel traces the events of David's administration across a period of about forty years.

This book is named for the prophet Samuel, the author of 1 Samuel (see the introduction to 1 Samuel on p. 411). But 2 Samuel could not have been written by him, since it reports on events that happened after Samuel's death (1 Sam. 25:1). Many scholars believe 2 Samuel was written by Abiathar, the high priest of the nation during David's administration (2 Sam. 15:24–35).

Unlike Saul, Israel's first king, who rejected God's counsel (see the introduction to 1 Samuel on p. 411), David followed the Lord and set a good example for his people. God rewarded him by giving him victory over all of Israel's enemies and expanding the borders of his kingdom. God even promised David that one of his descendants would always occupy the throne of Israel (7:1–17).

But even David had feet of clay. He committed adultery with Bathsheba and tried to cover up his crime by having her husband killed. When confronted by God's prophet, David repented of his sin and received God's forgiveness. But he would have to face the consequences of his sin through tragedies that would strike his own family (11:1–12:12).

Toward the end of David's reign, his son Absalom raised an army and tried to take the kingship from his father by force. David's army prevailed, but Absalom was killed in battle. The king mourned his son with some of the saddest words in the Bible: "O my son Abaslom, my son, my son Absalom! would God I had died for thee, O Absalom, my son, my son!" (18:33).

Some of the events from David's reign that appear in 2 Samuel are also reported in the book of 1 Chronicles. These events are cross-referenced to 1 Chronicles in the summary of 2 Samuel below.

Summary of 2 Samuel

1:1–16. David is informed of the death of Saul and Saul's son Jonathan at the hands of the Philistines.

1:17–27. David laments the death of Saul and Jonathan.

2:1–7. David is recognized as king by the tribe of Judah in southern Israel. He makes Hebron his headquarters city.

2:8–11. Abner, commander of Saul's army, makes Saul's son Ish-bosheth king over the other tribes of Israel. For seven and one-half years, two opposing kingships exist in Israel.

One faction recognizes David, and the other recognizes Ish-bosheth.

2:12–32. In an initial battle between the two factions, Ish-bosheth's forces under Abner are defeated by David's army under the leadership of Joab.

3:1–5. David's fortunes increase, while Ish-bosheth loses ground. Six sons from several different wives are born to David while he rules over the tribe of Judah at Hebron.

3:6–21. Abner offers to desert to David and to swing the support of the tribes that follow Ish-bosheth to David.

3:22–39. Joab assassinates Abner. David makes it clear that he had nothing to do with his death.

4:1–8. Ish-bosheth is assassinated by his two brothers; they cut off his head and present it to David.

4:9–12. David executes Ish-bosheth's assassins.

5:1–5. David is recognized by all the tribes as king over all Israel (1 Chron. 11:1–3).

5:6–10. David captures the city of Jerusalem from the Jebusites and turns it into his new headquarters city (Josh. 15:63; 1 Chron. 11:4–9).

5:11–16. Hiram, king of Tyre, pays honor to David as king of Israel (1 Chron. 14:1–2). Eleven sons from several different wives are born to David at Jerusalem (1 Chron. 14:3–7).

5:17–25. David defeats the Philistines in a major battle in the valley of Rephaim (1 Chron. 14:8–17).

6:1–11. David moves the ark of the covenant from the house of Abinadab to the house of Obed-edom. Uzzah is killed when he touches the ark while it is being moved (1 Chron. 13:1–14).

6:12–19. David dances before the ark of the covenant when it is moved from the house of Obed-edom to Jerusalem (1 Chron. 15:1–29).

6:20–23. David's wife Michal criticizes him for dancing before the ark of the covenant. David defends his behavior as an act of devotion and worship before the Lord.

7:1–17. God promises David that his kingship will be established forever—that a descendant of David will always occupy the throne of Israel (1 Chron. 17:1–15; Ps. 132:11).

7:18–29. David pours out his heart to God in a prayer of praise and thanksgiving (1 Chron. 16:7–36).

8:1–14. David extends his kingdom and

[10:1–19] A DOUBLE INSULT. *Hanun took David's servants, and shaved off the one half of their beards, and cut off their garments in the middle, even to their buttocks, and sent them away (2 Sam. 10:4).*

King David sent several ambassadors to Hanun, king of the Ammonites, to express his sympathy at the death of his father (2 Sam. 10:1–2).

Convinced these messengers were spies, Hanun humiliated them by cutting off their beards on one side of their faces. Israelite men were fond of their beards and considered them a symbol of manhood. To have only half a beard made these messengers objects of ridicule and scorn.

Israelite men also wore long outer robes and full-length undergarments (see the note "Not Quite Naked" on p. 415). To have these clothes cut off below the waist so their lower bodies were exposed added to the embarrassment they had already endured.

When David learned about these actions by Hanun, he took military action against the Ammonites (2 Sam. 10:7–9).

his influence by defeating the Philistines, Moabites, Syrians, Amalekites, and Edomites (1 Chron. 18:1–14).

8:15–18. The aides and chief officials in David's administration are listed (1 Chron. 18:15–17).

9:1–13. David provides for Mephibosheth, the lame son of his late friend Jonathan. David invites Mephibosheth to live in Jerusalem and to eat at his table like one of his own sons.

10:1–19. David's army, led by his commander Joab, defeats the allied forces of the Ammonites and the Syrians (1 Chron. 19:6–19).

11:1–5. David commits adultery with Bathsheba, the wife of Uriah the Hittite, while Uriah is away on duty with David's army. She informs David that she is pregnant with David's child.

11:6–13. David tries to cover his sin by granting Uriah a furlough to spend time with Bathsheba. But Uriah foils the king's scheme by refusing to spend the night with his wife.

11:14–25. David directs his commander, Joab, to move Uriah to the front of the battle so Uriah will be killed.

11:26–27. With Uriah disposed of, David takes Bathsheba as his own wife. She gives birth to a son by David.

12:1–9. Nathan the prophet condemns David for his sin and his crime against Uriah. Nathan convicts David of his sin by telling him a parable about a wealthy man (representing David) who stole a lamb from a poor man (representing Uriah).

12:10–12. Nathan announces God's judgment against David because of his sin with Bathsheba: David's own family will be afflicted with trouble and violence.

12:13–23. David repents of his sin and is assured by Nathan that he will not die. But the sickly child born to Bathsheba dies within a few days.

12:24–25. David comforts Bathsheba in the loss of their first child. She later gives birth to another son by David whom they name Solomon.

[11:1–5] TEMPTATION ON THE ROOF. *David arose from off his bed, and walked upon the roof of the king's house: and from the roof he saw a woman washing herself (2 Sam. 11:2).*

In Bible times the roofs of houses were flat. People used these rooftops, particularly in the evening, to catch a cooling breeze.

This is probably what King David was doing when he looked down and saw Bathsheba taking a bath. His casual "rooftop glance" turned to lust. He committed adultery with her and eventually arranged for her warrior husband to be killed in battle to cover up his sin (2 Sam. 11:4–27).

[12:13–23] DAVID'S BEREAVEMENT PATTERN. *Then said his servants unto him [David], What thing is this that thou hast done? thou didst fast and weep for the child, while it was alive; but when the child was dead, thou didst rise and eat bread (2 Sam. 12:21).*

The newborn child whom King David's servants referred to had been conceived during his adulterous affair with Bathsheba (see sidebar, "Temptation on the Roof," on p. 419).

David's servants were amazed because he reversed the normal pattern of grieving in Israelite culture. Following the death of a loved one, the survivors would stop all their normal activities and mourn and fast for a period of several days. Then they would be persuaded by other family members to return to their daily routine.

But David mourned for his newborn child for seven days before he died. He knew this child would die because the prophet Nathan had told him so (2 Sam. 12:13–17). He returned to his routine activities as soon as the child died.

12:26–31. David's commander, Joab, defeats the Ammonites at Rabbah, and they are made slaves in David's kingdom (1 Chron. 20:1–3).

13:1–19. Amnon, one of David's sons, rapes his half sister Tamar.

13:20–33. David's son Absalom, full brother of Tamar and half brother of Amnon, murders Amnon to avenge his crime against Tamar.

13:34–39. Absalom goes into hiding in Geshur and is greatly missed by his father, David.

14:1–24. David's commander, Joab, pleads with the king to let Absalom return to Jerusalem from Geshur. David agrees but refuses to have any contact with Absalom.

14:25–28. Absalom is portrayed as a handsome, vain, and arrogant man who takes great pride in his long, beautiful hair.

14:29–33. Absalom sets Joab's barley fields on fire to force him to arrange a meeting between him and the king. David and his son Absalom are finally reconciled after years of estrangement.

15:1–12. Absalom works behind the scenes to undercut his father's influence and to cultivate loyalty to himself throughout Israel. Absalom gathers a force at Hebron in opposition to David's kingship.

15:13–23. David and his family, his household servants, and the officials in his administration flee Jerusalem. They hide in the wilderness because of the threat from Absalom's rebellion.

15:24–29. David sends the priests Zadok and Abiathar back to Jerusalem with the ark of the covenant, since this city is considered its appropriate resting place.

15:30–37. David sends his friend and supporter Hushai the Archite into Jerusalem so he can spy on the rebellious Absalom.

16:1–4. Ziba, the servant of Mephibosheth, comes to the aid of the fleeing David and his officials by providing food and supplies.

16:5–14. Shimei, a distant relative of Saul, issues curses against David as he flees from Jerusalem.

[15:30–37] DUST ON THE HEAD. *Hushai the Archite came to meet him [David] with his coat rent [torn, NIV], and earth [dust, NIV] upon his head (2 Sam. 15:32).*

Hushai was a friend and supporter of King David. During Absalom's rebellion, Hushai expressed his sorrow at David's exile by tearing his clothes and throwing dust on his head.

Adam, the first man, was created by the Lord from "the dust of the ground" (Gen. 2:7), one of the most common substances on earth. Putting dust on one's head may have been a way of showing humility and helplessness in the face of sorrow.

The custom of putting dust on the head is also referred to in several other passages in the Bible (Josh. 7:6; 1 Sam. 4:12; 2 Sam. 1:2; 13:19; Neh. 9:1; Job 2:12; Lam. 2:10; Ezek. 27:30; Rev. 18:19).

16:15–19. Absalom enters Jerusalem with his supporters. The spy Hushai convinces Absalom he has switched loyalties from David to Absalom.

16:20–23. Ahithophel, a former aide of David, now supports Absalom's rebellion. Ahithophel advises Absalom to claim David's concubines as his own, an act that symbolizes Absalom is assuming the kingship.

17:1–14. Ahithophel advises Absalom to attack David and his forces while they are on the run. But the spy Hushai convinces him to wait until he has gathered a large army before pressing the attack.

17:15–22. Hushai sends messengers to warn David to flee into the wilderness, in case Absalom should decide to mount a surprise attack against him.

[17:15–22] HIDDEN IN A CISTERN. *They [Jonathan and Ahimaaz]...came to a man's house...which had a well in his court; whither they went down. And the woman took and spread a covering over the well's mouth, and spread ground corn [grain, NIV] thereon; and the thing was not known* (2 Sam. 17:18–19).

Jonathan and Ahimaaz were spies who reported on Absalom's activities to King David while David was in exile during Absalom's rebellion.

The "well" in which Jonathan and Ahimaaz were hidden was probably a cistern that was used to collect rainwater. It must have been dry at this time. With containers of grain or flour placed on top of its cover, this cistern was an ideal hiding place.

17:23. Ahithophel commits suicide because Absalom did not follow his advice to attack David immediately.

17:24–29. David and his forces hide out near the city of Mahanaim; here they are supplied with food and other necessities by local residents.

18:1–8. David's army, under three military leaders—Joab, Abishai, and Ittai—attack Absalom's forces in the forest of Ephraim. David instructs them not to harm his son Absalom.

18:9–18. Disregarding the king's orders, Joab kills Absalom after his long hair is entangled in the branches of a tree.

[18:19–33] DAVID'S SAD LAMENT. *The king [David] ...wept...O my son Absalom, my son, my son Absalom! would God I had died for thee* (2 Sam. 18:33).

David's outpouring of grief over his son Absalom is one of the saddest passages in the entire Bible. Apparently such expressions of sorrow over deceased loved ones were common in Bible times. When Jacob died, his family "mourned with a great and very sore lamentation" (Gen. 50:10).

18:19–33. David weeps bitterly for his son after a messenger informs him that Absalom is dead.

19:1–8. David's extreme and extended grief over his son Absalom comes across to his supporters as lack of appreciation for their loyalty. Joab confronts David about this problem, and David agrees to meet with his soldiers and constituents at the city gate.

19:9–14. David builds political support throughout Israel to prepare for his return to Jerusalem as king. He names his nephew Amasa, who had commanded Absalom's army (2 Sam. 17:25), an officer in his army in order to reach out to those who had supported Absalom.

19:15–43. David is acclaimed king by several different segments of Israelite society as he crosses the Jordan River and enters the city of Jerusalem. He forgives Shimei for insulting him as he was fleeing the city (2 Sam. 16:5–14).

[19:15–43] **CROSSING THE JORDAN RIVER.** *There went over a ferry boat to carry over the king's household* (2 Sam. 19:18).

This verse describes David's return from exile to take up his duties as king over Israel after Absalom's rebellion had been put down. David and the rest of the royal household crossed over the Jordan River back into Israelite territory.

Many interpreters question the KJV's use of the term *ferry boat* to describe this crossing. The Jordan River is not very deep in most places. It is generally crossed at shallow places known as fords by just wading across.

The NIV's rendering of this verse—"they crossed at the ford to take the king's household over"—is probably a better translation.

20:1–7. A man named Sheba of the tribe of Benjamin incites a rebellion against David among the northern tribes of Israel. David dispatches his army under Joab and Amasa to put down the rebellion.

20:8–13. Joab murders Amasa, apparently because he had doubts about Amasa's loyalty to the king.

20:14–22. Sheba's rebellion ends when he is assassinated by citizens of the city where he sought refuge from David's army.

20:23–26. The chief officials in David's administration are listed.

21:1–9. About 400 years before David's time, Joshua had made a treaty with the Gibeonites that guaranteed their safety (Josh. 9:3–27). But Saul had broken this treaty by killing some of the Gibeonites. David makes amends with the Gibeonites by allowing them to execute seven of the surviving descendants of Saul.

21:10–14. David retrieves the bones of Saul and his son Jonathan from the city of Jabesh-gilead and has them buried in Saul's family plot in the territory of Benjamin.

21:15–22. David's army kills several Philistine giants, some of whom were descendants of the giant Goliath whom David had killed several years before (1 Sam. 17:32–52).

22:1–51. David utters a prayer of thanksgiving to God for giving him victory over all his enemies. This psalm also appears in the Bible as Psalm 18.

[20:8–13] **GRASPING THE BEARD.** *Joab said to Amasa, Art thou in health, my brother? And Joab took Amasa by the beard with the right hand to kiss him* (2 Sam. 20:9).

Grasping a person's beard and kissing his cheek was a customary greeting among men of Bible times. But Joab used it as a cover to assassinate Amasa (2 Sam. 20:10) because Amasa had supported Absalom's rebellion.

23:1–7. Apparently near the end of his life, David issues these words of praise to God for His faithfulness and His promise that David would enjoy an eternal reign on the throne of Israel (2 Sam. 7:1–17).

23:8–39. The names and brave deeds of David's

[22:1–51] **A PSALM REPEATED.** *David spake unto the LORD the words of this song in the day that the LORD had delivered him out of the hand of all his enemies* (2 Sam. 22:1).

The remaining verses in 2 Samuel 22 contain the words of this psalm that David wrote. This psalm also appears in the Bible as Psalm 18. Although there are a few minor variations between these two recordings of the same psalm, it is essentially the same in both locations.

This verse shows that David wrote many of the psalms in response to specific events in his life. He wrote this psalm to praise the Lord for giving him victory over the enemies of Israel and for establishing him as king throughout the land.

24:16–25. Farmers in Israel about a century ago knock grain kernels loose on a threshing floor. David bought a stone threshing floor in Jerusalem and built a sacrificial altar there, where his son Solomon later built the temple.

"mighty men" are listed. These men may have been an elite group of warriors, perhaps David's personal bodyguards (1 Chron. 11:10–47).

24:1–9. David directs his commander, Joab, to take a census of all the fighting men throughout the tribes of Israel (1 Chron. 21:1–6).

24:10–15. The Lord sends a plague upon the people because of David's sin in ordering the census. Perhaps his sin was human pride over the kingdom he had built (1 Chron. 21:7–17).

24:16–25. David buys a threshing floor from Ornan/Araunah the Jebusite as the site for an altar on which sacrifices will be offered to God. These sacrifices bring an end to the plague (1 Chron. 21:18–30).

1 KINGS

OVERVIEW: The united kingdom splits into two factions: Judah (Southern Kingdom) and Israel (Northern Kingdom). The prophet Elijah challenges Israel's evil king Ahab.

Introduction to 1 Kings

The book of 1 Kings is so named because it traces the history of God's people through a succession of kings following the death of David about 970 B.C. and the succession of his son Solomon to the throne. But the pivotal event in the book is the split of the united kingdom into two rival factions—Judah (Southern Kingdom) and Israel (Northern Kingdom)—after the death of Solomon.

Solomon was noted for his wisdom and the expansion of his kingdom through international trade and diplomacy. But he was also very foolish about some things. He built his kingdom through burdensome taxation and even forced his subjects to work without pay on some of his lavish building projects.

The tribes in the northern section of Solomon's kingdom pulled away and formed their own nation (Israel) under their own king (Jeroboam). This happened when Solomon's son and successor, Rehoboam, vowed to continue—and even intensify—Solomon's oppressive policies (12:16–24).

First Kings does not name its author, and he remains unknown to this day. But we do know that he based his book at least partially on the official historical records of these two

rival nations. The unknown author of 1 Kings mentions "the book of the chronicles of the kings of Israel" (14:19) and "the book of the chronicles of the kings of Judah" (14:29).

Several kings of both Judah and Israel are mentioned in the book of 1 Kings. But the author gives major attention to Ahab of Israel and his evil wife, Jezebel. They were responsible for promoting worship of the pagan Canaanite god Baal throughout Israel. God raised up a fiery prophet named Elijah to condemn their idolatry and predict that God would punish their evil deeds. This prophecy is fulfilled in the final chapter of the book when Ahab is killed in his royal chariot during a battle with the Syrians (22:29–40).

Elijah's sudden appearance on the scene (17:1) to challenge the powerful king of Israel shows that God is never without a witness, even in the darkest of times. Over and over again in 1 Kings we are told that "the word of the LORD came to Elijah" (18:1). And this faithful prophet always "went and did according unto the word of the LORD" (17:5).

Accounts of many of the events in 1 Kings are duplicated in the book of 2 Chronicles. These events are cross-referenced to 2 Chronicles in the summary of 1 Kings below.

Summary of 1 Kings

1:1–4. David's health declines with age, and he is unable to carry out his duties as king.

1:5–10. Adonijah, a son of David and brother

of Absalom, plots to seize the throne as David's successor.

1:11–31. David's wife Bathsheba and Nathan the prophet persuade David to designate Bathsheba's son Solomon as the royal successor.

1:32–40. Solomon is officially anointed at Gihon as David's successor (1 Chron. 23:1).

1:41–53. Adonijah seeks sanctuary from Solomon at the altar. Solomon promises Adonijah that he will not kill him if he causes no trouble for the new king.

[1:41–53] SAFETY AT THE ALTAR. *Adonijah feared because of Solomon, and arose, and went, and caught hold on the horns of the altar* (1 Kings 1:50).

Adonijah, a son of David, had hoped to succeed his father as king of Israel (1 Kings 1:11). But this honor went to Adonijah's brother Solomon.

Adonijah sought protection from Solomon's wrath by grasping the four corners, or horns, of the altar in the tabernacle. This provided temporary asylum or protection for a person who had committed a crime until the charges against him were thoroughly investigated.

This same protection could be sought in one of the cities of refuge throughout the land (Deut. 4:41–42).

2:1–9. David charges Solomon to remain faithful to the Lord as the new king of Israel. David gives Solomon permission to take revenge against two of his political enemies—Joab and Shimei.

2:10–12. David dies after forty years as king—seven years as king of the southern tribe of Judah and thirty-three years as king over all the tribes of Israel (1 Chron. 29:26–27).

2:13–25. Solomon has Adonijah killed because he requested that a former wife of David be given to Adonijah as his own wife.

2:26–27. Solomon deposes Abiathar from the priesthood because he supported Adonijah's quest for the kingship.

2:28–35. Solomon assassinates Joab, former commander of David's army, because he supported Adonijah's attempt to seize the throne. Joab had also killed two innocent men: Abner and Amasa.

2:36–46. Solomon has Shimei assassinated when he disobeys the king's orders and leaves the city of Jerusalem.

3:1–2. Solomon marries the daughter of the pharaoh of Egypt to seal a political alliance with that nation.

3:3–15. Solomon has a dream while offering sacrifices to the Lord at Gibeon. In the dream, Solomon asks for great wisdom so he might be a wise and just king. God promises to honor his request and to give Solomon great riches and honor, as well (2 Chron. 1:1–13).

3:16–28. Solomon's wisdom is revealed as he settles a dispute between two women who claim to be the mother of the same child.

4:1–20. The aides and officials in Solomon's administration are listed.

[4:1–20] SUPPLIES FOR SOLOMON. *Solomon had twelve officers [district governors, NIV] over all Israel, which provided victuals [supplies] for the king and his household: each man his month in a year made provision* (1 Kings 4:7).

Taxes are nothing new. They existed as early as King Solomon's time (about 950 B.C.). He needed revenue to support his lavish building projects and the huge army and staff that he assembled.

For taxation purposes, Solomon divided the nation into twelve administrative districts. Each of these districts supplied the king with what he needed to run the central government for one month out of the year.

Each district had a governor or administrator appointed by the king. This official was responsible for gathering needed supplies from the people in his district.

4:21–28. Solomon becomes wealthy and extravagant as the ruler of a kingdom that stretches from Egypt in the south to the Euphrates River in the north (Ps. 72:8–11).

4:29–34. Solomon is also acclaimed for his great wisdom. He writes thousands of songs and proverbs.

5:1–18. Solomon makes a trade agreement with King Hiram of Tyre, a friend and supporter of his father, David. Solomon trades food for cedar trees as well as cut stone, which are available in Hiram's territory. These building materials are to be used in the construction of a magnificent temple for worship of the Lord in Jerusalem (2 Chron. 2).

6:1–38. Solomon's temple in Jerusalem is completed in seven years (2 Chron. 3).

7:1–12. Solomon spends thirteen years constructing his own royal palace and other administrative buildings in the capital city.

7:13–22. Solomon hires a metalworker from Tyre to construct two magnificent pillars of brass, or copper, in the temple.

7:23–51. This metalworker also fashions other furnishings for the temple, including a huge water basin ("molten sea," v. 23) for sacrificial washing of the priests; candlesticks that stand before the altar; and pots, shovels, and other utensils to be used by the priests in handling sacrificial offerings (2 Chron. 4).

8:1–11. The ark of the covenant is placed in the Most Holy Place in the inner court of the temple. The Lord shows His pleasure and His presence by filling the Most Holy Place with a cloud.

8:12–66. In an elaborate ceremony of dedication for the temple, Solomon prays a prayer of gratitude to the Lord and leads the people to make sacrificial offerings to show their

3:16–28. King Solomon orders a baby cut in half after two women claim the child belongs to them. Solomon then gives the boy to the one woman who objected.

[8:12–66] **HANDS LIFTED IN PRAYER.** *Solomon stood before the altar of the LORD in the presence of all the congregation of Israel, and spread forth his hands toward heaven* (1 Kings 8:22).

When King Solomon dedicated the newly constructed temple with a prayer to the Lord, he stood with his hands open and the palms lifted toward heaven. This stance was often taken when praying, especially in Old Testament times (Exod. 9:33; Ezra 9:5; Ps. 28:2; Isa. 1:15).

dedication and obedience (2 Chron. 5–6).

9:1–9. God makes Solomon the same conditional promise He had made to his father, David. If Solomon follows the Lord, his kingship over Israel will be established forever. But if Solomon turns away from God and leads His people astray, the Lord will reject Solomon and bring punishment upon the land (2 Chron. 7:12–22).

9:10–28. Solomon builds supply cities and chariot cities for military purposes and establishes a port for conducting trade with other nations (2 Chron. 8).

10:1–13. The Queen of Sheba visits Solomon and is impressed with his wisdom and great riches (2 Chron. 9:1–12).

10:14–29. Solomon's riches multiply as he develops trade relationships with other nations. Other rulers honor him for his wisdom and power (2 Chron. 9:13–28).

11:1–8. Solomon's dozens of foreign wives, many of whom he married to seal political alliances, cause him to turn from the Lord and worship pagan gods.

11:9–13. God declares that He will divide Solomon's kingdom because of his sin of idolatry. But He will allow one tribe to remain under the kingship of Solomon's son and successor because of His promise of an eternal kingship to Solomon's father, David (2 Sam. 7:1–17).

11:14–25. Several Israelite leaders oppose Solomon's kingship. These include Hadad and Rezon.

11:26–40. The most serious threat to Solomon arises from within his own administration. Jeroboam, one of Solomon's officials, rebels against the king. The prophet Ahijah promises Jeroboam that Solomon's kingdom will be split into two factions. The northern tribes will unite under Jeroboam against Solomon. The southern tribe of Judah will remain loyal to the dynasty of David and will be ruled by Solomon's son.

11:41–43. Solomon dies and is succeeded by his son Rehoboam (2 Chron. 9:29–31).

12:1–15. Rehoboam disregards the complaints of the northern tribes under Jeroboam and vows to intensify the harsh practices of his father, Solomon (2 Chron. 10:1–15).

12:16–24. The northern tribes revolt against Rehoboam and acclaim Jeroboam as their king. For the next several centuries of Israel's history, two opposing nations of the Jewish people exist—the northern tribes known as the nation of Israel (or the Northern Kingdom) and the southern tribes known as the nation of Judah (or the Southern Kingdom). God's promise of an eternal kingship through David and his descendants continues through the Southern Kingdom (2 Chron. 10:16–19).

12:25–33. King Jeroboam of Israel (Northern Kingdom) sets up sanctuaries for worship at the cities of Bethel and Dan in his territory. He wants to remove the temptation for the people of his kingdom to return to the temple at Jerusalem in Judah (Southern Kingdom) to worship God and offer sacrifices (2 Chron. 11:14–17).

13:1–10. God sends a prophet from Judah to King Jeroboam of Israel. This prophet delivers the prediction that Josiah, a descendant

[14:1–18] FOOD FOR A JOURNEY. *Take with thee [King Jeroboam's wife] ten loaves, and cracknels [cakes, NIV], and a cruse of honey, and go to him [the prophet Ahijah]* (1 Kings 14:3).

When King Jeroboam's son became sick, he sent his wife to ask the prophet Ahijah whether his son would get well. The journey to Ahijah's house must have been long, since the king's wife carried enough food for several days.

Cracknels were bread that had been baked into thin, hard biscuits. They probably held up better under traveling conditions than soft-baked bread.

of King David, will burn the bones of Jeroboam's priests upon the altar at Bethel at a distant future time.

13:11–32. The prophet who delivers this message to King Jeroboam is killed by a lion after he disobeys God's commands to return immediately to Judah.

13:33–34. King Jeroboam continues his practice of using unauthorized and unqualified persons as priests in the sanctuaries he has established in the Northern Kingdom.

14:1–18. A prophet at Bethel predicts that King Jeroboam's ill son will die and that Jeroboam will be punished for his sin and idolatry.

14:19–20. Jeroboam dies after reigning over Israel for twenty-two years and is succeeded by his son Nadab.

14:21–31. Rehoboam dies after serving as king of Judah for seventeen years and is succeeded by his son Abijam/Abijah (2 Chron. 12:13–16).

15:1–8. Abijam/Abijah dies after reigning over Judah for three years and is succeeded by his son Asa (2 Chron. 13:21–14:2).

15:9–24. King Asa pleases the Lord while ruling Judah. He removes the idols and pagan shrines that had been established in the land. After reigning for forty-one years, Asa dies and is succeeded by his son Jehoshaphat (2 Chron. 15; 16:13–17:1).

15:25–31. King Nadab of Israel is assassinated and succeeded by Baasha after a reign of only two years.

15:32–16:7. The prophet Jehu predicts that the dynasty of King Baasha of Israel will end. Baasha dies and is succeeded by his son Elah.

16:8–14. Elah is assassinated and succeeded as king of Israel by Zimri, one of his chariot commanders. Zimri also murders all the relatives of Baasha and Elah to end the royal dynasty of Baasha, as the prophet Jehu had predicted (1 Kings 16:1–7).

16:15–20. Zimri commits suicide after he

[18:20–40] A GOD WHO HEARS AND ACTS. *Elijah mocked them [the prophets of Baal], and said, Cry aloud: for he [Baal] is a god; either he is talking, or he is pursuing, or he is in a journey, or peradventure he sleepeth, and must be awaked* (1 Kings 18:27).

The prophet Elijah challenged the prophets of the pagan god Baal to a contest on Mount Carmel. They laid a sacrificial animal on a pile of wood. The prophets of Baal would call on their god, and Elijah would call on his. The god who answered by sending fire to consume the sacrifice would be declared the superior god (1 Kings 18:22–25).

Elijah ridiculed Baal because he did not answer the cry of his priests, even though they called to him for several hours. Perhaps he was silent, Elijah suggested, because he was preoccupied with other matters, was away on a journey, or was taking a nap.

When Elijah called on the Lord, fire fell immediately from heaven and consumed the sacrificial animal on the altar (1 Kings 18:38). This proved that God heard the prayers of His people and was superior to Baal.

18:20–40. Part of the Mount Carmel range, this lone hill overlooks the Jezreel Valley, also known as the Valley of Armageddon. On one of Carmel's hilltops, the prophet Elijah called down fire from heaven, winning a spiritual battle over 850 of Queen Jezebel's prophets.

realizes his forces face defeat at the hands of Omri. He is succeeded as king of Israel by Omri.

16:21–30. Omri builds Samaria and makes it the capital city of Israel. After an evil reign of twelve years, he dies and is succeeded by his son Ahab.

16:31–34. Ahab marries Jezebel, a worshiper of the pagan god Baal, and sets up a shrine to Baal in the capital city of Samaria.

17:1. The prophet Elijah predicts that a drought will strike Israel as punishment for Ahab's sins.

17:2–7. Elijah is kept alive by ravens as he hides from Ahab beside the brook Cherith.

17:8–16. During the drought, Elijah and a widow and her son are kept alive miraculously by the Lord through a small amount of meal and oil that never runs out.

17:17–24. The son of the widow dies, and

Elijah restores him miraculously to life.

18:1–14. God commands Elijah to meet King Ahab. The Lord assures Elijah that He will end the drought by sending rain. Elijah sends word through one of Ahab's servants that he wants to meet with the king.

18:15–19. Elijah talks with King Ahab and asks him to send the prophets of Baal to meet him on Mount Carmel.

18:20–40. Elijah prevails over the prophets of Baal in a dramatic encounter on Mount Carmel. The Lord sends a miraculous sign to show His superiority over all pagan gods. Elijah kills the prophets of Baal at the brook Kishon.

18:41–46. God ends the drought by sending rain in response to the prayer of Elijah (1 Kings 17:1).

19:1–18. Elijah flees to Mount Horeb to escape Jezebel's threat against his life. God directs him to return to Israel to anoint new kings for Syria and Israel and to select the prophet Elisha as his successor. The Lord assures Elijah in a still, small voice that many people in Israel remain faithful to Him.

19:19–21. Elisha follows Elijah after he is selected as the prophet's successor.

20:1–12. King Ben-hadad of Syria prepares to attack the forces of King Ahab of Israel at the capital city of Samaria.

20:13–21. Although outnumbered, Ahab's army defeats Ben-hadad because of the Lord's miraculous intervention.

20:22–34. Ahab defeats Ben-hadad a second time and spares his life.

20:35–43. A prophet of the Lord condemns King Ahab for not killing Ben-hadad when he had the opportunity.

21:1–4. Naboth refuses to sell his land with a vineyard to King Ahab.

[21:1–4] NO SALE. *Naboth said to Ahab, The Lord forbid it me, that I should give the inheritance of my fathers unto thee* (1 Kings 21:3).

Naboth's refusal to sell his land in which his vineyard grew shows the dedication of the Israelites to the land they had inherited from their ancestors. By law, Israelites were not to sell their land inheritance, except in cases of extreme poverty or financial hardship (Lev. 25:23, 25; Num. 36:7).

King Ahab eventually brought false charges against Naboth, had him killed, and took his land (1 Kings 21:7–13). The Lord sent the prophet Elijah to condemn these brazen acts and to tell the king that he would pay for these crimes with his life (1 Kings 21:17–22).

21:5–16. Jezebel and Ahab have Naboth executed on a false charge so they can take over his property.

21:17–29. The prophet Elijah announces to King Ahab that he and Jezebel will be killed and that dogs will lick up his blood and ravage Jezebel's corpse. This will be the Lord's punishment for their crime against Naboth and their encouragement of idol worship throughout Israel.

22:1–4. The kings of Israel (Ahab) and Judah (Jehoshaphat) propose a joint campaign against the Syrians to capture the city of Ramoth-gilead (2 Chron. 18:1–3).

22:5–12. Several false prophets assure King Ahab of a great victory if he and Jehoshaphat attack the Syrian forces (2 Chron. 18:4–11).

22:13–28. Micaiah, a true prophet of the Lord, announces that Ahab will be defeated if he goes against the Syrians (2 Chron. 18:12–27).

22:29–40. King Ahab is killed in the battle at Ramoth-gilead. Dogs lick up his blood when it is washed from his chariot, in fulfillment of the prediction of the prophet Elijah (1 Kings 21:19; 2 Chron. 18:28–34).

22:41–50. After twenty-five years as king of Judah, Jehoshaphat dies and is succeeded by his son Jehoram/Joram (2 Chron. 20:31–21:1).

22:51–53. Ahaziah succeeds his father, Ahab, as king of Israel and continues his evil and sinful policies.

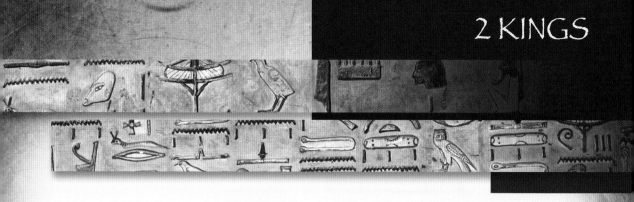

OVERVIEW: Elisha succeeds the prophet Elijah. Israel falls to Assyria, and Judah falls to the Babylonians.

Introduction to 2 Kings

The book of 2 Kings picks up where 1 Kings leaves off, continuing the account of the reigns of various kings of Judah and Israel. The same unknown author who wrote 1 Kings also wrote this book (see the introduction to 1 Kings on p. 424). Second Kings covers a period of about 260 years in the histories of these two nations.

Israel, the breakaway nation of the northern territory, began its history with questionable worship practices instituted by King Jeroboam. This pattern continued under most of the successive kings, with some encouraging and even lending state support to worship of pagan gods. God's punishment fell upon Israel in 722 B.C., when the Assyrians overran the nation and carried away many of its citizens as captives and slaves (17:5–23).

One bright spot in the nation of Israel was the prophet Elisha, who succeeded Elijah as God's spokesman to the kings of the North. He worked many miracles among the people and was an influential force for righteousness. But not even this stalwart prophet could turn Israel from its rush toward destruction.

The kings of Judah, since they were descendants of the great King David, were generally a better lot than the kings of Israel. Several kings of Judah, including Hezekiah (chaps. 18–20) and Josiah (22:1–23:30), led reform movements to purge idolatry from the land and turn the people back to worship of the one true God.

But Judah also had its share of evil kings. Two of the worst were Ahaz, who practiced child sacrifice (2 Chron. 28:1–4), and Manasseh, who built altars for pagan worship and participated in black magic and witchcraft (21:1–9). About 135 years after Israel fell to a foreign power, God sent the same punishment upon Judah. The leading citizens of the nation were carried into exile when Jerusalem fell to the Babylonians in 587 B.C.

The book of 2 Kings ends with Jerusalem in shambles and the beautiful temple destroyed and looted by a pagan army (25:8–21)—a far cry from the glory days of David and Solomon. Perhaps the writer of Proverbs had this situation in mind when he declared, "Righteousness exalteth a nation: but sin is a reproach to any people" (Prov. 14:34).

Many of the events described in 2 Kings are also recorded in the book of 2 Chronicles. These events are cross-referenced to 2 Chronicles in the summary of 2 Kings below.

Summary of 2 Kings

1:1–18. Ahaziah, son and sucessor of Ahab as king of Israel, dies after suffering injuries in an accident. Since he has no son, he is succeeded by his brother Jehoram, another son of Ahab.

2:1–11. Elisha asks that a double portion of Elijah's spirit be given to him as Elijah's successor. Elijah is taken into heaven by a whirlwind.

[2:1–11] SONS OF THE PROPHETS. *And the sons of the prophets that were at Bethel came forth to Elisha* (2 Kings 2:3).

These "sons of the prophets" knew that Elisha had been chosen as Elijah's successor, so they came out to see the two prophets together when Elijah and Elisha approached the city of Bethel.

Several different groups of "sons of the prophets" are mentioned in the book of 2 Kings (2:5, 7; 4:38, 43; 6:1–2). They were apparently disciples or followers of prophets such as Elijah and Elisha who assisted the prophets in their work and learned from their example and instruction.

A "company of prophets" is also mentioned in connection witht the ministry of the prophet Samuel (1 Sam. 19:19–20). Samuel may have been the founder of this prophetic guild.

2:12–18. Elisha is recognized by the sons of the prophets as Elijah's legitimate successor, with the Spirit of the Lord that filled Elijah.

2:19–22. Elisha miraculously purifies the bad waters of a spring at Jericho.

2:23–25. Elisha curses several children who were mocking and taunting him as God's prophet; they are attacked by two bears.

3:1–3. Ahab's son Jehoram becomes king of Is-rael and continues his father's evil practices.

3:4–20. Elisha predicts that the combined forces of Israel, Judah, and Edom will be victorious over the Moabites.

3:21–27. As Elisha predicts, the Moabites are defeated.

4:1–7. Elisha works a miracle for a poor widow whose sons are about to be sold into slavery. A jar of oil is multiplied until she has enough to pay her debts.

4:8–37. Elisha brings back to life the only son of a woman at Shunem who had provided food and lodging for the prophet.

4:38–44. Elisha miraculously purifies and mul-tiplies a meager supply of food to feed a large group of the sons of the prophets.

5:1–14. Naaman, commander of the Syrian army, is miraculously cured of his leprosy by the prophet Elisha (Luke 4:27).

5:15–27. Elisha refuses to accept the gifts of thanks offered by Naaman. But his servant Gehazi follows Naaman and claims the gifts. As punishment, Elisha declares that the leprosy that afflicted Naaman will fall on Gehazi.

6:1–7. Elisha miraculously causes an ax head to float so it can be retrieved from the Jor-dan River.

6:8–23. Elisha is miraculously delivered from a company of Syrian soldiers when the Lord strikes them blind.

6:24–7:20. The Syrians besiege Israel's capital

[8:7–15] SHOWING OFF WITH GIFTS. *So Hazael went to meet him [Elisha], and took a present with him, even of every good thing of Damascus, forty camels' burden, and came and stood before him* (2 Kings 8:9).

Hazael was a servant of Ben-hadad, king of Syria. When the prophet Elisha visited Damascus, Ben-hadad sent Hazael to meet him with royal gifts. Since the king was sick, he may have been trying to get Elisha to exercise his healing powers on his behalf.

In Old Testament times, even small gifts were often accompanied by great pomp and ceremony. The forty camels that greeted Elisha were probably not loaded down with all they could carry. Each camel may have carried only a small part of the total gift. The king wanted to impress Elisha with an extravagant outward display.

city of Samaria, and the people begin to run out of food. But Elisha predicts that the city will be saved through a miracle. The Lord sends panic and confusion among the Syrian army; the city is delivered, just as Elisha predicted.

8:1–6. The king of Israel restores the property of the woman of Shunem who had befriended Elisha (2 Kings 4:8–37) because of the prophet's reputation and influence.

8:7–15. Hazael assassinates and succeeds Ben-hadad as king of Syria. Elisha predicts that Hazael will commit many cruel acts against the nation of Israel.

9:14–29. Israel's King Jehu—a warrior who led the coup that ended Ahab's dynasty—bows before the Assyrian King Shalmaneser III.

8:16–24. Jehoram/Joram succeeds his father, Jehoshaphat, as king of Judah. After a reign of eight years, Jehoram/Joram dies and is succeeded by his son Ahaziah.

8:25–29. The allied forces of Israel and Judah go to war against King Hazael of Syria. King Jehoram/Joram of Judah is wounded in a battle at Ramoth-gilead.

9:1–13. Elisha sends a prophet to Ramoth-gilead to anoint Jehu, a commander in Israel's army, as the new king of Israel. Jehu is directed to execute all claimants to the throne from the line of Ahab.

9:14–29. Jehu assassinates King Jehoram/Joram of Israel, the son of Ahab. Jehu also kills Jehoram's ally and friend, King Ahaziah of Judah (2 Chron. 22:2–9).

9:30–37. Jehu kills Jezebel, the wife of Ahab. Her body is eaten by dogs, in fulfillment of the prophecy of Elijah (1 Kings 21:17–29).

10:1–17. Jehu assassinates all the descendants of Ahab to end the royal dynasty of this wicked and idolatrous king. Jehu also murders several relatives of King Ahaziah of Judah because of their connection with Ahab.

10:18–28. Jehu kills the worshipers of Baal throughout Israel and destroys the images of this pagan god.

10:29–31. Jehu fails to abolish the golden calves that King Jeroboam of Israel had established at Bethel and Dan. God promises to extend Jehu's royal dynasty to the fourth generation because of his obedience of God's command to end the dynasty of Ahab.

10:32–36. King Hazael of Syria wins many victories in Israel. Jehu dies and is succeeded as king of Israel by his son Jehoahaz.

11:1–3. After King Ahaziah of Judah is killed by King Jehu of Israel (2 Kings 9:27–29), Ahaziah's mother, Athaliah, seizes the throne. She does so by murdering her own grandsons, who were legitimate claimants to the throne. Joash/Jehoash, one of Ahaziah's sons, is saved from Athaliah's massacre and hidden away in the temple for six years (2 Chron. 22:10–12).

11:4–21. When Joash/Jehoash is seven years old, he is brought out of hiding by Jehoiada the priest and acclaimed as the new king of Judah. Athaliah is deposed as queen and assassinated (2 Chron. 23).

[11:4–21] A ROYAL CORONATION. *He [Jehoiada] brought forth the king's son [Joash], and put the crown upon him, and gave him the testimony [presented him with a copy of the covenant, NIV]; and they [the people] made him king, and anointed him; and they clapped their hands, and said, God save the king (2 Kings 11:12).*

This verse gives us insight into a royal coronation ceremony in Old Testament times. After the royal crown was placed on Joash's head, the king was presented with a copy of God's law. This was to serve as his guide in governing the people. He was then formally anointed for his task by having oil poured on his head (1 Sam. 16:13).

A royal coronation must have been a public affair. The people showed their approval of Joash's coronation by clapping and shouting, "God save the king [Long live the king, NIV]."

12:1–16. Joash/Jehoash follows the Lord under the counsel of the priest Jehoiada. Joash/Jehoash authorizes a special offering to be taken among the people designated for making needed repairs to the temple (2 Chron. 24:1–14).

12:17–18. Joash/Jehoash pays tribute to King Hazel of Syria to keep him from invading Judah's capital city of Jerusalem.

12:19–21. Assassinated by his own servants, Joash/Jehoash is succeeded as king of Judah by his son Amaziah (2 Chron. 24:25–27).

13:1–9. In the Northern Kingdom (Israel), Jehoahaz succeeds his father, Jehu, as king. Israel is ravaged by the Syrians during Jehoahaz's administration. After a reign of seventeen years, Jehoahaz is succeeded by his son Joash.

13:10–13. The evil reign of Joash ends after sixteen years, and he is succeeded as king of Israel by his son Jeroboam II.

13:14–19. The prophet Elisha predicts from his deathbed that the Northern Kingdom will win several key battles against the Syrians.

13:20–21. After Elisha's death and burial, a dead man is revived when his body touches the prophet's bones.

13:22–24. After oppressing Israel for several years, King Hazael of Syria dies and is succeeded by his son Ben-hadad.

13:25. King Joash of Israel takes back from the Syrians the cities they had captured when his father, Jehoahaz, reigned in Israel. This fulfills Elisha's prophecy (2 Kings 13:14–19).

14:1–7. Amaziah defeats the Edomites during his reign as king of Judah.

14:8–14. The kingdoms of Judah and Israel go to war against each other. Israel's king, Joash, seizes gold and silver items from Judah's capital city, Jerusalem, and carries them to Israel's capital, Samaria (2 Chron. 25:17–24).

14:15–22. King Joash of Israel dies; King Amaziah of Judah dies.

14:23–29. Jeroboam II succeeds his father, Joash, as king of Israel (2 Kings 13:10–13). His evil reign displeases the Lord.

15:1–7. Azariah/Uzziah succeeds his father, Amaziah, as king of Judah. Azariah/Uzziah dies and is succeeded by his son Jotham (2 Chron. 26:16–23).

15:8–12. Zachariah succeeds his father, Jeroboam II, as king of Israel. Zachariah is assassinated and succeeded by Shallum after a brief reign. This fulfills God's promise to Jehu that his royal dynasty would extend to the fourth generation (2 Kings 10:29–31).

15:13–16. After a reign of only one month, Shallum is assassinated and succeeded by Menahem as king of Israel.

15:17–22. During his reign as king of Israel, Menahem is forced to pay tribute to King Pul (Tiglath-pileser) of Assyria. Menahem dies and is succeeded by his son Pekahiah.

15:23–26. After a reign of two years, Pekahiah is assassinated and succeeded as king of Israel by Pekah, a commander in Pekahiah's army.

15:27–31. During Pekahiah's reign over Israel, King Tiglath-pileser of Assyria invades his territory and enslaves some of his subjects. Pekah is assassinated and succeeded by Hoshea as king of Israel.

15:32–38. Azariah's/Uzziah's son Jotham becomes king of Judah (2 Kings 15:1–7). Jotham dies and is succeeded by his son Ahaz.

16:1–4. King Ahaz encourages worship of false gods thoughout Judah, even committing the abominable practice of child sacrifice to pagan gods (2 Chron. 28:1–4).

16:5–9. Ahaz pays tribute to the Assyrian king, Piglath-pileser, who rescues Ahaz from his enemies.

16:10–18. Ahaz offers sacrifices on the altar of a pagan god and dismantles the altar in the temple devoted to worship of the one true God.

16:19–20. Ahaz dies and is succeeded as king of Judah by his son Hezekiah (2 Chron. 28:26–27).

17:1–4. Ahaz's son Hoshea reigns over Israel as a puppet king under the thumb of King Shalmaneser of Assyria. Hoshea is imprisoned by Shalmaneser after he quits paying tribute to Assyria and tries to form an aliance with Egypt to resist the Assyrian threat.

17:5–6. Assyria defeats Israel and carries away many of its citizens as captives to several Assyrian cities.

17:7–23. The end of Israel as a separate kingdom is attributed to the people's sin and rebellion against God and their worship of false gods.

17:24–41. Assyria settles people from pagan lands in the territory previously occupied by the citizens of Israel. The Israelites left in the land eventually adopt the pagan worship practices of these foreigners.

18:1–12. Hezekiah becomes king of Judah. Unlike his father, Ahaz (2 Kings 16:10–18), Hezekiah follows the Lord, tears down pagan altars, and leads the people to worship the Lord. At first, Hezekiah is able to resist the threat to his kingdom from Assyria.

18:13–37. Sennacherib, king of Assyria, captures several fortified cities of Judah. He stations his army outside Jerusalem and threatens to attack the city with a prolonged siege unless Hezekiah surrenders (2 Chron. 32:1–19).

19:1–7. King Hezekiah sends word about Judah's plight to the prophet Isaiah, who assures the king that God will deal with this threat from Assyria.

19:8–19. King Hezekiah receives a written threat from the Assyrian forces; he prays earnestly to the Lord for Judah's deliverance.

19:20–37. The prophet Isaiah assures King Hezekiah again of the Lord's protection. A mysterious plague strikes the Assyrian army, wiping out 185,000 warriors. Sennacherib returns to Assyria without attacking Jerusalem (2 Chron. 32:20–23; Isa. 37).

18:13–37. Confirming the Bible story that the Assyrian king Sennacherib never captured Jerusalem, his own record says only that he surrounded the city and trapped King Hezekiah inside.

20:1–11. King Hezekiah falls seriously ill and prays fervently to the Lord. The prophet Isaiah assures him that he will recover and live to reign as king of Judah for fifteen more years (Isa. 38). To confirm His promise of miraculous healing to the king, the Lord moves a sundial backwards by ten degrees (2 Chron. 32:24–26).

20:12–19. The prophet Isaiah reprimands King Hezekiah for showing his vast treasures of gold and silver to envoys from Babylonia. Isaiah predicts that these treasures will be captured and carried away someday by the Babylonians (2 Chron. 32:27–31).

20:20–21. King Hezekiah dies and is succeeded as king of Judah by his son Manasseh (2 Chron. 32:32–33).

21:1–9. As king of Judah for fifty-five years, Manasseh constructs altars for idol worship, performs child sacrifice to pagan gods, and participates in black magic and witchcraft. His long reign and acts of evil make him perhaps the worst king in the history of Judah (2 Chron. 33:1–10).

21:10–16. Because of Manasseh's wickedness and encouragement of pagan worship, God vows that He will punish the nation of Judah.

21:17–18. Manasseh dies and is succeeded as king of Judah by his son Amon (2 Chron. 33:20).

21:19–26. Amon continues the evil practices of his father, Manasseh. Amon is assassinated by his own servants after a reign of only two years and is succeeded by his son Josiah (2 Chron. 33:21–25).

22:1–7. As a faithful follower of the Lord, King Josiah authorizes repairs to the temple in Jerusalem (2 Chron. 34:8–13).

22:8–14. During the temple repairs, a copy of the book of the law (Genesis, Exodus, Leviticus, Numbers, and Deuteronomy) is discovered. Josiah realizes when this book is read that the people of Judah have wandered away from God's commands. He sends several priests to confer with a prophet to find out how God will deal with the sins of His people (2 Chron. 34:14–21).

22:15–20. Huldah the prophetess declares that the Lord will deal kindly with Josiah because of his determination to follow His will. But God will punish the nation of Judah for its waywardness and rebellion (2 Chron. 34:22–28).

23:1–3. King Josiah calls the leaders of Judah together to renew the covenant with the Lord (2 Chron. 34:29–33).

23:4–27. King Josiah launches a religious reform movement throughout Judah. He tears down pagan altars, destroys images of idols, puts to death pagan priests who were leading people astray, and reinstates observation of the Passover—a festival celebrating their deliverance from slavery in Egypt.

23:28–30. Killed in a battle with the Egyptians, Josiah is succeeded as king of Judah by his son Jehoahaz (2 Chron. 35:20–36:1).

23:31–37. After a reign of only three months, King Jehoahaz is captured and imprisoned by the Egyptians. The Egyptians put Eliakim, another son of Josiah, on the throne as a puppet king and demand that he pay tribute to the Egyptian government. The Egyptians also give Eliakim another name, Jehoiakim (2 Chron. 36:2–4).

24:1–7. During the reign of Eliakim/Jehoiakim, the Babylonians invade Judah. He dies and is succeeded by his son Jehoiachin.

24:8–19. King Nebuchadnezzar of Babylonia invades and subdues the nation of Judah. He takes King Jehoiachin and his royal household as well as all the key leaders of Judah to Babylon as captives. Nebuchadnezzar also places Mattaniah on the throne of Judah as a puppet king and renames him Zedekiah (2 Chron. 36:9–10).

24:20–25:7. Mattaniah/Zedekiah rebels against Babylonia. Nebuchadnezzar invades Jerusalem and takes the king to Babylon as a prisoner after forcing him to watch the murder of his sons.

[24:20–25:7] BLINDING OF PRISONERS. *They [the Babylonian army] slew the sons of Zedekiah before his eyes, and put out the eyes of Zedekiah, and bound him with fetters of brass [bronze shackles, NIV], and carried him to Babylon* (2 Kings 25:7).

Zedekiah was serving as king of Judah when the nation fell to the Babylonians in 587 B.C. The last thing he saw before being blinded by his captors was the death of his sons.

The blinding of prisoners was a cruel punishment often meted out by the Babylonians, Assyrians, and Persians. This was done by searing the pupils with a hot copper plate or by thrusting a sword or dagger into the eyes.

Samson was also blinded when he was captured by the Philistines (Judg. 16:21).

25:8–21. Nebuchadnezzar ransacks the city of Jerusalem, breaking down the city wall, burning the temple and other buildings, and carrying away gold and silver from the temple furnishings. Key leaders of Judah are murdered or enslaved and taken to Babylon, while peasants and farmers of Judah are left behind to cultivate the land.

25:22–26. A remnant of the citizens of Judah flees to Egypt after murdering Gedaliah, an official whom Nebuchadnezzar had appointed governor of Judah.

25:27–30. In Babylonia, Nebuchadnezzar is succeeded as king by his son Evil-merodach. The new king releases King Jehoiachin of Judah from prison and gives him a place of honor and privilege in the Babylonian court.

1 CHRONICLES

OVERVIEW: A chronicle of the reign of David as king of Israel. This book covers many of the same events as 2 Samuel.

Introduction to 1 Chronicles

The book of 1 Chronicles focuses on the reign of David as king of Israel. Many of the events in David's life covered in 2 Samuel are also included in 1 Chronicles. Why do two books of the Old Testament cover essentially the same territory?

Perhaps the best answer is that the author of 1 Chronicles wrote with a distinct purpose in mind. Many scholars believe it was written by Ezra the priest after the Jewish people returned to Jerusalem following their period of exile among the Babylonians and Persians. This was a time of great discouragement and disillusionment among God's people. Ezra wanted to give them hope by showing that God was with them. His promise that a descendant of David would always rule over His people (2 Sam. 7:1–17) had not been forgotten.

The books of 1 and 2 Chronicles were written originally as one unbroken book. Thus, Ezra began Chronicles with nine chapters of genealogical material that traced God's people all the way back to Adam. He ended Chronicles with the Jewish people returning from the Exile (2 Chron. 36:21–23). This "review of history" technique was a reminder that God had blessed His people in the past. He would continue to do so as they began to rebuild their lives back in their homeland.

First Chronicles does give us insights into David's character not found in 1 Samuel. For example, we learn that David organized the priests and Levites into several different groups and assigned them specific duties in the tabernacle (23:2–26:32). He gathered the materials for his son and successor, Solomon, to use in building the temple (28:9–29:19). David was more than a military king; he was also interested in honoring God through appropriate forms of worship.

Events from David's life in 1 Chronicles that also appear in 2 Samuel are cross-referenced to 2 Samuel in the summary below.

Summary of 1 Chronicles

1:1–4. Descendants of Adam up through Noah and his sons are listed.

1:5–7. Descendants of Noah's son Japheth are listed.

1:8–16. Descendants of Noah's son Ham are listed.

1:17–27. Descendants of Noah's son Shem up through Abraham are listed.

1:28–33. Descendants of Abraham's son Ishmael and other sons born to Abraham's concubine Keturah are listed.

1:34–54. Descendants of Abraham's son Isaac through Isaac's son Esau are listed.

2:1–2. The twelve sons of Isaac's son Jacob, or Israel, are listed.

2:3–15. Descendants of Jacob's son Judah up through King David are listed.

2:16–55. Other descendants of Judah are listed.

3:1–4. Sons of David born while he reigned at Hebron are listed.

3:5–9. Sons of David born while he reigned at Jerusalem are listed.

3:10–24. Descendants of David's son Solomon are listed.

4:1–23. Descendants of Jacob's son Judah are listed.

4:24–43. Descendants of Jacob's son Simeon are listed.

5:1–10. Descendants of Jacob's son Reuben are listed.

5:11–17. Descendants of Jacob's son Gad are listed.

5:18–26. A brief history is given of the tribes of Israel that settled on the eastern side of the Jordan River—Reuben, Gad, and one-half of the tribe of Manasseh (Josh. 22:1–9).

6:1–30. Descendants of Jacob's son Levi are listed. The Levites assisted the priests with sacrificial duties at the tabernacle and the temple.

6:31–48. Levites who assisted with the song service after David moved the ark of the covenant to Jerusalem are listed.

6:49–53. The son and successors of Aaron as priests of Israel are listed.

6:54–81. The cities assigned to the Levites throughout the territory of Israel are listed (Josh. 21:1–45).

7:1–5. Descendants of Jacob's son Issachar are listed.

7:6–12. Descendants of Jacob's son Benjamin are listed.

7:13. Descendants of Jacob's son Naphtali are listed.

7:14–19. Descendants of Jacob's grandson Manasseh are listed.

7:20–29. Descendants of Jacob's grandson Ephraim are listed.

7:30–40. Descendants of Jacob's son Asher are listed.

8:1–40. Descendants of Jacob's son Benjamin are listed. (This is a more detailed list than that given in 1 Chron. 7:6–12.)

9:1–9. Various Jewish leaders who lived in Jerusalem are listed.

9:10–34. Various priests and Levites who ministered in Jerusalem are listed.

9:35–44. Ancestors and descendants of Saul, the first king of Israel, are listed.

10:1–14. King Saul and his sons are killed in a battle against the Philistines on Mount Gilboa (1 Sam. 31:1–13).

> **[10:1–14] GOD KNOWS THE NEWS.** *They [Philistines] took his [Saul's] head, and his armour, and sent into the land of the Philistines round about, to carry tidings unto their idols* (1 Chron. 10:9).
>
> When the Philistines defeated King Saul and his army, they notified their fellow citizens to carry news about their victory to their pagan gods. This shows the weakness of idols and the superiority of the one true God, who sees all and knows all: "The eyes of the LORD are in every place, beholding the evil and the good" (Prov. 15:3).

11:1–3. David is acclaimed king over all Israel by all the tribes (2 Sam. 5:1–5).

11:4–9. David captures the fortified city of Jebus from the Jebusites. Later it becomes his capital city and is known as Jerusalem (2 Sam. 5:6–10).

11:10–47. The brave commanders and warriors among David's "mighty men" are listed (2 Sam. 23:8–39).

12:1–40. Warriors who joined David's forces while he was hiding from King Saul at Ziklag are listed.

13:1–14. David moves the ark of the covenant from the home of Abinadab to a temporary resting place at the house of Obed-edom. Uzza/Uzzah is killed when he reaches out to steady the ark and accidentally touches it (2 Sam. 6:1–11).

14:1–2. King Hiram of Tyre provides materials and workmen to build a house for David (2 Sam. 5:11–12).

14:3–7. Thirteen children are born to David at Jerusalem (2 Sam. 5:13–16; 1 Chron. 3:5–9).

14:8–17. David defeats the Philistines in a major battle in the valley of Rephaim (2 Sam. 5:17–25).

15:1–29. David makes plans for a great celebration with music and dancing as the ark of the covenant is moved to Jerusalem from the house of Obed-edom. This time the ark is moved as God directed—by Levites carrying it on their shoulders on poles inserted into rings on the ark (2 Sam. 6:12–19).

16:1–6. David presents burnt offerings and peace offerings to the Lord before the ark in the tent he has prepared for its dwelling place.

16:7–36. David offers a prayer of praise and thanksgiving to God for His wonderful works on behalf of His people (2 Sam. 7:18–29).

16:37–43. David appoints a group of Levites to minister continuously before the ark, offering burnt offerings and other sacrifices to the Lord.

17:1–15. David makes plans to build a house, or temple, devoted to worship of God. Instead, the Lord promises that He will build David a house, or memorial. He promises that David's kingdom will be established forever—that his descendants will reign from generation to generation on the throne of Israel (2 Sam. 7:1–17).

17:16–27. In a prayer of humility and gratitude, David praises God for His love and goodness.

18:1–14. David expands his nation's territory and power by defeating the Philistines, Moabites, Syrians, Amalekites, and Edomites (2 Sam. 8:1–13).

[18:1–14] CRIPPLING WAR HORSES. *David also houghed [hamstrung, NIV] all the chariot horses (1 Chron. 18:4).*

David extended his kingdom as far north as Syria by defeating Hadarezer, king of Zobah. He weakened Hadarezer's ability to wage war by capturing his chariots and crippling his chariot horses, probably by cutting a muscle or tendon in their legs.

Since David did not take the horses as booty, he probably had little use for chariots and horses in his own army. Chariots would have been impractical in the rocky and hilly terrain of Palestine.

18:15–17. Selected officials in David's administration are listed (2 Sam. 8:14–18).

19:1–5. David sends messengers to the Ammonites on a peaceful mission, but they are rejected and humiliated.

19:6–19. David's army, under the command of Joab, defeats the combined forces of the Ammonites and the Syrians (2 Sam. 10).

20:1–3. David seals his victory over the Ammonites by capturing their capital city, Rabbah (2 Sam. 12:26–31).

20:4–8. David's warriors are victorious over several Philistine giants, relatives of the giant Goliath whom David killed (1 Sam. 17:46–51).

21:1–6. David orders Joab, commander of his army, to take a census of all the fighting men throughout the tribes of Israel (2 Sam. 24:1–9).

15:1–29. A pair of bronze cymbals and a jar painted with a man holding a lyre, preserved from King David's time. David was a gifted musician who played the lyre, wrote many songs, and organized the music ministry at the Jerusalem worship center.

21:7–17. God sends a plague on the nation because of David's sinful pride that led him to order the census (2 Sam. 24:10–15).

21:18–30. David buys a threshing floor from Ornan/Araunah the Jebusite as the site for an altar on which sacrifices will be offered to the Lord. The plague ends when sacrifices are offered (2 Sam. 24:16–25).

22:1–19. God refuses to allow David to build the temple in Jerusalem because he has been

[25:1–31] **MUSIC FOR WORSHIP.** *All these were the sons of Heman the king's seer in the words of God, to lift up the horn* (1 Chron. 25:5).

David organized the priests and Levites into several different groups to serve at the tabernacle on a rotating basis. The Levites descended from Heman were to provide music for worship—specifically to play the horn, or trumpet.

Other Levite musicians were assigned to play different instruments, including cymbals, psalteries [lyres, NIV], and harps (1 Chron. 25:6).

a warrior king. But David gathers material for the project and challenges Solomon, his son and successor, to complete the task.

23:1. Solomon will succeed his father, David, as king of Israel (1 Kings 1:32–40).

23:2–32. David organizes the Levites into several different groups and assigns them specific duties as officers and judges, musicians, doorkeepers, and assistants to the priests.

24:1–19. David organizes the priests into twenty-four different groups that will officiate at the altar on a rotating basis.

24:20–31. Several different leaders of the divisions of the Levites are listed.

25:1–31. The Levites responsible for worship music are organized into twenty-four different groups to serve on a rotating basis.

26:1–19. Levites who serve as porters (doorkeepers and gatekeepers) for the tabernacle and temple are listed.

26:20–32. The Levites listed in these verses are responsible for storing and caring for offerings and sacrifices devoted to support and upkeep of the tabernacle and the temple.

27:1–15. David's military force is divided into twelve units of 24,000 warriors each. These units apparently served for one-month assignments on a rotating basis during the year. The captains of the twelve units are listed by name.

27:16–24. Leaders of the tribes of Israel during David's administration are listed.

27:25–34. Counselors, advisers, chief officials, and keepers of the royal herds in David's administration are listed (2 Sam. 8:14–18; 1 Chron. 18:15–17).

28:1–8. David gathers the leaders of Israel and informs them that his son Solomon will be his successor. He challenges them to remain faithful to the Lord as leaders of Israel.

28:9–21. David encourages his son Solomon to build the temple in Jerusalem, using the materials and funds that David has collected.

29:1–9. Encouraged by David, the leaders of Israel contribute additional gold and silver to pay for the temple's construction.

29:10–19. David offers a prayer of thanksgiving to God. He pledges all the money and supplies to construction of a temple that will bring glory and honor to the Lord.

29:20–25. The leaders of Israel offer sacrifices to God and acclaim Solomon as the new king of Israel.

29:26–30. David dies after forty years as king—seven years as king of the southern tribe of Judah and thirty-three years as king over all the tribes of Israel (1 Kings 2:10–12).

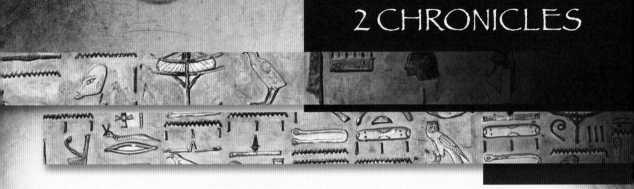

OVERVIEW: A chronicle of the reign of Solomon as king of Israel and division of the united kingdom into two nations. This book covers many of the same events as 1 and 2 Kings.

Introduction to 2 Chronicles

The book of 2 Chronicles picks up where 1 Chronicles ends—with Solomon's succession to the kingship following the death of his father, David, about 970 B.C. This book covers essentially the same period as the books of 1 and 2 Kings and repeats many of the events from these two books (see introductions to 1 and 2 Kings on pp. 424 and 431).

Ezra the priest was the author of both 1 and 2 Chronicles. His purpose for writing the books was to give hope to the Jewish people who were given permission to return to their homeland following the Exile (36:21–23; see the introduction to 1 Chronicles on p. 438).

One of the major differences between 2 Chronicles and the books of 1 and 2 Kings is that little attention is given to the kings of Israel (Northern Kingdom) in 2 Chronicles. This probably indicates that Ezra was concerned only with tracing the line of David and showing that Judah (Southern Kingdom) was the nation that remained loyal to the Lord.

Once the former residents of Judah were resettled in their homeland, Ezra may have been hinting that they needed to rebuild the temple. It was important to reestablish the traditions that proved they were the true worshipers of God.

Another striking difference between 2 Chronicles and 1 and 2 Kings is the role of the prophets Elijah and Elisha. They are prominent spokesmen for the Lord in 1 and 2 Kings, but Elijah is mentioned in only one verse in all of 2 Chronicles (21:12), and Elisha is not mentioned at all. This is explained by the fact that Ezra focused on Judah in 2 Chronicles, and Elijah and Elisha directed their prophecies against the kings of Israel.

Events from 2 Chronicles that also appear in 1 and 2 Kings are cross-referenced to these two books in the summary of 2 Chronicles below.

Summary of 2 Chronicles

1:1–13. As the new king of Israel, Solomon offers sacrifices to the Lord on an altar at Gibeon. He asks God for great wisdom in order to be a good leader. The Lord promises to honor this request and to give him riches and honor as well (1 Kings 3:3–15).

1:14–17. The symbols of Solomon's wealth include his chariots, chariot cities, gold and silver, and horses.

2:1–18. Solomon prepares to build the temple by securing cedar timber from King Hiram/Huram of Tyre (1 Kings 5). Hiram/Huram also provides skilled craftsmen for the project. Solomon presses into service thousands of non-Israelites who are living in his territory to serve as construction workers.

3:1–17. The huge, ornate temple compound built by Solomon is described (1 Kings 6).

[8:1–18] WALLED CITIES. *Also he [King Solomon] built Beth-horon the upper [Upper Beth Horon, NIV], and Beth-horon the nether [Lower Beth Horon, NIV], fenced cities, with walls, gates, and bars* (2 Chron. 8:5).

Cities of Bible times—like the twin cities of Upper and Lower Beth Horon—were surrounded by massive stone walls. Some of these structures were more than thirty feet high and ten to twelve feet thick. Residents of the city would retreat behind these walls when under attack by an enemy.

The attacking army would either scale the wall by using ladders or try to break down the city gate. The gate was made of heavy timbers, reinforced with iron. When closed, the gate would be secured by sliding heavy timbers or iron bars across its surface from the inside.

When in full lock-down mode, a heavily fortified or "fenced" city was an effective defense against an army of superior numbers. Often the besieging force would camp around the city for months and starve its citizens into submission.

4:1–22. The furnishings of the temple include the central altar, a huge water basin ("molten sea," v. 2), smaller basins, tables, candlesticks, and utensils used by the priests to handle sacrifices (1 Kings 7:23–51).

5:1–6:42. In an elaborate dedication ceremony, the ark of the covenant is placed in the completed temple. God's glory fills the temple in the form of a cloud. Solomon blesses the people gathered for the ceremony and praises God for His provision for His people. He prays that Israel will always remain faithful to the one true God (1 Kings 8:12–66).

7:1–3. Fire from heaven consumes a sacrifice that had been placed on the altar of the temple.

7:4–11. Additional sacrifices to the Lord are placed on the altar of the temple. This ceremony of thanksgiving continues for eight days.

7:12–22. The Lord renews with Solomon the covenant He had made with his father, David. Solomon's kingship over Israel will be eternal if he follows the Lord. But if Solomon does not obey God's commands, God will reject him and bring catastrophe upon the land (1 Kings 9:1–9).

8:1–18. Solomon builds storage cities and fortifies and equips other cities as defense outposts. He also establishes a port from which international trade is conducted (1 Kings 9:10–28).

9:1–12. Solomon receives a royal visitor, the Queen of Sheba, and impresses her with his wealth and wisdom (1 Kings 10:1–13).

9:13–28. Solomon multiplies his riches through international trade. He is honored by other nations for his power and wisdom (1 Kings 10:14–29).

9:29–31. Solomon dies after reigning for forty years and is succeeded as king by his son Rehoboam (1 Kings 11:41–43).

10:1–15. Rehoboam ignores the complaints of Jeroboam and the northern tribes about the harsh and oppressive practices of King Solomon. Rehoboam tells them he plans to multiply their misery (1 Kings 12:1–15).

10:16–19. The northern tribes revolt against Rehoboam and acclaim Jeroboam as their king. For the next several centuries of Israel's history, two opposing nations of the Jewish people exist—the northern tribes, known as the nation of Israel (or the Northern Kingdom), and the southern tribes, known as the nation of Judah (or the Southern Kingdom). God's promise of an eternal kingship through David and his descendants continues through the

Southern Kingdom (1 Kings 12:16–24).

11:1–4. God speaks through a prophet to prevent Rehoboam from going to war against the Northern Kingdom.

11:5–13. King Rehoboam fortifies cities as defense outposts in the Southern Kingdom.

11:14–17. Many priests and Levites in the Northern Kingdom move to the Southern Kingdom to be near the central place of worship at the temple in Jerusalem. King Jeroboam sets up rival sanctuaries for worship and appoints his own priests (1 Kings 12:25–33).

11:18–23. The wives and children of King Rehoboam of Judah are listed.

12:1–12. To punish King Rehoboam for his unfaithfulness, God allows Shishak of Egypt to invade Judah and carry away the royal treasures.

12:13–16. After reigning for seventeen years, King Rehoboam of Judah dies and is succeeded by his son Abijah/Abijam (1 Kings 14:21–31).

[16:13–17:1] WAS KING ASA CREMATED? *They [Israelites]...laid him [King Asa] in the bed [bier, NIV] which was filled with sweet odours and divers kinds of spices prepared by the apothecaries' art: and they made a very great burning for him [made a huge fire in his honor, NIV]* (2 Chron. 16:14).

Was the body of King Asa of Judah cremated by being burned on a platform, or bier, sprinkled with spices? Some interpreters say yes; others say no.

Some believe the spices were first burned as an offering, then the king's body was laid in a coffin on top of the ashes from these spices. Others believe the king's body was actually burned along with the spices. This verse lends itself to either interpretation.

What is certain is that cremation was practiced on occasion among the Jews in Old Testament times. The bodies of King Saul and his sons were burned (1 Sam. 31:12). The prophets Jeremiah (Jer. 34:5) and Amos (Amos 6:10) also mentioned the practice of cremation.

13:1–20. King Abijah/Abijam of Judah defeats the forces of King Jeroboam of Israel and captures several towns in the Northern Kingdom.

13:21–14:1. Abijah/Abijam dies and is succeeded as king of Judah by his son Asa (1 Kings 15:1–8).

14:2–8. Asa is a good king who follows the Lord and removes pagan altars and idols from the territory of Judah.

8:1–18. Walled Jerusalem, painted in 1870. King Solomon used his wealth to fortify cities throughout Israel, adding walls and military facilities.

14:9–15. God gives Asa a decisive victory over King Zerah of Ethiopia.

15:1–19. A prophet encourages Asa to follow the Lord. Asa responds by implementing a religious reform movement throughout Judah, tearing down pagan altars, smashing idols, and leading the people to renew the covenant with God (1 Kings 15:9–24).

16:1–6. King Asa forms an alliance with the Syrian king Ben-hadad, who delivers Judah from oppression by the forces of King Baasha of Israel.

16:7–12. The prophet Hanani rebukes Asa because he relied on the military might of Syria for deliverance rather than the power of God.

16:13–17:1. Asa dies after reigning for forty-one years and is succeeded as king of Judah by his son Jehoshaphat (1 Kings 15:9–24).

17:2–5. King Jehoshaphat continues to follow the Lord as his father, Asa, had done. God rewards him for his faithfulness.

17:6–19. Jehoshaphat sends Levites throughout the land to teach God's law to the people. His kingdom thrives, and other nations pay tribute to him and honor his accomplishments.

18:1–3. King Jehoshaphat agrees to join an alliance with King Ahab of Israel against the Syrians (1 Kings 22:1–4).

18:4–11. False prophets who served as "yes men" for the king of Israel assure Ahab and Jehoshaphat that an attack against the Syrians will be successful (1 Kings 22:5–12).

18:12–27. Micaiah, a true prophet of the Lord, warns Ahab and Jehoshaphat that their campaign against Syria will fail (1 Kings 22:13–28).

22:10–12. A killer granny, Queen Athaliah is driven from the worship center and executed. She had seized the throne after assassinating her grandchildren—to eliminate all blood rivals. She missed one, though—and when the boy surfaced a few years later, he was declared the legitimate king and Athaliah was killed.

18:28–34. King Ahab of Israel is killed in the battle with the Syrians at Ramoth-gilead (1 Kings 22:29–40).

19:1–11. King Jehoshaphat implements additional religious reforms throughout the kingdom of Judah.

20:1–30. After Jehoshaphat and the people pray fervently to God, He gives them a great victory over the combined forces of the Moabites and the Ammonites.

20:31–21:1. Jehoshaphat dies after a twenty-five year reign as king of Judah and is succeeded by his son Jehoram/Joram (1 Kings 22:41–50).

21:2–7. On becoming king of Judah, Jehoram/Joram kills all his brothers to remove any challenge to his kingship. He fails to honor the Lord with his leadership.

21:8–10. The Edomites revolt against Judah and try to reestablish themselves as an independent kingdom.

21:11–22:1. As the prophet Elijah predicts, King Jehoram/Joram dies of a mysterious disease. His reign over Judah lasts for eight years. He is succeeded by his son Ahaziah.

22:2–9. Ahaziah's reign fails to please the Lord because of his connections with Ahab, the wicked king of Israel. When Jehu assassinates Ahab and becomes the new king of Israel, he also has Ahaziah executed (2 Kings 9:14–29).

22:10–12. Athaliah seizes the throne of Judah when her son Ahaziah is assassinated. She attempts to execute all claimants to the throne. But one of Ahaziah's sons, Joash/Jehoash, is hidden in the temple for six years (2 Kings 11:1–3).

23:1–21. Jehoiada the priest brings Joash/Jehoash out of hiding, and the people acclaim him as the new king of Judah. Athaliah is executed (2 Kings 11:4–21).

24:1–14. Joash/Jehoash follows the Lord as long as the priest Jehoiada is alive. Joash/Jehoash authorizes a special offering to be taken among the people and designates it for making needed repairs to the temple (2 Kings 12:1–16).

24:15–22. After the death of the priest Jehoiada, King Joash/Jehoash turns away from the Lord and encourages idol worship in the land. He even has Jehoiada's son killed because he condemned the king's waywardness and idolatry.

24:23–24. To punish Joash/Jehoash, the Lord allows the Syrians to defeat Judah and carry away the king's treasures.

24:25–27. Assassinated by his own servants, King Joash/Jehoash of Judah is succeeded by his son Amaziah (2 Kings 12:19–21).

25:1–16. At the beginning of his reign, Amaziah pleases the Lord. But he sins by setting up shrines for worship of pagan gods after defeating the Edomites (2 Kings 14:1–7).

25:17–24. King Jehoash of Israel invades the kingdom of Judah and carries away gold and silver from the temple in Jerusalem (2 Kings 14:8–14).

25:25–26:1. King Amaziah of Judah dies and is succeeded by his son Uzziah/Azariah (2 Kings 15:1–7).

26:2–5. Uzziah/Azariah is a good king who follows the Lord and reigns for fifty-two years in Judah.

26:6–15. Uzziah/Azariah strengthens the nation of Judah during his long reign by improving Jerusalem's defenses, developing a strong army, and subduing the Philistines and the Ammonites.

26:16–23. Uzziah/Azariah is struck with leprosy when he attempts to burn incense at the altar—a task reserved for priests only. After his death, he is succeeded by his son Jotham (2 Kings 15:1–7).

27:1–9. After reigning over Judah for sixteen

[26:6–15] UZZIAH'S WAR MACHINES. *He [King Uzziah] made in Jerusalem engines [machines, NIV], invented by cunning [skillful, NIV] men, to be on the towers and upon the bulwarks [corner defenses, NIV], to shoot arrows and great stones* (2 Chron. 26:15).

King Uzziah of Judah made Jerusalem's city wall defenses even more effective by increasing the firepower of the warriors on the wall. In the defense towers on top of the wall, he placed mechanical war machines that were capable of hurling huge stones and shooting arrows in bulk on the enemy below.

These "engines" were probably similar to the catapults used so effectively by the Roman army in later centuries.

years, Jotham dies and is succeeded by his son Ahaz.

28:1–4. Ahaz is an evil king who encourages idolatry throughout Judah. He even sacrifices his own children to a pagan god (2 Kings 16:1–4).

28:5–25. The Lord punishes Judah because of King Ahaz's abominable acts. The nation is pillaged by the Syrians, the Edomites, and the Philistines, as well as the nation of Israel (Northern Kingdom).

28:26–27. Ahaz dies and is succeeded as king of Judah by his son Hezekiah (2 Kings 16:19–20).

29:1–36. Hezekiah orders the priests to restore and purify the temple, since it had been desecrated during the reign of his father, Ahaz. Hezekiah leads the people to rededicate the temple and to resume the practice of bringing sacrifices and offerings to the altar.

30:1–27. Hezekiah leads the priests and the people to reinstate celebration of the Passover—a major religious festival that had not been observed in the land for many years.

31:1. The people destroy pagan altars and idols that had been set up throughout the land.

31:2–21. Hezekiah orders the people to bring firstfruits and other offerings to provide a livelihood for the priests and Levites. He directs that the surplus goods be stored for future use.

32:1–19. King Sennacherib of Assyria surrounds the city of Jerusalem. He taunts the God of Judah and orders Hezekiah to surrender (2 Kings 18:13–37).

32:20–23. Hezekiah and the prophet Isaiah pray earnestly to the Lord. Judah is delivered miraculously from the Assyrian forces (2 Kings 19:20–37).

32:24–26. King Hezekiah is struck by a serious illness, but he recovers when he prays to God in a spirit of humility (2 Kings 20:1–11).

32:27–31. God blesses Hezekiah, and his wealth increases. But the king commits a serious error when he displays his treasures to envoys from Babylonia (2 Kings 20:12–19).

32:32–33. King Hezekiah dies and is succeeded as king of Judah by his son Manasseh (2 Kings 20:20–21).

33:1–10. Manasseh reverses the religious reforms of his father, Hezekiah, and reinstates pagan worship throughout the land. He even participates in black magic and witchcraft and sacrifices some of his own children to pagan gods (2 Kings 21:1–9).

33:11–19. As punishment, God allows the Babylonians to capture Manasseh. He eventually continues his kingship under their jurisdiction. Manasseh tries to stem the tide of idol worship in Judah that he had started, but the people continue in their misguided ways.

33:20. Manasseh dies and is succeeded as king of Judah by his son Amon (2 Kings 21:17–18).

33:21–25. King Amon continues the evil practices of his father, Manasseh. Assassinated by his own servants after a brief reign, he

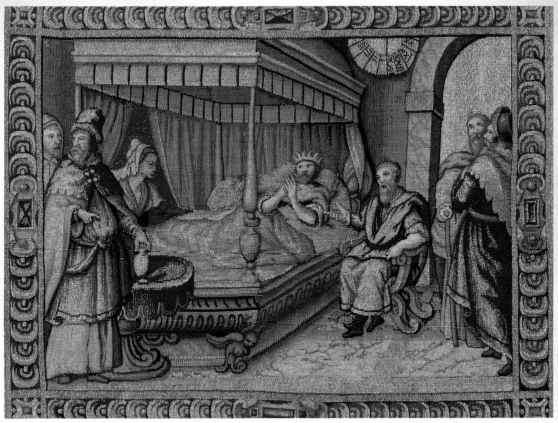

32:24–26. The prophet Isaiah has bad news for sick King Hezekiah. The king will die soon. But Hezekiah prays, and God extends his life for fifteen more years.

is succeeded by his son Josiah (2 Kings 21:19–26).

34:1–7. A good and godly king like his great-grandfather Hezekiah, Josiah tears down the pagan altars and images that had been placed throughout the land.

34:8–13. King Josiah orders that needed repairs be made to the temple in Jerusalem (2 Kings 22:1–7).

34:14–21. During the temple repairs, a copy of the book of the law (Genesis, Exodus, Leviticus, Numbers, and Deuteronomy) is discovered. Josiah realizes when this book is read that the people of Judah have wandered away from God's commands. He sends several priests to confer with a prophet to find out how God will deal with the sins of His rebellious people (2 Kings 22:8–14).

34:22–28. Huldah the prophetess declares that the Lord will deal kindly with Josiah because he has vowed to follow His will. But God will punish the nation of Judah for its sin and rebellion (2 Kings 22:15–20).

34:29–33. Josiah calls the elders of Judah and Jerusalem to meet at the temple to renew the covenant with the Lord (2 Kings 23:1–3).

35:1–19. King Josiah orders a nationwide observance of the Passover—a religious festival celebrating the deliverance of the Israelites from slavery in Egypt.

35:20–36:1. Josiah is killed in a battle with the Egyptians. Josiah's son Jehoahaz succeeds him as king of Judah (2 Kings 23:28–30).

[36:2–4] FROM ELIAKIM TO JEHOIAKIM. *The king of Egypt made Eliakim his [Jehoahaz's] brother king over Judah and Jerusalem, and turned [changed, NIV] his name to Jehoiakim (2 Chron. 36:4).*

Egypt siezed control of Judah, deposed King Jehoahaz, and installed Jehoahaz's brother Eliakim as king in his place. Then the Egyptian authorities changed the new king's name to Jehoiakim.

This renaming of the king sent a message to all the people that a new era in the life of their nation had begun—their subjection to Egypt. The power to change their king's name symbolized Egypt's supreme authority.

The nation of Judah was eventually overrun by the Babylonians. They carried away the leading citizens as captives, installed Mattaniah as a puppet king over what was left of the nation, and changed his name to Zedekiah (2 Kings 24:16–17).

36:2–4. Jehoahaz reigns only three months before he is captured by the Egyptians. They put Eliakim, another son of Josiah, on the throne as a puppet king and rename him Jehoiakim (2 Kings 23:31–37).

36:5–8. Judah is invaded by the Babylonian army under King Nebuchadnezzar during the reign of Eliakim/Jehoiakim. He is succeeded as king by his son Jehoiachin.

36:9–10. Jehoiachin reigns only three months and ten days before he is captured and deported to Babylonia. The Babylonians place Jehoiachin's brother Zedekiah/Mattaniah on the throne of Judah as a puppet king (2 Kings 24:8–19).

36:11–20. Zedekiah/Mattaniah rebels against the Babylonians, who ransack the city of Jerusalem and carry away all the temple treasures (2 Kings 24:20–25:21).

36:21–23. After seventy years as captives in a foreign land, the Jewish people are permitted to return to their homeland. This return is authorized by King Cyrus of Persia. This nation succeeds Babylonia as the dominant world power.

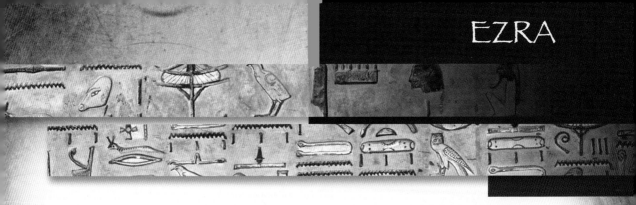

OVERVIEW: Ezra the priest leads the Jewish people to renew the covenant after their return from exile.

Introduction to Ezra

The book of Ezra belongs to the postexilic period of Israel's history—the time when God's people were allowed to return to their homeland following their years of exile in Babylonia and Persia.

Judah's leading citizens had been carried into exile by the Babylonians (2 Kings 25:8–21). But the Persians eventually defeated Babylonia. Persian policy was to allow subject peoples to live in their own territory and to worship their own god under a Persian-appointed military governor.

King Cyrus of Persia allowed the first group of Jewish exiles to return to Judah about 530 B.C. under the leadership of their duly-appointed governor, Zerubbabel (Ezra 2:1–2). The account of this group of exiles and their accomplishments is found in chapters 1–6 of Ezra.

About seventy years later, Ezra the priest returned to Jerusalem with another group of exiles. His accomplishments are related in chapters 7–10 of the book. Just as the first group of Jews rebuilt the temple, Ezra led the people to rebuild their commitment to God and His requirements in the law.

Ezra wrote the book that bears his name as well as the books of 1 and 2 Chronicles and Nehemiah (see the introductions to these books on pp. 438, 443, and 454. His book teaches an enduring message about the providence of God, who sometimes works through surprising circumstances—even the edict of a pagan Persian king—to accomplish His will in the lives of His people.

Summary of Ezra

1:1–4. King Cyrus of Persia conquers Babylonia, the nation that had overrun Judah and carried away captives to Babylon about seventy years before. In the first year of his reign, Cyrus allows the Jews who want to do so to return to their homeland and rebuild the city of Jerusalem and the temple (2 Chron. 36:22–23).

1:5–11. A group of Jewish leaders, along with priests and Levites, agree to return to Jerusalem to conduct the rebuilding project. Cyrus sends with them gold and silver and items from the temple that had been taken away by the Babylonians when they pillaged Jerusalem (2 Kings 24:13).

2:1–67. The leaders of the first group of Jewish exiles—more than 42,000—who return to their homeland under Zerubbabel (Hag. 2:20–23) are listed.

2:68–70. The returning exiles settle in various cities of their native land and contribute to a special rebuilding fund (1 Chron. 26:20).

3:1–6. People gather at Jerusalem from throughout their homeland to begin

[2:1–67] TEMPLE SERVANTS. *The Nethinims: the children of Ziha, the children of Hasupha, the children of Tabbaoth (Ezra 2:43).*

This verse begins a listing of all the Nethinims, or temple servants, who returned to Jerusalem under Zerubbabel after the Babylonian captivity. The Nethinims were a distinct class of people of non-Jewish background. Many were captives of war or former Canaanites such as the Gibeonites (Josh. 9:21–27) who had been made lowly servants.

The Nethinims assisted the Levites in the temple by doing such menial jobs as cleaning sacrificial utensils and carrying water and wood to the altar.

rebuilding. They offer sacrifices of thanksgiving to God on the altar of the temple when it is restored.

3:7–13. Skilled workmen are enlisted, and materials are gathered to lay the foundation of the temple. Some of the Israelites are saddened that this new temple is not as ornate and beautiful as the first temple built by Solomon.

4:1–3. Zerubbabel, governor of Judah under appointment by the Persian king, refuses to allow non-Israelites to join in the rebuilding project.

4:4–16. These non-Jews take revenge for this rejection by trying to stop the construction project. They send a false report to King Artaxerxes of Persia, Cyrus's successor, that the Jews are plotting a rebellion against the Persian government.

4:17–24. Artaxerxes orders the work on the reconstruction of Jerusalem to stop until this charge against the Jews is investigated. The work does not resume until the accession of Darius to the Persian throne.

5:1. The prophets Haggai and Zechariah urge the people to resume work on the temple.

5:2–17. The leaders of Israel petition King Darius of Persia to allow the work on the temple to resume.

6:1–12. Darius permits the Jews to begin building again. He orders the enemies of the Jews to quit interfering with their building efforts. He sends gold and silver and building materials to assist in the construction work so they can resume their worship in the temple.

6:13–22. The temple is completed, the priests and Levites are organized for service at the altar, and celebration of the Passover festival is reinstated.

7:1–10. Ezra, a priest and scribe, prepares to leave Persia and join his countrymen who have already returned to their homeland. As an expert in the law of the Lord, he plans to teach the law to his fellow Israelites, probably because it had been neglected during their years in exile (Neh. 2:8, 18).

7:11–26. Ezra carries with him a letter from King Artaxerxes of Persia, giving him permission to return to Israel and to lead his countrymen in renewing their commitment to the law of the Lord. Artaxerxes also gives Ezra gold and silver and other valuable commodities to assist him in this restoration effort.

7:27–28. Ezra gives thanks to God for selecting him for this important task.

[6:1–12] ZERUBBABEL'S TEMPLE. *Cyrus the king made a decree.... Let the house be builded, the place where they offered sacrifices (Ezra 6:3).*

One of the reasons King Cyrus of Persia allowed the Jewish exiles to return to Jerusalem was to rebuild the temple. This central place of worship for the Jewish people had been destroyed by the Babylonian army about sixty years before.

Work on this temple began under Zerubbabel, Persian-appointed governor of Jerusalem. Thus, it is known as Zerubbabel's Temple. It was built on the site of the first temple, known as Solomon's Temple (1 Kings 6).

8:1–14. The exiles who returned to Jerusalem with Ezra are listed.

8:15–23. Ezra sends word for Levites to join his group of travelers. Several answer the call, and Ezra proclaims a fast of dedication to God before they begin the trip.

8:24–36. Ezra delivers the gold and silver and vessels from the temple to a group of priests for safekeeping. These were sent to Jerusalem as a gift from the Persian king Artaxerxes.

9:1–2. The leaders of Israel inform Ezra that many Jewish men have defiled themselves during the exile by marrying women from pagan backgrounds (Exod. 34:16).

9:3–15. In an eloquent prayer of confession and repentance, Ezra asks the Lord to forgive His people for their transgression.

10:1–17. All the Israelite men who have married women from pagan backgrounds gather at Jerusalem and agree to give up these wives.

10:18–44. The names of Israelite men who gave up their pagan wives are listed.

7:1–10. A priest and a scholar, Ezra taught the laws of Moses to Jews who returned from exile in what is now Iraq.

NEHEMIAH

OVERVIEW: Nehemiah leads the people to rebuild the walls of Jerusalem after their return from exile.

Introduction to Nehemiah

The book of Nehemiah emerged from the same background and circumstances that are reflected in the book of Ezra (see the introduction to Ezra on p. 451).

Nehemiah was a servant of King Artaxerxes of Persia. When he heard about the hardships of his fellow Jews who had returned to their homeland, he gained the king's permission to go there to assist in the rebuilding effort. His great accomplishment was leading his people to rebuild the defensive wall around Jerusalem. He also assisted Ezra the priest in his moral and legal reform movements among the people.

Nehemiah is a good case study in effective leadership. Under his supervision, the people rebuilt Jerusalem's wall in fifty-two days (6:15–19). He accomplished this challenging job by first seeking God's guidance and praying for the people of Judah. He took the time to do a careful analysis of the work to be done and to organize his workforce for maximum effectiveness.

Throughout the building project, Nehemiah also motivated and encouraged his workers and solved problems as soon as they arose with an aggressive leadership style. He persevered in the task and led the people to stay the course, even when their enemies threatened to attack them while they worked on the wall.

The world needs more courageous, visionary leaders like Nehemiah!

Summary of Nehemiah

1:1–3. In Persia, Nehemiah learns of the plight of the people who were left behind in Jerusalem when the Babylonians ransacked the nation of Judah many years before (2 Kings 25:1–4).

1:4–11. Nehemiah prays for his homeland and pleads with the Lord to forgive the sin and rebellion of His people.

> **[1:4–11] A ROYAL CUPBEARER.** *For I [Nehemiah] was the king's cupbearer* (Neh. 1:11).
>
> A cupbearer was one of the most important servants in the household of a king. His task was to taste the king's wine before he drank it to make sure it had not been poisoned by his enemies.
>
> Although Nehemiah was a Jew, he had risen to a position of prominence in the Persian court. Artaxerxes, the king, trusted him and allowed him to return to Jerusalem to rebuild the walls of the city (Neh. 2:3–7).

2:1–10. Nehemiah is the cupbearer for King Artaxerxes of Persia (Neh. 1:11). The king gives Nehemiah permission to go to Jerusalem to help rebuild the devastated city.

2:11–16. After arriving in Jerusalem,

Nehemiah surveys the broken defensive wall of the city under the cover of darkness to determine the repairs needed.

2:17–18. Nehemiah challenges the rulers of Jerusalem to rebuild the wall around the city.

2:19–20. Several enemies of the Jews scoff at Nehemiah's plan to rebuild the wall. But he insists that the project will be completed with the help of the Lord.

3:1–32. The names of several people who worked with Nehemiah on this building project are listed.

4:1–3. Sanballat and Tobiah, enemies of the Jews, ridicule Nehemiah's attempt to rebuild the wall of Jerusalem.

4:4–6. Nehemiah answers their taunts with a prayer for God's guidance and protection in the building project.

4:7–12. Sanballat and Tobiah and other enemies of the Jews vow to stop the building project with military force.

4:13–23. Nehemiah organizes a defensive force and arms his workers so they can protect themselves against an enemy attack. Many workers labor on the wall with their construction tools in one hand and their weapons in the other.

5:1–5. Some of the people complain to Nehemiah about their economic hardship. Their own fellow Jews are charging them excessive interest on money they have borrowed and are even holding their children in slavery as collateral against their debts (Ezra 4:13).

5:6–13. Nehemiah confronts the wealthy Jews who are exploiting their poor neighbors. They agree to restore the land and children that are being held as collateral.

5:14–19. Nehemiah is serving as governor of Judah under appointment by the Persian king. But he refuses to use his position and power to line his own pockets.

6:1–14. The enemies of the Jews continue their

2:1–10. A worker in Jerusalem repairs a model of what the Holy City looked like in Bible times. Nehemiah led the work of repairing Jerusalem's walls after Babylonian invaders tore it down.

[5:6–13] AN EMPTY POCKET. *I [Nehemiah] shook my lap [shook out the folds of my robe, NIV], and said, So God shake out every man from his house, and from his labour, that performeth not this promise, even thus be he shaken out, and emptied* (Neh. 5:13).

The "lap" in this passage was a pocket in the loose outer robe where people carried items such as money or important papers. It served the same purpose as a man's wallet in modern times.

Nehemiah had just received a promise from the wealthy Jews of Jerusalem that they would no longer mistreat and defraud their poorer fellow Jews. When he shook out the pocket in his robe, he was saying to the wealthy, "God will make you just as empty as this pocket if you fail to keep the promise you have made."

plots to stop the building project. They even hire a false prophet to lure Nehemiah into an error in order to undermine his leadership. But Nehemiah is not fooled by their tricks.

6:15–19. The defensive wall around Jerusalem is rebuilt in fifty-two days—to the disappointment of Tobiah and other enemies who had tried to stop the project.

7:1–4. Nehemiah selects priests and Levites to preside over sacrifices in the temple. He also appoints civil leaders to provide security for the city of Jerusalem.

7:5–69. The Jewish tribes who have returned to Judah under the leadership of Zerubbabel (Hag. 2:20–23) are listed by clans and family groups.

7:70–73. Contributors to a special fund to assist in the rebuilding effort in Jerusalem are listed.

8:1–12. The people gather in the streets of Jerusalem and listen reverently as Ezra reads the book of the law (Genesis, Exodus, Leviticus, Numbers, and Deuteronomy). The priests and Levites are stationed among the crowd to explain these commands from God.

8:13–18. Ezra reads God's directions from the book of the law on how the Feast of Booths, or Tabernacles, is to be observed (Lev. 23:39–43). The people cut branches from trees and build themselves huts, or booths, to remember their living conditions during the years of wandering in the wilderness.

9:1–38. All the people, including civil leaders, priests, and Levites, repent and confess their sins to God. They vow to keep the covenant between the Lord and Israel.

10:1–27. The names of the leaders who sealed the covenant between the Lord and the Israelites are listed.

10:28–39. The people agree to follow God's commands from the book of the law. They agree to resume the practice of bringing tithes, offerings, and sacrifices to the priests and Levites in the temple.

11:1–2. The leaders of Israel cast lots (Matt. 27:35) to determine the settlement of the returned exiles in the land. Ten percent are to settle in Jerusalem, and the remaining 90 percent will live in other cities throughout Judah.

11:3–24. The people selected to live in Jerusalem are listed.

11:25–36. Other cities of Judah where the exiles will settle are listed.

12:1–26. The names of priests and Levites who returned from the exile under Zerubbabel are listed (Ezra 2:1–67).

12:27–43. The names of priests and Levites whom Nehemiah appointed for a special function are listed. They lead the celebration at the dedication of the restored defensive wall of Jerusalem.

12:44–47. Nehemiah appoints priests and Levites to store the goods offered by the people for the support of the priesthood. He also organizes the priests and Levites to serve at the altar in the temple on a rotating basis. This restores the procedure established by David and Solomon (1 Chron. 25:1–26:32).

13:1–31. Nehemiah institutes religious reforms throughout the land of Judah. He restores the sanctity of the Sabbath, casts foreigners out of the temple, and forbids the Jewish people from marrying people from pagan backgrounds.

[10:28–39] **WOOD FOR THE ALTAR.** *We cast the lots among the priests, the Levites, and the people, for the wood offering, to bring it into the house of our God, after the houses of our fathers, at times appointed year by year, to burn upon the altar of the Lord our God* (Neh. 10:34).

Supplying wood for priests to use in offering burnt sacrifices on the altar was a task assigned to the Nethinims, or temple servants (see sidebar, "Temple Servants," on p. 452). But not enough of these servants returned from the Exile in Babylonia and Persia to handle this task.

Nehemiah solved the problem by assigning other people from among the Levites and the general population to do this work. He cast lots to set up a rotating system under which wood would be supplied for this purpose throughout the year.

ESTHER

OVERVIEW: Esther delivers her people, the Jews, from their enemies while they are living among the Persians.

Introduction to Esther

Following their years of exile among the Babylonians and Persians, the Jewish people were allowed by the Persians to return to their homeland (see the introduction to Ezra on p. 451). But the book of Esther shows clearly that not all the Jews took advantage of this opportunity. Many chose to remain in Persia, probably because this had become home to them during their long separation from Judah, their native land.

Esther, the young Jewish woman for whom

7:1–10. Queen Esther expresses her despair to her husband, the king of Persia, informing him that his second in command has plotted genocide against her people, the Jews.

the book is named, rose to the position of queen under the Persian king, Ahasuerus. Her cousin Mordecai was also an important official who served at the king's palace.

King Ahasuerus reigned from about 485 to 465 B.C., so the book of Esther can be dated to this time period. This was about forty years after the Persians allowed the first group of exiles to return to Judah. The author of the book is unknown.

The main characters in the book of Esther are King Ahasuerus; his wife, Queen Esther; his top official, an evil man named Haman; and Mordecai, Esther's cousin, who was also a palace official and a leader among the Jewish people who were living throughout Persia.

Haman developed a hatred for the Jews because he felt they did not pay him the respect he deserved as a high official of the Persian government. He tricked the king into issuing an order for their wholesale execution. But Queen Esther, at Mordecai's encouragement, used her influence with the king to expose Haman's plot. Haman was hanged on the gallows that he had built for Mordecai's execution, and Mordecai was promoted by the king to a higher position.

The Jewish people were allowed to resist their enemies, and they were granted victory by the Lord. The book ends with their celebration of this miraculous deliverance through a special holiday known as the Feast of Purim.

Summary of Esther

1:1–9. King Ahasuerus of Persia invites the leaders throughout his kingdom to a lavish banquet at his royal palace in Shushan.

1:10–12. The king asks his queen, Vashti, to appear before his guests to showcase her beauty, but she refuses.

1:13–22. On the advice of his aides, King Ahasuerus decrees that Vashti will be deposed as queen and replaced by another woman.

2:1–4. Ahasuerus begins a search throughout his kingdom for a woman to replace Vashti as queen.

2:5–18. Esther, also known as Hadassah, is a beautiful young Jewish woman who was adopted by her cousin Mordecai after the death of her parents. She wins the king's favor and replaces Vashti as the queen.

2:19–23. Mordecai, who serves in the palace of King Ahasuerus (Esther 2:5), saves the king's life when he stops an assassination plot.

3:1–6. Haman, a high official in King Ahasuerus's administration, is enraged when Mordecai refuses to bow before him and show him honor and respect.

3:7–15. In order to kill Mordecai, Haman devises a plan to destroy all the Jews. He convinces King Ahasuerus that the Jewish people are reckless and dangerous revolutionaries who refuse to abide by the king's laws. Ahasuerus issues an order that all the Jews throughout his kingdom are to be wiped out on a

---

[1:10–12] HAREM CARETAKERS. *The seven chamberlains [eunuchs, NIV] that served in the presence of Ahasuerus the king* (Esther 1:10).

A chamberlain was a male servant in a king's court who was responsible for the king's harem. To minimize the danger to these women, a chamberlain was emasculated. King Ahasuerus of Persia must have had a large harem, since he had seven of these servants.

Sometimes these male servants rose to positions of prominence as advisers in the king's administration. This must have been the case with two chamberlains of King Ahasuerus, since they participated in a plot to assassinate the king (Esther 2:21–23).

Other references to chamberlain or eunuchs include 2 Kings 9:32; Jer. 29:2; and Dan. 1:10.

specific day in the future.

4:1–9. Mordecai mourns for the Jewish people in front of the royal palace. He sends word to Esther that she must use her influence with the king to save the Jews from destruction.

4:10–17. Esther reminds Mordecai of the law that any person who approaches the Persian king without authorization runs the risk of being executed. But she promises Mordecai that she will take this risk on behalf of her own people, the Jews.

5:1–2. Esther makes an unauthorized appearance before the king. He agrees to receive her by extending his royal scepter for her to touch.

5:3–8. Esther asks the king to invite Haman to a banquet that she has prepared. At this banquet, she asks the king, along with Haman, to attend another banquet that she is preparing for the next day. During this second banquet she will make known her request to King Ahasuerus.

5:9–14. Filled with pride, Haman boasts to his wife and friends about his achievements and his special invitation to attend a banquet with the king and Queen Esther the next day. But Haman admits that all these achievements mean little as long as Mordecai refuses to bow down and show him honor. At his wife's suggestion, he builds a gallows on which he plans to have Mordecai hanged.

[4:10–17] DON'T BOTHER THE KING. *Whosoever… shall come unto the king…who is not called, there is one law…to put him to death, except such to whom the king shall hold out the golden sceptre* (Esther 4:11).

Mordecai asked Esther to seek an audience with King Ahasuerus of Persia to plead for the Jewish people. In this verse, Esther reminded Mordecai that anyone who approached the king without a personal invitation ran the risk of immediate execution.

The purpose of this harsh law may have been to keep the king from being pestered by grumblers and favor-seekers. He had the option of granting an audience to uninvited visitors by touching them with his royal scepter.

Esther did decide to approach the king—uninvited—on behalf of her people, the Jews. The king touched her with his scepter and agreed to hear her request (Esther 5:1–2).

6:1–14. While reading the royal archives, Ahasuerus discovers the account of Mordecai's intervention on the king's behalf (Esther 2:19–23). The king orders Haman to prepare and lead a tribute to Mordecai for his brave action. Haman's humiliation at being forced to honor the Jew grows deeper when his wife predicts that he will fall before Mordecai.

7:1–10. During the banquet with Haman and the king, Queen Esther exposes Haman's plot to have the Jews destroyed. King Ahasuerus orders that Hamon be put to death. He is hanged on the gallows he

[9:20–32] A CELEBRATION OF DELIVERANCE. *Wherefore they [the Jews] called these days Purim after the name of Pur* (Esther 9:26).

The Jewish people celebrated their deliverance from the death edict issued by Haman (Esther 3:5–15) with a special holiday known as the Feast of Purim.

The Hebrew word *purim* means "lots." The feast was named for the lots that Haman cast to determine the time when the Jews would be annihilated (Esther 3:7). Thanks to the brave actions of Esther and Mordecai, Haman was annihilated and the Jewish people prospered throughout the land.

9:1–19. Throughout the kingdom of Persia, the Jews destroy many of their enemies, including ten sons of Haman. Mordecai, on the other hand, grows in popularity and power.

9:20–32. Mordecai and Esther proclaim the fourteenth and fifteenth days of the month of Adar as an official religious holiday among the Jews. Known as Purim, it memorializes God's deliverance of His people from their enemies.

10:1–3. The Jewish Mordecai becomes an important and highly respected official under King Ahasuerus. He is also respected and honored by his own countrymen throughout the kingdom of Persia.

9:20–32. Jews today read aloud the book of Esther at the springtime festival of Purim, celebrating the holocaust she prevented. Noisemakers drown out the name of the villain. One rattle is in the shape of a gallows, on which the villain was hanged.

had prepared for Mordecai's death (Esther 5:14).

8:1–2. Mordecai is promoted to a high position in King Ahasuerus's administration.

8:3–8. Queen Esther pleads with the king to spare her countrymen, the Jewish people.

8:9–17. King Ahasuerus issues a decree that authorizes the Jews to resist when their lives are threatened under the earlier order issued by Haman (Esther 3:13).

CHAPTER 3
BOOKS OF POETRY
AND WISDOM

One of the most beloved books in the entire Bible—the book of Psalms—is included among the books of poetry and wisdom of the Old Testament. Other books in this category are Job, Proverbs, Ecclesiastes, and Song of Solomon.

Old Testament poetry does not include such elements as rhyme and alliteration, which we normally associate with poetic writings. Rather, the main feature of Old Testament poetic literature is parallelism. In this form of literary construction, the content of one line is advanced, contrasted, or repeated by the content of the next line. (See the introduction to the book of Psalms on p. 467 for a more detailed explanation of the technique of parallelism.)

Writings in this section of the Old Testament that deal with issues such as the meaning of life, the nature of human suffering, and how to have a happy and successful life are known as wisdom literature. The books of Job, Proverbs, and Ecclesiastes fall into this category. Several of the individual psalms are also classified as wisdom psalms: 1, 19, 37, 49, 104, 107, 112, 119, 127, 128, 133, 147, and 148.

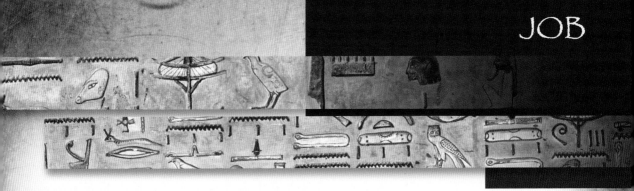

OVERVIEW: In debates with his three friends, Job examines the problems of evil and human suffering.

Introduction to Job

The book of Job, written in the form of a dramatic poem by an unknown author, deals with a question as old as humankind: Why do the righteous suffer? Although Job was a righteous man who worshiped God and shunned evil (1:1), God allowed Satan to take away everything he owned, as well as his children.

As Job cried out to God in his misery, three friends arrived to offer comfort. But they actually drove Job into deeper despair because of their outspoken conviction that Job was being punished by the Lord because of his sins. Job protested that he was a righteous man and that God was treating him unjustly.

After Job and his friends had debated this question for a long time, God Himself finally spoke from a whirlwind. Revealing Himself as the powerful, all-knowing God, He declared that He could be trusted to do what was right, although His ways might seem strange and puzzling.

Humbled by this outpouring of God's power, Job finally learned to trust God, in spite of his imperfect understanding. He stopped questioning God and His ways and declared, "I abhor myself, and repent in dust and ashes" (42:6). God was pleased with this profession of faith and trust. He restored Job's fortunes and gave him additional children to replace those he had lost.

The book of Job teaches us that it is futile to try to understand the reason behind our suffering. It is enough to know that God is in control and that He is our refuge and strength in times of trouble. Like Job, we also need to learn that God is not bound by our understanding or by our lack of it. He is free and subject to no will but His own. He does not owe us an explanation for His actions.

Summary of Job

1:1–5. Job is a righteous and upright man who has been abundantly blessed by the Lord. He owns large herds of livestock and has many sons and daughters.

> **[1:1–5] A MAN OF MEANS.** *His [Job's] substance also was seven thousand sheep, and three thousand camels, and five hundred yoke of oxen, and five hundred she asses [female donkeys, NKJV]* (Job 1:3).
>
> In Old Testament times, a man's wealth was measured by the size of his flocks and herds. Job was a rich man by these standards. Female donkeys are mentioned in this passage because they were more valuable than male donkeys. The milk produced by females was a valuable food substance.

1:6–12. In a dialogue with God, Satan charges that Job serves Him for selfish reasons—what is in it for him. God gives Satan permission to test Job to determine if his charge is true.

1:13–22. In one disastrous day, Job loses everything: his large herds of livestock, his servants, and his own sons and daughters. But Job remains faithful to God.

2:1–10. Satan tells God that Job will certainly deny Him if he is afflicted with physical suffering. With God's permission, Job is struck with boils and sores. But still he refuses to cry out against God.

2:11–13. Three of Job's friends—Eliphaz, Bildad, and Zophar—hear about Job's misfortune. They come to mourn with Job and to comfort him in his anguish and pain.

3:1–26. Before his friends say a word, Job issues a plaintive cry of self-pity. He curses the day of his birth and wishes he had never been born. This chapter begins the first cycle of debate between Job and his friends. This cycle continues through chapter 14, with Eliphaz responding to Job (chaps. 4–5); Job replying to Eliphaz (chaps. 6–7); Bildad's first speech to Job (chap. 8); Job's response to Bildad (chaps. 9–10); Zophar's first speech to Job (chap. 11); and Job's reply to Zophar (chaps. 12–14).

4:1–5:27. In his response to Job's outburst, Eliphaz reminds his friend that the innocent do not suffer like Job is suffering. He calls on Job to turn to God and repent; then his troubles will go away.

6:1–7:21. Job protests that he is innocent. How can God be punishing him when he has done nothing wrong?

8:1–22. Bildad steps up the tempo when he enters the debate. God always acts with justice and fairness, he declares. Is Job suggesting otherwise by claiming that God is punishing an innocent man?

9:1–10:22. Job expresses his confusion and frustration. He agrees in theory with Bildad that God is just. But in Job's case He seems to be punishing a person who is righteous. Job laments his condition and again wishes he had never been born.

11:1–20. Zophar now jumps into the debate and turns it up a notch. He attacks Job personally and accuses him of being filled with pride and of uttering meaningless words. He charges that there must be some hidden sin in Job's life. God knows about it and is giving Job what he deserves.

12:1–14:22. Job grows angry and sarcastic with his know-it-all friends. He declares that he knows as much about God and how He works as they do. He appeals his case directly to God and calls on Him to declare him innocent. He also laments the brevity of life and the lot of all human beings on earth: "Man that is born of a woman is of few days, and full of trouble" (Job 14:1).

15:1–35. Eliphaz replies to Job's outburst, calling him a vain man whose stomach is filled with the east wind (in other words, a windbag!). His speech kicks off the second cycle of debate in the book of Job. This cycle continues through chapter 21, with Job's response to Eliphaz (chaps. 16–17); Bildad's second speech to Job (chap. 18); Job's

---

[9:1–10:22] MESSAGES ON FOOT. *My [Job's] days are swifter than a post [runner, NIV]: they flee away, they see no good* (Job 9:25).

Job complained about the brevity of human life by declaring that his days went by faster than a swift runner. He was probably referring to the fleet-footed messengers used by Old Testament kings to carry important messages to distant places.

King Hezekiah of Judah restored several important religious practices, including observance of the Passover, which had been neglected by the people. He sent "posts [couriers, NIV]...with...letters...throughout all Israel and Judah" (2 Chron. 30:6), summoning all citizens to gather at Jerusalem for this solemn occasion.

reply to Bildad (chap. 19); Zophar's second speech to Job (chap. 20); and Job's response to Zophar (chap. 21).

16:1–17:16. Job continues his complaining. He calls his friends "miserable comforters" (16:2) because of their lack of sensitivity and compassion.

18:1–21. Bildad insists that Job is being punished for his sin. He describes the destiny of the wicked in graphic terms, apparently to frighten Job into repentance.

19:1–29. Broken and depressed, Job begs his friends to have pity on him. They have become accusers and tormentors instead of comforters, accusing him unfairly and providing no answers to his probing questions.

3:1–26. Having lost his health, children, and flocks, Job moans in self-pity, cursing the day of his birth.

[19:1–29] CAUGHT IN GOD'S NET. *God hath overthrown me [Job], and hath compassed [surrounded, NKJV] me with his net (Job 19:6).*

Birds and other animals were often trapped with nets. These were also effective weapons in combat. A warrior would restrain an enemy by throwing a thick net around him. Then he would finish him off with a sword or spear.

In his suffering and struggles with God, Job compared himself to an animal or a man trapped in a net. He believed God was wielding the net. As an innocent sufferer, he thought he was being punished by God for no reason.

20:1–29. Zophar picks up the subject that Bildad had discussed in chapter 18: the terrible fate of the wicked. The implication of his remarks is that Job is being punished by God for his wickedness.

21:1–34. Job agrees with Zophar and the others that the wicked are ultimately punished, but he insists that they often prosper and flourish during this life.

22:1–30. Eliphaz intensifies his assault on Job.

He accuses him of serious sins, including oppression of the poor. His speech launches the third and final cycle of debate between Job and his friends. This cycle continues through chapter 26, with Job's response to Eliphaz (chaps. 23–24); Bildad's third speech to Job (chap. 25); and Job's reply to Bildad (chap. 26).

23:1–24:25. Job wishes he could stand in God's presence and present his case directly to Him. He protests that life is not fair—that God sometimes seems to punish the righteous and reward the wicked.

25:1–6. Bildad feels compelled to defend God against Job's accusations. He declares that man has no right to question God's actions.

26:1–14. Job ends the three cycles of debate with a strong affirmation about God: He is all-powerful, and His ways are beyond human understanding: "The thunder of his power who can understand?" (v. 14).

27:1–31:40. In these five chapters, Job issues his final defense against his accusers. He looks back on his days of plenty and compares them with his present state of poverty. But through it all he has kept his integrity before God. He claims, as he has throughout the debate, that he is an innocent sufferer.

32:1–37:24. These six chapters contain the angry outburst of a young man named Elihu. Apparently he had listened to the debate between Job and his three friends and was not pleased with what they were saying. Job was wrong because he had justified himself rather than God. And his three friends had failed to convince Job of the error of his ways. Elihu feels he needs to defend God's honor and set the record straight. In his long speech, he upholds God's works, wisdom,

[38:1–41:34] SEALING WITH CLAY. *It [the earth] is turned as clay to the seal* (Job 38:14).

This verse is part of God's response to Job's charge against Him that He was unjust and unfair for causing Job to suffer.

In Bible times clay tablets or clay bricks were often stamped or sealed with a symbol that identified their owner or creator. God declared to Job that He was the all-powerful, omnipotent Lord who had created the earth and stamped it with His own seal. He did not owe Job an explanation for His actions.

and justice. He declares that Job is getting what he deserves because of his sin.

38:1–41:34. Elihu's diatribe is not dignified by a response from either Job or God. Instead, God finally replies to Job after Job's whining throughout the book. God does not give Job an explanation for his suffering. But He reminds Job that He is the sovereign, all-powerful, omnipotent Creator of the universe whose ways are beyond human understanding. He does not have to justify and defend His actions to mere mortals (Hab. 2:2–20).

42:1–6. Job's prideful desire for understanding and justification gives way to trust and submission. With faith and humility he declares, "I have heard of thee by the hearing of the ear: but now mine eye seeth thee. Wherefore I abhor myself, and repent in dust and ashes" (vv. 5–6).

42:7–17. The Lord reprimands the three friends of Job because He is not pleased with their treatment of Job. Then He restores Job's fortunes by giving him twice as much as he had before (Isa. 40:2).

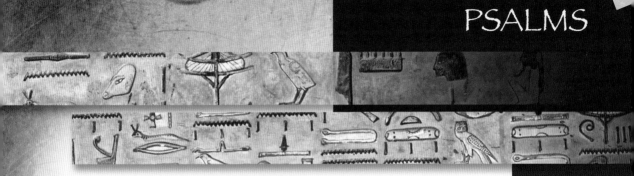

OVERVIEW: Prayers of praise, joy, and agony of soul addressed to God.

Introduction to Psalms

Several things about the book of Psalms make it unique among the books of the Bible: (1) It is the longest book of the Bible, (2) it was written by many different authors across a period of several centuries, and (3) parts of the book were used as a hymnal in the worship services of God's people, the Israelites.

The name of David appears in the titles of 73 of the 150 individual psalms in this book. But several other people are named in the titles of other psalms, and at least 50 psalms have no authors identified in the titles.

From the content of the individual psalms, it is clear that they were written by many different people across a long period of time. They were eventually compiled as a book of 150 psalms by an unknown editor. Musical terms in some of the psalms (for example, "To the chief

Making music in his tent, a Bedouin herder plays a lyre—a common instrument in Bible times. Psalms is a collection of ancient Jewish songs.

Psalm 8. A full moon rises over a hilltop known as Masada, in southern Israel. Many ancient Jewish songs praise the wonder of God's creation.

Musician," Ps. 46 title) show that many of the psalms were chanted or sung during worship services in the tabernacle or temple.

All the psalms were written in poetic form. Many of these poems demonstrate the nature of Hebrew poetry. The psalm writers used a technique known as parallelism rather than rhyme or rhythm. In parallelism, one phrase is followed by a second phrase that repeats, adds to, or contrasts with the first phrase. Here are two examples of parallelism from the Psalms:

> For I will declare mine iniquity;
> I will be sorry for my sin.
> (repetition; Ps. 38:18)

> For the LORD knoweth the way of the righteous:
> but the way of the ungodly shall perish.
> (contrast; Ps. 1:6)

Several of the psalms look forward to the coming of the Messiah. Psalm 22 predicts the suffering of the Savior on the cross (Ps. 22:1; fulfilled in Matt. 27:46). Other psalms indicate that He would pray for His enemies (Ps. 109:4; fulfilled in Luke 23:34) and that His reign would last forever (Ps. 45:6; fulfilled in Heb. 1:8).

The book of Psalms is one of the most beloved books of the Bible, perhaps because it expresses the thoughts about God that believers sometimes feel in their hearts but can't seem to put into words. For example, these words from Psalm 95 are an appropriate prayer of praise for every circumstance of life: "O come, let us sing unto the LORD: let us make a joyful noise to the rock of our salvation. Let us come before his presence with thanksgiving, and make a joyful noise unto him with psalms. For the LORD is a great God, and a great King above all gods" (Ps. 95:1–3).

Summary of Psalms

Psalm 1. Blessed is the person who walks in accordance with the word of God (Prov. 4:14).

Psalm 2. A messianic psalm that declares that God's ultimate rule over the world will be established by His Son.

Psalm 3. God is a shield who protects the believer in troublesome times. This psalm was written by David when he fled from the rebellion of his son Absalom (2 Sam. 15–16).

Psalm 4. God hears the prayers of believers and grants peace and rest in the dark experiences of life.

Psalm 5. The Lord will reward the righteous and punish the wicked.

Psalm 6. A prayer for God to show mercy to the psalmist and to punish his enemies.

Psalm 7. This psalm focuses on righteousness. David wants God to know that he has lived a righteous life. He asks God to deliver him from wicked enemies.

Psalm 8. As he meditates on the wonders of God's physical creation, the psalmist realizes that man is weak and insignificant. But God has placed him in a position of honor and glory.

Psalm 9. A psalm of praise for the mercy and grace shown by the Lord to the nation of Israel. The psalmist also declares that God will punish the pagan nations.

Psalm 10. The wicked are persecuting and cheating the poor. The psalmist calls on the Lord to rise to their defense.

Psalm 11. God is in control, and the psalmist affirms his confidence in His wisdom and guidance.

Psalm 12. Surrounded by those who speak false, flattering words, the psalmist declares that "the words of the LORD are pure words" (v. 6). He can be trusted to be honest and fair.

Psalm 13. Although he is feeling lonely and abandoned, the psalmist vows to "sing unto the LORD, because he hath dealt bountifully with me" (v. 6).

Psalm 14. Wicked, depraved people who live as if God does not exist are fools (v. 1). The apostle Paul quoted the first two verses of this psalm to show that no person is sinless in God's eyes (Rom. 3:10–12).

Psalm 15. The psalmist gives a brief description of the godly person who walks in the ways of the Lord.

Psalm 16. This is a messianic psalm because of its reference to the resurrection of Christ (vv. 9–11; see Acts 13:35–37).

Psalm 17. Overwhelmed by his enemies, the psalmist looks to God for guidance and deliverance.

Psalm 18. This psalm of thanksgiving from David celebrates his deliverance by the Lord from threats against his life by King Saul. It closely parallels David's song of deliverance in 2 Samuel 22.

Psalm 19. A majestic celebration of God's revelation of Himself through nature and the law, God's written Word.

Psalm 20. This is a public prayer for the king of Israel, encouraging him and the people to trust in the Lord rather than military might.

Psalm 21. A prayer for victory over Israel's enemies under the leadership of the nation's earthly, political king.

Psalm 22. A well-known messianic psalm. Christ quoted from it while He was on the cross: "My God, my God, why hast thou forsaken me?" (v. 1; see Matt. 27:46).

Psalm 23. Because it portrays God as a tender, caring shepherd, this beloved psalm is known as the "Shepherd Psalm."

Psalm 24. As worshipers traveled to the temple in Jerusalem, they may have chanted

[56] GOD KNOWS OUR TEARS. *Thou [God] tellest my wanderings: put thou my tears into thy bottle: are they not in thy book?* (Ps. 56:8).

David may have been referring in this psalm to an ancient custom observed by mourners at funerals. They would collect the tears they shed for departed loved ones in small flasks and place them in their tombs as memorials of their love.

This was David's way of saying that God knows all about us. He even keeps a record of the tears we shed in our moments of sorrow and sadness. Jesus expressed the same truth when He declared, "The very hairs of your head are all numbered" (Matt. 10:30).

Psalm 58. This psalm calls for God's judgment on leaders who use their authority to defraud and cheat the innocent.

Psalm 59. David recalls the time when King Saul posted soldiers around his house to ambush and kill him (1 Sam. 19:11–18). He denounces his enemies and affirms his trust in God.

Psalm 60. Although Israel suffers from temporary setbacks, the psalmist is convinced that God will give them the ultimate victory over their enemies.

Psalm 61. A prayer for the earthly king of Israel. He and the psalmist will find security and safety in "the rock that is higher than I" (v. 2).

Psalm 62. The psalmist urges all people to put their trust in God, not riches or prestige. He is a never-failing source of strength and power.

Psalm 63. In "a dry and thirsty land" (v. 1), David longs for God's presence rather than water. This psalm may reflect the time when David was hiding in the wilderness from King Saul (1 Sam. 24).

Psalm 64. The psalmist expresses his conviction that God will protect him from his enemies and give them what they deserve.

Psalm 65. A hymn of thanksgiving for God's physical creation (Gen. 1:1–25) and the abundant crops He provides throughout the land.

Psalm 66. An eloquent expression of praise and thanksgiving for the Lord's mighty acts on behalf of His people.

Psalm 67. A call to worship that invites everyone, even the nations beyond Israel, to join in joyous praise of the Lord.

Psalm 68. This psalm is a battle march or victory hymn celebrating Israel's defeat of its enemies under the leadership of God.

Psalm 69. This messianic psalm, with its graphic description of human suffering, portrays the agony of Christ (compare Ps. 69:9 with John 2:17 and Ps. 69:21 with Matt. 27:34, 48).

Psalm 70. An urgent prayer for God's speedy deliverance. This psalm closely parallels Psalm 40:13–17.

Psalm 71. The psalmist thanks God for walking with him since his youth. He expresses confidence in the Lord's continuing presence in his senior years.

Psalm 72. A messianic psalm that looks toward the time when God will rule with righteousness throughout the world.

Psalm 73. Although the ungodly seem to be winning at the present time, they will eventually be judged and punished by the Lord. The righteous will be rewarded for their faithfulness.

Psalm 74. A plea for God to punish the enemies of Israel who destroyed the temple in Jerusalem (2 Kings 25:1–12). This psalm was probably written during Israel's period of exile in Babylon.

Psalm 75. A hymn of warning to the wicked. God is portrayed as the righteous judge.

Psalm 76. A hymn of victory celebrating God's deliverance of Israel from its enemies.

Psalm 77. A historical psalm that reviews

Psalm 82. This psalm is directed to rulers or leaders. God will judge those who use their authority to oppress and cheat others (Isa. 28).

Psalm 83. The psalmist calls on God to exercise His sovereignty and defend His people against their enemies.

Psalm 84. A hymn sung by worshipers as they approached God's temple: "My soul longeth, yea, even fainteth for the courts of the LORD" (v. 2).

Psalm 85. An optimistic psalm that looks to the future under God's leadership.

Psalm 86. Out of a deep sense of spiritual need ("O LORD, hear me: for I am poor and needy," v. 1), the psalmist pleads for God's mercy and forgiveness.

the Lord's wondrous acts on behalf of His people.

Psalm 78. Looking back on Israel's history, this psalm warns future generations to remain loyal to God and His commands.

Psalm 79. This psalm describes a time of national disaster, perhaps the destruction of Jerusalem and the temple by the Babylonians (2 Kings 25:1–12). The psalmist calls on God to deliver Israel from its shame and humiliation.

Psalm 80. Israel was once like a healthy vine (vv. 8–11; see Isa. 5:1–7), but now it has been cut down and defeated. The psalmist asks the Lord to restore the nation to its former glory.

Psalm 81. The psalmist paints a graphic contrast between God's faithfulness and the waywardness of Israel.

Psalm 82. Assyrian officials are profiled in art from the 700s B.C., when their vicious empire dominated the Middle East. Psalm 82 vows judgment on rulers who oppress others. Assyria was overrun by Babylonian invaders in 612 B.C.

Psalm 87. A short psalm on the glories of Jerusalem, referred to as Zion (v. 2).

Psalm 88. This is perhaps the most desperate of all the psalms, prayed by a person who was seriously ill. But the Lord did not seem to hear his plea. The tone of this psalm is similar to that of the book of Job.

Psalm 89. This psalm refers to the everlasting covenant that God made with David (2 Sam. 7:1–17). But tragic events since that time make the psalmist wonder if God has given up on Israel.

Psalm 90. This is the only psalm in the book of Psalms attributed to Moses. He contrasts the eternity of God with the brief human life span.

Psalm 91. This is one of the most beloved of the psalms. God is a refuge and fortress for the believer: "He that dwelleth in the secret place of the most High shall abide under the shadow of the Almighty" (v. 1).

Psalm 92. A majestic hymn of praise and thanksgiving for God's goodness to His people.

Psalm 93. A short psalm that celebrates God's reign over the world in glory and majesty.

Psalm 94. The Lord is a God of justice. He will ultimately judge the wicked and reward those who follow His law.

Psalm 95. A call to worship: "O come, let us sing unto the Lord: let us make a joyful noise to the rock of our salvation" (v. 1).

Psalm 96. The psalmist calls on all the earth to sing praises to God. This psalm is one of the greatest affirmations in the Bible of the believer's missionary witness.

Psalm 97. The Lord is to be praised because He is superior to all other gods.

Psalm 98. The Lord is to be praised with music and song because of His salvation and righteousness.

Psalm 99. The Lord is to be praised because He is a holy God who has remained faithful to His people.

Psalm 100. A short psalm of praise to God because "the Lord is good; his mercy is everlasting; and his truth endureth to all generations" (v. 5).

Psalm 101. The psalmist pledges to remain faithful to God and not to associate with evil and ungodly people.

Psalm 102. In anguish and affliction, the psalmist pours out his heart to God. He prays that the Lord will have mercy on Jerusalem, or Zion. This psalm may have been written during Israel's period of exile under the Babylonians.

Psalm 103. This is a psalm of overflowing gratitude to God for His goodness, mercy, and love: "Bless the Lord, O my soul: and all that is within me, bless his holy name" (v. 1).

Psalm 104. The psalmist marvels at the display of God's glory in the universe that He has created (Ps. 8).

Psalm 105. This psalm reviews God's mighty acts on behalf of His people Israel, especially His dealings with Abraham and His miracles during the Exodus.

Psalm 106. This psalm also reviews the history of Israel's relationship with God, but it emphasizes the sin and disobedience of the people.

Psalm 107. People in many different situations experience anguish and suffering, but God is the great comforter of all who walk in His ways.

Psalm 108. A psalm of praise to the Lord, who has formed Israel into His own people. This psalm is made up of verses from Psalm 57:7–11 and Psalm 60:5–12.

Psalm 109. The psalmist describes his distress because of persecution by his enemies. He asks God to take up his case against them.

Psalm 110. This messianic psalm looks toward

[110] GOD GIVES THE VICTORY. *Sit thou at my [God's] right hand, until I make thine enemies thy footstool (Ps. 110:1).*

A footstool was a piece of furniture, similar to a modern ottoman, on which a person rested his or her feet while in a reclining or resting position. To treat one's enemies as a footstool was to defeat them and bring them into total subjection. Thus, God assured the psalmist that he would be victorious over his enemies if he trusted in the Lord.

This passage has been interpreted as a reference to the Messiah. Following His victory over death and the grave, Jesus is now seated at God's right hand as our Savior and Mediator (Acts 2:32–35; 1 Cor. 15:27).

Lord is the beginning of wisdom" (v. 10).

Psalm 112. The person who respects and follows the Lord will be safe and secure, having nothing to fear from the forces of evil.

Psalm 113. A psalm of praise to God because He lifts up the poor and showers them with mercy.

Psalm 114. The psalmist praises the Lord because of His deliverance of Israel from slavery in Egypt during the Exodus (Exod. 12:31–42).

Psalm 115. This psalm describes the futility of trusting in false gods and the wisdom of trusting in the Lord.

Psalm 116. Delivered from the snares of death, the psalmist vows to serve God and to present sacrifices and offerings before Him in the temple.

Psalm 117. A two-verse psalm of praise—the shortest of all the psalms.

Psalm 118. A messianic psalm. Jesus quoted this psalm to show that He had been

the reign of the coming Messiah, who will be exalted as "a priest for ever after the order of Melchizedek" (v. 4; see Heb. 5:6).

Psalm 111. The psalmist praises the Lord for His goodness and His gracious deeds. He reminds the people that "the fear of the

Psalm 125. "As the mountains are round about Jerusalem, so the Lord is round about his people from henceforth even for ever" (v. 2).

rejected by His own people: "The stone which the builders refused is become the head stone of the corner" (v. 22; see Matt. 21:42).

Psalm 119. This psalm on the written Word or law of God is the longest of the psalms and the longest chapter in the entire Bible. It is divided into twenty-two sections of eight verses each, with each section identified by a different letter of the Hebrew alphabet. The eight verses in each section begin with their respective Hebrew letter.

Psalm 120. The psalmist prays for deliverance from lies and slanderous words that are being uttered against him by his enemies.

Psalm 121. Pilgrims traveling to the temple at Jerusalem for worship may have sung this prayer for safety along the way.

Psalm 122. A prayer for the peace and prosperity of the city of Jerusalem.

Psalm 123. A short psalm imploring the Lord's mercy.

Psalm 124. The psalmist admits that Israel would not have been victorious over its enemies without the Lord's help.

Psalm 125. Just as the hills and mountains surround Jerusalem, God places His love and mercy around His people.

Psalm 126. This psalm is associated with the return of Jewish exiles to their homeland following the exile in Babylon (2 Chron. 36:22–23). The people are overwhelmed with joy.

Psalm 127. A psalm that celebrates family life, particularly the joys of children.

Psalm 128. This psalm may have been recited as a blessing on the groom at a wedding: "Thy wife shall be as a fruitful vine by the sides of thine house: thy children like olive plants round about thy table" (v. 3).

Psalm 129. This psalm celebrates the victories of the Israelites over their enemies.

Psalm 130. The psalmist waits patiently and

expectantly before the Lord as he pleads for mercy and forgiveness.

Psalm 131. A brief prayer of quiet and humble trust in the Lord's goodness.

Psalm 132. This messianic psalm rejoices in God's promise to David of an eternal kingship (2 Sam. 7:1–17).

Psalm 133. A brief psalm celebrating unity and brotherly love.

Psalm 134. The psalmist encourages the priests and Levites who are on watch duty in the temple at night.

Psalm 135. God's mighty acts in history display His greatness and show that He is superior to all pagan gods.

Psalm 136. This psalm was probably a responsive hymn sung in the temple. As the choir or priests recited the main part of the hymn, the people responded, "His mercy endureth for ever."

Psalm 137. This psalm from the exile in Babylon shows how the Israelites missed their homeland: "By the rivers of Babylon...we wept, when we remembered Zion" (v. 1).

Psalm 138. A prayer of thanksgiving for God's kindness, truth, and mercy.

Psalm 139. The psalmist celebrates God's unlimited knowledge and universal presence. There is nothing God doesn't know—even the psalmist's unexpressed thoughts (v. 2).

Psalm 140. Dangerous people are threatening the life of the psalmist, and he prays for God's protection.

Psalm 141. The psalmist prays that he will not use the same tactics against his enemies that they are using against him—and thus fall into sin.

Psalm 142. A prayer of David for protection when he was hiding in a cave from King Saul (1 Sam. 22:1–5).

Psalm 143. A plaintive cry for God's guidance and direction: "Teach me to do thy will" (v. 10).

[150] PRAISE WITH CYMBALS. *Praise him [God] upon the loud cymbals; praise him upon the high sounding cymbals* (Ps. 150:5).

The cymbals of Bible times were similar to our modern cymbals. Two circular plates of brass were struck against each other to produce a clanging or ringing sound.

Two different types of cymbals are apparently mentioned in this verse. "Loud" cymbals were probably similar to the large metal plates used in modern marching bands. The "high sounding" cymbals may have been similar to our modern castanets. Worn on the fingers of both hands, these were struck together rapidly to produce a distinctive rattling or rhythmic sound.

Psalm 144. A battle song asking for victory under the leadership of the Lord. The army of Israel may have sung or chanted psalms like this as it went into battle.

Psalm 145. A psalm of pure praise to God for His wondrous works: "Great is the LORD, and greatly to be praised; and his greatness is unsearchable" (v. 3).

Psalm 146. The psalmist celebrates God's universal reign and calls on people to place their trust in Him.

Psalm 147. A hymn of praise focusing on God as protector of His people Israel and as Creator of the universe.

Psalm 148. A hymn of universal praise. Let everything praise God: angels, sun and moon, heavens, waters, mountains, animals, kings, men, women, and children.

Psalm 149. The psalmist exhorts all the people of Israel to praise the Lord, their faithful and mighty King.

Psalm 150. The book of Psalms ends with a ringing affirmation of praise to God: "Let every thing that hath breath praise the LORD" (v. 6).

PROVERBS

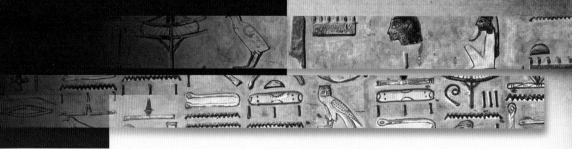

OVERVIEW: Wise sayings and observations on life designed to motivate believers to walk in the way of wisdom.

Introduction to Proverbs

The book of Proverbs is one of three books in the Old Testament classified as wisdom literature. The other two are Job and Ecclesiastes. They are known as books of wisdom because they deal with philosophical issues such as the meaning of life and behavior that leads to happiness and contentment in daily living.

Proverbs is the most practical of these three books. It contains wise sayings on how to live in harmony with God as well as other people. The underlying theme of Proverbs is that true wisdom consists of showing respect for God and living in harmony with His commands.

The very first verse of Proverbs identifies its author as "Solomon the son of David, king of Israel" (1:1). Even among other nations beyond Israel, Solomon was noted for his great wisdom (1 Kings 4:29–34). So he certainly had good qualifications for writing this book.

But some chapters within the book are attributed to other writers, including Agur (30:1) and King Lemuel (31:1). Solomon probably wrote the basic core of Proverbs but added some writings from other sources and gave proper credit to their writers.

The book of Proverbs is the most practical, down-to-earth book in the Old Testament. It reads like a manual of instructions for daily living, even using occasional humor to make an important point: "Even a fool, when he holdeth his peace, is counted wise: and he that shutteth his lips is esteemed a man of understanding" (17:28).

In this realistic book you will find advice on the importance of home and family, dealing with pride, getting along with others, the perils of adultery, getting ahead through hard work, the dangers of strong drink, treating the poor with kindness and compassion, and dealing honestly and forthrightly with others in business relationships.

Summary of Proverbs

1:1–7. This brief introduction to the book of Proverbs states its purpose: to give instruction in wisdom.

1:8–33. The phrase "my son" (v. 8) is repeated often throughout Proverbs. The authors of Proverbs are imparting good advice and practical rules for living, as a father might do with his son. Those who heed the counsel of wisdom will not fall into evil.

2:1–22. The Lord is the true source of wisdom. Those who seek Him will avoid the pitfalls of sin and will not be enticed into adulterous relationships.

3:1–12. It is best to trust God for insight and direction and not to depend on human understanding: "In all thy ways acknowledge him, and he shall direct thy paths" (v. 6).

3:13–26. Happy is the person who finds

1:1–7. King Solomon, famous for his wisdom, probably wrote most of Proverbs. The Bible says Solomon composed 3,000 proverbs and 1,005 songs (1 Kings 4:32).

wisdom and understanding. He will have nothing to fear, since his confidence is in the Lord.

3:27–35. Treat your neighbors with kindness. Do not envy or copy the ways of the wicked.

4:1–27. Avoid evil and the company of those who commit evil deeds. Follow the straight and narrow path of righteousness. Do not criticize others or speak idle words.

5:1–23. Marriage is sacred in the eyes of the Lord. Stay away from extramarital affairs, and cultivate your relationship with your spouse.

6:1–5. Do not enter into contracts carelessly or make foolish promises to others.

6:6–15. Idleness and laziness lead to poverty. Follow the example of the ant; it works diligently without having to be hounded by a supervisor!

[6:6–15] FROM NAUGHTY TO WORTHLESS. *A naughty person [scoundrel, NIV], a wicked man, walketh with a froward [corrupt, NIV] mouth* (Prov. 6:12).

The word translated as "naughty person" or "scoundrel" in this verse literally means "son of Belial." In the Hebrew language, *Belial* means "worthless" or "useless." Thus, one mark of a worthless person is the evil or corrupt speech that comes from his or her mouth.

People in the Bible who were called "worthless" or "son of Belial" include the evil sons of Eli the priest (1 Sam. 2:12), those who supported Jeroboam's rebellion against the southern tribes of Israel (2 Chron. 13:7), and those who gave false testimony against Naboth at the urging of Jezebel (1 Kings 21:11–13).

6:16–19. A list of seven things that the Lord hates: pride, lying, murder, wickedness, the spreading of gossip, the bearing of false witness, and the stirring up of trouble among people.

6:20–35. A second exhortation to avoid adulterous relationships (Prov. 5).

7:1–27. A third exhortation to avoid adulterous relationships (Prov. 5; 6:20–35).

8:1–36. In this hymn of praise, wisdom is exalted as something that is more valuable than gold and silver or precious stones. Wisdom was present with God when He created the world. This is another way of saying that God is the author of all wisdom.

9:1–18. Both foolishness and wisdom are personified as women. They illustrate the two different approaches to life.

10:1–32. These proverbs draw a contrast between the wise/righteous/godly and the foolish/unrighteous/wicked: "The mouth of a righteous man is a well of life: but violence covereth the mouth of the wicked" (v. 11).

11:1–31. The contrast between the wise and the foolish continues: "He that trusteth in his riches shall fall: but the righteous shall flourish as a branch" (v. 28).

12:1–28. The contrast between the wise and the foolish continues: "Lying lips are abomination to the LORD: but they that deal truly are his delight" (v. 22; see Rev. 22:15).

13:1–25. The contrast between the wise and foolish continues: "Every prudent man dealeth with knowledge: but a fool layeth open his folly" (v. 16).

14:1–35. The contrast between the wise and the foolish continues. But some of these proverbs have a touch of humor: "The poor is hated even of his own neighbour: but the rich hath many friends" (v. 20).

15:1–33. The contrast between the wise and the foolish continues: "The thoughts of the wicked are an abomination to the LORD: but the words of the pure are pleasant words" (v. 26; see Ps. 37:30).

16:1–33. These proverbs give moral and ethical advice on various subjects: "Pride goeth

[17:1–28] KEEP THE GATE LOW. *He that exalteth his gate [builds a high gate, NIV] seeketh destruction* (Prov. 17:19).

The typical house of Bible times consisted of four to six rooms built around a central courtyard. This courtyard was similar to a modern hallway. First you entered the courtyard through the front door, or gateway. Then you used the courtyard to gain access to all the rooms in the house.

The gateway into a house was normally only about four feet high. These low entrances may have been designed to keep thieves from riding horses into the courtyard. Thus, the writer of Proverbs states that anyone who built his gate high was asking for trouble. This was a symbolic way of saying that pride or self-exaltation also leads to destruction.

23:1–35. More proverbs with moral and ethical advice: "Let not thine heart envy sinners: but be thou in the fear of the Lord all the day long" (v. 17; see Ps. 37:1).

24:1–34. More proverbs with moral and ethical advice: "Be not a witness against thy neighbour without cause; and deceive not with thy lips" (v. 28; see Eph. 4:25).

25:1–28. More proverbs with moral and ethical advice: "Confidence in an unfaithful man in time of trouble is like a broken tooth, and a foot out of joint" (v. 19; see Job 6:15).

26:1–28. More proverbs with moral and ethical advice: "Answer not a fool according to his folly, lest thou also be like unto him" (v. 4).

before destruction, and an haughty spirit before a fall" (v. 18; see Jer. 49:16).

17:1–28. More proverbs with moral and ethical advice: "A reproof entereth more into a wise man than an hundred stripes into a fool" (v. 10).

18:1–24. More proverbs with moral and ethical advice: "Death and life are in the power of the tongue: and they that love it shall eat the fruit thereof" (v. 21; see Matt. 12:37).

19:1–29. More proverbs with moral and ethical advice: "House and riches are the inheritance of fathers: and a prudent wife is from the Lord" (v. 14).

20:1–30. More proverbs with moral and ethical advice: "Bread of deceit is sweet to a man; but afterwards his mouth shall be filled with gravel" (v. 17).

21:1–31. More proverbs with moral and ethical advice: "The horse is prepared against the day of battle: but safety is of the Lord" (v. 31).

22:1–29. More proverbs with moral and ethical advice: "Train up a child in the way he should go: and when he is old, he will not depart from it" (v. 6; see Eph. 6:4).

[25:1–28] BEAUTIFUL WORDS. *A word fitly [aptly, NIV] spoken is like apples of gold in pictures [settings, NIV] of silver* (Prov. 25:11).

This verse refers to the beautiful metal engravings that were displayed in the homes of kings and the wealthy in Bible times. "Apples of gold" were probably carvings of apples that were made from gold or painted to look like gold. These were placed in a highly polished silver frame to give the entire work of art an ornate appearance.

The point of this proverb is that an appropriate word spoken at just the right time is a thing of beauty. Or to put it another way, "A wholesome tongue is a tree of life" (Prov. 15:4).

27:1–27. More proverbs with moral and ethical advice: "Let another man praise thee, and not thine own mouth; a stranger, and not thine own lips" (v. 2).

28:1–28. More proverbs with moral and ethical advice: "He that covereth his sins shall not prosper: but whoso confesseth and forsaketh them shall have mercy" (v. 13; see Job 31:33).

31:10–31. A herder's wife, photographed in the early 1900s. Proverbs, a book written especially for young men, closes by praising the value of a good wife.

31:1–9. People in positions of authority should avoid strong drink, lest it impair their judgment. They also have the responsibility to treat the poor and helpless with fairness and compassion.

31:10–31. The book of Proverbs ends with words of praise for a wife of noble character. She works hard to take care of her household, and she performs acts of kindness in her community. A wife like this is a priceless asset to her family: "Her price is far above rubies" (v. 10).

29:1–27. More proverbs with moral and ethical advice: "The fear of man bringeth a snare: but whoso putteth his trust in the LORD shall be safe" (v. 25).

30:1–9. God has infinite wisdom. Consider His wonderful works. By comparison, humans are weak and foolish.

30:10–33. The natural order reveals the wisdom and power of God. Humans are awestruck by many things in nature that they cannot understand (Ps. 104).

[30:10–33] CHURNING UP ANGER. *The churning of milk bringeth forth butter…so the forcing of wrath [stirring up anger, NIV] bringeth forth strife* (Prov. 30:33).

In Bible times butter was produced by placing milk in a bag made from an animal skin and shaking it vigorously back and forth until the butter fat separated from the milk.

This proverb has a "just as" construction. Just as surely as shaking milk produces butter, giving vent to one's anger will cause strife and trouble. The phrase "stirring up anger" suggests that a person can feed his or her anger until it becomes uncontrollable.

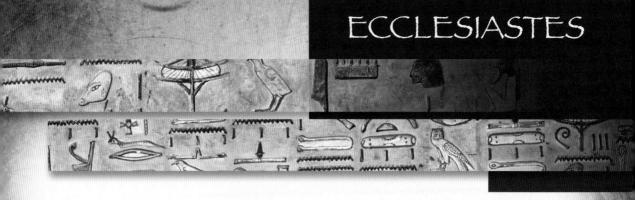

Overview: A philosophical essay on the futility and emptiness of life apart from God.

Introduction to Ecclesiastes

The book of Ecclesiastes takes its title from the Greek word *ekklesiastes*, meaning "assembly" or "congregation." The author of the book identifies himself as "the Preacher" (1:1), or one who assembles a congregation.

This author reveals the theme of Ecclesiastes in the second verse of his book: "Vanity of vanities; all is vanity" (1:2). He wants us to understand what he has learned through his own experience—that all human achievements are empty and unfulfilling when pursued as ends in themselves.

He repeats this phrase throughout the book, showing how wisdom, hard work, wealth, learning, fame, and pleasure—in and of themselves—do not bring happiness. Life's highest good, he delares at the conclusion of the book, is to "fear God, and keep his commandments" (12:13).

This preacher of the-things-in-life-that-really-matter further identifies himself as "the son of David, king in Jerusalem" (1:1). This must have been Solomon, the king who was noted for his superior wisdom and great riches (1 Kings 4:29–34; 10:14–23). He probably wrote Ecclesiastes near the end of his life as he looked back and measured the meaning of all his achievements.

This book shows that earthly possessions, popularity, and great accomplishments do not bring lasting happiness. True joy is a result of serving God and following His will for our lives.

Summary of Ecclesiastes

1:1–11. The author of the book identifies himself as the Preacher (probably Solomon). He observes that life is vain and meaningless, and it seems to go around and around in an endless circle.

1:12–18. Even the accumulation of much learning and wisdom does not give meaning and purpose to life.

2:1–3. The pursuit of fun and pleasure fails to satisfy (Prov. 14:13).

2:4–11. Great wealth and accomplishments in themselves are empty and meaningless.

2:12–23. Both the wise man and the foolish man are destined to die—and neither of them knows what will happen after they are gone. Man's brief life on earth is filled with pain and sorrow (Job 14:1–2; James 4:13–14).

2:24–26. Perhaps the most sensible thing a person can do while on earth is to enjoy life's simple pleasures and take pride in his work.

3:1–8. There is an appropriate time for everything in life: "a time to keep silence, and a time to speak" (v. 7).

3:9–15. God's gift to man is his ability to take pleasure in the daily routine and to enjoy his work.

3:16–22. God judges the righteous and the

2:4–11. The Queen of Sheba visits King Solomon and is awed by his wealth. But the writer of Ecclesiastes, probably Solomon, moans that wealth is meaningless. We die, he says, and others spend whatever we've accumulated.

wicked. Eventually all life turns to dust, the substance from which man was originally created (Gen. 2:7).

4:1–16. The vanity of life is multiplied by man's idleness, envy, and greed.

5:1–7. Do not make a vow to God unless you intend to keep your promise and follow through on your commitment (Gen. 28:20–22).

5:8–20. A rich person doesn't sleep as soundly as a working man. The man of means is always worrying about what might happen to his possessions.

6:1–12. Another problem with wealth is that rich people are never satisfied with what they have. The more possessions they acquire, they more they want. Thus, they are ruled by their desires (Luke 18:18–30).

7:1–22. These verses consist of miscellaneous proverbs on many different subjects. They are similar to the sayings in the book of Proverbs.

7:23–29. While wisdom does not bring meaning to life, acting wisely is preferable to acting foolishly.

8:1–5. Wise people respect the king and bow to his authority (Dan. 4:35).

8:6–17. Solomon complains that life is not fair. Sometimes the righteous suffer while the wicked flourish and prosper.

9:1–10. Solomon laments the plight of those who have died. They are soon forgotten by the living. He exhorts the living to enjoy their brief days on earth.

9:11–18. Wisdom is better than brute strength and the weapons of war.

10:1–20. Miscellaneous proverbs on various subjects, particularly careless speech: "The

[9:1–10] **DRESSED IN WHITE.** *Let thy garments be always white* (Eccles. 9:8).

In the hot climate of Palestine, white was a sensible color for clothes. So it was only natural for Solomon, the author of Ecclesiastes, to express this wish for others.

The wearing of white clothes was also a symbol of purity and holiness—a characteristic of God and those who follow His commands. When Daniel saw God in a vision, He was dressed in white clothes (Dan. 7:9). In the end time, the redeemed are also to be "arrayed in white robes" (Rev. 7:13).

words of a wise man's mouth are gracious; but the lips of a fool will swallow up himself" (v. 12).

11:1–6. Solomon's advice in these verses is twofold: Don't put all your eggs in one basket ("Give a portion to seven, and also to eight," v. 2), and have a backup strategy in case your original plan does not work out ("Thou knowest not whether [it] shall prosper," v. 6).

11:7–12:7. Old age, with the inevitable loss of physical strength, arrives sooner than one expects. In their youthful years, people should enjoy life and honor their Creator.

12:8–14. Solomon concludes his search for meaning in life with this ringing affirmation: "Fear God, and keep his commandments: for this is the whole duty of man" (v. 13).

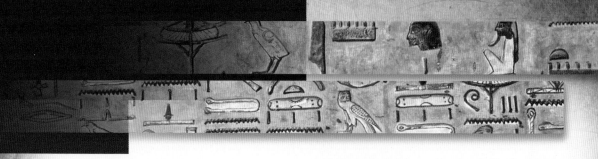

SONG OF SOLOMON

OVERVIEW: A love song celebrating human love relationships and God's love for His people.

Introduction to the Song of Solomon

This book is also called the "Song of Songs" because the author, Solomon, claimed it was his favorite or the most important among all the songs he wrote (1:1). This is significant, because Solomon is reported to have written 1,005 songs (1 Kings 4:32).

Perhaps this was Solomon's favorite song because it describes his love for a young woman who is referred to as a "Shulamite" (6:13). This wealthy king had hundreds of wives and concubines in his harem (1 Kings 11:3). But many of his marriages were political arrangements to seal treaties with other nations.

Is it possible that Solomon's marriage to the Shulamite—a peasant vineyard keeper whose skin had been darkened by long exposure to the sun—was the only meaningful and intimate marriage relationship he ever experienced?

Many people are shocked by the frank language of physical attraction between a husband and wife that appears in the Song of Solomon (7:1–9). But the physical side of marriage is a beautiful part of God's plan. God created man and woman for each other and declared, "Therefore shall a man leave his father and his mother, and shall cleave unto his wife: and they shall be one flesh" (Gen. 2:24).

Like the Book of Genesis, the Song of Solomon says a bold yes to the sanctity of marriage and the physical side of the husband-wife relationship.

Summary of the Song of Solomon

1:1. Introduction to Solomon's Song.

1:2–7. The bride expresses her love for her groom. She is dissatisfied with her appearance, since she is a girl from the country whose skin has been darkened by the sun (vv. 5–6).

[1:2–7] A MIDDAY REST. *Tell me, O thou whom my soul loveth, where thou feedest, where thou makest thy flock to rest at noon* (Song 1:7).

These are the words of King Solomon's bride as she searched for her beloved, the king. She referred to a common practice in Bible times of shepherds protecting their sheep by having them rest at midday in order to avoid the oppressive heat.

David may have referred to this practice when he compared God to a watchful shepherd: "The LORD is my shepherd; I shall not want. He maketh me to lie down in green pastures" (Ps. 23:1–2).

1:8–11. The groom reassures his bride that he is pleased with how she looks: "Thy cheeks are comely with rows of jewels" (v. 10).

1:12–17. Both bride and groom continue to express their affection for each other.

2:1–17. The setting for these verses is springtime in the country (vv. 11–13). The couple

1:8–11. Solomon's "song of songs," perhaps his favorite of the many he wrote, is an intimate love song in which a man and a woman express their devotion to each other. Some scholars say musicians may have performed this song at the king's wedding.

as pillars of marble, set upon sockets of fine gold" (v. 15).

6:1–3. In answer to the question "Whither is thy beloved gone?" (v. 1), the bride says he is with her, referring to herself as "his garden" (v. 2).

6:4–13. The groom describes the beauty of his one true love. All the queens and concubines in a king's harem do not compare to her.

7:1–13. The bride and groom express their mutual love and devotion to each other. They take great delight in the time they spend together.

8:1–14. The Song of Solomon ends with the bride and groom united in their mutual love for each other. The writer declares that true love is eternal: "Many waters cannot quench love, neither can the floods drown it" (v. 7).

express their joy that they are committed in love to each other: "My beloved is mine, and I am his" (v. 16).

3:1–6. The bride dreams about her groom and expresses sorrow over their separation.

3:7–11. The groom, symbolized by King Solomon in a royal procession, arrives for the wedding ceremony.

4:1–16. The groom expresses great delight in the beauty of his bride.

5:1–8. The bride has another dream that she is separated from her groom. She asks other people to join her frantic search for him.

5:9–16. The bride takes great pleasure in the appearance of her groom: "His legs are

[3:7–11] SOLOMON'S PORTABLE CHAIR. *King Solomon made himself a chariot of the wood of Lebanon. He made the pillars [posts, NIV] thereof of silver, the bottom thereof of gold, the covering of it of purple (Song 3:9–10).*

The Hebrew word translated as "chariot" in this passage actually refers to a palanquin—a portable couch or chair in which kings were carried from place to place by royal servants. Poles were fastened to each side of the palanquin. Four servants would then hoist the king in his chair and place the poles on their shoulders.

Solomon's gold and silver palanquin had a purple awning or cover to protect him from the sun. Purple was the color that signified royalty.

CHAPTER 4
BOOKS OF THE
MAJOR PROPHETS

The last seventeen books of the Old Testament are classified as books of prophecy. Five of these books—Isaiah, Jeremiah, Lamentations, Ezekiel, and Daniel—are known as major prophets, while the remaining twelve are called minor prophets.

These terms do not mean that some of these books are more important than others. Rather, as the Old Testament was compiled, the longer—or major—books were placed first in the prophetic section, while the shorter—or minor—books were placed second. The exception is Lamentations, a short book of only five chapters. This book was placed after Jeremiah because the prophet Jeremiah wrote Lamentations.

The word *prophet* comes from two Greek words that mean "to speak for." The prophets of the Old Testament received God's message by direct revelation and passed it on to others in written or spoken form. They literally spoke for God and prevailed upon His people to remain obedient and loyal to Him.

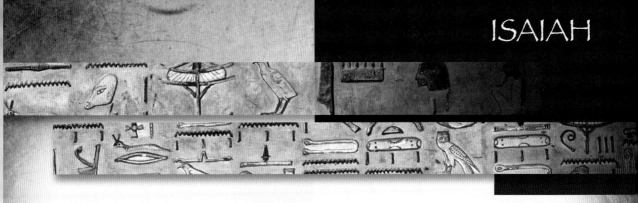

OVERVIEW: God will punish His people for their rebellion, but He also promises to send the Messiah, who will save them from their sins.

Introduction to Isaiah

The book of Isaiah is the best known prophetic book of the Old Testament, probably because of its emphasis on the theme of salvation and its prophecies about the coming Messiah. Because of its anticipation of the coming of Jesus Christ and His message of redemption, Isaiah is sometimes called the fifth Gospel.

Isaiah was called to the prophetic ministry "in the year that king Uzziah died" (6:1; about 740 B.C.) in a dramatic vision of the Lord in the temple. He preached God's message of judgment and hope to the people of the Southern Kingdom (Judah) for the next forty years.

In the early part of Isaiah's ministry, Judah's sister nation, the Northern Kingdom (Israel) fell to the Assyrians because of its sin and rebellion against God (2 Kings 17:5–23). Isaiah

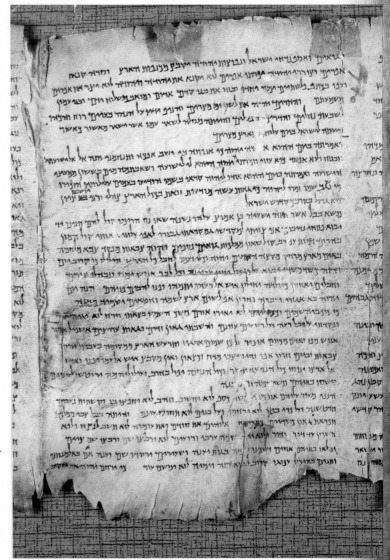

Isaiah's prophecy was one of many sacred Jewish writings preserved among the famous Dead Sea Scrolls. Scribes made this copy of the prophecy some 200 years before Jesus. That makes this scroll about 1,000 years older than copies used to translate the King James Version of the Bible.

[28:1–29] **METHODS OF THRESHING GRAIN.** *The fitches [caraway, NIV] are not threshed with a threshing instrument, neither is a cart wheel turned about upon the cummin; but the fitches are beaten out with a staff, and the cummin with a rod* (Isa. 28:27).

In this verse Isaiah contrasts two different methods of separating grain from the stalk in Bible times.

Small grains such as caraway and cummin were threshed by beating them with a stick. This method was also used when theshing a small amount of grain (Ruth 2:17). Dragging a stone threshing sledge ("threshing instrument") over the grain was the preferred method for threshing wheat or barley in large quantities.

Isaiah's point is that God knows us, and He knows our needs. He will use whatever method is appropriate as His discipline to keep us focused on Him.

28:1–29. Isaiah condemns both Judah (Southern Kingdom) and Israel (Northern Kingdom) because they have turned away from the Lord to worship false gods. He has harsh words especially for the leaders of these nations who have led the people astray (Jer. 8).

29:1–24. A woe is pronounced against Ariel, or Jerusalem, "the city where David dwelt" (v. 1). God is not impressed with those who flatter Him with words but refuse to obey His commands.

30:1–31:9. Through Isaiah the prophet, the Lord condemns the leaders of Judah who have formed an alliance with Egypt against the Assyrian threat. They should be turning to the Lord instead for protection against their enemies.

32:1–20. Isaiah calls on the people to look for the Messiah, the coming King, who will "reign in righteousness" (v. 1). But before this King arrives, the people must turn from their sinful and complacent ways.

33:1–24. The Lord alone is the hope and salvation of His people: "The LORD is our judge, the LORD is our lawgiver, the LORD is our king; he will save us" (v. 22; see Ps. 77:1–2).

34:1–17. Isaiah returns to the theme of God's judgment against the foreign nations (chaps. 13–23).

35:1–10. This chapter portrays a future time when God will redeem and restore His people. They will return to Jerusalem ("Zion," v. 10) with songs of joy and gladness.

36:1–22. King Sennacherib of Assyria invades Judah and captures several walled cities. He sends word to King Hezekiah of Judah that Assyria will attack with a superior force unless Judah surrenders.

37:1–38. King Hezekiah and the prophet Isaiah pray to the Lord, asking Him to save Judah from the Assyrian threat. God miraculously delivers the nation by destroying 185,000 warriors in Sennacherib's army (2 Kings 18:13–19:37).

[40:1–31] **GET READY FOR THE KING.** *Prepare ye the way of the LORD, make straight in the desert a highway for our God.... The crooked shall be made straight, and the rough places plain* (Isa. 40:3–4).

Roads of Bible times were little more than paths, rough and crude by modern standards. When a king traveled, his servants would go ahead of him, removing stones, filling in low places, and straightening curves so the king's journey would be more pleasant.

Isaiah found in this practice a spiritual principle. The people needed to prepare the way for the coming of the Lord in a new and fresh way—a reference to the future Messiah. In the New Testament, this passage was applied to John the Baptist, who prepared the way for the ministry of Jesus Christ (Luke 3:4–5).

49:1–55:13. Jesus endures a beating, a punishment that New Testament writers said fulfilled Isaiah's prophecy of a Suffering Servant: "wounded for our transgressions. . .and with his stripes we are healed" (Isa. 53:5).

38:1–22. King Hezekiah of Judah is seriously ill, and Isaiah tells him he will die. But Hezekiah prays humbly to the Lord, who graciously extends the king's life for fifteen more years (2 Kings 20:1–11).

39:1–8. Hezekiah foolishly shows off his royal riches to a messenger from the king of Babylon. Isaiah predicts that the Babylonians will defeat the nation of Judah and carry off these treasures at some future time (2 Kings 20:12–19).

40:1–31. The prophet Isaiah follows his prediction of disaster for Judah with words of encouragement. The Lord is the great comforter who never stops loving His people. He gives power and strength to those who depend on Him.

41:1–29. In contrast to lifeless idols that are fashioned by human hands, God is the living, awesome Lord who brought all of creation into being (Gen. 1:1–24). He alone is worthy of worship.

42:1–9. This is one of several "Servant" passages or "Servant Songs" in Isaiah (chaps. 49–55). The nations of Judah and Israel have failed to carry out the mission of world redemption that God intended. Therefore, He will accomplish this through one person—His coming Servant, the Messiah, His Son, Jesus Christ.

42:10–16. This redemptive mission of God's Servant is reason for rejoicing: "Give glory unto the Lord, and declare his praise in the islands" (v. 12).

42:17–25. In contrast to the faithfulness of God's Servant, the nations of Judah and

Israel have rejected the Lord and followed their own desires.

43:1–44:5. In spite of the unfaithfulness of His people, God forgives. He will walk with them in their humiliation and suffering.

44:6–20. These are some of the most striking verses in the Bible on the worship of false gods. How foolish it is for a person to worship something he has conceived in his mind and fashioned with his hands (Jer. 10:1–25).

44:21–28. In contrast to lifeless and powerless idols, the one true God is the living and powerful redeemer of His people.

45:1–13. The Lord promises to restore His people to their homeland after a period of exile in Babylonia and Persia. This will be accomplished by the Lord, who will use King Cyrus of Persia as an instrument in His plan (v. 1; see 2 Chron. 36:22–23).

45:14–25. The entire world will eventually turn to God because He alone offers salvation: "Look unto me, and be ye saved, all the ends of the earth: for I am God, and there is none else" (v. 22).

46:1–13. Isaiah reminds the people that the worship of idols is futile, since they are weak and helpless and offer no hope.

47:1–15. The nation of Babylonia will be devastated by the Lord because of its wickedness and pride.

48:1–22. Throughout their history the nations of Judah and Israel have rejected God. But He continues to love them and call them back from their wayward ways.

49:1–55:13. These seven chapters of Isaiah contain more of the prophet's famous "Servant Songs" (Isa. 42:1–9). At times the prophet seems to speak of the nations of Judah and Israel as God's servant. But in other places in these passages, it is clear that he is referring to the Servant who is to come—the

[47:1–15] NO HELP FROM STARGAZERS. *Let now the astrologers, the stargazers, the monthly prognosticators, stand up, and save thee from these things that shall come upon thee* (Isa. 47:13).

The words *astrologers, stargazers,* and *monthly prognosticators* refer to people who studied the stars and the movement of the moon in order to foretell the future. This was especially popular among the ancient Babylonians.

In Babylonia the astrologers were members of a specific caste. Persons born into this caste continued to practice the star-gazing and sign-reading skills inherited from their ancestors. Astrologers were among the people with magical powers summoned by King Nebuchadnezzar of Babylonia to interpret his strange dream (Dan. 2:2).

Isaiah declared that God would judge the people of Judah for their sins, and nothing could thwart His purpose. He—the Creator of the moon and stars—was more powerful than those who read the moon and stars.

Messiah. Chapter 53 is clearly messianic in nature. It portrays the "Suffering Servant"—Jesus Christ—who gave His life to secure redemption for others: "He was wounded for our transgressions, he was bruised for our iniquities: the chastisement of our peace was upon him; and with his stripes we are healed" (v. 5).

56:1–12. God is bringing a new age of salvation for His people. But He expects them to live as people who belong to Him, keeping His laws and practicing justice.

57:1–21. The Lord's people cannot worship the one true God and participate in idol worship at the same time. He demands their exclusive loyalty (Josh. 24:15).

58:1–14. True religion does not consist of observing rituals such as fasting and offering sacrifices. The Lord honors such things as obeying His commands and treating others with justice and fairness (Amos 5:18–27).

59:1–21. The prophet catalogs the wicked and sinful actions that have separated the people of Judah from the Lord: lying, vanity and pride, murder of innocent people, and rebellion against God.

60:1–62:12. In these three chapters, Isaiah gives us a glimpse of the future glory of Jerusalem. God will take delight in His people. They will shine like a beacon of righteousness, drawing all nations of the earth to bow before the Lord. Jesus quoted from Isaiah 61:1–2 when He identified Himself as the Messiah who had been sent by God "to preach good tidings unto the meek...to bind up the brokenhearted, to proclaim liberty to the captives" (v. 1; see Luke 4:18–19).

63:1–64:12. But before these blessings fall upon God's people, He must punish them for their sin and rebellion. This leads Isaiah to

63:1–64:12. A rider tours the ruins of Jerusalem, which was destroyed by Babylon in 586 B.C.—as predicted in Isaiah 63.

[60:1–62:12] AN OPEN GATE POLICY. *Therefore thy gates shall be open continually; they shall not be shut day nor night* (Isa. 60:11).

The gates of walled cities (see the note "Walled Cities" on p. 444) were closed and bolted at night as a security measure. Residents of the city who didn't make it back inside before darkness fell were forced to spend the night outside.

Isaiah portrayed a future time under the reign of the Messiah when city gates would never be closed. God would be all the protection the people would need.

offer a beautiful prayer that God will uphold and sustain them during their days of trouble and suffering (2 Kings 25:1–12).

65:1–66:24. Isaiah ends his book by drawing a contrast between two different destinies. Total destruction awaits those who continue in their sin and refuse to turn to God. But a life of joy and peace is the destiny of those who follow the Lord.

JEREMIAH

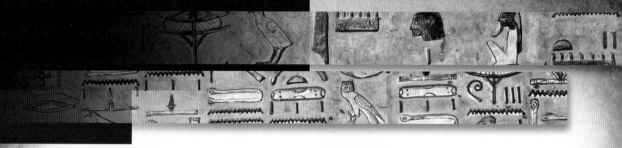

OVERVIEW: The Lord will use the pagan Babylonians as His instrument of judgment against Judah (Southern Kingdom).

Introduction to Jeremiah

For about forty years, the prophet Isaiah had tried to turn the Southern Kingdom (Judah) from its sinful ways (see the introduction to Isaiah on p. 489). About seventy-five years after Isaiah died, God raised up another spokesman, the prophet Jeremiah, to continue delivering His message to His people. Like Isaiah, Jeremiah also ministered in Judah for a period of forty years—from about 625 to 585 B.C.

4:1–31. Michelangelo's Jeremiah, a portrait of sadness. God instructed Jeremiah to tell the people of Jerusalem that their nation would fall. It was a prophecy Jeremiah lived to see.

But these two prophets were very different in the type of message they were called on to deliver. Isaiah was a prophet of hope, but Jeremiah was a prophet of despair. By Jeremiah's time the nation of Judah had degenerated into such a godless state that its destruction was assured. It was Jeremiah's task to deliver this bad-news message from the Lord: As punishment for its sin and idolatry, Judah would be defeated by the pagan Babylonians.

When God called Jeremiah to the prophetic ministry, He made it clear that his job would not be easy. But He promised to strengthen and protect him: "I have made thee this day a defenced city, and an iron pillar...against the kings of Judah....And they shall fight against thee; but they shall not prevail...for I am with thee...to deliver thee" (1:18–19).

Jeremiah needed this assurance and protection because he was mocked, criticized, and abused by his own people throughout his entire ministry.

As the power of the Babylonians grew, Jeremiah was accused of treason because he called on the leaders of Judah to surrender, since their fate was already sealed by the Lord. Citizens of his own hometown threatened his life. He was imprisoned several times for delivering the Lord's unpopular message.

This faithful prophet's message from the Lord was verified with the fall of Jerusalem to the Babylonian army in 587 B.C. Jeremiah will always be remembered as a prophet who spoke God's truth without compromise, in spite of strong opposition.

Summary of Jeremiah

1:1–3. This brief introduction to the book tells us that Jeremiah prophesied during the reigns of three different kings of Judah—Josiah, Jehoiakim, and Zedekiah—or a period of about forty years.

1:4–19. God calls Jeremiah to his prophetic ministry. His task is to proclaim God's forthcoming judgment against the nation of Judah because the people are worshiping false gods. The prophet's vision of a budding almond tree shows that God's judgment is coming soon. The vision of a boiling pot facing toward the north indicates the direction from which this judgment will come.

2:1–37. God led His people out of slavery in Egypt and brought them into the Promised Land (Exod. 12:32–42). But they have rejected Him to serve the pagan gods of the surrounding nations. God's charge against them through the prophet Jeremiah is that "they have forsaken me the fountain of living waters, and hewed them out cisterns, broken cisterns, that can hold no water" (v. 13).

[2:1–37] DRINKING FROM A CISTERN. *They have forsaken me [God] the fountain [spring, NIV] of living waters, and hewed them out cisterns, broken cisterns, that can hold no water* (Jer. 2:13).

Cisterns of Bible times were little more than deep pits dug in the ground or shallow reservoirs carved out of limestone rock. Rainwater was directed into these holding tanks and stored for use during the dry season.

Compared to a spring from which fresh groundwater flowed, a cistern left a lot to be desired. The water could get contaminated, or the cistern could lose its water supply because of a leak.

Jeremiah criticized the foolish people of Judah for drinking water from a cistern when fresh springwater was available. They had forsaken the living Lord and were worshiping lifeless pagan gods.

3:1–25. The Lord compares the idolatry of Judah with the sin of adultery (Hosea 2:1–13). God's people promised to remain faithful to Him alone. But they have gone back on their promise and are committing spiritual adultery through their worship of idols.

4:1–31. God's declaration that He will devastate the land of Judah leads Jeremiah to inspect the destruction and to lament the fate of his fellow citizens: "I beheld, and, lo, the fruitful place was a wilderness, and all the cities thereof were broken down at the presence of the LORD, and by his fierce anger" (v. 26).

5:1–6:30. God reveals that He will use a foreign power as His instrument of judgment against His people. This mighty and ancient nation will invade Judah, destroy crops and livestock, and overrun all its walled cities.

7:1–34. The Lord commands Jeremiah to stand in the entrance to the temple in Jerusalem. Here he denounces their sin and calls on them to turn back to the Lord before it is too late. The people have substituted religious rituals, such as offering sacrifices at the temple, for obedience of God's commands. But God is not fooled by such practices. He demands total loyalty and commitment from His people.

8:1–22. The leaders of Judah have led the people astray. For this, they will be judged severely by the Lord: "They shall not be gathered, nor be buried; they shall be for dung upon the face of the earth" (v. 2; see Isa. 28; Zech. 10–11).

9:1–26. This chapter is a graphic portrait of the depths to which people can sink when they turn their backs on God. The sins of Judah enumerated by Jeremiah include lying, slandering, and bearing false witness against others.

10:1–25. People who worship idols are vain and foolish. They bow down before a wooden statue decorated with gold that they have made with their own hands. Such gods are

---

[9:1–26] NOT A RUNAWAY. *Oh that I [Jeremiah] had in the wilderness a lodging place of wayfaring men [travelers, NIV]; that I might leave my people, and go from them! (Jer. 9:2).*

Jeremiah is known as the "weeping prophet" because it broke his heart to see his countrymen rejecting the Lord and following false gods. In this verse he expressed his desire to leave his familiar surroundings, escape to the desert, and live among strangers. Then he would not be exposed every day to the sin and rebellion of the nation of Judah.

But Jeremiah never acted on his desire. For about forty years he stayed at the prophetic task to which God had called him. He is one of the Bible's best examples of faithfulness and obedience to the Lord.

---

weak and powerless. But the Lord is the one true God, awesome in majesty and power, who is able to deliver and protect His people (Isa. 44:6–20).

11:1–17. The Lord charges His people with breaking the covenant they had formed with Him in their early history. They have turned from Him and worshiped other gods. They will be punished for their waywardness.

11:18–23. Jeremiah learns that certain "men of Anathoth" (v. 21), his hometown, have plotted to kill him because of his prophecies against Judah. But God promises to protect the prophet and to punish these people for their actions.

12:1–17. Jeremiah complains to God because the wicked people in the land seem to be prospering, while the righteous followers of the Lord are suffering. God assures the prophet that this situation will be remedied when He exercises His judgment throughout the land.

13:1–11. The Lord commands Jeremiah to place a linen girdle (belt or sash) among the rocks on the bank of the Euphrates River. The prophet retrieves it some time later after it has rotted. Just as the girdle was ruined, God declares, He will eventually "mar the pride of Judah, and the great pride of Jerusalem" (v. 9).

13:12–27. At God's command, Jeremiah tells the people of Judah that "every bottle shall be filled with wine" (v. 12). But this is not a symbol of prosperity. It actually means that the inhabitants of Jerusalem will be as if they were drunk, helpless to defend themselves against the coming invasion from a foreign nation.

14:1–22. Jeremiah complains that false prophets are denying his message that God will punish Judah through a great disaster. They are predicting peace and prosperity for the land (1 Kings 22:1–28). God assures Jeremiah that he is the true prophet who is delivering the message He intends for His people.

15:1–21. Jeremiah reminds the Lord that he has been mocked and persecuted by his own people for proclaiming God's message of forthcoming judgment. He wonders how much longer he can stand up under the pressure. And what will happen to him when Jerusalem falls? God assures His faithful prophet of His strength and protection: "I will make thee unto this people a fenced brasen wall: and they shall fight against thee, but they shall not prevail against thee: for I am with thee to save thee and to deliver thee" (v. 20).

16:1–21. The Lord tells Jeremiah that he will not be permitted to marry and have children. To do

so would be futile, since children have no future in a land marked for destruction.

17:1–8. Jeremiah declares that the sin of the people of Judah is no surface problem. It has infected and corrupted their total being. They can be delivered from their evil only if they repent and turn to God.

17:9–27. Judah is so corrupt that the people have stopped observing the Sabbath (Exod. 20:8–11). Such ungodly behavior will be punished severely by the Lord.

18:1–17. A potter at work in Israel. After Jeremiah watched a potter reshape a marred vessel, God said He would do the same with the Jewish nation.

18:1–17. Jeremiah watches a potter reshape a piece of clay until he makes exactly the vase or bowl he had in mind. Just like this human craftsman, God has the right to shape the nation of Judah into the people He wants them to be. If they refuse His shaping influence, He will discipline them by scattering them before their enemies.

[18:1–17] A LESSON FROM THE POTTER. *Then I [Jeremiah] went down to the potter's house, and, behold, he wrought a work on the wheels* (Jer. 18:3).

The Lord instructed Jeremiah to watch a potter at work and He would give the prophet a special message for the people. Ancient potters made pots by shaping wet clay with their hands as it turned on a foot-powered pedestal.

As Jeremiah watched the potter, the vessel he was making collapsed. The potter massaged the clay into a lump and began to form it into another pot. The message for the people was that Judah was like clay in the hands of God. They should allow Him to shape them into a vessel of His own choosing (Jer. 18:6).

18:18–23. The enemies of Jeremiah threaten his life again (11:18–23). He prays a bitter prayer of vengeance against them. This prayer is similar to outcries against the enemies of the psalmist in the Psalms (Ps. 59).

19:1–15. At God's command the prophet breaks a bottle, or jug, before the people of Judah. This object lesson is a warning that God will shatter the nation unless the people forsake their worship of pagan gods and turn back to God.

20:1–6. Pashur, son of Immer the priest, beats Jeremiah and puts him in shackles because he is proclaiming God's message of judgment against Judah. The prophet predicts that Pashur and his household as well as other citizens of Judah will be carried away as captives by the Babylonians.

20:7–18. Jeremiah cries out to God because of the burden he bears as a spokesman for the Lord against his country. This is such a difficult job for the prophet that he laments the day he was born (Job 3:1–4).

21:1–14. The setting for this chapter is apparently the final siege of Jerusalem by the Babylonians while Zedekiah was king of Judah (2 Kings 25:1–12). Resistance against the Babylonians is futile, the prophet tells the king. Their only hope for survival is to surrender.

22:1–30. This chapter contains Jeremiah's prophecies of disaster against three different kings of Judah: Shallum (vv. 11–17), Jehoiakim (vv. 18–23), and Coniah, or Jehoiachin (vv. 24–30). Chronologically, these prophecies were delivered before the events described in Jeremiah 21.

23:1–8. Jeremiah predicts that a faithful remnant of God's people will return to their homeland after their period of captivity by a foreign nation is over. He also speaks of the future Messiah, "THE LORD OUR RIGHTEOUSNESS" (v. 6). This prophecy was fulfilled with the birth of Jesus about 600 years after Jeremiah's time (Luke 2:1–7).

23:9–40. Jeremiah denounces the false prophets of Judah who are telling the leaders of the nation what they want to hear rather than declaring the word of the Lord (Jer. 14).

24:1–10. God shows Jeremiah a basket of good figs and a basket of spoiled figs. The good figs represent the faithful remnant of God's people whom He will return to their homeland after the Babylonian captivity is over (2 Chron. 36:22–23). But the spoiled figs represent King Zedekiah of Judah and his sons, who will be wiped out when the nation is defeated (2 Kings 25:1–12).

25:1–38. Because of their idolatry, the people of Judah will be carried away as captives to

Babylon for a period of seventy years. The nations that surround Judah will also fall to the Babylonian invasion.

26:1–19. After Jehoiakim becomes king of Judah, God sends Jeremiah to proclaim His message to the people: Jerusalem will fall because of the sin of the people. The leaders of Judah push for Jeremiah's execution, but he is spared when a group defends his prophetic ministry.

26:20–24. King Jehoiakim has Urijah the prophet executed because he is proclaiming God's forthcoming judgment just like Jeremiah. The prophet Jeremiah must have wondered if he would be next in line for the executioner.

27:1–22. The setting for this chapter is the continuing Babylonian threat against Judah. The Babylonian army had already defeated King Jeconiah/Jehoiachin, ransacked Jerusalem, carried some citizens into exile, and robbed the temple treasures (vv. 18–20). Jehoiakim was ruling over Judah (v. 1). God directed Jeremiah to put on a yoke—a symbol of submission—and to wear it in the city of Jerusalem to show that the nation's only hope for survival was unconditional surrender to Babylonia.

28:1–17. Hananiah, a false prophet, denies Jeremiah's prophecy that the Babylonians will defeat the nation of Judah. Instead, Hananiah predicts peace and prosperity for the land. As Jeremiah predicts, Hananiah dies within a short time because he delivered a false prophecy in the Lord's name and led the people astray (Jer. 14; 23:9–40).

29:1–9. Jeremiah writes a letter to the Jewish captives who had already been taken to Babylon (see summary of 27:1–22). He advises them to settle down and make the best of life in Babylon, since they will be there for many years (25:11).

29:10–19. God promises that a faithful remnant of His people will eventually return from captivity to their homeland.

29:20–32. The Lord pronounces judgment against several false prophets who have been leading the people to trust in a lie.

30:1–31:40. Even in the midst of the punishment of His people, God will show mercy. A remnant will be saved and restored to their homeland. At the same time, God will establish a new covenant with those who belong to Him. This new spiritual covenant, written on their hearts, will replace the covenant of law, which they were unable to keep. Ultimately, this promise of a new covenant was fulfilled with the coming of Jesus Christ and His sacrificial death and offer of eternal life for all who accept Him as Lord and Savior (Heb. 9:11–15).

32:1–44. While the Babylonians are attacking Jerusalem, Jeremiah buys a plot of land in Anathoth, his hometown. This shows his confidence in the promise of the Lord that the land throughout Judah will eventually be valuable again. This will happen when the remnant of God's people return from captivity to their homeland.

33:1–26. This chapter is messianic in nature. The Lord reminds His people of the promise He had made to David several centuries before—that one of David's descendants would always occupy the throne of Judah (2 Sam. 7:12–16). Jesus as the "son of David" (Matt. 1:1) is the ultimate fulfillment of this prophecy.

34:1–7. The Lord sends Jeremiah to King Zedekiah of Judah with a message while Jerusalem is under siege. The message is that the city will fall to Babylonia and Zedekiah will be captured by the enemy.

34:8–22. God expresses His displeasure that the citizens of Judah have broken His law about enslavement of their own countrymen. They are keeping Jewish slaves in perpetual slavery rather than freeing them after seven years, as the law commands (Deut. 15:12–15).

35:1–19. A group of people known as the Rechabites seeks refuge in Jerusalem because of the Babylonian threat. Their refusal to drink wine—a commitment they had made many years before—emphasizes the failure of the people of Judah to keep their covenant with the Lord.

36:1–10. Jeremiah enlists a scribe named Baruch to write down his prophecies of God's judgment against the nation of Judah. Baruch then reads the prophet's words to the people in the temple.

36:11–26. King Jehoiakim of Judah sends for the scroll after he hears about Jeremiah's written message. To show his contempt for the prophet, he burns the scroll bit by bit as it is read by one of his aides.

36:27–32. Jeremiah reproduces the destroyed scroll by dictating God's message again to

---

[36:11–26] BARUCH'S INK AND PAPER. *Then Baruch answered them, He [Jeremiah] pronounced all these words unto me with his mouth, and I wrote them with ink in the book [scroll, NIV]* (Jer. 36:18).

Baruch was the faithful scribe of Jeremiah who wrote down the messages of the prophet in order to preserve them for future generations.

The ink used by Baruch and other ancient scribes was made by mixing soot, lampblack, or ground charcoal with water and gum. The scroll on which he wrote Jeremiah's prophecies was probably made from the papyrus plant or from animal skins.

While this writing was primitive by modern standards, it held up well. The manuscripts in the collection known as the Dead Sea Scrolls, discovered in 1947, were still legible, even though they had been written about 2,000 years before.

Baruch. He also expands the original message of judgment. The Lord declares that King Jehoiakim will be judged severely for destroying the scroll.

37:1–21. Jeremiah is imprisoned on the false charge that he is deserting his own people to seek refuge among the Babylonian army. King Zedekiah asks him if he has any word from the Lord for Judah, since the nation is under attack by the enemy. Jeremiah's reply is not what the king wants to hear: "Thou shalt be delivered into the hand of the king of Babylon" (v. 17).

38:1–13. Jeremiah's enemies throw him into a dungeon or pit—perhaps a cistern with mud in the bottom—and leave him to die. With King Zedekiah's permission, Ebed-melech, a servant of the king, pulls the prophet out of the pit.

38:14–28. King Zedekiah summons Jeremiah in secret and asks him what he should do. Jerusalem is running out of food and water because of the prolonged Babylonian siege. The prophet tells him the only way to save himself and the city is to surrender to the Babylonian army.

39:1–10. Just as Jeremiah had predicted for many years, the Babylonians conquer Judah. After a long siege, they break down the walls of Jerusalem and burn the city. King Zedekiah and his sons are captured when they try to escape. The proud king of Judah is forced to watch as his sons are executed. Then the Babylonians put out his eyes and carry him away in chains to their capital city. Also forced into exile are the elite members of Jewish society. The peasants are left behind to cultivate the land (2 Kings 25:1–12).

39:11–14. King Nebuchadrezzar of Babylon releases Jeremiah from prison, treats him with kindness, and allows him to remain in Judah.

36:27–32. A scribe named Baruch recorded the prophecies that Jeremiah dictated to him. In a day when most people couldn't read or write, scribes were often hired to draft contracts and other important documents.

39:15–18. Jeremiah assures Ebed-melech, who had pulled him out of a cistern (38:1–13), that his life will be spared because of his trust in the Lord.

40:1–6. The Babylonians treat Jeremiah with kindness and allow him to decide whether he wants to go to Babylon or stay in Jerusalem. He decides to stay with the poor of the land who have been left behind.

40:7–41:18. The Babylonians place Gedaliah in charge of affairs in Judah. Ishmael, a Jewish zealot, incites a mob and assassinates Gedaliah, along with several Babylonian citizens who were helping to keep order in the land (2 Kings 25:22–25).

42:1–22. Representatives of the Jewish remnant left in Judah ask Jeremiah what they should do. They are apparently afraid of retaliation from the Babylonians for Gedaliah's assassination; they wonder if they should seek safety in Egypt. Jeremiah predicts they will be destroyed if they flee to Egypt. He advises them to stay in Judah.

43:1–7. Disregarding Jeremiah's advice, the Jewish remnant seeks refuge in Egypt, carrying Jeremiah and Baruch with them.

43:8–44:30. Jeremiah warns the Jewish remnant in Egypt that it is futile to try to hide from God's judgment in a foreign land. The Babylonians will eventually conquer Egypt, and they will be carried into exile to join their Jewish countrymen who have already been settled in Babylon.

45:1–5. Jeremiah assures his faithful scribe, Baruch, that Baruch's life will be spared in the devastating events that lie ahead.

[46:1–51:64] JUDGMENT AGAINST MOAB. *Moab… hath not been emptied from vessel to vessel…therefore his taste remained in him, and his scent is not changed* (Jer. 48:11).

This verse refers to a step in the process of making wine when it was poured from one jar to another to improve its taste. Jeremiah declared that Israel's enemy, Moab, had not yet experienced devastation by an enemy nation—or being "emptied from vessel to vessel."

But this would change in the future when Moab would be judged by the Lord for its sin. God would "empty his [Moab's] vessels, and break their bottles" (Jer. 48:12).

46:1–51:64. These five chapters contain Jeremiah's prophecies against the nations. God's judgment will be poured out against the nations that surround Judah as well as Judah itself. Marked for destruction because of their idolatry are Egypt (chap. 46), the Philistines (chap. 47), Moab (chap. 48), the Ammonites (49:1–6), Edom (49:7–22), Damascus (49:23–27), Kedar and Hazor (49:28–33), Elam (49:34–39), and Babylonia (chaps. 50–51).

52:1–34. The book of Jeremiah ends with a review of one of the greatest tragedies in the history of God's people: the fall of Jerusalem to the Babylonian army. This chapter covers the same events as those described in chapter 39 (see also 2 Kings 24–25). Perhaps Jeremiah revisited this national tragedy to remind his readers of the perils of refusing to follow the Lord.

OVERVIEW: Jeremiah laments the fall of Jerusalem to the Babylonian army.

Introduction to Lamentations

A lament is a cry of despair. Thus, Lamentations is appropriately named because it expresses great despair over the destruction of Jerusalem by the Babylonian army in 587 B.C.

This book was probably written by the prophet Jeremiah. He had warned Judah for many years that they would be defeated by a foreign power unless the people repented of their idol worship and turned back to the one true God (see the introduction to Jeremiah on p. 496).

Lamentations shows the sensitive side of Jeremiah's personality. He loved the city of Jerusalem and his native land, although he was compelled by the Lord to deliver a harsh message of judgment against his fellow citizens. When the inevitable finally happened, he was overcome with grief and despair: "For these things I weep; mine eye, mine eye runneth down with water, because the comforter that should relieve my soul is far from me: my children are desolate, because the enemy prevailed" (1:16).

Summary of Lamentations

1:1–22. Jerusalem, capital of the nation of Judah, was once a proud and prosperous city. But now it lies in ruins, devastated and looted by the Babylonian army. Its streets

---

[1:1–22] TRAMPLED BY GOD'S JUDGMENT. *The Lord hath trodden the virgin, the daughter of Judah, as in a winepress* (Lam. 1:15).

Jeremiah referred to the city of Jerusalem as "the virgin, the daughter of Judah." He lamented the destruction of the city by the Babylonian army in 587 B.C.

Jerusalem had been trodden down like grapes in a winepress. In Bible times the juice was extracted from grapes to make wine by crushing them underfoot in a vat, or winepress, carved out of solid rock.

God's judgment is also described as a winepress in Isaiah 63:3 and Revelation 14:19–20; 19:15.

---

were once filled with people, but now it is almost deserted. The Babylonians have carried the leading citizens of Judah into captivity, leaving behind only a few peasants and farmers (2 Kings 25:1–12). The city is like a destitute widow who mourns for her family.

2:1–22. Why did this happen? The prophet Jeremiah declares that Jerusalem has only itself to blame for its predicament. The Lord had warned Judah for many years that the nation would be defeated by a foreign enemy unless it forsook its worship of false gods and turned back to the one true God. Now God has "thrown down, and hath not pitied: and he hath caused thine enemy to rejoice over thee" (v. 17).

3:1–42. Out of his despair over Jerusalem's plight, Jeremiah sees a glimmer of hope.

After all, the Babylonians have spared the lives of most of the Jewish people (v. 22). Perhaps through God's mercy and grace they will survive their ordeal of captivity in Babylon and be restored to their homeland at some future time.

3:43–66. Once again, Jeremiah is overwhelmed by the suffering and humiliation of the people of Judah. Their enemies had laughed and cheered when Jerusalem fell. The prophet asks God to pay them back for their cruelty.

4:1–20. These verses contain more stark pictures of the devastation of Jerusalem. Jeremiah condemns the priests and prophets for failing to lead the people back to God. This would have kept divine judgment from falling on the city.

1:1–22. The saddest book in the Bible, Lamentations tells the graphic and horrifying story of invaders laying siege to Jerusalem and then slaughtering the people.

4:21–22. The nation of Edom, an enemy of the Israelites for many years, apparently participated in the capture and destruction of Jerusalem (see the book of Obadiah). Jeremiah predicts that Judah will eventually be restored, but Edom will be permanently wiped out by the Lord.

5:1–22. Jeremiah reviews the numerous sufferings of the people of Judah. Then he prays for God to grant them restoration and forgiveness: "Turn thou us unto thee, O Lord, and we shall be turned; renew our days as of old" (v. 21).

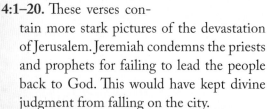

[5:1–22] FOXES IN JERUSALEM. *Because of the mountain of Zion, which is desolate, the foxes walk upon it* (Lam. 5:18).

Jeremiah used this word picture to show the desolation of Jerusalem (referred to as "Zion") after it was captured, plundered, and destroyed by the Babylonians.

The city was virtually empty, since the leading citizens of Judah had been carried away to Babylon as captives. Once-thriving Jerusalem was now the haunt of foxes and other wild animals.

The Hebrew word for "foxes" is often rendered as "jackals" (see the NIV). These animals, similar to wild dogs, were scavengers. Jackals prowling through Jerusalem gives an even more vivid portrait of the plight of the city.

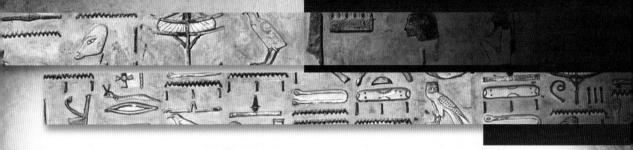

OVERVIEW: Prophecies of judgment and hope to God's people while they are in exile in Babylon.

Introduction to Ezekiel

The prophet Ezekiel received his messages from God through a series of visions. He addressed his prophecies to the Jewish exiles in Babylon across a twenty-year period, from about 593 to 573 B.C.

Ezekiel himself was one of those exiles. He was carried away from Judah about 597 B.C. during the first Babylonian invasion of his nation. Ten years later the Babylonians returned to Judah and destroyed the city of Jerusalem. Thus, Ezekiel's messages to the Jewish exiles

2:1–10. Ezekiel was a prophet who ministered while exiled in the Babylonian Empire in what is now Iraq. From there, he predicted that God would destroy the Jewish nation for its persistent sinning.

referred to tragedies that had already happened as well as those that would happen in the future.

Their period of exile in Babylon was a time of great disillusionment for the Jewish people. Now that they were reaping the fruits of their sins, there was little need for harsh condemnation. Ezekiel's major task was to encourage the people and give them hope for the future.

In the first part of Ezekiel's book, the prophet reminded the people of their sins and the losses they had suffered and predicted other disasters. But beginning with chapter 36, he began to give them assurance that better days were ahead. God would lead them back to their homeland and establish His univeral rule among His people through a descendant of David. This prophecy was fulfilled when Jesus was born in Bethlehem more than five hundred years after Ezekiel's time (Luke 2:1–7).

One of the great contributions of the book of Ezekiel is the doctrine of personal accountability. The Jewish people had such a strong sense of group identity that they often glossed over their personal sins. Ezekiel told the exiles that each of them was responsible for his or her own sin. They must stand before God and take responsibility for their wrongdoing.

The book of Ezekiel has an important message for modern believers. We cannot depend on the beliefs of our parents, a church, or a denomination to give us favor in God's sight. He demands that we stand before Him and make our own personal, deliberate choice to follow His will and obey His commands.

Summary of Ezekiel

1:1–28. Ezekiel has a vision of four winged creatures known as cherubim. God's glory appears among these creatures.

2:1–10. The Lord informs Ezekiel that He has called him as His messenger to the Jewish exiles in Babylon.

3:1–27. Ezekiel eats a roll, or scroll, on which God's message to His rebellious people is written. This symbolizes the prophet's acceptance of God's message and mission to the Jewish exiles.

4:1–17. At God's command, Ezekiel uses a clay tile and an iron pan to enact the Babylonian siege against Jerusalem. He eats tiny amounts of food for several days to show the starvation conditions that existed in Jerusalem before the city fell.

[4:1–17] A RECORD IN CLAY. *Son of man [Ezekiel], take thee a tile [clay tablet, NIV], and lay it before thee, and pourtray upon it the city, even Jerusalem (Ezek. 4:1).*

God made a strange request of the prophet Ezekiel. He asked him to draw upon a clay tablet a picture of the city of Jerusalem under siege by the Babylonian army. This was to serve as a warning to the people about the forthcoming judgment of God against Jerusalem and the nation of Judah.

In Bible times clay tiles or tablets about six by nine inches in size were often used as writing material, just like paper is used today. Characters were etched into these tablets with a metal pen while the clay was soft. When hardened in a kiln, the writing on these tiles was virtually indestructible.

Archaeologists have discovered many of these clay tablets in the ruins of ancient cities. They shed light on the culture and customs of the ancient world.

5:1–17. Ezekiel shaves his beard and his head with a sword. Then he burns the hair to show that God has judged His people with the sword of the Babylonians because of their unfaithfulness.

6:1–14. God's destruction has fallen upon the mountains of Judah and those who worshiped false gods upon these high places.

7:1–27. The doom that God has promised against Judah because of the idolatry of the people is now unleashed in full force against the land: "According to their deserts will I judge them; and they shall know that I am the LORD" (v. 27).

8:1–18. Ezekiel is transported in a vision to the temple in Jerusalem. Here God shows him how the temple has been desecrated through the worship of false gods.

9:1–11. God commands that a special mark be placed on every person in Jerusalem who is grieved by the desecration of the temple. They will be saved when Jerusalem falls, but everyone without this mark will be destroyed (Rev. 9:4; 14:1).

10:1–22. Ezekiel has a vision of the same four winged creatures, or cherubim, that he had in chapter 1. God's glory leaves the temple and rests above these cherubim. This signifies that God's glory will eventually leave the temple because His people have polluted this holy place with their pagan worship practices.

11:1–25. Ezekiel speaks against certain leaders of Jerusalem who are predicting prosperity rather than disaster for the city. He declares that the future of God's people rests with the Jewish exiles in Babylon. God will eventually restore His remnant to their homeland (2 Chron. 36:22–23).

12:1–28. At God's command, Ezekiel acts out the fall of Jerusalem and the exile of the people to Babylon.

13:1–23. Ezekiel denounces false prophets who are telling the people what they want to hear rather than proclaiming God's message of judgment (Jer. 28). He also condemns false prophetesses who are leading the people astray through witchcraft and the reading of signs to foretell the future.

14:1–23. God will not tolerate the worship of false gods by His people. He demands their exclusive loyalty (Josh. 24:15). He will judge the nation of Judah for their false worship.

15:1–8. God's people were often compared to a vine (Isa. 5:1–7; Hosea 10:1), but their idolatry has turned them into a vine that bears no fruit. They will be cut down and burned by the fire of God's judgment (Luke 13:6–9).

16:1–63. This long chapter is a parable about

[15:1–8] USELESS AS A WILD VINE. *Shall wood be taken thereof [from a vine] to do any work? or will men take a pin of it to hang any vessel thereon?* (Ezek. 15:3).

Ezekiel compared the nation of Judah to a wild vine. Just as a vine of this type yields no lumber—not even as much as a pin or peg to hang a pot on—so Judah had become useless to the Lord because of the sin and rebellion of the people.

Domestic vines such as the grape are useful because of the fruit they produce. Throughout their history the Israelites were often spoken of as a fruitful vine (Gen. 49:22). But even a grapevine is useless if it fails to produce grapes (Jer. 2:21). Ezekiel looked in vain for the fruits of righteousness and holiness among the people of his time.

God's relationship with His people Israel. The Lord adopted Israel when she was an orphan, lavishing her with His love and care. But she rejected Him and turned to the worship of pagan gods. While Israel will receive its deserved punishment, God will not give up on His people. He remains faithful to His covenant promises: "I will establish my covenant with thee; and thou shalt know that I am the LORD" (v. 62).

17:1–24. The two eagles in this chapter represent Babylonia and Egypt. The vine represents the nation of Judah, which broke its oath of allegiance to Babylonia and turned to Egypt for help. God will punish Judah for this act of disobedience, but He will eventually rebuild His people through a faithful remnant who follow His commands.

18:1–32. The people of Judah were sometimes

fatalistic in their attitudes, blaming their ancestors for their current problems. Ezekiel declares that each person is accountable for his or her own sins: "The soul that sinneth, it shall die. The son shall not bear the iniquity of the father, neither shall the father bear the iniquity of the son" (v. 20).

19:1–14. In this mournful poem, Ezekiel laments the kings who ruled Judah during the tragic period just before the nation fell to the Babylonians.

20:1–44. Several leaders of Judah ask Ezekiel if he has a message from the Lord. The prophet responds by giving them a history lesson, showing that the Israelites have tended to be sinful and rebellious from the very beginning of their existence as a nation.

20:45–21:32. Because of their rebellious history, God will send His wrath against His people. His agent of judgment will be the Babylonians, who will destroy Jerusalem as well as the capital of the Ammonites.

22:1–31. Jerusalem was supposed to be the "holy city." Instead, it has become the "bloody city" (v. 2) because of its sin, idolatry, and denial of justice to the poor. Jerusalem will be judged severely by the Lord for its corruption.

23:1–49. In this parable of two adulterous sisters, Ezekiel portrays the nation of Israel (Northern Kingdom) as Aholah and the nation of Judah (Southern Kingdom) as Aholibah. Their lust leads them to pursue their lovers with reckless abandon. Judah saw Israel punished with defeat and exile because of Israel's sins, but in spite of this warning, Judah continued her sinful ways.

24:1–14. Ezekiel portrays Jerusalem as a cooking pot. Its citizens will be stewed like meat in the fire of God's judgment when the Babylonians besiege the city (2 Kings 25:1–12).

24:15–27. God warns Ezekiel that his wife will soon die, but he is not to mourn her death. This is a sign to the Jewish exiles in Babylon that they will soon be cut off from their relatives in Jerusalem when the city is overrun by the Babylonians.

25:1–32:32. These chapters contain Ezekiel's prophecies of God's judgment against the nations: Ammon (25:1–7); Moab (25:8–11); Edom (25:12–14); the Philistines (25:15–17); Tyrus, or Tyre (26:1–28:19); Zidon, or Sidon (28:20–26); and Egypt (chaps. 29–32).

33:1–20. The Lord tells Ezekiel that the duty of a watchman is to sound a warning in times of danger. This is also the mission of a true prophet of God.

[20:45–21:32] BABYLONIAN SIGN-READING. *The king of Babylon stood...at the head of the two ways [at the junction of the two roads, NIV], to use divination [seek an omen, NIV]: he made his arrows bright, he consulted with images, he looked in the liver* (Ezek. 21:21).

Ezekiel told the people of Judah that the king of Babylonia was coming into their territory on a mission of conquest. He would stop at a fork in the road and decide whether to take the road toward Jerusalem or to go the other way and attack the capital city of the Ammonites (Ezek. 21:19–20).

To decide which road to take, the king would read the signs by using one of three possible methods. He might cast lots by drawing an arrow out of his quiver and throwing it down to see which way it pointed. He could consult his pagan gods. Or he could have one of his priests "read" the liver of a sacrificial animal and advise him on which city to attack.

Such superstitious sign-reading was practiced by the pagan nations of Bible times. But God declared black magic and divination off-limits to His people (Deut. 18:10–11).

37:1–14. Ezekiel's most famous vision takes place in a valley filled with human skeletons that suddenly grow flesh and come to life. God says He will do the same for Israel, resurrecting the dead nation.

33:21–33. News that the city of Jerusalem has fallen reaches Ezekiel. He passes this on to the other Jewish exiles in Babylon.

34:1–31. The leaders of Judah will be punished because they have exploited and misled the people rather than guiding them in the ways of the Lord. In contrast to such undependable human leaders, God is a true shepherd. He will eventually bring His people back to their homeland to feed on fertile pastures.

35:1–15. The nation of Edom, referred to as "mount Seir" (v. 2) by Ezekiel, joined in the humiliation of Judah when Jerusalem fell to the Babylonians. God will repay this callous act. The prophet Obadiah also condemned Edom for these acts of treachery (see the book of Obadiah).

36:1–38. This chapter represents a turning point in the book of Ezekiel. Up to now, the prophet has spoken mainly of God's judgment against the nation of Judah. But now that God's judgment has reached its climax with the fall of Jerusalem, Ezekiel will spend the rest of his book giving hope to the Jewish exiles in Babylon. In the future God will restore His people to their homeland. He will give them a new heart and fill them with a new spirit.

37:1–14. Ezekiel has a vision of a valley filled with dry, lifeless bones. God's Spirit enters the bones, and they spring to life. This symbolizes the forthcoming spiritual restoration of the nation of Israel.

37:15–28. At God's command, Ezekiel picks up two sticks. These represent the two separate nations of Israel (Northern Kingdom) and Judah (Southern Kingdom). The prophet

[37:15–28] MESSAGES ON WOOD. *The sticks whereon thou [Ezekiel] writest shall be in thine hand before their [Israel's and Judah's] eyes* (Ezek. 37:20).

God told Ezekiel to write messages on two separate sticks, representing the nations of Judah (Southern Kingdom) and Israel (Northern Kingdom). Then he was to place the two sticks together. This represented the time when the two nations would become one again and be ruled over by the messianic king.

Messages were often written on long, narrow strips of wood in Bible times. The practice is referred to as early as the time of Moses (Num. 17:2–3).

declares that God will unite His people into one kingdom under one king—"David my servant" (v. 24). This is a title for the promised Messiah. This prophecy was fulfilled with the coming of Jesus.

38:1–39:29. Ezekiel looks into the future and predicts a great battle between the forces of evil and the people of God. Several evil nations, under the leadership of Gog, attack God's people, but they are defeated when God intervenes. The apostle John, writing in the book of Revelation, uses Gog's evil forces to represent all who oppose God in the final battle in the end times under the leadership of Satan (Rev. 20:8).

40:1–48:35. The book of Ezekiel ends with the prophet's glorious vision of a new temple rebuilt on the site of Solomon's temple in Jerusalem. This must have brought hope to the Jewish exiles in Babylon, since Solomon's temple had been destroyed when Jerusalem fell to the Babylonian army.

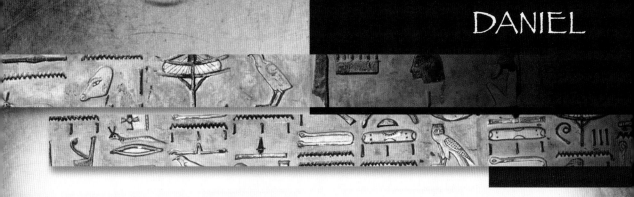

OVERVIEW: Daniel and his three friends model faithfulness to God while living among pagan nations. Daniel also issues prophecies of the future and the end-time.

Introduction to Daniel

The prophet Daniel, author of the book that bears his name, was taken into exile about 600 B.C., along with other citizens of Judah, when the Babylonians invaded his country. He was probably in his late teens at the time.

The events recorded in the book of Daniel show that he remained in exile for at least fifty years. Daniel served as an aide in the administration of King Nebuchadnezzar of Babylonia soon after he was carried away (2:46–49). Eventually Babylonia was defeated by the Persians. Daniel also served under the Persian king Darius (6:1–13). This king brought the exile to an end when he allowed Jewish captives who wished to do so to return to their homeland (2 Chron. 36:22–23).

One of the problems that confronted the Jewish captives in Babylonia and Persia was how to remain faithful to God in the midst of pagan surroundings. Was this possible? Two episodes recorded by Daniel gave a bold yes to this question.

Three of Daniel's friends were thrown into a hot furnace because they refused to worship an image of the Babylonian king. When they emerged unharmed because of God's miraculous intervention, the Babylonians developed a reverent respect for this awesome God (3:8–27).

This respect for God grew even stronger when Daniel was miraculously delivered from a den of lions, where he was thrown when he continued to pray to his own God rather than the pagan Persian gods. The Lord had demonstrated that He was superior to all other gods.

The book of Daniel serves as an inspiration for modern believers. In a critical and unbelieving world, we can rest assured of God's presence and protection if we remain faithful to Him.

Summary of Daniel

1:1–7. Daniel and his three friends—Shadrach, Meshach, and Abednego—are carried to Babylon as captives after Judah

---

[1:1–7] LOOTING OF THE TEMPLE. *He [King Nebuchadnezzar] brought the vessels into the treasure house of his god* (Dan. 1:2).

When the Babylonian army captured and plundered the city of Jerusalem, King Nebuchadnezzar siezed the golden utensils, spices, jewels, and other valuable items that belonged to the Jewish temple. He carried these valuables to Babylon, where he deposited them in the treasure house of a temple devoted to the worship of a pagan Babylonian god.

This fulfilled a prophecy that Isaiah had issued to the people of Judah about 100 years before: "The days come, that all...which thy fathers have laid up in store...shall be carried to Babylon" (Isa. 39:6).

3:19–30. An ancient drawing from Roman catacombs tells a famous Bible story: Shadrach, Meshach, and Abednego survive a walk in Babylonian King Nebuchadnezzar's fiery furnace.

is defeated by the Babylonians under King Nebuchadnezzar (2 Kings 25:1–12). These four young Jewish men are selected for training in Babylonian customs and culture before being placed in government service in Babylon.

1:8–21. Daniel and his three friends refuse to defile themselves with the rich foods and strong wine they are required to eat while in training for government service. Eating only vegetables ("pulse," v. 12) and water, they grow stronger than all the other young men in the training program.

2:1–11. King Nebuchadnezzar of Babylonia has a dream that he is not able to recall. None of his wise men or magicians can tell him what he dreamed.

2:12–45. Daniel is able to tell Nebuchadnezzar what he dreamed and what it meant. The prophet tells the king that he will continue for a while as a mighty ruler over a broad territory. But his successors will not be able to hold this kingdom together.

2:46–49. King Nebuchadnezzar appoints Daniel to a high position in his administration. Also promoted are Daniel's three friends: Shadrach, Meshach, and Abednego.

3:1–7. King Nebuchadnezzar fashions a statue of himself from gold and has it set up at a prominent site in Babylonia. He orders all the people in his kingdom to bow down and worship the image at his command.

3:8–18. Enemies of Daniel's three friends inform the king that these young Jewish men will not worship the golden image. When Nebuchadnezzar questions them about this, they reply: "O king...we will not serve thy gods, nor worship the golden image which thou hast set up" (v. 18).

3:19–30. Because of their disobedience of the king's order, Shadrach, Meshach, and Abednego are thrown into a hot furnace. But an angel protects them, and they emerge untouched and unharmed by the flames. King Nebuchadnezzar is so impressed by this miracle that he orders everyone in Babylonia to be respectful toward the God whom they worship. He also promotes Shadrach, Meshach, and Abednego to higher positions in his administration.

4:1–37. Daniel interprets another dream of King Nebuchadnezzar—and it happens just as Daniel predicts. Toward the end of his reign, the king is struck by a strange disease—perhaps mental illness. Convinced he is an animal, he forages in the pastures, eating grass with the livestock. But he apparently recovers from this illness long enough to recognize Daniel's God as the one true God (vv. 34–37).

5:1–12. Belshazzar, successor of Nebuchadnezzar as king of Babylonia, is partying with friends and officials of his administration. In the midst of the merrymaking, a hand appears and writes some words on the wall. None of his wise men or magicians can make sense of the message.

5:13–31. Called to interpret the handwriting, Daniel gives Belshazzar the bad news: The days of the Babylonian kingdom are numbered. God will deliver the nation into the hands of the Medes and Persians. That very night Belshazzar is killed, and the glory days of Babylonia come to an end.

6:1–13. Daniel wins the favor of the new Persian regime and the victorious king, Darius,

[6:1–13] UNCHANGEABLE PERSIAN LAWS. *O king, establish the decree...that it be not changed, according to the law of the Medes and Persians, which altereth not* (Dan. 6:8).

The enemies of Daniel in Persia asked King Darius to issue a law against worshiping any god other than the king himself. They knew this would trap Daniel, since he would refuse to bow down to any god other than the supreme Lord of the universe.

The ancient Medes and Persians considered their laws infallible and irreversible. Once a decree was ordered by the king, it could not be changed or wiped off the books. For example, the Persian law authorizing the extermination of the Jews in Esther's time was not canceled. But the king issued another decree warning the Jews about the death warrant and authorizing them to act in self-defense against their enemies (Esther 8:5–11).

who names him to a high position in his administration. But Daniel has some political enemies, and they conspire to have him killed. They persuade King Darius to issue a decree making it unlawful for anyone to pray to any god except the king. Daniel continues his practice of praying to God as he has always done.

6:14–28. Because of his disobedience, Daniel is thrown into a den of lions. The next day Darius finds him standing among the lions unharmed because God sent an angel to protect him. The king issues an order for all the people to "tremble and fear before the God of Daniel" (v. 26).

7:1–28. Daniel has a vision that foretells events of the future. He sees four beasts that represent four future earthly kings. The fourth beast will triumph over all the nations of the earth. A horn on the fourth beast represents a ruler who will oppose God and persecute those who follow the Lord. But eventually God's eternal kingdom will be established.

8:1–27. Daniel has a vision of a ram and a goat. The ram, representing the kingdoms of Media and Persia, is defeated by a goat. This foretells the rise of Alexander the Great and the Greek Empire that he would establish. At Alexander's death, his empire would be divided among his generals: "Four kingdoms shall stand up out of the nation" (v. 22).

9:1–19. Daniel realizes that the seventy-year captivity of the Jewish people by the Babylonians and Persians is almost over (Jer. 29:10). So he prays a beautiful prayer of intercession and deliverance for his people.

9:20–27. These verses contain the famous "seventy weeks" prophecy of Daniel, revealed to him by the angel Gabriel. Most interpreters believe these seventy weeks should be interpreted as seventy times seven years—or a period of 490 years. Thus, this prophecy refers to the coming of the Messiah, Jesus Christ, about 490 years from the time when the Jews were allowed to return to Jerusalem from the exile to resettle their homeland.

10:1–11:45. This vision is revealed to Daniel after a period of fasting and prayer while he stands by the Hiddekel (Tigris) River in Persia. Strengthened by an angel after his period of fasting, Daniel falls into a trance and receives a revelation of events of the future. He foresees a struggle between a "king of the south" and a "king of the north." Many interpreters believe this refers to the battle for supremacy between two generals of Alexander the Great after Alexander's death about 300 years after Daniel's time.

12:1–13. An angel reveals to Daniel that the Jewish people can expect a period of tribulation in the future. But those who persevere will experience joy and a new beginning in the Lord. Even Daniel is not given perfect understanding of events that will happen in the end-time (vv. 8–9). But he is assured of God's eternal presence as he waits for Him to act: "Go thou thy way till the end be: for thou shalt rest, and stand in thy lot at the end of the days" (v. 13).

CHAPTER 5
BOOKS OF THE
MINOR PROPHETS

The last twelve books of the Old Testament are known as the minor prophets. This does not mean they are of minor importance. The title refers to the short length of the books and the fact that they were placed after the major prophets (Isaiah, Jeremiah, Lamentations, Ezekiel, and Daniel) in the compilation of the Old Testament.

If all the minor prophets were compiled into one book, their total length would be about equal to that of the book of Isaiah. Though brief, the books and the prophets who wrote them delivered God's powerful message to several different situations over a period of about 400 years.

Amos and Hosea preached to the Northern Kingdom before that nation fell to the Assyrians in 722 B.C. Six of the minor prophets—Obadiah, Joel, Micah, Nahum, Zephaniah, and Habakkuk—ministered in the Southern Kingdom. God sent the prophet Jonah to preach judgment and repentance to the pagan nation of Assyria. Three of these prophets—Haggai, Zechariah, and Malachi—encouraged and challenged the Israelites after they returned to their homeland following the exile among the Babylonians and Persians.

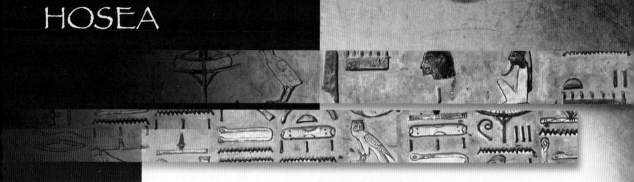

HOSEA

OVERVIEW: Hosea's own tragic marriage to an unfaithful wife shows that God's people have rejected Him to worship false gods.

Introduction to Hosea

The book of Hosea paints a beautiful picture of God's faithful love for His people. It was written by the prophet Hosea, who ministered in the nation of Israel (Northern Kingdom) during a period of forty years, from about 755 to 715 B.C.

Hosea declared to the people of his homeland that they were marked for destruction by the Lord because of their sinful ways, especially their worship of false gods. As the prophet predicted, Israel fell to the Assyrians in 722 B.C.

But the message for which Hosea is most remembered is his declaration that God had not given up on His people. Even though they were sinful and rebellious, He still loved them and worked patiently to restore them to their favored status as His special people.

This truth about God was demonstrated in Hosea's own life. At the Lord's direction, the prophet married a prostitute. Several children were born into this marriage. But just as it appeared that his wife had given up her sinful ways, she left Hosea and returned to her life of prostitution.

Hosea searched for his wayward spouse and found that she had been sold into slavery. He bought her from her master and restored her as his wife. This object lesson showed that God had not rejected Israel, although the people had turned their back on Him by worshiping false gods.

The message of Hosea is that God's punishment of His people is motivated by His love. He loves us too much to let us continue in our wayward ways. His goal is to restore us to full fellowship with Him.

Summary of Hosea

1:1–11. God calls Hosea to deliver His message to the wayward nation of Israel (Northern Kingdom). At God's command, Hosea marries a prostitute named Gomer. She bears three children, and they are given symbolic names that represent God's intention to punish Israel.

2:1–13. Just as Gomer had committed adultery before she married Hosea, so has Israel been guilty of spiritual adultery in God's sight (Isa. 3:1–25). The people have worshiped false gods and have been unfaithful to the one true God. He will judge them for these rebellious acts.

2:14–23. After God has punished and disciplined His people, He promises to restore them to His favor. His kindness and mercy will be showered upon them once again.

3:1–5. Hosea's wife, Gomer, apparently returns to her life as a prostitute and is sold as a slave. God directs Hosea to buy her back. This shows God's redemptive love. For a while, the people of Israel will also lose their

[3:1–5] INDULGENT WORSHIP. *The children of Israel... look to other gods, and love flagons of wine [sacred raisin cakes, NIV] (Hosea 3:1).*

The prophet Hosea condemned the people of the Northern Kingdom for their worship of Baal, a pagan fertility god. He described them as indulgent worshippers who loved "flagons of wine."

The Hebrew word rendered as "flagons of wine" by the KJV is translated as "sacred raisin cakes" by the NIV. This is probably a more accurate translation, since cakes made of raisins, or dried grapes, were considered a delicacy in Bible times. They may have been eaten in connection with immoral worship ceremonies at the altars of Baal.

freedom to an enemy nation as punishment for their sin. But God will eventually redeem them and restore them as His people.

4:1–19. God gives a detailed list of the sins that Israel has committed. These include killing, stealing, lying, and committing adultery. But their greatest sin is worshiping false gods.

5:1–15. Even the priests have turned away from following God and are leading the people astray. Hosea also declares that the nation of Judah is just as guilty as Israel of forsaking the Lord and going its own way (v. 10).

6:1–7:16. Some of the people of Israel have been convicted of their sin and have turned back to God. But their repentance was a sham, and they have fallen right back into idolatry. Hosea declares that their goodness "is as a morning cloud, and as the early dew it goeth away" (6:4).

8:1–14. The nation of Israel will experience God's law of sowing and reaping. They will reap God's terrible punishment for the sins they have sown: "They have sown the wind, and they shall reap the whirlwind" (v. 7).

9:1–10:15. Hosea announces the specific punishment that God has in store for Israel.

Because of their idolatry, the people will be carried away as captives by the Assyrians (10:6; see 2 Kings 18:9–12).

11:1–12. This chapter shows God's everlasting love for His people. He compares the nation of Israel to a little child whom He guided and taught as He led them out of slavery in Egypt. Now Assyria will rule over them for a time, but the Lord will eventually restore His people through His grace.

[11:1–12] RELIEF FROM THE YOKE. *I [God] drew them [Israelites] with cords of a man, with bands of love: and I was to them as they that take off the yoke on their jaws (Hosea 11:4).*

In this verse Hosea portrays the love of God for His special people, the Israelites. Although they had rebelled against Him again and again, He kept pulling them back into His fellowship with "bands of love."

Hosea also compared the love of God to relief given to oxen when they were wearing heavy wooden yokes while working in the fields. These yokes had to be lifted up by their masters to enable the animals to lower their heads so they could eat or drink.

God is the great "yoke lifter" who shows mercy and love to His people.

12:1–13:16. These chapters return to the theme of God's judgment against Israel because of the people's worship of false gods. The prophet declares that Samaria (captial city of Israel) "shall become desolate; for she hath rebelled against her God" (13:16).

14:1–9. Hosea closes his book with a plea for Israel to repent and return to the Lord before it is too late. The path to forgiveness and restoration is open if the people will turn from their rebellious ways.

JOEL

OVERVIEW: A plague of locusts serves notice that God will judge His people for their sin and rebellion.

Introduction to Joel

This brief prophetic book paints a disturbing picture of the coming judgment of God against His people because of their sin. It was written by the prophet Joel about 590 B.C., during the dark days before the nation of Judah fell to the Babylonians.

Joel begins his book with a description of the devastation of Judah by a swarm of locusts. These destructive insects, similar to grasshoppers, destroyed all the crops and stripped the leaves from shrubs and trees. This was a foretaste of the judgment of God that would fall upon the land unless the people repented and turned from their wicked ways.

Along with this message of judgment, Joel also had words of hope. God promised to bless His people if they would turn to Him and obey

2:1–11. Locusts swarm an island beach in November 2004. Billions struck throughout the Middle East and northern Africa during the month. The prophet Joel apparently used such an infestation to warn that an even worse disaster was coming. Invaders would destroy the Jewish nation for its sins.

His commands. He would renew their zeal and commitment through a great outpouring of His Spirit (2:28–29). The entire world would be impressed as He gathered His people in Jerusalem to serve as their sovereign ruler (3:2).

The prophecy about the outpouring of God's Spirit was fulfilled several centuries later during the days of the early church. The Holy Spirit came in great power upon the followers of Jesus while they were in Jerusalem praying for God's guidance (Acts 2:16–21).

This same Spirit is alive and well today in the lives of those who belong to Christ.

Summary of Joel

1:1–20. The land of Judah is invaded by a huge swarm of locusts. The flying insects, similar to grasshoppers, destroy all the vegetation in their path, even stripping leaves and bark from the trees (Exod. 10:12–15). With their crops destroyed, the people face the prospect of starvation. Joel calls on the priests to proclaim a fast and to gather the people to God's house for prayer and repentance.

2:1–11. The prophet declares that this locust plague is only a shadow of what the approaching "day of the Lord" (v. 1) will be like. This time of God's judgment and punishment will be "a day of darkness and of gloominess, a day of clouds and of thick darkness" (v. 2; see Jer. 46:10).

2:12–17. But it is not too late for Judah to repent. Joel calls on the people to forsake their sinful ways and turn to the Lord.

2:18–27. In response to the repentance of His people, God will withhold His judgment and give them many blessings instead. He will send the rains and give them an abundant harvest, more than enough to replace the crops devastated by the locusts.

2:28–32. Even more abundant are the spiri-

[1:1–20] DESTRUCTION BY LOCUSTS. *That which the palmerworm hath left hath the locust eaten; and that which the locust hath left hath the cankerworm eaten; and that which the cankerworm hath left hath the caterpiller eaten (Joel 1:4).*

A locust plague, such as the one described by Joel in this verse, was one of the worst disasters that could happen in the agricultural society of Bible times. Millions of these insects, similar to grasshoppers, would descend on the land and devour the crops. Scarcity of food—and even widespread starvation—could follow.

The eighth plague that God sent against the Egyptians to convince Pharaoh to release the Hebrew slaves was a swarm of locusts (Exod. 10:12–15).

Joel's account of a swarm of locusts in his time details the four stages in the development of this destructive insect: (1) a hatchling emerges from the egg (palmerworm); (2) it develops wings and begins to fly (locust); (3) it becomes strong enough to begin eating vegetation (cankerworm); and (4) as a fully grown adult, it flies in a swarm with millions of others to do its most destructive work (caterpiller).

tual blessings that God will send upon His people if they remain faithful to Him. He promises to send His Spirit "upon all flesh" (v. 28)—not just on prophets and priests but on ordinary people. The apostle Peter quoted this passage on the day of Pentecost to show that God had fulfilled this promise by sending His Spirit to empower the early Christian believers (Acts 2:16–21).

3:1–21. Joel looks into the future to the day of messianic blessing for the people of God. But this will also be a day of judgment for the pagan nations as well as individuals who have refused to acknowledge Jesus as Savior and Lord: "Multitudes, multitudes in the valley of decision: for the day of the LORD is near in the valley of decision" (v. 14).

AMOS

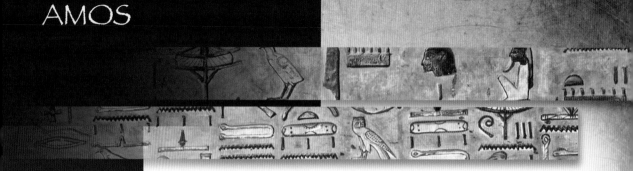

OVERVIEW: Genuine religion consists of treating others with justice and mercy rather than observing rituals and offering sacrifices.

Introduction to Amos

Like Hosea, Amos was also a prophet to the Northern Kingdom (Israel). But Amos was a native of Judah (Southern Kingdom). He was sent by the Lord into Israel to denounce the sin and corruption of the people. Amos's prophecy is dated at about 760 B.C., a few years before Hosea began his public ministry (see the introduction to Hosea on p. 518).

Amos is known as the great prophet of righteousness and social justice of the Old Testament. He condemned the wealthy people of Israel who were cheating the poor. He criticized the wives of the rich leaders of the nation for their selfishness and greed. The prophet also declared that the religion of the people was shallow and meaningless. Worship had degenerated into empty rituals and ceremonies that had no relationship to daily life.

According to Amos, authentic religion results in holy and righteous behavior. True worship does not consist of offering burnt offerings, observing all the religious holidays, and worshiping at the temple. Worship that honors God will lead people to treat others with justice and to follow the Lord's commands.

Amos was a lowly shepherd from the tiny village of Tekoa in Judah (1:1) who left his flocks to serve as the Lord's spokesman among the affluent classes in another country. God often surprises us with the people whom He calls out as His special servants.

Summary of Amos

1:1–2. Amos is from the village of Tekoa in Judah (Southern Kingdom). But he is sent to proclaim God's judgment against Israel (Northern Kingdom).

1:3–2:5. God's judgment is first pronounced against the cities and nations surrounding Israel: Damascus (1:3–5), Gaza (1:6–8), Tyrus, or Tyre (1:9–10), Edom (1:11–12), Ammon (1:13–15), Moab (2:1–3), and Judah (2:4–5).

2:6–16. God lists the sins for which the nation of Israel will be punished. These include worshiping idols instead of the one true God, cheating the poor, and persecuting the prophets whom God sends as His spokesmen.

3:1–15. The Lord reminds the citizens of Israel that He brought them out of Egypt when they were a slave people and made them into a nation that belongs to Him (Exod. 12:33–42). But He will just as surely punish them unless they turn from their rebellious ways.

4:1–3. Amos refers to the wives of the wealthy Israelites as "kine [cows] of Bashan" (v. 1). They are just as guilty as their husbands because they encourage the men to oppress the poor to support their extravagant lifestyle.

4:4–13. God has punished Israel for its sin and

[2:6–16] BAD NEWS FOR THE WEALTHY. *They [wealthy class of Israel] sold the righteous for silver, and the poor for a pair of shoes* (Amos 2:6).

Two of God's highest expectations for His people, the Israelites, were that they would practice righteousness and show compassion toward the poor. In this verse Amos charged the wealthy class of Israel—the Northern Kingdom—with violating both these commands.

They were so calloused toward righteousness that they thought they could buy and sell it like any other commodity. Rather than treating the poor with fairness and justice, they were selling them into slavery because they could not pay their debts. Sometimes these debts were no more than the minor sum required to buy a cheap pair of sandals!

Amos declared that God would judge the wealthy for such greed and lack of compassion.

extravagance in many different ways. But these reprimands have failed to turn the people back to Him.

5:1–17. Amos issues a lament against Israel, as if the nation has already fallen to a foreign oppressor and experienced God's judgment. But he also declares that the people can avoid this fate if they will turn to God: "Seek the LORD, and ye shall live" (v. 6).

5:18–27. Commitment to the Lord must go deeper than worship rituals such as bringing offerings to the altar and singing songs of praise. God requires genuine repentance and righteous living from His people: "Let judgment run down as waters, and righteousness as a mighty stream" (v. 24; see Isa. 58).

6:1–14. Amos makes it clear what will happen to Israel if the people do not turn from their sinful ways. They will be taken away as captives into a foreign land.

7:1–9. Amos sees three visions of judgment promised by the Lord against Israel: grasshoppers (vv. 1–3), fire (vv. 4–6), and a plumb line (vv. 7–9). The plumb line is a dramatic demonstration that Israel does not measure up to God's standards.

7:10–17. Amaziah the priest rejects Amos's message and tells him to go back to Judah. Amos pronounces God's judgment against Amaziah because he refuses to hear the word of the Lord.

[7:10–17] AMOS AND SYCAMORE FIGS. *I [Amos] was no prophet, neither was I a prophet's son; but I was an herdman, and a gatherer of sycomore fruit* (Amos 7:14).

Amos was a lowly shepherd from the tiny village of Tekoa (Amos 1:1) in Judah (Southern Kingdom). But he was called to declare God's judgment against the rich people of the neighboring nation, Israel (Northern Kingdom). This verse shows that he did not claim to be a learned and sophisticated messenger. His only credential was his call from the Lord.

The "sycomore fruit" that Amos mentioned was a type of wild fig that grew in his native Judah. These figs were inferior in quality to the domesticated figs that are mentioned several times in the Bible (Num. 13:23; 1 Sam. 25:18; Mark 11:12–21). Only the poorest people of the land grew and ate sycamore figs.

8:1–14. Amos sees a vision of a basket of ripe fruit. This shows that Israel is ready for God's judgment, just as ripe fruit is ready to eat.

9:1–15. God's judgment falls on Israel. Although the people try to hide, He hunts them down. But God's grace is also evident in the midst of His judgment. He promises to preserve a faithful remnant of people who will eventually return to their homeland.

OBADIAH

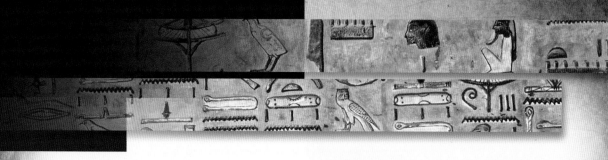

OVERVIEW: God will punish the Edomites for participating in the humiliation of Jerusalem.

Introduction to Obadiah

Obadiah is the shortest book in the Old Testament, containing only twenty-one verses. The author is identified in the first verse of the book, but this is all we know about him.

Obadiah's brief prophecy was against the Edomites, ancient enemies of the nation of Israel. They had participated in the destruction and looting of the city of Jerusalem when it fell to the Babylonian army in 587 B.C. Because of this despicable act, the Edomites would be destroyed by the Lord.

The message of Obadiah's book is that God keeps faith with His people. He had promised many centuries before Obadiah's time that He would guide and protect His people and deal harshly with anyone who tried to do them harm (Gen. 12:1–3). God is the rock to whom we can flee in times of trouble and distress.

Summary of Obadiah

Verse 1. The Lord gives Obadiah the prophet a message of judgment that he is to speak against the nation of Edom.

Verses 2–5. God condemns the pride and vanity of Edom. The Edomites considered themselves invincible in their fortress cities—particularly the capital of Sela. But the Lord makes it clear through Obadiah that He will bring them down (Ezek. 25:12–14).

Verses 6–9. References to Esau in these verses show the ancestry of the Edomites. They were descendants of Esau, the twin brother of Jacob (Gen. 25:9–28). The problems between the nations of Israel and Edom had begun with the conflict between these two brothers many centuries before Obadiah's time (Gen. 25:19–28; 27:1–41).

Verses 10–16. The Lord will use an enemy nation to defeat Edom. Such punishment is deserved because of Edom's treatment of Judah. The Edomites stood by when foreigners attacked Jerusalem. They even carried away spoils from the city and prevented Jewish fugitives from fleeing to safety.

Verses 17–21. In contrast to the humiliation and defeat of Edom, God will bless His people Israel. After the exile in Babylon, they will return and possess the land that God has promised to Abraham and his descendants.

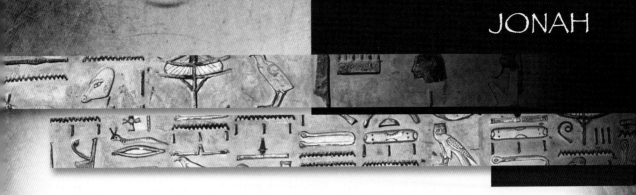

OVERVIEW: God uses a prejudiced prophet to show that He loves all people, even the enemies of the Israelites.

Introduction to Jonah

The book of Jonah shows that God can use a negative example to teach a positive lesson.

The negative example is the prophet Jonah, whom God called to preach to the citizens of Nineveh. This great city was the capital of the Assyrian Empire. The Jews hated the Assyrians because they were their sworn enemies who worshiped pagan gods. So Jonah tried to run away from God's call.

Eventually Jonah did travel to Nineveh and preach to the Ninevites, as God commanded him to do. But when they repented and turned to God, he sulked and pouted because the Lord refused to destroy them.

The positive lesson taught through this negative prophet is that God loves everyone, not just the Jewish people. Their religious pride led them to the false belief that they had an exclusive claim on God's love. But no one is outside the scope of His grace.

One positive thing we can say about Jonah is that he did dare to tell the truth about himself and his prejudice by writing the book that bears his name. It was probably written about 760 B.C. during the glory days of the Assyrian Empire. Jonah ministered during the days of King Jeroboam II of Israel (Northern Kingdom), who reigned about 793–753 B.C. (2 Kings 14:25).

Summary of Jonah

1:1–3. God calls Jonah to pronounce judgment against Nineveh, capital city of the Assyrian Empire. But Jonah runs from God and catches a ship bound for Tarshish in the opposite direction from Nineveh.

1:4–16. A violent storm strikes the ship. The superstitious crew casts lots to determine who is responsible for the storm. The lot falls on Jonah, who admits he is running from God's call. He advises the sailors to toss him overboard to appease the Lord's anger.

[1:4–16] SUPERSTITIOUS SAILORS. *Come, and let us [sailors on Jonah's ship] cast lots, that we may know for whose cause this evil is upon us* (Jon. 1:7).

Sailors of ancient times tended to be very superstitious because of their constant exposure to the dangers of the sea. When a storm struck the ship in which Jonah was escaping from the call of the Lord, they assumed the pagan gods were punishing them because of their displeasure with one person on board.

To find out who this person was, they cast lots—a custom similar to rolling dice or drawing straws in modern times. These lots may have been round stones or flat sticks of various lengths. Exactly what they looked like is not known.

The casting of lots as a method of decision making is mentioned several times in the Bible (Lev. 16:8–10; Num. 33:54; Josh. 14:2; 1 Chron. 25:8–9; Acts 1:26).

1:4–16. Sailors throw Jonah overboard in an effort to calm a storm that is about to sink the ship. The storm halts as Jonah is swallowed by a big fish, not necessarily a whale.

1:17. God saves Jonah by sending a great fish to swallow him and keeping him alive for three days in the stomach of the fish (Matt. 12:40).

2:1–10. Jonah prays an eloquent prayer for deliverance. The Lord hears his prayer and has him ejected from the fish unharmed and placed on the shore.

3:1–4. The Lord calls on Jonah again to proclaim His message to the city of Nineveh. This time Jonah obeys and delivers God's message of judgment against the Ninevites (Luke 11:32).

3:5–10. The citizens of Nineveh repent of their wicked ways and turn to the Lord in repentance. God withholds the disaster He had threatened against the city.

4:1–3. Jonah gets angry because the Lord extends mercy and forgiveness to the Ninevites. In self-pity, he asks God to take his life.

4:4–8. Jonah builds a hut on the eastern side of Nineveh. Here he waits to see what will happen to the city. God causes a vine to grow up over his head to shelter him from the sun and to cool his anger. Then the Lord causes the vine to die, and Jonah is miserable in the sun and hot wind. He again wallows in self-pity and wishes he were dead.

4:9–11. God condemns Jonah because he is more concerned about a vine than he is about the people of the city of Nineveh. He reminds Jonah that He is a merciful and forgiving God who loves all people, even the pagan Assyrians.

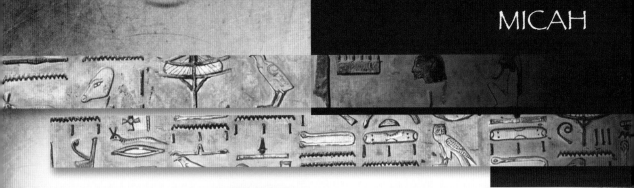

OVERVIEW: God's judgment will fall, but better days are ahead for God's people. He will send the Messiah, who will be born in Bethlehem.

Introduction to Micah

The prophet Micah delivered God's message to the citizens of both Judah (Southern Kingdom) and Israel (Northern Kingdom). He mentioned the reigns of three kings of Judah—Jotham, Ahaz, and Hezekiah (1:1)—a period that stretched from about 750 to 687 B.C. He must have written his book toward the end of this period.

Like most of the prophets of the Old Testament, Micah's book included prophecies of both judgment and promise. God would send His punishment upon His people because of their sin. But He was just as determined to bless them to fulfill the promises He had made to Abraham many centuries before (Gen. 12:1–5).

Micah made it clear that the people of both Judah and Israel would be punished by the Lord for their sin and rebellion. But in the future, God would restore His people through a remnant of those who would remain faithful to Him.

The book of Micah is best known for its promise of the coming Messiah. Micah even foretold the place where He would be born: the village of Bethlehem (5:2). This is one of the most remarkable messianic prophecies in the entire Old Testament.

Summary of Micah

1:1–16. God announces through the prophet Micah that He will judge the cities of Samaria and Jerusalem (v. 1). Jerusalem was the capital city of Judah (Southern Kingdom), while Samaria was the capital of Israel (Northern Kingdom). God plans to punish both nations because they have turned away from Him to worship false gods.

2:1–11. Micah condemns the wealthy people of Judah and Israel because they are

5:1–15. Priests pause for a photo in Bethlehem's Church of the Nativity, built over a cave where ancient tradition says Jesus was born. Micah predicted that God would send a Savior who would be born in Bethlehem.

cheating the poor. He accuses them of lying awake at night, making plans to strip the poor of their houses and fields. But God is also making plans. He intends to send disaster against the rich and proud.

2:12–13. Judah and Israel will be defeated by a foreign nation. But God will preserve a small group of people—a faithful remnant—who will remain loyal to Him. He will use this minority to rebuild His people.

3:1–4. Many of the problems of Judah and Israel can be traced to their political leaders. They have lost the ability to distinguish between good and evil, so they lead the people astray (Ezek. 11:3).

3:5–7. Even the prophets fail to follow the Lord. They are called to be the moral conscience of the people. But instead they are prophesying that good times will continue and that Judah and Israel have nothing to fear (Jer. 14).

3:8–12. The Lord repeats His promise of judgment against the two nations because of their widespread sin and corruption.

4:1–13. This chapter mixes the themes of judgment and blessing in reverse order. Judah will be defeated and carried into exile by the pagan nation of Babylonia (vv. 9–13; see 2 Kings 25:1–12). But after the exile is over, the Jewish people will return to their homeland (2 Chron. 36:22–23). They will enjoy an era of peace and prosperity. From Jerusalem, God will extend His witness and influence to all the nations (vv. 1–8).

5:1–15. This chapter foretells the defeat of Israel (Northern Kingdom) by the Assyrians. But in the midst of this prophecy is another look into the future that has universal implications. A deliverer or "ruler in Israel" (v. 2) will be born in Bethlehem. This

[4:1–13] SITTING IN THE SHADE. *They shall sit every man under his vine and under his fig tree; and none shall make them afraid* (Mic. 4:4).

Micah used these word pictures to portray the future for God's people. After the coming of the Messiah, they would enjoy peace and prosperity, symbolized by resting in the shade.

In the hot, dry climate of Palestine, people often escaped from the sun's oppressive heat by sitting under a grapevine or fig tree. Its thick branches and broad leaves made the fig tree an ideal shade.

When Philip found Nathanael and brought him to Jesus, Nathanael was sitting under a fig tree. He was probably resting in its shade and meditating on God's Word (John 1:45–51).

messianic prophecy was fulfilled with the birth of Jesus about 700 years after Micah's time (Luke 2:1–7).

6:1–16. The Lord rehearses all the mighty deeds He has performed for His people. What does He expect in return? Not burnt offerings, fasting, and empty rituals—but obedience to His commands and commitment to His principles of love and justice: "What doth the LORD require of thee, but to do justly, and to love mercy, and to walk humbly with thy God?" (v. 8).

7:1–20. Micah mourns ("Woe is me!" v. 1) when he reviews the sins of Judah and Israel. He wonders if there is one righteous person left in the land. This drives him to place his trust in the holy and righteous God. He is also a God of justice and forgiveness. After His people receive their deserved punishment, He will shower them with mercy and love: "He will have compassion upon us; he will subdue our iniquities; and thou wilt cast all their sins into the depths of the sea" (v. 19).

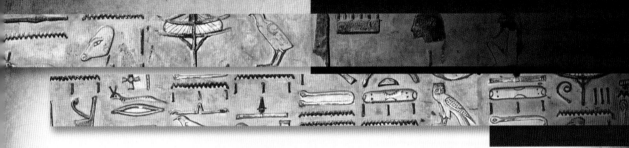

OVERVIEW: Nineveh, capital city of the Assyrian Empire, will fall before God's judgment.

Introduction to Nahum

The book of Jonah shows that God loved the pagan Assyrians (see the introduction to Jonah on p. 525); this book shows that He held them accountable for their sins, just like everyone else.

Nahum consists of a prophecy written by the prophet Nahum about 615 B.C. that Nineveh—capital city of the Assyrian Empire—would fall as a result of God's judgment against its rebellion and cruelty. This happened in 612 B.C., just as the prophet predicted, when the Assyrians were defeated by the Babylonians.

Assyria had been the dominant world power for more than a century when Nahum

1:1. Gruesome art of Assyrian soldiers impaling Jewish captives. The stone engraving was recovered from palace ruins at Nineveh, capital of the Assyrian Empire. The prophet Nahum warned that God would destroy Nineveh.

proclaimed his prophecy against it. God's judgment does not always come quickly, but it is thorough and efficient when it does arrive.

Summary of Nahum

1:1. The prophet Nahum receives a message of judgment from God. This message is to be proclaimed against Nineveh, capital of the Assyrian Empire.

1:2–8. Nahum paints a graphic picture of a powerful God who will judge the pagan city of Nineveh. But at the same time, those who serve Him have nothing to fear: "The Lord is good, a strong hold in the day of trouble" (v. 7).

1:9–15. God will destroy the idols and images of the pagan Assyrian religious system. But He will restore the nation of Judah and its system of worship of the one true God.

2:1–13. This chapter describes Nineveh under siege as God's judgment falls upon the city. Once known as "the dwelling of the lions" (v. 11), Nineveh is now weak and helpless as it cowers before its enemies. Just as Assyria had once robbed and looted other nations, now it will be stripped of its treasures.

3:1. Nahum declares, "Woe to the bloody city!" Assyria was known for its violence and cruelty in warfare. They disabled captive enemy soldiers by cutting off their hands. Rival political leaders were often impaled on stakes. Now these acts of cruelty will be carried out against the Assyrians.

3:2–19. Nahum continues his description of the defeat of Nineveh. Its streets will be littered with corpses, and it will be ransacked and burned. Not a single person will mourn the fall of Nineveh, because everyone has felt the effects of its evil and wickedness during its glory days.

[2:1–13] ASSYRIAN TERROR. *The shield of his mighty men is made red, the valiant men are in scarlet: the chariots shall be with flaming torches in the day of his preparation* (Nah. 2:3).

Nahum's description of Assyrian warriors and their battle gear shows why they struck terror in the hearts of those who faced them in battle.

The uniforms of Assyrian soldiers were scarlet in color, and they carried shields painted red, or perhaps overlaid with copper. They may have used these colors to make the blood from their wounds hard to see. In hand-to-hand combat, they wanted to give no sign that would infuse the enemy with hope and courage.

The "flaming torches" on their war chariots may have been whirling blades on the axles designed to damage and immobilize the wheels of enemy chariots. Or this could refer to the weapons in their chariots that flashed in the sunlight, giving the appearance of burning torches.

Assyria was noted for its cruelty in warfare. Their warriors would cut off the feet and hands of captives as a terror tactic to intimidate nations into surrendering to their rule (see the note "Mutilation of Captives" on p. 404).

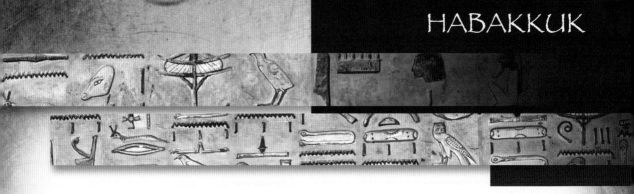

OVERVIEW: Because God is sovereign, He can use any agency He desires—even a pagan enemy nation—to bring judgment upon His people.

Introduction to Habakkuk

Habakkuk was a prophet to the Southern Kingdom (Judah) who wrote his book about 600 B.C. Like Job, he had the audacity to question the ways of God (see the introduction to Job on p. 463).

First, the prophet thought God was being lenient for not punishing the people of Judah for their sin. The Lord assured him that punishment was coming in the form of the Babylonian army from the north.

Then Habakkuk questioned whether it was just and fair for the Lord to use a pagan nation as an instrument of His judgment. Weren't they more sinful than those whom God was sending them against?

The Lord told Habakkuk that He was the sovereign ruler of the universe who could do as He pleased. He did not owe the prophet an explanation for His actions. Habakkuk finally accepted this truth about the Lord and His ways in submissive faith.

One of the great truths from the book of Habakkuk is that God has no problem with honest questions from His followers. He does not reject us if we bring our doubts and questions to Him. He will listen and sympathize and help us in the struggle to learn more about Him and His sometimes mysterious ways.

Summary of Habakkuk

1:1–4. Habakkuk begins his book not with a declaration of the word of God to others but with a question directed to God Himself. The prophet wants to know why God allows His people, the nation of Judah, to continue committing sin without subjecting them to judgment.

1:5–11. The Lord assures Habakkuk that He does intend to hold His people accountable for their wrongdoing. Even now He is raising up an enemy nation, the Chaldeans (Babylonians), who will serve as His instrument of punishment against the people of Judah. When He does judge His people, it will be harsh and effective. The Babylonians are a "bitter and hasty nation" (v. 6) known to be "terrible and dreadful" (v. 7).

[1:12–2:1] BABYLONIAN WEAPONS WORSHIP. *They [Babylonian warriors] sacrifice unto their net, and burn incense unto their drag [dragnet, NIV]* (Hab. 1:16).

This verse apparently refers to the practice among the pagan Babylonians of worshiping and offering sacrifices to their weapons of war. The Babylonians were on a mission of world conquest in Habakkuk's time. Bowing down to these weapons was the Babylonians' way of strengthening and dedicating them for this purpose.

This pagan practice made it difficult for Habakkuk to accept the reality that God would use the Babylonians as an instrument of judgment against His own people, the nation of Judah.

1:12–2:1. The Lord's answer presents Habakkuk with another dilemma. The Babylonians are unrighteous people who worship pagan gods. Are they not more evil and wicked than those whom God will send them against? How can God use them to carry out His will? The prophet climbs upon a tower to wait for God's answer to this question.

2:2–20. God honors Habakkuk's question with a forthright answer. He is using the Babylonians not because of who they are or are not but because He can work His sovereign will as He desires. After He finishes with the Babylonians, He will also judge them for their evil ways. The Lord ends His answer to the prophet with a gentle rebuke that shows He does not have to justify His actions to anyone: "The LORD is in his holy temple: let all the earth keep silence before him" (v. 20; see Job 42:1–6).

3:1–19. In a beautiful prayer of submission, Habakkuk accepts the judgment of God against His people and the method He will use to bring it about. Praising God for His wonderful works, he declares, "I will rejoice in the LORD, I will joy in the God of my salvation" (v. 18).

1:1–4. A Bedouin family begs for money in this photo taken in 1899. The prophet Habakkuk complained to God that wicked people prosper while good people suffer. God respond by promising to send invaders who would punish the Jewish nation for its sin.

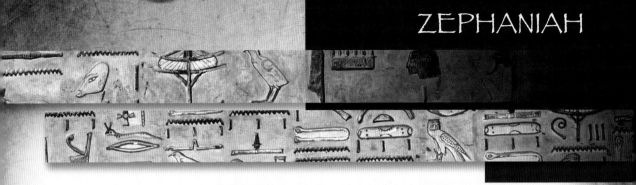

Overview: Judah (Southern Kingdom) will fall to a foreign enemy because the people are bowing down to idols.

Introduction to Zephaniah

The prophet Zephaniah tells us more about himself and his background than any of the other minor prophets of the Old Testament. He traces his ancestry back to his great-great-grandfather King Hizkiah (Hezekiah) of Judah (1:1; see 2 Chron. 29:3–36).

Zephaniah also reveals that he ministered during the days of Josiah (1:1), a godly king who reigned in Judah from about 641 to 609 B.C. Zephaniah probably wrote his book about 627 B.C.

The prophet addressed his prophecies to the nation of Judah (Southern Kingdom), which was soon to be punished by the Lord for its sin and idolatry. His prophecies were fulfilled when the nation was overrun by the Babylonian army several years after he issued his warning.

Even as the Lord was punishing His people and sending them into exile, Zephaniah declared, He would preserve a remnant who would remain faithful to Him. These would eventually inherit the promise God made to Abraham hundreds of years before (Gen. 12:1–5). People of all nations would gather in Jerusalem to worship the Lord when the remnant of Judah returned to their homeland. The King of kings, the Messiah would rule among them (3:9–13).

Summary of Zephaniah

1:1. During the days of King Josiah of Judah, God calls the prophet Zephaniah to deliver His message of judgment.

1:2–18. Judah has turned away from the Lord and is worshiping false gods. Punishment for this serious sin will come upon Judah on the great day of the Lord. This will be "a day of trouble and distress, a day of wasteness and desolation...a day of clouds and thick darkness" (v. 15). No one in Judah will escape this time of judgment.

2:1–3. But even while preaching God's coming judgment, Zephaniah holds out hope. He urges the people of Judah to seek the Lord and follow His commands. Those who do so may possibly "be hid in the day of the LORD's anger" (v. 3).

2:4–15. God's wrath will extend beyond the land of Judah to the surrounding pagan nations. He will also punish the Philistines (vv. 4–7), the Moabites (vv. 8–11), the Ethiopians (v. 12), and the Assyrians (vv. 13–15).

3:1–7. As the capital city of Judah, Jerusalem will suffer the same fate as the rest of the nation. Because it has been polluted through worship of false gods, it will fall to foreign oppressors (2 Kings 25:1–12).

3:8–20. Although God is angered by Judah's idolatry, He has not given up on His people. He will preserve a faithful remnant who will remain loyal to Him. God will use them to resettle the land and bear witness of Him to others when they return from their time of captivity in a foreign land.

HAGGAI

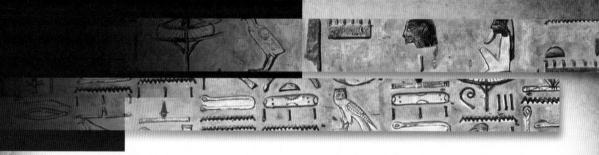

OVERVIEW: A message of hope for the Jewish exiles who have returned to Jerusalem and a call for them to complete the task of rebuilding the temple.

Introduction to Haggai

Haggai is one of three prophets in the Old Testament known as postexilic prophets. The other two are Zechariah and Malachi. They wrote their books during the turbulent period after the return of the Jewish exiles to Judah following their period of captivity by the Babylonians and Persians.

The years after the exile were discouraging times for God's people. They literally had to rebuild their lives following an absence from their homeland of more than fifty years. Neglected farmland had to be cleared before it could be cultivated. Destroyed homes had to be rebuilt. Customs and traditions had to be reestablished.

Haggai wrote his book to encourage the people to remain faithful to God, to rebuild the Jewish temple as a central place for worship, to practice holiness and righteousness in the midst of tough times, and to look forward to the coming of the Messiah and the establishment of His kingdom.

The book of Haggai emphasizes the truth that all of us need encouragement at times. One of the greatest ministries we can perform is to serve as encouragers to others.

Summary of Haggai

1:1–11. The Lord commands the prophet Haggai to address the people who have returned to Jerusalem after the exile in Babylon (2 Chron. 36:22–23). He is to challenge them to resume the task of rebuilding the temple. Haggai declares that they are suffering hard times because they have not rebuilt God's house as a place of worship.

1:12–15. The people respond to Haggai's challenge by beginning the work. The prophet delivers God's promise that He will be with them during the reconstruction project.

[2:10–19] THIRTY VESSELS SHORT. *When one came to the pressfat [wine vat, NIV] for to draw out fifty vessels out of the press, there were but twenty (Hag. 2:16).*

The Hebrew word rendered as "pressfat" by the KJV refers to a winepress or an olive press. These stone presses were used in Bible times to squeeze the oil out of olives for making fuels to burn in lamps or to press the juice out of grapes for making wine.

What Haggai is saying is that God will give the people less harvest than they expect unless they get their priorities straight and resume the task of rebuilding the temple. We can't shirk our responsibility to God and expect Him to shower us with blessings.

2:1–9. God realizes some of the people will be discouraged because the rebuilt temple will not be as large or as beautiful as the original temple. So Haggai encourages the people not to make such comparisons. What really matters is whether the temple brings glory and honor to God. The Lord promises to fill it with His presence so "the glory of this latter house shall be greater than of the former" (v. 9).

2:10–19. Haggai declares to the priests that a defiled object cannot be made clean through contact with a holy object. In the same way, the completed temple will have no magical qualities. The people should not think they will be made clean through contact with the temple. Holiness comes through devoting oneself to God and following His commands.

2:20–23. Haggai encourages Zerubbabel, a Jewish leader who has been appointed governor of Judah by the Persians (Hag. 1:1). God makes it clear that Zerubbabel has

[2:20–23] ZERUBBABEL AS A SIGNET RING. *In that day...will I [God] take thee, O Zerubbabel...and will make thee as a signet: for I have chosen thee, saith the LORD of hosts* (Hag. 2:23).

In ancient times a signet ring functioned much like a personal signature does today. A king or other high official would stamp an official document with the symbol on his ring to establish its legality and show that it was issued under his authority.

God compared Zerubbabel, the Jewish governor of Jerusalem, to a signet ring. He had invested Zerubbabel with the highest honor and would use him as His representative to bring about His purposes in the city of Jerusalem.

When the pharaoh of Egypt appointed Joseph to a high position in his administration, he gave Joseph his signet ring to show that he had the authority to act in his behalf (Gen. 41:42).

been placed in this important position for a good reason. He will use the governor to bring many blessings to His people.

ZECHARIAH

OVERVIEW: God will bless His people in the future by sending the Messiah. Meanwhile, the returned Jewish exiles need to rebuild Jerusalem and the temple.

Introduction to Zechariah

Zechariah addressed his prophecy to the same situation faced by Haggai (see the introduction to Haggai on p. 534). Like Haggai, he also encouraged the people to complete the task of rebuilding the temple in Jerusalem.

This building had been destroyed by the Babylonian army when it ransacked the city in 587 B.C. The temple was the center of religious life for the nation of Judah. So it was imperative that it be rebuilt as quickly as possible.

But the greatest contribution of Zechariah's book is his description of the coming Messiah. He described a coronation scene (6:9–15), in which a priest named Joshua, symbolizing the Messiah, is crowned as king as well as priest. He declared that the Messiah would reign in justice from the city of Jerusalem (8:3, 15–16).

Zechariah even described the manner in which the Messiah would enter the city: "He is just, and having salvation; lowly, and riding upon an ass, and upon a colt the foal of an ass" (9:9). This prophecy was fulfilled when Jesus rode into Jerusalem on a young donkey just a few days before His crucifixion (Matt. 21:5).

Summary of Zechariah

1:1–6. Zechariah calls upon the people to repent and turn from their sinful ways back to the Lord (James 4:8).

1:7–17. The prophet has a vision of four horsemen, or watchmen, who report that "all the earth...is at rest" (v. 11). This is a sign that it is time for the Jewish exiles to return from Persia to their homeland to rebuild the city of Jerusalem (2 Chron. 36:22–23).

[1:7–17] MONTH OF SEBAT. *Upon the four and twentieth day of the eleventh month, which is the month Sebat [Shebat, NIV], in the second year of Darius (Zech. 1:7).*

Zechariah had eight visions that he recorded in his book. In this verse he tells us the exact month and day on which his first vision occurred. The Jewish month of Sebat closely parallels our month of February.

Many scholars believe this vision of the prophet—a man on a red horse among the myrtle trees (1:8)—can be precisely dated at February 24, 519 B.C., by using the phrase "the second year of Darius." We know from secular history that King Darius began his reign over Persia about 521 B.C.

1:18–21. The four horns in Zechariah's vision in these verses represent the nations that had defeated Judah. These foreign nations have been defeated, so the return of Jewish exiles to Jerusalem can now proceed with no interference.

2:1–13. In this vision, Zechariah sees a man with a measuring line who is preparing

9:9–17. With crowds cheering Him, Jesus rides into Jerusalem on a donkey—just as the prophet Zechariah predicted.

to measure the wall of Jerusalem. But this measurement is not necessary, since God will serve as the protector of the city: "I, saith the Lord, will be unto her a wall of fire" (v. 5).

3:1–10. The high priest Joshua is cleansed and restored to his office in this vision of Zechariah. This prepares the way for the coming of the Messiah, who is referred to as "the BRANCH" (v. 8; see also 6:9–15).

4:1–14. In this vision, Zechariah sees a golden candlestick, or lamp stand, with an olive tree on the left side and another olive tree on the right side. The message of the vision is that God will provide the resources to enable Zerubbabel, the governor of Jerusalem, to complete the rebuilding of the temple (Hag. 2:20–23).

5:1–4. Zechariah's vision of the flying scroll ("roll," v. 1) represents God's curse against any person who steals from others or swears falsely.

5:5–11. The basket ("ephah," v. 6) in this vision represents the cleansing of the land of

Judah. The sins of the people are in the basket, which is taken away to Babylonia.

6:1–8. Zechariah's vision of the four chariots is similar to his first vision (1:7–17). God is in control, and He exercises His sovereignty over the entire world.

6:9–15. A crown is placed on the head of Joshua the high priest. He symbolizes the promised Branch, or the Messiah (chap. 3).

7:1–8:23. These chapters address the question of fasting among God's people. Since the temple is being rebuilt, should the people continue to fast? God replies that He intends to bless His people and to turn their fasts into occasions of joy.

9:1–8. God declares that He will punish the pagan nations surrounding Judah because of their worship of false gods.

9:9–17. These verses describe the arrival of the long-promised messianic King, riding on a young donkey. This passage was fulfilled by Jesus when He made His triumphant entry into Jerusalem in this fashion (Matt. 21:5).

10:1–11:17. The earthly leaders of Judah have led the nation astray (Jer. 8). God promises that He will guide His people; they can count on Him to lead them with justice and mercy.

[13:1–14:21] HOLINESS AND HORSES. *In that day shall there be upon the bells of the horses, HOLINESS UNTO THE LORD* (Zech. 14:20).

In this verse Zechariah foresees a future time when all the nations will acknowledge and worship the one true God. The praise of the Lord will be so widespread that even horses will have "HOLINESS UNTO THE LORD" inscribed on the bells on their harnesses. These are the same words embroidered on the hat worn by the high priest of Israel (Exod. 28:36).

It was customary among the nations of Bible times to hang bells on the harnesses of their warhorses. This gave them a regal, military appearance. The noise produced by the bells also may have conditioned the horses for the noise of battle.

12:1–14. God empowers His people for a great battle against the nations, and victory is assured. The phrase "They shall look upon me whom they have pierced" (v. 10) has been interpreted as a reference to Christ and His suffering (John 19:37).

13:1–14:21. In the final days, the Lord will cleanse and bless Jerusalem and establish His eternal rule throughout the world.

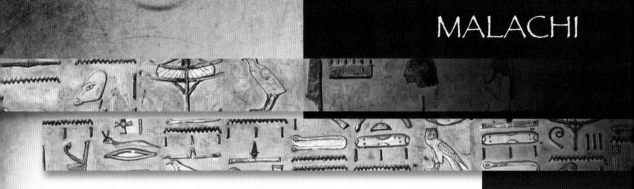

OVERVIEW: A prophetic call for spiritual renewal among the Jewish exiles who have returned to Jerusalem.

Introduction to Malachi

Malachi was a postexilic prophet, so he faced the same situation as Haggai and Zechariah (see the introduction to Haggai on p. 534). The name Malachi means "messenger of the Lord," and he was bold and forthright as God's appointed spokesman.

The prophet Malachi delivered his messages to God's people about 450 B.C., or about 100 years after their return from captivity. This was a time of great moral laxity and indifference in the nation of Judah.

Many of the people stopped bringing their tithes and offerings to the temple. Others offered defective animals as sacrifices rather than the finest from their flocks, as the Lord demanded. Intermarriage with pagan people was commonplace. Even the priests grew careless and indifferent in presiding over ceremonies at the temple.

Malachi declared that these lax practices were unacceptable to the Lord. Unless the people and the leaders changed their ways, they would face His punishment.

To make God's message more forceful, Malachi wrote parts of his book in a debate format. God made a statement of truth that was denied by the people. The Lord then overturned their argument to emphasize the truth of His original statement (1:2–7; 2:10–17; 3:7–10).

It is futile to argue with God; He always has the last word!

Summary of Malachi

1:1–5. Malachi begins his message to the exiles who have returned to Jerusalem by assuring them of God's love. His love for Israel is evident because He allowed the Jewish exiles to return and resettle their land (2 Chron. 36:22–23). God continues to honor the covenant He made centuries ago with Abraham (Gen. 12:1–5). By contrast, the land of Edom has been destroyed and will not be reclaimed by the Edomites.

1:6–14. But God is displeased with the response of the people to His love. They have grown cold and casual in their devotion to Him. They are bringing sick and defective animals to offer as sacrifices rather than presenting the best from their flocks. This is a flagrant violation of His commands (Lev. 22:20).

2:1–9. Even the priests are neglecting their responsibilities. As spiritual leaders, they are supposed to be leading the people in the ways of the Lord. But they are actually leading people astray through their waywardness and neglect.

2:10–16. The spiritual condition of the people is reflected in their family problems. Many Israelite men have married women from the surrounding nations who worship pagan gods (Ezra 10:10–17). And some of the older men are divorcing the wives of their youth to marry younger pagan women. God is displeased with these practices.

2:17–3:5. The Lord declares that He is getting tired of the whining of the people about His apparent lack of judgment against the ungodly. He assures them that He is aware of the actions of the wicked and He will deal with them as they deserve when the time is right.

3:6–10. God declares that the people are guilty of withholding tithes and offerings that belong to Him. This is another example of their lack of commitment and spiritual zeal.

3:11–18. Apparently, some Israelites were complaining that their service to God had not been rewarded. God seemed to bless the unrighteous while bringing suffering upon the righteous. The Lord rebukes this pessimistic attitude. Those who truly belong to Him, He says, will "discern between the righteous and the wicked, between him that serveth God and him that serveth him not" (v. 18).

1:6–14. A shepherd counts his sheep as they enter the pen for the evening. The prophet Malachi complained that worshipers were bringing diseased and crippled animals as sacrifices to God, when Jewish law required only the best animals.

[3:11–18] GOD'S BOOK OF REMEMBRANCE. *A book of remembrance was written before him [God] for them that feared the LORD* (Mal. 3:16).

God promised through the prophet Malachi that He would write in a "book of remembrance" the names of all the people who honored and worshiped Him.

This metaphor probably comes from the ancient Persian custom of keeping an official record of those who rendered special service to the king. King Ahasuerus of Persia was looking through such a book when he discovered that Mordecai the Jew had saved him from an assassination plot (Esther 6:1–2).

4:1–3. The coming day of the Lord, when God exercises His judgment, will have two different realities. To the wicked, it will be like a consuming hot oven. But those who belong to God will experience joy when they see "the Sun of righteousness arise with healing in his wings" (v. 2; see Joel 2:1–11).

4:4–6. These verses form a fitting conclusion not only to Malachi but to the entire Old Testament. They look back to God's law that was revealed to Moses many centuries before. But they also look forward to the fulfillment of this law with the coming of Christ. Four hundred years after the end of Malachi, God sent one final prophet known as John the Baptist to prepare the way for the promised Messiah. Jesus identified John as the Elijah who is promised in verse 5 (Matt. 17:10–13).

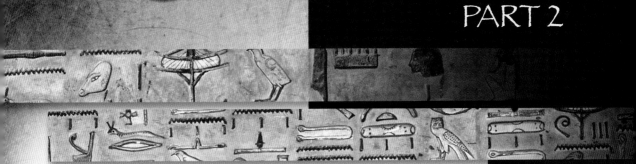

PART 2

THE NEW TESTAMENT

The second grand division of the Bible is the New Testament. Unlike the Old Testament, which was written over a period of many centuries, the twenty-seven books of the New Testament were inspired by God and written down by human authors across a period of about sixty years.

The great event that brought the New Testament into being was the life and ministry of Jesus Christ. He fulfilled the promises that God made to His people in the Old Testament by establishing a new covenant (the word *testament* means "covenant") based on the spiritual principles of grace and forgiveness rather than the keeping of the law. This new covenant between God and His people was sealed with the atoning death of His own Son.

The four major divisions of the New Testament are (1) the four Gospels, accounts of the life and ministry of Jesus; (2) the Acts of the Apostles, a book of history that traces the growth of the early church after the death and resurrection of Jesus; (3) the thirteen epistles, or letters, of the apostle Paul; and (4) the eight letters classified as general epistles, written by early church leaders other than Paul to various churches and individuals. These divisions of the New Testament are discussed in the following chapters.

CHAPTER 6
THE GOSPELS

Jesus Christ is the cornerstone of the church and the Christian faith, so it is appropriate that the New Testament opens with not one account but four separate records of His life and ministry—the Gospels of Matthew, Mark, Luke, and John. These reports were written either by Jesus' apostles who witnessed His work firsthand (Matthew and John) or by persons who recorded the eyewitness testimony of those who had known Jesus in the flesh (Mark and Luke).

These Gospels are selective accounts rather than complete biographies of the life of Jesus. The Gospel writers focused on the final three years of Jesus' life when He conducted His teaching and healing ministry. Their purpose was to show how God revealed Himself supremely in the life of His Son. Even with their narrow three-year focus, they tell us only a few of the things He did. The apostle John declared in his Gospel: "There are also many other things which Jesus did, the which, if they should be written every one, I suppose that even the world itself could not contain the books that should be written" (John 21:25).

The Gospels of Matthew, Mark, and Luke are known as the Synoptic Gospels. This designation comes from the Greek word *synopsis*, which means "seeing together." There is a great deal of overlap and repetition among these three Gospels. They report many of the same events from the life of Jesus, using a similar chronology and even repeating the information almost word for word in many cases. Of course, each of these Gospels also contains material about Jesus not found in any other account.

In contrast to the Synoptic Gospels, the Gospel of John takes a unique approach to the life of Jesus. The apostle John does more than just tell us about the things that Jesus said and did. He goes beyond the obvious to give us the theological meaning behind His teachings and miracles.

We are fortunate to have four separate Gospel witnesses to the Jesus event. While they overlap and repeat one another at certain points, together they enrich and expand our understanding of who He was and what He did.

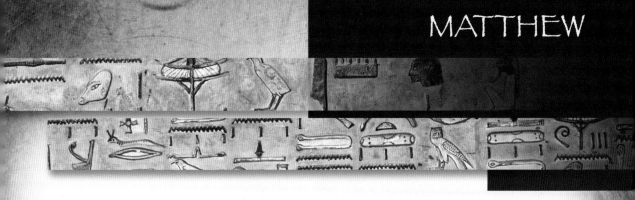

OVERVIEW: As the teacher who is greater than Moses, Jesus is the fulfillment of the Old Testament Scriptures.

Introduction to Matthew

The Gospel of Matthew is an ideal bridge between the Old Testament and the New Testament. It was written to show that Jesus is the fulfillment of Old Testament prophecy. For centuries the Jewish people had looked forward to the coming of the Messiah. Matthew affirmed that Jesus is this long-awaited Savior and King.

Matthew is never identified by name as the author of this Gospel. But since the early days of the church, he has been accepted as the writer. Matthew, also known as Levi (Mark 2:14), was called away from his duties as a tax collector to become one of the twelve disciples, or apostles, of Jesus (9:9–13).

Several clues in the Gospel of Matthew indicate that it was written to a Jewish audience to show that Jesus is the Messiah. Matthew quoted more than seventy times from the Old Testament—more than all the other three Gospels combined—using the refrain "that it might be fulfilled" (1:22) to show that Jesus fulfilled the prophecies of the Old Testament. Matthew also began his Gospel by tracing Jesus' ancestry back to Abraham, the father of the faith (1:1–2).

Another characteristic of this Gospel is its emphasis on the teaching ministry of Jesus.

The Sermon on the Mount (chaps. 5–7) summarizes the ethical standards that Jesus established for those who belong to the kingdom of God. In addition to these teachings, other important pronouncements of Jesus are grouped into major sections that end with a refrain such as "when Jesus had ended these sayings" or "when Jesus had finished these parables" (see 7:28; 11:1; 13:53; 19:1; 26:1).

Some accounts of Jesus' life and ministry in Matthew also parallel events reported in Mark, Luke, and John. These parallel passages are identified in the following summary of Matthew. The parallel passages in bold type with "see" references refer to pages in this book where expanded summaries of specific Gospel accounts may be found.

Summary of Matthew

1:1–17. Matthew begins his Gospel by tracing Jesus' genealogy through forty-two generations from Abraham up to Joseph and Mary. (For a different genealogy of Jesus, see Luke 3:23–38.)

1:18–25. Joseph is disturbed when Mary becomes pregnant while they are betrothed to each other. But an angel assures him that this pregnancy is of divine origin. Joseph marries Mary, and they name their firstborn son Jesus.

2:1–12. Wise men from the east arrive in Jerusalem to worship the newborn "King of the Jews" (v. 2). They are sent to Bethlehem,

[1:18–25] JOSEPH AND MARY'S BETROTHAL. *When as his mother Mary was espoused [pledged to be married, NIV] to Joseph, before they came together, she was found with child of the Holy Ghost* (Matt. 1:18).

In Bible times a marriage was arranged through a legal agreement between the parents of the groom and the bride. The groom's parents selected a woman for their son to marry, then paid the bride's parents a dowry, or bride price, to compensate them for the loss of her services as a daughter.

The period between the time of this legal agreement and the actual marriage of the couple was known as the betrothal. The future groom and bride were espoused or pledged to each other during this time in a formal agreement that was as legally binding as marriage itself. The betrothal could be broken only by a legal proceeding similar to a divorce.

It was during the time of her betrothal to Joseph that Mary discovered she was pregnant. This was certainly grounds for Joseph and his family to dissolve their marriage agreement with Mary and her parents.

But Joseph was informed by an angel that Mary's pregnancy was due to the miraculous action of the Holy Spirit. This child from her womb would be the Messiah, the Son of God, who would "save his people from their sins" (Matt. 1:21).

Joseph believed this message from the Lord, and he went forward with his plans to take Mary as his wife (Matt. 1:24).

Nazareth, the ancestral home of Mary and Joseph (parallel passage: Luke 2:39–40).

3:1–12. In the wilderness of Judea, the forerunner of Jesus, John the Baptist, begins preaching his message of repentance and the coming kingdom (parallel passages: Mark 1:1–8; **Luke 3:1–20**, see p. 572).

3:13–17. Jesus is baptized by John the Baptist in the Jordan River. God shows His approval by declaring, "This is my beloved Son, in whom I am well pleased" (v. 17) (parallel passages: Mark 1:9–11; Luke 3:21–22).

4:1–11. At the beginning of His public ministry, Jesus faces a series of temptations from Satan (parallel passages: Mark 1:12–13; **Luke 4:1–13**, see p. 572).

4:12–17. Leaving His hometown of Nazareth, Jesus moves to Capernaum in Galilee and launches His public ministry. He continues the message that John the Baptist, His forerunner, had been preaching: "Repent: for the kingdom of heaven is at hand" (v. 17) (parallel passages: Mark 1:14–15; John 4:45).

4:18–22. Jesus calls two different pairs of brothers—Peter and Andrew, James and John—away from their fishing nets to become His followers and disciples (parallel passages: Mark 1:16–20; **Luke 5:1–11**, see p. 572).

where the Scriptures predicted this king would be born (Mic. 5:2). In Bethlehem, the wise men present gifts of gold, frankincense, and myrrh to the young Jesus.

2:13–18. The jealous and paranoid King Herod of Judah slaughters all the male children under two years of age around Bethlehem in an attempt to kill the young Jesus. But Joseph is warned in a dream to take the boy and His mother to a safe place in the land of Egypt.

2:19–23. After Herod dies, Jesus and His family return to Judah. They settle in the city of

[5:1–7:29] SALT OF THE EARTH. *Ye [followers of Jesus] are the salt of the earth: but if the salt have lost his savour [loses its saltiness, NIV], wherewith shall it be salted? it is thenceforth good for nothing* (Matt. 5:13).

Salt added flavor to food, and it was also used to preserve meat in a society in which refrigeration and cold storage did not exist.

Jesus used the imagery of salt to describe His followers. If they did not demonstrate their distinctive purity and holiness as His people, they would have no influence in the world. Christians have no higher calling than to serve as the "salt of the earth" in a sinful and decadent culture.

4:12–17. A monument built over Peter's house in Capernaum reflects in its window the synagogue ruins just a few yards away. Jesus selected the fishing village of Capernaum, hometown of several of His disciples, as His ministry headquarters.

4:23–25. Jesus travels throughout the region of Galilee, preaching the gospel of the kingdom of God and healing the sick. As His fame spreads, crowds flock to Him from as far away as Judea and the city of Jerusalem in southern Palestine (parallel passages: Mark 1:35–39; Luke 4:42–44).

5:1–7:29. Jesus delivers His famous Sermon on the Mount to His followers. It describes the type of behavior expected of those who are true citizens of the kingdom of God. Jesus covers several distinctive themes in these teachings:

(1) The Beatitudes (5:3–12). The word *blessed*, meaning "happy," describes the rewards in store for those who live as citizens of God's kingdom.

(2) Salt and light (5:13–16). Christian living by citizens of God's kingdom bears a positive witness in the world.

(3) Authentic righteousness (5:17–48). We must go beyond rituals and external appearances and live by the deeper meaning of God's laws.

(4) The dangers of hypocrisy (6:1–18). Matters of worship such as giving, praying, and fasting must grow out of the right motives.

(5) Getting priorities in order (6:19–34). Anxiety over lesser matters will disappear when we put God's kingdom first.

(6) Not judging (7:1–6). The citizens of God's kingdom must not judge and condemn people with a harsh, critical attitude.

(7) The importance of prayer (7:7–12). We may claim the blessings of prayer that God has promised to those who follow Him.

(8) The two ways (7:13–14). Believers must choose the narrow way that leads to life, not the broad and popular way that leads to certain destruction.

(9) Fruit-bearing (7:15–20). A genuine follower of the Lord will perform deeds and render service that bring honor and glory to Him.

(10) Actions versus words (7:21–23). Obeying God is more important than a long speech about how committed we are to Him.

(11) The solid foundation (7:24–29). Jesus' parable about the man who built his house on a rock shows how important it is to plant our lives on the unshakable foundation of the Lord and His Word.

8:1–4. Jesus heals a man with leprosy (parallel passages: **Mark 1:40–45**, see p. 560; Luke 5:12–16).

8:5–13. Jesus expresses His surprise at the faith of a centurion, a Roman military officer. He heals the man's servant at a distance (parallel passage: Luke 7:1–10).

8:14–17. Many sick people from Capernaum seek Jesus for healing after He heals Peter's mother-in-law (parallel passages: Mark 1:29–34; Luke 4:38–41).

8:18–22. Jesus challenges His followers to be fully committed to Him (parallel passage: Luke 9:57–62).

8:23–27. Jesus calms a storm on the Sea of Galilee. The disciples are amazed at His power (parallel passages: Mark 4:35–41; Luke 8:22–25).

8:28–34. Jesus casts demons out of two wild men among the tombs (parallel passages: **Mark 5:1–20**, see p. 562; Luke 8:26–39).

9:1–8. Several scribes accuse Jesus of blasphemy after He heals a paralyzed man and forgives his sins (parallel passages: **Mark 2:1–12**, see p. 560; Luke 5:17–26).

9:9–13. Jesus calls Matthew, a tax collector, to leave his tollbooth and follow Him and become His disciple (parallel passages: Mark 2:13–17; **Luke 5:27–32**, see p. 572).

9:14–17. Jesus is asked why He and His disciples do not fast. He replies that fasting is an

[9:1–8] TOTAL PARALYSIS. *Then saith he [Jesus] to the sick of the palsy [the paralytic, NIV], Arise, take up thy bed* (Matt. 9:6).

The word *palsy* is used in the KJV to describe a person who is totally paralyzed. The Gospels use this word only of the man whose friends let him down through the roof of a house on a blanket so he could be healed by Jesus (Matt. 9:1–6; see also Mark 2:1–12; Luke 5:17–26).

Matthew's Gospel eliminates the details about this man being let down through the roof. But scholars believe this is the same healing miracle—with these details added—reported by Mark and Luke.

The apostle Peter also healed a man who was totally paralyzed (Acts 9:32–34).

external law or rite that is being displaced by spiritual principles. The kingdom of God that has arrived in Jesus cannot conform to the rituals of the Pharisees (parallel passages: Mark 2:18–22; Luke 5:33–39).

9:18–26. Jesus heals a woman with a hemorrhage and raises the daughter of a synagogue ruler from the dead (parallel passages: **Mark 5:21–43**, see p. 562; Luke 8:40–56).

9:27–31. Jesus heals two blind men and orders them not to tell anyone about this miracle.

9:32–35. Jesus heals a demon-possessed man who is unable to speak. The Pharisees charge Him with performing miracles through the power of Satan.

9:36–38. The spiritual needs of the people move Jesus to compassion. He prays for more workers to minister to these needs.

10:1–4. From among all His followers, Jesus selects twelve men to serve as His disciples (parallel passages: Mark 3:13–19; **Luke 6:12–16**, see pp. 572–74).

10:5–42. Jesus sends His twelve disciples out to preach the gospel of the kingdom of God and to heal the sick. He warns them that they will be rejected and persecuted in

some places. But they can depend on God's promise of guidance and protection (parallel passages: Mark 6:7–13; Luke 9:1–6).

11:1–19. After being imprisoned by King Herod, John the Baptist wonders if Jesus really is the Messiah whom he has announced in his preaching. He sends two of his followers to Jesus to find out. Jesus assures John that He is indeed the spiritual deliverer whom God has sent. He also commends John for his faithfulness to the task of paving the way for His work (parallel passage: Luke 7:18–35).

11:20–24. Jesus condemns the cities of Chorazin, Bethsaida, and Capernaum in the region of Galilee for their spiritual stubbornness and lack of belief in Him and His teachings.

11:25–30. Jesus commends the common people ("babes," v. 25), who are open to His teachings, in contrast to the proud Pharisees ("the wise and prudent," v. 25), who are critical of His ministry. He invites all who are burdened down by a religion of legalistic rule-keeping to find relief and rest in Him.

12:1–8. The Pharisees criticize Jesus and His

[12:1–8] EATING GRAIN OFF THE STALK. *His [Jesus'] disciples were an hungered, and began to pluck the ears of corn [heads of grain, NIV], and to eat* (Matt. 12:1).

While passing by a field of wheat or barley on the Sabbath, Jesus' disciples stripped some grain from the stalks. They rubbed it in their hands to remove the outer husks, then popped the grain into their mouths.

Wheat or barley was usually ground into flour, then baked into bread. But when bread was not available, eating grain right off the stalk was a quick way to satisfy one's hunger.

The Old Testament law permitted hungry travelers to pick and eat handfuls of grain from fields along the road (Deut. 23:25).

disciples for picking grain on the Sabbath to satisfy their hunger. According to their interpretation, this breaks the law that prohibits working on the Sabbath (Exod. 31:14). Jesus replies that human needs must take precedence over ritual laws. Besides, as the Messiah, God's Son, He is "Lord even of the sabbath day" (v. 8) (parallel passages: Mark 2:23–28; Luke 6:1–5).

12:9–14. Jesus heals a man's withered hand in the synagogue on the Sabbath. The Pharisees again accuse Him of breaking the Sabbath law and begin to plot His destruction (parallel passages: Mark 3:1–6; Luke 6:6–11).

12:15–21. Jesus heals many sick and diseased people among the crowds that follow Him. Matthew the Gospel writer identifies Jesus with the Suffering Servant in the book of Isaiah (vv. 17–21; see Isa. 42:1–4) (parallel passage: Mark 3:7–12).

12:22–23. Jesus heals a demon-possessed blind man who cannot speak.

12:24–37. The Pharisees charge that Jesus heals people by the power of Satan. He responds by stating that Satan would not act against himself by casting demons (satanic beings) out of a person. He turns this charge back on the Pharisees by showing that they are committing blasphemy by attributing the work of God to Satan (parallel passage: Mark 3:20–30).

12:38–45. The scribes and Pharisees ask Jesus to show them some spectacular sign to prove that He is the Messiah. He refuses, knowing that no sign will be strong enough to overcome their unbelief. He does tell them that they will be given a continuing sign at some future time—His resurrection from the dead after three days in the grave.

12:46–50. According to Jesus, His true relatives, in a spiritual sense, are those who "do the will of my Father" (v. 50) (parallel passages: **Mark 3:31–35**, see p. 561; Luke 8:19–21).

13:1–9. Jesus delivers the parable of the sower to a crowd beside the Sea of Galilee. The sower threw seed on four different types of soil: wayside soil (v. 4), rocky soil (v. 5), soil where thorns grew (v. 7), and good soil (v. 8) (parallel passages: Mark 4:1–9; Luke 8:4–8).

13:10–17. Jesus explains to His disciples why He speaks in parables. These stories drawn from everyday life communicate spiritual truths to people with open minds. But they conceal truth from proud know-it-alls such as the Pharisees who are not open to new revelation from God (parallel passages: Mark 4:10–12; Luke 8:9–10).

13:18–23. Jesus tells His disciples that the four types of soil in the parable of the sower represent the different responses that people make to the claims of the kingdom of God (parallel passages: Mark 4:13–20; Luke 8:11–15).

13:24–30. The parable of the wheat and the tares (weeds) teaches that good and evil will exist in intermingled fashion until the final judgment. Then they will be separated. Good will be rewarded, and evil will be punished.

13:31–35. These two parables—mustard seed and leaven—teach the same truth: The kingdom of God may seem small and insignificant in the beginning, but it will grow to render an effective influence throughout the world (parallel passage: Luke 13:18–21).

13:36–43. Jesus explains the meaning of the parable of the wheat and the tares (weeds) to His disciples.

13:44–46. These two parables—the hidden treasure and the pearl of great price—teach that a person should be willing to pay any price to claim the blessings of God's kingdom.

9:27–31. Healing miracles, such as curing the blind, draw crowds of people to Jesus. His rising popularity made Jewish leaders jealous.

14:13–21. Jesus feeds a crowd of more than 5,000 with just five loaves of bread and two fish.

13:47–50. This parable of the net is similar to the parable of the wheat and the tares (weeds). The kingdom of God, symbolized by the net, will inevitably collect people who are both good and bad. But they will be separated at the final judgment.

13:51–52. This brief parable depicts a householder or landowner mixing both old and new to provide for his family. With His fresh teachings, Jesus brings many new insights to the traditions from the past. Both are essential for those who belong to the kingdom of God.

13:53–58. Jesus returns to His hometown of Nazareth, where He teaches in the local synagogue. But He is rejected because of the "hometown boy" syndrome. He declares that "a prophet is not without honour, save in his own country, and in his own house" (v. 57) (parallel passage: Mark 6:1–6).

14:1–12. John the Baptist is imprisoned by King Herod because he condemned Herod's adulterous marriage to his brother Philip's wife, Herodias. She succeeds in having John the Baptist executed (parallel passage: Mark 6:14–29).

14:13–21. Jesus multiplies a little bread and a few fish to feed more than 5,000 hungry people (parallel passages: **Mark 6:30–44**, see p. 562; Luke 9:10–17; John 6:1–14).

14:22–33. Jesus walks on the water to join His disciples in a boat on the Sea of Galilee. Peter tries his "water legs" but sinks because of a lack of faith. The disciples are amazed and declare that Jesus is "the Son of God" (v. 33) (parallel passages: Mark 6:45–52; John 6:15–21).

14:34–36. Jesus heals many sick and diseased people in the land of Gennesaret (parallel passage: Mark 6:53–56).

15:1–20. Several scribes and Pharisees criticize Jesus because He and His disciples do not perform a ritual washing of their hands before eating. He replies that externals such as food that go into the body do not defile a person. The impure thoughts and ideas that come from within a person are the real sources of defilement (parallel passage: Mark 7:1–23).

15:21–28. Jesus heals the daughter of a Gentile woman and expresses amazement at her great faith (parallel passage: Mark 7:24–30).

15:29–39. Jesus feeds a hungry crowd of more than 4,000 people by miraculously multiplying seven loaves of bread and a few fish (parallel passage: Mark 8:1–10). This miracle was performed for non-Jews in Gentile territory. Earlier He had fed more than 5,000 Jews in Jewish territory (see Matt. 14:13–21).

16:1–12. Jesus condemns the hypocrisy of the Pharisees and Sadducees and warns His disciples to avoid their teachings (parallel passage: Mark 8:11–21).

16:13–20. In the region of Caesarea-Philippi, Jesus commends the apostle Peter for his faith after he proclaims Jesus as the Messiah and the Son of God (parallel passages: Mark 8:27–30; Luke 9:18–20).

16:21–28. Jesus reveals to His disciples that He will be killed by the religious leaders and then resurrected. He condemns Peter for refusing to believe this prediction (parallel passage: Mark 8:31–9:1).

17:1–13. Jesus demonstrates His future glory by being transfigured before three of His disciples—Peter, James, and John. God speaks from a cloud, "This is my beloved Son, in whom I am well pleased; hear ye him" (v. 5) (parallel passages: Mark 9:2–13; Luke 9:28–36).

17:14–21. Jesus casts a stubborn demon out of a boy. He expresses disappointment in His disciples because their lack of faith prevented them from healing the boy (parallel passages: Mark 9:14–29; Luke 9:37–42).

17:22–23. Jesus again predicts His death and resurrection (parallel passages: Mark 9:30–32; Luke 9:43–45).

17:24–27. Jesus miraculously produces a coin to pay the yearly temple tax for Himself and Peter.

[17:24–27] A TAX FOR THE TEMPLE. *They [temple officials] that received tribute money came to Peter, and said, Doth not your master [Jesus] pay tribute?* (Matt. 17:24)

This verse refers to the annual tax designated for maintenance and support of the temple in Jerusalem. Every Jewish male was required to pay this tax. Perhaps the temple officials who collected this tax approached Peter about paying it because Jesus and His disciples were hard to pin down. Their teaching and healing ministry kept them moving from place to place.

The NIV translates the Greek word for "tribute money" in this verse as "two-drachma tax." The standard Greek coin of that time was the drachma. It took two of these coins to pay the tax.

The drachma was roughly equivalent to the Roman coin known as the denarius. A common laborer of Bible times would often be paid one denarius for a full day's work.

18:1–10. Jesus uses a child as an illustration to teach His disciples about the meaning of humility and service to others (parallel passages: Mark 9:33–50; Luke 9:46–50).

18:11–14. Through the parable of the lost sheep, Jesus shows His disciples that His mission is to seek and save lost and hurting people.

18:15–22. Jesus teaches His disciples just how far citizens of the kingdom of God should go to reclaim those who have wronged them. Love and forgiveness have no limit.

18:23–35. Through the parable of the unforgiving servant, Jesus teaches that all who have been forgiven should extend forgiveness to others.

19:1–12. In answer to a question from the Pharisees, Jesus discusses the meaning of marriage and the issue of divorce (parallel passage: Mark 10:1–12).

19:13–15. Jesus welcomes and blesses little children (parallel passages: **Mark 10:13–16,** see p. 564; Luke 18:15–17).

19:16–30. The rich young ruler turns away with regret because his wealth is more important to him than becoming a follower of Jesus (parallel passages: Mark 10:17–31; Luke 18:18–30).

20:1–16. This parable is known as the workers in the vineyard. The laborers worked for different lengths of time, but all were paid the same. The message is that God relates to citizens of His kingdom with mercy and grace and gives us more than we deserve.

20:17–19. On His way to Jerusalem, Jesus again tells His disciples that He will be executed in that city—but He will be resurrected on the third day after His death (parallel passages: Mark 10:32–34; Luke 18:31–34).

20:20–28. The mother of James and John, two of Jesus' disciples, asks Him to give her sons prominent places in His kingdom. He teaches the disciples that His kingdom is spiritual rather than physical in nature (parallel passage: Mark 10:35–45).

20:29–34. Jesus heals two blind men at Jericho (parallel passages: Mark 10:46–52; Luke 18:35–43).

21:1–11. Jesus is acclaimed by the crowds as the long-expected Messiah when He rides into Jerusalem on a donkey. Riding a lowly donkey fulfills the prophecy of Zechariah 9:9 and also shows that Jesus is a spiritual king, not the political deliverer whom the people were expecting (parallel passages: Mark 11:1–11; Luke 19:28–44; John 12:12–19).

21:33–46. Rich farmland lays a pattern of bounty on the fields of northern Israel, where Jesus once ministered. There, Jesus told many parables about farming. These parables were a way of teaching the people about God and His kingdom. One story was about tenant farmers who killed the landowner's son—a metaphor of Jesus' coming crucifixion.

[21:12–22] COMMERCIALISM IN THE TEMPLE. *Jesus went into the temple…and cast out all them that sold and bought in the temple, and overthrew the tables of the moneychangers, and the seats of them that sold doves* (Matt. 21:12).

These commercial activities that upset Jesus were being conducted in an outer court of the Jewish temple during the observance of the Passover in Jerusalem.

All male Jews were expected to attend this festival, even if they lived a long distance from Jerusalem. The moneychangers were probably exchanging foreign coins of these pilgrims for the appropriate coins with which to pay the temple tax (see the note "A Tax for the Temple" on p. 551).

These pilgrims were also expected to provide animals for sacrifice on the altar of the temple during this celebration. Merchants were selling animals for this purpose as a convenience so pilgrims would not have to bring them along on their trip to the holy city.

Jesus was angry about the crass commercialism of the scene. Temple officials may have been profiting personally from the buying and selling. He quoted Isaiah 56:7 ("Mine house shall be called an house of prayer") and accused the merchants of defiling the temple: "But ye have made it a den of thieves" (Matt. 21:13).

21:12–22. Jesus drives out merchants who are buying and selling in the temple. He pronounces a curse on a fig tree that is bearing no fruit. The barren fig tree symbolizes the dead traditions of the Pharisees and other religious leaders of the nation (parallel passages: Mark 11:12–26; Luke 19:45–48).

21:23–27. Jesus answers the objections of the Pharisees and asserts His divine authority over the temple (parallel passages: Mark 11:27–33; Luke 20:1–8).

21:28–32. In this parable of the vineyard workers, a contrast is drawn between the Pharisees and the sinners. The Pharisees were supposed to be doing God's work (they promised to work in the vineyard but did not), but their stubbornness and traditions kept them from entering God's kingdom. But the sinners were open and teachable (they refused to work in the vineyard at first but then did so) and thus able to become citizens of the kingdom.

21:33–46. The wicked husbandmen, or tenant farmers, in this parable represent the religious leaders of Israel. They are rejecting Jesus as God's Son, so God will turn to others—even Gentiles (Acts 13:46)—and offer them the opportunity to become citizens of God's kingdom (parallel passages: Mark 12:1–12; Luke 20:9–19).

22:1–14. This parable of the marriage feast teaches essentially the same truth as the parable of the wicked husbandmen (Matt. 21:33–46). The Jewish people who have rejected the Messiah will be turned away from the messianic feast, and Gentiles will be brought in to take their place at the table (Rom. 15:16).

22:15–22. The Pharisees and Herodians try to trap Jesus with a question about paying taxes to the Roman government. Jesus silences them by pointing out that people have a dual obligation—to the state or civil government as well as to God, the ultimate authority (parallel passages: Mark 12:13–17; Luke 20:20–26).

22:23–33. Jesus also deals skillfully with a question from the Sadducees that is designed to make Him look foolish. Whose wife would a woman be in the afterlife if she had been married to several different men? Jesus tells the Sadducees they are assuming the afterlife will be like life here on earth. But the spiritual realities of the life beyond will be different: "In the resurrection they neither marry, nor are given in marriage, but are as the angels of God in heaven" (v. 30) (parallel passages: Mark 12:18–27; Luke 20:27–40).

22:34–40. Jesus tells a teacher of the law that the command to love your neighbor as yourself (Lev. 19:18) is just as important as the command to love God (Deut. 6:4–9) (parallel passage: Mark 12:28–34).

22:41–46. In a discussion with the Pharisees, Jesus rejects the popular thinking of the day that the Messiah would be a human descendant of King David (2 Sam. 7:8–16). Jesus identifies Himself as the Messiah and the divine Son of God (parallel passages: Mark 12:35–37; Luke 20:41–44).

23:1–36. Jesus condemns the scribes and Pharisees because of their hypocrisy, dishonesty, pride, spiritual blindness, and preoccupation with external matters in religion (parallel passages: Mark 12:38–40; Luke 20:45–47).

23:37–39. Jesus expresses His sorrow over the city of Jerusalem because of its failure to accept Him as the Messiah (parallel passage: Luke 13:34–35).

24:1–51. This chapter is known as Jesus' great prophetic discourse. He predicts the destruction of the temple in Jerusalem and discusses events that will take place in the end-time before His second coming (parallel passages: Mark 13:1–37; Luke 21:5–38).

25:1–13. Through the parable of the ten virgins, Jesus teaches His followers to be in a state of watchful readiness at all times. His second coming may occur at any time—probably when it is least expected (1 Thess. 5:1–11).

25:14–30. In the parable of the talents, two servants multiplied the money entrusted to them by their master. But one was lazy and earned no interest on his talent. This parable teaches that we are to be good stewards of the gifts and abilities granted to us by the Lord.

25:31–46. Jesus compares the separation of people at the final judgment to the work of shepherds, who would separate the sheep from the goats in their flocks at the end of the day. Jesus identifies so closely with people in extreme need—the lonely, hungry, and imprisoned—that ministry to such people will be counted as service to Christ Himself.

26:1–5. Members of the Jewish Sanhedrin meet to plot how they can capture Jesus and have Him executed. They realize they must do this discreetly because of Jesus' popularity among the people (parallel passages: Mark 14:1–2; Luke 22:1–2).

26:6–13. A woman (according to the Gospel of John, it was Mary of Bethany) anoints the head of Jesus with an expensive perfume. Jesus interprets this as an anointing in preparation for His death and

[23:1–36] PHYLACTERIES AND TASSELS. *They [the Pharisees] make broad their phylacteries, and enlarge the borders [tassels, NIV] of their garments* (Matt. 23:5).

In this verse, as in all of Matthew 23, Jesus denounced the scribes and Pharisees for their hypocrisy and legalism.

The Pharisees were noted for their attempts to keep the Old Testament law in every minute detail. Over the centuries they had added their own interpretations of the law that they considered as binding as the original law itself.

Phylacteries were little boxes containing strips of parchment on which portions of the law were written. The Pharisees wore these boxes on their foreheads and hands as a literal obedience of the Lord's command, "Thou shalt bind them [God's laws] for a sign upon thine hand, and they shall be as frontlets between thine eyes" (Deut. 6:8). Tassels were decorative fringes that the Pharisees wore on their clothes to remind them of God's laws (Deut. 22:12).

The problem with these displays of piety among the Pharisees is that they were done just for show. Jesus declared that they worked hard to observe the externals of religion while omitting "the weightier matters of the law, judgment, mercy, and faith" (Matt. 23:23).

burial (parallel passages: Mark 14:3–9; John 12:1–8).

26:14–16. Judas, a disciple of Jesus, agrees to betray Jesus for thirty pieces of silver and lead the religious leaders to Him at an opportune time (parallel passages: Mark 14:10–11; Luke 22:3–6).

26:17–19. Jesus instructs His disciples to make preparations for a meal that they will eat together to observe the Jewish Passover (parallel passages: Mark 14:12–16; Luke 22:7–13).

26:20–25. During the Passover meal, Jesus identifies His disciple Judas as His betrayer (parallel passages: Mark 14:17–21; Luke 22:21–23; **John 13:21–30**, see p. 587).

26:26–30. Jesus observes the Last Supper with His disciples (parallel passages: Mark 14:22–26; **Luke 22:14–20,** see pp. 579–80).

26:31–35. Jesus predicts that all His disciples will abandon and deny Him during His arrest and trial (parallel passages: Mark 14:27–31; **Luke 22:31–38,** see p. 580; John 13:31–38).

26:36–46. Jesus agonizes in prayer in the Garden of Gethsemane about His forthcoming suffering and death. His disciples fall asleep and fail to support Him in His hour of need (parallel passages: Mark 14:32–42; Luke 22:39–46).

26:26–30. Jesus and His disciples share one final meal in celebration of Passover. After this meal, known as the Last Supper, Jesus went to a garden to pray. He was arrested that night and hanging from a cross by nine the next morning.

[26:47–56] **CHIEF PRIESTS.** *Judas, one of the twelve, came, and with him a great multitude...from the chief priests and elders of the people* (Matt. 26:47).

The phrase "chief priests" in this verse probably refers to the leaders or directors of the twenty-four groups of priests into which the priesthood was divided in David's time (1 Chron. 24:1–5). These twenty-four divisions of the priesthood probably presided at the altar in the tabernacle or temple on a rotating basis.

In New Testament times, these "chief priests" may have included the high priest as well as priestly members of his immediate family.

26:47–56. Judas leads a group of temple guards sent by the Sanhedrin to the place where Jesus is praying in the Garden of Gethsemane. He identifies Jesus by greeting Him with a kiss. Jesus is arrested and taken away (parallel passages: Mark 14:43–52; Luke 22:47–53; John 18:1–12).

26:57–68. Jesus appears before the high priest Caiaphas and the rest of the Jewish Sanhedrin. Peter follows and waits outside the house of the high priest to see what will happen. The Sanhedrin declares Jesus guilty of blasphemy when He admits He is the Son of God (parallel passages: Mark 14:53–65; Luke 22:63–71).

26:69–75. Outside the house of the high priest, Peter denies that He knows Jesus when he is questioned by three different people. The crowing of a rooster makes Peter realize that Jesus' prediction of his denial has come true (parallel passages: Mark 14:66–72; Luke 22:54–62; John 18:15–27).

27:1–2. The Sanhedrin finds Jesus guilty of blasphemy under the Jewish law. Determined to have Him executed, they take Him to Pontius Pilate, the Roman provincial governor of Judea. Only the Romans had the authority to pronounce and carry out the death sentence (parallel passages: Mark 15:1; Luke 23:1).

27:3–10. Judas has a change of heart when he realizes his actions have condemned an innocent man. He returns the betrayal money and then commits suicide (Acts 1:16–20).

27:11–26. Jesus appears before Pontius Pilate, the Roman governor. Pilate realizes Jesus is an innocent man. But he is also under pressure from the religious leaders, who are determined to have Him executed. He tries to get Jesus released by using the custom of setting one prisoner free at the whim of the people during a major Jewish holiday. But the people call for the release of another prisoner named Barabbas instead. Finally, Pilate condemns Jesus to death by crucifixion (parallel passages: Mark 15:2–15; Luke 23:13–25; John 18:28–19:16).

27:27–31. Jesus is mocked and abused by Roman soldiers before they lead Him away to the crucifixion site (parallel passage: Mark 15:16–20).

27:32. A bystander, Simon of Cyrene, is pressed into service to carry the cross of Jesus (parallel passages: Mark 15:21; **Luke 23:26–31,** see p. 580).

27:33–37. Jesus is crucified at a site known as Golgotha ("place of the skull") just outside the walls of Jerusalem (Heb. 13:12). The placard on His cross that specifies His crime reads, "THIS IS JESUS THE KING OF THE JEWS" (v. 37). This indicates that He was probably executed on the false charge that He was a political revolutionary who challenged the power and authority of the Roman government (parallel passages: Mark 15:22–26; Luke 23:32–38; John 19:17–24).

27:38–44. Jesus is mocked and ridiculed by people in the crowd as well as two thieves

28:16–20. After His crucifixion and resurrection, Jesus gives His disciples the Great Commission, commanding them to take His message to people throughout the world.

who are being crucified at the same time (parallel passages: Mark 15:27–32; **Luke 23:39–43**, see p. 581).

27:45–54. Jesus' suffering and death are accompanied by several mysterious events, including an earthquake at the moment when He dies (parallel passages: **Mark 15:33–39**, see p. 567; Luke 23:44–48).

27:55–56. Several women from Galilee who are followers of Jesus are among the crowd at the crucifixion site (parallel passages: Mark 15:40–41; Luke 23:49; **John 19:25–27**, see p. 588).

27:57–60. Joseph of Arimathea buries the body of Jesus in his own tomb (parallel passages: Mark 15:42–46; Luke 23:50–54; **John 19:38–42**, see p. 589).

27:61. Mary Magdalene and "the other Mary" (probably the mother of Jesus' disciple James, the son of Alphaeus), followers of Jesus, mourn at the tomb where Jesus is buried (parallel passages: Mark 15:47; Luke 23:55–56).

27:62–66. After talking to Pilate, the religious leaders station guards at the tomb where Jesus is buried and seal the entrance with a large stone.

28:1–10. Mary Magdalene and "the other Mary" (see Matt. 27:61) visit the tomb of Jesus on Sunday morning after His death and burial two days before. They are greeted by an angel, who tells them He has been raised from the dead. The angel instructs them to tell His disciples this good news. Then Jesus Himself greets the women to assure them and calm their fears (parallel passages: Mark 16:1–8; Luke 24:1–8; John 20:1–2).

28:11–15. The Jewish Sanhedrin bribes the guards who were on duty at Jesus' tomb in an attempt to deny the claims of His resurrection. These guards spread the rumor that Jesus' disciples took His body out of the grave before daybreak on Sunday morning.

28:16–20. Jesus meets with His disciples in Galilee and charges them with His Great Commission (Acts 1:8). They are to continue His mission of bringing people into the kingdom of God (parallel passages: Mark 16:14–18; Luke 24:44–49).

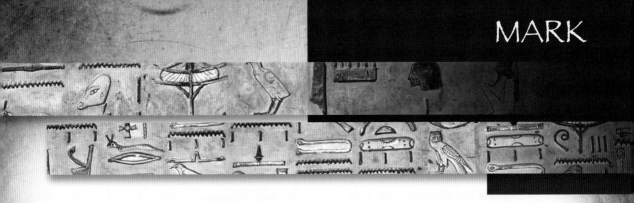

OVERVIEW: Probably the first Gospel written, Mark focuses on the power of Jesus and presents Him as the Suffering Servant.

Introduction to Mark

Mark is the shortest and most concise of the four Gospels—only sixteen chapters in length. It's the Gospel of choice for those who want a quick, to-the-point overview of the life and ministry of Jesus.

Most scholars believe that Mark was the first Gospel written. It appeared about A.D. 60—about thirty years after the death and resurrection of Jesus. Matthew and Luke were written after Mark. These two Gospels apparently included material from Mark as well as additional accounts of Jesus' life from other sources. A careful study of these three Synoptic Gospels (see the introduction to the Gospels on p. 542) shows that all but a few verses from Mark appear in Matthew and Luke.

The author of Mark was John Mark, the young man who turned back to Jerusalem after accompanying Paul and Barnabas for a while on their first missionary journey (Acts 13:1–3). Mark later overcame this initial failure in Christian service and was associated with the apostle Peter in his ministry (1 Pet. 5:13). Before his death, Peter must have recounted events that he remembered from his experience as one of the twelve disciples of Jesus. John Mark wrote these eyewitness accounts down in the Gospel that bears his name.

While the Gospel of Matthew was written to a Jewish audience (see the introduction to Matthew on p. 543), Mark's Gospel has a Gentile orientation. Mark was careful to translate Jewish terms into Roman equivalents (for example, he indicated that the Aramaic word *Boanerges* meant "the sons of thunder," 3:17) and to explain Jewish customs to his non-Jewish audience. Mark also emphasized the miracles of Jesus rather than His teachings. Jesus comes across in this Gospel as a person of action who has power over sickness, the natural order, and the forces of evil.

Above all, Mark tells us about a Savior who was obedient to the will of His Father, even to the point of becoming the Suffering Servant on our behalf. Even the Roman centurion at the cross recognized this when he declared, "Truly this man was the Son of God" (15:39).

Some accounts of Jesus' life and ministry in Mark also parallel events reported in Matthew, Luke, and John. These parallel passages are identified in the following summary of Mark. The parallel passages in bold type with "see" references refer to pages in this book where expanded summaries of specific Gospel accounts may be found.

Summary of Mark

1:1–8. John the Baptist, forerunner of Jesus, begins preaching (parallel passages: Matt. 3:1–12; **Luke 3:1–20**, see p. 572).

1:9–11. Jesus is baptized by John (parallel

passages: **Matt. 3:13–17**, see p. 544; Luke 3:21–22).

1:12–13. Jesus is tempted by Satan (parallel passages: Matt. 4:1–11; **Luke 4:1–13**, see p. 572).

1:14–15. Jesus begins preaching in the region of Galilee (parallel passages: **Matt. 4:12–17**, see p. 544; John 4:45).

1:16–20. Jesus beckons Peter and Andrew and James and John to follow Him (parallel passages: Matt. 4:18–22; **Luke 5:1–11**, see p. 572).

1:21–28. Jesus casts demons out of a man in the synagogue at Capernaum on the Sabbath. The people are amazed at His power and authority (parallel passage: **Luke 4:31–37**, see p. 572).

1:29–34. Jesus heals Peter's mother-in-law; many sick people come to Him for healing (parallel passages: Matt. 8:14–17; Luke 4:38–41).

1:35–39. Jesus preaches and heals throughout Galilee (parallel passages: **Matt. 4:23–25**, see p. 546; Luke 4:42–44).

1:40–45. Jesus heals a man with leprosy. He ignores Jesus' instructions not to tell anyone about his miraculous healing, and people from a wide area flock to Jesus (parallel passages: Matt. 8:1–4; Luke 5:12–16).

2:1–12. Four men lower their paralyzed friend through the roof to Jesus for healing. Jesus also forgives his sins and is accused of blasphemy by a group of scribes (parallel passages: Matt. 9:1–8; Luke 5:17–26).

2:13–17. Jesus calls the tax collector Matthew, also known as Levi, to become His disciple (parallel passages: Matt. 9:9–13; **Luke 5:27–32**, see p. 572).

2:18–22. Jesus explains to the Pharisees why He and His disciples do not observe the ritual of fasting (parallel passages: **Matt. 9:14–17**, see pp. 546–47; Luke 5:33–39).

2:23–28. The Pharisees condemn Jesus for violating the law against working on the Sabbath (Exod. 20:8–11) by picking grain to eat (parallel passages: **Matt. 12:1–8**, see pp. 547–48; Luke 6:1–5).

3:1–6. Jesus angers the Pharisees by healing a man's withered hand on the Sabbath (parallel passages: **Matt. 12:9–14**, see p. 548; Luke 6:6–11).

3:7–12. People from many distant cities flock to Jesus because they have heard about His ability to heal (parallel passage: **Matt. 12:15–21**, see p. 548).

3:13–19. Jesus chooses twelve followers to serve as His disciples (parallel passages: Matt. 10:1–4; **Luke 6:12–16**, see p. 572–74).

3:20–30. Jesus answers the charge of the Pharisees that He is healing people who are possessed by demons through the power of

---

[2:1–12] GOING THROUGH THE ROOF. *They [four friends of the paralyzed man] uncovered the roof where he [Jesus] was: and when they had broken it up, they let down the bed wherein the sick of the palsy [paralyzed man, NIV] lay* (Mark 2:4).

This verse shows the determination of the friends of a disabled man to get him to Jesus for healing. They brought their friend in a blanket or pallet to the house where Jesus was teaching. Unable to get into the building because of the crowd, they climbed an exterior stairway to the roof. After ripping a hole in the roof, they lowered him down to Jesus.

The roofs of most houses in Bible times were built in three steps. First, beams or logs were laid across the tops of the exterior walls. These beams were then overlaid with thatch, consisting of tree branches and straw. Finally, the thatch was topped with a layer of clay that was hardened in the sun. In a climate in which rainfall was minimal, these roofs would hold up well if the clay was rolled and hardened on a regular basis.

Tearing through a roof like this was a simple matter. It was also easy to repair.

4:30–32. A ridge of yellow mustard plants grows wild in Israel. Jesus said that God's kingdom is like the tiny mustard seed, which starts small but grows large.

Satan (parallel passage: **Matt. 12:24–37,** see p. 548).

3:31–35. Jesus' mother and brothers come to the place where He is teaching. They send word that they would like to see Him. Jesus affirms that His true relatives are those who do the will of God (parallel passages: Matt. 12:46–50; Luke 8:19–21).

4:1–9. Jesus delivers the parable of the sower from a fishing boat on the Sea of Galilee (parallel passages: **Matt. 13:1–9,** see p. 548; Luke 8:4–8).

4:10–12. In answer to a question from His disciples, Jesus explains why He teaches through parables (parallel passages: Matt. 13:10–17; Luke 8:9–10).

4:13–20. Jesus explains the meaning of the parable of the sower to His disciples (parallel passages: **Matt. 13:18–23,** see p. 548; Luke 8:11–15).

4:21–25. Citizens of the kingdom of God should let their influence penetrate the world, just as a candle or lamp is placed on a stand to light a room (parallel passage: Luke 8:16–18).

4:26–29. This parable of the seed growing quietly is found only in the Gospel of Mark. It teaches that the kingdom of God is God's work. He allows us as His followers to sow the seed, but God causes the seed to grow and produce a harvest.

4:30–32. Jesus in this parable compares the kingdom of God to a mustard seed. Although it is a tiny seed, it grows into a large plant. The kingdom of God is also destined to grow from obscurity into an influential force throughout the world.

4:33–34. Jesus continues to speak in parables and to explain their meaning to His disciples.

4:35–41. Jesus calms a storm and rebukes His disciples for their lack of faith (parallel passages: Matt. 8:23–27; Luke 8:22–25).

5:1–20. Jesus casts numerous demons out of a wild man who lived among the tombs in the country of the Gadarenes. The demons enter a herd of pigs, and they drown in the Sea of Galilee. Jesus sends the healed man into the cities of that region to tell others what Jesus has done for him (parallel passages: Matt. 8:28–34; Luke 8:26–39).

[5:1–20] LIVING AMONG THE DEAD. *There met him [Jesus] out of the tombs a man with an unclean spirit, who had his dwelling among the tombs* (Mark 5:2–3).

This man who met Jesus was possessed by demons. He may have been driven out of the villages of "the country of the Gadarenes" (Mark 5:1) and forced to live a life of isolation in a cemetery because of his violent, unpredictable behavior (Mark 5:5).

The "tombs" mentioned in this passage were probably natural caves or burial chambers that had been dug out of solid rock. Tombs like this were commonly used by the upperclass families of Bible times.

This poor, deranged man may have been living among the bones of the dead in one of these burial caves. The NIV states specifically that he was living "in the tombs," not "among the tombs."

5:21–43. Jesus heals a woman with a hemorrhage who slips through the crowd to touch the edge of His robe. He also raises from the dead the daughter of a synagogue ruler named Jairus (parallel passages: Matt. 9:18–26; Luke 8:40–56).

6:1–6. Jesus is rejected by the unbelieving citizens of His hometown of Nazareth (parallel passage: **Matt. 13:53–58,** see p. 550).

6:7–13. Jesus sends His disciples out to preach and heal (parallel passages: **Matt. 10:5–42,** see p. 547; Luke 9:1–6).

6:14–29. Herodias, the wife of King Herod, uses her daughter's influence with the king to have John the Baptist executed. Herodias wanted John killed because he had condemned her adulterous affair with the king (parallel passage: Matt. 14:1–12).

6:30–44. A huge crowd follows Jesus to an isolated area when He withdraws to rest and pray. As the day draws to a close, He has compassion on them because they have not eaten all day. He multiplies five loaves of bread and two fish to feed the crowd of more than 5,000 people. So thorough is this miracle that twelve baskets of food are left over (parallel passages: Matt. 14:13–21; Luke 9:10–17; John 6:1–14).

6:45–52. Jesus joins His disciples in a boat on the Sea of Galilee by walking on the water (parallel passages: **Matt. 14:22–33,** see p. 550; John 6:15–21).

6:53–56. Jesus and His disciples put ashore at the land of Gennesaret, where He heals many people (parallel passage: Matt. 14:34–36).

7:1–23. Jesus explains to the scribes and Pharisees why He and His disciples do not perform ritualistic hand-washings before eating (parallel passage: **Matt. 15:1–20,** see pp. 550–51).

7:24–30. Jesus heals a Gentile woman's daughter (parallel passage: **Matt. 15:21–28,** see p. 551).

7:31–37. Jesus heals a deaf man with a speech impediment, and he begins to speak clearly.

8:1–10. Jesus performs a second feeding miracle—this one for Gentiles (parallel passage: **Matt. 15:29–39,** see p. 551).

8:11–21. Jesus warns His disciples to stay away from the Pharisees and their teachings (parallel passage: Matt. 16:1–12).

8:22–26. Jesus heals a blind man outside the city of Bethsaida.

6:45–52. *A lone fisherman at sunrise rows along the shoreline of the Sea of Galilee. Much of Jesus' ministry took place along the shores of this freshwater lake. And in one dramatic miracle, Jesus walked on these waters.*

[7:1–23] **JESUS AND THE SCRIBES.** *Then came together unto him [Jesus] the Pharisees, and certain of the scribes [teachers of the law, NIV]* (Mark 7:1).

The scribes and Pharisees are often mentioned together as if they were united in their opposition to Jesus (see Matt. 15:1; Luke 5:21; John 8:3).

The office of scribe developed in Old Testament times when they were charged with the responsibility of copying the Scriptures. Laboriously copying a sacred document by hand was the only way to reproduce and pass on God's commands in written form.

By New Testament times scribes had assumed the task of interpreting and teaching God's law as well as copying it. This is why they are mentioned often with Pharisees as those who were opposed to Jesus. Both were committed to preserving the traditions that had grown up around the original written law. They considered these additions as binding as the law itself (see the note "Phylacteries and Tassels" on p. 554).

Jesus criticized these "sacred traditions," broke many of them Himself during His teaching and healing ministry, and insisted they were not as authoritative as God's law in its original form (Matt. 15:5–6; Mark 7:5–6; Luke 6:1–5).

8:27–30. Peter confesses Jesus as the Christ, God's Anointed One. Jesus cautions them to tell no one that He is the Messiah (parallel passages: **Matt. 16:13–20,** see p. 551; Luke 9:18–20).

8:31–9:1. Jesus informs His disciples about His future death and resurrection (parallel passage: **Matt. 16:21–28,** see p. 551).

9:2–13. Jesus is transfigured before three of His disciples, and He talks again about His forthcoming death (parallel passages: **Matt. 17:1–13,** see p. 551; Luke 9:28–36).

9:14–29. Jesus encourages the faith of the father of a demon-possessed boy. Then He casts out the stubborn demon and heals his son (parallel passages: Matt. 17:14–21; Luke 9:37–42).

9:30–32. Jesus again predicts He will be killed and then resurrected (parallel passages: Matt. 17:22–23; Luke 9:43–45).

9:33–50. Jesus teaches His disciples the meaning of true greatness for those who are citizens of God's kingdom (parallel passages: Matt. 18:1–10; Luke 9:46–50).

10:1–12. Jesus discusses with the Pharisees the meaning of marriage and the problem of divorce (parallel passage: Matt. 19:1–12).

10:13–16. The disciples try to keep children away from Jesus, but He welcomes and blesses them and declares that a citizen of the kingdom must become "as a little child" (v. 15) (parallel passages: Matt. 19:13–15; Luke 18:15–17).

10:17–31. The rich young ruler refuses to follow Jesus (parallel passages: **Matt. 19:16–30,** see p. 552; Luke 18:18–30).

10:32–34. Jesus again speaks with His disciples about His forthcoming death (parallel passages: **Matt. 20:17–19,** see p. 552; Luke 18:31–34).

10:35–45. Jesus' disciples James and John ask for places of prominence and honor in His kingdom (parallel passage: **Matt. 20:20–28,** see p. 552).

10:46–52. On His way to Jerusalem, Jesus heals a blind man named Bartimaeus at Jericho (parallel passages: Matt. 20:29–34; Luke 18:35–43).

[11:12–26] **STRAIGHT-UP PRAYER.** *When ye [Jesus' followers] stand praying, forgive, if ye have aught against any* (Mark 11:25).

This teaching of Jesus on prayer and forgiveness shows that standing was one common stance while praying in Bible times. The person would address his prayer to God by lifting his hands toward heaven with the palms up.

This is the way King Solomon prayed when he dedicated the newly constructed temple in Jerusalem to the Lord (1 Kings 8:22).

11:1–11. Jesus makes His triumphal entry into Jerusalem (parallel passages: **Matt. 21:1–11**, see p. 552; Luke 19:28–44; John 12:12–19).

11:12–26. Jesus places a curse on a barren fig tree and drives out merchants who are conducting business in the temple (parallel passages: **Matt. 21:12–22**, see p. 553; Luke 19:45–48).

11:27–33. Jesus assures the Pharisees of His divine authority over the temple (parallel passages: Matt. 21:23–27; Luke 20:1–8).

12:1–12. In this parable, Jesus compares the religious leaders of Israel to wicked husbandmen, or tenant farmers (parallel passages: **Matt. 21:33–46**, see p. 553; Luke 20:9–19).

12:13–17. The Pharisees and Herodians question Jesus about paying taxes to the Roman government (parallel passages: **Matt. 22:15–22**, see p. 553; Luke 20:20–26).

12:18–27. Jesus deals with a question from the Sadducees about the resurrection (parallel passages: **Matt. 22:23–33**, see p. 553; Luke 20:27–40).

12:28–34. Jesus answers a question from a teacher of the law on which is the greatest commandment (parallel passage: **Matt. 22:34–40**, see p. 554).

12:35–37. Jesus challenges the thinking of the Pharisees about the Messiah who would spring from the line of David (parallel passages: **Matt. 22:41–46**, see p. 554; Luke 20:41–44).

12:38–40. Jesus denounces the Pharisees for their pride and hypocrisy (parallel passages: **Matt. 23:1–36**, see p. 554; Luke 20:45–47).

12:41–44. Jesus praises a poor widow for her sacrificial offering (parallel passage: Luke 21:1–4).

13:1–37. Jesus predicts the destruction of the temple in Jerusalem and discusses end-time events (parallel passages: **Matt. 24:1–51**, see p. 554; Luke 21:5–38).

14:1–2. The Jewish Sanhedrin plots to arrest Jesus and have Him executed (parallel passages: **Matt. 26:1–5**, see p. 554; Luke 22:1–2).

14:3–9. A woman anoints Jesus with an expensive perfume (parallel passages: **Matt. 26:6–13**, see p. 554–55; John 12:1–8).

14:10–11. Judas makes arrangements to betray Jesus (parallel passages: **Matt. 26:14–16**, see p. 555; Luke 22:3–6).

14:12–16. Two of Jesus' disciples select a location where they will partake of a Passover meal with Jesus (parallel passages: Matt. 26:17–19; Luke 22:7–13).

14:17–21. Jesus predicts that one of His disciples will betray Him (parallel passages: Matt. 26:20–25; Luke 22:21–23; **John 13:21–30**, see p. 587).

[14:17–21] BREAD OF BETRAYAL. *He [Jesus] answered... It is one of the twelve, that dippeth with me in the dish* (Mark 14:20).

People of Bible times did not use utensils such as forks and spoons to eat their meals. They picked up the food with their hands. But some dishes such as stew or gravy had to be scooped up with a piece of bread. This is the method of eating to which Jesus referred in this verse.

In John's Gospel this bread used to pick up liquid food is call a "sop." Jesus handed the bread to Judas, clearly identifying him as the betrayer (John 13:26).

14:22–26. Jesus institutes the memorial meal (1 Cor. 11:23–26), known today as the Lord's Supper (parallel passages: Matt. 26:26–30; **Luke 22:14–20**, see pp. 579–80).

14:27–31. Jesus predicts that all His disciples, including Peter, will deny Him (parallel passages: Matt. 26:31–35; **Luke 22:31–38**, see p. 580; John 13:31–38).

15:22–26. After a secret, all-night trial, Jesus is crucified on Friday morning.

14:32–42. Jesus prays with a heavy heart in the Garden of Gethsemane (parallel passages: **Matt. 26:36–46**, see p. 555; Luke 22:39–46).

14:43–52. Jesus is arrested in the Garden of Gethsemane (parallel passages: **Matt. 26:47–56**, see p. 556; Luke 22:47–53; John 18:1–2).

14:53–65. Jesus is declared guilty of blasphemy when He appears before the Jewish Sanhedrin (parallel passages: Matt. 26:57–68; Luke 22:63–71).

14:66–72. Peter denies that he knows Jesus (parallel passages: **Matt. 26:69–75**, see p. 556; Luke 22:54–62; John 18:15–27).

15:1. The Sanhedrin delivers Jesus to the Roman governor in an attempt to have Him sentenced to death (parallel passages: **Matt. 27:1–2**, see p. 556; Luke 23:1).

15:2–15. Pilate, the Roman governor, sentences Jesus to death by crucifixion (parallel passages: **Matt. 27:11–26**, see p. 556; Luke 23:13–25; John 18:28–19:16).

15:16–20. Jesus is mocked by Roman soldiers (parallel passage: **Matt. 27:27–31**, see p. 556).

15:21. Simon of Cyrene, a bystander, carries the cross of Jesus to the crucifixion site (parallel passages: Matt. 27:32; **Luke 23:26–31**, see p. 580).

15:22–26. Jesus is crucified at a site known as Golgotha (parallel passages: **Matt. 27:33–37**, see p. 556; Luke 23:32–38; John 19:17–24).

15:27–32. As He hangs on the cross between two thieves, Jesus is taunted by the crowd (parallel passages: Matt. 27:38–44; **Luke 23:39–43**, see p. 581).

15:33–39. For three hours before Jesus dies, darkness covers the earth. He quotes from Psalm 22:1 and cries out in despair, "My God, my God, why hast thou forsaken me," (v. 34). Upon His death, the huge curtain in the temple is ripped from top to bottom. Shaken by these mysterious happenings, a Roman centurion declares, "Truly this man was the Son of God" (v. 39) (parallel passages: Matt. 27:45–54; Luke 23:44–48).

15:40–41. Several women stand watch at the cross as Jesus is crucified (parallel passages: Matt. 27:55–56; Luke 23:49; **John 19:25–27**, see p. 588).

15:42–46. Jesus is buried in the tomb of Joseph of Arimathea (parallel passages: Matt. 27:57–60; Luke 23:50–54; **John 19:38–42**, see p. 589).

15:47. Women mourn at the tomb where Jesus is buried (parallel passages: Matt. 27:61; Luke 23:55–56).

16:1–8. Women discover that Jesus is gone when they visit the tomb to anoint His body on Sunday morning (parallel passages: Matt. 28:1–10; Luke 24:1–8; John 20:1–2).

16:9–11. The resurrected Jesus appears to Mary Magdalene (parallel passage: **John 20:11–18**, see p. 589).

16:12–13. Jesus appears to two of His followers on their way to Emmaus (parallel passage: **Luke 24:13–35**, see p. 582).

16:14–18. Jesus commissions His disciples (Acts 1:8) to continue His work (parallel passages: **Matt. 28:16–20**, see p. 558; Luke 24:44–49).

16:19–20. Jesus ascends to His Father (Acts 1:9), and His disciples continue His ministry, as they were commanded (parallel passage: Luke 24:50–53).

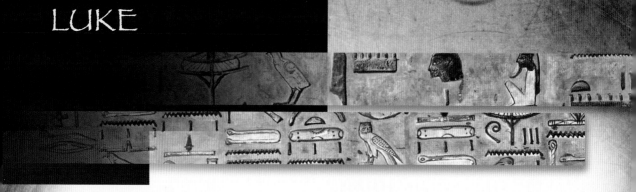

LUKE

OVERVIEW: The most complete account of the life and ministry of Jesus, Luke was written for Gentiles.

Introduction to Luke

Perhaps the most unique characteristic of the Gospel of Luke is that it has a sequel in the book of Acts. Both books are addressed to a person named Theophilus (1:3; Acts 1:1). This name means "lover of God," and Theophilus was probably a Roman of high rank. In this Gospel, Luke apparently wanted to show Theophilus and other Roman citizens like him the truth about Jesus and His ministry and those who had become His followers.

Luke did not identify himself as the author of this Gospel, but early church tradition ascribed this writing to him. Luke was a physician (Col. 4:14) and a missionary associate of the apostle Paul (2 Tim. 4:11; Philem. 24). Luke was not an eyewitness of the ministry of Jesus. But he tells us in the opening words of Luke that he had access to information from actual eyewitnesses that he included in the Gospel that bears his name (1:1–4).

The Gospel of Luke gives us the most complete picture we have of the life of Jesus. It is the only Gospel that tells us anything about the birth of Jesus (2:1–12). We also learn only in Luke that Jesus was aware of His unique mission as God's Son as a twelve-year-old boy (2:41–52).

With the exception of Matthew, which records the visit of the wise men to Jesus when He was a two-year-old child (Matt. 2:1–12), we find nothing in the other Gospels about Jesus' childhood years. Many of Jesus' most beloved parables appear only in the Gospel of Luke— for example, the lost coin and the lost son, also known as the prodigal son (chap. 15).

Luke is also the most inclusive of all the Gospels. He portrays Jesus associating with people of all classes—the poor, outcasts, sinners, women, and tax collectors. The hero of one of Jesus' parables is even a compassionate Samaritan—a member of a race of half-breeds whom the Jewish people despised (10:25–37).

More than the other Gospels, Luke also emphasizes the Holy Spirit in the life and ministry of Jesus (4:14; 10:21) and portrays Jesus as a person of prayer (3:21; 6:12; 9:29; 22:39–46).

Some accounts of Jesus' life and ministry in Luke also parallel events reported in Matthew, Mark, and John. These parallel passages are identified in the following summary of Luke. The parallel passages in bold type with "see" references refer to pages in this book where expanded summaries of specific Gospel accounts may be found.

Summary of Luke

1:1–4. Luke begins his Gospel by addressing his friend Theophilus. He wants Theophilus to hear from him the truth about Jesus and His work. Luke also wrote the book of

2:15–20. Bethlehem shepherds come to see the baby Jesus, who was born in a place where livestock were kept. Early church tradition said he was born in a cave that now rests like a basement beneath the oldest church in the world: Bethlehem's Church of the Nativity.

Acts. He also began this book with a word to Theophilus (Acts 1:1).

1:5–7. An elderly priest named Zacharias and his wife, Elisabeth, are godly, righteous people. But they have not been able to have children.

1:8–17. The angel Gabriel appears to Zacharias while he is burning incense in the temple. He informs the elderly priest that he and Elisabeth will be blessed with a son whom they are to name John. He will grow up to become a great prophet who will prepare the way for the coming of the long-expected Messiah.

1:18–25. Zacharias expresses doubt that this will happen. The angel informs him that he will be punished for his disbelief by not being able to speak until the child is born.

1:26–33. The angel Gabriel also visits Mary, a young woman who lives in the city of Nazareth in the region of Galilee. Gabriel informs Mary that she will become pregnant and give birth to the long-expected Messiah. She is to give Him the name Jesus, which means "Savior."

1:34–38. Mary wonders how this birth can happen, since she is a virgin. The angel assures her that her pregnancy will occur supernaturally through the power of the Holy Spirit. The angel also informs Mary of the pregnancy of her cousin Elisabeth in the region of Judea.

1:39–56. Mary visits her cousin Elisabeth. They rejoice together about God's actions in their lives. Mary sings a beautiful song of thanksgiving known as the Magnificat (vv. 46–55). It expresses her joy that God will fulfill His promise of a Messiah for Israel through this child who will come from her womb.

1:57–66. The child of their old age is born to Zacharias and Elisabeth. Following the orders of the angel Gabriel, they name him John. The punishment for Zacharias's doubt is lifted, and he is able to speak again.

1:67–80. In this prophetic song known as the Benedictus, Zacharias expresses his thanks to God for the coming of the Messiah and the role his son, John, will play in preparing the way for His mission.

2:1–5. Mary and Joseph, the man to whom Mary is engaged, travel from Nazareth to the city of Bethlehem, Joseph's ancestral home, to register in a census. This registration for taxation purposes had been ordered for all residents throughout the Roman Empire by the emperor, Augustus Caesar.

2:6–7. While Mary and Joseph are in Bethlehem, Jesus is born in a stable. Their accommodations are crude because all the inns are filled with people in town for the census. Jesus' first crib is a feeding trough for livestock.

2:8–14. Angels announce the birth of Jesus to a group of shepherds who are watching over their sheep in the fields outside Bethlehem.

2:15–20. The shepherds hurry into Bethlehem, where they find Mary and Joseph and the baby Jesus. These humble shepherds become the first to announce the birth of "a Saviour, which is Christ the Lord" (Luke 2:11) to others.

2:21–24. When Jesus is eight days old, His parents take Him to the temple in Jerusalem for circumcision and dedication to the Lord, in accordance with Jewish custom (Gen. 17:12; Lev. 12:3).

2:25–35. When Jesus is brought into the temple, an aged man named Simeon recognizes Him as the long-expected Messiah. He prophesies that Jesus will be a light for Gentiles as well as the Jewish people (Eph.

[4:16–30] **READING IN A SYNAGOGUE.** *He [Jesus] went into the synagogue on the sabbath day, and stood up for to read* (Luke 4:16).

This synagogue in which Jesus read the Old Testament Scriptures was in Nazareth, his hometown in the province of Galilee. Synagogues were built in towns and cities throughout Palestine. Their purpose was not to replace the temple in Jerusalem that served as the central place of worship and sacrifice for all Israel. Synagogues existed to teach the law to local people.

A community synagogue was presided over by a leader who had been elected by its members. Priests had no official role in synagogues, although they often attended and were honored by being asked to read the Scriptures during the service.

Jesus was not a priest or a member of the religious establishment. His reading in the Nazareth synagogue shows that common, everyday "laypeople" who were known in the community were often asked to participate in the service. In addition, His ministry as a teacher and healer had begun to attract attention throughout Galilee (Luke 4:14–15).

Jesus read from the book of Isaiah and identified Himself as the Servant of the Lord whom the prophet had written about (Luke 4:17–21).

2:11–22). He also declares that His mother's heart will be broken by the suffering He is destined to endure.

2:36–38. An aged prophetess named Anna overhears Simeon's prophecy. She joins in with thanksgiving to God for sending redemption to Israel through this newborn Messiah.

2:39–40. Jesus grows up under the nurture of His earthly parents, Mary and Joseph, in the village of Nazareth in the region of Galilee (parallel passage: Matt. 2:19–23).

2:41–52. These verses in Luke give us the only information we have about Jesus' childhood years. When He is twelve years old, He accompanies His parents to Jerusalem to observe the Passover festival (Josh. 5:10–12). On their way back to Nazareth, Mary and Joseph discover that

4:1–13. *After His baptism and before launching His ministry, Jesus retreats for a time of solitude and prayer into the wilderness badlands of what is now southern Israel.*

Jesus is missing. Returning to Jerusalem, they find Him sitting among the learned interpreters of the Scriptures, both learning from them and contributing His own ideas. It is obvious to everyone that this is no ordinary twelve-year-old boy.

3:1–20. John the Baptist, forerunner of Jesus, launches his preaching ministry (parallel passages: Matt. 3:1–12; Mark 1:1–8). He challenges the people to repent of their sins and get ready for the coming of God's kingdom. Many of his hearers think John is the Messiah, but he makes it clear that he is preparing the way for "one mightier than I" (v. 16) who is the deliverer sent from God.

3:21–22. Jesus is baptized by John (parallel passages: **Matt. 3:13–17,** see p. 544; Mark 1:9–11).

3:23–38. Luke's genealogy of Jesus begins with Joseph and goes all the way back to Adam. (For a different genealogy of Jesus, see Matt. 1:1–17.)

4:1–13. Beginning in the wilderness, Satan presents a series of temptations to Jesus at the beginning of His public ministry. Jesus rises above these temptations through the power of prayer and the Scriptures (parallel passages: Matt. 4:1–11; Mark 1:12–13).

4:14–15. Jesus begins His preaching ministry in the region of Galilee.

4:16–30. Jesus preaches in the synagogue in His hometown of Nazareth. He identifies Himself as God's Suffering Servant depicted in the book of Isaiah (Isa. 61:1–2). The townspeople are enraged because they consider this blasphemous, so they try to kill Jesus. But He slips away and leaves the town.

4:31–37. Jesus makes Capernaum in the region of Galilee His headquarters city. He heals a demon-possessed man in the synagogue on the Sabbath. His reputation grows as people express amazement at His power and authority (parallel passage: Mark 1:21–28).

4:38–41. Jesus heals Peter's mother-in-law in Capernaum (parallel passages: **Matt. 8:14–17,** see p. 546; Mark 1:29–34).

4:42–44. Jesus preaches and heals in other cities throughout the region of Galilee (parallel passages: **Matt. 4:23–25,** see p. 546; Mark 1:35–39).

5:1–11. Jesus astonishes Peter by producing a miraculous catch of fish after Peter and his partners had worked all night without catching anything. Then Jesus calls Peter and his partners, the brothers James and John, to leave their fishing nets and become His followers (parallel passages: Matt. 4:18–22; Mark 1:16–20).

5:12–16. Jesus heals a man with leprosy (parallel passages: Matt. 8:1–4; **Mark 1:40–45,** see p. 560).

5:17–26. Jesus heals a paralyzed man and forgives his sins (parallel passages: Matt. 9:1–8; **Mark 2:1–12,** see p. 560).

5:27–32. Jesus calls Matthew (also known as Levi), a tax collector, to become His disciple. Scribes and Pharisees criticize Him for associating with tax collectors and sinners. Jesus explains that His mission is "not to call the righteous, but sinners to repentance" (v. 32) (parallel passages: Matt. 9:9–13; Mark 2:13–17).

5:33–39. Jesus tells why He and His disciples do not fast (parallel passages: **Matt. 9:14–17,** see pp. 547–48; Mark 2:18–22).

6:1–5. Jesus answers the charge that He is desecrating the Sabbath; He claims to be "Lord also of the sabbath" (v. 5) (parallel passages: **Matt. 12:1–8,** see pp. 547–48; Mark 2:23–28).

6:6–11. The Pharisees are enraged because Jesus heals a man's withered hand on the Sabbath (parallel passages: **Matt. 12:9–14,** see p. 548; Mark 3:1–6).

6:12–16. After spending all night in prayer,

7:36–50; 8:1–3. Jesus has compassion on various sinful women throughout His ministry, including one woman with a bad reputation who anointed His feet and Mary Magdalene, possessed by demons.

13:1–9. *Green figs ripen on the tree. Jesus told a parable about a fig tree that didn't produce fruit, saying the farmer vowed to cut it down unless it started producing. The implication was that God's people should produce the fruit of godliness and behave as though they are citizens of God's kingdom.*

overly concerned about their physical needs but to seek first "the kingdom of God; and all these things shall be added unto you" (v. 31).

12:35–48. Through the parable of the unfaithful servant, Jesus teaches His followers to be watchful and ready for His second coming (1 Thess. 5:1–11).

12:49–59. Jesus makes it clear that the time of His death is drawing near. People should be aware of this critical moment and turn to God in repentance and faith.

13:1–9. Jesus' parable of the barren fig tree teaches that the Jewish people have failed in their mission as God's special people. But He is giving them one last chance to show their obedience by accepting His Son Jesus and becoming citizens of His kingdom.

13:10–17. A synagogue ruler criticizes Jesus after He heals a woman with a crooked back on the Sabbath. Jesus points out that the Jewish law allowed livestock to be led to water on the Sabbath. Wasn't this woman more important than an ox or a donkey?

13:18–21. The parables of the mustard seed and the leaven show that the kingdom of God will eventually become a strong force in the world (parallel passage: Matt. 13:31–35).

13:22–30. The Jewish people thought they had an exclusive claim on God's love and generosity and that all non-Jews were excluded. But Jesus declares that the kingdom of God belongs to those who turn to Him in repentance and faith.

13:31–33. Jesus ignores a warning from the Pharisees to leave Galilee because of a supposed threat from Herod, the Roman ruler in the region.

13:34–35. Jesus predicts that the city of Jerusalem will be punished by the Lord because it has refused to accept Him as the Messiah (parallel passage: Matt. 23:37–39).

14:1–6. Jesus defends His healing of a man with the dropsy (a condition that causes a buildup of fluid in the body) on the Sabbath.

[14:1–6] DINING WITH A PHARISEE. *He [Jesus] went into the house of one of the chief Pharisees to eat bread on the sabbath day (Luke 14:1).*

Jesus' clash with the Pharisees throughout the Gospels may lead us to believe that all Pharisees were bad or that Jesus condemned them all. But this verse shows us otherwise.

A leader among the Pharisees apparently invited Jesus to dine in his home on the Sabbath, and He accepted the invitation. Jesus used the occasion to teach this man and several other Pharisees about His healing mission and His superiority over the Sabbath (Luke 14:3–6).

Two other Pharisees in the Gospels are also worthy of commendation. Nicodemus was a Pharisee who was known for his inquiring mind and seach for truth (John 3:1–12). Joseph of Arimathea was probably a Pharisee since he was a member of the Sanhedrin. He claimed the body of Jesus and buried it in his own new tomb (Mark 15:43–46; Luke 23:53; John 19:38).

14:7–14. Citizens of the kingdom of God should not seek positions of glory and honor for themselves. Humble service to others should be their main concern.

14:15–24. This parable of the great supper shows that the nation of Israel has refused God's glorious invitation to enter His kingdom. Now God is establishing a covenant relationship with the Gentiles—those once considered outsiders and sinners. Any person who accepts God's invitation and turns to Him in repentance and faith is included in God's kingdom, no matter what his or her race or ethnic background (Acts 15:19).

14:25–35. Following Jesus involves sacrifice. A person should consider the cost before making a commitment to discipleship.

15:1–32. Two of the three parables in this chapter about something lost—a lost coin and a lost son—are unique to the Gospel of Luke. The parable of the lost sheep also appears in Matthew's Gospel (Matt. 18:11–14). These parables show that God's love has no limits. He is relentless in His efforts to seek and restore to His favor those who are lost.

16:1–18. The dishonest manager in this parable is shrewd enough to look ahead and prepare for his future security. Believers should show the same foresight in their preparation for eternal life in fellowship with God.

16:19–31. The parable of the rich man and Lazarus shows the tragedy of a life devoted to earthly pleasures with no concern for spiritual values. The rich man's lifestyle of indulgence shuts him off from fellowship with God—an eternal separation that continues in the afterlife.

17:1–10. Jesus teaches that the lives of those who are citizens of God's kingdom should be characterized by forgiveness and service (Eph. 6:7). We serve others not for reward or commendation but because service is what God has called us and equipped us to do.

17:11–19. Jesus heals ten men with leprosy while on His way to Jerusalem. He commends the one man among the ten—a Samaritan—who seeks Jesus out to express His gratitude.

17:20–37. Jesus tells the Pharisees that the kingdom of God is already present. He stands among them as God's Son, the Messiah, the personification of the kingdom that God is building in the hearts of those who believe in Him. He also discusses the final consummation of this kingdom in the future, when He will return as the victorious King over all creation in His second coming (1 Thess. 4:13–17).

18:1–8. This parable of the persistent widow teaches an important lesson about prayer: We should be consistent and persistent in the prayer requests we present to God.

18:9–14. Through this parable of the Pharisee and the publican (tax collector), Jesus teaches about humility in prayer. God rejects the self-righteous prayer of the proud Pharisee, but He accepts the prayer of the publican because he admits his sin and unworthiness.

[18:9–14] TWICE-A-WEEK FASTING. I *[self-righteous Pharisee] fast twice in the week, I give tithes of all that I possess* (Luke 18:12).

These are the words of the self-righteous Pharisee in Jesus' parable about the Pharisee and the tax collector. The Pharisee tried to justify himself in God's sight by claiming he had kept the letter of the law. But the tax collector realized he was a sinner and cast himself on God's mercy (Luke 18:9–14).

Fasting twice a week, as the Pharisee claimed to do, was not commanded in the Law of Moses. This was probably a custom instituted by the Pharisees as an addition to the law that they practiced scrupulously.

The message of this verse is that we can't buy our way into heaven by observing certain rituals. We are justified in God's sight only through faith in Jesus Christ and His atoning death on our behalf.

18:15–17. Jesus welcomes little children (parallel passages: Matt. 19:13–15; **Mark 10:13–16,** see p. 564).

18:18–30. Jesus challenges the rich young ruler to sell all his possessions and follow Him (parallel passages: **Matt. 19:16–30,** see p. 552; Mark 10:17–31).

18:31–34. Jesus again tells His disciples that He will be executed in Jerusalem, then resurrected (parallel passages: **Matt. 20:17–19,** see p. 552; Mark 10:32–34).

18:35–43. Jesus heals a blind man near Jericho (parallel passages: Matt. 20:29–34; Mark 10:46–52).

19:1–10. A tax collector named Zacchaeus climbs a tree to get a better look at Jesus as He passes through Jericho. Confronted by Jesus, he vows to give half of his possessions to the poor and to repay fourfold any excess taxes he has collected "by false accusation" (v. 8).

19:11–27. This passage is known as the parable of the pounds. Ten servants are given one pound (a sum of money) each to manage for their master while he is gone. The servant who plays it safe and fails to increase his pound is criticized by his master. This parable teaches that we are held accountable for our management of God's resources.

19:28–44. Jesus is greeted and praised by the crowds as He rides into Jerusalem (Zech. 9:9). He weeps over the city because of its unbelief (parallel passages: **Matt. 21:1–11,** see p. 552; Mark 11:1–11; John 12:12–19).

19:45–48. Jesus drives out the merchants who are buying and selling in the temple (parallel passages: **Matt. 21:12–22,** see p. 553; Mark 11:12–26).

20:1–8. Jesus responds to the charge of the Pharisees by claiming that He has authority over the temple (parallel passages: Matt. 21:23–27; Mark 11:27–33).

20:9–19. Jesus condemns the religious leaders of Israel by comparing them to wicked husbandmen, or tenant farmers (parallel

19:45–48. Swinging a whip, Jesus drives merchants out of the temple's main courtyard. This courtyard was as close to the sanctuary as non-Jewish worshipers could go—it was their sacred space to worship God.

passages: **Matt. 21:33–46,** see p. 553; Mark 12:1–12).

20:20–26. Jesus is questioned by His enemies about paying taxes to the Roman government (parallel passages: **Matt. 22:15–22,** see p. 553; Mark 12:13–17).

20:27–40. Jesus avoids a trick question from the Sadducees about the resurrection (parallel passages: **Matt. 22:23–33,** see p. 554; Mark 12:18–27).

20:41–44. Jesus uses Scripture to show the scribes that the Messiah from the line of David is more than an earthly king (parallel passages: **Matt. 22:41–46,** see p. 554; Mark 12:35–37).

20:45–47. Jesus condemns the Pharisees for their pride and dishonesty (parallel passages: **Matt. 23:1–36,** see p. 554; Mark 12:38–40).

21:1–4. A sacrificial offering in the temple by a poor widow draws Jesus' praise (parallel passage: Mark 12:41–44).

21:5–38. Jesus discusses events that will occur in the end-time before His second coming (parallel passages: **Matt. 24:1–51,** see p. 554; Mark 13:1–37).

22:1–2. The Jewish Sanhedrin plots the death of Jesus (parallel passages: **Matt. 26:1–5,** see p. 554; Mark 14:1–2).

22:3–6. Judas makes a deal with the Sanhedrin to betray Jesus (parallel passages: **Matt. 26:14–16,** see p. 555; Mark 14:10–11).

22:7–13. Jesus sends Peter and John to find a room where He and His disciples can partake of the Passover meal together (parallel passages: Matt. 26:17–19; Mark 14:12–16).

22:14–20. Jesus turns the Passover meal with His disciples into a supper that memorializes His forthcoming sacrificial death (1 Cor. 11:23–26). He institutes the new covenant with all believers by declaring that the bread represents His broken body and the wine represents His blood, "which is shed for you" (v. 20) (parallel passages: Matt. 26:26–30; Mark 14:22–26).

22:21–23. Jesus reveals to His disciples that one of them will betray Him (parallel passages: Matt. 26:20–25; Mark 14:17–21; **John 13:21–30,** see p. 587).

22:24–30. Jesus' disciples begin to argue over which of them is the most important. Jesus teaches them that the greatest citizen in the kingdom of God is the one who is self-giving in service to others.

22:31–38. Jesus tells Peter that he will face great temptation from Satan during the next several hours. He predicts that Peter will deny Him three times before the rooster crows at daybreak (parallel passages: Matt. 26:31–35; Mark 14:27–31; John 13:31–38).

22:39–46. Jesus pours out His heart to God in agonizing prayer in the Garden of Gethsemane (parallel passages: **Matt. 26:36–46,** see p. 555; Mark 14:32–42).

22:47–53. Jesus is betrayed by Judas and arrested by the Jewish Sanhedrin (parallel passages: **Matt. 26:47–56,** see p. 556; Mark 14:43–52; John 18:1–12).

22:54–62. Peter follows Jesus when He is led away to the house of the Jewish high priest for interrogation by the Sanhedrin. Questioned outside the house by three different people, he denies that he knows Jesus (parallel passages: **Matt. 26:69–75,** see p. 556; Mark 14:66–72; John 18:15–27).

22:63–71. Jesus is found guilty of blasphemy by the Jewish Sanhedrin when He admits He is the Son of God (parallel passages: Matt. 26:57–68; Mark 14:53–65).

23:1. Determined to have Jesus executed, the Sanhedrin delivers Him to Pontius Pilate, the Roman governor of Judea (parallel passages: **Matt. 27:1–2,** see p. 556; Mark 15:1).

23:2–12. After questioning Jesus, Pilate is convinced He is innocent. Trying to shift responsibility for a ruling in His case, Pilate sends Jesus to Herod, the Roman governor of Galilee, who is visiting Jerusalem during the Passover celebration. Herod refuses to get involved and sends Jesus back to Pilate.

23:13–25. Pilate finally gives in to the cries of the crowd and sentences Jesus to death by crucifixion (parallel passages: **Matt. 27:11–26,** see p. 556; Mark 15:2–15; John 18:28–19:16).

23:26–31. A citizen of Cyrene named Simon carries Jesus' cross to the crucifixion site. Addressing a group of women in the crowd, Jesus prophesies that great calamity will fall upon the nation of Israel in the future. He may have been referring to the destruction of Jerusalem by the Roman army in A.D. 70 (parallel passages: Matt. 27:32; Mark 15:21).

23:32–38. Jesus is crucified at a site known as Calvary (Latin for "Golgotha") (parallel passages: **Matt. 27:33–37,** see p. 556; Mark 15:22–26; John 19:17–24).

23:39–43. Jesus is crucified between two criminals. One of these men ridicules Jesus, but the other turns to Him in repentance and faith and is assured that he will be with Jesus in paradise (parallel passages: Matt. 27:38–44; Mark 15:27–32).

23:44–48. Jesus' suffering and death are accompanied by several supernatural events that can only be explained as acts of God (parallel passages: Matt. 27:45–54; **Mark 15:33–39,** see p. 567).

23:49. Several women from Galilee watch from a distance as Jesus is crucified (parallel passages: Matt. 27:55–56; Mark 15:40–41; John 19:25–27).

23:50–54. A wealthy man from Arimathea named Joseph claims the body of Jesus and buries it in his own tomb (parallel passages: Matt. 27:57–60; Mark 15:42–46; **John 19:38–42,** see p. 589).

23:55–56. Women followers from Galilee note the tomb where Jesus is buried so they can anoint His body with spices after the Sabbath is over (parallel passages: Matt. 27:61; Mark 15:47).

24:1–8. Several women visit the tomb on

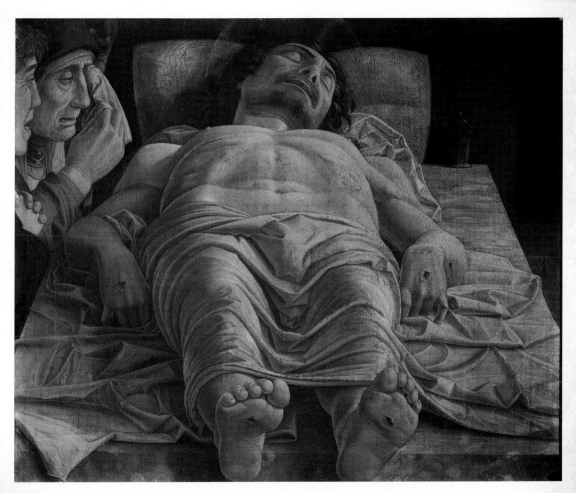

23:55–56. Women followers of Jesus mourn His death, which took place as Friday evening approached, the beginning of the Sabbath. Jews were forbidden to work on the Sabbath—even to prepare a body for burial. By the time the women returned to the tomb on Sunday morning, Jesus was once again alive.

[24:44–49] THE JEWISH SCRIPTURES. *All things must be fulfilled, which were written in the law of Moses, and in the prophets, and in the psalms, concerning me [Jesus]* (Luke 24:44).

Jesus spoke these words to His disciples when He appeared among them in Jerusalem after His resurrection. He declared that He had fulfilled all the things foretold about the Messiah in the Jewish Scriptures.

The Scriptures used by the Jews in Jesus' time included the books in our present Old Testament, but they were arranged differently than in our modern Bibles. Jesus mentioned the three major divisions of the Jewish Scriptures.

1. The Law of Moses. This is what we refer to today as the Pentateuch—Genesis, Exodus, Leviticus, Numbers, and Deuteronomy.

2. The Prophets. This section included Joshua, Judges, 1 and 2 Samuel, 1 and 2 Kings, and all the prophets except Daniel.

3. The Psalms. Included in this section were the Psalms, the book for which the entire section was named, as well as Proverbs, Job, Song of Solomon, Ruth, Lamentations, Ecclesiastes, Esther, Daniel, Ezra, Nehemiah, and 1 and 2 Chronicles.

Sunday morning to anoint Jesus' body. Two angels inform them that Jesus has been raised from the dead (parallel passages: Matt. 28:1–10; Mark 16:1–8; John 20:1–2).

24:9–12. The disciples are skeptical when informed by these women that Jesus has been resurrected. Peter runs to the tomb to check out their story. But he is not certain what to believe when he finds the tomb empty (parallel passage: John 20:3–10).

24:13–35. The risen Christ talks with two of His followers as they walk along the road to the village of Emmaus. He vanishes as they prepare to have a meal together, and they realize this was the resurrected Lord. They report this appearance of Jesus to His disciples in Jerusalem (parallel passage: Mark 16:12–13).

24:36–43. Jesus appears among His disciples. He convinces them they are not seeing a vision or a ghost by showing them His hands and feet and eating a meal in their presence.

24:44–49. Jesus charges His disciples to continue His mission by preaching "repentance and remission of sins...among all nations" (v. 47) (parallel passages: **Matt. 28:16–20,** see p. 558; Mark 16:14–18).

24:50–53. Jesus blesses His disciples and ascends to His Father (parallel passage: Mark 16:19–20).

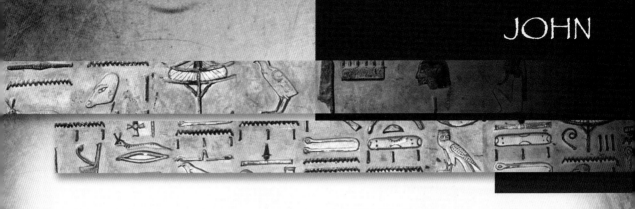

OVERVIEW: Presents Jesus as the divine Son of God who came to earth in human form.

Introduction to John

John was the last of the Gospels to be written, probably as late as about A.D. 90. The author of this Gospel had probably studied Matthew, Mark, and Luke, so he chose to write a different type of Gospel. Rather than just reporting on events in Jesus' life and ministry, John's Gospel majors on the theological meaning of these events. In John, Jesus is portrayed as the eternal Word of God who existed before the world was created (1:1), as the divine Son of God who came to earth in human form.

The author of this Gospel was the apostle John, the son of Zebedee and the brother of James. These two brothers left their fishing business with their father to become two of the twelve disciples of Jesus (Matt. 4:18–22). Along with Peter, John and James developed an "inner circle" relationship with Jesus. They were often involved in important events in the ministry of Jesus when none of the other disciples were present (Matt. 17:1–2; 26:37; Mark 5:37).

Beyond this, John described himself in his Gospel as "the disciple whom Jesus loved" (21:20). He was the only one of the Twelve who dared to follow Jesus to the cross and witness the crucifixion. Jesus committed His mother, Mary, to the care of John just before He died (19:25–27).

In contrast to the other Gospels, John contains little of the teachings of Jesus on such subjects as prayer, the kingdom of God, and how to treat others. Instead, Jesus gives extended monologues about His reason for coming into the world and His inevitable return to the Father. A full five chapters (13:1–17:26) are devoted to Jesus' farewell discourses to His disciples. These reveal the inner mind of Jesus and His own conception of His mission and destiny more clearly than the material in any of the other Gospels.

John's Gospel is also unique because it tells us why it was written. John declared, "These [things] are written, that ye might believe that Jesus is the Christ, the Son of God; and that believing ye might have life through his name" (20:31). Clearly, John wanted to do more than give his readers the facts about Jesus. His goal was to lead us to acknowledge Jesus as the Messiah sent from God and to accept His offer of forgiveness of sin and His gift of eternal life.

Some accounts of Jesus' life and ministry in John also parallel events reported in Matthew, Mark, and Luke. These parallel passages are identified in the following summary of John. The parallel passages in bold type with "see" references refer to pages in this book where expanded summaries of specific Gospel accounts may be found.

Summary of John

1:1–5. John begins his Gospel with the creation, affirming that Christ, God's Son ("the Word," v. 1), participated with the

1:19–34. John the Baptist, a distant relative of Jesus, baptizes Him in the Jordan River. Several weeks later, after spending time alone in the barren wilderness, Jesus starts His ministry.

Father in the creation of the world (Gen. 1:1, 26).

1:6–8. John the Baptist was sent to prepare the way for Jesus and to announce His coming into the world (Mark 1:1–8).

1:9–18. Christ left His place of honor with the Father and was born into the world in the form of a man in order to bring people to God (Phil. 2:5–8).

1:19–34. Jesus meets John the Baptist at the place where he is preaching and baptizing. John identifies Him clearly as the long-expected Messiah.

1:35–42. Andrew, a disciple of John the Baptist, follows Jesus. Andrew brings his brother Simon Peter and introduces him to Jesus.

1:43–51. Jesus calls Philip and his friend Nathanael to become His disciples.

2:1–11. Jesus performs His first miracle by turning water into wine at a wedding cel-

---

[1:19–34] HUMILITY OF JOHN THE BAPTIST. *He [Jesus] it is…whose shoe's latchet [thongs, NIV] I [John the Baptist] am not worthy to unloose* (John 1:27).

Although John the Baptist was divinely selected to serve as the forerunner of Jesus (Luke 1:76), he was aware of his unworthiness of such an honor. He declared in this verse that he was not even worthy to bend down and untie the leather thongs that held Jesus' sandals on His feet.

But Jesus recognized John's greatness and commended him for his faithfulness: "Among them that are born of women there hath not risen a greater than John the Baptist" (Matt. 11:11).

ebration in the town of Cana in the region of Galilee.

2:12. Accompanied by His mother and His brothers, Jesus visits the city of Capernaum in the region of Galilee.

2:13–25. Jesus drives out merchants who are conducting business in the temple during the Passover celebration. He charges them with desecrating the house of His Father.

3:1–21. Jesus explains the meaning of the new birth to Nicodemus, a ruler of the Pharisees.

3:22–24. Jesus and His disciples minister in the region of Judea, not far from the place where John the Baptist is preaching and baptizing.

3:25–36. John the Baptist points people to Jesus as the Messiah, the Son of God, who holds the keys to eternal life.

4:1–4. Jesus leaves the region of Judea in the south to travel to the region of Galilee in the north. During this journey He chooses deliberately to pass through the territory of the Samaritans.

4:5–44. Jesus stops at a well outside a Samaritan village and asks a woman for a drink of water. He talks with her about her life of sin and reveals to her that He is the long-expected Messiah. She brings many people from her village to meet Jesus, and they also become believers.

4:45. Jesus finds a receptive audience when He begins preaching in the region of Galilee (parallel passages: **Matt. 4:12–17**, see p. 544; Mark 1:14–15).

4:46–54. A nobleman, or royal official, from Capernaum seeks out Jesus in the town of Cana about twenty miles away. He begs Jesus to heal his sick son. Jesus heals the boy at a distance while his father is traveling back to Capernaum.

5:1–15. Jesus is criticized for healing a lame man on the Sabbath at the pool of Bethesda in Jerusalem.

5:16–47. Jesus defends His healing on the Sabbath by declaring that He has been given all authority as God's Son. Furthermore, He is doing the work that His Father has sent Him to do.

6:1–14. Jesus multiplies a boy's lunch of five pieces of bread and two fish to feed more than 5,000 hungry people (parallel passages: Matt. 14:13–21; **Mark 6:30–44**, see p. 562; Luke 9:10–17).

6:15–21. Jesus walks on the water to join His disciples in a boat on the Sea of Galilee (parallel passages: **Matt. 14:22–33**, see p. 550; Mark 6:45–52).

[6:15–21] SUDDEN STORMS ON LAKE GALILEE. *The sea arose by reason of a great wind that blew* (John 6:18).

Jesus' disciples were crossing the Sea of Galilee in a small fishing boat when they were caught in a sudden storm.

This freshwater lake, about thirteen miles long by eight miles wide, is fed by the Jordan River. It sits about seven hundred feet below sea level in an area surrounded by high mountains. Cool winds frequently rush down from these mountains and mix with the warm air on the surface of the lake. The result is a sudden, violent storm such as that which overwhelmed the disciples.

6:22–65. Many people look for Jesus, expecting a handout because they hear He has fed more than 5,000 hungry people. He teaches them that He is God's Son, the true "bread of life" who offers eternal life to all who place their faith in Him.

6:66–71. Many of Jesus' followers turn away when He does not live up to their expectations of the Messiah. Peter, speaking for the other disciples, declares that they will continue to be His faithful followers. Jesus predicts that one of the Twelve will betray Him.

7:1–9. The brothers of Jesus do not believe that Jesus is the Messiah. In a mocking and skeptical tone, they urge Him to attend the Feast of Tabernacles in Jerusalem where He can declare openly that He is the Messiah.

7:10–52. Jesus decides to attend the celebration in Jerusalem without revealing that He is the Messiah. But His teachings and His reputation as a healer and miracle worker cause a division among the people. Some believe He is the Messiah, while others deny this possibility. Nicodemus, a Pharisees who had talked with Jesus earlier (John 3:1–21), urges his fellow Pharisees not to condemn Jesus for blasphemy until they have more solid evidence against Him.

7:53–8:11. Jesus forgives a woman who is accused of adultery and condemns the self-righteousness of her accusers: "He that is without sin among you, let him first cast a stone at her" (8:7).

8:12–30. Jesus angers the Pharisees by claiming

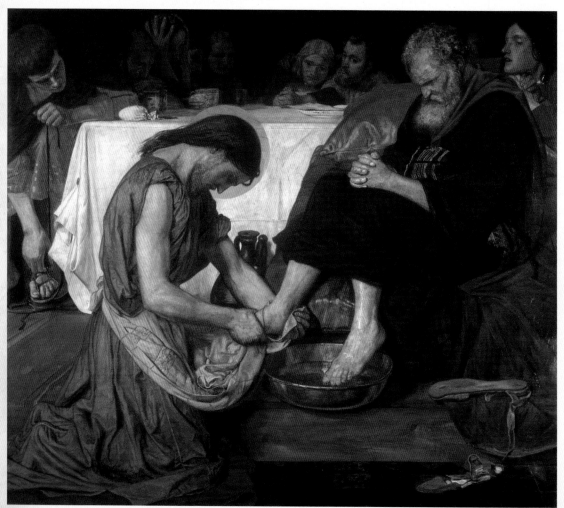

13:1–20. Though Peter doesn't feel worthy, Jesus takes on the role of a servant and washes Peter's feet. This took place at the Last Supper. Jesus washed the feet of each disciple and then urged them to become servants, too.

to be the Son of God and the light that God has sent to deliver the world from darkness (1 John 1:7).

8:31–59. Jesus further angers the Pharisees by questioning their claim that they are "children of Abraham." If they were truly Abraham's descendants, He declares, they would be doing the works of Abraham rather than plotting to have Him killed. As the eternal, preexistent Son of God, He is superior to Abraham: "Before Abraham was, I am" (v. 58).

9:1–41. Jesus heals a man who had been blind all his life. The Pharisees question Jesus' credentials, since He had sinned, according to their legalistic laws, by performing this healing on the Sabbath. They question the man about this healing, and he stands his ground in defense of Jesus. After this healed man becomes a believer, Jesus declares that the Pharisees are the real blind people in this situation; they fail to see the truth because of their sin and prejudice.

10:1–21. This is one of Jesus' "I am" statements in the Gospel of John. He compares Himself with a shepherd who watches over his sheep. As the good shepherd, Jesus will make the ultimate sacrifice for those who follow Him: "The good shepherd giveth his life for the sheep" (v. 11).

10:22–42. Jesus declares to the religious leaders of Israel that He is the Christ, the Son of God. They accuse Him of blasphemy and try to execute Him by stoning. But He slips away to an isolated spot in the wilderness of Judea to rest and pray.

11:1–44. Jesus is informed that His friend Lazarus of Bethany has died. After two days He goes to Bethany, where He is met by Lazarus's sister Martha. He declares to Martha, "I am the resurrection, and the life" (v. 25), then raises Lazarus from the dead.

11:45–57. Jesus' raising of Lazarus and His claim to be God's Son drive the Pharisees and the Jewish Sanhedrin into a frenzy. They begin to plot how they can arrest Him and have Him executed.

12:1–8. Mary of Bethany, sister of Lazarus and Martha, anoints Jesus with an expensive perfume (parallel passages: **Matt. 26:6–13,** see pp. 554–55; Mark 14:3–9).

12:9–11. The religious leaders continue their plot against Jesus, even including Lazarus in their accusations because he is responsible for causing many people to believe in Jesus.

12:12–19. Jesus makes His triumphal entry into Jerusalem on a young donkey (parallel passages: **Matt. 21:1–11,** see p. 552; Mark 11:1–11; Luke 19:28–44).

12:20–50. A group of Greeks (Gentiles or non-Jews) ask to see Jesus. They had probably heard about His miracles and unique teachings in regions beyond the Jewish nation. Jesus takes this as a sign that the time of His death is drawing near. He declares that He is the light sent by God to provide salvation for Gentiles as well as Jews—that is, the entire world (Rom. 3:29).

13:1–20. Jesus and His disciples observe the Passover by eating a meal together. He teaches them the meaning of humble service by washing their feet. This was a menial chore that only the lowliest slave would perform for household guests.

13:21–30. During the Passover meal, Jesus predicts that one of His disciples will betray Him. He identifies this disciple by dipping a piece of bread in a bowl of food and giving the bread to Judas (parallel passages: Matt. 26:20–25; Mark 14:17–21; Luke 22:21–23).

13:31–38. Jesus gives His disciples a new commandment: "As I have loved you...ye also love one another" (v. 34). He also predicts

[13:21–30] RECLINING WHILE EATING. *There was leaning on Jesus' bosom [breast] one of his disciples, whom Jesus loved* (John 13:23).

This verse describes the time when Jesus was eating the Last Supper with His disciples on the night before He was crucified. They were not seated at a high table, as some popular paintings show, but they were reclining around a low table, in accordance with the custom of that time.

Each person thrust his legs out to the side and leaned on his elbow while taking food from the table. This is how it was possible for John, the "disciple whom Jesus loved," to be leaning back against the bosom, or breast, of Jesus, who was immediately behind him.

that Peter will deny Him three times (parallel passages: Matt. 26:31–35; Mark 14:27–31; **Luke 22:31–38,** see p. 580).

14:1–16:33. Jesus delivers an extended farewell to His disciples. He tells them He is going to prepare a place for them (14:3–4), promises to send the Holy Spirit to guide them after He is gone (14:16–18, 26; 16:7–13), encourages them to abide in Him as the true vine (15:1–8), and assures them that the persecution they will experience in the world will be bearable since He has overcome the world (16:32–33).

17:1–26. These verses are known as Jesus' High Priestly Prayer. He prays for Himself, that He will glorify the Father in His suffering and death that are now just a few hours away (vv. 1–5), for His disciples (vv. 6–19), and for all future believers (vv. 20–26).

18:1–12. Jesus is arrested by officers from the Jewish Sanhedrin after Judas leads them to the spot where He can be found—probably the Garden of Gethsemane (parallel passages: **Matt. 26:47–56,** see p. 556; Mark 14:43–52; Luke 22:47–53).

18:13–14. Jesus appears first before Annas, father-in-law of Caiaphas the high priest.

18:15–27. Jesus next appears before Caiaphas the high priest and the rest of the Jewish Sanhedrin (v. 24). Standing outside the house of the high priest, Peter denies that he knows Jesus (parallel passages: **Matt. 26:69–75,** see p. 556; Mark 14:66–72; Luke 22:54–62).

18:28–19:16. Jesus appears before the Roman governor Pontius Pilate, who sentences Him to death by crucifixion (parallel passages: **Matt. 27:11–26,** see p. 556; Mark 15:2–15; Luke 23:13–25).

19:17–24. Jesus is crucified at a site known as Golgotha (parallel passages: **Matt. 27:33–37,** see p. 556; Mark 15:22–26; Luke 23:32–38).

[19:17–24] CARRYING THE CROSS. *And he [Jesus] bearing his cross went forth* (John 19:17).

A cross strong enough to hold the weight of a man and long enough to be placed in the ground and have the victim elevated at the same time would probably be too heavy for a person to carry.

Thus, Jesus probably carried only the horizontal beam to the crucifixion site. Here he was stripped naked, laid on the ground, and nailed to the beam, which was then raised and attached to the upright post.

This form of execution was so cruel and degrading that it was never imposed by the Roman government against its own citizens.

19:25–27. Jesus' mother and two other women—Mary the wife of Cleophas and Mary Magdalene—look on as Jesus is crucified. Jesus commends His mother to the care of His disciple John ("the disciple standing by, whom he loved," v. 26) (parallel passages: Matt. 27:55–56; Mark 15:40–41; Luke 23:49).

19:28–30. Jesus dies on the cross after the soldiers give Him vinegar to drink as a painkiller.

20:26–31. Doubting Thomas touches the spear wound in Jesus' side. Thomas was gone when the resurrected Jesus appeared earlier to the disciples. Thomas told the men he wouldn't believe Jesus was alive again unless he saw it for himself.

19:31–37. After Jesus dies, soldiers pierce His side with a sword to make sure He is dead. Jesus had died quickly, so it was not necessary for the soldiers to break His legs to hasten His death. This fulfills the Scripture that no bones of the sacrificial lamb offered during Passover were to be broken (Exod. 12:46; Num. 9:12).

19:38–42. Joseph of Arimathea, a secret follower of Jesus, claims His body to give it an appropriate burial. Joseph is assisted by Nicodemus (John 3:1–21), who brings perfume and spices to anoint the body. They bury Jesus in a new tomb that has never been used (parallel passages: Matt. 27:57–60; Mark 15:42–46; Luke 23:50–54).

20:1–2. Mary Magdalene discovers the body of Jesus is missing when she visits the tomb on Sunday morning. She reports this to His disciples Peter and John (parallel passages: Matt. 28:1–10; Mark 16:1–8; Luke 24:1–8).

20:3–10. Peter and John rush to the tomb to check out Mary's report that Jesus' body has been taken away (parallel passage: Luke 24:9–12).

20:11–18. Mary Magdalene remains outside the tomb after Peter and John leave. Two angels tell her that Jesus has been resurrected from the dead. Then Jesus appears before Mary and reveals Himself clearly as the risen Christ. She reports this to His disciples (parallel passage: Mark 16:9–11).

20:19–25. The resurrected Jesus appears to His disciples in a place where they are hiding because of their fear of the Jewish religious leaders. He convinces them He is the risen Christ by showing them the wounds on His hands and side. Jesus' disciple Thomas is not present during this appearance. He refuses to believe that Jesus is alive until he can see Him with his own eyes.

[20:19–25] SUPERNATURAL PEACE. *The same day at evening…came Jesus and stood in the midst, and saith unto them [His disciples], Peace be unto you* (John 20:19).

According to John's Gospel, this was Jesus' first appearance to His disciples after His resurrection. His first word to them was the common greeting used by the Jewish people of that day—a wish for their peace, wholeness, and well-being.

When Jesus greeted them with these words, perhaps the disciples remembered a promise of His supernatural peace and presence that He had made to them while training them for the task of carrying on His work: "Peace I leave with you, my peace I give unto you: not as the world giveth, give I unto you. Let not your heart be troubled, neither let it be afraid" (John 14:27).

20:26–31. Jesus appears among His disciples again—this time when Thomas is present. He deals with Thomas's skepticism by inviting Him to touch the wounds in His hands and side. Believing, Thomas declares, "My Lord and my God" (v. 28).

21:1–14. Jesus appears to seven of His disciples at the Sea of Galilee. He prepares and eats a meal with them to prove they are not seeing a ghost or a vision.

21:15–19. Jesus forgives Peter for his denials and reinstates him to full service as His disciple, charging him to "feed my sheep" (v. 17). He predicts that Peter will suffer persecution and death because of his faithfulness to the risen Lord.

21:20–23. Jesus deals with Peter's question about how long His disciple John ("the disciple whom Jesus loved," v. 20) will live.

21:24–25. Jesus' disciple John, the author of this Gospel, vows that the things he has written about Jesus are authentic eyewitness accounts. He also declares that Jesus did many things he has not included in this Gospel. If he had written about all these events, John says, "the world itself could not contain the books that should be written" (v. 25).

CHAPTER 7
ACTS, A HISTORY OF THE
EARLY CHURCH

Acts is a one-of-a-kind book in the New Testament. It is not a Gospel, since it contains only a few verses about the life and ministry of Jesus (Acts 1:1–10). Neither is Acts an epistle, or letter, to early Christians or churches, like the rest of the books in the New Testament canon. Acts is in a class by itself, and that is why it is treated here as a major section of God's Word.

The full title of Acts in the King James Version is "The Acts of the Apostles." But it could also be called "The Acts of the Holy Spirit," since it reports on the actions of the Spirit in the birth and development of the church. Jesus promised His followers that they would be empowered by His Spirit to carry on His work (Acts 1:8). This is exactly what happened as believers lived out their faith and shared the gospel in the pagan culture of their time.

ACTS

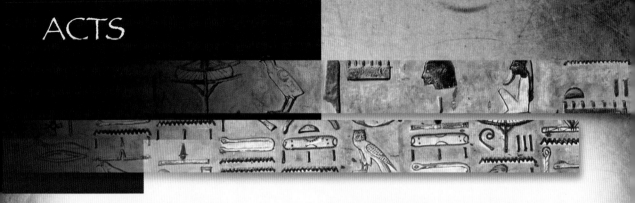

OVERVIEW: Traces the expansion of Christianity from a movement localized in Jerusalem that appealed mainly to Jews to a worldwide faith that included Gentiles.

Introduction to Acts

The book of Acts picks up where the Gospels end—with Jesus' ascension to the Father and His commission to his followers to take the gospel into all the world (Matt. 28:19; Luke 24:47). As the only book of history in the New Testament, Acts recounts how Jesus' commission was accomplished. In about thirty-five years (A.D. 33–68), the Christian faith spread from Jerusalem to the city of Rome, capital of the Roman Empire. More significantly, it grew from a movement that appealed mainly to Jews into a universal faith that included people of all ethnic backgrounds.

Acts was written by Luke, a physician and early church leader, as a sequel to the Gospel of Luke (see the introduction to Luke's Gospel on p. 568). Luke accompanied the apostle Paul on some of his missionary tours. Luke identified himself with the personal pronoun "we" when recounting some of Paul's experiences in which he was involved (16:10–17; 20:5–21:18; 27:1–28:16).

In addition to firsthand observation, Luke must have interviewed many of the people about whom he wrote and drawn on other reputable sources in order to compile his account of the spread of the church during its first thirty-five years. The book of Acts is known for its careful attention to detail and historical accuracy. It mentions ninety-five different people from thirty-two countries, fifty-four cities, and nine islands in the Mediterranean Sea.

The two dominant personalities of Acts are Peter and Paul. In chapters 1–12, Peter takes the lead in proclaiming the gospel to nonbelievers, mostly of Jewish background, in and around Jerusalem. But Paul becomes the leading witness in chapters 13–28, after his dramatic conversion in an encounter with the living Christ on the road to Damascus. As the "apostle to the Gentiles," he traveled throughout the Mediterranean world, calling people to faith in Christ and founding churches to serve as outposts of righteousness in a pagan world.

The book of Acts ends with Paul under house arrest by the Roman authorities in the city of Rome. But even his imprisonment fails to stop the advance of the gospel. He continues to witness for Christ "with all confidence, no man forbidding him" (28:31).

Summary of Acts

1:1–5. Luke, the author of Acts, reminds his friend Theophilus (v. 1) of the things he wrote about Jesus in his other book, the Gospel of Luke. Theophilus is also mentioned by Luke in the opening verses of his Gospel (Luke 1:3).

1:6–9. Jesus ascends to His Father after assuring His followers that they will receive power

[1:12–15] A SHORT WALK. *Then returned they [early Christian believers] unto Jerusalem from the mount called Olivet, which is from Jerusalem a sabbath day's journey (Acts 1:12).*

Jesus ascended to heaven from the Mount of Olives after delivering a farewell message to these believers (Acts 1:6–9). This hill east of Jerusalem is just a few minutes' walk from the city. This tells us that a "sabbath day's journey" was probably less than a mile.

The prohibition against working on the Sabbath (Exod. 20:8–11) led to this regulation about a Sabbath day's journey. Walking farther than this short distance permitted on the day of worship was considered work, and thus a violation of the Sabbath law.

Jesus may have had this regulation in mind when He told His followers they might have to flee to escape persecution in the end-time: "Pray ye that your flight be not…on the sabbath day" (Matt. 24:20).

from the Holy Spirit to witness for Him throughout the world (Mark 16:19–20).

1:10–11. Two angels tell His followers that Jesus will return to earth again someday.

1:12–15. About 120 followers of Jesus, including His disciples and several women, meet together in Jerusalem.

1:16–26. Under the leadership of the apostle Peter, also known as Simon (Mark 1:16–18), this group of followers selects Matthias to replace Judas as one of the twelve apostles.

2:1–13. While celebrating the festival of Pentecost (Lev. 23:15–21) in Jerusalem, Jesus' apostles are filled with the Holy Spirit. Their normal spoken language is either Aramaic or Greek. But these followers of Jesus begin to speak in several different languages that are recognized by Jews from different parts of the world who are gathered at Jerusalem for the Pentecost celebration. Some

of these Jews are amazed at this display, but others accuse the apostles of being drunk with "new wine" (Acts 2:13).

2:14–42. In a great speech known as his "Pentecost Sermon," the apostle Peter assures the crowd that their strange speech is a fulfillment of the ancient prophecy of Joel 2:28–32. He turns their attention to Jesus, who has empowered the apostles with the Holy Spirit. Then he declares, "Repent, and be baptized every one of you in the name of Jesus Christ for the remission of sins, and ye shall receive the gift of the Holy Ghost" (v. 38). Three thousand people turn to Jesus in repentance and are baptized.

2:43–47. The apostles perform wonders and signs among the people in Jerusalem. The followers of Jesus pool their resources to care for the needy among their fellowship.

3:1–11. Peter and John heal a lame man outside the temple in the name of Jesus.

3:12–26. Peter preaches another strong sermon to the people of Jerusalem. He urges them to repent and be baptized in the name of Jesus—the one whom they have rejected but whom God has raised and designated as the Prince of Life.

4:1–22. Peter and John are arrested and questioned by the Jewish Sanhedrin about their healing of the lame man outside the temple. They are released after they declare boldly that the man was healed through the power of Jesus. But the Sanhedrin warns them not to continue to speak or teach in the name of Jesus.

4:23–31. Peter and John meet with other believers. Together, they pray for strength and boldness to continue to preach about Jesus, in spite of the threats from the Jewish Sanhedrin. God honors their prayers by strengthening them again with the Holy Spirit (John 14:16–18; Acts 2:1–13).

2:1–13. The Holy Spirit descends on the followers of Jesus, giving them the boldness and miracle-working power to establish a new religious movement that eventually takes its name from Christ: Christianity.

4:32–37. These early believers continue their practice of pooling their resources in order to care for the needy among their fellowship (Acts 2:43–47). Barnabas sells his land and places the proceeds in the common treasury.

5:1–11. Ananias and his wife, Sapphira, sell a field and pretend to place all the proceeds in the common treasury of the church. But they actually keep part of the money for themselves. They pay with their lives for lying to God.

[5:1–11] IMMEDIATE BURIAL. *The young men arose, wound him [Ananias] up [wrapped up his body, NIV], and carried him out, and buried him (Acts 5:6).*

Ananias, an early Christian believer, was struck dead when he lied about his contribution to the church's common treasury. He was buried immediately by his fellow believers.

Burial on the day of death was the customary practice in Palestine in New Testament times. Embalming was not practiced by the Jews, and a body would deteriorate quickly in the sweltering climate.

Bodies were often prepared for burial by being wrapped with strips of cloth. This procedure is suggested by the NIV translation of this verse. Spices were sometimes placed among these layers of cloth. This is how Joseph of Arimathea and Nicodemus prepared the body of Jesus for burial (John 19:38–40).

5:12–16. The apostles perform signs and wonders, including healing the sick, among the people of Jerusalem. The church continues to grow with the addition of many believers (Acts 2:41).

5:17–32. The apostles are imprisoned by the Sanhedrin for continuing to preach about Jesus. Released by an angel, they go right back to bearing witness about Jesus and His resurrection. They are dragged before the Sanhedrin again, only to declare, "We ought to obey God rather than men" (v. 29).

5:33–42. Gamaliel advises the other members of the Sanhedrin to release the apostles, with the observation that their work will come to an end if it is not in God's will. After a beating, the apostles return to their preaching, "rejoicing that they were counted worthy to suffer shame for his name" (v. 41).

6:1–7. Greek-speaking members of the early church complain that their widows are not receiving their fair share in the church's food-distribution efforts. The church selects seven men of Greek-speaking background to coordinate this ministry.

6:8–15. Stephen, one of the seven men selected to coordinate food distribution for the church, speaks boldly for Jesus in a debate with a group of Jewish zealots. They accuse him of blasphemy and drag him before the Jewish Sanhedrin for trial.

7:1–53. In a long speech before the Sanhedrin, Stephen reviews the history of the Jewish people. He accuses the religious leaders of rejecting God's messengers and disobeying His commands at every turn. This includes their rejection of Jesus as the Messiah.

7:54–60. Enraged by these accusations, the Jewish leaders execute Stephen by stoning him to death.

8:1–4. A Pharisee named Saul (later known as the apostle Paul) is a consenting bystander when Stephen is killed. Stephen's death stirs open persecution from the Jewish religious leaders against the church in Jerusalem. Saul is one of the ringleaders in these efforts to stamp out the church. Many believers flee Jerusalem and carry the message of Jesus wherever they go.

8:5–17. Philip, one of the seven men selected to distribute food to the needy, preaches the gospel in the region of Samaria. Many

10:9–16. *Model of a flat-roofed house from Bible times. People treated the roofs like patios. While Peter was praying on a roof one day, he experienced a vision that convinced him it was all right to preach to non-Jews. Previously, Jews avoided contact with Gentiles.*

Samaritans believe on Jesus Christ and are baptized. Peter and John come to Samaria from Jerusalem to help Philip in this evangelism effort.

8:18–25. Peter condemns Simon the magician for trying to buy the power of the Holy Spirit with money.

8:26–40. Philip witnesses in the desert to a eunuch from Ethiopia, an official under Candace the queen. The eunuch is baptized by Philip on his testimony of faith that "Jesus Christ is the Son of God" (v. 37).

9:1–7. Saul the persecutor is converted to Christianity in a dramatic encounter with the risen Christ on the road to Damascus, Syria (Acts 22:4–10).

9:8–18. Saul is struck with blindness for three days following his conversion experience. God sends a believer named Ananias to find Saul in Damascus and to restore his sight. The Lord makes it clear that Saul is a part of His plan to reach the Gentiles with the gospel (Acts 13:44–50).

9:19–25. Saul angers the Jews in Damascus by preaching about Jesus in the synagogue. They attempt to kill him, but Saul escapes when his fellow believers let him down in a basket over the city wall.

9:26–31. Returning to Jerusalem, Saul attempts to join the Christian fellowship. But he is met with suspicion and distrust because of his previous persecution of the church. Barnabas speaks up for Saul and convinces them he is a genuine believer. Saul eventually returns to Tarsus, his hometown, because of threats against his life from the unbelieving Jews in Jerusalem.

9:32–35. In Lydda Peter heals a man named Aeneas of the palsy.

9:36–43. Peter raises Dorcas, a female believer who "was full of good works" (v. 36), from the dead, in Joppa.

10:1–8. Cornelius, a Roman centurion and thus a Gentile, is a godly man who worships the one true God. In a vision, God instructs Cornelius to send for the apostle Peter, who will tell him what he should do. Cornelius obeys and sends three servants to Joppa to find Peter at the house of Simon the tanner.

10:9–16. As Cornelius's servants draw near the city of Joppa, Peter is praying in the outdoor space on top of Simon's house. In a vision, Peter sees a group of unclean animals that are forbidden as food for the Jews (Lev. 11:1–47). But God instructs Peter to kill and eat these animals. When Peter protests, God declares, "What God hath cleansed, that call not thou common" (v. 15). This is God's way of telling Peter that Gentiles are included in God's plan of salvation. No one

is to be excluded from His love and grace.

10:17–23. Just then, Cornelius's three servants arrive. Peter learns they want him to go to Caesarea to talk with Cornelius. Then he invites them in to spend the night.

10:24–48. The next day Peter travels to the home of Cornelius and preaches the gospel to him and his entire household. They repent, turn to Jesus, receive the Holy Spirit, and are baptized. This is dramatic evidence of God's inclusion of the Gentiles in His redemptive plan (John 12:20–50).

11:1–18. Leaders of the church in Jerusalem question Peter about the conversion of Cornelius and other Gentiles. One faction in the church is upset that Peter associated with uncircumcised Gentiles. But when Peter explains what happened, most of the church leaders are pleased. They declare, "Then hath God also to the Gentiles granted repentance unto life" (v. 18).

11:19–24. God blesses the work of a new church that has been planted among the people of Greek-speaking background in the city of Antioch in Syria. The Jerusalem church sends Barnabas to guide this new work, and it grows dramatically under his leadership.

11:25–26. Barnabas travels to Tarsus (Acts 9:27–30) and enlists Saul/Paul to help him in the church at Antioch.

11:27–30. A severe famine strikes the Mediterranean area, as foretold by the prophet Agabus. Barnabas and Saul/Paul deliver a relief offering from their area to the suffering Christians in Judea around Jerusalem.

12:1–5. Herod Agrippa I, Roman ruler over Palestine, executes the apostle James (Mark 1:19–20) and imprisons the apostle Peter.

12:6–19. Peter is miraculously delivered from prison by an angel and reunited with believers who are praying for his release.

[10:9–16] PRAYING ON THE HOUSETOP. *Peter went up upon the housetop to pray about the sixth hour [about noon, NIV]* (Acts 10:9).

This may seem to us like a strange place to pray, but it made perfect sense to Peter.

The roofs of houses in Bible times might be compared to our modern patios. They were flat and easily accessible by an exterior stairway. People often went to the roof for rest and relaxation, particularly at night to catch a cooling breeze (see the note "Guardrails on the Roof" on p. 396).

Peter probably went to the roof so he could be alone in prayer, since he was a visitor in the house of Simon the tanner (Acts 10:5–6).

12:20–25. Herod is struck dead by the Lord for allowing himself to be elevated to the status of a god in the eyes of the people.

13:1–3. The Holy Spirit selects Barnabas and Saul/Paul for missionary work. The church at Antioch obeys the Spirit's leading by sending them out after praying and fasting and commissioning them to this task through the laying on of hands. The work of Barnabas and Paul described in Acts 13:4–14:28 is known as the apostle Paul's first missionary journey.

13:4–12. On the island of Cyprus, Paul and Barnabas witness to the governor of the region, and he becomes a believer. Paul rebukes a magician or sorcerer named Bar-jesus when he tries to hinder their work.

13:13. Leaving Cyprus, Paul and Barnabas stop at the city of Perga in the province of Pamphylia. John Mark, who has been accompanying them on the trip, decides to return to Jerusalem.

[13:14–43] THE SYNAGOGUE LEADER. *The rulers of the synagogue sent unto them [Paul and Barnabas], saying…if ye have any word of exhortation…say on* (Acts 13:15).

During Paul's first missionary journey, he and his associate, Barnabas, attended worship services at the local synagogue (see the note "Reading in a Synagogue" on p. 571) in Antioch of Pisidia. They were invited to speak to the other worshipers by the rulers or presiding officers of the synagogue.

A synagogue ruler was elected to his position by other members of the congregation. His responsibility was to plan the services, enlist readers and speakers, and preside at the worship proceedings.

Most mentions of this synagogue officer in the New Testament refer to only one ruler (Mark 5:36–38; Luke 13:14). But this passage in Acts mentions more than one ruler. Perhaps a division of responsibilities was required in larger synagogues.

13:14–43. Paul preaches about Jesus in the Jewish synagogue in the city of Antioch in the province of Pisidia. The staunch Jews are skeptical of his message, but it is well received by Gentiles (Acts 10:45) and religious proselytes.

13:44–50. On the next Sabbath a crowd gathers in the city to hear Paul speak again. This time the Jews openly condemn Paul and accuse him of blasphemy. They expel Paul and Barnabas from the city. The two missionaries declare: "It was necessary that the word of God should first have been spoken to you [Jews]: but seeing ye put it from you, and judge yourselves unworthy of everlasting life, lo, we turn to the Gentiles" (v. 46; see Rom. 3:29). This represents a turning point in the ministry of Paul. From now on he will direct most of his evangelistic efforts to the Gentiles because of their openness to the gospel message.

13:51–14:5. Many Gentiles and Jews of Greek-speaking background turn to the Lord in Iconium. But Paul and Barnabas are eventually forced to leave the city because of strong opposition from the Jews.

14:6–20. In the province of Lycaonia, Paul and Barnabas preach in the cities of Lystra and Derbe. When Paul heals a lame man, the superstitious citizens of Lystra think the missionaries are gods. At Lystra Paul is also delivered miraculously by the Lord from a mob of Jewish zealots who try to stone him to death.

14:21–28. Paul and Barnabas return to their sending church at Antioch of Syria. This brings Paul's first missionary journey to a close. On the return trip the missionaries stop at the places they had visited, "confirming the souls of the disciples, and exhorting them to continue in the faith" (v. 22). They also appoint elders (Acts 20:17) to lead the

13:13. *Sunlit mountains tower over a bay in southern Turkey—the bay that Paul and Barnabas sailed into during their first missionary trip.*

churches they had founded. The church at Antioch rejoices when they learn that God has "opened the door of faith unto the Gentiles" (v. 27) through the ministry of Paul and Barnabas.

15:1–6. A faction within the church insists that Gentiles must convert to Judaism and be circumcised in accordance with the Law of Moses before they can be saved. Leaders of the church meet at Jerusalem to consider the matter.

15:7–35. The apostle Peter, followed by Paul and Barnabas, speaks against circumcision as a requirement for Gentile believers. James, the half brother of Jesus and a leader in the church, issues the church's opinion that all persons, Jews and Gentiles alike, are saved through faith alone (Rom. 3:21–31). Paul and Barnabas deliver this good news to the church at Antioch.

15:36–41. Paul and Barnabas prepare to set out on a second missionary journey. But they disagree on whether to take John Mark, who had left them and returned home on their first trip (Acts 13:13). Finally, the two missionaries agree to go their separate ways. Barnabas takes John Mark and sails for the island of Cyprus. Paul travels north through the provinces of Syria and Cilicia, accompanied by Silas, a believer in the church at Antioch.

16:1–3. Paul and Silas strengthen believers in Derbe and Lystra, two cities where Paul had preached during his first missionary tour (Acts 14:6–20). This stop begins Paul's second missionary journey, which continues through Acts 18:22. At Lystra Paul meets a young believer named Timothy, whom he enlists as a helper in his missionary work (1 Tim. 1:1–2).

16:4–10. After traveling through several provinces, Paul and Silas are persuaded by the Holy Spirit not to enter the regions of Asia and Bithynia. Through a vision they are beckoned instead into the province of Macedonia.

16:11–15. In the city of Philippi (Phil. 1:1) in Macedonia, a businesswoman named Lydia and her entire household become believers.

16:16–24. Paul and Silas heal a demented slave girl. They are thrown into prison on charges from her master, who was profiting from her fortune-telling abilities.

16:25–40. As they sing praises to God, Paul and Silas are freed miraculously from prison by an earthquake. The jail keeper and his entire household are baptized by Paul after they turn to the Lord.

17:1–9. Unbelieving Jews create an uproar in the city of Thessalonica after Paul preaches in the Jewish synagogue. But several Gentiles become believers.

17:10–14. Paul finds an open and eager audience in the city of Berea: "They received the word with all readiness...and searched the scriptures daily, whether those things were so" (v. 11). But enraged Jews who have followed Paul and Silas from Thessalonica drive them out of the city.

17:15–34. While waiting for Silas and Timothy to join him in Athens, Paul preaches to the philosophers and intellectuals in this cultured Greek city. Most are skeptical, especially about the resurrection of Jesus (1 Cor. 15:1–11). But a few are receptive and turn to the Lord.

18:1–18. Paul travels from Athens to Corinth, where he joins forces with a Christian couple, Aquila and Priscilla. They support themselves as tentmakers for eighteen months while witnessing for Christ and establishing a church in this pagan city (1 Cor. 1:1–9).

18:19–22. After preaching for a while in the city of Ephesus, Paul returns to his home base—the church at Antioch. This brings to an end his second missionary journey.

18:23. Paul begins his third and final missionary journey by traveling through the provinces of Galatia and Phyrgia, encouraging new believers and strengthening their churches. This journey will end with his return to Jerusalem in Acts 21.

18:24–28. Apollos, a zealous new believer from Alexandria, Egypt, preaches in the church at Ephesus. After instructions in the faith

19:24–41. The many-breasted goddess Diana was the favorite deity of Ephesus. Craftsmen and merchants made a good living selling figurines of her—until Paul arrived and convinced many people to stop worshiping idols. With their livelihood threatened, the merchants responded with a riot.

from Aquila and Priscilla, he moves on to the province of Achaia to minister in the church at Corinth.

19:1–7. Paul arrives in Ephesus, where he finds several believers who were followers of John the Baptist (John 4:1). He instructs them about Jesus and baptizes them in His name.

19:8–23. Paul continues his work in Ephesus and the surrounding province of Asia. In addition to preaching and teaching, he performs miraculous healings among the people. Black magic and superstition yield to the power of the Word of God.

19:24–41. Believers in Ephesus are threatened by a mob under the leadership of Demetrius, a silversmith. The gospel was cutting into the profits of those who made and sold miniature replicas of the pagan goddess Diana. But the crowd disperses quietly when calmed down by the town clerk.

20:1–5. Paul takes several believers on a preaching and witnessing tour through the provinces of Macedonia, Greece (Achaia), and Asia.

20:6–12. In the city of Troas, Paul preaches late into the night in an upstairs room. A young man named Eutychus goes to sleep and falls from the window. Paul revives him and stays with him until he regains his strength.

20:13–16. Paul decides to go to Jerusalem in time to celebrate the feast of Pentecost. He catches a ship headed for Miletus, a seaport city not far from Ephesus.

20:17–38. Paul sends word for the elders of the church at Ephesus to meet him at Miletus. He delivers a tearful farewell address and predicts that this is the last time they will see one another. He encourages them to remain true to the gospel that he has planted in their midst. Paul also tells the church elders about his feeling that trouble awaits

[19:24–41] PAGAN CHARMS. *A certain man [of Ephesus] named Demetrius, a silversmith, which made silver shrines for Diana [Artemis, NIV], brought no small gain unto the craftsmen* (Acts 19:24).

Paul worked in the city of Ephesus for almost three years—longer than he stayed at any other one place. A city of about 300,000 people, it was a strategic center for the planting of the gospel in the Gentile world.

The pride of Ephesus was a large, ornate temple devoted to the worship of Diana, or Artemis, a pagan goddess. Demetrius and other craftsmen of the city made their living by making and selling miniature replicas of this pagan goddess. These were probably worn as charms on necklaces or bracelets by worshipers of this goddess.

When the citizens of Ephesus began turning to the Lord and quit buying these pagan charms, Demetrius incited a riot against Paul (Acts 19:24–29). Religious tolerance was out of the question when pagan profits were at stake.

him in Jerusalem: "I go...not knowing the things that shall befall me there" (v. 22).

21:1–9. After sailing across the Mediterranean Sea, Paul's ship docks at the coastal city of Tyre, about 100 miles north of Jerusalem. At Tyre he meets and encourages other believers, then travels south to the city of Caesarea, the home of Philip the evangelist (Acts 8:5–17, 26–40).

21:10–15. At Tyre Paul is warned by a prophet named Agabus that he will be arrested by the Jews if he goes to Jerusalem. But Paul pushes on and finally arrives in the city. This brings to an end Paul's third missionary journey.

21:16–26. Paul greets the leaders of the church at Jerusalem. They rejoice over the acceptance of the gospel by the Gentiles under his ministry. At their suggestion, Paul agrees to serve as sponsor for several men who are undergoing purification rituals in the Jewish temple.

21:27–36. Paul is grabbed by an angry mob of Jews. They jump to the conclusion that he has taken a Gentile into an area of the temple reserved only for Jews—and thus polluted the holy sanctuary. A quick-acting detachment of Roman soldiers rescues Paul from the angry crowd.

21:37–22:22. Paul addresses the crowd, telling them he was a zealous Jew just like them until he was converted in a dramatic encounter with Jesus Christ (Acts 9:1–7). But the crowd renews their cry that he deserves to die for his blasphemous actions.

22:23–29. The Roman soldiers take Paul away to one of their own prisons where he will be safe from the Jewish mob. They prepare to force him to talk by giving him a scourging (beating), but Paul reveals that he is a Roman citizen. This guarantees that he will be treated with respect and fairness while in Roman custody.

22:30–23:10. Paul appears before the Jewish Sanhedrin. He causes dissension among the members of this body when he declares that Jesus was resurrected from the dead. The Roman soldiers return Paul to their own prison for his protection.

23:11. The Lord appears to Paul and informs the apostle that he will bear witness of Him in Rome, capital city of the Roman Empire (Acts 28:17–31).

23:12–22. Paul's nephew warns the Roman commander of a plot by Jewish zealots to kill the apostle.

23:23–35. The Roman commander, Claudius Lysias, sends Paul to the seat of the Roman provincial government at Caesarea. Here Paul is to stand trial before Felix, governor of the province.

24:1–21. The Jews from Jerusalem present their charges of blasphemy against Paul before Felix. Speaking eloquently in his own defense, Paul shows the charges to be false.

24:22–27. Felix holds Paul in prison at Caesarea for two years, hoping the apostle will buy his freedom with a bribe.

25:1–12. Festus succeeds Felix as the Roman provincial governor over Judea. He asks Paul if he is willing to have his case heard before the Jewish Sanhedrin in Jerusalem. The apostle realizes he cannot receive a fair trial in such an arrangement, so he appeals his case to Rome—the right of every Roman citizen.

25:13–27. While Paul is waiting to go to Rome, Festus discusses Paul's case with Herod Agrippa II, another Roman ruler over the Jewish territories. Agrippa asks for Paul to be brought before him so he can hear his story firsthand. Festus is glad to comply. He hopes this appearance by Paul will give him some specific charge against the apostle that he can send with him to Rome.

26:1–32. Paul makes a passionate defense speech before Festus and Agrippa. He recounts his conversion experience and tells how he was called by the Lord to serve as an apostle

---

[25:1–12] PAUL'S RIGHT OF APPEAL. *Festus… answered, Hast thou [Paul] appealed unto Caesar? unto Caesar shalt thou go* (Acts 25:12).

Festus was the Roman governor of Judea who agreed to hear the charges against Paul brought by the Jewish leaders. When Festus suggested that the apostle be sent back to the Jewish court, Paul invoked his rights as a Roman citizen. He appealed his case to Rome, the capital city, where he would be assured of a fair trial (Acts 25:10–11).

In Paul's time, a person could become a Roman citizen by birth or by buying this special status. Roman officials often granted these rights to non-Romans who had rendered special service to the empire. Although Paul was a Jew, he had been born a Roman citizen (Acts 22:28). How his parents had obtained their citizenship rights is unknown.

[27:27–38] PERILS OF THE SEA. *Fearing lest we [Paul and shipmates] should have fallen upon rocks, they [sailors] cast four anchors out of the stern, and wished for the day* (Acts 27:29).

Acts 27 reports on the voyage of Paul to Rome and the wreck of his ship in a ferocious storm. Ancient sailing ships were at the mercy of the winds. This verse reports that the crew tossed out four anchors from the rear of the ship to keep it from being broken to pieces on the rocky shore.

This chapter of Acts also tells us that the captain of this ship was pushing his luck by sailing to Rome so late in the year. Most ships that sailed the Mediterranean Sea apparently docked in a protected bay or inlet until the storms of winter were over (Acts 27:7–12).

Several actions were taken to save the ship when the storm struck with its full fury. The crew pulled ropes or cables tightly around the hull to keep it from breaking apart (Acts 27:17). They also lightened the ship by throwing the cargo and even its pulleys and ropes for hoisting the sails into the sea (Acts 27:19, 38).

to the Gentiles (Acts 9:1–7). Agrippa is so moved by Paul's remarks that he declares, "Almost thou persuadest me to be a Christian" (v. 28). Both Festus and Agrippa agree that Paul is innocent of the charges against him. But since he has appealed his case to Caesar, to Rome he must go.

27:1–13. Paul sails for Rome as a prisoner of the Roman Empire. The first part of their journey takes them several hundred miles to an area near the island of Crete in the Mediterranean Sea. The captain of the ship plans to land at a port known as Phoenix to wait out the approaching winter storms.

27:14–20. But the ship never reaches Crete. Struck by a violent winter storm, it drifts off course as it is buffeted by the crashing waves. The crew throws part of the ship's tackle overboard to give it more stability in the rough seas.

27:21–26. Paul assures the crew and the other passengers that no lives will be lost in this storm. This has been revealed to him in a vision by a messenger from the Lord. But the ship will be wrecked and they will be "cast upon a certain island" (v. 26).

27:27–38. As the ship drifts into shallow water, Paul urges everyone to eat so they will have strength to escape when they run aground.

27:39–44. The ship is torn apart by the violent waves when it hits land. But everyone on board escapes to the shore, as Paul had predicted.

28:1–6. The passengers and crew find themselves on the island of Melita (now know as Malta). Paul impresses the native islanders by surviving a bite from a poisonous snake.

28:7–11. Paul conducts a healing ministry during his three months on the island.

28:12–16. Paul sets sail again, making several stops along the way before finally arriving at Rome, capital city of the Roman Empire.

28:17–29. Paul takes the initiative to meet with a group of Jews in Rome. His message about Jesus is received by some but rejected by others.

28:30–31. For two years, while under house arrest in Rome, Paul preaches the message of Christ to many people (Phil. 1:12–13). He witnesses "with all confidence, no man forbidding him" (v. 31).

CHAPTER 8
EPISTLES OF THE APOSTLE PAUL

As a proud Pharisee, the apostle Paul (also known as Saul) was a zealous persecutor of the Christian movement during its early years (Acts 7:58). But he was converted to Christianity in a dramatic encounter with the living Lord on the road to the city of Damascus about A.D. 35 (Acts 9:1–8). From then until his death about thirty years later, he preached the gospel and founded churches with a holy passion. His travels in the service of Christ took him hundreds of miles throughout the ancient world. Toward the end of his ministry, he even traveled by ship to the city of Rome, capital of the Roman Empire (Acts 28:14–16).

Because Paul's ministry covered such a large area, he used epistles, or letters, to communicate with the churches he founded as well as with the members of these new congregations. In these epistles he dealt with problems in the churches, instructed new believers in the essentials of the Christian faith, and encouraged local church leaders to remain faithful to their calling.

Thirteen of these Pauline letters are included in the New Testament. Nine were written to churches: Romans, 1 and 2 Corinthians, Galatians, Ephesians, Philippians, Colossians, and 1 and 2 Thessalonians. Four were written to individuals: 1 and 2 Timothy, Titus, and Philemon.

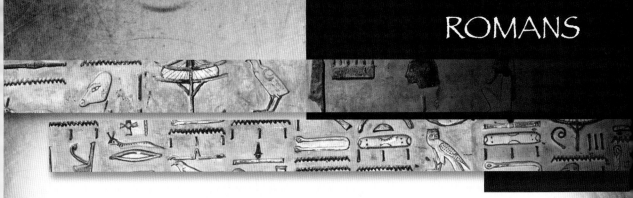

ROMANS

OVERVIEW: A thorough exploration of the doctrine of justification by faith alone.

Introduction to Romans

Most of Paul's letters were written to congregations that he had founded. But Paul had never visited the church at Rome. Indeed, one of his reasons for writing to this congregation may have been to pave the way for a personal visit to the believers in that city (1:11). Perhaps he wanted to generate their support for a missionary visit he hoped to make

A model of ancient Rome shows the circular Coliseum and the oblong chariot racecourse dominating the cityscape, alongside the Tiber River.

7:1–13. Keeping God's law was the criterion by which righteousness was measured in Old Testament times (Deut. 6:1–3). But the law had only succeeded in stimulating people to greater sin. Humanity's sinful nature has not been changed by the law.

7:14–25. Paul gives his own personal testimony to illustrate the stubbornness of man's sinful nature. In his own strength, he was unable to overcome the sins of the flesh. The harder he tried to keep the law, the lower his tendency to sin dragged him down.

8:1–27. But believers who have found new life in Christ have a different story to tell. Energized by the power of the Holy Spirit, they are not victimized by sin and death. God's indwelling presence strengthens Christians and enables them to walk in the path of holiness and righteousness.

[8:1–27] ADOPTION AND SALVATION. *Ye [believers in Christ] have received the Spirit of adoption [sonship, NIV], whereby we cry, Abba, Father* (Rom. 8:15).

Paul compared the process by which believers are justified to the process of adoption in Roman culture.

If a Roman man had no son by biological birth, he could adopt one. One of his slaves might even be adopted as a son. The adopted son took the name of the father and had all the rights that would have been extended to a biological child.

Paul also made this comparison between adoption and salvation in his letter to the Galatians. After being delivered from bondage to sin and adopted into God's family, the believer is "no more a servant, but a son; and if a son, then an heir of God through Christ" (Gal. 4:7).

8:28–39. Reflecting on God's goodness and the redemption provided in His Son causes Paul to break out in a glorious song of praise. In spite of all the testings and troubles that confront God's people, they can rest assured that they are "more than conquerors" (v. 37) through Christ who loves them.

9:1–11:36. In these three chapters, Paul addresses the question of why the Jews, his own people, have rejected the gospel. His conclusion is that they missed the mark by stubbornly seeking justification with God by keeping the law. But some among the Jews have seen the light and have accepted Jesus by faith as the only way to salvation. This remnant of the saved gives Paul hope for the future of the Jewish people.

12:1–2. Total commitment to the Lord leads believers to have a new outlook on life. Resisting the temptations of the world, we make doing God's will our main concern.

12:3–8. God has given different spiritual gifts to the members of His body, the church. We should use these gifts not to bring honor to ourselves but to glorify the Lord and to enrich and build up the congregation (1 Cor. 14).

12:9–21. Love toward others, particularly fellow church members, gives evidence of our new life in Christ. Christian love is such a powerful force that it enables us to "overcome evil with good" (v. 21; see 1 Cor. 13).

13:1–7. Paul encourages his readers to respect the civil authorities, to pay their taxes (Matt. 22:15–22), and to live as good citizens of their nation (Luke 20:20–26). He believes human government is used by the Lord as a restraining influence on sin and disorder.

13:8–14. All the commandments, Paul declares, are summed up in this: "Thou shalt love thy neighbour as thyself" (v. 9; see Matt. 22:35–40). He also encourages the Roman Christians to be on the watch for Christ's return.

14:1–23. Believers should live in harmony with one another. Apparently, some of the Roman Christians were critical of their fellow believers for eating certain food. Paul urges

8:1–27. A portrait in stone preserves the image of a Roman family, displayed in a tomb. Paul used the example of Roman adoption to convey the idea that by faith we become adopted into the family of God—much like a slave can become a son.

them not to judge one another on such trivial issues. "For the kingdom of God is not meat and drink," he declares, "but righteousness, and peace, and joy in the Holy Ghost" (v. 17).

15:1–13. The foundation of Christian unity consists of mutual respect and acceptance among all believers. Paul holds up Christ as an example because He "received us to the glory of God" (v. 7).

15:14–33. Paul is confident that his readers will continue to serve as faithful witnesses in the capital city of the Roman Empire, just as he has shared the gospel as a traveling missionary. He intends to make a missionary trip to Spain, and he will visit them in Rome when he passes through.

16:1–2. Paul commends Phebe to the church at Rome. She may have carried this letter from him to the Roman believers.

16:3–16. Paul extends personal greetings to several believers in the Roman church, including Priscilla and Aquila (v. 3; see Acts 18:1–3).

16:17–20. Some problem had caused divisions in the church at Rome. Paul urges the believers to deal decisively with the troublemakers.

16:21–27. Paul extends personal greetings to the church from several of his missionary associates. He concludes with a beautiful doxology of praise to God for His faithful love.

1 CORINTHIANS

OVERVIEW: God's guidance for various problems that plagued the church at Corinth.

Introduction to 1 Corinthians

Paul's first epistle to the church at Corinth gives us a realistic view of the early church. Just like churches today, this first-century congregation had its problems and shortcomings.

The apostle dealt with these problems head-on in an attempt to make the church a more effective witness for Jesus Christ.

The church at Corinth was a product of Paul's own missionary efforts. He spent about eighteen months in the city of Corinth in A.D. 50–52. During this time he gathered a large congregation of believers (Acts 18:1–8).

Ruins, such as these pillars from what was once the Temple of Apollo, are all that remain of the ancient port city of Corinth.

Eventually he moved on to other fields of service, leaving this church under the direction of other leaders. About five years later he received word about difficulties in the Corinthian church. He wrote 1 Corinthians about A.D. 57 to address these problems.

Most of the believers at Corinth had been converted from a pagan background. They seemed to be struggling to leave their past behind and commit themselves totally to Christian ethical standards. They also had questions or misunderstandings about some of the doctrines of the faith, including marriage, the Lord's Supper, spiritual gifts, and the afterlife. These concerns were also dealt with by the apostle in 1 Corinthians.

Summary of 1 Corinthians

1:1–9. Paul opens his letter with traditional greetings to believers in the church at Corinth (Acts 18:1–11), wishing them grace and peace.

1:10–17. Strife and division marred the Corinthian church. Some claimed to be following Apollos, while others were loyal to Cephas (Peter) and Paul. Perhaps those of the "Christ" party (v. 12) were claiming to be "super Christians."

1:18–31. Paul declares that people who follow their own drives and desires will always end up at odds with one another. The Corinthians should seek God's wisdom to help them achieve unity and peace, because "the foolishness of God is wiser than men" (v. 25).

2:1–5. Paul declares that he preached the gospel with simplicity when he ministered among the Corinthians. The results prove that God's power energized his message.

2:6–16. Human beings cannot discover God's wisdom on their own. But God has given us His written Word that tells us about Him and His nature. The Holy Spirit enables us to interpret His written Word. These two gifts from God lead us to understand "the mind of Christ" (v. 16).

3:1–9. The quarreling of the Corinthians over human leadership shows they are immature in their spiritual development. God, not human leaders, is the source of wisdom and spiritual growth.

3:10–15. Jesus is the foundation on which every believer's life should be built. Anything less than Him and His divine purpose will not stand the test of time (Matt. 7:24–27).

3:16–23. Each believer is a temple of the Holy Spirit, a place where God dwells. Jesus should be the focus of our lives. In Him alone—not human leaders—should we place our trust.

4:1–7. Human leaders in the church should find their joy in serving as "ministers of Christ" (v. 1). The standard by which He will judge their work is whether they are faithful to Him. God has given us different gifts to be used in His service (Rom. 12:3–8). We should exercise these gifts to His glory.

[4:8–13] GLADIATOR APOSTLES. *I [Paul] think that God hath set forth us the apostles last, as it were appointed to death: for we are made a spectacle unto the world, and to angels, and to men (1 Cor. 4:9).*

In this verse Paul compares himself and the other apostles of the New Testament to the gladiators who were "set forth…last" in the Roman arena. These were slaves or criminals who were forced to fight experienced gladiators or wild animals without weapons and who were quickly "appointed to death."

Paul was saying that he and the other apostles of New Testament times had made sacrifices to advance the gospel—and the Corinthian believers had been blessed by their witnessing efforts.

Paul's words were prophetic. Most of the apostles of the early church, including this great missionary to the Gentiles, were eventually martyred for their faith.

4:8–13. Spiritual leaders should not build little empires for themselves. It is their duty to accept suffering, if necessary, in the service of God and His people (1 Pet. 2:18–25).

4:14–21. Paul makes a personal appeal for unity in the church at Corinth. He was a spiritual father to many of them because they had been converted under his ministry. He urges them to follow his example as a faithful disciple of Christ.

5:1–8. In these verses Paul deals with the problem of sexual sin. A believer in the church at Corinth was involved in a sexual relationship with his "father's wife" (v. 1)—probably his stepmother. The apostle criticizes the Corinthian Christians for ignoring the problem and allowing it to continue. He advises the church to exercise discipline by expelling the unrepentant sinner.

5:9–13. Paul makes a distinction between relating to nonbelievers and associating with fellow believers. We are not to judge nonbelievers and isolate ourselves from them. Rather, we are to bear our witness for Jesus before them. But we are called to withdraw from fellow believers who continue in willful sin. Church discipline is designed to reclaim and restore those who have wandered away from the Lord (Matt. 18:15–22).

6:1–11. The apostle expresses disappointment that some of the believers at Corinth are taking one another to civil courts, perhaps to settle financial claims. He urges them to settle their differences through committees of their fellow believers.

6:12–20. Paul declares that sexual relationships outside the bonds of marriage are a perversion of God's plan. Sexual immorality is actually a sin against one's own body because of the Bible's teaching on the one-flesh relationship (Gen. 2:24). Believers should view their bodies as a temple, or residence, for the Holy Spirit of the Lord.

7:1–40. In this chapter Paul answers questions from the Corinthians on the nature and meaning of marriage. The married state is the best option for most people, he declares, but singlehood also has advantages for those who can control their sexual passions. Believers who are married to unbelievers should remain married. But if the unbeliever should leave the relationship, the Christian is released from the bonds of marriage and is free to get married again (vv. 12–16). All believers should live with happiness and contentment in the lifestyle in which God has placed them (vv. 17–24).

8:1–13. In this chapter Paul addresses the problem of meat sacrificed to pagan gods in the city of Corinth. Some believers felt that eating this meat after it had been sacrificed was no problem for worshipers of Christ. But others thought this practice was an act of idolatry. The apostle agreed, in principle, that it was acceptable to eat this meat because all creation belongs to God (v. 6). But he urged believers to abstain from eating

---

[9:1–27] DISCIPLINE AND TRAINING. *Every man that striveth for the mastery is temperate in all things* (1 Cor. 9:25).

This is one of many references in Paul's writings to the Greek games that were similar to our modern Olympics. An athlete who expected to win at these games had to be "temperate in all things," or undergo a strict regimen of discipline and training.

Paul was comparing the Christian life to the discipline required of these Greek athletes. Believers are saved to a life of service in the cause of Christ. Every day should bring us closer to the goal of total commitment to Christ and His work: "That the man of God may be perfect, thoroughly furnished unto all good works" (2 Tim. 3:17).

11:2–16. A young woman from ancient Pompeii, near modern-day Naples, Italy, wears jewelry and a fashionable hairstyle. Paul asked Christian women to dress modestly and to cover their heads during worship.

such meat if the practice offended weaker Christians (vv. 9–11).

9:1–27. This chapter consists of Paul's testimony about his motivation for ministry. He was not just preaching about the principles of making personal sacrifices and living as an example for the Corinthians. He had given up his freedom to do as he pleased and had accommodated himself to the needs of others in order to bring them to the Lord: "I am made all things to all men, that I might by all means save some" (v. 22).

10:1–22. Paul warns the Corinthian believers to stay away from idol worship. He uses the example of the Israelites during the wilderness wandering years to show how easy it is to give in to the temptation to worship pagan gods (Num. 25:1–18).

10:23–11:1. Paul returns to the issue of meat sacrificed to idols (see 1 Cor. 8:1–13). Such meat is neither good nor bad in itself. But our freedom in the Lord should not blind us to the fact that we must avoid certain activities that hinder our Christian witness before others. We bring glory to God when we seek the good of others, not our individual rights.

11:2–16. According to Paul, female believers in Corinth were to cover their heads during public worship and men were to worship with their heads uncovered. This was apparently the accepted custom in Corinthian society. He saw no need for believers to reject these customs if they did not hinder the worship of Christ.

11:17–34. The Corinthians were desecrating the Lord's Supper by turning it into a feast. The rich were eating like gluttons while the poor were getting shoved aside because they had no food to bring. This added to the problem of factions in the church (see 1 Cor. 1:10–17). Paul exhorted the church to stop this feasting and to make the Lord's Supper an occasion for remembering the sacrificial death of Jesus Christ on their behalf (Luke 22:14–20).

12:1–31. In this chapter Paul addresses the issue of spiritual gifts. The more spectacular gifts—such as speaking in tongues, prophecy, and teaching—are not more important than the other, more subdued gifts. All work together to edify and build up the body of Christ. The apostle compares the church to a human body, pointing out that all parts of the body contribute to the healthy operation of the whole.

13:1–13. This is known as the "love chapter" of the Bible. No matter how gifted or talented a person may be, he is nothing but "sounding brass" or "a tinkling cymbal" (v. 1) if he

[13:1–13] SPEECH BASED ON LOVE. *Though I [Paul] speak with the tongues of men and of angels, and have not charity [love, NIV], I am become as sounding brass [a resounding gong, NIV], or a tinkling [clanging, NIV] cymbal (1 Cor. 13:1).*

The Greek word translated as "charity" or "love" in this verse is *agape*—self-giving love that asks for nothing in return. No matter how eloquent in speech a person may be—even if he speaks several languages—this amounts to nothing if his words are not spoken in love.

Pagan worship in Paul's time was often accompanied by strange noises, the clang of gongs and cymbals, and loud blasts on trumpets. Paul declared that the speech of the Corinthian believers was no better than these meaningless rituals unless spoken in love.

does not exercise these gifts in the spirit of love (Rom. 12:9–21).

14:1–40. Some believers in the Corinthian church were elevating the gift of speaking in tongues above all other gifts. Paul declares that prophecy is actually the most important gift because it builds up and edifies the church. Speaking in tongues should be practiced only if an interpreter is present to clarify the meaning of the message to others. Paul's concern was that everything should be done "decently and in order" (v. 40) in a public worship service.

15:1–11. Some Corinthian Christians had doubts about the bodily resurrection. Paul insists on the reality of the resurrection of Jesus because He was seen alive by several different groups after He was raised from the dead (Mark 16:9–11; Luke 24:13–43; John 20:19–29). To Paul, Jesus' resurrection—and its promise of the future resurrection of all believers—is one of the cornerstones of the Christian faith.

15:12–34. The offering of firstfruits was presented by worshipers to the Lord on the first day of the week following Passover. This offering guaranteed the coming harvest (Lev. 23:9–11). This was true of Christ's resurrection as well. His bodily resurrection guaranteed the resurrection of all believers.

15:35–58. Paul insists that believers will experience resurrection with a body that is suitable for its new spiritual environment in the world beyond (1 Thess. 4:13–18). The hope of a future resurrection gives believers the courage to bear up under hardship and suffering for the sake of Christ. In Him we experience victory over sin and death.

16:1–4. Paul encourages the Corinthian Christians to give to an offering he is receiving for the impoverished believers in Jerusalem.

16:5–20. The apostle tells about his plans for a future visit to Corinth. He instructs them to receive Timothy when he visits, and he commends Stephanas and his fellow workers. Paul also sends personal greetings from Aquila and Priscilla (Acts 18:1–3).

16:21–24. Paul closes the letter with a benediction of grace and love to the Corinthian believers.

2 CORINTHIANS

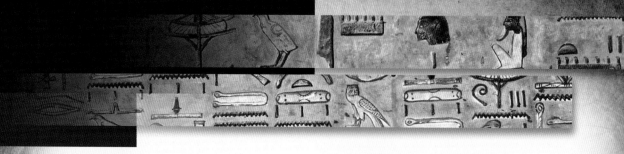

OVERVIEW: Paul gives a vigorous defense of his credentials as an apostle.

Introduction to 2 Corinthians

Paul's second letter to the Corinthians is a follow-up letter to his first Corinthian correspondence (see the introduction to 1 Corinthians on p. 610). Apparently the believers at Corinth had responded appropriately to some of his admonitions in the first letter, and he wrote to express his appreciation for their actions (2 Cor. 2:1–11; chap. 7). He probably wrote this epistle about A.D. 58.

But at several places in this letter, Paul reveals that all was still not well in the Corinthian church. His credentials as a minister were being questioned by some people in Corinth. Paul defended his calling and ministry, assuring the church that his work among them was motivated by love for Christ and his concern for their welfare.

Second Corinthians is one of the most personal and emotional writings of the apostle Paul. He admitted he suffered from some physical malady that he called his "thorn in the flesh" (12:7). He also cataloged the various sufferings he had endured as a traveling missionary in the cause of Christ (11:16–33). Although he was weak and imperfect, he rejoiced that his shortcomings revealed "that the excellency of the power may be of God, and not of us" (4:7).

Summary of 2 Corinthians

1:1–2. Paul begins his letter with greetings of grace and peace to the Corinthian church (Acts 18:1–13).

1:3–11. The apostle uses his experience of suffering to comfort the Corinthian believers. He had also experienced God as the source of comfort in his afflictions. He assures them that God will comfort them in their sufferings for the sake of the gospel.

1:12–24. Paul had promised to make a personal visit to the Corinthian church (1 Cor. 16:3–6). In these verses he explains why he has not yet fulfilled his promise: "To spare you I came not as yet unto Corinth" (v. 23). He apparently wanted to give them time to respond to the instructions he had given them in his previous letter—1 Corinthians.

2:1–4. Paul's love for the Corinthian believers was another factor in his delay of his visit. He hopes the church will respond positively to his previous letter so they can rejoice together when he finally visits them at Corinth.

2:5–11. In his previous letter, the apostle had instructed the church to deal with a man who was living in an immoral sexual relationship (1 Cor. 5). The church had apparently done so, and the man had repented. Now Paul encourages the church to forgive the man and restore him to full Christian fellowship.

[2:12–17] **TRIUMPHANT IN CHRIST.** *Thanks be unto God, which always causeth us to triumph [leads us in triumphal procession, NIV] in Christ* (2 Cor. 2:14).

In this verse Paul compares the victory of Christ over death to a Roman military procession. A victorious general and his army would return from a battle with captives and spoils of war in tow. The entire city of Rome would turn out to welcome the warriors with loud shouts and joyful music.

To Paul, Christ's victory over the grave was more impressive than Roman military triumphs that led to such lavish displays. And more significantly, all believers share in this victory procession of Christ.

2:12–17. To Paul, the favorable response of the Corinthians to his instructions was like a sweet fragrance. He expresses thanks to God for the victorious ministry that He gives to His servants.

3:1–3. Paul's credentials as a minister were apparently being questioned by some people in the Corinthian church. He insists that changed lives as a result of his work were all the endorsement his ministry required.

3:4–18. Paul claims to be a minister of the new covenant of grace, which is far superior to the old covenant of law (Heb. 8:1–10:18). Anyone who questions the apostle's ministry must take its superior nature into account.

4:1–18. Paul compares himself as a human minister to an earthen vessel (v. 7), or a clay pot. But God had filled this common, unworthy container with His treasure, or the glory of the gospel. The sufferings Paul faced in living out his calling were light when compared with the glory God was storing up for him as an eternal reward.

5:1–21. God sent His Son Jesus Christ to reconcile sinners to Himself through His atoning death on the cross. Paul sees his ministry as a part of this divine plan. He serves as an ambassador for Christ, imploring others, "Be ye reconciled to God" (v. 20).

6:1–13. Paul reminds the Corinthians of the suffering he has endured as a minister of the gospel. He wants them to understand that troubles and tribulations are a natural result of serving Christ (1 Pet. 4:12–17).

6:14–18. The apostle makes an eloquent plea for the Corinthian believers to throw off evil and unbelief and to follow the commands of Christ. They are not to be "unequally yoked together with unbelievers" (v. 14).

7:1–16. Titus apparently brought a report to Paul that the Corinthians had responded favorably to his words of rebuke and instruction in his previous letter—1 Corinthians. Paul expresses his joy at the news of their repentance.

8:1–9:15. In these two chapters, Paul discusses in detail the offering he had mentioned in his previous letter (1 Cor. 16:1–4). This was an offering he was taking among the churches of the province of Macedonia to assist the Christians in Jerusalem who were suffering from a famine. To motivate the

[6:14–18] **GIVE UP THE PAST.** *Be ye [Corinthian believers] not unequally yoked together with unbelievers* (2 Cor. 6:14).

Paul was probably alluding in this verse to a familiar prohibition in the Mosaic Law: "Thou shalt not plow with an ox and an ass [donkey] together" (Deut. 22:10).

The reason for this law was that a donkey was an unclean animal, while the ox was among the clean animals that Jews were permitted to eat. What's more, they would have been out of step with each other in their pull against the plow.

Paul's point is that the believers of Corinth should leave the patterns and habits of their old life of unbelief behind. They should live in accordance with their new status as members of God's family.

Corinthian believers to give to this fund, Paul reminds them of Jesus' example of giving His life unselfishly on their behalf (Phil. 2:1–11). He also set before them the method by which they should give: "Every man according as he purposeth in his heart, so let him give; not grudgingly, or of necessity: for God loveth a cheerful giver" (9:7).

10:1–11. Apparently, a rebellious element in the Corinthian church was critical of Paul and resistant to his authority. In these verses Paul answers their charge that he is a weak and timid leader. He assures them that his leadership approach is consistent, whether addressing them by letter or speaking to them face-to-face.

10:12–18. Paul refuses to buy into the game of his opponents in Corinth. They were claiming to be superior to Paul in their leadership ability. Rather than arguing the point, Paul declares that God's assessment is the only thing that matters.

[11:16–33] PAUL'S ESCAPE IN A BASKET. *Through a window in a basket was I [Paul] let down by the wall* (2 Cor. 11:33).

The event to which Paul refers in this verse is reported in the book of Acts (9:22–25). Paul traveled to the city of Damascus to persecute Christians. But after his dramatic conversion, he witnessed for Christ among the Jews of the city. Other believers had to help him escape over the city wall when the Jews determined to kill him.

The window out of which Paul escaped may have been in a house that was built into or on top of the defensive wall of Damascus. Such "wall houses" were common in some cities. This was the type of house in which Rahab the prostitute lived. She helped several Israelite spies escape over the city wall from the window in her house in Jericho (Josh. 2:15).

11:1–6. Paul warns against deceitful teachers who would lead the Corinthian believers to follow them rather than point the church to Christ.

11:7–15. Paul had supported himself while preaching the gospel in the Corinthian church (Acts 18:1–3). He expresses his frustration that his enemies have criticized him even for this. He charges these critics with trying to undermine his leadership by using false and deceitful tactics.

11:16–33. In these verses the apostle lists the various troubles he has suffered as a minister of the gospel. This litany of tribulations proves that he is a true follower of Christ. The same cannot be said of those who are questioning his leadership.

12:1–10. This passage contains Paul's famous "thorn in the flesh" statement (v. 7). This disability, possibly an eye disease, helped the apostle to come to the realization that God's power is made perfect in human weakness. In their human frailties, servants of the Lord must depend on His never-failing strength.

12:11–21. Paul has spoken boldly to the Corinthians to build them up in their faith. He assures them that he is not interested in their money or possessions. He has poured himself out gladly on their behalf.

13:1–10. The apostle promises the Corinthian Christians that he will visit them soon. He warns them that he will deal forthrightly with any who are in willful rebellion against the Lord.

13:11–14. Paul closes his letter with a beautiful benediction, praying that God's love and grace will abide with the Corinthian believers.

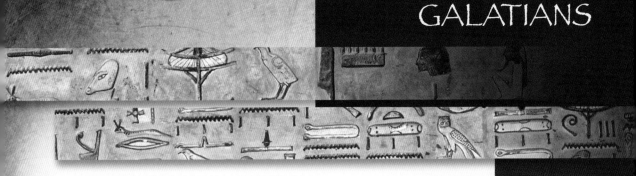

OVERVIEW: Jesus sets believers free from bondage to the law by granting them salvation by grace through faith.

Introduction to Galatians

Paul's epistle to the Galatians was not written to a specific church but to the *"churches of Galatia"* (1:2, emphasis added). The apostle visited several cities of this region during his first missionary journey about A.D. 47, founding several churches. He wrote this letter to these young churches about two years later, in A.D. 49. Of Paul's thirteen letters that are preserved in the New Testament, Galatians was probably the first to be written.

After the Galatian churches had gotten off to such a good start, the apostle was saddened to learn "that ye are so soon removed from...the grace of Christ unto another gospel" (1:6). A group of false teachers known as the Judaizers had won them over to the view that faith in the grace of Christ was not sufficient for salvation. They taught that it was also necessary to obey the Jewish law, which involved submitting to circumcision and observing Jewish holy days.

Paul condemned these false teachers and informed the Galatians that they were foolish indeed if they returned to the bondage of the law from which the grace of Christ had set them free (3:1; 5:1).

Summary of Galatians

1:1–5. Paul opens his letter to the Galatian Christians with wishes for grace and peace in the name of Jesus Christ.

1:6–10. The apostle expresses his disappointment that the Galatians have turned away from the true gospel he has preached to them; they are now following a false gospel.

1:11–24. Apparently the Judaizers at Galatia were claiming that Paul had no authority to preach the gospel among them. In response to this charge, Paul reviews the facts about his conversion and call from God to serve as an apostle (Acts 9:1–20).

[1:11–24] "UP" TO JERUSALEM. *After three years I [Paul] went up to Jerusalem to see Peter* (Gal. 1:18).

Paul indicates in the previous verse that he was in Damascus, Syria (Gal. 1:17), when he traveled to Jerusalem to see Peter.

Damascus was north of Jerusalem. Why didn't Paul say that he went "down" to the city to see Peter? To most people today, "up" refers to northern locations and "down" to southern sites.

Jerusalem was built on high hills in a mountainous territory about 2,500 feet above sea level. To the Jews, whatever the direction from which they approached Jerusalem, it was always "up" (Luke 2:42).

2:1–10. At first, early leaders of the church, such as Peter, James, and John, were hesitant to accept Paul because he had been a persecutor of the church. But they eventually

1:11–24. Jerusalem, in a painting from 1825. Located on a ridge in the hills, Jerusalem was often described as "up." People would say they were going "up" to Jerusalem. That's because no matter what direction they came from, they always had to climb to reach the city.

recognized his call from God and his apostleship (Acts 9:26–30).

2:11–14. Paul tells the Galatians how he rebuked Peter and Barnabas because they were led astray by a group of zealous Jews in the church at Antioch. Apparently Peter and Barnabas gave in to their demands that Gentiles had to be circumcised and keep the Jewish law before they could become Christians. On this issue, Paul declares, he "withstood him [Peter] to the face" (v. 11).

2:15–21. Paul declares that repentance and faith alone justify a person in God's sight. Nothing else is to be added to these basic requirements for salvation (Rom. 3:28).

3:1–4:31. In these two chapters, Paul contrasts the freedom that believers experience in Christ with the restrictions of the Jewish law. Anyone who would exchange the grace of Jesus Christ for keeping the Jewish law, as the Galatians were tempted to do, was foolish indeed. The Judaizers have been insisting on making Gentiles sons of Abraham through the rite of circumcision. But Paul declares that Gentile Christians are already Abraham's sons because they share the faith that he demonstrated (3:7, 29).

5:1–15. Freedom in Christ is not a license to live as one pleases. We are saved to a life of love and service toward others. Believers are compelled by God's grace to follow only one law—the royal law of love: "All the law is fulfilled in one word...Thou shalt love thy neighbour as thyself" (v. 14).

5:16–6:10. In these verses Paul gives some specific examples of behavior that should characterize the believer: "love, joy, peace, long-suffering, gentleness, goodness, faith, meekness, temperance" (5:22–23). These attitudes and characteristics are "the fruit of the Spirit" (5:22) in the believer's life—a natural result of God's grace and love in the human heart. Following a list of do's and don'ts in the law is a poor substitute for such a radiant pattern of life.

6:11–18. Paul closes his letter to the Galatians by reminding them that Jesus and His death on the cross are the central focus of the salvation story—not whether a person should be circumcised: "For in Christ Jesus neither circumcision availeth any thing, nor uncircumcision, but a new creature" (v. 15).

> **[6:11–18] MARKS OF PERSECUTION.** *I [Paul] bear in my body the marks of the Lord Jesus* (Gal. 6:17).
>
> In Paul's time slaves were branded with distinctive marks to show that they belonged to their masters, much as cattle are branded in modern times. Paul declared that his body bore marks from the persecution he had endured in Christ's service. These showed that he belonged to the Lord Jesus.
>
> The apostle named some of these marks of persecution in 2 Corinthians 11:24–25: "Five times received I forty stripes save one. Thrice was I beaten with rods, once was I stoned."

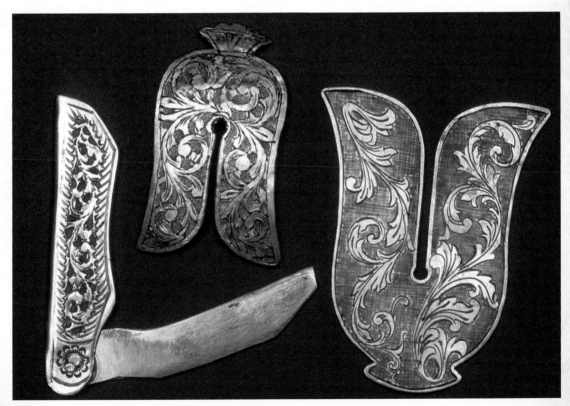

2:11–14. Circumcision tools include a sharp knife and a knife guide. Excessive foreskin is pulled through the guide slit and then cut off. Some Jewish Christians insisted that non-Jewish Christians had to observe this and other Jewish traditions, such as rules about kosher food. Paul strongly objected.

EPHESIANS

OVERVIEW: All who belong to Christ are bound together as one in His love and in His church.

Introduction to Ephesians

Ephesians, along with Philippians, Colossians, and Philemon, was written by the apostle Paul while he was in prison. Most scholars believe he wrote Ephesians near the end of his life, about A.D. 62, while he was under house arrest in Rome (Acts 28:16, 30).

Paul founded the church at Ephesus and spent three years among the believers in this city (Acts 19:1–41)—longer than he stayed at any other place during his ministry. He developed a close relationship with the Ephesian believers. The leaders of this church traveled to Miletus to greet him at the end of his third missionary journey. They sent the apostle away with sadness when they learned that he was determined to return to Jerusalem and face the dangers that awaited him there (Acts 20:17–38).

In this epistle Paul describes the exalted Christ, who is Lord of the church, the world, and the entire created order. As the living Lord, He is completing through His body—the church—what He began during His days on earth. Those who belong to Christ, both Jews and Gentiles, are united as one body in His church to serve as agents of reconciliation to a lost world.

Summary of Ephesians

1:1–2. Paul opens his letter by referring to the Ephesian Christians as "saints" (v. 1). This word as used in the New Testament means those who have been set aside for God's exclusive use (Rom. 1:7; Phil. 1:1).

1:3–14. God's redemptive plan for humankind from the beginning involved sending His Son to die for our sins. Paul marvels at such love and grace expressed in the life and sacrificial death of Jesus Christ.

1:15–23. The apostle expresses his thanks for these Ephesian Christians. He wants them to grow in their understanding of the riches of Christ's grace.

2:1–10. Paul reminds the Ephesian believers of the wonder of their salvation in Christ. They were dead in their "trespasses and sins" (v. 1), but God redeemed them and filled their lives with joy. This came about solely through God's grace, not because of any goodness or good works on their part: "By grace are ye saved through faith; and that not of yourselves: it is the gift of God: not of works, lest any man should boast" (vv. 8–9; see Rom. 3:21–31).

2:11–22. Jesus is the great equalizer who has broken down the barriers between different classes and ethnic groups in society (Rom. 1:14–16). All who belong to Him are bound together as one in His love and in His church.

3:1–13. Paul declares that in times past, God's promises have been interpreted as applying mainly to the Jewish people. But this

[1:3–14] SEALED BY THE SPIRIT. *After that ye [Ephesian Christians] believed, ye were sealed with that holy Spirit of promise* (Eph. 1:13).

Paul refers in this verse to the distinct mark of identification that was placed on a letter, contract, or other legal document in Bible times. This seal proved the document's authenticity.

Likewise, believers are sealed or authenticated by the Holy Spirit after their conversion. His mark in our lives results in holy and righteous living. God also gives us His spirit as His pledge of our future inheritance of eternal life (2 Cor. 1:22).

changed with the coming of Christ and His offer of salvation to the Gentiles, as well (Rom. 3:28–29). Paul is pleased that he was selected to help inaugurate this new phase of world redemption: "Unto me...is this grace given, that I should preach among the Gentiles the unsearchable riches of Christ" (v. 8).

3:14–21. Again, Paul prays for the Ephesian Christians—this time that they might be strengthened in their faith and in their commitment to Christ.

4:1–6. Paul encourages the Ephesian believers to express through their actions the underlying unity that exists in the body of Christ (1 Cor. 1:10). This calls for patience and humility on the part of all members of the body.

4:7–16. God in His wisdom has given many different gifts to the people in His church. They exercise their gifts as apostles, prophets, evangelists, pastors, and teachers. All these gifts are needed if the church is to function properly (Rom. 12:3–8).

4:17–5:20. This passage is known as the practical section of Ephesians because it deals with the way believers should live. Paul calls on the Ephesians to "put on the new man" (4:24) and to copy the character of God in their daily behavior.

5:21–6:9. Relationships should also reflect the lordship of Christ. Paul has advice on godly living for wives (5:22–24), husbands (5:25–33), children (6:1–3), fathers (6:4), servants (6:5–8), and masters (6:9).

6:10–20. Paul recognizes that living a godly life in a godless world is not an easy task. He urges the Ephesians to put on their spiritual battle gear and to get ready to "stand against the wiles of the devil" (v. 11).

6:21–24. Paul closes his letter with wishes of grace and peace for the Ephesian believers.

[6:10–20] SPIRITUAL BATTLE GEAR. *Take unto you [Christian believers] the whole armour of God, that ye may be able to withstand in the evil day* (Eph. 6:15).

Paul told the Ephesian believers they needed to equip themselves for spiritual battle, just as the Roman soldiers of his day put on their battle gear to get ready for war.

The apostle compared the breastplate of righteousness to the armor that protected a soldier's upper body. The hobnail shoes that soldiers wore symbolized the believer's sure footing in the gospel. Believers should also carry with them into battle the "shield of faith," the "helmet of salvation," and the "sword of the Spirit, which is the word of God" (Eph. 6:16–17).

These items will assure victory in the spiritual battles that believers face in the world.

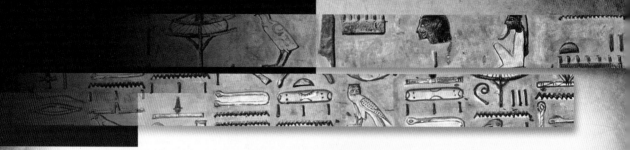

PHILIPPIANS

OVERVIEW: A joyful letter from prison in which Paul thanks God for the fellowship and support of the Christians at Philippi.

Introduction to Philippians

Paul's letter to the Philippians is one of his four "prison epistles" (see the introduction to Ephesians on p. 622). He sent it to the church at Philippi while he was being held a prisoner in Rome about A.D. 62 or 63.

Unlike most of Paul's other letters, this epistle was not written specifically to deal with a church problem, to warn against false teachers, or to correct the behavior of the recipients. He does make a passing reference to dangers from false teachers (3:1–11) and urges two church members to settle their differences (4:2–9). But Philippians is best characterized as a "friendship letter." Paul expressed his warm thoughts toward the Philippian believers and assured them of his appreciation for their support

Greece's seaside city of Philippi takes its name from the father of Alexander the Great: Philip II of Macedonia. His image is preserved in stone and on a gold coin (at right).

624

of his ministry (1:3–11; 4:10–23).

The apostle founded the church at Philippi about A.D. 52, at the beginning of his second missionary journey. A businesswoman named Lydia became one of his first converts in this city (Acts 16:13–15). The keeper of the prison from which Paul and Silas were delivered at Philippi also came to faith in Christ, along with the members of his household (Acts 16:25–34).

Summary of Philippians

1:1–2. Paul begins his letter with greetings from himself and his helper, Timothy (Acts 16:1–3), to the church at Philippi (Acts 16:12–40).

1:3–11. Paul prays a beautiful prayer of thanksgiving for the Philippian believers. He remembers them with joy because of their kindness to him and their faithful support of the gospel.

1:12–26. Although Paul is in prison, he wants the Philippian Christians to realize that God has brought something good out of

> **[2:12–30] POURED OUT FOR THE LORD.** *If I [Paul] be offered upon the sacrifice and service of your [Philippian believers'] faith, I joy, and rejoice with you all* (Phil. 2:17).
>
> The NIV translates this verse, "Even if I am being poured out like a drink offering on the sacrifice and service coming from your faith." Paul was comparing himself and his life to a sacrifice known as the drink offering.
>
> In this ceremony the worshiper poured wine on top of the animal that had been sacrificed as a burnt offering. The wine was vaporized as steam when it hit the hot carcass. This symbolized the rising of the offering to God (Exod. 29:38–41; Hosea 9:4).
>
> Paul viewed his life as a drink offering. He rejoiced that it was being poured out in sacrifical service on behalf of the Philippians and other early believers.

this experience (Rom. 8:28). It has actually brought greater opportunity for the proclamation of the gospel and the growth of new believers. The apostle is content in this situation, whether he lives or dies: "To me to live is Christ, and to die is gain" (v. 21).

1:27–30. Paul encourages the believers at Philippi to remain loyal to Christ, even if they should be persecuted for their faith.

2:1–11. Paul uses the example of Christ to motivate the Philippians to live holy and righteous lives in the midst of a selfish world. Verses 6–11 are probably a hymn or confession of faith on the nature of Jesus used in worship services by early believers. Christ was God's Son—fully divine—but He came to earth in the form of a man—fully human—to bring salvation and eternal life to all who believe.

2:12–30. The Philippian believers are encouraged to continue the good work they have started. To help them, Paul promises to send two of his coworkers—Timothy and Epaphroditus.

3:1–11. Paul warns against the corrupting influence of the Judaizers. This group was teaching that Gentile converts must be circumcised and keep the Jewish law before they could become Christians. Paul declares that he was once a strict observer of all Jewish traditions, but he has learned that true righteousness comes only through faith in Jesus Christ.

3:12–4:1. Paul urges his fellow Christians at Philippi to "stand fast in the Lord" (4:1). He points to himself as the example they should follow, since he continues to "press toward the mark for the prize of the high calling of God in Christ Jesus" (3:14).

4:2–9. Apparently there was some problem with divisions in the church at Philippi (1 Cor. 1:11–13). Paul makes a personal appeal for unity to those who are causing trouble and urges the entire church to seek the guidance and counsel of the Lord.

4:10–23. Paul concludes by thanking his Christian brothers and sisters at Philippi for their generous support of him and his ministry. Their gifts had apparently been sent through Epaphroditus while the apostle was in prison (v. 18).

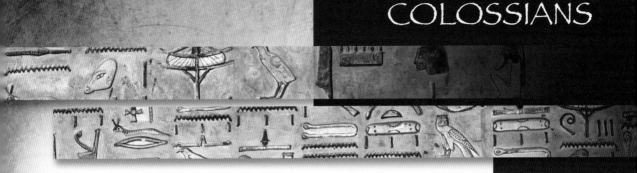

OVERVIEW: The salvation of believers is perfect and complete in Jesus Christ.

Introduction to Colossians

As one of Paul's four "prison epistles" (see the introduction to Ephesians on p. 622), Colossians was written to a church that the apostle had never visited. Epaphras, one of Paul's missionary associates, may have founded the church (1:7–8). He brought word to Paul about false teachers who had infiltrated the church at Colosse. To deal with this situation, the apostle sent this letter about A.D. 62 or 63, while he was imprisoned at Rome.

These false teachers were adding to the simple gospel that Paul and others had preached by claiming it was necessary to observe certain Jewish rules and regulations (2:16) and to assign a prominent role to angels in their worship (2:18). Paul corrected this misunderstanding by showing that Christ is the all-inclusive and all-sufficient Savior. He alone is the basis of our hope for salvation and eternal life.

Summary of Colossians

1:1–14. Paul opens his letter to the believers at Colosse with a prayer of thanksgiving for the faith and love of these brothers and sisters in the Lord. Paul had never visited this church, but he apparently knew about them through his missionary associate Epaphras (Philem. 23), who had ministered among them (v. 7).

1:15–23. The Colossian believers were being led astray by false teachers, who were challenging the divinity and supremacy of Jesus Christ. The apostle corrects this error by declaring that Jesus is the divine Son of God, the head of the church, and the one in whom God the Father is fully revealed.

1:24–29. Through the church as His body, Jesus is still at work in the world. Paul is pleased to be a minister who labors among the churches as a representative of the living Christ (2 Cor. 5:20).

2:1–23. Paul reminds the Colossian believers of the new life they have experienced as a result of their acceptance of Christ. He encourages them to continue their daily walk in obedience to His commands and to stay anchored to the truth in their doctrinal beliefs. They didn't need some mystical experience to perfect their salvation, as the false teachers were

[2:1–23] SALVATION AND CIRCUMCISION. *In whom [Jesus] also ye [Colossian believers] are circumcised with the circumcision made without hands* (Col. 2:11).

Circumcision—the removal of the foreskin from the male sex organ—was a mark of the covenant between God and His people, the Israelites (Rom. 4:11).

In this verse Paul compares the death of Christ on the cross to this ritual. This "circumcision" of Jesus was the event that provided for the salvation of believers. We are also "circumcised" when we die to our sins by committing ourselves to Him as our Lord and Savior.

claiming. Their deliverance from sin was "complete in him [Christ]" (v. 10).

3:1–4:6. In these verses Paul contrasts the old way of life with the new patterns of behavior that should characterize a person who has come to know Christ as Lord and Savior. The apostle has practical advice on Christian living for wives (3:18), husbands (3:19), children (3:20), fathers (3:21), servants (3:22), and masters (4:1).

4:7–9. Paul mentions his coworker Tychicus (v. 7), who may have delivered this letter to the Colossian Christians. Tychicus may have been accompanied by the runaway slave Onesimus (v. 9; see Philem. 10).

4:10–18. Paul closes his letter by sending greetings from several of his missionary associates and coworkers.

2:1–23. A Roman statue of a man strikes the pose of a teacher addressing his students. Paul warned Christians in Colosse to watch out for false teachers spreading a distorted gospel.

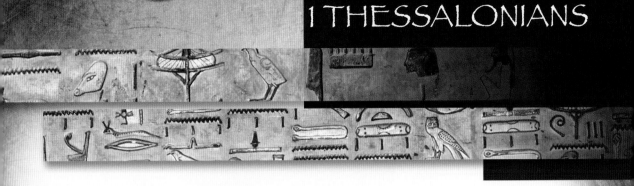

OVERVIEW: Answers to questions about the end times and the second coming of the Lord.

Introduction to 1 Thessalonians

Thessalonica was the capital city of the Roman province of Macedonia. Paul and his missionary associates witnessed in this city during his second missionary journey. Opposition from a group of fanatical Jews drove them out of Thessalonica after a short stay, but not before several Gentiles came to faith in Jesus Christ (Acts 17:1–9). These faithful few became the nucleus of the church to which the apostle wrote this letter.

First Thessalonians is one of Paul's earliest epistles, probably written about A.D. 51 or 52, while he was working at Corinth. Paul mentioned Silas (Silvanus) and Timothy (Timotheus) in the greeting of the letter (1:1). This suggests that these two missionary associates worked with Paul to encourage and strengthen this young congregation.

The theme of this epistle is the second coming of Christ. Every chapter contains some reference to this important future event (1:10; 2:19; 3:13; 4:13–18; 5:1–11, 23).

Summary of 1 Thessalonians

1:1–10. Paul commends the believers at Thessalonica (Acts 17:1, 11–13) for their faith and love, as well as their testimony to the power of the gospel. Because of Paul's work among them, they had "turned to God from idols to serve the living and true God" (v. 9).

2:1–16. Paul reminds these fellow believers of the time he had spent among them proclaiming the gospel. He had spoken the truth about Christ with all sincerity, not appealing to their pride or trying to win their favor with flattering words.

2:17–20. Paul has not forgotten these new believers, although he has not seen them for a while. He considers them his "glory and joy" (v. 20).

3:1–13. On a previous occasion while visiting Athens (Acts 17:13–15), Paul had sent his coworker Timothy to check on the new converts at Thessalonica. Timothy brought the apostle a good report about their growth in the Lord. Paul is grateful for this good news, and he offers a prayer of thanksgiving for the Thessalonian Christians.

[5:1–11] PROTECTED BY FAITH AND LOVE. *Let us…be sober [self-controlled, NIV], putting on the breastplate of faith and love* (1 Thess. 5:8).

In his letter to the Ephesian Christians, Paul instructed them to put on the "breastplate of righteousness" (see the note "Spiritual Battle Gear" on p. 623). Here he exhorts the Thessalonian believers to put on the "breastplate of faith and love."

The breastplate, or body armor, of a Roman soldier protected the vital organs of the upper body. Likewise, believers are protected from giving in to temptation when we focus on His love for us and exercise faith in His promises.

4:1–12. The apostle reminds his fellow believers of the behavior expected of those who belong to Christ. They are to stay sexually pure, to practice justice, to love one another, and to bear their witness for Christ in a quiet and humble way.

4:13–18. In these verses Paul addresses a question that had been raised by some of the Thessalonian Christians. Apparently some of them expected Jesus to return during their lifetime. What would happen to those believers who had not lived to experience this great event? The apostle assured them that "the dead in Christ shall rise first: Then we which are alive and remain shall be caught up together with them in the clouds, to meet the Lord in the air" (vv. 16–17).

5:1–11. Paul goes on to address the question of when the Lord will return. No one knows. But we can be sure He will return suddenly—and when we least expect it. We should be ready (Matt. 24:42–51).

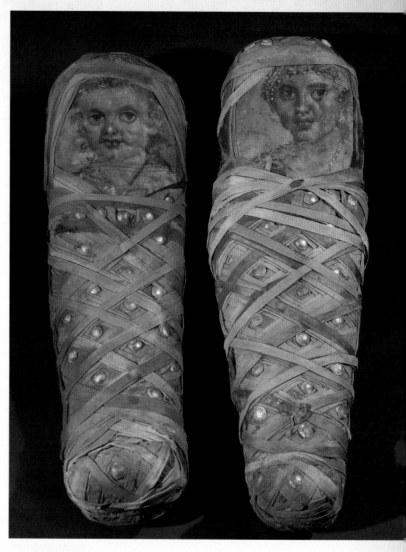

4:13–18. Funeral portraits of children who died in about A.D. 50. That's about the time Paul wrote to Christians in Thessalonica, assuring them that believers who die before Jesus returns are already with their Savior and that their bodies will be raised at the Second Coming.

5:12–24. With a series of short exhortations, Paul tells the Thessalonian believers how they should be living while waiting for the Lord's return.

5:25–28. Paul closes his letter by asking for the grace of the Lord to fill their lives and requesting that they continue to pray for him and his coworkers.

OVERVIEW: Believers should not be waiting in idleness for the Lord's second coming.

Introduction to 2 Thessalonians

This short letter of only three chapters is closely related to Paul's first letter to the believers at Thessalonica (see the introduction to 1 Thessalonians on p. 629). It was probably written within a few months of the first letter. Thus, the date for 2 Thessalonians is about A.D. 51 or 52, and the apostle wrote it while he was ministering among the believers in Corinth.

Second Thessalonians is a letter of encouragement as well as rebuke. Paul encouraged the believers in this church to remain faithful to the Lord in the midst of the persecution they were experiencing. He also exhorted those who were idly waiting for the return of the Lord to get back to work.

This epistle teaches us that idle speculation about the return of the Lord accomplishes nothing. We should be busy about His work while we wait for His return.

Summary of 2 Thessalonians

1:1–2. Paul opens his second letter to the Christians at Thessalonica (Acts 17:1, 11–13) with greetings from himself as well as Silas ("Silvanus," v. 1) and Timothy.

1:3–12. Paul thanks God that the Thessalonian Christians are continuing to grow and mature in their faith. This growth is helping them to endure the persecution they are experiencing. He reminds them that the roles of persecutor and persecuted will one day be reversed. In the final judgment, believers who have been persecuted in this life will be rewarded by the Lord with eternal life. But persecuting unbelievers will be punished "with everlasting destruction from the presence of the Lord" (v. 9).

2:1–2. Apparently the Thessalonians had been told by false teachers that the day of the Lord or the second coming of Christ had already occurred.

2:3–12. Paul corrects this falsehood. He assures the believers at Thessalonica that the second coming of Christ has not yet happened. This will not occur until after the appearance of "that man of sin...the son of perdition" (v. 3). Paul was referring to the Antichrist.

2:13–15. Paul exhorts the Thessalonians to "stand fast" (v. 15) and not be led astray by false teachings about the end times and their eternal inheritance. Their salvation has been purchased by Jesus Christ and sealed by the Holy Spirit because of their belief of the truth.

2:16–17. In a beautiful benediction, Paul prays that these believers will be strengthened in their faith and belief.

3:1–5. Paul urges the Thessalonian believers to pray for him in his work of planting and nurturing the gospel.

3:6–15. Jesus returns to earth. To believers in Thessalonica who were obsessed with the Second Coming—some of whom had quit their jobs—Paul told them to get on with their lives.

3:6–15. Some of the Thessalonian Christians had apparently quit working to wait for the second coming of Christ. They may have been expecting others to support them as they waited for the Lord's return. Paul criticized such idleness and exhorted these people to get back to work. Christians are to share the gospel message with diligence until Jesus returns (Acts 1:8–11).

3:16–18. Paul closes with wishes of grace and peace for the believers at Thessalonica.

[3:16–18] PAUL'S OWN HANDWRITING. *The salutation of Paul with mine own hand, which is the token in every epistle: so I write (2 Thess. 3:17).*

In Bible times many people wrote letters by dictating them to a secretary—a professional amanuensis, or scribe. This apparently was done occasionally by Paul, the most prolific letter writer of the New Testament (see introduction to the epistles of Paul on p. 604).

To prove to the recipients of 2 Thessalonians that this letter was from him—even though it had been written by someone else—Paul wrote the final words in his own handwriting. He also closed 1 Corinthians (16:21) and Colossians (4:18) in the same way.

In Paul's letter to the Romans, his secretary identified himself and included his own greeting to the Roman Christians: "I Tertius, who wrote this epistle, salute you in the Lord" (Rom. 16:22).

1 TIMOTHY

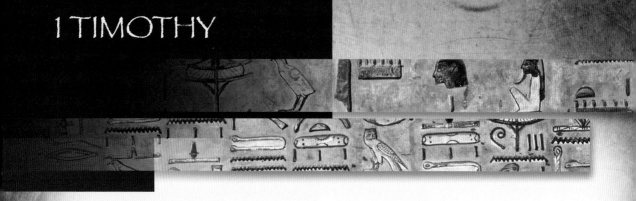

OVERVIEW: A vigorous call for Timothy to be faithful to his calling as a church leader and to oppose false teachings in the church.

Introduction to 1 Timothy

First Timothy is one of three of Paul's letters classified as pastoral epistles (along with 2 Timothy and Titus). All three were written to individual church leaders rather than churches. They deal with issues of church leadership—thus the term "pastoral epistles." They show the apostle's concern for effective church organization and administration.

Paul met Timothy in the city of Lystra during his second missionary journey (Acts 16:1–3). Timothy may have been converted under Paul's ministry, since the apostle referred to him in later years as his "beloved son" (1 Cor. 4:17) and his "son in the faith" (1 Tim. 1:2). Timothy became one of Paul's missionary associates, accompanying him on his second and third missionary journeys (Acts 16:3–4; 19:22).

After establishing a church in the city of Ephesus and ministering there for about three years (Acts 20:31), Paul left Timothy in charge and moved on to other locations to preach the gospel and plant churches. He apparently wrote this letter to Timothy while Timothy was still working with the Ephesian church (1 Tim. 1:3). It was written about A.D. 63 or 64, near the end of Paul's life.

Timothy was a young and inexperienced church leader. Paul counseled him to do his job and act responsibly in spite of his immaturity ("Let no man despise thy youth," 4:12) and to deal forcefully with false teachers who were stirring up trouble in the church.

Summary of 1 Timothy

1:1–2. Paul opens this letter to Timothy (1 Cor. 4:17) by addressing him as his "own son in the faith" (v. 2).

1:3–11. Paul had left Timothy in the church at Ephesus while he moved on to preach the gospel at other places. The apostle urges Timothy to stay at Ephesus so he can oppose false teachings that are beginning to appear in the church.

1:12–20. Paul had once been a persecutor of the church (Acts 9:1–2). He expresses his amazement to Timothy that God is now using him to spread the gospel.

2:1–8. Prayer is one of the most important functions of the church. Prayers should be offered for kings and others in authority as well as a church's own members.

2:9–15. Paul reminds Timothy that a specific code of conduct is expected of female believers in the church.

3:1–7. Those believers who serve as bishops or elders in the church must meet certain qualifications (Titus 1:5–9).

3:8–13. High standards are also established for those who would serve as deacons.

3:14–16. Paul expresses his hope that he will soon be able to visit Timothy at Ephesus.

1:3–11. *Christians were once baptized in this cross-shaped pool located in what was once a church in Ephesus. Timothy was a pastor in Ephesus when Paul wrote him the letter now known as 1 Timothy.*

4:1–16. With strong words, Paul condemns those in the church at Ephesus who are teaching false doctrine. He urges Timothy to stand firmly against these false teachings and to exercise discipline against the troublemakers. Although Timothy is young and inexperienced, he should exercise the authority that has been delegated to him by the Lord and officials of the church.

[5:1–16] ABOVE-AND-BEYOND HOSPITALITY. *If she [a widow] have lodged strangers, if she have washed the saints' feet* (1 Tim. 5:10).

In this verse Paul gave Timothy some criteria by which he could determine if a widow in the church was a sacrificial servant of the Lord who should receive financial assistance from her fellow believers.

One mark of her character was that she had shown hospitality to strangers. Throughout the New Testament the grace of welcoming strangers into one's home is commended (Rom. 12:13; 1 Pet. 4:9).

Another thing that Timothy should look for is whether a widow had gone beyond what was expected in the hosting of strangers. Washing a guest's feet was considered the job of a lowly slave.

5:1–16. The early church offered financial support to widows, many of whom were destitute (Acts 6:1–7). Paul instructs Timothy on how to conduct this ministry in the church at Ephesus. Older widows are more likely to need this assistance. The families of some widows can help their own. The church should make sure its resources go to those in dire need.

5:17–25. Elders, or pastors, should be selected by the church with great care. Once placed in positions of leadership, they should be treated with respect and compensated for their work.

6:1–10. Paul offers advice for masters and slaves and the rich and the poor. He warns against the blind pursuit of riches (Eccles. 2:8–11) and encourages believers to be content with what they have: "Godliness with contentment is great gain" (v. 6).

6:11–21. Paul closes this letter to Timothy with a charge to be faithful to his calling and to continue to oppose false teachings in the church.

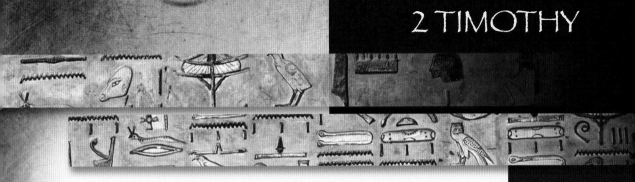

OVERVIEW: A letter of love and affection to Paul's son in the ministry.

Introduction to 2 Timothy

Paul wrote this second letter to his young missionary associate Timothy in A.D. 66—about two years after he wrote 1 Timothy (see the introduction to 1 Timothy on p. 634).

Imprisoned for the second time in Rome, Paul expected to be executed at any time. He wrote to encourage Timothy to stand firm in his commitment to Christ in the midst of troubling times for the church.

This letter is classified as one of Paul's pastoral epistles (see the introduction to 1 Timothy on p. 634). But it is also one of his most personal letters. He expressed deep affection for Timothy and looked back with no regrets over his life that had been poured out for Christ.

Summary of 2 Timothy

1:1–7. Paul opens this letter by expressing deep love for Timothy, whom he calls "my dearly beloved son" (v. 2; see 1 Cor. 4:17). The apostle also remembers Timothy in his prayers and has a great desire to see his young coworker.

1:8–18. Although Paul is imprisoned in Rome, he has no regrets about the course his life has taken. He reflects on his years as a witness for Christ and rejoices in the assurance of His presence in all of life's circumstances: "I know whom I have believed, and am persuaded that he is able to keep that which I have committed unto him against that day" (v. 12).

2:1–26. Paul knew better than anyone that staying the course as a Christian minister requires determination, prayer, and commitment to holiness and righteousness in one's daily walk. He counsels Timothy to "flee...

[2:1–26] HARDSHIP AND SACRIFICE. *Thou [Timothy] therefore endure hardness [hardship, NIV], as a good soldier of Jesus Christ. No man that warreth entangleth himself with the affairs of this life; that he may please him who hath chosen him to be a soldier [his commanding officer, NIV]* (2 Tim. 2:3–4).

Paul continues his imagery from the Roman military (see the notes "Spiritual Battle Gear" on p. 623 and "Protected by Faith and Love" on p. 629) by referring to the discipline and singleness of purpose required of a Roman soldier.

The ordinary foot soldier in the Roman military was loaded down with his armor and weapons, tools, and rations that would last him for several days. He was sworn through strict discipline and training to obey the orders of his commanding officer without question.

Paul was telling Timothy that the Christian life—while it has its rewards—is not an easy path. It requires discipline and sacrifice.

1:8–18. As his execution approached, Paul wrote Timothy one last letter. Paul wrote from this Roman prison, if an ancient tradition is correct. That tradition says Paul and Peter were both held in the dungeon beneath Mamertinum Prison.

youthful lusts" and to "follow righteousness, faith, charity, peace" (v. 22).

3:1–13. According to Paul, perilous times are ahead for the church. As the time for Jesus' return draws near, evil will grow stronger, even within the fellowship of the church.

3:14–17. In the midst of such challenging times, Timothy is to stick to the truths revealed in God's written Word. It is a trustworthy and reliable guide for believers (Ps. 119:105).

4:1–8. Paul expects to be executed in Rome at any time. But he can look back over his life with the assurance that he has been faithful to his divine calling: "I have fought a good fight, I have finished my course, I have kept the faith" (v. 7).

4:9–22. Paul closes his second letter to Timothy by mentioning several coworkers who have supported him to the very end, as well as some who have let him down. He sends greetings to "Prisca [Priscilla] and Aquila, and the household of Onesiphorus" (v. 19).

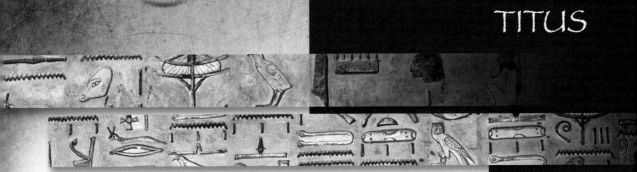

OVERVIEW: Paul gives instructions for the way that church leaders, including Titus, should conduct themselves.

Introduction to Titus

Like the epistles of 1 and 2 Timothy, Titus was also written to a person, not a church, and it is also known as one of the apostle Paul's pastoral epistles (see the introduction to 1 Timothy on p. 634).

Paul wrote this epistle about A.D. 63 to his missionary associate Titus, whom he had sent to work with the church on the island of Crete in the Mediterranean Sea. This was a tough assignment, since the residents of Crete were known for their depraved behavior (1:12). But Paul had confidence that Titus could handle the situation. In his second letter to the Corinthians, the apostle described Titus as a reliable, hardworking, and dependable leader (2 Cor. 7:6; 8:16–17).

In his letter to Titus, Paul instructed him to appoint leaders for the Cretan church, to discipline those who were teaching false doctrine, and to lead the believers to practice godly behavior.

Summary of Titus

1:1–4. Paul greets Titus (Gal. 2:1–3) as "mine own son after the common faith" (v. 4) and wishes for him God's "grace, mercy, and peace" (v. 4).

1:5–9. Paul reminds Titus that he has given him the responsibility of appointing elders or pastors to serve the church on the island of Crete. Church leaders such as elders and bishops must be mature people of high moral character who are devoted to the Lord (1 Tim. 3:1–7).

1:10–16. Paul has harsh words for false teachers who are hindering the work of the Lord. His advice to Titus is to "rebuke them sharply" (v. 13) so they will be turned back to the truth.

2:1–10. Titus should overlook no segment of the church in his instructions on how to live the Christian life. Godly behavior is expected of aged men (v. 2), aged women (v. 3), young women (vv. 4–5), young men (vv. 6–8), and servants (vv. 9–10).

2:11–15. All believers are to live "soberly, righteously, and godly" (v. 12) in the world because of the example set for believers by Jesus Christ (Phil. 2:5–8).

3:1–8. What a difference Christ makes in the lives of believers, Paul declares. We who were "foolish, disobedient, deceived" (v. 3) have been delivered from our sin and filled with the "kindness and love of God" (v. 4). Good works are the outgrowth of this new life in Christ.

3:9–11. Paul warns Titus to shun those people who deal in foolish questions and argue about the merits of the Old Testament law. They condemn themselves by such vain and senseless behavior.

3:12–15. Paul plans to send someone to Crete as Titus's replacement. Then he wants Titus to join him.

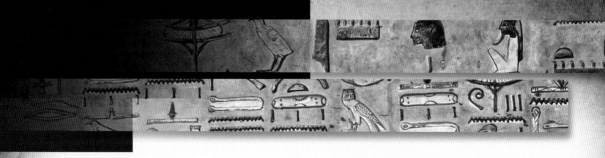

PHILEMON

OVERVIEW: A plea for mercy and forgiveness for a runaway slave who has become a believer.

Introduction to Philemon

Paul's letter to Philemon, containing only twenty-five verses, is the shortest of his epistles. The apostle wrote it while in prison in Rome about A.D. 63. The purpose of the letter was to appeal to Philemon, a believer in the church at Colosse, to forgive and welcome back his runaway slave named Onesimus, who had been converted under Paul's ministry in Rome.

Philemon had the legal right as a slave owner in the ancient world to punish and even kill Onesimus for his act of betrayal. But Paul expressed confidence that he would welcome him back as a fellow believer, "a brother beloved" (v. 16) in the Lord.

This beautiful letter shows the warm and caring side of Paul's personality. It reminds us that Jesus Christ has the power to transform all human relationships.

[Verses 1–7] PHILEMON'S HOUSE CHURCH. *To the church in thy [Philemon's] house: Grace to you, and peace* (Philem. 2–3).

Paul sent greetings in this verse to the believers who met in Philemon's house. Groups of believers in New Testament times did not have church buildings, so they usually met in private homes. Priscilla and Aquila apparently made their home available as a meeting place in both Rome (Rom. 16:5) and Ephesus (1 Cor. 16:19). Early believers also met in the home of Nymphas (Col. 4:15–16).

Summary of Philemon

Verses 1–7. Paul, writing from prison in Rome (Acts 28:16, 30–31), greets his fellow believer Philemon in the church at Colosse. Philemon's home may have been the meeting place for the Colossian church, since Paul mentions "the church in thy house" (v. 2).

Verses 8–11. Paul begins his appeal on behalf of Philemon's runaway slave Onesimus by referring to Onesimus as "my son" (v. 10). Apparently Paul had led Onesimus to Christ, and he considered him a Christian brother who was as close to him as a son.

Verses 12–17. Although he preferred to keep Onesimus with him in Rome, Paul was sending him back to Philemon in Colosse. The apostle uses his influence and reputation to persuade Philemon to receive Onesimus back not as a slave but as a brother in Christ: "If thou count me therefore a partner, receive him as myself" (v. 17).

Verses 18–21. Paul even offers to repay Philemon for anything Onesimus might have taken from his master when he ran away. But the apostle also appeals to his spirit of forgiveness and generosity, confident that Philemon will "do more than I say" (v. 21).

Verses 22–25. Paul closes by sending greetings to Philemon from believers who had served as his helpers in the ministry. He also expresses hope that he might be released from prison and come to Colosse for a visit.

CHAPTER 9
THE GENERAL EPISTLES

The last nine books of the New Testament are known as the "general epistles" because they were addressed to broad, general audiences rather than to specific churches or individuals. The exceptions to this categorization are the letters of 2 and 3 John, which were addressed to specific people.

Most of these letters were written during the final years of the first Christian century, about A.D. 65–95. By this time false teachings had begun to creep into the Christian movement. Many of these epistles were written to correct or condemn these heretical doctrines.

These nine general letters—Hebrews; James; 1 and 2 Peter; 1, 2, and 3 John; Jude; and Revelation—are often called the "catholic (universal) epistles." They portray a Savior whose strength can sustain us in the midst of life's problems.

HEBREWS

OVERVIEW: Jesus Christ is superior to the Old Testament sacrificial system. He is the great High Priest, who sacrificed His life to atone for our sin.

Introduction to Hebrews

Hebrews is unique among the New Testament epistles because it does not give a single clue about its author. It omits the greeting and the conclusion that are typical of all the other letters contained in the New Testament, and it reads more like a sermon or an essay than a personal letter.

In the early years of the church, many people assumed that the apostle Paul wrote Hebrews. But this assumption has been rejected by modern scholarship because Hebrews does not fit the Pauline mold. Possible authors who have been suggested include several early believers mentioned in the book of Acts: Luke, Barnabas, or Apollos. But the bottom line is that no one knows who wrote the epistle to the Hebrews.

The date when this book was written is also a mystery, but we can assume that it was written before A.D. 70. In that year the Roman army destroyed the temple in Jerusalem during their campaign against a rebellion of the Jewish people. The author of Hebrews does not refer to this event, although he mentions Jewish temple sacrifices several times. It seems likely that he would have discussed the temple's destruction if he had written this epistle after A.D. 70.

While the author and date of Hebrews are a mystery, there is no doubt about the purpose of this epistle. It was written to people from a Jewish background who had become Christians. They were wavering in their commitment and were even considering returning to their former Jewish customs and beliefs. Hebrews declared to these weak believers that Jesus Christ had replaced Judaism as God's perfect revelation of Himself and that they should stand firm in their commitment to Him.

Summary of Hebrews

1:1–4. The epistle begins by affirming that God has spoken in the past, during Old Testament times, through the prophets. But He has revealed Himself supremely through the life and ministry of His Son, Jesus Christ.

1:5–14. Several Old Testament passages are quoted to show that Jesus is superior to all previous ways in which God has revealed Himself. He is especially superior to angels, messengers who often spoke for God in Old Testament times (Gen. 18:9–10; Exod. 14:19–20).

2:1–4. This is the first of four warning messages in the epistle to the Hebrews (see Heb. 5:11–6:12; 10:19–39; 12:12–29). This message warns believers to pay attention to the salvation offered by Jesus Christ.

2:5–18. Although Christ was God's Son, He was human and thus subject to all the temptations that people face. He is a Savior with whom we can identify: "In that he himself hath suffered being tempted, he is able to succour them that are tempted" (v. 18).

3:1–6. Moses was the great hero of the Jewish people. They considered him greater than the angels, since he had passed on God's law to His people. But Jesus is greater even than Moses. He is like the builder and owner of a house, while Moses is just a butler or servant in the house.

3:7–19. When the Jewish people were wandering in the wilderness, they rebelled against Moses and committed idolatry (Num. 14:1–35). This shows the danger of unbelief. It is an even more serious matter to reject Jesus, since He is superior to Moses.

4:1–13. The writer of Hebrews probably had Joshua in mind when he referred to the Israelites as failing to find rest in the land of promise (v. 1). The implication is that Jesus is superior to Joshua, because He provides rest for all who place their faith in Him.

4:14–16. Jesus Christ is the great High Priest for all believers. Although He was tempted just like we are, He never gave in to sin (Luke 4:1–13). He identifies with us in our temptations because He has experienced all the human emotions that we feel. When we commit ourselves to Him, we will be received with grace and mercy.

5:1–10. Jesus' comparison to Melchisedec (Gen. 14:17–20) is explained more fully in Hebrews 7. As our great High Priest, Jesus suffered on our behalf and became "the author of eternal salvation unto all them that obey him" (v. 9).

5:11–6:12. These verses contain the second warning to the readers of Hebrews (see also Heb. 2:1–4; 10:19–39; 12:12–29). This message cautions those who had professed faith in Christ to press on to maturity in their commitment. As new Christians, they were

[4:14–16] BOLD ACCESS TO THE KING. *Let us therefore come boldly unto the throne of grace, that we may obtain mercy, and find grace to help in time of need* (Heb. 4:16).

As a person becomes famous or rises to a high position, he limits his accessibility to others for his own protection. Many kings of Bible times, for example, could not be approached by anyone but their most trusted advisors. The Persians had a law that anyone who came into their king's presence without his permission could pay with their lives (see the note "Don't Bother the King" on p. 460).

This verse from Hebrews, when seen against the background of these "unapproachable" kings, makes us realize what a revolutionary Savior Jesus is. Although He is exalted to the highest position as God's Son, He is still as approachable to us as a member of the family or a close friend.

We can bring our needs boldly to Jesus and expect to be received joyfully into His presence.

in the elementary stages of their faith. But they should continue growing in their faith. A mature faith results in works of mercy and righteousness.

6:13–20. Abraham is an example of a person to whom God "made promise" (v. 13; Gen. 12:1–3). But Abraham had the responsibility to obey God in order to bring this promise to fruition. Human obedience is still a vital ingredient in God's plan for His people.

7:1–28. This entire chapter picks up on the topic of Melchisedec, first mentioned in Hebrews 5:6–10. Melchisedec was the mysterious priest and "king of Salem" who received tithes from Abraham (Gen. 14:17–20). The Bible gives no information about the genealolgy or death of Melchisedec. He simply appears out of nowhere, and this implies that his priesthood was eternal. But the priesthood of Christ is greater even

8:1–10:18. Though Jews no longer offer sacrifices, since they have no temple, a small community of Samaritans in Israel still sacrifices lambs at Passover. The writer of Hebrews, however, said Jesus was the sacrifice to end all sacrifices.

than that of Melchisedec. With His atoning death, the Old Testament sacrificial system was abolished. Human priests were no longer needed to offer animal sacrifices to atone for sin. Jesus took care of this "when he offered up himself" (v. 27).

8:1–10:18. This long passage describes the new covenant that was established by Christ. The old covenant between God and His people required them to offer animal sacrifices and to follow prescribed rituals to take away the stain of sin (Lev. 4:1–35). These rituals had to be repeated again and again. But under the new covenant, Jesus offered His own life as a permanent, once-for-all sacrifice for sin.

10:19–39. This is the third warning to the readers of Hebrews (see also Heb. 2:1–4; 5:11–6:12; 12:12–29). This message cautions them to persevere in the commitment they had made to follow Jesus Christ. The author of Hebrews also exhorts them to meet together for regular worship in order to encourage and strengthen one another in the faith. He uses the certainty of Jesus' second coming to motivate them to stand firm in their faith.

11:1–40. This is known as the great "faith chapter" of the Bible. Several heroes of the faith from the Old Testament are mentioned to encourage the readers of Hebrews to remain strong in their own faith. Personalities singled out for their faith include Noah (v. 7), Abraham (vv. 8–10, 17), Jacob (v. 21), Joseph (v. 22), and Moses (vv. 23–29).

12:1–2. Endurance and faithfulness are exemplified by Jesus, who followed the path of obedience all the way to the cross (Phil. 2:8). We as believers should also overcome every obstacle in our path in order to remain faithful to the Lord's call.

12:3–11. Chastening, or God's discipline, is something to be expected by all believers (1 Pet. 4:12–17). Trials and troubles teach us that we are not self-sufficient and that we should look to God for strength and guidance.

12:12–29. These verses contain the fourth and final warning to the readers of the book of Hebrews (see also Heb. 2:1–4; 5:11–6:12;

[11:1–40] EXECUTION BY SAWING. *They were stoned, they were sawn asunder [sawed in two, NIV], were tempted, were slain with the sword* (Heb. 11:37).

This verse appears in the famous "roll call of the faithful" chapter in Hebrews. The writer pays tribute to the people of past generations who remained faithful to God in spite of great persecution.

Execution by being sawed in two is cruel and inhumane by modern standards, but this form of capital punishment was apparently practiced in the ancient world. It was not out of character for the cruel Assyrians, who were known to cut off the ears and hands of their victims just for sport (see the note "Mutilation of Captives" on p. 404).

But even King David of Judah may have practiced this form of torture and execution against the Ammonites. After capturing their capital city, Rabbah, he "brought out the people that were in it, and cut them with saws, and with harrows of iron, and with axes" (1 Chron. 20:3).

10:19–39. *Jews in Jerusalem gather for prayer at their most sacred site, the Western Wall. Once a retaining wall that held up the dirt sides of a hilltop on which the temple rested, this wall is all that remains of the temple. Hebrews was a book written for Jewish Christians who were leaving the faith because of persecution and returning to Judaism. The writer warned that there was nothing to return to because Jesus brought the prophesied new covenant between God and humanity.*

[12:1–2] **A LIFETIME RACE.** *Let us [Christian believers] lay aside every weight, and the sin which doth so easily beset us, and let us run with patience [perseverance, NIV] the race that is set before us* (Heb. 12:1).

In this verse Paul compares the Christian life to the foot race in which Christians competed in the Greek games (see the note "Discipline and Training" on p. 612). The foot race was one of the most popular of the Greek games that were held every year in Athens.

To prepare themselves for these races, runners underwent rigorous training, trimming down their bodies to eliminate every ounce of excess fat. On race day they wore light clothing—perhaps no clothes at all—to give themselves every possible advantage in the competition against other runners. These races covered various distances—from short sprints where speed was called for, to longer runs where stamina and endurance were more important.

In Paul's thinking the Christian life is like a marathon. It's important for us to remain faithful to Christ during a lifetime of service so we can say with him at the end of the race, "I have finished my course, I have kept the faith" (2 Tim. 4:7).

10:19–39). This message cautions them against developing a stubborn attitude and disobeying the commands of Jesus. God has dealt forcefully with such sin and rebellion in the past, and He will do so again.

13:1–17. Believers are to demonstrate the character of Christ in their lives by loving one another, keeping themselves sexually pure, serving others, and praising and giving thanks to God.

13:18–25. The author of Hebrews closes with a benediction of God's grace and peace for his readers.

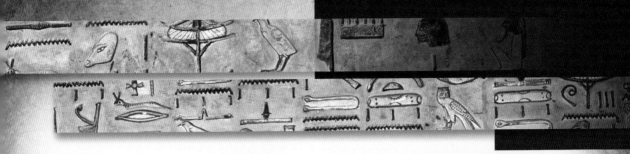

JAMES

OVERVIEW: How genuine faith expresses itself in daily life.

Introduction to James

The epistle of James is one of the most practical books in the Bible. It shows there is a connection between what we believe and how we behave. Jesus summarized this principle in one succinct sentence: "The tree is known by his fruit" (Matt. 12:33).

The James who wrote this epistle was probably the half brother of Jesus, one of four sons born to Mary and Joseph after Jesus was born (Matt. 13:55; Mark 6:3). At first James was skeptical about Jesus and His claim to be the Messiah. But he apparently became a believer after the resurrection and ascension of the Lord. James eventually became a leader in the church at Jerusalem (Acts 15:2–21; 21:18).

The epistle of James is known for its direct and forthright declaration on the behavior expected of those who follow the Lord. For James the supreme test of religion is how we act rather than what we profess to believe.

Summary of James

1:1. The "twelve tribes...scattered abroad" to which James wrote this letter were probably Jewish Christians who were living outside Palestine.

1:2–18. James encourages these Christians of Jewish background who are being persecuted for their faith. He also cautions them

> **[1:2–18] AN ETERNAL CROWN.** *Blessed is the man that endureth temptation: for...he shall receive the crown of life, which the Lord hath promised to them that love him* (James 1:12).
>
> Crowns were worn by kings as symbols of authority and power (2 Sam. 1:10). James compared the believer's inheritance of eternal life through the atoning death of Jesus Christ to a crown.
>
> This crown, unlike earthly and physical status symbols, will never grow tarnished or lose its luster because of changing cultural standards. It has an "eternal lifetime" warranty from the King of kings and Lord of lords (Rev. 21:5–7).

to remain faithful to God, even when they are tempted to do wrong.

1:19–27. The best way to stay true to God and to hold up under persecution is to live out one's faith: "Be ye doers of the word, and not hearers only" (v. 22).

2:1–13. The way of the world is to cater to rich people and to discriminate against the poor. But this is not how believers should relate to people. Everyone should be treated with equal respect, regardless of economic means, social status, or race (Rom. 1:14–16).

2:14–26. In these verses James is not teaching that a person is saved by his or her works. His point is that genuine faith will result in good works. If a person claims to be a believer but does not live righteously or perform acts of service toward others, we have

2:1–13. The Roman emperor Hadrian. James warned fellow Christians not to show favoritism to the rich and famous. Instead, believers are to treat everyone with full and equal respect.

to question whether he or she has really experienced saving faith.

3:1–12. The greatest challenge any person faces is controlling the tongue (Prov. 21:23). Although it is one of the smallest organs of the body, it has the potential to build up as well as to destroy. Only God can give us the self-discipline it takes to tame the tongue.

3:13–4:10. Being wise in the ways of the Lord is different from being wise in the ways of the world. Worldly wisdom leads to strife, conflict, and ungodly lust. But seeking the Lord and His wisdom results in righteousness and treating others with justice and mercy (Zech. 7:9).

4:11–17. James warns his readers about the sin of presumption—making plans with no regard for God and assuming that we have unlimited time in this life. He reminds us that life is only a vapor or a cloud "that appeareth for a little time, and then vanisheth away" (v. 14).

5:1–6. Those who grow rich by cheating the poor will be judged harshly by the Lord. The accumulated riches that they thought would bring them pleasure will actually bring them misery and unhappiness.

5:7–12. James encourages his readers to display persistent devotion to the Lord in the midst of their persecution and suffering.

5:13–18. One key to bearing up under persecution is persistent prayer (Luke 18:1–8). This is one of the most eloquent passages in the Bible on the power of prayer: "The effectual fervent prayer of a righteous man availeth much" (v. 16).

5:19–20. James closes his letter with a plea to his readers to try to reclaim their fellow believers who have strayed from the truth.

[5:7–12] PATIENT WAITING. *The husbandman [farmer, NIV]...hath long patience for it [the harvest], until he receive the early and latter rain* (James 5:7).

The land of Palestine, known for its dry climate, had limited rainfall. Moisture for crop production was supplemented by heavy dews (Deut. 33:13).

But every farmer knew that at least two major rainfalls during the year were essential for crops to grow. The early rain in October and November softened the soil for planting. The latter rain of March and April brought a needed boost for the crops before they ripened fully for the harvest.

James declared that just as farmers waited patiently from the early rain to the latter rain for their crops to mature, so believers must wait patiently for the second coming of Jesus (2 Tim. 4:8).

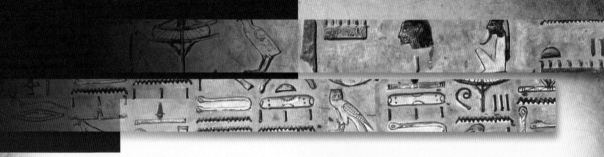

1 PETER

OVERVIEW: Encouragement to believers who are suffering persecution because of their faith.

Introduction to 1 Peter

By about A.D. 65 the Christian faith had grown so dramatically that it was becoming a threat to the Roman Empire. Believers were feeling the first wave of persecution for their faith, and this seemed destined to grow stronger in the decades ahead. The first epistle of Peter was written to encourage Christians in these trying times.

This epistle was written by the apostle Peter, the disciple of Jesus who became the leader of the Christian movement during its early days in Jerusalem (Acts 2:14–41). Peter eventually traveled to Rome, capital city of the Roman Empire. From Rome, he addressed his letter to believers who had been "scattered throughout Pontus, Galatia, Cappadocia, Asia, and Bithynia" (1:1–2). Perhaps harassment from Roman officials had forced Christians to flee to these distant territories.

Peter encouraged these suffering believers to follow the example of Christ. His persecution and death—and subsequent resurrection—provided assurance and hope for the future.

Summary of 1 Peter

1:1–2. Peter addresses this letter to believers scattered throughout five distant regions of the Roman Empire.

1:3–25. The basis of the believer's hope is Jesus

[1:3–25] CLEAR THINKING. *Gird up the loins of your mind, be sober* (1 Pet. 1:13).

Both men and women of Bible times wore full-body outer robes that extended almost to the feet (see the note "Not Quite Naked" on p. 415). If a person needed to run or do strenuous work, he would tuck the bottom part of his robe into the belt or sash around his waist. This gave him greater freedom of movement.

This practice is described by the KJV as "girding up the loins." In this verse, Peter described the need for believers to do constructive thinking as girding up the "loins of your mind." The NIV translates it, "Prepare your minds for action." Peter means that believers should think clearly and reject the hindrances and temptations of the world by focusing on God and His grace.

Tucking the robe into the belt is sometimes referred to in the Bible in a figurative sense to denote strength and determination (Job 40:7; Pss. 65:6; 93:1).

Christ and His resurrection from the dead. He alone provides salvation and the promise of eternal life.

2:1–17. Jesus is the living stone who serves as the foundation for the faith of believers. Although He was rejected by His own people, God made Him the cornerstone of salvation for the world (Eph. 2:20). Those who place their faith in Him are delivered from their sins. They become part of God's "royal priesthood, an holy nation" (v. 9) that bears witness of Him and His kingdom to others.

4:12–19. *Peter is crucified upside down in Rome. This story isn't in the Bible, but church leaders in the early centuries said Peter didn't feel worthy to be crucified the way Jesus was.*

2:18–25. Peter uses the example of Jesus and His suffering to motivate believers. Just as He suffered to purchase salvation for them, they should endure persecution for His sake with a willing and joyous spirit.

3:1–7. Husbands and wives have a special responsibility to live in obedience to the commands of Christ. Husbands should love and honor their wives, and wives should "be in subjection to your own husbands" (v. 1; see Eph. 5:22–28). Such respectful and humble behavior by wives might lead their unbelieving husbands to the Lord.

3:8–17. Peter appeals to his readers to be united in the Lord, to practice humility and love, and to resist the temptation to seek revenge against those who are causing them pain and suffering.

3:18–22. Jesus was the ultimate sufferer— a case of the just suffering for the unjust "that he might bring us to God" (v. 18). After purchasing our salvation, He is now exalted at God's right hand. All earthly powers and authorities are subject to Him (Rev. 19:1–6).

4:1–11. Again, the example of Christ provides a demonstration of the way believers should live. Peter appeals to his readers to practice love and hospitality toward others, thus serving as "good stewards of the manifold grace of God" (v. 10).

4:12–19. It should not surprise Christians that they are called to suffer persecution for their faith. According to Peter, suffering is actually a badge of honor (Heb. 12:3–11). Just as Christ's suffering was the prelude to His glorification with the Father, so it will be for all believers.

5:1–4. Peter has a special word for the leaders ("elders," v. 1) of the churches to whom he is writing. The elders must have a loving, shepherd spirit and not a dominating attitude toward those whom they serve.

5:5–9. All the members of the churches are to respect their leaders and to show a kind and humble spirit. They should be on guard against the temptations of Satan (James 4:7).

5:10–14. Peter closes with a benediction, commending his readers to the grace of God. He also sends greetings from his coworkers Silvanus ("Silas," v. 12; see also Acts 15:40) and Marcus (v. 13; probably John Mark; see also Acts 13:13; 2 Tim. 4:11).

[5:1–4] JESUS THE CHIEF SHEPHERD. *When the chief Shepherd [Jesus] shall appear, ye shall receive a crown of glory that fadeth not away* (1 Pet. 5:4).

In Bible times wealth was often measured by the size of one's flocks and herds of livestock (see the note "A Man of Means" on p. 463). Some wealthy people had hundreds of sheep, and this required the services of several shepherds. These shepherds would be supervised by a chief shepherd or master shepherd (1 Sam. 21:7).

Peter compared Jesus Christ to a chief shepherd. This title is similar to His designation as "that great shepherd of the sheep" in Hebrews 13:20.

All ministers who lead God's people should remember that they are undershepherds who work under the supervision of the Great Shepherd or Chief Shepherd—Jesus Christ. He enables then to take care of God's people with wisdom and kindness.

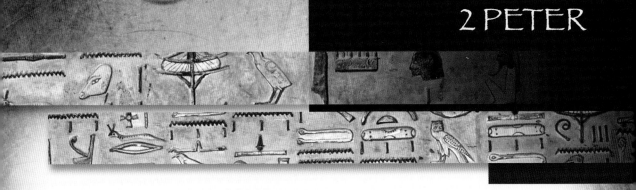

OVERVIEW: A warning to be on guard against false teachers within the church.

Introduction to 2 Peter

This brief epistle of only three chapters was also written by the apostle Peter (see introduction to 1 Peter on p. 650). But unlike 1 Peter, the author named no audience for his second epistle. It was probably written from Rome just before Peter's martyrdom in that city about A.D. 68.

The problem that Peter addressed in this letter was not persecution from without but troubles from within. False teachers were leading people astray with their views of the nature of Christ and His second coming. Peter corrected these false views and advised the leaders of the church to deal firmly with these heretical teachers.

Summary of 2 Peter

1:1–2. Peter opens his letter with wishes for grace and peace to his readers.

1:3–11. These are some of the greatest verses in the New Testament on the need for growth in the Christian life. Growing more like Christ involves faith, temperance, patience, godliness, kindness, and love.

1:12–21. The Christian faith does not grow out of hearsay and myth. It is grounded in historical facts and the testimony of eyewitnesses who were with Jesus in the flesh (1 John 1:1–7). We can also trust God's revelation of truth through His written Word.

2:1–22. Peter warns that false teachers from within the church will rise up in the future to lead believers astray. The church should be on guard against such heresies. God will punish such false prophets, just as he has done in the past. They will "utterly perish in their own corruption" (v. 12).

3:1–10. These verses declare the certainty of the second coming of Jesus and the final judgment (1 Thess. 4:13–17). These will happen in God's own time. The fact that they haven't yet happened doesn't mean that God is slow or apathetic. Rather, He is loving and patient, waiting for others to respond to His offer of salvation. He is "not willing that any should perish, but that all should come to repentance" (v. 9).

3:11–18. While waiting for the Lord to return, how should believers conduct themselves? Peter declares that they should live as holy and godly people, continuing to "grow in grace, and in the knowledge of our Lord and Saviour Jesus Christ" (v. 18; see 2 Thess. 3:6–15).

1 JOHN

OVERVIEW: Jesus was fully human as well as fully divine.

Introduction to 1 John

The first epistle of John does not name an author, but there seems little doubt that it was written by the apostle John, the disciple of Jesus who also wrote the Gospel of John (see introduction to the Gospel of John on p. 583).

First John has many similarities to John's Gospel. Both contain numerous contrasts between "love" and "hate," "life" and "death," and "darkness" and "light." The opening verses of the Gospel and 1 John are also similar, and the author of 1 John claims that he was personally acquainted with Jesus during His earthly ministry (1 John 1:1–4).

John probably wrote his first epistle about A.D. 92, shortly after writing his Gospel. A leader in the church at Ephesus, he was in his eighties by this time. During this same general period, he also wrote 2 and 3 John and the book of Revelation.

One reason why John wrote his first epistle was to refute false teachers who were denying that Jesus had come to earth in human form. They believed that Jesus was a divine spirit who only seemed to exist in the flesh. But John affirmed that with his own eyes he had seen Jesus walk the earth as a man: "That which we have seen and heard declare we unto you" (1:3). This is a central doctrine of the Christian faith that the church has affirmed throughout

its history: Jesus was the God-man. In some mysterious way that the human mind cannot fully understand, Jesus was both fully human and fully divine.

Another important theme of 1 John is love. John declared that God is love (4:8, 16), and He acts in love on our behalf (4:9–10). We show our love for God by loving others (2:9–11; 3:10).

Summary of 1 John

1:1–7. John declares that he was an eyewitness of the earthly ministry of Jesus. As one of the Twelve, he saw Jesus' miracles with his own eyes and listened to His teachings with his own ears. Thus, John is qualified to bear witness about Christ to others (2 Pet. 1:12–21).

1:8–10. Even believers will fall into sin. Rather than denying our wrongdoings, we should confess them and bring them to Jesus for forgiveness.

2:1–6. True believers abide in Christ and keep His commandments.

2:7–17. Another characteristic of believers is love for others (1 Cor. 13). A person who harbors hate toward others is walking in darkness rather than in the light of God's salvation.

2:18–29. John declares that the Antichrist—the embodiment of evil and the archenemy of Christ—will appear during the last days when the return of Jesus draws near.

4:1–6. Jesus suffers through isolation and temptation during the several weeks He spent in the wilderness before starting His ministry. John warned believers not to listen to false teachers who said Jesus was just a spirit who only pretended to be human and to suffer.

Many false teachers ("many antichrists," v. 18) were denying that Jesus was the Messiah. John interprets this as a sign that the final judgment is close at hand.

3:1–10. John declares that true believers will not continue in a habitual state of sin. God's love guides believers to recognize their sins as soon as they are committed and to seek His forgiveness day by day.

3:11–24. John again encourages believers to love one another. This is the great lesson that Jesus taught His followers (John 13:34).

4:1–6. These verses refute the claim of some false teachers that Jesus did not come to earth in human form. They taught that Jesus was a spirit and that He only seemed to have a physical body. John declares, "Every spirit that confesseth not that Jesus Christ is come in the flesh is not of God" (v. 3).

4:7–21. These verses declare that God's essential character is love and that He is the author of all love (John 3:16). It is logical to John that if God loved us enough to grant us salvation and eternal life, then "we ought also to love one another" (v. 11).

5:1–12. The foundation of the Christian's hope for eternal life is faith in Jesus as God's Son. John boils it down to one simple statement:

"He that hath the Son hath life; and he that hath not the Son of God hath not life" (v. 12).

5:13–21. John closes his letter by assuring his readers that they can know with assurance that Jesus is who He claimed to be. They can also pray to Him with full confidence that He will hear and answer in accordance with their needs (James 5:16).

[3:11–24] BOWELS OF COMPASSION. *Whoso...seeth his brother have need, and shutteth up his bowels of compassion from him, how dwelleth the love of God in him?* (1 John 3:17).

In Bible times the bowels were considered the seat of emotions and feelings. According to the apostle John in this passage, a person who shuts his "bowels of compassion" has no pity or empathy toward those in need. In our modern figure of speech, we would probably say that a person like this does not have a compassionate heart.

The apostle John makes it clear throughout this epistle that love and compassion toward others is one of the marks of an authentic Christian believer: "This commandment have we from him, That he who loveth God love his brother also" (1 John 4:21).

5:13–21. *During the Transfiguration, Jesus meets with Moses and Elijah while His body glows with the celestial radiance of divinity. John wanted his readers to believe that Jesus was both fully human and fully divine, even though it's impossible to comprehend how He could be both.*

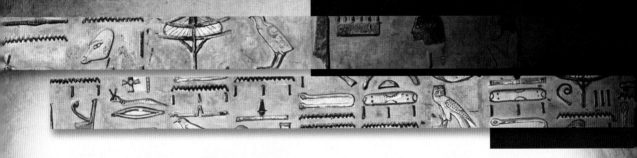

OVERVIEW: A warning to shun false teachers who deny that Jesus came in the flesh.

Introduction to 2 John

Like his first epistle, 2 John was also written by the apostle John about A.D. 92, when he was more than eighty years old (see introduction to 1 John on p. 654).

Second John is the shortest book in the New Testament, containing only thirteen verses. It was written to warn believers and churches against showing hospitality to false teachers (v. 10). John also encouraged Christians to obey the commandments of Jesus Christ and to love one another.

Summary of 2 John

Verses 1–3. The author of this letter refers to himself as "the elder" (v. 1). This was probably a title of authority or respect for the apostle John, one of the twelve disciples of Jesus. Nothing is known about the "elect lady" (v. 1) to whom this epistle is addressed. Was John referring to a church or a person? No one knows.

Verses 4–6. John is delighted to learn that the elect lady and her children are walking in love (1 Cor. 13). He repeats the commandment that he learned from Jesus: "Love one another" (v. 5; see John 13:34).

Verses 7–11. John warns the elect lady to shun false teachers who deny that Jesus Christ came in the flesh (1 John 4:1–6). These were probably members of a heretical sect known as the Gnostics. They taught that Jesus came to earth in spirit form and that He only seemed to suffer and die on the cross.

Verses 12–13. John extends closing greetings, with the hope that he will soon be able to make a personal visit.

3 JOHN

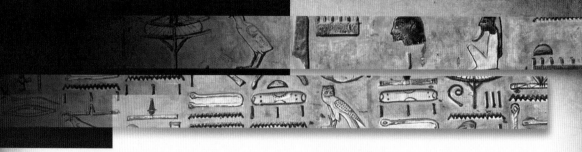

OVERVIEW: Words of criticism and commendation for early church leaders.

Introduction to 3 John

The third epistle of John was written by the apostle John about A.D. 92 (see introduction to 1 John on p. 654) to a believer named Gaius. John referred to himself as "the elder" (v. 1). This identified him as a leader in a local church, probably the church at Ephesus.

In this letter John has words of criticism for one prideful church leader but words of praise for Gaius and Demetrius, who were leading in the Spirit of Christ.

Summary of 3 John

Verses 1–8. John writes to a fellow believer named Gaius, who was probably a leader in one of the churches of Asia Minor. John commends Gaius for standing for the truth and for showing hospitality to evangelists who traveled from church to church preaching the gospel.

Verses 9–10. John has harsh words for Diotrephes, a believer who apparently had taken control of a local church and refused to receive the apostles and other traveling ministers.

Verses 11–12. John endorses a believer named Demetrius and assures Gaius that Demetrius can be trusted to follow the Lord and walk in the truth.

Verses 13–14. John extends personal greetings to other believers associated with Gaius and promises to visit him soon.

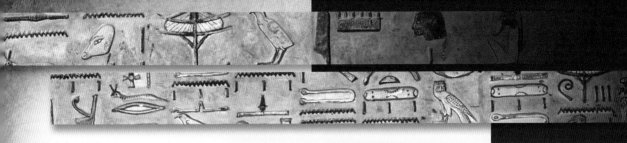

OVERVIEW: A strong warning against false teachers in the church.

Introduction to Jude

The epistle of Jude addresses the same problem as 2 Peter: false teachers within the church who were leading believers astray (see introduction to 2 Peter on p. 653). The author probably wrote this letter about A.D. 82 to warn church leaders to beware of these heretical teachers and their dangerous doctrines.

Who was this Jude who wrote this brief epistle? The most likely candidate is one of the half brothers of Jesus who is mentioned in Matthew 13:55 ("Judas") and Mark 6:3 ("Juda"). Like Jesus' other half brothers, Jude was skeptical of Jesus and His mission while He was conducting His earthly ministry. But he apparently became a believer after Jesus' resurrection and ascension.

Jude identified himself in the opening verse of his

A child kisses the newborn Jesus. Jude may have been one of Jesus' older brothers. An ancient church tradition says that Jesus' brothers and sisters, mentioned in the Bible, were older than Him—children of Joseph from a previous wife who had died.

[Verses 3–16] **THE LOVE FEAST.** *These are spots in your feasts of charity, when they feast with you, feeding themselves without fear* (Jude 12).

The "feasts of charity" to which Jude refers in this verse was probably the love feast, a meal that early Christians ate together as part of their observance of the Lord's Supper. The purpose of this meal was to remember the sacrifice of Christ, since he was eating the Passover meal with His disciples when He turned it into a memorial of His sacrificial death (Luke 22:14–20).

In its early years, the love feast was also known as the agape meal. It became a charity meal for the poor in some Christian traditions. Most Christian groups today have dropped this communal meal from their observance of the Lord's Supper.

epistle as a "brother of James" (v. 1). This was probably another half brother of Jesus who wrote the epistle of James (see introduction to that epistle on p. 647).

Summary of Jude

Verses 1–2. Jude identifies himself as "the servant of Jesus Christ, and brother of James" (v. 1). His brother James, at first a skeptic like Jude, eventually became a believer and assumed a prominent leadership role in the early church at Jerusalem (Acts 15:13).

Verses 3–16. Jude urges his fellow believers to "earnestly contend for the faith" in opposition to certain people who were hindering the work of the church. These people were particularly dangerous because they were working from within the fellowship of the church (2 Pet. 2:1–3). Jude describes them as "murmurers, complainers" who were "walking after their own lusts" (v. 16). Apparently they were using the grace of God as a cover for their lifestyles of sin and wickedness.

Verses 17–23. Jude contrasts the ungodly behavior of these people with the characteristics of true believers. Those who truly know God reflect the love of Christ (1 John 3:11–24). They are strengthened for godly living through the power of prayer.

Verses 24–25. Jude closes with a beautiful benediction that should comfort and strengthen all believers. Jesus is able to keep us from falling and to present us justified before God.

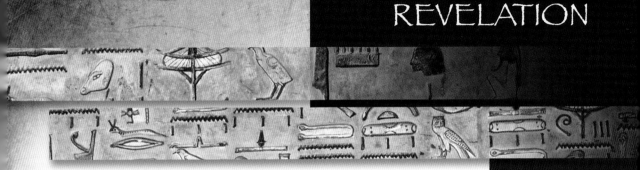

REVELATION

OVERVIEW: A prophecy of the end times and God's ultimate triumph over the forces of evil.

Introduction to Revelation

Revelation is the only book of apocalyptic literature in the New Testament. This was a distinctive type of writing in biblical times that used symbols and numbers to depict the end of the present age and the coming of God's future kingdom. Revelation is similar to apocalyptic writings in several books of the Old Testament: Daniel (chaps. 7–12), Ezekiel (chaps. 37–41), and Zechariah (chaps. 9–12).

The book of Revelation was written about A.D. 95 by the apostle John, one of the twelve disciples of Jesus (see introduction to the

1:9–20. Exiled on this tiny island of Patmos, off the coast of Turkey, the apostle John wrote the last book in the Bible: Revelation.

1:1–3. *John sees one of many visions he experiences on the island of Patmos. Revelation is a collection of those visions.*

Gospel of John on p. 583). At this time he was imprisoned by the Roman authorities on Patmos (1:9), a rocky and barren island off the coast of Asia Minor (modern Turkey).

John wrote this book during a time of intense persecution of the Christian movement under the Roman emperor Domitian. The apostle probably used symbolism in his writing to hide the meaning of his message from the Roman enemies of the church. Christian "insiders" understood the images that John used, but the Roman persecutors did not have the "key" that enabled them to decode John's message.

The book of Revelation came to John under divine inspiration through a series of visions. In spite of the persecution that believers were experiencing, John affirmed that the all-powerful Lord would fulfill His promises and accomplish His purpose in history. Jesus Christ would be victorious over the forces of Satan, and He would reign forever as King of kings and Lord of lords.

Summary of Revelation

1:1–3. These verses indicate that the book of Revelation was revealed to the apostle John (Mark 1:17–20) through an angel. But it came directly from the Father through His Son, Jesus Christ. John chose to write this revelation down in the form of a letter. It was probably intended to be read publicly in local congregations.

1:4–8. John addresses this letter to the churches in seven cities that represent the major centers of Christianity in the region of Asia (modern-day Turkey). The theme of his letter is "victory in Jesus." God has guaranteed that His Son, Jesus Christ—"Alpha and Omega, the beginning and the ending" (v. 8)—will reign ultimately over the entire earth (Phil. 2:11).

1:9–20. While in exile on the island of Patmos, John had a vision of the risen Lord. He was told to write down what he saw and to send his message to the seven churches, represented by seven candlesticks. Jesus appeared among these candlesticks; this represented His presence with these congregations. In His hands Jesus held seven stars. These represented "the angels of the seven churches" (v. 20), perhaps angels with responsibility for and authority over these churches.

2:1–7. John writes a specific message to the believers in the church at Ephesus (Acts 19:1–40). Their initial love and enthusiasm for the Lord had cooled, and they needed to rekindle their zeal.

2:8–11. John encourages the church at Smyrna, which was undergoing great persecution. Their faithfulness would be richly rewarded by the Lord.

2:12–17. The church at Pergamos was accused of indulging in idol worship. Unless they repented immediately of their evil, the Lord promised to confront them and to fight against them with the sword of His mouth.

[2:12–17] A STONE FOR THE WINNER. *To him that overcometh will I give…a white stone* (Rev. 2:17).

This imagery of a white stone has been explained in various ways by interpreters: as a badge of acquittal in a legal case, as an expression of welcome by a host to his guests, or as a voting token used by a voter to indicate his choice of a candidate.

Perhaps the most believable explanation is that the apostle John, the author of Revelation, was referring to a white stone given to the winner of an athletic contest. This stone was an admission ticket to the winner's celebration at a later time. This may refer to the time when the faithful, persevering Christian believer will receive his ticket to eternal life and the Lord's great victory celebration in heaven.

2:18–29. Tolerating immorality and false teaching was the problem of the church at Thyatira. This congregation was exhorted to return to the truth.

3:1–6. The believers in the church at Sardis had lost their spiritual zeal. They needed to wake up and "strengthen the things…that are ready to die" (v. 2) so they could bring honor and glory to the Lord.

3:7–13. The church at Philadelphia is the only one of the seven churches that receives no rebuke. In spite of great persecution, this congregation remained faithful to the Lord.

3:14–22. The church at Laodicea is condemned more severely than all the other churches. The problem of these believers was spiritual apathy. They were "neither cold nor hot" (v. 16) about spiritual matters. God promised to deal with this church severely unless they repented of their waywardness.

4:1–11. This chapter describes a vision in which John saw the Lord in heaven, seated on a throne. Seated around the throne were twenty-four elders, representing angels who administered God's rule throughout the universe. The four creatures described as "beasts" (v. 6) were actually seraphim (Isa. 6:1–3), winged beings, or another order of angels who helped to administer the rule of God in the universe. God's unquestioned rule and authority are clear when these twenty-four elders and four seraphim fall down in worship before Him.

5:1–14. This chapter continues John's vision of God seated on a throne. In His hand God holds a book, or scroll, that is sealed with seven wax seals. One of the elders around the throne declares that only the risen Christ—represented by a Lamb—is worthy to remove the seven seals and open the scroll. God hands the scroll to Jesus. This symbolizes that He has delegated to His crucified and risen Son all authority in heaven and earth. The elders and angels who had previously bowed down to God now fall down in adoration and worship at the feet of Jesus.

6:1–8:1. This section of Revelation describes the events of God's judgment represented by the seven seals when Jesus removed them from the scroll. Seals 1 through 4 (6:2–8) show the horrors of war, including famine, devastation, and death. Seal 5 (6:9–11) represents the reward of believers who are martyred for their faith. Seal 6 (6:12–17) shows the earthshaking events that will happen before the second coming of Christ. The opening of the seventh seal (8:1) causes an eerie silence in heaven, as all the earth awaits the coming judgment of the Lord.

Chapter 7 of Revelation is inserted between the opening of seal 6 and seal 7. This chapter describes a great multitude of people who fall down before God and the Lamb in reverence and worship. These people have been redeemed by the Lamb, and they are in God's presence in heaven.

[Chapter 7] SYMBOLS OF VICTORY AND JOY. *A great multitude…stood before…the Lamb, clothed with white robes, and palms in their hands* (Rev. 7:9).

The "palms" held by this great multitude of believers were palm branches. These were considered symbols of victory and joy (Lev. 23:40; Neh. 8:15).

Jesus was welcomed on His triumphant entry into Jerusalem by the crowds waving palm branches (John 12:13). In the New Jerusalem, or heaven, believers will acclaim Jesus as the triumphant Lamb or Savior by waving these same symbols of victory and gladness.

8:2–11:19. This section describes the seven trumpet judgments, or God's judgment against the earth and those who have rejected Him. These trumpets are sounded by seven angels.

Trumpet 1 (8:7) brings hail and fire on the earth. Trumpet 2 (8:8–9) brings the destruction of sea life and ships. At the sound of trumpet 3 (8:10–11), a meteorite poisons earth's rivers and streams. Many of the heavenly bodies are darkened with the sounding of trumpet 4 (8:12). Trumpet 5 (9:1–12) brings torment and misery on earth's inhabitants. With trumpet 6 (9:13–21), widespread death occurs. The sounding of the seventh and final trumpet (11:15–19) indicates that the kingdoms of this world will become the kingdoms over which Christ will rule.

10:1–11:14 is inserted between the sounding of trumpets 6 and 7. Chapter 10 reaffirms the call of the apostle John. He is told to eat a book, or scroll. This recalls the experience of the prophet Ezekiel (Ezek. 2:1–3:11).

In Revelation 11:1–14, the apostle John sees the city of Jerusalem trampled for forty-two months. Two unnamed witnesses are raised up by the Lord to prophesy in His name. After their persecution and death, they are resurrected and called up to heaven. Faithfulness in God's service will be rewarded (Matt. 25:14–29).

12:1–17. John sees a vision of a woman who gives birth to a male child. Satan, represented by a red dragon, tries to kill the child. But the child is protected and delivered from harm by the Lord. The message of this chapter is that God will protect His church from Satan's threats.

13:1–18. The vision in this chapter shows that Satan continues his efforts to destroy the church. John sees a beast emerge from the sea. He is the Antichrist, the archenemy of Christ, who is determined to destroy the church and all who follow the risen Lord.

John also sees a second beast emerge from the earth. As a servant of the first beast, he uses miraculous signs and economic threats to try to turn believers away from loyalty to Christ and to convince them to worship the Antichrist. The symbol for this second beast is the number 666. Six was the number for evil, so triple sixes shows that this beast was thoroughly evil in his personality and intentions.

14:1–20. Several short visions of John are recorded in this chapter. He sees the Lamb, Jesus Christ (John 1:36), who has returned to earth and is standing with a multitude of the redeemed on Mount Zion. John also sees several angels, who deliver messages of encouragement to God's people in the midst of persecution and assure them that doom is coming for those who worship the beast.

15:1–16:21. Different aspects of God's judgment have already been revealed through the seven seals (6:1–8:1) and the seven trumpets (8:2–11:19). In this section, yet

---

[15:1–16:21] THE NUMBER SEVEN. *And I [John the apostle] saw another sign in heaven…seven angels having the seven last plagues* (Rev. 15:1).

The Jewish people thought of seven as a sacred number. It is used often in the Bible to show fullness, completion, and perfection (Gen. 2:2–3; Dan. 9:25).

The apostle John uses the number seven throughout the book of Revelation: seven churches (1:4), seven stars (2:1), seven lamps (4:5), seven seals (5:1), seven angels with seven trumpets (8:2), seven thunders (10:4), a beast with seven heads (13:1), seven vials, or bowls (17:1), and seven kings (17:10).

By using this number, John declared that God will bring about His perfect judgment in the end-time. All believers will participate in the full and complete victory of Christ over the forces of evil.

8:2–11:19. *Most trumpet blasts that John wrote about in Revelation signalled monumental events, usually disasters and plagues. Christians, however, look forward to the day when "the Lord himself shall descend from heaven with a shout, with the voice of the archangel, and with the trump of God" (1 Thess. 4:16).*

[19:11–21] A KING WITH MANY CROWNS. *His [the reigning Christ's] eyes were as a flame of fire, and on his head were many crowns* (Rev. 19:12).

John borrowed this imagery from the custom of kings who ruled over more than one country. They would wear several crowns to represent all the nations under their control. For example, the kings of Egypt wore a two-in-one crown to represent the unification of Upper and Lower Egypt under their rule.

To the apostle John in this verse, the many crowns worn by Jesus show His universal reign as Savior and Lord throughout the world. The hymn writer expressed it like this:

Crown Him with many crowns,
The Lamb upon His throne;
Hark! How the heavenly anthem drowns
All music but its own!

Awake, my soul, and sing
Of Him who died for thee;
And hail Him as thy matchless King
Thro all eternity.

—Matthew Bridges, "Crown Him with Many Crowns"

another dimension of His judgment is communicated through John's vision of the seven vials (cups or bowls) of God's wrath poured out on the earth by seven angels. These events happen when the contents of the bowls are poured out: Sores break out on the followers of the beast (bowl 1; 16:2); all sea creatures die (bowl 2; 16:3); fresh waters of the earth turn to blood (bowl 3; 16:4–7); the sun scorches the earth (bowl 4; 16:8–9); darkness and suffering strike the earth (bowl 5; 16:10–11); the Euphrates River dries up (bowl 6; 16:12); and storms and a great earthquake devastate the land (bowl 7; 16:17–18). These bowl judgments give a graphic picture of the wrath of God poured out against unbelievers and an evil world.

17:1–18. In this vision John sees a despicable prostitute seated on a scarlet beast. Her name is Babylon, probably a code name symbolizing the forces of evil that are arrayed against God and the forces of righteousness. She was responsible for the continuing persecution of God's people. An angel explains to John that the beast on which she is seated is the Antichrist.

18:1–24. This vision is a continuation of John's vision in chapter 17. An angel appears and shouts, "Babylon the great is fallen" (v. 2). To John the term *Babylon* symbolized all the evil forces of the world that were allied against God. The Lord has won the victory over Babylon, but pride, idolatry, and immorality have also contributed to its downfall.

19:1–5. The twenty-four elders and the four seraphim around God's throne (see Rev. 4:1–11) fall down and worship God. Thanksgiving is offered for the destruction of Babylon.

19:6–10. John portrays the relationship with Christ that believers would soon begin to experience in terms of a marriage. Christ is the Lamb (Acts 8:32), and the church is His bride (Eph. 5:25–33), and "blessed are they which are called unto the marriage supper of the Lamb" (v. 9).

19:11–21. As "KING OF KINGS, AND LORD OF LORDS" (v. 16), Jesus will return to earth in victory. In a final battle against the forces of evil, He will defeat the Antichrist and the beast that worships him (see Rev. 13:1–18). Then He will cast them alive into "a lake of fire burning with brimstone" (v. 20).

20:1–15. Looking into the future, John predicts the events of the final days. Satan will be bound and sealed up in the bottomless pit for a period of one thousand years. Then he will be released to work his deception among the nations for a time. Finally, he will be defeated and cast into the lake of fire and brimstone to suffer eternally, along with the Antichrist and the beast. After this the great white throne judgment will occur. The unredeemed—those people whose names do not appear in the Book of Life—will also be cast into the lake of fire.

21:1–8. John foresees that believers will enter a final state of blessedness characterized by a new heaven and a new earth. Grief and pain will be no more. God will live among His people, and they will enjoy continuous fellowship with Him.

21:9–22:5. John's final vision is of the heavenly Jerusalem, where believers will live in the eternal state with God and His Son. No temple exists in this city, "for the Lord God Almighty and the Lamb are the temple of it" (21:22). Its gates are never shut at night as a security measure, because night and darkness do not exist. A river of pure water, representing the water of life (John 7:38), issues from God's throne. Along this river grows the tree of life. John is describing spiritual realities with physical metaphors that his readers could understand.

22:6–21. John concludes Revelation by stating that he has reported accurately the prophecies that God has revealed to him in a series of visions. He urges his readers to remain faithful to the One who is "Alpha and Omega, the beginning and the end, the first and the last" (v. 13; see Rev. 1:8). Thus, the Bible comes to a close with an affirmation of the supremacy of the Lord Jesus Christ.

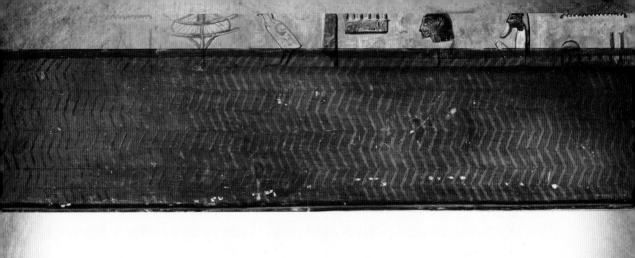

Maps

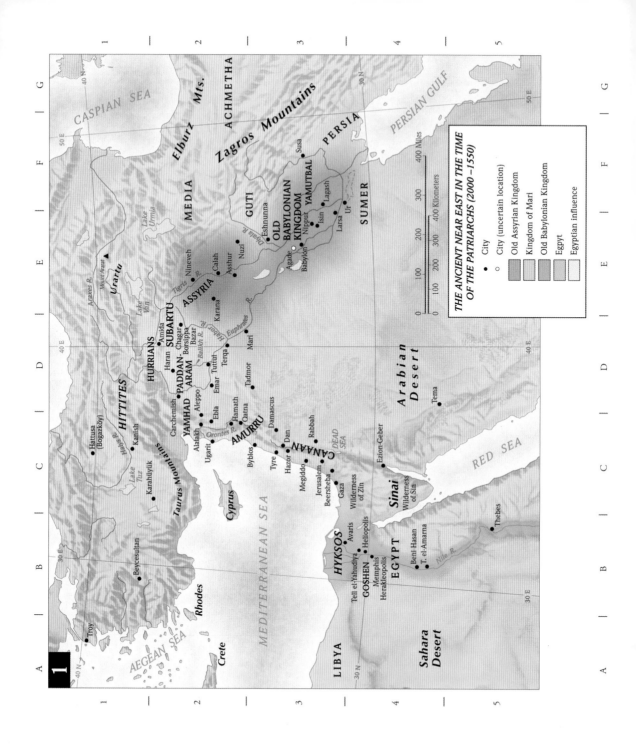

THE ANCIENT NEAR EAST IN THE TIME
OF THE PATRIARCHS (2000–1550)

- City
- City (uncertain location)
- Old Assyrian Kingdom
- Kingdom of Mari
- Old Babylonian Kingdom
- Egypt
- Egyptian influence

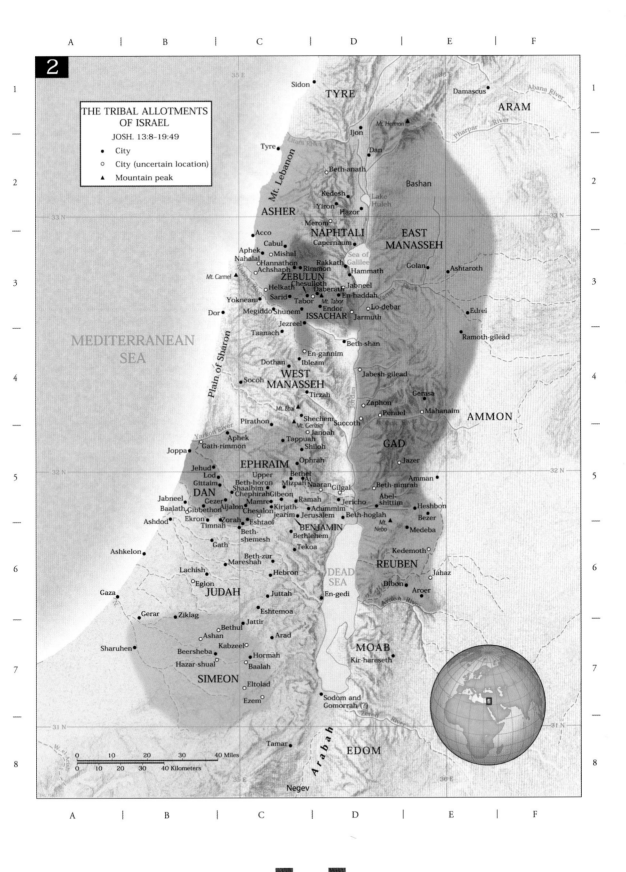

THE TRIBAL ALLOTMENTS OF ISRAEL

JOSH. 13:8–19:49

- • City
- ○ City (uncertain location)
- ▲ Mountain peak

2

A B C D E F

TYRE

Sidon

Damascus

ARAM

35 E

Ijon

Mt. Hermon ▲

Tyre

Dan

Abana River

Utah River

Beth-anath

Pharpar River

Mt. Lebanon

Kedesh

Bashan

33 N

ASHER

Yiron

Hazar

Merom

Acco

Cabul

NAPHTALI

Capernaum

EAST MANASSEH

Aphek

Mishal

Nahalal

Hannathon

Rakkath

Sea of Galilee

Golan

Ashtaroth

Achshaph

Rimmon

Hammath

Mt. Carmel ▲

ZEBULUN

Chesulloth

Helkath

Daberath

Jabneel

Sarid

Tabor

Mt. Tabor ▲

En-haddah

Yokneam

Shunem

Endor

Lo-debar

Dor

Megiddo

ISSACHAR

Jarmuth

Edrei

Jezreel

Taanach

Beth-shan

Ramoth-gilead

MEDITERRANEAN SEA

En-gannim

Dothan

Ibleam

Jabesh-gilead

WEST MANASSEH

Socoh

Gerasa

Tirzah

Plain of Sharon

Zaphon

Penuel

Mahanaim

AMMON

Mt. Ebal ▲

Pirathon

Shechem

Mt. Gerizim ▲

Janoah

Succoth

Yarkon River

Aphek

Tappuah

Gath-rimmon

Shiloh

GAD

Joppa

Ophrah

Jazer

Jehud

EPHRAIM

Bethel

Amman

32 N

Lod

Upper

Ai

Beth-nimrah

Gittaim

Beth-horon

Mizpah

Naaran

Gilgal

Shaalbim

Gibeon

Jabneel

DAN

Chephirah

Abel-shittim

Gezer

Mamre

Ramah

Jericho

Heshbon

Baalath

Gibbethon

Aijalon

Kirjath-jearim

Adummim

Bezer

Ashdod

Chesalon

Jerusalem

Beth-hoglah

Medeba

Ekron

Zorah

Eshtaol

Mt. Nebo ▲

Timnah

BENJAMIN

Beth-shemesh

Bethlehem

Gath

Tekoa

Kedemoth

Ashkelon

Beth-zur

REUBEN

Lachish

Mareshah

Hebron

Jahaz

Eglon

DEAD SEA

Dibon

Aroer

Gaza

JUDAH

Juttah

En-gedi

Arnon River

Gerar

Ziklag

Eshtemoa

Jattir

Bethul

Arad

MOAB

Sharuhen

Ashan

Kabzeel

Kir-hareseth

Beersheba

Hormah

Hazar-shual

Baalah

SIMEON

Eltolad

Ezem

Sodom and Gomorrah (?)

31 N

Tamar

Arabah

EDOM

Wadi el-Arish

0 10 20 30 40 Miles

0 10 20 30 40 Kilometers

35 E

36 E

Negev

Zered River

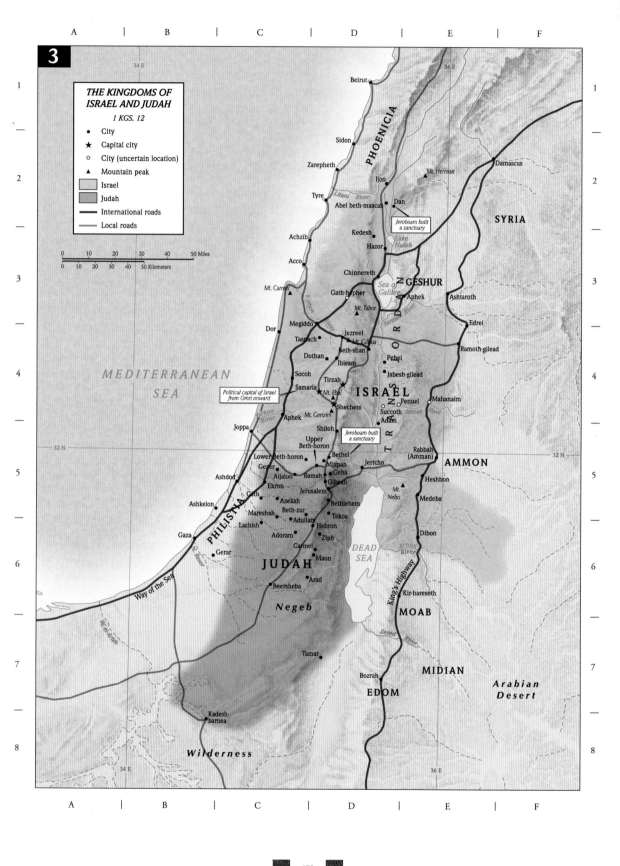

3

THE KINGDOMS OF ISRAEL AND JUDAH
1 KGS. 12

- • City
- ★ Capital city
- ○ City (uncertain location)
- ▲ Mountain peak
- Israel
- Judah
- —— International roads
- —— Local roads

0 10 20 30 40 50 Miles
0 10 20 30 40 50 Kilometers

MEDITERRANEAN SEA

PHOENICIA

Beirut

Sidon

Zarepheth

Tyre
Litani River

Achzib

Acco

Dor

Mt. Carmel ▲

Megiddo

Taanach

Dothan

Socoh

Samaria ★

Aphek

Joppa

Lower Beth-horon
Upper Beth-horon

Gezer

Ashdod

Aijalon
Ramah

Ekron

Ashkelon

Gath

Azekah
Beth-zur
Mareshah

Lachish

Adoram

Adullam

Gaza

Gerar

Carmel

Maon

Beersheba

Arad

JUDAH

Negeb

Tamar

Kadesh-barnea

Wilderness

Ijon

Abel beth-maacah

Kedesh

Hazor

Chinnereth

Gath-hepher

Mt. Tabor ▲

Jezreel
Mt. Gilboa ▲
Beth-shan
Ibleam

Tirzah

Mt. Ebal ▲
Shechem
Mt. Gerizim ▲

Shiloh

Bethel

Mizpah
Geba
Gibeah
Jerusalem

Bethlehem

Tekoa

Hebron

Ziph

Mt. Hermon ▲

Dan

Jeroboam built a sanctuary

Lake Huleh

Sea of Galilee

GESHUR

Aphek

Ashtaroth

Edrei

Ramoth-gilead

Pehel

Jabesh-gilead

Penuel

Succoth
Adam

Mahanaim

Rabbah (Amman)

AMMON

Jericho

Mt. Nebo ▲

Heshbon

Medeba

Dibon

DEAD SEA

King's Highway

Kir-haresceth

MOAB

Arnon River

Zered River

Bozrah

EDOM

MIDIAN

Arabian Desert

Damascus

SYRIA

ISRAEL

JORDAN

TRANS

Jordan River

Yarmuk River

Jabbok River

Political capital of Israel from Omri onward

Jeroboam built a sanctuary

Way of the Sea

N. Besor

W. Arish

PHILISTIA

34 E

36 E

34 E

36 E

32 N

32 N

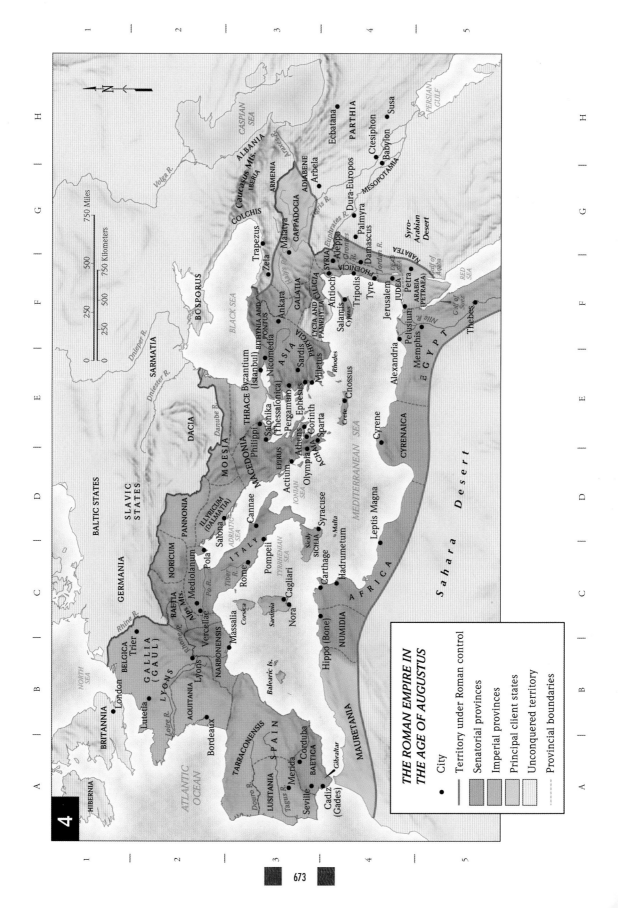

THE ROMAN EMPIRE IN THE AGE OF AUGUSTUS

- City
- Territory under Roman control
- Senatorial provinces
- Imperial provinces
- Principal client states
- Unconquered territory
- Provincial boundaries

4

HIBERNIA

BRITANNIA
London
Lutetia

GERMANIA
BALTIC STATES
SLAVIC STATES
SARMATIA

GALLIA (GAUL)
BELGICA
Trier
AQUITANIA
Bordeaux
LYONS
Lyons
NARBONENSIS
Massalia
Vercellae
Mediolanum
RAETIA
NORICUM
PANNONIA
DACIA
MOESIA

SPAIN
TARRACONENSIS
LUSITANIA
Merida
Seville
BAETICA
Corduba
Cadiz (Gades)
Gibraltar

Balearic Is.
Corsica
Sardinia
Nora
Cagliari

ITALY
Pola
Salona
ILLYRICUM (DALMATIA)
Cannae
Rome
Pompeii
Sicily
Carthage
Hadrumetum
Syracuse
Malta
Leptis Magna

MAURETANIA
NUMIDIA
Hippo (Bone)
AFRICA

Sahara Desert

EPIRUS
Actium
MACEDONIA
Philippi
Thessalonica
Salonika
THRACE
Byzantium (Istanbul)
BITHYNIA AND PONTUS
Nicomedia
Ankara
GALATIA
Zela
Trapezus
Malatya
CAPPADOCIA
ARMENIA
IBERIA
ALBANIA
COLCHIS
Caucasus Mts.

ASIA
Pergamum
Sardis
PHRYGIA
Ephesus
Miletus
LYCIA AND PAMPHYLIA
CILICIA
Antioch
SYRIA
Aleppo
PHOENICIA
Palmyra
Damascus
Dura-Europos
MESOPOTAMIA
ADIABENE
Arbela
Ecbatana
PARTHIA
Ctesiphon
Babylon
Susa

Athens
Olympia
ACHAEA
Corinth
Sparta
Crete
Cnossus
Rhodes
Salamis
Cyprus
Tyre
Tripolis
JUDEA
Jerusalem
Pelusium
ARABIA
Petra
NABATEA (PETRAEA)
Syro-Arabian Desert

Cyrene
CYRENAICA
Alexandria
Memphis
EGYPT
Thebes

MEDITERRANEAN SEA
BLACK SEA
BOSPORUS
ADRIATIC SEA
IONIAN SEA
TYRRHENIAN SEA
CASPIAN SEA
RED SEA
PERSIAN GULF
Gulf of Suez
Gulf of Aqaba
NORTH SEA
ATLANTIC OCEAN

Rhine R.
Rhône R.
Loire R.
Tagus R.
Douro R.
Po R.
Tiber R.
Danube R.
Dniester R.
Dnieper R.
Volga R.
Araxes R.
Halys R.
Tigris R.
Euphrates R.
Orontes R.
Jordan R.
Nile R.

Alps Mts.

N

0   250   500   750 Kilometers
0   250   500   750 Miles

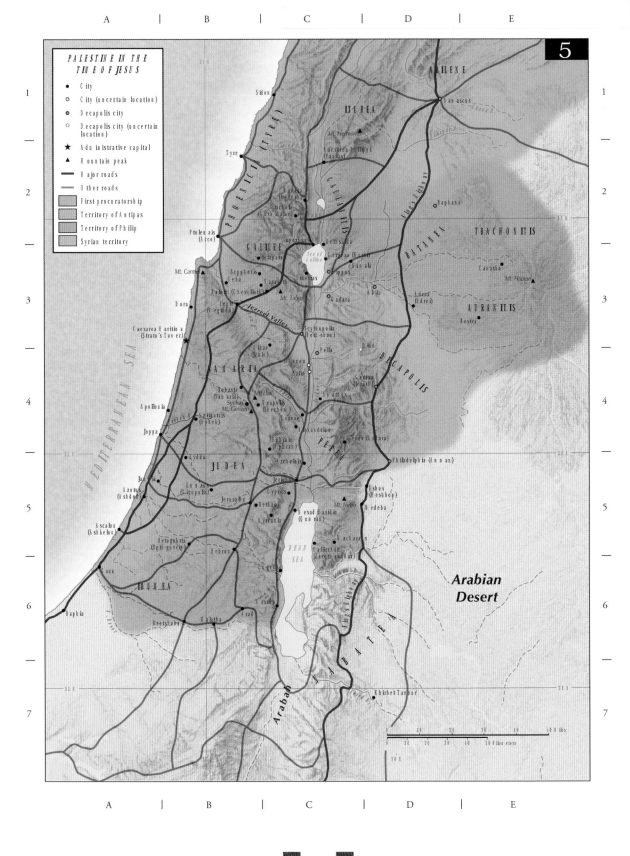

PALESTINE IN THE TIME OF JESUS

- • City
- ○ City (uncertain location)
- ◉ Decapolis city
- ○ Decapolis city (uncertain location)
- ★ Administrative capital
- ▲ Mountain peak
- —— Major roads
- ----- Other roads
- First procuratorship
- Territory of Antipas
- Territory of Philip
- Syrian territory

5

Sidon

ABILENE

Damascus

ITUREA

Mt. Hermon ▲

Caesarea Philippi
(Paneas)

Tyre

PHOENICIA (TYRE)

GAULANITIS

Raphana

BATANEA

TRACHONITIS

Ptolemais
(Acco)

GALILEE

Jotapata

Sea of
Galilee

Bethsaida

Gergesa (Kursi)

Capernaum

Hippos

Gadara (Umm)

Canatha

Mt. Hauran ▲

AURANITIS

Mt. Carmel ▲

Sepphoris

Geba

Nazareth

Tiberias

Abila

Adraa
(Edrei)

Dora

Yaloth (Chesulloth)

Mt. Tabor ▲

Jezreel valley

Gadara

Bostra

MEDITERRANEAN SEA

Caesarea Maritina
(Strato's Tower) ★

Legio
(Megiddo)

Scythopolis
(Beth-shean)

Ginae
(Jenin)

Pella

Dion

DECAPOLIS

SAMARIA

Sebaste
(Samaria)

Aenon

Salim

Gerasa
(Jerash)

Apollonia

Sychar
Mt. Ebal ▲
Neapolis
(Shechem)
Mt. Gerizim ▲

Korea

Amathus

Antipatris
(Aphek)

Ephraim
(Ophrah)

PEREA

Gedor (Gadara)

Joppa

Philadelphia (Amman)

Lydda

JUDEA

Archelais

Jamnia

En az an
(Nicopolis)

Jericho

Cyprus

Eshus
(Heshbon)

Azotus
(Ashdod)

Jerusalem

Bethany

Medeba

Ascalon
(Ashkelon)

Betogabris
(Beit-guvrin)

Hebron

Hyrcania

Mt. Nebo ▲

Mesad Hasidim
(Qumran)

DEAD
SEA

Machaerus

Callirhoe
(Zereth-shahar)

Gaza

IDUMEA

Engedi

Masada

Arabian
Desert

Raphia

Beersheba

Malatha

Arad

NABATEA

King's Highway

Arabah

Khirbet Tannur

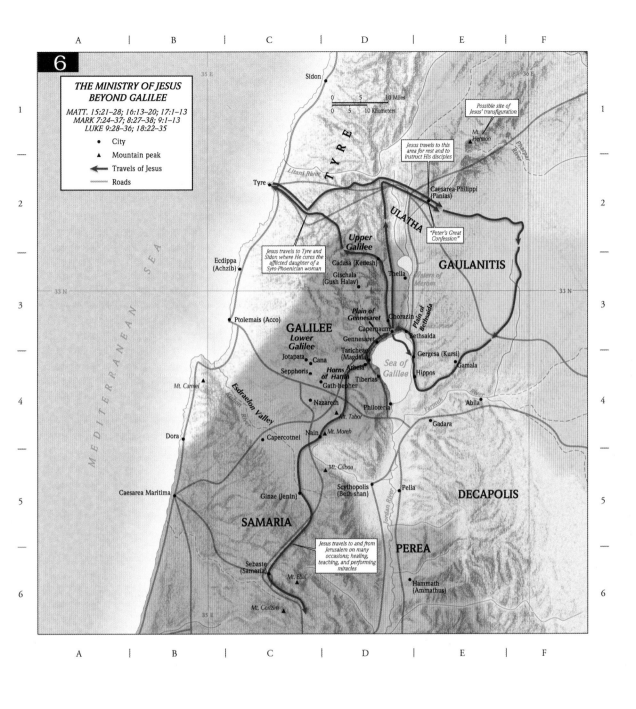

THE MINISTRY OF JESUS
BEYOND GALILEE

MATT. 15:21–28; 16:13–20; 17:1–13
MARK 7:24–37; 8:27–38; 9:1–13
LUKE 9:28–36; 18:22–35

- • City
- ▲ Mountain peak
- ← Travels of Jesus
- Roads

0   5   10 Miles
0   5   10 Kilometers

Sidon

TYRE

Litani River

Pharpar River

Mt. Hermon

Possible site of
Jesus' transfiguration

Jesus travels to this
area for rest and to
instruct His disciples

Tyre

Caesarea-Philippi
(Panias)

ULATHA

"Peter's Great
Confession"

Jesus travels to Tyre and
Sidon where He cures the
afflicted daughter of a
Syro-Phoenician woman

Upper
Galilee

GAULANITIS

Ecdippa
(Achzib)

Cadasa (Kedesh)

Gischala
(Gush Halav)

Thella

Waters of
Merom

Ptolemais (Acco)

Plain of
Gennesaret

Chorazin

Plain of
Bethsaida

GALILEE

Lower
Galilee

Capernaum

Gennesaret

Bethsaida

Jotapata

Cana

Taricheae
(Magdala)

Gergesa (Kursi)

Sepphoris

Horns
of Hattin

Arbela

Sea of
Galilee

Hippos

Gamala

Gath-hepher

Tiberias

Mt. Carmel

Esdraelon Valley

Kishon River

Nazareth

Mt. Tabor

Philoteria

Abila

Yarmuk River

Dora

Capercotnei

Nain

Mt. Moreh

Gadara

Mt. Gilboa

Caesarea Maritima

Ginae (Jenin)

Scythopolis
(Beth-shan)

Pella

DECAPOLIS

SAMARIA

Jordan River

PEREA

MEDITERRANEAN SEA

Jesus travels to and from
Jerusalem on many
occasions; healing,
teaching, and performing
miracles

Sebaste
(Samaria)

Mt. Ebal

Hammath
(Ammathus)

Mt. Gerizim

35 E

36 E

33 N

35 E

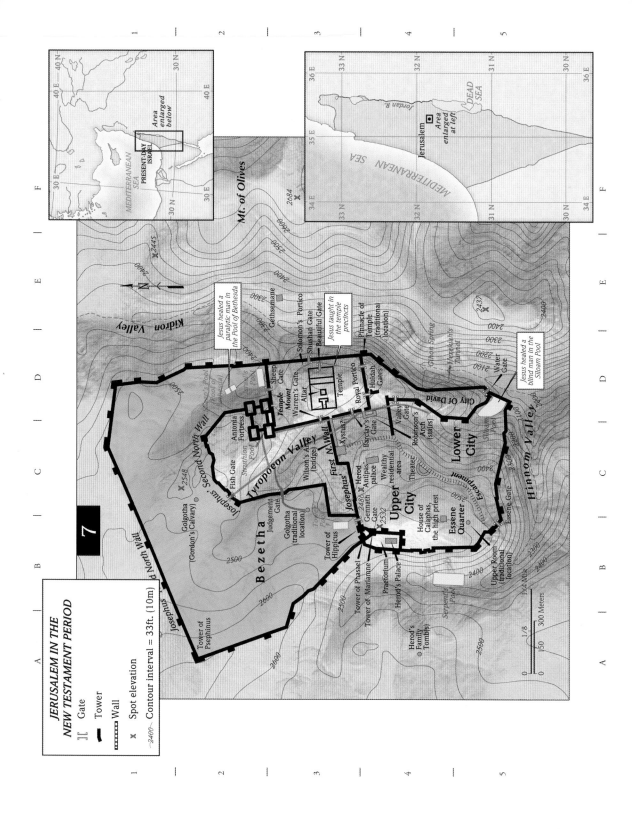

JERUSALEM IN THE
NEW TESTAMENT PERIOD

⊥L Gate

━━ Tower

▬▬▬▬ Wall

✕ Spot elevation

~2400~ Contour interval = 33ft. (10m)

7

Mt. of Olives

Kidron Valley

✕ 2084

Gethsemane

Jesus healed a
paralytic man in
the Pool of Bethesda

Pool of Bethesda

Israel's Pool

Sheep Gate

Solomon's Portico

Shushan Gate

Beautiful Gate

Jesus taught in
the temple precincts

Pinnacle of
Temple (traditional
location)

Second North Wall

✕ 2548

Fish Gate

Antonia Fortress

Struthion Pool

Warren's Gate

Temple Mount

Altar

Temple

Royal Portico

Huldah Gates

Gihon Spring

Hezekiah's Tunnel

✕ 2437

Water Gate

Jesus healed a
blind man in the
Siloam Pool

Bezetha

Tyropoeon Valley

First N. Wall

Wilson's Arch (bridge)

Xystus

Barclay's Gate

Robinson's Arch (stairs)

City Of David

Lower City

Valley Gate

Hinnom Valley

Golgotha
(Gordon's Calvary)

Josephus'

Judgement Gate

Golgotha
(traditional
location)

Tower of Hippicus

Theater

Antipas' palace

Herod's palace

Wealthy residential area

Escarpment

Upper City

House of
Caiaphas,
the high priest

Essene Quarter

Essene Gate

2400

Gennath Gate

✕ 2532

✕ 2484

Tower of Phasael

Tower of Mariamne

Praetorium

Herod's Palace

Upper Room
(traditional
location)

2400

Serpent's Pool

Herod's
Family
Tomb(s)

Third North Wall

Josephus'

Tower of Psephinus

2600

2500

2500

2400

N

1/4 Mile

1/8

0 150 300 Meters

0 300 Meters

676

Mt. of Olives

Kidron Valley

MEDITERRANEAN SEA

PRESENT-DAY ISRAEL

Area enlarged below

DEAD SEA

Jordan R.

Jerusalem

Area enlarged at left

MEDITERRANEAN SEA

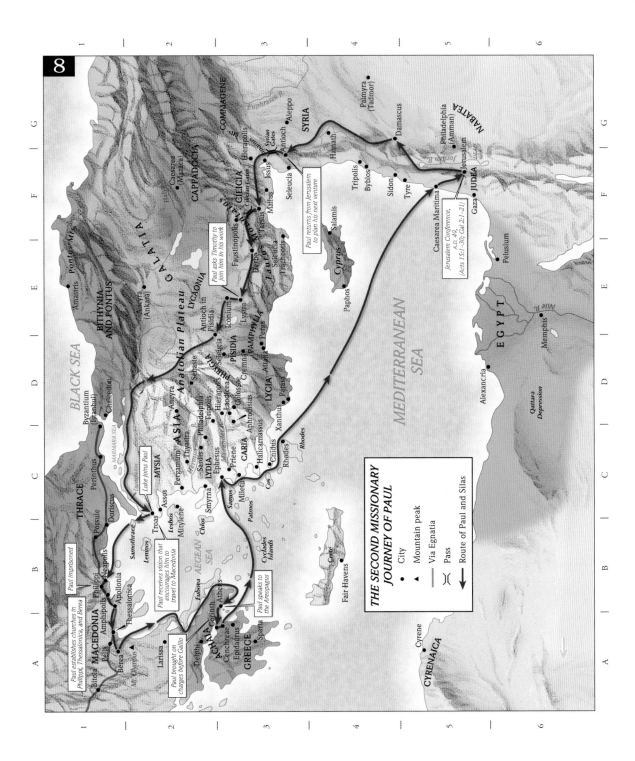

THE SECOND MISSIONARY
JOURNEY OF PAUL

- City
- ▲ Mountain peak
- Via Egnatia
-)(Pass
- ↓ Route of Paul and Silas

Paul establishes churches in
Philippi, Thessalonica, and Berea

Paul Imprisoned

Paul receives vision that
encourages him to
travel to Macedonia

Luke Joins Paul

Paul brought on
charges before Gallio

Paul speaks to
the Areopagus

Paul asks Timothy to
join him in his work

Paul returns from Jerusalem
to plan his next venture

Caesarea Maritima

Jerusalem Conference,
A.D. 49,
(Acts 15:1–30; Gal 2:1–21)

BLACK SEA

THRACE

BITHYNIA
AND PONTUS

MACEDONIA

GALATIA

Anatolian Plateau

CAPPADOCIA

COMMAGENE

ASIA

MYSIA

LYCAONIA

PISIDIA

PHRYGIA

CILICIA

SYRIA

LYDIA

CARIA

PAMPHYLIA

LYCIA

GREECE

ACHAIA

AEGEAN
SEA

Cyclades
Islands

MEDITERRANEAN
SEA

Cyprus

NABATEA

JUDEA

EGYPT

CYRENAICA

Crete

Fair Havens

Byzantium
(Istanbul)

Chalcedon

Perinthus

Doriscus

Poiséle

Neapolis

Philippi

Amphipolis

Apollonia

Thessalonica

Pella

Berea

Larissa

Mt. Olympus ▲

Delphi

Corinth

Cenchreae

Epidaurus

Sparta

Athens

Eubœa

Troas

Assos

Mitylene

Lesbos

Chios

Samos

Miletus

Priene

Ephesus

Smyrna

Pergamum

Thyatira

Sardis

Philadelphia

Tripolis

Hierapolis

Laodicea

Colossae

Aphrodisias

Halicarnassus

Cnidus

Cos

Rhodes

Rhodes

Xanthus

Patara

Attalia

Perga

Cremna

Antioch in
Pisidia

Iconium

Lystra

Derbe

Seleucia

Faustinopolis

Tyana

Caesarea
(Mazaca)

Ancyra
(Ankara)

Amastris

Pontus Mts.

Taurus Mts.

Anti-Taurus Mts.

Cilician Gates

Tarsus

Mallus

Issus

Syrian
Gates

Seleucia

Antioch

Hierapolis

Aleppo

Palmyra
(Tadmor)

Hamath

Tripolis

Byblos

Sidon

Tyre

Damascus

Philadelphia
(Amman)

Jerusalem

Gaza

Pelusium

Alexandria

Memphis

Cyrene

Qattara
Depression

Euphrates R.

Jordan R.

Nile R.

MARMARA SEA

Propontis

Hermus R.

Salamis

Paphos

Seleucia

Tracheotis

prophecies of, 195, 282; and sins of Israel, 194

Amos, book of, **32, 522–523;**
as minor prophet, 225
reference to stars, *324*

Amoz, 170

Anak, **33,** 39

Anakim, 33, 39, 113, 136

Anakites, 33

Anammelech, **33**

Ananias, believer at Jerusalem, **33**

Ananias, believer at Damascus, **33,** 595, 596

Anathoth, **33,** 498, 501

Andrew, disciple, **38,** 58, 73, 133, 134, 156, **174,** 313, 347, 544, 560, 584

Angel(s), **34,** *120,* 153; Abaddon, **17,** 34; Apollyon, 17, **38,** 34; appearing, *34;* to Abraham, *21;* to Balaam, *34,* 49; to Gideon, 249; to Hagar, 171; to Isaac, *21;* to Jacob, *34,* 57, 212; to Joseph, 24; to Mary, 187, 216, 319, 353; names Israel, 172; wrestles Jacob, 174; archangel, **40;** Gabriel, 132, *236;* Michael, 34, 40, 222; at Ascension, 593; blowing trumpets, 290; bring judgment, 667; of bottomless pit, 17, 34; carry messages, 405, 663, 665, *666;* cherubims, **78;** of death, 342; fallen, 34; Gabriel, 24, 34, 132, *132;* inferior to Jesus, 642, 643; legion of, 201; of the Lord, **34;** not to be worshiped, 627; other appearances of, *34;* Pharisees' unbelief of, 296; as principality, 275; surround God's throne, 664, 667; symbolic meaning of, 290, 324

Anger, **34,** 277, 362

Animal(s),
bees, 356; blood of sacrificial, 336; buzzard, 353; camel, *224;* dog, 360; eagles, 359; ferret, **124,** 135; as food, 351; food for, 326; fox. *See* Animal(s), jackal; goad for, 323; grazing, 326; greyhound, **145;** hawk, *353;* hind, **157;** horse, **161,** 323, 355; jackal, **174;** kid, **193;** kine, **194;** lamb, **196;** leopard, **201;** lizard, **206;** mole, 356; moth, **230,** 360; mouse, **230;** oxen, 355; poisonous, 351; polecat, 356; ram, 338; red kite, 353; for sacrificial offering, 283, 295, 314 , *330,* 336, 344, 356; scorpion, 351; shark, 357; sheep, 360; shelter for, 323; skins of, 331, 362; snake, 351; tortoise, 343; **trapping,** 318; unclean, 279, 325, 331, 343, 353, 356; unicorn, 349; vulture, 353, *353;* whale, 357; wild ox, 349; wolf, 360; worm, 362; and yoke, 363; **young,** 327

Anise, **35,** 101

Anna, **35,** 277, 344, 571

Annas, 588

Anointing, **35,** *35,* 38, 71, 298, 246, 300, 414

Anointed One, 180

Ant, **36**

Antediluvians, **36**

Anthropomorphisms, **36**

Antichrist, **36,** 37, 103, 631, 654, 665, 667, 668; characteristics, 37; final abode of, 260

Antinomianism, **37**

Antioch of Pisidia, **37,** 133; **Paul's preaching in,** 267, 598; Antioch of Syria, 26, **37;** church of, 37, 79, 258, 597; and Judaizers, 620; and Jerusalem Council, 180; and missionaries, 199, 599; Paul visits, 261, 600; Antiochus IV Epiphanes, 19–20, **37,** 211; Antipatris, **37;** Antonia, fortress of, 75; Anvil, **37**

Anxiety, 305, 328

Ape, **37**

Apis, 71, 380

Apocalypse/Apocalyptic literature, *36,* **37,** 94, *120*

Apocrypha, **37**

Apollos, 28, **37,** 600, 611, 642

Apollyon, 17, 34, **38**

Apostle(s), *34,* **38,** 142. *See also* Disciple(s); accused by Sanhedrin, 87–88; choose Matthias, 218; **and divine purpose,** 290; doctrine of, 189; Jesus' **appearance to,** 289; and Mary Magdalene,

216; miracles of, 225; proclaim resurrection, 289; Simon Peter, 313; Simon Zelotes, 314; Apothecary, **38**

Appian Way. *See* Appii Forum

Appii Forum, **38,** 130, 332

Aquila, 37, **38,** 270, 293, 600, 601, 609, 615, 638, 640

Arabah, **28**

Arabia, **39,** 50, 249, 491; ancestors of, 309; country of, 295; and Midianites, 222; and myrrh, 232; people of, 72, 136, 172; and queen of Sheba, 39; Aram, **39,** 329. *See also* Syria

Arameans, 309

Aramaic, 58, 72, 115

Ararat, Little, *39*

Ararat, Mount, **39,** *39,* 40, 41

Araunah, **39**

Arba, **39**

Archaeology, **39,** 148. *See also* Bible, and archaeology

Archelaus, **40**

Archevites, **40**

Arcturus, **40**

Areopagus, **40,** 45, 101

Argob, **40**

Ariel, **40,** 492

Arimathaea/Arimathea, **40.** *See also* Joseph of Arimathea

Aristarchus, **40**

Ark, Noah's, 39, **40,** *41,* 127

Ark, **building of,** 142, 372, *373,* 242; Ark of the covenant/Ark of the testimony, **41;** captured, 165, 310; crossing Jordan, 400, 412, 413; destruction of, 334; and Jerusalem, 176, 240, 418, 420, 439; and Kohathites, 196; lumber for, 311; penalty for touching, 350; places kept, 19, 58, 195, 440; pictured, *220;* in temple, 93, 111, 334, 426, 444; and Ten Commandments, 394

Armageddon, **41.** *See also* Archangel

Armenia, 39, **41**

Armor of God, 153, 623

Armour, **41,** 145, 153, 309

Armourbearer, **41**

Army, 128, 158; Assyrian, 332; Babylonian, 237; David's, 158, 176, 183, 350; Egyptian, 225; Roman, 172, 180; Saul's, 222; Syrian, 233; Arnon, **41**

Aromatic cane, **41,** 71

Arphaxad, **41**

Arrogance, 274

Arrow, **41,** 269, 281

Artaxerxes I, **41,** 262, 452, 453, 454

Artemis, **42,** 140. *See also* Diana

Artificer, **42**

Asa, **42,** 56, 428, 445, 446; battle at Mareshah, 214; and Hilkiah, **157;** son of, 177; Asahel, **42**

Asaph, **42**

Ascension of Christ, **42,** *43,* 289, 313. *See also* Jesus Christ; and evangelism, 185

Asenath, **42,** 248, 376

Aser, 42

Ashdod, **42,** 47, 93, 265, 413

Asher. *See also* Tribes of Israel, Asher; son of Jacob, **42,** 366, 388, 397, 402, 405, 439; territory of, 22, 225; Asherah, 44, 140, 280

Ashes, **42**

Ashima, **42**

Ashkelon, **42**

Ashtaroth/Ashtoreth, **42,** 44, 140, 146, 280

Ashurbanipal, 44

Asia, 24, **44,** 262, 338, 339, 600, 601, 650

Asia Minor, 37, 44, 61, 80, 114, 133, 252, 658, 663; cities of, 165, 264, 299; Bithynia, **61;** Cilicia, **80;** Ephesus, **114,** 140; Galatia, **133;** Laodicea, 198; Lycaonia, 210; Miletus, 223; and Paul, 265, 267, 258; Pisidia, 37, 133; **Priscilla and Aquila's home,** 270; **and seven churches,** 261, 264, 306, 318, 338; Tarsus, 80

Askelon, 42, **44,** 265

Asnapper, **44**

Asp, **44**

Ass, **44,** 127

Assembly, **44,** 79, 85, 86

Asshur, **44,** 242

Assos, 291

Assur, **44**

Assurance, 337

Assyria, **44,** 45, 74, 110, 151, *473,* 489, 490, 491, 492, 517, 519, 526; allies of, 329; ancestry of, 44, 309; Ava, 46; Calah, 71; capture of Samaria, 304; cruelty in warfare 437, 529, *529,* 530; defeat of Northern Kingdom (Israel), 33, 40, 42, 73, 92, 98, 101, 115, 143, 148, 149, 172, 297, 306, 327, 331, 332, 398, 431, 435, 528; defeat of Syria, 329; gods of, 24, 33, 42; idolatry of, 238; Nisroch, 242; Halah, 148; Hara, 149; and Hosea, 161; and Judah, 170, 237; kings of, 27, 44; Esar-haddon, 115; Sargon, 218, 299; Sennacherib, 115, 197, 242, 282, 312; Shalmaneser, 44, 163, 238; Sennacherib, 45; Tigleth-pileser III, 151, 219, 339; Nineveh, 186, 242, 525, *529;* people of, 44, 45, 56, 98, 101; Avites, 240; prophecies concerning, 529, 530, 533; downfall of, 233; by Isaiah, 212; siege at Millo, 224; siege Jerusalem, 156

Astrologer, **45,** 276, 494. *See also* Magic; Witchcraft; Wise men

Aswan, **45.** *See also* Sinim

Athaliah, 28, 45, 434, *446,* 447; daughter of Ahab, 248, 27; Joash hidden from, 177, 183; family of, 28; Atheism, **45**

Athena, *45*

Athens, **45,** *45,* 101, 115, 145, 600, 629, 646; philosophers of, 40, 45, 101, 115

Athletics, 612, 646, 663

Atonement **45,** 46, *46,* 50, 62, *66,* 90, 114, 122, 131, 142, 153, 383, 384, 389; and Gentiles, 222; by sacrifice, 295

Atonement, Day of, **46,** *46,* 159, 385; and high priest, 300; and laying on of hands, 199; and mercy seat, 220; sin offering, 314

Augustus, **46,** 70, 292. *See also* Caesar

Aul, **46**

Author, 73

Authority, 321, 338

Autumn rain, **46,** 129

Ava, **46**

Aven, **46,** 248

Avenger of blood, **46,** 80

Avims 393

Avites, 240

Awl, **46**

Axe, **47**

Azariah/Abed-nego, 18, **47**

Azariah/Ahaziah, 28, **46-47,** 188, 195

Azariah, prophet, **47**

Azariah/Uzziah, **47,** 434, 447

Azazel, **47,** 300. *See also* Scapegoat

Azotus, 42, **47**

Azzah, **47,** 135

B

Baal, 27, **48,** 48, *48,* 74, *109,* 110, 140, 405, 406, 424, 429, 433, 519; and Ahab, *178;* and Elijah, 165; and Jezebel, 183; prophets of, 195; worship of, 177; Baalah, **48**

Baal-berith, **48**

Baali, 171

Baalim, **48,** 48

Baal-peor, **48**

Baal-perazim, **48** *See also* Perazim

Baal-zebub, **48,** 265

Baasha, **49,** 178, 233, 271, 428, 446

Babel, Tower of, **49,** 136, 228, 316, 366, 373

Baboon, **49.** *See also* Peacock

Baby, 328

Babylon, **49**, 120, *196*, 305, 667
Babylonia/Babylonian Empire, **49**, 262. *See also* Exile, Babylonian/Persian
and Abraham, 20; Ahava, **27**; allies of, 329; ancient, 328; and astrology, 324, 494; as pagan people, 45, 93, 147; Babylon, capital city, 120; captures Manasseh, 214; Chebar, **77**; conquers Assyria, *473*, 529; conquers Egypt, 504; conquest/captivity of Judah (Southern Kingdom), **74**; and books of Chronicles, 79; captives made, 288, 437, 450; and Daniel, 93, 513; Ezekiel prophesies, 120; as God's judgment, 147, 496–497, 528, 531-532; and Hezekiah, *156*, 436, 448, 493; and Jeremiah; prophecies of, 148, 500, 502; remains in Jerusalem, 178; treated kindly, 504; and Jerusalem, 135, 431, 454, 536; conquest of, 177, 180, 237, 331; and Joel, 520; and Obadiah, 524; by Nebuchanezzar, 176; psalms of, 472, 473; return from, 398; and 2 Kings, 195; Cuth/Cuthah, 92; defeated, 92, *94;* destruction of ark of the covenant, 334; destruction of Nineveh, 242; destruction of Jerusalem, 198; destruction of temple, 334; and Dispersion, 223; Dura, 105; Euphrates River, 117; gods of, 49, 221; and Jews, 238, 365; judgment of, 276, 290, 491; king(s) of, 96; Belshazzar, **55**, *55;* Berodach-baladan, 56; called Lucifer, 209; Evil-Merodach/Merodach-baladan, 119; Hammurabi, 148; Nebuchadnezzar, 18, 41, 49, 55, 104, 105, 119, 237, 365; and Mesopotamia, 221; music in, 105; and Nebuchadnezzar's family, 297; and Nimrod, 242; and Northern Kingdom, 148; plain of Dura, 105; Prince Nergal-Sharezer, 238; prophecy concerning, 147, 504, 515; provided colonists, 92; renamed Jews, 221; Shinar, 22, 49; tower of Babel, **49**, *49*, 136, *373*, *373;* towns of, 27; Ur, 20
Babylonish garment, **49**
Backsliding/apostasy, 38, 49
Badger, **49**, 85
Bag, **49**. *See also* Scrip
Bagpipe, 105
Balaam, 27, *34*, **49**, 50, 241, 260, 263, 267, 391. *See also* Prophecy, by Balaam
Balak/Balac, 49, **50**, 260, 391
Balance, **50**
Balm of Gilead, *50*, **138**, 151, 218
Balsam, **50**
Banner, **50**, 114, 323
Banquet, **50**, *128*
Baptism, 41, *50*, 180, 249; of eunuch, 264; and John the Baptist, 185, 296; of Jesus, 187, 319, 345; as sacrament, 295; Barabbas, **51**
Barak, **51**, 97, 151, 404, 405; as Issacharite, 172; Deborah sends out, 331; defeat of Canaanites, 190, 331; defeats king of Hazor, 173; victory over Sisera, 219
Barbarian, **51**, 606
Bar-jesus, **51**, 111, 598
Bar-jona, **51**
Barley, **51**, 127, 254, 277
Barnabas, **51**, 92, 99, 559, 595, 596, 597, 598, 599, 620, 642; called Joses, 188; called Jupiter, 190, 191; confirmed as missionary, 199; in Iconium, 165; and Jerusalem Council, 188; and Mark, 215; and miracles, 336; and Paul, 258, 261, 296, 303; testimony of, 336; and Simeon, 313
Barracks, **51**, 75
Barren, **51**, 78
Barrier, **51**
Bartholomew/Nathanael, **51**, 133, 347
Bartimaeus, **51**, 564
Baruch, **52**, 168, 502, *503*, 504
Barzillai, **52**
Bashan, 40, **52**, 108, 246, 391, 394, 522
Basin/Bason, **52**

Bat, **52**
Bath, **52**
Bathing, **52**
Bath-sheba/Bathsheba, **52**, 95, 419, 420, 425, 471; and David, 234, *234*, 350; mother of Solomon, 280; son Nathan, 234
Bath-shua, 52
Battlement, **52**
Battle of Armegeddon, 183
Bdellium, **52**
Beans, 277
Bear, **52**
Beard, **52**
Beast, the, 290
Beatitudes, the, **53**, *53*, 546. *See also* Principles, biblical; Chapel of the Beatitudes
Beautiful Gate, the, **53**, 81
Bedan, **53**
Bedchamber, **53**
Bedouins *532*
Beeliada, 110
Beelzebub/Beelzebul, 48–49, **53**
Beersheba, altar, *31*
Beer-sheba, city, **53**
Beer-sheba, well, **53**, 374, 375
Beer-sheba, wilderness of, **53**
Beggar, **54**
Behavior, 333-334, 341
Beheading, **54**
Behemoth, **54**
Bekah, **54**
Bela, **54**, 80. *See also* Zoar
Belial, **54**, 480
Belief, 326
Believer(s), **55**. *See also* names of individual believers; access to God, 275, 329; accountability of, 22; as ambassadors, 31, 285; Apollos, 378; attitude of, 318; and forgiveness, 288; love test for, *208;* patience of, 258; avoid sin, 198, 210, 130, 151, 256; and baptism, 51; behavior of, 333-334; Bereans, 56; called Christians, 79; Christ's love for, 277; and Christ's return, 337; and Christ's victory, 275; Cleopas, 82; commitment to Christ, 361; Demas, 98; duty to God, 334; and edification, 107; equipped for missions, 226; and eternal life, 117, 152, 228, 289, 314; faith of, 292; and false prophets, 122; fellowship of, 124; foundation in Christ, 293; fruitfulness of, 131; Gentile, 180; gifts bestowed on, 323; God's care for, 148; and God's commandments, 78, 80, 185; God's grace to, 143; God's household, 163; and God's kingship, 194; greeted, 209; and guilt, 146; and Hebrews, 153; as heirs, 303; holiness of, 225, 298; and Holy Spirit, 106; and Jesus, 90, 139; and judgment, 190-191; and justice, 191; Paul's letters to, 87, *87*, 114, 174; as priests, 275; meeting with Paul, 332; and new covenant, 240; and obedience, 346; purification of, 286; resisting Satan, 334; rewards for, 285, 304; and resurrection, 182; righteousness through God, 291; salvation of, 168, 240, 275, 285; service for God, 353; set apart for God, 296; sharing Christ's reign, 362; transformed minds, 358; "walk worthy," 353; as witnesses for Christ, 360
Bellows, **55**. *See also* Smith
Belshazzar, **55**, *55*, 515
Belt, **55**, 138
Belteshazzar, **56**. *93*
Benaiah, **56**
Ben-ammi, **56**
Benedictus, 570
Ben-hadad, 434
Ben-hadad I, **56**, 446
Ben-hadad II, 27, **56**, 430, 433
Ben-hadad III, **56**
Benjamin, **56**, *56*, 375, 376, 377, 388, 402, 408, 413, 414, 439. *See also* Tribes of Israel, Benjamin

held hostage, 313; and Judah, 189; son of Jacob, 282; territory of, 365; Benjamite, 258, 310
Berea/Beroea, **56**, 56, 600
Bernice, **56**
Berodach-baladan, **56**
Beryl, **57**, 74, 79
Bethabara, **57**
Bethany, **57**, 57
Bethel, *30*, **57**, 71, 108, 156, 179, 375, 427, 428, 433
Bethesda, pool of, **57**
Beth-horon, **57**, 444
Bethlehem, **57**, 70, *70*, 95, 115, 410, *527;* birthplace of Jesus, 182, 187, 216, 527, 528, 543–544, 570; Church of the Nativity, *25*, *73;* City of David, 57, 81; and Izban, 165; Naomi returns to, 234, 294; wise men visit, 359
Bethlehem-judah, 57
Beth-millo, **57**
Beth-peor, **57**
Bethphage, **57**
Bethsaida, 33, **58**, 547, 562
Bethshan, **58**
Beth–shan, 473
Beth-shean, 58
Beth–shemesh, **58**
Beth-shemesh, 58
Beth-zatha, 57, **58**
Beth-zur, **58**
Betrayal. *See* Judas Iscariot, betrayal of Christ
Betrothal, **58**, *59*, 103, 115
Beulah, **58**
Bezaleel, 381
Bezer, **58**, 80, *80*
Bible, **58**, 60, *60*, 64, 140. *See also* Old Testament; New Testament, and archaeology, **39**, 40, 114, 116, 148; apocalyptic literature, *120;* Apocrypha, **37**; Geneva, 60; God's revelation through, 360-361; King James Version, 60; on laziness and work, *361;* Pentateuch, 64; Law of Moses, 64, 102, 119; redemptive message, 60
Bier, 60
Bildad, **60**, 110, 184, 311, 464–466
Bilhah, **60**, 168, 234
Bird. *See also* Vulture; cuckow, 90; crane, 325; dove, **103**, 347; ibis, 328; of prey, **61**, 106. *See also* Speckled bird; sparrow, 322; stork, 325; swallow, 328; swan, 328; turtledove, 347; water hen, 328; white owl, 328
Birthright, **61**, 108, 115, *116*, 126; Christian, 168; Jacob's, 174; and laying on of hands, 199; lost by Reuben, 290; sold by Esau, 201
Bishop, **61**, 244, 250, 256
Bithynia, **61**, 600, 650
Bitter herbs, **61**
Bitter water, **61**
Bittern, **61**
Bitumen, **61**. *See also* Slime
Blacksmith. *See also* Smith
Black Sea, 270, 301
Black vulture, **61**, 250
Blains, **61**
Blasphemy, 325, 349, 385
Bless(ing[s]), **62**; God's, 276, 287, 305, 341; sacrifice as thanks for, 336; for service, 353; spiritual, 296; tongue used for, 342; when reviled, 290
Blood,
avenger of, **46**, 80; of Christ, 19, *46*, 62, 91, 275, 336; field of, *125;* on Israelites' doorpost, 342
Boanerges, **63**, 559
Boar, **63**
Boaz, 57, **63**, 139, 149, 409, 410
as kinsman-redeemer, 195; marriage of, 202, 234; and Ruth, 294
Boils, 61, **63**
Bondage, **64**. *See also* Israelites, as slaves
Bondservant, **64**, 176
Bone(s), **64**, 351
Book, **64**

Onion, **248**
Onycha, **248**
Onyx, **248**. *See also* Sardonyx
Ophel, **248**
Ophir, son of Joktan, **249**
Ophir, territory, **249**, 256
Ophrah, 179, **249**
Oppressor, **249**
Oracle, **249**
Orchard, 134, **249**
Ordain, **249**
Ordinances, **249**, 295
Organ, 127, 232, **249**. *See also* Pipe
Orion, **249**
Ornament(s), 243, **249**, 291, 316
Ornan/Araunah, *34*, **39**, 423, 440. *See also* Araunah.
Orontes, **249**
Orpah, **249**
Orphans, **249**
Orthodox Jew, *273*
Osee, **249**
Oshea, **250**
Osnappar, 44
Ospray, 61
Osprey, 137
Ossifrage, **250**
Ostrich, **250**
Othniel, 80, **250**, 404
Ouches, 140, **250**
Outcasts, **251**
Oven, **251**
Overseer, **251**
Owl, 145, **251**
Owner, **251**
Ox/Oxen, 139, 155, **251**, 269
Ox Goad, **251**
Ozias, **251**. *See also* Uzziah

P
Pace, **252**
Padan-Aram, **252**
Paddle, **252**
Pagan. *See* Gods, false; Altar
Paint, **252**
Palace, **252**
Palestina, **252**
Palestine, **252**, 265
 animals of, 52, 72, 85, 139, 256; boundaries with, 292; Arabian tribes in, 193; and archeology, 39; cities of, 80, 93; Caesarea, 70–71, 124, 156; Caesarea Philippi, 71; coins of, 227; crops of, 100, 144; customs of, 320; Dead Sea, 96; and Edom, 108; fuel in, 105; inhabitants of, 288; Iturea, 172; Jordan River, 187; Judea, 182, 189; Kishon River, 195; Lebanon, 201; Maccabean revolt, 211; Mount Carmel, 74, *109*. *See also* Carmel, Mount; Mount Hermon, 93. *See also* Hermon, Mount; Mount Hor, 160
Paul's journey to, 291
Plants/trees of, 126, 152, 232, 246, 248, 269
 places in, 48, 57, 356, 320; provinces of, 97, **133**; road through, 356; and Rome, 292; rulers of, 56, 155, 180, 185, 264, 278; tribes of, 78, 93, 148
Palm, **252**, 664
Palmer worm, 73, **252**
Palsy, **252**, 254
Pamphylia, **252**, 261, 598
Pan, 145, **252**
Pantheism, **252**
Paper, 68, **252**
Paphos, 51, **252**, 258
Paps, 66, **254**
Papyrus, 64, 68, 301, 312, 362. *See also* Bulrush
Parable(s), **200**, *200*, **254**, 276, 321, 548, 550, 551, 552, *552*, 553, 554, 561, *561*, 565, 568, 576, 577, 578
Paraclete, 83, 88, 153, **254**

Paradise, 152, 153, **254**
Paradox, **254**
Paralytic, **254**, 339
Paramour, 84, **254**
Paran (Mount), 111, **254**
Parapet, 52, **254**
Parched corn, **254**
Parched grain, **254**
Parchment, **254**
Pardon, 129, **255**
Parents, 78, 86, 94, 101, 245, 249, **255**
Parlour, **254**
Parthians, **254**
Partiality, **254**
Partition, 222, 334. *See also* Middle Wall of Partition
Partridge, **256**
Parvaim, **256**
Paschall Lamb, **256**
Pashur, **256**, 500
Passover, 61, 86, 106, 124, 154, **256**, *256*, *266*, 274, 328
 and Feast of Unleavened Bread, 124, 154; holy family attends, 216; and Lord's Supper, 182, 207; and new covenant, 240; observed by Jesus, 555, *555*, 565, 571, 579, 587; observed by Hezekiah, 156; in Old Testament times, *297*, 342, 385, 389, 395, 437, 448, 449, 452, 580, 615; and Pentecost, 260; and trial of Jesus, 266
Pastor, 61, 127, 244, **256**, 332
Pastoral epistles, **256**
Pasture, **256**
Pasture lands, **256**. *See also* Suburbs
Path, **256**
Pathros, **256**
Patience, 184, **258**, 344
Patmos, isle of, *34*, 185, **258**, *661*, *662*, 663
Patriarch(s), 136, 170, 199, 228, **258**, 269
Paul, 80, 101, 133, 134, 254, *256*, 263; angel appeared to, *34*
 as apostle, 38, 56, 87, 98, *99*, 117, 126, 130, 133, **258**; and believers, 332; birthplace of, 332; called Hermes, 190, 220; confirmed as missionary, 199; church plantings, 156, 337; commends believers, 206, 209, 216, 264; contemporaries of; Agabus, 26–27; Ananias, 33; Annas, 35; Apollos, 37–38; Areopagus council, 40, 101; Barnabas, 303; Claudius Lysias, 81; Crispus, 90; Demas, 98; Epaphras, 114; Epicurians, 115; Eutychus, 117; Felix, 124, 125; Festus, 125; Galatians, 133; Gallio, 134; Herod Agrippa, 156; Jason, 175; Lucius, 209; Lydia, 338; Mark, 215; Onesimus, 248, 264; Paulus, Sergius, 258; Philemon, 264; Phygellus, 265; Rufus, 293; Silas, 264, 337; Simeon (Niger), 313; Timothy, 55, 340, 357; Titus, 341; Trophimus, 345; conversion of, 33, 38, 51, 80, 93, 258, 300, 329, 404, 595, 596, 602, 604; converts of, 248, 258, 264; in Ephesus, 347; epistles of, 38, 115, 256, 258, 276, 338, 340, **604**, 642; Paul, epistles of; Colossians, 82–83, **627–628**; Corinthians, 78, 87, **610–615, 616–618**; Ephesians, 114, **622–623**; Galatians, 133, **619–621**; Philippians, 71, *114*, 274, **624–626**; Romans, 75, 292, 293, **605–609**; Thessalonians, 337, **629–630, 631–633**; Timothy, **634–636, 637–638**, 340; Titus, 341, **639**; Philemon, 316, **640**; excommunication by, 164; founded churches, 37, 86, 115, 249; and God's mercy, 220; healings by, 117, 127, 210, 598; and the Holy Spirit, 61, 62; and Hosea, 161; in Iconium, 165; imprisonment/trial, 258, 276; arrest for preaching, 320; at Antipatris, 37; appealed to Nero, 70; before Felix, 105, 124; before Festus, 125; before Herod Agrippa II, 56, 71, 156; at Jerusalem, 75, 88, 338; at Phillippi, 211, 264; prophecy of, 27; in Rome, 23, 114, *114*, *275*, 592, 603, 293; epistles written, 276, 622, 624,

627, 637, *638*, 640; intercession of, 169; and Jerusalem Council, 180; Jesus' appearance to, 289; journeys of, 22, 24, 28, 37, 38, 40, 45, *45*, 51, 56, 61, 75, 81, 86, *87*, 89, 92, 99, 100, 117, 121, *121*, 123, 133, **166**, 252, 258, 261, 291, 296, 297, 303, 313, 320, 325, 329, 340, 345, 347, 559, 592, 598, 599, 600, 634; and Judiazers, 189; letters from. *See* Paul, epistles to; in Macedonia, 211; and mariners, 214; martyred, 238, 258, 293, 325; and Mediterranean Sea, 218; miracles of, 279, 301, 336; as missionary, 38, 44, 45, *45*, 51, 75, 87, *87*, 92, 99, 104, 133, 264, 338; and Mnason, 226
 ; at Philippi, 210, 237, 274, 363; persecution of Christians, 329; preaching of, 37, 40, 44, *87*, 98, 100, 115, 117, 258, 267, 274, 329, 337, 592, 598, 606, 629, 634; prophecy by Agabus, 26, 27; shipwrecked, 219, 279; and Silas, 337; teachings of, 18, 21, 24, 29, 31, 37, 54, 56, 66, 67, 75, 78, 80, *82*, 83, 84, 85, 86, 87, 89, 102, 103, 114, 131, 139, 153, 155, 246, *248*, *256*, *258*; on Christ's return, 337; on eternity, 289; on giving, 341; on God's will, 358; on intermarriage, 170; on intermediate state, 170; on labor, 316, 337; on lasciviousness, 199; on the Law, 301; on liquor, 205; on magicians, 174, 175; on marriage, 163, 215; on meekness, 219; on mind, 224; on moderation, 227; on mystery, 232; on neighbors, 238; on novices, 244; on persecution, 340; on personal accomplishments, 286; on prayer, 169, 328; on righteous living, 261, 337; on sacrifice, 304; on sexual morality, 337; on sin, 354; on steadfastness, 262; on stumblingblock, 326; on tongues, 342; on vocation, 353; on women 614, 635, 636; as spiritual father, 634, 637, 639, 640; sufferings of, 258, 336, 343, 400, 602, 603, 613, 616, 617, 621, 625, 637; as tentmaker, 336; testimony of, 336; in Thessalonica, 337; and thorn in the flesh, 338; in Tyre, 347; and "yokefellow," 363
Paulus Sergius, 254, **258**
Pavement, the, 132, **259**
Pavilion, 105, **259**
Peace, 191, 218, **259**, 268, 278
Peacemaking, 53, 85, 110
Peace offering, 152
Peacock, 49, **259**
Pearl, **259**, 293
Peck, 69
Peg, *315*, 316
Pekah, 27, **259**, 435
Pekahiah, 219, **259**, 435
Peleg, **259**
Pelethites, **259**
Pelican, 87, 100, **259**
Pen, **259**
Peniel, 173, **260**
Penknife, **259**
Penny, 99, 123, **260**
Pentateuch, 64, 100, 199, 370, **260**
Pentecost, 86, 124, 149, 252, 254, **260**
 day of, , 342 521, 593, 265; feast of, 385, 601; Joel's prophecy of, 184; Spirit's power, 159
Penuel, 172
People of God, **260**
Peor, **260**
Perazim, 48
Perdition, 93, **260**
Perea (Roman province), 133, 138, 215, **260**
Perez, 262, 331
Perfection, **261**
Perfume, 167, 205, 232, 246, **261**, *261*, 322
Perfumer, 38
Perga, 252, **261**, 598
Pergamos, church of, 241, **261**, 306
Pergamos, city of, 44, 663
Pergamum. *See* Pergamos
Perrizites, 262

Principles, biblical, 67, 133, 149, 328, 334, 341
Prison, 80, 105, **275**, *275*, 355
Prisoners, 293, *302*
Priscilla/Prisca, 37, 38, 270, 293, 600, 601, 609, 615, 638, 640
Privy, **276**
Proclamation, **276**
Proconsul, 99, **276**
Prodigal Son, the, **276**, 568
Prognosticator, **276**
Promise, **276**
Promises, God's. S*ee* God, promises of
Promised Land, The, 17, *71*, 138, 252, 297, 343, 378, 387, 390, 391, 393, 397, 399, 497
  Hivites in, 158; and Jericho, 179; and Joshua, 188; and Kadesh, 192; and Moses' death, 237; and Nun, 244; Hebrews enter, 180; Prophecy. *See also* Israel, prophecy against; Judah, prophecy against; by Agabus, 26, 27; by Ahijah, 28; by Amos, 32, 56, 195; of the Antichrist, 36; by Balaam, 27, **49**, 50; by Daniel, 20, 36, 55, *55*, 93, 94, 104, 319; by Elijah, 28, 110, 177, 183; by Ezekiel, 120, *120*, 311, 323, 347; of God's future kingdom, 37; by Habakkuk, 147; by Haggai, 147, *147;* by Hosea, 352; by Isaiah, 49; Israel's punishment, 287-288; Jesus' birth, 352; Messiah, 305; potter and clay analogy, 271; regarding Tubal, 346; and ruins of Babylon, 299; the Savior's ministry, 300; Shebna's death, 307; by Jeremiah, 30, 49*, 52*, 101, 168, 177, 242, 305; by Jesus, 180; about Jesus, 24, 42, 57, 127, 182, 246; by Joseph, 104; of Messiah, 180; by Noadiah, 242; Old Testament, 228; as spiritual gift, 323; by the stars, 45, 276
Prophets, 44, 145, 251, 265, 274, **277**, 290, 325. *See also* names of prophets
  false, 48, 51, *109*, **122**, *122*, 349, 360; on Israel as mother, 230; of Judah, 184, 309; killed by Jezebel, 183; minor, 225; teachings of, 196; visions of, 355
Prophetess, **277**
Prophetic books, 268
Propitiation, 220, **277**
Proselyte, **277**
Prostitute, 149
Prostitution, 269
Provender, 128, **277**
Protection, 281, 298, 307, 309
Protestants, 295
Proverbs, book of, 165, 268, **277**, 342, 348, 359, 478–**482**, 484
Providence, **278**
Province, **278**
Provision, **278**, 358
Prudent, **278**
Pruninghook, **278**
Psalmist, the, 44, 45, 281, 318, 336
Psalms, book of, 98, 268, **278**, 289, 303, 309, 359, 362, 467–**477**. *See also* Music, Musicians
Psaltery, 149, 232, **278**, 352
Ptolemais, 22, 264
Ptolemy, **278**
Publican, **279**
Publius, 127, **279**
Pul, 435. *See also* Tiglath-Pileser III
Pulse, **279**
Punishment, 95, 149, **279**, 303, 325, 360; God's, 289; method of, 301, 302, *325;* tongue used for, 342
Purification, 42, 66, 81, 164, 202, **279**, 346, 356
Purim, Feast of, **279**, 459, 460, 461
Purity, 303, 355
Purple, **279**, 487
Purpose, **278**
Purse, 90, **279**

Put. *See* Phut
Pygarg, **279**

Q

Quails, **280**, *280*, 314
Quarternion, **280**
Quartz, 27, 76, 90, 127
Queen, **280**
Queen Athalia. *See* Athaliah
Queen, of Heaven, **280**
Queen of Sheba, 39, 226, 259, 295, 427, 444, *484*. *See also* Sheba
Quicken, **281**
Quicksands, **281**
Quilts, 267
Quirinius, 92
Quiver, **281**
Qumran, 97, 116, **281**

R

Raamses, 344. *See also* Rameses
Rabbah, **282**, 323, 420, 440
Rabbath, *See* Rabbah
Rabbi, **282**
Rabbit, 149
Rabboni. *See* Rabbi
Rabbouni. *See* Rabbi
Rab-Shakeh, **282**
Raca, **282**
Race, **282**
Rachab. *See* Rahab
Rachel, 60, **282**
  barrenness of, 51; death of, 56; father, Laban, 197, 336; husband, Jacob, 174; son Joseph, 187
Rahab, *150*, **282**, 400
Rahel. *See* Rachel
Raid. *See* Road
Rain, 127, 148, **282**, 372, 380, 394, 429, 649. *See also* Autumn rain; Early rain; Former rain
Rainbow, **282**, 329
Raisins, **283**
Ram, **283**, 338
Ramah, 233, 234, **283**, 412, 415, 416. *See also* Rama; Ramoth-Gilead
Rameses, **283**
Ramoth. *See* Ramoth-Gilead
Ramoth-Gilead, 27, 80, *80*, **283**, 430, 433, 447
Ramparts, 68, **284**
Ramses II, 76
Ram's Horn, **284**
Ransom, **284**
Rapture, the, **284**
Raven(s), 78, **284**
Razor, **284**
Ready, **284**
Reap, **284**
Reaper, 149
Reaping, *161*
Rebecca. *See* Rebekah
Rebekah, 170, 174, 197, 211, 244, **284**, 249, 374, 375
Rebellion
  against God, 314; of children, 325; man's, 289; signal of, 311; turning from, 288; of Zedekiah, 365
Rebirth, 195
Rechab, **285**
Rechabites, 502
Recompense, **285**
Reconciliation, 219, 225, **285**, 296, 617, 622
Record, **285**
Recorder, **285**
Red Dragon, **285**
Red heifer, **285**
Red kite, 139. *See also* Vulture
Redeem, **286**

Redeemed, 274, 303
Redemption, 114, 168, 195, **275**, 292, 319, 362
Red Sea, 38, 72, 111, 119, 120, *130, 241*, 244, **285**, *285*, 311, 380
Reed, 68, **286**
Refiner, **286**
Refuge, cities of. *See* Cities of refuge
Refuse, **286**
Regeneration, 240, **286**
Register, 123, 135, **286**
Rehoboam, 58, **286**, 309, 424, 427, 444, 445
  built Mareshah, 214; and divided kingdom, 172; as king, 24, 189; son, Abijah, 19; father, Solomon, 24, 286; rebellion against, 179, 332; successor of, 19; warned not to attack Israel, 309
Reins, **286**
Rejoice, **287**
Religion, 357
Remission, **287**
Remnant, 170, *222*, 242, **287**, 365
Remphan, **288**
Rend, **288**
Repent, **288**
Repentance, 46, 49, 50, 62, 86, 129, 136; believers', 287; expression of, 295
  God's command for, 166; and God's longsuffering, 206; of Israel, 293; Jewish religious gathering of, 318; and John the Baptist, 185; after judgment, 190; and kingdom, 182, 195; for laciviousness, 199; sign of, 288; for sins of ignorance, 166
Rephaim, **288**
Rephaim, Valley of, 288, 418, 440
Rephaims, 137
Rephan, *See* Remphan
Rephidim, **288**
Reproach, **288**
Reprobate, 97, 99, **288**
Reproof, **288**
Resin, *130*
Resources, 325
Respect, 290, 357
Responsibility, 325
Restitution, **289**, 344
Restraint, 258, 340
Resurrection, **289**, 296. *See also* Jesus Christ, resurrection
Resurrection of Christ, **289**. *See also* Jesus Christ, resurrection
Retribution, **289**, 290
Reuben, **290**, 380, 388, 392, 394, 399, 401, 402, 439
  Bezer, **58**; and Judah, 189; inheritance of, 168; sin of, 167; territory of, 58; tribe of. *See* Tribes of Israel, Reuben
Reuel, 379
Revelation, book of, 21, *36*, 37, 44, 93, *120*, 140, 641, **661**–**668**
  and Laodicean church, 198; writing of, 185
Revelation, 37, 139, **290**
Revelation, book of, 258, 261, 264, **290**, 306
Revenge, **290**
Reverence, **290**
Reviler, **290**
Reward, 290, **291**, 303
Rezin, 27
Rezon, 427
Rhoda, **291**
Rhodes, **291**
Rich robe. *See* Stomacher
Riches, **291**. *See also* Wealth
Riddle, **291**
Rie, 126, **291**
Righteous, **291**, 337
Righteousness, 210. *See also* Righteous; of God, 292
  and John the Baptist, 185; and justice, 191; Jesus fulfilled, 182; Noah preaches, 242; of Joseph, 187; and suffering, 184; theme of Romans, 292

Right hand, **292**
Rimmon, **291**
Ring, **291**
Rituals. *See* Ceremonial rites
River, **291**
River of Egypt, **292**
Rizpah, *292*
Road, **292**
Robe, **292**, 325
Roboam, 186. *See also* Rehoboam
Rock, **292**
Rod, **292**
Roe, 135, **292**
Roebuck. *See* Roe
Roasted grain, **250**
Roll, 64, **292**
Roman Catholics, **295**
Roman Empire, 39, 46, 70, 278, **292**
  control of Syria, 329; emperors of, 207, **238**;
  and Italy, 172; law of, 156; Lycaonia, 210;
  Mamertinum Prison, *275*; mythology, 75, 140;
  objects/artifacts, *91*, 114, 123; **portrayed as
  Babylon,** 293; rule over Israel, 185
Roman road, 38
Romans, *273*, 278, *302*. *See also* Roman Empire
Romans, epistle to, 216, **292**, 293, 604, **605–609,**
  633
Rome, 28, 38, 72, 75, 86, 89, 108, 114, *114*, 117,
  121, *121*, 140, **293**, *605*, 606, 650, 653. *See also*
  Caesar; Caesarea; Achaia, 134; Appii Forum/
  Appian Way, **38**, 130
  army of, 201; Asia (Minor), province of, 24, 61,
  73, 114, 133; authorities of, 56, 70, 71, 87, 90,
  92, 98, 105, 124, 125, 134, 143, 155, 156. *See also*
  Caesar; Pilate; Governor; Herod; Caesarea, **70**,
  124, 156; Caesarea Philippi, 71; capital city, 172;
  captivity of Jews, 203, 352, *354;* church of, 38,
  209; coins of, 227; Decapolis, province of, **97;**
  embraces Christianity, 592; Galilee, **133**, 133,
  155; and gospel, 210, 293; government, 276, 279;
  governors, 254, 272; great fire of, 238, *239;* and
  Jesus, 182; judgment of, 290; measurements of,
  223; Onesimus' escape to, 248; pagan worship in,
  190, 191, 220, 293; Paul in, *257*, 258, 264, 340,
  602, 603, 604, 605, 640; Perea, province of, 133,
  138; province of Judea, 189; rule over Palestine,
  180, 365; soldiers of, 75, 81, 87, 292; spiritual
  gifts in, 323; Timothy in, 340
Romulus, 292
Roof(s), 339, 560, *596*, 597
Root, 293
Rope, 86, **293**
Rose, 90, **293**
Royal deputy, 77
Rubbish, 105. *See also* **Refuse**
Ruby, 86, **293**
Ruddy, 293
Rue, 293
Rufus, 293
Ruhamah, 293
Ruler(s), 143, 146, **324**. *See also* Prince
Ruler of Evil, Satan, 275
Runner, 128
Rush, 126, **294**
Rust, 294
Ruth, 57, 63, 110, 139, 149, **294;** husband Mahlon,
  212
  Levirate marriage of, 202; as Moabite, 226, 409,
  410, *410;* and Naomi, 234, 294; redeemed by
  Boaz, 195
Ruth, book of, **294**, 398, **409–410**
Rye, 126

S
Sabaoth, 295
Sabbath, 86, 105, 274, **295; breaking,** 325; day of
  rest, 381, 385, 390

ignored by Judah, 457, 499; Jesus' teachings on,
  547–548, 572; Jews' worship on, *346*
Sabbath Day's journey, 295
Sabbatical year, 295
Sabeans, **295**
Sackbut, **295**
Sackcloth, **295**
Sacrament, **295**
Sacredness, of life, 328
Sacrifice(s), 19, 20, *21*, 40, 66, 76, 105, *109*, 115,
  126, 127, 131, *147*, **295**, *330*
  abolished by Jesus 383, 644; and altar, 161;
  animal, 18, 19, *31*, 46, 62, 68, 69, 71, 126, 127,
  139, 153, *194*, 286, 307, 329, 336, 344, 347, 356,
  383, *644;* and laver, 199; meat offering, 218, 285;
  priests' portion, 218; wrong practices, 213; child,
  19, 24, 48, 78, 325; in Hinnom Valley, 158; of
  Christians, 225; **and worship of many gods,** 269;
  for Christ, 304; Christ's, 46, *46*, 146, 153; Day
  of Atonement, 159; human, 342; in giving, 226;
  of Isaac, 177, 228; Jesus as, 157, 197, 218, 275,
  295; and new moon, 228
Sadducees, 551, 553, 565, 579, **296**
Saffron, 296
Sage(s), 277
Saint, 79, **296**
Salamis, **296**
Salem, 180, *219*, 219. *See also* Melchizedek
Salim, 296
Salome, 296
Salt, **296**, 544, 546
Salt, City of, **296**
Salt Sea, 96, 97, **296**
Salt, Valley of, **296**
Salutation, 296
Salvation, 49, 64, 65, 86, *87*, 89, 97, 103, 110, 117,
  121, 133, 135, 139, 140, 142, 143, 147, 149, 254,
  296–297; assurance of, 287; **eternal,** 274
  God's plan of, 321, 371, 372, 489, 494, 536,
  587, 597, 606, 608, 619, 620, 622, 623, 625,
  627, 631, 642, 643, 650, 652, 653, 655; through
  Jesus Christ, 300, 319, 351; Jesus' sacrifice, 218;
  proclaimed by Joel, 184; **theme of Romans,**
  292; **thanksgiving for,** 336; "**well**" as, 357; of
  Zacchaeus, 364
Samaria, **297;** Assyrian colonists, 24, 40, 42, 46, 98,
  101, 115
  Avites in, 240; building of, 341; capital of Israel,
  172, 309, 429, 430, 433, 434, 519; Christian
  witness in, 23, 264; city in, 329; **district of,**
  297; Ebal, *106*; evangelized, 596; fall of, 143,
  299, 304; gods of, 24, 33, 42; Jesus in, 575, 585;
  people of, 24, 40, 42, 98, 101, 115; prophecies
  against, 527
Samaritan(s), 40, 46, 98, 101, 115, 135, 136, **297**,
  297
  good, 568, 575; and Jesus, 209
Sanballat, 298
  territory of, 260; woman, 174, 355
Samgar-Nebo, 297
Samos, **297**
Samothrace. *See* **Samothracia**
Samothracia, **297**
Samson, 98, **297–298**, 406, 407, 408, 437; angel
  appearing to parents, *34;* and Delilah, 98
  death of, 135; as Nazarite, 237; and Philistines,
  135, 174, 190, *291;* strength of, 98, 135
Samuel, 110, 149, 233, **298**, *411*, 412, 413, 414, 415,
  416, *416*, 417
  anoints David, 18, 180; birth of, 149; books of,
  298, 398, **411–416, 417–423;** boyhood of, 110;
  builds altar, 107; as judge, 327, 337; as Nazarite,
  237; sons, 18, 184; spirit of, 123, 360; and witch
  of Endor, 212
Sanballat, **298**, 342, 455
Sanctification, 158, 202, **298**, 292
Sanctuary, 80, 88, 159, 271, **298**, 330, *333*. *See also*

Refuge, cities of
Sand, 299
Sandals, 299
Sanhedrin, 87, 88, 134, 258, 337, 344, 554, 556, 558,
  565, 566, 577, 579, 580, 587, 588, 593, 595, 602
Sapphira, **299**
Sapphire, 174, **299**
Sapphira 595
Sara, *See* Sarah
Sarah, **299**, 373, 374; death and burial, 20, 153,
  156, 193, 211; husband, 19, 20, 136, 147, 153,
  170, 350
  and king Abimelech, 19, 136; name change, 20;
  once barren, 20, 51; servant, Hagar, 20, 147, 171;
  son, Isaac, 20
Sarai, *See* Sarah
Sardine, 299
Sardis, **299**, 306, 664
Sardius, 299
Sardonyx, 299
Sarepta. *See* Zarephath
Sargon, **299**
Saron. *See* Sharon
Satan, 97, 118, **299;** affects believers, 38, 334, 290;
  afflicts Job, 183, 299, 463–464
  and Antichrist, 36; battles archangel Michael,
  40; battles Christ, 663, 665, 668; chief of
  demons, 575; Christ's miracles attributed to, 62,
  349; demise of, 118, 331; as fallen angel, 34, 285;
  and lake of fire, 197; names of/terms describing,
  24, 49, 53, **54**, 97, 100, 103, 118, 203, 275, 285;
  overthrown, 183; power of, 348; tempts Jesus,
  182, 267, 544, 560, 572; ways of, 97, 99, 100
Satrap, 299
Satyr, 140, **299**
Saudi Arabia, *59*, *128*
Saul, 30, *56*, 66, 149, **300**, 439
  and Abinadab, 19; and Abner, 19, 42; and
  Ahimelech, **28**, 103; battles of, 31, 138, 142, **300**;
  burial of, 301, **331**, 365; and David,; as harpist,
  231; Jonathan's friend, *186*; pursues, 233, 316,
  320, 366, 415, 416, 469, 471, 472, 476; struggles
  with, 17, 22, 95, 113, 298; daughter Michal, 222;
  death of, 58, 79, 138, **300**, 412, 416, 417, 418, 445,
  473; defends Jabesh-Gilead, 173; descendants
  of, 219; disobedience to God, 27, 95; failures of,
  411, 413, 414, 416, 417; and Heman, **154**; and
  Jonathan, 19, 95; kills priests, 243; king of Israel,
  138, 194, 413, 422; kingdom of, **137;** loses God's
  favor, 27; overseer Doeg, 103; and Philistia, 265;
  and Rizpah, 292; and servants, 366; sons; **death
  of,** 300; Ish-Bosheth, 171; Jonathan, 186; Malchi-
  shua, 213; as warrior, 176; and witch of Endor,
  113, 123, 212, 360;
Saul/Paul, 258, 300, 595, 596. *See also* Paul,
  conversion of; Savior, **300;** dependence on
  Father, 182; and "I am," 156; from David's line,
  180; Jesus as, 221; promise of, 276

Saw, 300
Scab, 300
Scabbard. *See* **Sheath**
Scales. *See* Balance
Scall, 300
Scapegoat, 46, 47, 199, **300**
Scarlet, 90, **300**
Scented wood. *See* Thyine wood
Sceptre, 301
Sceva, 301
Schechem, 223
School, 301
Schoolmaster, 101, **301**
Scorpion, 301
Scourging, 127, **301**, *302*
Screech owl, 61, **301**
Scribe(s), 78, 87, 120, 168, **301**, 564
Scribe's knife. *See* Penknife

Yokefellow, 84, **363**
Yom Kippur, 46

Z

Zabulon. *See* Zebulun
Zacchaeus, 279, 289, **364**, 578
Zachariah, **364**, 435
Zacharias, *34*, 132, **364**, 569, 570. *See also* Zechariah
Zadok, 28, **364**, 420
Zalmunna, 406
Zamzummim. *See* Zamzummims
Zamzummims, 137, **364**
Zamzummites. See Zamzummims
Zaphanath-Paaneah, 187
Zarephath, **364**
Zeal, **364**
Zealot. *See* Zelotes
Zealots, 72, 180
Zebah, 406
Zebedee, 63, 174, 184, **364**, 583
Zeboim, **364**
Zeboiim, 80. *See also* Zeboim
Zebulun, 135, 172, 344, **364**, 388, 402, 405
Zechariah, book of, 225, **365**, **536–538**, 661
Zechariah/Zacharias, *34*, 185
Zechariah, prophet, *34*, 364, **365**, 452, 517, 534, 536, 537, 539
Zedekiah, 178, 237, **365**, 437, 450, 497, 500, 501
Zela. *See* Zelah
Zelah, **365**
Zelophehad, **365**, 391, *392*
Zelotes, 72, **365**
Zephaniah, book of 225,, **365**, 517, **533**
Zerah, 214, 331, 446
Zerubbabel, 180, 334, 341, **366**, 451, 452, 456, 535, 537
Zeus, 75, 190. *See also* Jupiter
Ziba, **366**, 420
Zidon. *See* Sidon
Zidonians, 407
Zif, **366**
Ziggurat, 49, **366**
Ziklag, **366**, 416, 439
Zilpah, 42, **366**
Zimri, 108, 265, **366**, 428
Zin, **366**
Zinc, 66
Zion, **366**, 471, 474, 476, 492
    Mount, 252, 506, 665
Zipporah, 182, 230, **366**, 379
Ziv. *See* Zif
Zoar, 54, 56, 80, **366**
Zobah, 147, 440
Zophar, 110, 184, 464–465, **366**
Zorobabel. *See* Zerubbabel
Zuzim, **366**
Zuzites. *See* Zuzim

ART CREDITS